The MIND of

Charles Hartshorne

Charles Hartshorne by Michelle Bakay (based on a 1981 photo)

The MIND of

Charles Hartshorne

A Critical Examination

Donald Wayne Viney
George W. Shields

PROCESS
CENTURY
PRESS

ANOKA, MINNESOTA 2020

The Mind of Charles Hartshorne: A Critical Examination

Process Century Press
RiverHouse LLC
802 River Lane
Anoka, MN 55303

Process Century Press books are published in association with the International Process Network.

Cover: Susanna Mennicke

ISBN 978-1-940447-44-5
Printed in the United States of America

CONTENTS

ABBREVIATION FOR BOOK TITLES

AD   *Anselm's Discovery: A Re-examination of the Ontological Proof for God's Existence* (La Salle, IL: Open Court, 1965).

AW   *Aquinas to Whitehead: Seven Centuries of Metaphysics of Religion* (Milwaukee, WI: Marquette University Publications, 1976).

BH   *Beyond Humanism: Essays in the Philosophy of Nature* (Chicago: Willett, Clark & Company, 1937). Republished in 1975 by Peter Smith.

BS   *Born to Sing: An Interpretation and World Survey of Bird Song* (Bloomington: University of Indiana Press, 1973).

CAP   *Creativity in American Philosophy* (Albany: State University of New York Press, 1984).

CE   *Creative Experiencing: A Philosophy of Freedom*, edited by Donald Wayne Viney and Jincheol O (Albany: State University of New York Press, 2011).

CH   Santiago Sia (ed.) *Charles Hartshorne's Concept of God: Philosophical and Theological Responses* (Dordrecht, the Netherlands: Kluwer Academic Publishers, 1990).

CS   *Creative Synthesis and Philosophic Method* (La Salle, IL: Open

Court, 1970).

DL   *The Darkness and the Light: A Philosopher Reflects Upon His Fortunate Career and Those Who Made it Possible* (Albany: State University of New York Press, 1990).

DR   *The Divine Relativity: A Social Conception of God* (New Haven, CT: Yale University Press, 1948).

EA   John B. Cobb, Jr. and Franklin L Gamwell (eds.) *Existence and Actuality: Conversations with Charles Hartshorne* (Chicago: University of Chicago Press, 1984).

HB   Auxier, Randall E. and Mark Y. A. Davies (eds.) *Hartshorne and Brightman on God, Process, and Persons: The Correspondence, 1922-1945* (Nashville: Vanderbilt University Press, 2001).

HP   Robert Kane and Stephen H. Phillips (eds.) *Hartshorne, Process Philosophy and Theology* (Albany: State University of New York Press, 1989).

IO   *Insights and Oversights of Great Thinkers: An Evaluation of Western Philosophy* (Albany: State University of New York Press, 1983).

LP   *The Logic of Perfection and Other Essays in Neoclassical Metaphysics* (La Salle, IL: Open Court, 1962).

MVG   *Man's Vision of God and the Logic of Theism* (Chicago: Willett, Clark and Company, 1941).

NT   *A Natural Theology for Our Time* (La Salle, IL: Open Court, 1967).

OO   *Omnipotence and Other Theological Mistakes* (Albany: State University of New Press, 1984).

PCH   Lewis Edwin Hahn (ed.) *The Philosophy of Charles Hartshorne*, The Library of Living Philosophers Volume XX (La Salle, IL: Open Court, 1991).

PPS   *The Philosophy and Psychology of Sensation* (University of Chicago Press, 1934). Republished in 1968 by Kennikat Press.

PSG   *Philosophers Speak of God*, with William L. Reese (University of Chicago Press, 1953). Republished in 2000 by Humanity Books.

RSP   *Reality as Social Process: Studies in Metaphysics and Religion* (Boston: Beacon Press, 1953).

WM   *Wisdom as Moderation: A Philosophy of the Middle Way* (Albany: State University of New York Press, 1987).

WP   *Whitehead's Philosophy: Selected Essays, 1935-1970* (Lincoln: University of Nebraska Press, 1972).

WVR   *Whitehead's View of Reality*, with Creighton Peden (New York: Pilgrim Press, 1981). Republished in 2010 by Cambridge Scholars Publishing.

ZF   *The Zero Fallacy and Other Essays in Neoclassical Philosophy*, edited by Mohammad Valady (Peru, IL: Open Court Publishing Company, 1997).

KEY TO LOGICAL SYMBOLS USED IN THE TEXT

$\sim p$	not-p
$p \wedge q$	p and q
$p \vee q$	p and/or q
$p \supset q$	if p then q
$p \equiv q$	p if and only if q, or $(p \supset q) \wedge (q \supset p)$
$\square\, p$	necessarily p
$\lozenge\, p$	possibly p
$p \rightarrow q$	p strictly implies q, or $\square\, (p \supset q)$
$p \leftrightarrow q$	p and q strictly imply each other, or $\square\, (p \equiv q)$
$\exists$	Existential quantifier

The modal operators are interdefinable: $\square\, p = df. \sim \lozenge \sim p$

$$\lozenge\, p = df. \sim \square \sim p$$

৵ PREFACE ৵

CHARLES HARTSHORNE is widely regarded as an important figure in twentieth-century philosophy. His wide-ranging and diverse contributions encompass both philosophy and science—aesthetics, metaphysics, the history of philosophy, philosophical theology, numerous topics of applied philosophy, psychology, and ornithology. He championed the aspirations of metaphysics when it was unfashionable, and the metaphysic he championed helped change some of the fashions of philosophy. Metaphysics, he said, has a future as well as a past (RSP 168; CS 22).[1] He counted some well-known scientists among his friends, and he embraced the deliverances of modern science; he never questioned, for example, the truth of evolution. He insisted, however, that metaphysics and empirical science have different aims and methods, each ensuring in its own way a disciplined objectivity.[2] His "neoclassical" or "process" metaphysics is in the same family of speculative philosophy as what one finds in the works of Charles Sanders Peirce and the later writings of Alfred North Whitehead. Although he did not style himself a disciple of Peirce or of Whitehead, he made significant contributions to the study of these philosophers even as he developed his own views. Like them, Hartshorne endeavored in his own metaphysical thinking to give full weight to the dynamic, relational, temporal, and affective dimensions of the universe. He emphasized, as few before him had, in logic and in the processes of nature, the foundational nature of asymmetrical relations.

Throughout his long career, Hartshorne was a severe critic of some forms of belief in God, but he was an enthusiastic defender of what he called neoclassical or dipolar theism. Much of the criticism of theism in his lifetime was aimed not so much at the truth of theism as at its coherence. These anti-theistic arguments came from quarters as various as logical positivism and Sartrean existentialism. Hartshorne found the key to the logic of theism in what he called "Anselm's discovery," that God's *existence* could not be contingent. Hartshorne's name is inseparable from the revival of the ontological or modal argument for God's existence. He devoted twenty-three articles and the better part of two books to the topic. He continually and consistently insisted, however, that it was unavailing to appeal to the ontological argument (or any theistic argument) as support for theism without first rethinking the concept of deity. He argued that thinking about God had been handicapped by lack of attention to the logically possible forms of theism (e.g., MVG Ch. 1). He averred that there would be fewer atheists if theists had done a better job of making sense of the concept of God (CS xvi). Hartshorne's response to this situation was to replace the concept of the unmoved mover of classical theology with what he called "the most, *and best*, moved mover," a phrase borrowed, in part, from Abraham Heschel (ZF 6, 39).[3] He made a distinction in logical type between the *existence* of God as necessary and the *actuality* of God as contingent; in this way, he advocated a "dipolar" God. Hartshorne sought a "panentheism" in which God includes the creatures without negating their distinctiveness. He argued that no putative inerrant revelation or infallible institution could negate the effects of the inherent fallibility of human knowledge. He occasionally worried that his "highly rationalized" form of theism would not have wide appeal; on the other hand, it was precisely a God of love and the love of God that were ever his "intuitive clue[s]" in philosophy (HB 14; CS xviii; IO 231; PHC 700). His ideas about deity changed both philosophy of religion and theology, for it became necessary to take seriously an alternative to classical understandings of God that—Hartshorne argued—avoided their shortcomings while rendering coherent their best insights.

While most of Hartshorne's philosophical work concerned metaphysical issues, he had a good deal to say on matters of applied philosophy. He never wrote a systematic treatment of moral philosophy, but from early in his career various questions in ethics concerned him. For example, between 1929 and 1936 he published fourteen book reviews and two articles in the *International Journal of Ethics*. During the years of the Second World War he wrote on questions of war, peace, pacifism, and democracy. In the last thirty years of the century, he published articles on abortion, animal rights, environmental ethics, and technology. He advocated the ideals of being creative and fostering creativity in others and of love considered as sympathetic understanding of others and an active promotion of their welfare. He considered an ethics based merely on self-interest to be not only mistaken but also not conducive to mental health. He called his own ethical view *contributionism*, the idea that life is made meaningful by contributing to what is greater than ourselves which, as Hartshorne argued, is the divine life.

Hartshorne did not devote all of his intellectual energies to philosophy. His first book ventured empirical hypotheses about sensation, a subject to which he returned intermittently throughout his career. Also of note is that, from an early age, he was interested in birds. He became known among ornithologists as a serious student of oscines. His efforts as a scientist studying a possible aesthetic sense in songbirds culminated in 1973 with the publication of his empirically rich and quantitatively analytical treatise *Born to Sing: An Interpretation and World Survey of Bird Song*. Hartshorne's psychological and ornithological theories do not presuppose his metaphysical views, but they are consistent with them and they show the relevance of metaphysical considerations in forming novel empirical and scientific hypotheses that take account of the qualitative dimensions of experience.

The present book is designed to be a more comprehensive overview of Hartshorne's thought than has hitherto been available. There is a great deal of detailed scholarly interest in Hartshorne's work that highlights various aspects of his thinking. The works of Daniel Dombrowski are particularly noteworthy in this regard, and the authors of this work have devoted a good deal of energy to these topics.[4] However, the closest anticipation of the present work is *Hartshorne and Neoclassical Metaphysics*, the classic study of Eugene H. Peters (1929–1983), which appeared in 1970 when Hartshorne was seventy-three years old.[5] For many philosophers, an account of their thought at such a late stage in their career could be expected to adequately summarize their contributions to philosophy.

Hartshorne, however, lived another thirty years and remained intellectually active and productive for most of that time. Indeed, he contributed to the festschrift published in honor of Peters upon his death.[6] Peters had access to most of Hartshorne's works prior to 1970 as well as manuscript notes that served as the basis of Hartshorne's *Creative Synthesis and Philosophic Method,* which appeared the same year as Peters's book. Counting *Creative Synthesis,* that is ten books. Hartshorne would go on to write another eleven books after 1970, ten of which were published during his lifetime. In addition, in the later period of his life, he contributed to four large volumes of essays devoted to the critical examination of his thought. Moreover, his important correspondence with Edgar Sheffield Brightman, which spanned twenty-three years, was published in 2001. Hartshorne referred to his longevity as his "secret weapon" for it allowed him to refine and expand upon an already novel and fruitful philosophical system. On the other hand, his publications became so numerous that he worried philosophers would have a difficult time staying abreast of his work.[7] The present book takes account of the total body of Hartshorne's work and the critical reception of it. We give more attention than is usual to Hartshorne's theory of sensation, but we treat his study of birdsong only as it relates to philosophical issues.[8]

We've had two main aims in writing this volume. First, we endeavor to give a reasonably comprehensive account of Hartshorne's philosophy with an eye to presenting his best arguments and correcting what we see as some misunderstandings of his views appearing in the critical literature. Our second goal is to update the field of Hartshorne scholarship by including within our purview later work by Hartshorne himself and more recent criticism, including criticism that Hartshorne did not address. We have aspired to formulate the best responses to criticisms that would be consistent with his central principles, but we do not hesitate to make critical comments of our own when we think them warranted. Of course, we cannot address all criticisms—explicit and implicit—that have appeared in the mountain of books, articles, and dissertations that have discussed Hartshorne's thought. Even for a book-length project this would be impractical. Rather, we have selected those critical arguments, interpretations, and observations that we consider most pressing and about which we think we have clear and well-grounded things to say. Our readers can decide whether we have succeeded, but we hope to have produced an updated, wide-ranging, and sustained *critical overview* of Hartshorne's thinking, the kind of project not seen since Peters's landmark study half a century ago.

Sometime in the early 1980s Hartshorne became sensitive to the feminist critique of language, including religious language, and he began using inclusive language in speaking of the creatures and of God. We shall document in this study that he was always a strong supporter of full political equality between the sexes; we will see, moreover, that he saw great value in female images of the divine as a way of expressing his own philosophical theology. In view of these attitudes it is not surprising that when the problem of sexist language was brought to his attention, he changed his linguistic habits to match his political and philosophical beliefs. He indicated that if he had it to do over again, he would have titled his third book *Our Vision of God* rather than *Man's Vision of God*. (HB 8, 159). We trust that the reader will not be confused if, when quoting Hartshorne's words prior to the 1980s, we do not make the corrections that he would have made of his exclusive language had he been given the opportunity to do so.

When it comes to God-talk, Hartshorne considered himself to be developing and defending the concept of a being worthy of worship that reflects what is best in theistic religion. It is traditional to capitalize "God" if nothing more than as an indication that one is talking about One that is indeed worthy of worship and is not an idol. In some quarters, it has become fashionable to use a lowercase *g* in writing on the subject of God. An example is the title of the popular book by the late Christopher Hitchens, *god is not Great*. We will not follow this practice; rather, we take a clue from David Hume in distinguishing divine-like beings that are products of nature's powers—as in stories of the origins of the deities in the Greek pantheon—and a divine being that is, in some fashion, responsible for nature's powers. We denote the former beings with a lowercase *g*, as in "gods" and "goddesses" and we denote the latter sort of being as "God." The traditional understanding of "God" is that it does not properly admit of a plural. Of course, this is a point that must be argued, and classical theists gave arguments to this effect. As we shall see, Hartshorne also does not lack for arguments for monotheism as against polytheism. In any event, he viewed the distinction between these ideas as something more than a theological nicety; for Hartshorne, the questions of the nature and the existence of God are at the very heart of sound metaphysical thinking.

A word is in order about the collaboration between the authors of this book. Since at least the mid-1980s, we have recognized that our interests in Hartshorne's philosophy have often been on parallel tracks. Neither of us were ever formally Hartshorne's students, but we both knew the man and both of us did our doctoral work on Hartshorne's global argument.[9] Each of us has offered different formalizations of Hartshorne's central argument against "classical theism," and we've both written on Hartshorne's solution to the problem of God's knowledge of future contingents—this latter interest culminated in a coauthored article on the subject in a book edited by Shields. The current book began as an article written for the *Internet Encyclopedia of Philosophy* (IEP). First inquiries were made in August 2010 by Viney to the editors of IEP concerning a possible article on Hartshorne to be co-authored with Shields. By the autumn of 2011 we had submitted the article for review. James Fieser, the founding editor of IEP remarked that the article was, in truth, a monograph and that it exceeded IEP guidelines for length of articles. He suggested that we cut the work up into briefer articles. This we did and the four articles first appeared in the IEP in August 2015. Fieser's remark made us realize that we wanted to see the work presented in the form of a book, to add material (sometimes of a more technical nature), and to expand the references. In July 2015, we were in attendance at the Tenth International Whitehead Conference at Pomona College in Claremont, California. It was there that we happened upon Jeanyne Slettom, who had recently launched Process Century Press. She expressed interest in our project and the rest, as one says, is history. We thank Dr. Slettom for her encouragement and for the opportunity to publish with her press.

The current book follows the plan of our original article for IEP, but expands considerably upon it. Each of us took primary responsibility for different chapters, but both of us offered substantial additions to or revisions of every chapter. The chapters on the new atheism, on divine temporality and cosmology, and the two chapters on Hartshorne's applied philosophy were not part of the IEP material. In addition, we deemed it important to include a revised and updated version of the primary bibliography of Hartshorne's philosophical works that originated with Dorothy Hartshorne and was later augmented by Viney and Randy Ramal. Secondary sources are included in the extensive endnotes. We hope that the primary bibliography and the secondary sources, along with extensive exposition and critical assessment of the wide reach of Hartshorne's work as well as its reception, will be of genuine help to students, process and Hartshorne scholars, and the educated public at large. Above all we hope to stimulate further reflection and scholarly research on this truly great and long-lived genius of American philosophical thought.

We wish to express gratitude to Andrew Schwartz, Chase Kirkham, and Steve Hulbert at the Center for Process Studies for their generous help in locating some of Hartshorne's unpublished manuscripts. We are also grateful to David Ray Griffin, John Quiring, Jorge Nobo, and Robert Kane for sharing anecdotes and reminiscences about Hartshorne and to David Basinger for sharing his correspondence with Hartshorne.

For their helpful comments on material appearing in this book which was presented in original drafts by the authors in various conference papers and lectures, we thank the following persons: Timothy Eastman, Michael Epperson, Gary Herstein, and H. P. Stapp (co-Research Fellows with Shields at the Center for Philosophy and the Natural Sciences at Cal State-Sacramento), Daniel Dombrowski, the late Frederick Ferré and Lewis S. Ford; also Franklin I. Gamwell, Derek Malone-France, Leemon B. McHenry, William L. Power, Randy Ramal, Kevin Schilbrack, James McBain, Hyatt Carter, and Jeanine Diller. Also, special thanks are due the General Editors of IEP James Fieser and Bradley Dowden and the former IEP American Philosophy section editor Aaron Preston and an anonymous reviewer for detailed comments on the original IEP articles.

ONE

The Career and Personality
of Charles Hartshorne

A FULL-LENGTH BIOGRAPHY OF CHARLES HARTSHORNE drawing
on archival material, extant letters, news articles, letters to the
editor, interviews, audio and video recordings, and the like, has yet to
be written. Hartshorne himself wrote several articles focusing on his
intellectual development, and his autobiography, *The Darkness and the
Light*, is a treasure trove, both informative and entertaining.[1] The most
complete article length biography of Hartshorne is the entry on him in
the *Dictionary of Literary Biography*, an article that was twelve years in
the making; Hartshorne read two prepublication versions of the article
and he advised on its contents.[2] In what follows, we draw on these
sources plus a few more that became available after Hartshorne's death,
in particular some reflections from his daughter, Emily Hartshorne
Schwartz. What we hope to accomplish in this chapter is to highlight
the significant moments of his career and life, to give some sense of his
intellectual development, and to provide insight into his personality
through his personal memories and the memories of those who knew
him, the most reliable anecdotes that have circulated about him, and
occasionally our own experiences.[3]

Charles Hartshorne (pronounced "Harts-horne"; literally, "deer's
horn") was born June 5, 1897, in Kittanning, Pennsylvania, the second

of six children of Francis Cope Hartshorne (1868–1950), an Episcopal minister, and Marguerite Haughton Hartshorne (1868–1959). He and his brother Richard (1899–1992)—who achieved fame as a geographer—attended Yeates Boarding School (1911–1915). In his second year at Yeates, a case of peritonitis sent him to surgery. Afterwards, he found himself wanting to write poetry, a desire he traced to the peaceful feelings he experienced from both the ether and his having fasted prior to the operation. Although philosophy became his vocation, he developed a lifelong interest in literature and poetry (DL 84–85). At Yeates he read Matthew Arnold's *Literature and Dogma* and Emerson's *Essays*. After reading Emerson, he resolved "to trust reason to the end" (LP viii). It was also at Yeates that he acquired a lifelong interest in ornithology, a subject to which he eventually devoted several articles and a book, *Born to Sing* (1973).

Later, Hartshorne attended Haverford College (1915–1917) where he was a student of Rufus Jones, a pioneer in the study of the history of mysticism and a Quaker reformer.[4] Thanks to Jones, he read Josiah Royce's *The Problem of Christianity* and became convinced, once and for all, that self-interest is neither the sole nor the basic human motivation, nor did he believe that it can form the basis of a sound ethical system. Jones also sensitized Hartshorne to the limits of human reason saying, "In every philosophical system there is an impasse somewhere" (DL 120). Jones's mysticism put its mark on Hartshorne's philosophy; he accepted the Jonesian thesis that, if God is omnipresent, then the difference between mystics (those with a sense of the presence of God) and non-mystics is only a matter of degree.[5]

With America's entry into the First World War imminent and conscription a near certainty, Hartshorne considered his options for military service, prompted by recruiters from the U.S. Medical Corps who came to Haverford (PCH 16). For a brief period, he had been an extreme pacifist as a result of reading Tolstoy, but he had decided against strict pacifism by the time President Wilson declared war. Nevertheless, he did not take easily, as he put it, to the idea of killing people, and he realized the immediate need for volunteers to the medical service. Consequently, he volunteered for the medical corps and spent the war years (1917–1919) in Le Tréport, France, as an orderly in a British hospital, working primarily in an isolation unit for soldiers with communicable diseases. Hartshorne remarked that tales of wartime experiences often involve killing and being killed but for the unit with which he worked, it was "rather the opposite" (DL 143). Reflecting on his decision in later years he summed up the situation: "I am a man of thought and feeling rather than of action . . . A soldier in an actual war is a man of action if anyone is" (DL 125).

For Hartshorne the war years were "pervaded by the sense of religious change" (DL 147). While crossing the Atlantic, he had "close to a mystical experience" while contemplating the idea of a finite God expressed in the novel, *Mr. Britling Sees It Through* by H. G. Wells. As Wells's story develops, England goes to war with Germany, and the main character, Mr. Britling, loses a son and close friends, including a fallen soldier on the German side. The sense of the title of the novel is that Mr. Britling sees a way through the horror and apparent futility of the war, in part, by finding solace and strength in a God of limited power. Mr. Britling explains to another character, named Letty, who is an atheist:

> It is a theologian's folly. God is not absolute; God is finite. . . . A finite God who struggles in his great and comprehensive way as we struggle in our weak and silly way—who is *with* us—that is the essence of real religion.[6]

This God, being a conscious spirit, is greater than nature and necessity, but does not control them. As Letty reflects on this idea, she says to herself that it is not nonsense to say of such a God that God is "love" and that God could be "a friend and companion."[7] Letty's atheism loses its motive force as she contemplates this concept of God. For H. G. Wells, these ideas were a phase in his movement towards agnosticism or, perhaps, a veiled atheism.[8] For Hartshorne, however, they were an important step towards what he considered to be a more adequate concept of God than what he found in much of religion. As we shall see in subsequent chapters, Hartshorne would considerably refine these ideas and incorporate them into his own philosophical theology. He came to accept that God is, in different respects, both finite and infinite. In addition, he rejected the idea that any single being, including God, does or *could* determine every detail of the world process. This is not because divine power is limited but because the very concept of an all-determining omnipotence is conceptually incoherent.

As the references to influences from literary figures such as Arnold, Emerson, and Wells suggest, Hartshorne was throughout his life, like

Whitehead, an avid and discerning reader of novels and poetry. He once observed that reading literary works not only informs us about life but in and by itself can be a way of "*intensely living*, as we read them" (ZF 35, our emphasis). His literary corpus contains numerous references to all manner of fictional characters and scenarios, literary masterpieces and poetic flourishes ranging from Omar Khayyam and Dante to Wordsworth and Melville, from Jane Austin and Mark Twain to Camus and Japanese novels. Heidegger's "turn" to poetics is applauded by Hartshorne as a corrective to the comparative lack of aesthetic sensibility in *Sein und Zeit* and the narrow cognitive concerns of Husserl's search for the *wesenschau* of the objects of experience in the phenomenological projects of the *Ideen* and *Cartesian Meditations* (IO 331). Not only literature, but the fine arts and music are profoundly evocative and truth-bearing in a most direct intuitive way, especially music: Mozart's *La Clemenza di Tito*, says Hartshorne, leads us to an encounter with higher dimensions of reality "more directly and more intimately than metaphysics can do" (EA 77). There is thus no doubt that Hartshorne's deep concerns with aesthetics and aesthetic sensibilities were well-honed by his wide-ranging encounter with literature and the arts. A philosopher of the "whole brain," he counseled that ideally philosophers ought to be *both* logicians *and* poets (CS xvii).[9]

Working in the hospital, Hartshorne was free from the dangers of the trenches. He spent his free time reading books he had taken with him. Among his books were Augustine's *Confessions* and William James's *The Varieties of Religious Experience*. The reading of James reinforced the idea that God cannot be merely absolute and that all actualization of value is finite. The reading of Augustine, on the other hand, seemed to have no appreciable effect on Hartshorne. Arnold's book had already been the occasion of his break with traditional forms of Christianity. In brief, although he regarded Jesus as a "supreme symbol" of God's sympathetic participation in the sufferings and joys of the creatures (RSP 24), Hartshorne did not accept that Jesus was literally God incarnate and thus he did not worship him (DL 147).[10] In addition, he ceased to believe in an afterlife in which one continues to accumulate new experiences, in heaven, in hell, or elsewhere. Although as a young man he seemed to have believed in some kind of personal afterlife (DL 149), the influences that originally led him to reject the belief were not clear to him.[11] He would later argue that only a divine being could tolerate the endless transformations of experience implied by personal immortality without destroying the fabric of one's individuality (LP 253; WM 51f). He considered it a "mistake in the history of religions" to refuse to accept birth and death as the beginning and ending of life respectively, and he was critical of Christians and Muslims for believing in rewards and punishments doled out in an afterlife, but he honored the ancient Jews for rejecting the same (ZF 70).[12] The form of immortality in which he believed, and which he considered to be adequate for religious purposes, was contributing to the divine life and being remembered by God, a view he called *contributionism.*

Hartshorne was under no illusions about the desire felt by many that there be an unending life beyond the grave, or as he sometimes called it, a "posthumous career" (ZF 57). He remarked that "it takes a high level of self-transcendence to find sufficient the preservation of one's experiences, not ultimately in one's own experiences, or even in those of other human persons, but in those of deity."[13] While he definitely rejected the idea that one could endlessly acquire new experiences beyond death, he apparently did not rule out the possibility of a limited postmortem existence (RSP 143). This is confirmed by David Griffin, who reported to Shields in 1994 that Hartshorne told him in personal conversation that he did not dismiss out of hand a potential empirical case for such postmortem existence that might be made through parapsychological evidence. This brings Hartshorne close to Whitehead who was "neutral" on the question of personal survival of death, but who did believe in the probable veracity of some psi phenomena such as telepathy (which would be theoretically underpinned by his non-sensationist doctrine of perception). Hartshorne emphasized, however, that evidence for postmortem existence would be empirical and could not establish an unending postmortem career. "Supposing natural life to be followed by supernatural life, supernatural life could end in some equally supernatural death."[14]

Hartshorne's departures from traditional Christianity notwith-standing, he found the seeds of his own theology clearly present in his father's thinking and the values that his parents embraced (DL 48–49). In his autobiography, Hartshorne reprints a letter (1926) and the end of a public address from his father (1950), both of which very clearly outline the trajectory of his father's theological thinking (DL 183–88; DL 191–94). F. C. Hartshorne viewed fundamentalism as hopelessly out of touch with the best thinking in both science and religion. For example, he wrote concerning an evolution exhibit in a museum, "If the biblical account [of creation] should be illustrated in the museum they should set up a model of the firmament, with windows in it, etc." (DL 188); or again, he believed that Thomas Huxley got the better of William Gladstone in their public exchange on Genesis (DL 192)[15]; finally, he was happy to have witnessed in his lifetime the diminishment of ideas of original sin, inherited guilt, and an angry God that locks the gates of heaven and holds open the gates of hell (DL 194).

The liberal form of Christianity preached by his father saved him from doubts about the general theory of evolution. Hartshorne reports, "I have never consciously not been an evolutionist" (EA xii). The same could be said of theism, although the exact form of theism he accepted underwent development. In any event, it is clear that he never felt obliged to choose between theistic religion and science. In April 1984, Viney spoke with Hartshorne in Lincoln, Nebraska, at a research conference in the philosophy of religion. During lunch on the 14th, Viney asked Hartshorne whether he considered himself a Christian. Hartshorne replied that he believed the great commandments to love God with all of one's heart, mind, soul, and strength and to love your neighbor as yourself to express the essential truth in religion (cf. CS xviii; OO 106).[16] "If you can call that Christian," he said, "then maybe I'm a Christian." Hartshorne's daughter recalled that, as an adult, she had made a collection of famous quotations about love. When her father read them, he marked a quotation from George Sand: "There is only one happiness in life, to love and be loved."[17]

In the conversation with Viney, Hartshorne further clarified his attitude towards Christian orthodoxy. He said that he did not believe in the divinity of Jesus or that Jesus ought to be worshipped. Nor, he said, did he accept the idea of a personal career after death or any kind of afterlife in which rewards and punishments are apportioned. He expressed similar views in a position paper he wrote at the request of Randal Auxier in May 1993. He mentioned his break with his father on the subjects of the Trinity, the Incarnation, and the afterlife and he spoke of giving up "the lingering bits of superstition about the resurrection of Jesus."[18] Hartshorne did not clarify whether the "superstition" was to believe that Jesus rose from the dead in some sense or whether it had to do with inferring a literalistic account of the resurrection from the rather confusing details in the New Testament Gospel accounts. We shall return to this question in our fourth chapter. For now, suffice it to say that belief in the resurrection of Jesus was not in any obvious sense part of Hartshorne's religion.

During the Great War, Hartshorne not only began to clarify his ideas about deity and religion, he also formulated an answer to the question of the immediate data of experience. He had been considering whether the world could be divided between mind (which includes feeling) and matter (in the sense of substance devoid of feeling). On such a dualistic view, affective qualities are wholly products of the mind even if they are often projected by us onto the world. While enjoying a beautiful French landscape, it occurred to Hartshorne that the dualistic view (also a merely materialist view) is entirely inadequate as a description of what is given in experience. While he agreed that we sometimes project our emotions onto the world, it is also the case that our experience of the world is never lacking in affective qualities. As he says in his autobiography, "No, the colors I was experiencing were themselves feelings, and they were as truly given, experienced as facts, as anything at all" (DL 151). As with his initial thoughts on God, he would develop these reflections on experience and incorporate them into his mature philosophy. He eventually came to the view that experience is to be analyzed as "feeling of feeling"—a phrase he borrowed from Whitehead—most clearly evident in the experience of memory and less clearly evident, but no less real, in the experience of one's own body.[19]

What Hartshorne referred to as "the second period" of his intellectual development began when he enrolled at Harvard in 1919.[20] He majored in philosophy and minored in English literature. Among his teachers were James Haughton Woods (named after Hartshorne's maternal grandfather), W. E. Hocking, H. M. Sheffer, Ralph Barton Perry, C. I. Lewis, and the psychologist L. T. Troland. It was a rich intellectual environment in which to be nurtured. Among other things, it provided him with his first systematic introductions to formal logic and the history of philosophy. The more or less inchoate but clearly unorthodox ideas about deity with which he had been struggling took on further definition. Hocking convinced Hartshorne that God is not entirely immutable (EA xv).[21] After a class period, Hartshorne argued with Hocking that if the future is outside God, then God cannot be an all-inclusive being. Hocking quickly revealed the flaw in the reasoning by pointing out that, insofar as the future is partially indeterminate, there is no definite object of knowledge that could be outside of God's awareness (CAP 155). Put in more positive terms, as Hartshorne would later do, omniscience is by definition perfectly adequate to its objects, so it must include knowledge of the extent to which the future is or is not open given the restrictions of antecedent conditions. Admit the reality of temporal process and there must be a temporal aspect to an omniscient deity.

Hartshorne was awarded a Sheldon Traveling Fellowship for the years 1923–1925, so he had to decide whether or not to rush his dissertation to completion. A friend of his, Stuart Mudd, encouraged him to think through his options carefully. Hartshorne decided to finish the dissertation before leaving the country. In little over a month he had completed a dissertation of 306 pages titled *An Outline and Defense of the Argument for the Unity of Being in the Absolute or Divine Good* for which he was awarded the Ph.D. in May 1923 (DL 174). The broad outlines of his later thought are evident in the dissertation. He later referred to it as "a fantastically bold and comprehensive project" (EA xv) and he remarked that it was a form of process philosophy that was "somewhat naïve and best forgotten" (CAP 103).[22] Of course, it is not best forgotten if one wishes to trace the arc of Hartshorne's philosophical development. Although he never published any part of the dissertation, he was enormously productive throughout his career, writing twenty-one books and over five hundred articles and reviews appearing in many of the most prestigious journals in philosophy and religious studies.

One illustration may serve to contrast Hartshorne's dissertation with his later philosophy. In the dissertation, Hartshorne addressed the question of the compatibility of divine power and human freedom. He maintained that "an omnipotence incapable of providing for itself the power of watching over the development of genuine and hence in some degree self-active individuals is a shorn and assuredly a contradictory all-powerfulness." He goes on to speak of a "voluntary self-limitation of the Perfect Control over finite beings" as a "reasonable exercise of infinitely good Omnipotence."[23] These views prefigure, to some extent, Hartshorne's ideas that (a) each genuine individual is to some extent self-creative[24]; and (b) a power that wholly determines the decisions of partially self-determined creatures is a contradiction in terms— the perfection of power is found in the capacity to foster creativity in others (OO 17-18). Hartshorne's mature philosophy diverges from the dissertation in considering it best to drop the word "omnipotence" (OO 26; although see CH 269). In addition, the idea of God's voluntary self-limitation ceased to be a part of Hartshorne's thought. Since, as Hartshorne asserts in the dissertation, the identity of non-divine beings as separate from God "depends upon their reality as agents,"[25] it makes no sense to speak of God as refraining from exercising a power over beings that would render them nonexistent in the first place.

After graduation, Hartshorne left for Europe as a Sheldon Traveling Fellow. His first stop, in the summer of 1923, was England where he spent some weeks, then to Vienna and eventually to Germany, where he spent most of his time.[26] He also visited France. He was fluent in German and spoke French reasonably well. Although he says he foolishly missed an opportunity to meet Henri Bergson in 1923 (ZF 14), his travels were rich with intellectual stimulation. He encountered Moritz Schlick, Heinrich Gomperz, Lucien Lévy-Bruhl, Edouard Le Roy, Lucien Laberthonnière, Samuel Alexander, R. G. Collingwood, J. S. Haldane, G. E. Moore, G. F. Stout, Harold H. Joachim, Richard Kroner, Oskar Becker, Julius Ebbinghaus, Max Scheler, Max Planck, Adolf Harnack, Jonas Cohn, Paul Natorp, and Nicolai Hartmann. Two of the most famous philosophers he met and with whom he studied were Edmund Husserl and Martin Heidegger. On his return to the United States Hartshorne wrote the first English language review of Heidegger's *Sein und Zeit* (*Being and Time*); the review appeared in the *Philosophical Review* and was published as part of the penultimate chapter of his second book, *Beyond Humanism*. Hartshorne later wrote three articles on Husserl's philosophy.[27] The sojourn in Europe familiarized Hartshorne with the current thinking on the other side of the Atlantic, but he did not believe that the exposure to Husserl and Heidegger produced any "explicit new convictions" for him.[28] Philosophically, he was closer to Heidegger than to Husserl since he did not think it possible to simply "bracket the world"; he also argued that Husserl too readily accepted that value qualities in experience are tertiary.[29] His most complete statement on his relation to phenomenology, written late in life, is in the chapter in *Creative Experiencing* titled "My Eclectic Approach to Phenomenology" (CE 11–26).

For the next three years (1925–1928), Hartshorne was an Instructor and Research Fellow at Harvard, where he was simultaneously exposed to the two thinkers with whose philosophies he felt the most affinity,

Charles Sanders Peirce (1839–1914) and Alfred North Whitehead (1861–1947). Boxes of Peirce's unpublished manuscripts were donated to the Harvard library by Peirce's widow. Hartshorne was given the assignment of editing these papers. The daunting nature of editing the Peirce papers for the young philosopher was indicated in a vivid dream:

> I was introduced to [Peirce] as the man who was editing his writings. He looked at me with disapproval and said coldly, "What makes you think you are competent to edit my writings when you don't know science and mathematics?"[30]

In 1927 Paul Weiss (1901–2002) joined Hartshorne on the project. *The Collected Papers of Charles Sanders Peirce* was published in six volumes between 1931 and 1935 and became the standard edition of Peirce's work throughout the century. Although Hartshorne published enough articles on Peirce to fill a book—a total of seventeen—neither he nor Weiss thought of becoming Peirce scholars.

Hartshorne's duties at Harvard also included helping to grade papers for Whitehead, who joined the faculty in 1924 while Hartshorne was still in Europe. Hartshorne was never Whitehead's student in the technical sense, for he had been awarded the Ph.D. two years prior to meeting Whitehead and serving as his assistant. In this capacity, however, he witnessed the Englishman develop "the philosophy of organism" that found expression in Whitehead's Gifford Lectures, published in 1929 as *Process and Reality*, the year after Hartshorne left Harvard.[31] This book, as well as others written by Whitehead during this period, formed much of the foundation of twentieth-century process philosophy. The only work of Whitehead that Hartshorne had read prior to this time was *The Concept of Nature* (1920), which he quoted in his dissertation. For this reason, he remarked in an early article that his "first acquaintance with most of [Whitehead's] ideas was by means of the spoken rather than the written word."[32] Later, Hartshorne qualified this statement: his first acquaintance with *some* of Whitehead's ideas was through the spoken word (WP 21). Elsewhere he says that he "learned Whitehead's philosophy chiefly from his books."[33] Of course, the occasion of Hartshorne's reading most of Whitehead's books was the fact that he was stimulated by his personal encounter with the man.

Hartshorne's earliest writings, prior to meeting Whitehead, emphasize process and relativity as metaphysically basic; for this reason, he characterized his relation to Whitehead (also to Peirce) as one of pre-established harmony.[34] As he would write much on Peirce's philosophy, so he promoted Whitehead's importance in thirty-nine articles and reviews. Thirteen of these articles are collected in *Whitehead's Philosophy: Selected Essays 1935–1970* (1972). For a time Hartshorne considered himself a Peircean and a Whiteheadian, in each case, as he said, "with reservations"—in later years he tended to emphasize the reservations.[35] It is clear, in any event, that the exposure to Peirce and Whitehead helped focus his thinking. From Peirce (but contrary to Whitehead) Hartshorne accepted the idea that the realm of possibility is best conceived as a continuum with no least member. From Whitehead (but contrary to Peirce), Hartshorne accepted that actuality is atomic or discontinuous, composed of momentary flashes of experience, which Whitehead called actual occasions and Hartshorne called dynamic singulars. In Hartshorne's words, "Without Whitehead I should still have been a process philosopher, but probably one unable to extricate himself from the Zeno paradoxes."[36]

We have already mentioned Hartshorne's fondness for the expression "feeling of feeling," which he borrowed from Whitehead. He considered Whitehead's concept of prehension to be revolutionary in the way it brings together, within the scope of a single idea, causation, temporal asymmetry, perception, and memory (CAP, Ch. 9).[37] Hartshorne made measured use of Whitehead's technical vocabulary for expressing his own metaphysics that in some respects overlaps with Whitehead's, but, in other respects, is very different from it. For the most part, Hartshorne expressed himself in quite ordinary language, and the only prerequisites for understanding his meaning are a familiarity with the general tool kit of philosophical terms and the problems that philosophers address. In the fullness of time, Hartshorne's differences from Whitehead led some scholars to complain of an overly Hartshornean slant to Whitehead studies, thus bearing testimony to Hartshorne's dominance. According to one of Hartshorne's more well-known students, Hartshorne "associated his thought so much with Whitehead that his students often had difficulty distinguishing them. Today it is clear that there are extensive differences as well as extremely important agreements."[38] It seems clear that Hartshorne's deeper motivation was less to promote another philosopher's ideas than to express his own philosophy, and to enlist the help of others when it furthered this aim. Hartshorne referred to the years between 1925 and 1958 as his "third period" to highlight the significant influence of Peirce and Whitehead on his thinking.[39]

Hartshorne wrote, "I came to know Whitehead well, visiting him and his wife in their summer cottage in Vermont, and saw him later on several visits to Harvard after going to Chicago for my first full time teaching engagement."[40] Whether Hartshorne influenced Whitehead is a matter of speculation, but there is some enticing evidence.[41] Hartshorne wrote a review of Whitehead's *Symbolism: Its Meaning and Effect* (1927) in which he made two constructive criticisms.[42] First, he suggested that "sympathetic rapport" in social influence is as fundamental as time in the analysis of the present conforming to the past; second, he argued that emotional coloring is as intrinsic to the data of conscious sensory awareness (Whitehead's "presentational immediacy") as it is to the largely unconscious and vague feelings we have of our bodies and of the environment (Whitehead's "causal efficacy"). Whitehead read Hartshorne's review and his views in *Process and Reality*, published two years later, moved in the directions that Hartshorne suggested. Although Whitehead introduced the concept of prehension in *Science and the Modern World* (1925), the explicit identification of prehensions with "feelings" and the concept of the "subjective form of a prehension" do not appear until *Process and Reality* (1929). In *Process and Reality*, Whitehead holds that the primal element in physical experience is "sympathy." Likewise, he wrote, "the separation of the emotional experience from the presentational intuition is a high abstraction of thought."[43] It must be emphasized, however, that there is no documentation that Whitehead was influenced by Hartshorne's review nor did Hartshorne claim such an influence. It may be the case that Hartshorne's review nudged Whitehead to be more explicit about what was already implicit in his thinking. Hartshorne developed his own views of sensation and feeling at greater length in his first book, *The Philosophy and Psychology of Sensation* (1934), a book which Whitehead read.[44]

When Harvard announced that they had "no job" for Hartshorne after his third year of teaching and research, he took a position in 1928 at the University of Chicago, where he was a faculty member in the Department of Philosophy until 1955. He eventually held a joint appointment as a member of the Meadville Theological School (1943–1955). Shortly after the move to Chicago he married Dorothy Eleanore

Cooper (1904–1995), his lifelong companion, and the person he characterized as "the dearest friend I could ever have" (DL 44). By all accounts, it was a happy, somewhat traditional, and stable marriage. Hartshorne remarked, "Rarely can two people have been so serenely confident that they wanted each other" (DL 211).

The Hartshorne's only child, Emily (mentioned above), was born in 1940. Eventually, the Hartshornes had two grandchildren, Charles Andrew Goodman (b. 1975) and Eleanor Amy Goodman (b. 1979). At her father's memorial service, Emily's eulogy characterized her parents as forming a team.

> Dorothy contributed to Charles Hartshorne's career in many ways—as housewife and hostess, but also as editor and bibliographer. It is difficult to imagine his professional career without her. Emotionally they were invaluable to each other, providing support and reassurance.

Hartshorne often commented on his wife's editorial expertise.[45] The book published immediately after Dorothy was no longer able to help with editing—*Wisdom as Moderation* (1987)—sadly shows the evidence of her absence in several typos, garbled sentences, and missing footnotes. At no point do these mistakes seriously affect comprehension, but they are a reminder of this aspect of Dorothy's importance to her husband's career. For later books Hartshorne received editorial help from others. Emily's eulogy also provides insight into the quality of her parents' marriage:

> Their marriage allowed for the differences between them. My father understood how important musical performance was to my mother. She belonged to various choral groups and played the piano with other musicians. When I was a teenager, I developed an intense dislike for a man who shared my mother's passion for music. They seemed to have much too good a time together. I thought my father should do something about this friendship. He heard me out, and then he said, "I think I am not going to worry about it." He was right, of course.

Emily also commented on her father's parenting style:

> My father was not a disciplinarian by nature, but he could let

me know his disapproval if I misbehaved. One time, however, words failed him. I have no idea what I did, but I remember what I saw: My father was standing facing me, his fists clenched, and his fists were moving up and down, rapidly. He was angry, but not even the provocation of a child's defiance could cause him to hit that child. Gentle by nature, he was also influenced by the values he was taught by Episcopalian and Quaker relatives when he was growing up.

Emily indicated in her eulogy that her father did not expound his philosophy to her. However, it is of interest that Emily's son, Charles Goodman, became a philosopher with expertise in Buddhism.[46]

During his twenty-seven years at Chicago Hartshorne truly became his own philosopher, and his reputation grew nationally and internationally. His name appeared repeatedly as the author of articles (numbering 71), comments (25), and book reviews (79) in the premier journals of philosophy and religion such as *The Monist, The International Journal of Ethics, The Journal of Philosophy, Philosophy of Science, Philosophical Review, The Journal of Religion, Hibbert Journal, Philosophy and Phenomenological Research, Journal of Liberal Religion, Journal of the History of Ideas, The Personalist,* and *The Review of Metaphysics.* His articles were also featured in Germany, in *Philosophisches Jahrbuch,* and in France, in *Revue de Métaphysique et de Morale* and *Les Études Philosophique.* (In later years, he would also publish in *Environmental Ethics* and in the Oxford University journal *Mind,* among numerous others.) His earliest focus, reflected in his first book and in several articles, was to argue that sensory qualities are inherently value-laden and that they form an affective continuum. He quickly moved to the problems of metaphysics, outlining its methods and defending its claims against the fashionable positivism of the day. In addition to the Peirce papers, mentioned above, he published six books, including the wide-ranging survey of philosophical theology titled *Philosophers Speak of God* (1953), edited with his student William L. Reese. His other books during this period were: *Beyond Humanism: Essays in the Philosophy of Nature* (1937), *Man's Vision of God and the Logic of Theism* (1941), and *Reality as Social Process: Studies in Metaphysics and Religion* (1953). One finds in his articles and books a mature thinker who knows what he's about, developing a distinctive system of speculative philosophy that he would eventually call neoclassical metaphysics.

Shortly after arriving at Chicago, Hartshorne was admitted to the X-Club, a group of scientists that met on a monthly basis for dinner and to share their research. It was here that he made the acquaintance of the geneticist Sewell Wright, who he called "the finest scientific mind I have ever known intimately" (DL 228). Hartshorne reports that the X-Club allowed one philosopher to be a member—he was the replacement for E. A. Burtt who left Chicago in 1932 for Cornell University (PCH 31)—but this seems to be contrary to the official files that are kept at the University of Chicago Library's special collections department.[47] According to the files, only in the 1960s did the X-Club expand to include scholars from the Humanities, but this was after Hartshorne's departure for Emory in 1955. This suggests that Hartshorne was elected to the X-Club because of his work in empirical psychology. Given the earlier inclusion of Burtt, author of the celebrated *The Metaphysical Foundations of Modern Science*, it is also possible that they considered philosophers who were logicians and philosophers of science, like Rudolph Carnap, to be in fields not really distinguishable from mathematics and physics. Many philosophers of science were trading in papers that showed much competence in theoretical physics. Hartshorne was assigned to teach Symbolic Logic because of his training with Sheffer and Lewis prior to Carnap's arrival, and he published in the second volume of the University of Chicago's journal *Philosophy of Science,* so he might have been elected to the club for one or both of these reasons. It is more likely that his reputation as a psychologist was the main reason for his inclusion. In 1981, at the University of Chicago, at a conference celebrating Hartshorne's achievements, R. M. Martin said that Hartshorne was already well regarded for his work on the psychology of sensation when he was invited to Oxford to speak at the famous 1930 International Congress of Philosophy meeting.[48] The paper that Hartshorne presented at the Oxford conference, titled "Sense Quality and Feeling Tone," outlines themes that would become prominent in his first book, published four years later. At that time, he was not primarily associated with theology or philosophical theology.[49] Indeed, Hartshorne's first published piece specifically addressing the question of theism did not appear until 1934.[50] Hartshorne's dissertation notwithstanding, his first notoriety came as a philosopher interested in the psychology of sensation.

Hartshorne was also a member of the informal group of faculty largely sympathetic to Whitehead's philosophy called "the Chicago school," which originally included Henry Nelson Wieman, and later included Daniel Day Williams, Bernard Meland, and Bernard Loomer.[51] His many opportunities for travel included being a visiting faculty at Stanford University in 1937 and spending the 1941–42 academic year at the New School in New York. During 1948–49 he taught at Goethe University in Frankfurt. While in Germany, Jean Wahl arranged for Hartshorne to give lectures in Paris. On February 4, 1949, he spoke at the Sorbonne on "The Philosophical Principle of Relativity in Whitehead" which he wrote in French using a German dictionary.[52] Concerning the lecture, Hartshorne wrote:

> Giving the French lecture to the Sorbonne philosophers—I also gave it to another group—was the hardest two hours work I ever did. Or at least the part of the time spent fielding questions in French was that. It seemed a matter of sheer will to keep my attention on the questions and grope about in my mind for French words with which to answer them. My reward came several years later. I happened upon a French report of the occasion with the following concluding sentence: 'The many questions only served to show the speaker's mastery of the subject.' So if I had tried hard, it was not in vain. (DL 240–41)

The year 1949 also saw Hartshorne serve as President of the Western Division of the American Philosophical Association. He was a Fulbright Lecturer at Melbourne, Australia, during 1951–52. Also of note during Hartshorne's Chicago years is that during the summers of 1952 and 1953, with his wife's encouragement, Hartshorne did his first systematic scientific research on birdsong. At the end of the first summer, he hit upon the hypothesis of a "monotony threshold" in oscines, the hypothesis that song birds with more varied repertoires generally have shorter pauses between songs than those with less varied repertoires. This would tend to confirm the idea that birds have a primitive aesthetic sense. During the second summer, Hartshorne tested the hypothesis and found it confirmed (PCH 29–30). This was the beginning of Hartshorne's career as a professional, and later published, ornithologist.

Some of the most delightful anecdotes about Hartshorne concern his love of birds and his knowledge of oscines. Robert Kane and his wife knew Hartshorne from the time that the Kanes arrived at the University of Texas in 1970. Kane recounts the following:

In the fall, many different kinds of birds migrate through Austin heading south for the winter. My wife used to hang many feeders outside of the window over the kitchen sink. And when a bird fed there she did not recognize, she would call Charles on the phone. He would ask her to put the phone up to the open window so he could hear the bird, and invariably he would tell her what kind of bird it was.[53]

David A. Pailin, who helped represent process philosophy and theology in England, had this to say about Hartshorne and his fondness for birds:

> There is no schizophrenic break between this man and his beliefs, and it seems to me typical of both that the only 'payment' he wanted for giving a lecture in my department at Manchester was to be taken into the countryside to hear and enjoy bird song—not, as it happened, an easy payment to meet on a damp and misty autumn afternoon![54]

George Shields heard of a humorous miscommunication when the French philosopher Paul Ricoeur visited the University of Chicago.[55] While sitting together in the lobby of Swift Hall awaiting a meeting, Ricoeur asked Hartshorne, "What have you been working on lately?" Hartshorne responded, "Birdsong." Ricoeur, whose English was not quite fluent and who spoke with a strong French accent, became quite animated and responded, "Oh, oui, yes, Bergson! His philosophy is still important!" This set off a few confused exchanges with both philosophers in a state of obvious incomprehension. A graduate student who was standing nearby and overheard the exchange finally leaned in and said in a staccato fashion, "No, forgive me Prof. Ricoeur, but he is talking about bird-song, not Bergson." This was followed by hearty, bemused laughter. It would be difficult to find a more amusing illustration of Hartshorne's view that it is extremely easy, for numerous reasons, for philosophers to miscommunicate. Notwithstanding, doubtless, Hartshorne was equally interested in discussing Bergson.

Ralph K. M. Haurwitz, writing an obituary notice for Hartshorne in the *Austin-American Statesman*, told the following story, which, one may infer from the article, came from John Silber:

> Once, about 30 years ago [1974], he flew to Australia to be honored at a conference of philosophers. But the Australian

ornithological society, hearing about his impending arrival, sent a delegation to the airport and spirited him away to its own meeting. . . . The philosophers eventually caught up with him.[56]

The birds themselves could contribute to the humor. A serendipitous coincidence occurred in 1987 during the question-and-answer period after Hartshorne had given a talk. A woman wished to be reminded of something Hartshorne had said to her the previous day about the songs of birds. As she asked her question, a bird could be heard chirping in the background. Whether Hartshorne heard the bird is a fair question, but his response evoked laughter.

> Oh, in the sermons of Kierkegaard . . . he said we should consider the birds, those creatures who not only sing at their business but whose business it is to sing. So we should sing praises to God [Hartshorne chuckled] Kierkegaardian. . . . I treasure that because we know that there is a sense in which singing at least for a certain part of the year may be the main business almost that a male bird does. Sometimes a female does a lot of it too, especially in the tropics. That's one reason I like the tropics— the females sing more there [Laughter].[57]

Another anecdote concerning birds came from Philip Schwartz, Emily's husband. He told Don Viney this story: Philip asked Hartshorne what he thought of John Dewey; Hartshorne's terse reply was, "He didn't like birds." Of course, as a philosopher, Hartshorne had much more to say about Dewey, for he devoted two chapters in his books to his thought (BH Ch. 3; CAP Ch. 8).

In 1936 Hartshorne served as secretary (i.e., chairperson) of the department of philosophy, during which time Rudolf Carnap was hired. The hiring of Carnap was especially ironic since he was the most famous of the logical positivists and Hartshorne was one of positivism's greatest critics. It should also be noted, however, that Hartshorne combined criticism with appreciation, saying that the "new metaphysics" has more to learn from the positivists "than any other group of contemporary thinkers" (BH 295). He was friendly to the general semantic thesis that there is an *essential* connection between experience and meaning. Hartshorne reported that, despite his and Carnap's profound differences in philosophical outlook, their engagement was cordial and fruitful (in fact, Hartshorne was instrumental in supporting Carnap's appointment at Chicago). The German helped him to formalize his objection to the classical understanding of divine foreknowledge in his book *The Divine Relativity*. Carnap was important in another way because he helped to orchestrate Bertrand Russell's brief sojourn at Chicago during the winter of 1938–39. During this time, Hartshorne had several conversations with the Englishman (DL 311–14).

One can tell from the titles of Hartshorne's books that questions surrounding the idea of God and of religion were his major preoccupation. He told the story of a conversation in a men's room at the University of Chicago. A fellow member of the X club asked him, "Hartshorne, are you still working on God?" Immediately, the voice of Robert Maynard Hutchins (president of the university) was heard to reply, "He ought to let God work on him" (DL 323). Hartshorne also relates how Charner Perry advised him not to talk about God in his APA presidential address of April 29, 1949. He followed the advice (DL 242; cf. RSP Ch. 5). Nevertheless, in his larger corpus, he continued to reflect upon the idea of a God that brings order to the universe but who is affected by creaturely decisions and faces a relatively open future. It was during his Chicago years that he carried on a lively correspondence with the great Personalist philosopher, Edgar Sheffield Brightman (1884–1953). Hartshorne, while still at Harvard, first wrote to Brightman in 1922, but their dialogue began in earnest only in 1933 and it finally trailed off in 1945. Randall Auxier and Mark Davies, with some input from Hartshorne, shepherded the correspondence toward publication in the late 1990s. Their scholarly notes and essays for the published volume do much to contextualize and clarify what divided and what united the two philosophers (HB).[58] Two issues dominated the discussion between Hartshorne and Brightman: the manner of God's relation to the creatures and the question of pacifism—the latter issue obviously quite topical during the war years when the correspondence was carried on.

The fact that Hartshorne was a philosopher eager to tackle the problems of theism may explain why he attracted so many graduate students from Chicago's three federated seminaries. Two of these students became well-known theologians, John B. Cobb, Jr. (b. 1925) and Schubert Ogden (1928–2019) and one of them, Eugene H. Peters (1929–1983), became one of the first important interpreters of Hartshorne's life and thought.[59] Hartshorne was unhappy, however, that few graduate students in philosophy studied with him. Four of the most well-known students in Hartshorne's classes were Huston Smith (1919–2016), William P. Alston (1921–2009), William L. Reese (b. 1921), and Richard Rorty (1932–2007). Three of this group became known for defending views at odds with Hartshorne's ideas; Smith in religious studies, and Alston and Rorty in philosophy. Smith adhered to the perennial philosophy that Hartshorne was at pains to reject.[60] Alston also inclined to a timeless view of God, but he sought to incorporate into this classical view Hartshorne's idea of bilateral relations between God and the world (EA 78–98). For his part, Rorty disagreed sharply with his former teacher, but he made it clear that he never ceased to admire Hartshorne's intellectual passion and generosity of spirit.[61] Reese was co-editor with Hartshorne of *Philosophers Speak of God*. He downplayed his role in the book when he wrote that "All the ringing sentences of the book belong to Professor Hartshorne" (PCH 187).

Hartshorne and his family left Chicago and moved to Atlanta, Georgia, in 1955, where he taught at Emory University until 1962. His days at Emory coincided with the early days of the civil rights movement in Atlanta (1955–1962). Emory, at the time, did not admit people of color. It was a private school and its trustees argued that this exempted Emory from the 1954 Supreme Court decision of Brown v. Board of Education.[62] An additional motive for resisting integration was a 1917 state law that Georgia's private institutions risked forfeiture of their tax-exempt status if they admitted both white and black students.[63] Hartshorne sided with liberal anti-racists and acted on these convictions by submitting editorials on desegregation that were published in the *Atlanta Constitution*. As a consequence, he and wife Dorothy suffered hateful phone calls. Given the tenor of the South in those days, this was a brave thing to do, as threats were all too often hardly idle. Hartshorne also participated in some of the civil rights speaking events of Martin Luther King, Sr. and Benjamin Mays, then President of Morehouse College, whom the Hartshornes knew from Mays's time as a graduate student at the University of Chicago (DL 287–89). Hartshorne strongly believed that access to higher education was critical to the procurement of skills that would lead to the economic enfranchisement of persons of color, and that only economic enfranchisement would lead to genuine political equality. This much resembles the argument of W. E. B. DuBois in his famous "Atlanta compromise" essay published in DuBois's *The Souls of Black Folk*.

At Emory University, Bowman Clarke (1927–1996), Lewis S. Ford (1933–2018), and Rem B. Edwards (b. 1934) were Hartshorne's most well-known students. All made significant contributions to process philosophy and theology. In 1958 Hartshorne taught at the University of Washington and visited Kyoto, Japan, as a Fulbright Lecturer, where he learned more about Buddhism, which he called the first process philosophy.[64] It was also in Japan that he began a more intense focus on Anselm's ontological argument for God's existence. The argument had been a fixture of Hartshorne's thinking since his dissertation. He had published on the subject while at Chicago and had already identified two forms of the argument in Anselm (PSG 96). In his final year at Emory, however, he published, in the second chapter of *The Logic of Perfection* (1962), for the first time in the history of philosophy, a formalization of the argument using modal symbolism (LP 50–51). Soon afterwards came *Anselm's Discovery* (1965), which includes an overview of treatments of the argument in the works of various philosophers and theologians. Hartshorne described this time in his life as the beginning of his "fourth period," as he gained more critical distance from the philosophies of Peirce and Whitehead.[65]

Now in his sixties, Hartshorne faced mandatory retirement at Emory in a few years when he would turn 68. In 1962 John Silber, then at the University of Texas at Austin, invited Hartshorne to Texas. Hartshorne had just published *The Logic of Perfection*, which won the Lecomte du Noüy Award and was creating quite a stir with its unique application of modal logic to the ontological argument; numerous philosophers with training in logic were moved to respond in the professional journals. The University of Texas was awash in cash during an oil and gas boom, and Silber was an ambitious department chair dedicated to the Austin school's mission to become an elite research institution, a veritable "Harvard of the South." He recognized that Hartshorne was a "star" and so was determined not to take "no" for an answer. Silber sweetened the deal by offering the availability of housing near the University aviary. After some initial reluctance, and with Dorothy's blessing, Hartshorne accepted the invitation. Thus, in 1963, he became the Ashbel Smith Professor of Philosophy; he taught full time until his official retirement in 1978, and part time for a few years thereafter.

By the time Hartshorne arrived in Austin he was something of a philosophical celebrity, at least among those familiar with the world of professional philosophy. Jorge Nobo, who became a noted Whitehead scholar, came to the University of Texas in part to study with Hartshorne. He describes his first encounter in these words:

> I did not meet Hartshorne until the first day of his fall of 1966 seminar on Spinoza and Leibniz. Since he was one of the main reasons for my going to Texas, I was both eager and nervous to meet this giant of process philosophy. I think other first-year students in the seminar were equally nervous. There was a palpable tension in the room as we waited for Hartshorne to appear. Suddenly, a small secretary-chair rolled into the seminar room and came to a stop exactly at the head of the seminar table. A few seconds later, Hartshorne walked into the room, sat on the secretary-chair and began to discuss the requirements of the course and some key ideas of Spinoza and Leibniz. I don't know if it was Hartshorne's intention, but that secretary-chair rolling unattended into the seminar room was a rather funny event that did much to ease the tension in the room. Later Hartshorne would explain why he would push, pull, or "throw" that little chair into whatever meeting room he needed to be in. The chair was perfectly adjusted to the length of his torso and legs. It enabled him, a short man grown shorter with age, to comfortably maintain good posture—something he was not able to do with standard-sized chairs and sofas. Here he entered into a sustained critique of a furniture industry that, with a one size fits all philosophy, neglected the health and comfort of people whose height was significantly below or above average. He made it clear that, until he first tried a secretary-chair, he had suffered from frequent neck, back, and leg pains.[66]

When Nobo began teaching as a graduate student he shared an office with Hartshorne for at least one semester; this led to frequent conversations and shared meals where the two would discuss philosophy as well as issues of the day.

Nobo learned that Hartshorne and his wife did not own an automobile, so he offered his services to chauffeur them to doctor's appointments and the like. Hartshorne was particularly pleased with Nobo's Volkswagen Beetle. In Nobo's words:

He praised the Beetle as a comfortable but reasonably sized car. He compared it most favorably with the huge gas-guzzling cars Detroit was putting out at that time. Oil, he held, is a valuable but finite resource. It should not be wasted.[67]

Hartshorne's ideas about the Beetle and the consumption of oil were part of a larger concern with moderation and the American tendency to value oversized products, be it automobiles, furniture, or food portions at restaurants. Here again are Nobo's words:

> Americans' love of large gas-guzzling cars was one of the reasons Hartshorne gave for claiming that moderation was a neglected virtue in our culture. Another reason was the building of ever larger, energy wasting homes with ever bigger water-wasting yards to match. But the most important reason, the one that bothered him the most, was our culture's casual waste of vast quantities of food. Grocery stores, restaurants, and homes threw out perfectly edible foods that did not look fresh. Immoderately large servings were the norm in restaurants and in no small number of homes. Large portions of such servings remained untouched and were thrown out with the garbage. When millions of people, at home or abroad, go hungry or starve on a daily basis, any needless wasting of food is an immoral act. Hartshorne acted as he preached, perhaps to an extreme. Servings on his plate were always modest in size and, at the end of the meal, his plate would be empty—literally. Anything too small for fork or spoon, he would have mopped up with bread or picked up with his knife or fingers. He was particularly adept at using an index finger to pick up a grain of rice here or a crumb of bread there.[68]

Nobo's memory of Hartshorne's preoccupation with the evils of wasting resources and with the virtues of moderation are echoed in Hartshorne's 1987 book *Wisdom as Moderation*. We shall see in our penultimate chapter that Hartshorne was not opposed to technological innovation and modernization, but he believed they should be tempered by moderation and a concern for overall human well-being.

Nobo remembers that Charles and Dorothy Hartshorne were in the habit of hosting two dinners at their house, one for students and one for faculty. According to Nobo, "generosity, kindness, and hospitality were much in evidence."[69] Nobo's report matches that of Norman Pittenger, a noted Whitehead scholar who knew the Hartshornes well. According to Pittenger:

> Their home in Austin, Texas, is a lovely place, where friends and other guests are always welcome and where anyone who visits them is aware of a loving care which surely is a manifestation of the divine charity. If a basic metaphysic ought to reflect itself in human behavior, the insistence that God is sheer Love in act, upon which Charles Hartshorne has written and spoken so much and always with the help and support of his wife, is vividly and compellingly expressed in the Hartshornes' generosity, unfailing kindness, and gracious hospitality.[70]

Hartshorne says that he was sometimes accused of liking everyone. He indicated that this was not true, but he explained: "What is true is that those I have disliked are a small minority" (DL 20). In a letter to Robert Corrington he wrote:

> It has been my experience that if I ever like a person I usually do right away. The best people are usually for me transparently good. Few people are transparently bad and it was years before it dawned on me why. Wickedness soon learns it has to hide, or knows that from the start.[71]

If Hartshorne liked most of those he met, it is a fair guess that most of those he met also liked him, a fact to which the authors of this book can attest.

Robert Kane, Hartshorne's colleague at the University of Texas, attests to his friend's magnanimity. Kane indicates that he shared common ground with Hartshorne in his sympathy for process theology and his critique of classical ideas about God. In the 1980s and 1990s, Kane often invited Hartshorne to his philosophy of religion classes. Kane recounts an episode which reveals something of Hartshorne's character:

> One time when I picked him up at his house to take him to my graduate class, my car was blindsided in the heavy traffic by another car that smashed into the passenger side where Charles was sitting. An ambulance had to be called and I went with him

in it to the hospital, since my car had to be towed. When the ambulance bed was wheeled into a corridor awaiting admission to the emergency room, Charles looked up to me and saw that I had tears in my eyes. I was shaken by the whole incident and felt it was somehow my fault; and when I looked down at his frail man well into his 90s, I couldn't stop the tears. When he saw this, he reached his hand out from under the white cover, grabbed my hand and said: "Don't worry. I'll be all right. It was not your fault. I'm just sorry we missed your class." It turned out he had a broken collarbone and some other broken bones. But the kindness he showed to me, despite the pain he must have been in, is something I will never forget.[72]

Hartshorne's kindness was also on display when Kane's son died at the age of twenty-seven in 1993 in a tragic accident. Kane says that Hartshorne was one of those leading the way in offering comfort to the family.[73]

During Hartshorne's years at Texas he taught and traveled widely—throughout the United States, including two summer sessions at Colorado College (1977 and 1979), but also to India and Japan on a third Fulbright (1966), Australia (1974), the University of Louvain, Belgium (1978), and again to Japan and Hawaii (1984). Throughout his life, Hartshorne's travels took him to every continent, although he never visited any part of Russia, and he visited Kenya and Uganda in Africa only as an ornithologist.[74] Hartshorne's productivity in the last three decades of his life was prodigious, beginning with four major works; these included the aforementioned book on Whitehead, the book on birdsong, as well as *A Natural Theology for Our Time* (1967) and *Creative Synthesis and Philosophic Method* (1970), the latter being his most comprehensive and systematic presentation of neoclassical metaphysics.[75] After becoming an octogenarian, he published dozens of articles, reviews, and forewords, and completed numerous books. He once remarked that he was trying to write the best philosophy of anyone in their eighties.[76] He gave his most complete assessment of Western philosophy in *Insights and Oversights of Great Thinkers: An Evaluation of Western Philosophy* (1983) and in *Creativity in American Philosophy* (1984). *Omnipotence and Other Theological Mistakes* (1984) is a nontechnical introduction to his philosophical theology. The posthumously published *Creative Experiencing: A Philosophy of Freedom* (2011), completed during the 1980s, complements *Wisdom as Moderation: A Philosophy of the Middle Way* (1987), and more or less rounds out the technical metaphysical work begun in *Creative Synthesis*.

While Hartshorne's philosophical and political views remained relatively stable throughout his life, he was neither inflexible nor dogmatic. This is nowhere more evident than in the change he made late in life from using exclusive language for the creatures and God to using inclusive language. We do not know what triggered the change, but it was something about which he felt passionately. We quoted above from the 1987 question-and-answer session after one of his talks; another exchange from that session illustrates both his humor and his passion about the subject. Viney was at the talk and noticed that several times during the delivery of the paper, Hartshorne slipped into his former exclusivist language. A woman in the audience began to comment on this by saying, "I noticed that you've chosen the masculine pronoun for God . . ." Before she could finish the sentence, Hartshorne replied, obviously upset with himself. "I never . . . I hardly use it at all . . . I didn't mean to use it at all. I'm sorry. I never do that very deliberately. I'm against that." He continued, still a bit flustered:

> I'm a feminist in those things. [Laughter] I didn't mean to do it. I didn't know I had. I tried to avoid it—repeat the word 'God'. I usually now prefer . . . I used to write . . . when I wrote, I did it, I admit. That's one thing I repent of in my writings. [Laughter] No, you can't . . . I have no intention of being an anti-feminist in any way, whatever. That is one of the things that makes me ashamed of my sex.[77]

We shall see in Chapter Nine that Hartshorne's feminism extended well beyond a mere change of pronouns. Feminism is a subject on which his views did not waver.

The last of Hartshorne's books to appear during his lifetime, *The Zero Fallacy and Other Essays in Neoclassical Philosophy* (1997), published in the year of his centenary, was edited by Muhammad Valady, a philosopher he met in 1985. Valady made a thorough study of Hartshorne's works and engaged him in conversation on a regular basis over lunch. Valady compiled the essays in *The Zero Fallacy* to reflect the full range of Hartshorne's thinking, including his empirical work on sensation and on birdsong. Approximately half of the book is comprised of essays not previously published. The book opens with a "brisk dialogue" between Hartshorne and Valady that conveys both the charm of a conversation with the aging philosopher as well as the keenness of his mind in dealing with philosophy. Robert Kane also attests to Hartshorne's mental clarity late in life.

> He remained quite clear and lucid and explaining his own views in these graduate classes and in our discussions of the issues even up through the 90s when he himself was in his 90s. He did have some short memory lapses towards the end in the 90s, so that if the students asked multiple questions, he would have to be reminded what the questions were. But as soon as reminded, he would go right into a lengthy discourse on the required subject without any missed steps.[78]

The last letter that Viney received from Hartshorne, dated April 2, 1995, confirms Kane's observations. The letter is handwritten, but quite legible. Hartshorne wrote, "I can still think, but it takes more time & only my *SCM* word processor makes it possible. Typing no longer possible, too many mistakes, clumsy fingers."[79]

Hartshorne achieved an unofficial status as being in the pantheon of twentieth-century philosophers when the Library of Living Philosophers devoted the twentieth volume to him (PCH).[80] This volume was preceded by three other books that were devoted exclusively to his thought (EA, HP, CH). Hartshorne contributed to each of these books, giving detailed replies to a total of sixty-two essays by fifty-six scholars. His responses fill approximately one-fourth of the pages in these volumes. In addition, as we have already mentioned, in his nineties, he gave editorial advice on the first published volume of his correspondence (HB). With good reason, as noted in the preface, he expressed concern that philosophers might find it difficult to stay abreast of his writing.

Hartshorne's productivity late in life was all the more remarkable in view of the circumstances at home. Emily says that her parents seemed to have an "inexhaustible vitality" long past retirement as they traveled the world. Sometime during 1985, however, Dorothy Hartshorne began to slow down. In Emily's words:

> My mother started to have symptoms of dementia. At that time I lived far away and had children who needed me, so I couldn't

do much to help. I have always admired my father, but never more than when he undertook to manage the household and care for his mentally disabled wife. It was obvious to him that it was his duty to do so, but living up to it was a terrible strain for him. Always slim, he lost ten pounds in the years that he cared for my mother at home. Finally, her condition deteriorated to such an extent that friends and family were able to persuade him that she would be better off in a nursing home, with professional care.[81]

Dorothy Hartshorne passed away at the age of ninety-one on November 21, 1995. Her husband would live another five years.

In his final years, Hartshorne's productivity came to an end as he was increasingly unable to manage his affairs, but his mind remained very clear and sharp for most of this time, as is evident from interviews he gave in April 1997 (two months from his one-hundredth birthday) and in October 1998.[82] In October 1997 he made a brief appearance at a birthday celebration and symposium at the University of Texas arranged by Robert Kane. At that gathering he said, "Old age is almost a disease itself. I have no nameable disease . . . I can't think as fast as I used to. I can't do anything as fast."[83] He was cared for partly by his daughter and by a full-time caregiver, Charles Richey. Richey and Hartshorne lived together in the house along with a dog named Plato. In September 1999, Richey sent out a report on the process philosophy listserve on Hartshorne's daily routines. He explained that Hartshorne was free of pain and disease, slept most of the day, and had lost the vitality characteristic of his earlier years. He still entertained visitors for brief periods. He also enjoyed having his hair trimmed at a local barbershop, The Sportsman, which Richey described as an old-fashioned male bastion stuffed with local game trophies. The barbers made a fuss over him, carrying on for his amusement, calling him "Perfessor." That Hartshorne retained his wit is indicated by Richey's remark, "He now refers to the place as the greatest institution he knows, indeed, the greatest possible." Charles Hartshorne died in his sleep on Yom Kippur, October 9, 2000 (incorrectly reported as October 10th by *The New York Times*).[84]

Anyone who knew Charles Hartshorne has a favorite story about him. Many of these stories involve his absentmindedness. Hartshorne knew of his reputation as an absentminded professor and commented on it.

A few of the stories that came back to me did happen. I did dismiss a two-hour seminar once at the end of the first hour but returned on remembering, at the bottom of the stairs, what the situation was and found the students still in the room discussing the matter. Once I accepted a cigarette from a certain physicist, put it in my mouth, then snatched it out again and said, "But, I don't smoke." The explanation, however, makes sense. I did for some twenty years smoke slightly, off and on, never a lot, but some months prior to the incident in question, I had decided once for all to give up smoking. I had had no appreciable addiction and felt no special trouble carrying out this decision. Momentarily, I had forgotten it, and any way, talking with a physicist of competence I had my mind on something more interesting than my relation to tobacco. (DL 19–20)

Hartshorne was not amused by all of the stories that circulated about him. In February 1988, the authors attended a conference given in Hartshorne's honor at the University of Texas at Austin. During one of the sessions, Hartshorne was sitting next to Viney as a speaker related a story about Hartshorne asking a student about the child in her baby carriage. According to the speaker, the student replied, "But Professor Hartshorne, I'm your babysitter and that's Emily."[85] Hartshorne, clearly annoyed, whispered to Viney, "That never happened. I'd never forget my own baby."[86] In his autobiography Hartshorne calls such stories "absurd" (DL 20).

Some anecdotes involving absentmindedness might just as well be described as examples of his single-minded focus on philosophical questions. The authors cannot verify the following, but it has a ring of truth about it. According to the tale, Hartshorne was crossing campus and stopped to speak with someone. After the conversation he asked, "From which way did I walk?" The other person pointed the direction and Hartshorne replied, "Oh, good, then I must have had lunch already." Some stories involve Hartshorne's reputation for being witty and others are simply charming in the light they cast on his personality. The authors attended a conference in Atlanta, Georgia, in March 2002 and heard the following. Hoyt Oliver, who taught at Oxford College at Emory University and took a class on Whitehead from Hartshorne, recounted this story: Hartshorne had been lecturing and wiped chalk on his blue jacket. A few minutes later he noticed the chalk and said, "I must get a chalk-colored jacket." William L. Power, who teaches in the Religion Department at the University of Georgia, was a graduate student when Hartshorne was teaching at Emory. Power was making money by working at an Atlanta clothing store. Hartshorne entered the store, wearing his usual frumpy and somewhat ill-fitted clothes. He became fascinated with a dark colored coat with white buttons. According to Power, the coat was the oldest in the store and the management had despaired of selling it. Hartshorne looked at the coat for quite some time. Finally, the manager whispered to young William, "We need to get that bum out of the store." Power did not say what he said to the manager, but he did relate that Hartshorne bought the coat.

One particularly memorable episode that illustrates how passionate Hartshorne could be about philosophical argument was related by Alan Gewirth at the 1981 University of Chicago conference that honored Hartshorne.[87] Gewirth and Hartshorne, who were colleagues at Chicago, would sometimes share a meal at Ida Noyes Hall and discuss philosophy. Gerwirth recounted that, at one point in his career, he was convinced that Aristotle's theory of substance was correct. He and Hartshorne debated the issue with Hartshorne criticizing Aristotle and defending instead an ontology of events. After a particularly lively exchange, Gewirth dismissed himself in order not to be late to class. As Gewirth was walking back to Cobb Hall to lecture he heard rapid foot steps behind him. He turned and to his astonishment it was Hartshorne who promptly threw a fistful of crunched corn flakes at him. As Gewirth told the story, Hartshorne's voice was rising in a pique of anger as he exclaimed, "How many substances do I have now, Gewirth? How many now?"

Hartshorne could be totally unflappable and remarkably focused during public disputations. On one occasion witnessed by Shields, he was presenting a commentary on Robert Neville's then just-published book on *Creativity and God* (1980) at an American Academy of Religion Symposium on the philosophy of religion. Hartshorne spoke before a large audience that filled a hotel auditorium to capacity. About midway through his presentation, without any warning and in mid-sentence, Hartshorne suddenly dropped to the floor. A horrified gasp was audible from the audience. Given his advanced age, surely many were wondering whether or not they had just witnessed Hartshorne's death by heart attack or stroke. However, as the podium participants (including Neville and Lewis Ford) immediately came to his aid, Hartshorne arose and gently swept his jacket. Without the slightest sign of embarrassment or hesitation or explanation or comment or coughing or breathing difficulty of any kind, he continued reading his paper at the exact place he had left off prior to his fall. Had it not been so potentially serious, the scenario would have been almost comical. No doubt the audience members were glad to learn of Hartshorne's safety, but were amazed at his total intellectual concentration. It was as if he was saying to the audience through his actions, "what matters is philosophy and my train of thought, not the position of my body in space!"

Hartshorne enjoyed the repartee and the give-and-take of philosophical discussion at professional conferences. In 1984, at the University of Nebraska, Hartshorne commented on a paper by James Ross.[88] He stood up from his chair and prefaced his remarks by saying, "Your paper is well argued and, I think, mostly correct. This is the second time I have heard you deliver such a fine paper. It has been some time since I heard the other paper." When the laughter subsided, he asked Ross whether he believed that his position entailed that God does not know future free decisions. Ross replied, with as much wit as respect, "With your commendation, I don't want to risk saying something I may later regret." Hartshorne, who had been seated next to Viney, sat down and whispered to him, "He is a capable fellow."[89]

Hartshorne was self-confident and understood his importance to philosophy, but he was not condescending. He respected those who presented reasoned arguments against him or could show him a flaw in his reasoning, including his students. His account of an exchange with his one-time student Norman Martin is instructive:

> Once I put a formal argument on the board: with a cordial smile Norman showed me the fallacy. Next day I tried again. Again a smiling identification of a mistake. The third time, the argument in its revised form was accepted. I am always charmed by students who can correct me without fear or conceit, and with a smile. (DL 234)

Martin recounts the same events in his contribution to The Library of Living Philosophers volume on Hartshorne. His reflections reveal something of the character of his teacher:

> The beauty of this exchange lay not only in his ability to

take criticism from students . . . but that the whole exchange was carried out with total good humor and a total lack of defensiveness or hostility, certainly on his part and I hope also on mine. What was important to Hartshorne was the truth of the matter and it bothered him not at all that the criticism came from a baby-faced novice with more experience in directing artillery fire than arguing points on philosophy. (PCH 340)

When Martin was later a candidate for a position at the University of Texas, Hartshorne enthusiastically supported his appointment, in large part because of his memory of his earlier exchange with Martin. Reflecting on his time in Texas as Hartshorne's colleague, Martin said, "The last twenty years have taught me that this experience is in no way a 'fluke'; Hartshorne is not only admirable in the creativeness of his thought, but also in the beauty of his soul" (PCH 340).

If Hartshorne could accept criticism from others, he could also be devastating in criticizing others, even unintentionally so. Emily Schwartz shared with Viney a letter that Hartshorne received from a university press concerning a foreword he had written for another author's book. The publisher opened the letter by saying that he had "some rather awkward news to communicate." He explained that the press had decided not to publish Hartshorne's essay because it was "just too damned good." According to the publisher, Hartshorne had penetratingly analyzed the author's arguments, refuted them, and offered a compelling alternative. After Hartshorne's foreword, no reader "would feel inclined to read the work itself." The book was published, but with another scholar's foreword. Hartshorne was hardest on those he believed had not done their historical and philosophical homework. He expressed great frustration with what he took to be the carelessness with which Anselm's ontological argument had been treated. Far too many readers of Anselm, he claimed, had proceeded no further than Chapter Eleven of *Proslogion*, while lionizing Gaunilo's reply on behalf of the fool, and declared Anselm refuted. According to Hartshorne, "A grosser failure of scholarship will not, I think, be found, considering that it went without effective challenge for centuries" (AD 4).

Few people are as fortunate or as gifted as Charles Hartshorne to have lived as long and productive a life as he did. He never failed to emphasize the extent to which luck played a role in his success. At the age of 76 he wrote, "To what do I owe my success, such as it is? Five words sum it up: good luck and good management. If asked which element predominates, I reply, the luck."[90] The subtitle of Hartshorne's autobiography also neatly encapsulates this idea: "A Philosopher Reflects Upon His Fortunate Career and Those Who Made It Possible." No one chooses their parents, their genetic endowment, the conditions of their upbringing, or even the larger swath of paths initially available in their life. The lottery of life gave Hartshorne good parents, a healthy constitution, a solid upbringing, conscientious teachers, and a society where his talents could be explored and developed. He generally made decisions that promoted his welfare and those of others, but he also dodged the accidents and tragedies that can cut life short. During his time as an orderly in France he choked on a piece of meat and a fellow orderly named Jabot performed the Heimlich maneuver (before it acquired that name), thereby saving his life. Hartshorne called it "fake theology" to suppose that God had providentially intervened to save his life at that moment. "I have no use for the notion that God cares about *me* yet not about the ones for whom there is no Jabot in the moment of need" (DL 139–40). Hartshorne had another close call in 1975. Dorothy sent a message to the journal *Process Studies* that on November 7th, he had been knocked down by a car on his way to a Ph.D. examination, resulting in five broken bones and twenty lacerations and contusions.[91] About twenty years later, he suffered more broken bones in the accident with Kane. The second piece of Hartshorne's formula for success—good management—is also, to a great extent, a matter of luck. For most of us, instruction from parents, friends, and especially role models of those who have successfully managed their affairs, are preconditions of whatever success we may enjoy. Hartshorne was no exception.

Hartshorne emphasized that it was precisely good fortune that afforded him certain philosophical advantages. He referred to his longevity as his secret weapon. In conversation with Muhammad Valady, he said:

> [Of] all the philosophers who have ever lived a long life, I may well be the one who has had by far the greatest opportunity to profit from critical evaluations while still able to react energetically to these appraisals. (ZF 41)

He was confident of his judgments, a confidence that some believed verged on conceit, as Hartshorne well knew (DL 308). He certainly had the ability to laugh at himself, but he was not amused by a parody of him by students at Chicago which portrayed him as an eccentric philosopher without ideas. "Eccentric I may be, make fun of my ideas if you please, but to accuse me of having no ideas . . . Show me a living philosopher in this country with more" (DL 249). Of course, the world of philosophy is a world where ideas matter, so the parody was tantamount to characterizing him as a fool who took himself to be a thinker. In his own assessment, "Stupidity has never been my problem."[92] As for the parody, it was Hartshorne who had the "last laugh" as his influence has arguably outshone virtually every member of the University of Chicago Philosophy Department at the time this parody took place. For example, in a 1990–91 survey of the state of the discipline, Nicholas Rescher listed Hartshorne as among the most referenced of American philosophers.[93] Another example: in 1998, at a (belated) celebration of Hartshorne's centenary, George R. Lucas, Jr. noted that Hartshorne is cited in *The Philosopher's Index* at "rates characteristic of Wittgenstein, Whitehead, Heidegger, Sartre, and other acknowledge giants of the century."[94] Lucas also reported that it was well known at the State University of New York Press, which published six of Hartshorne's books (and several others about him), that Hartshorne's books would be "best sellers" in the sense that enough copies would be sold to subtend the works of less successful authors. One can be confident that these facts do not reflect a man who lacked ideas.

When asked for his opinion of Hartshorne, Karl Popper reportedly responded, "Well . . . he is a theologian . . . but he argues" (PCH 650). Hartshorne took Popper's comment as a compliment, even though he did not consider himself a theologian.[95] In an unpublished and untitled statement of little over two pages, Hartshorne wrote, "Am I a theologian? The obvious and in a sense right answer is, no." He went on to explain, among other things, that he was influenced by what could be called revealed theology, but that he came closest to being a theologian in doing natural theology. But Popper was accurate to say that Hartshorne gave arguments. Hartshorne prided himself on seeking out and being able to accurately represent the best objections to his own views—in short, to avoid the straw man / straw woman fallacy.[96] In reference to Thomas Aquinas, he said, "When I compare my opportunities to think adequately with those of any thirteenth century writer, especially one with so short a life as Thomas's, I think I must be stupid if I have done no better than he" (CH 276). Hartshorne's boasts, however, only came after he had allowed his arguments to do the heavy lifting. If he did not lack for ideas, he also did not lack for arguments. He considered himself in the company of Peirce and Whitehead, two philosophers who he characterized as being "in the general neighborhood of basic metaphysical truth."[97] Nevertheless, in confronting the impasses that he found in his own philosophy, and recognizing the many obstacles to communication and clear thinking, he was undeniably a fallibilist; he asked, "And if we cannot agree, can any of us have the right to be sure?"[98]

The life of a modern academic is only rarely a life of intrigue and action and Hartshorne's life was no exception. His adventures were what Whitehead called "adventures of ideas." Nevertheless, those who knew the man have recognized that there was no dichotomy between his life and his philosophy. As he thought about life, so he endeavored to live it. John Wild, a philosopher with whom he had sharp disagreements, had this to say about Hartshorne:

> All who know him are aware of his amazing capacity to bring out the meaning of a haphazard incident that arises during a taxi ride to an official meeting, or on a casual walk through a city park. He can bring basic aspects of his philosophy to bear on the call of a bird or the flavor of Indian tea. His reflections are not isolated in a separate compartment of his mind. They are merged and fused with his life. I believe that what he says and what he writes wells up from a deep personal concern for life, and for the current problems, aesthetic, moral, and religious, of living man. I think of him as a philosopher who is engaged, concerned.[99]

As we shall have occasion to see in Chapter Nine, while Hartshorne is often cubbyholed as a metaphysician with a penchant for abstraction and rationalism (and a special fondness for and knowledge of songbirds), his philosophy in fact meets the criteria of being what Jean Wahl called "a philosopher of existence."[100]

What is evident in a study of Hartshorne's life and writings is that his was a unique chemistry of genuine kindness, epistemic humility, argumentative rigor, and speculative audacity.

TWO

The Affective Continuum
and the Theory of Sensation

HARTSHORNE'S FIRST PUBLISHED BOOK was *The Philosophy and Psychology of Sensation* (1934), the result of his intense philosophical interest in aesthetic motifs proffered by Peirce and Whitehead, and his longstanding interest in empirical psychological inquiries into sensation begun under Troland at Harvard. This interest in empirical inquiries continued with Hartshorne's study of some European experimental psychologists such as Julius Pikler, whose name is sometimes paired with Hartshorne's in the literature on sensation.[1] Hartshorne argues for a theory that, in his view, integrates leitmotifs of evolutionary biology with experimental and phenomenological data found in intersensory analogies, with aesthetic and religious values, and with an overall enhancement of intelligibility or the "unity of knowledge." The work was written when interest in sensation had dwindled under the influence of American behaviorist theory, when the odd indifference of William James to considerations of sensation was still lingering, and when psychologists were little interested in grand theoretical integrations, including integrations with evolutionary theory. Hartshorne once referred to his first book as the work of an amateur, but it is clearly not amateurish (RSP 80). The work, arguably ahead of its time, can be much better appreciated now than when it was first published.

Hartshorne began thinking seriously about sensation after an experience he had while serving as an orderly in France during the Great War. As he stood on a cliff looking over a scene of great natural beauty, George Santayana's phrase "beauty is objectified pleasure" came to him. Hartshorne rejected that slogan on the basis of what he was experiencing. It seemed to him that the pleasure was not experienced in himself as a subject and only then projected onto nature; rather, the pleasure was itself *given as in the object*. He concluded that experience, all experience, is saturated with affect, given in emotional terms. In his words, "Nature comes to us as constituted by feelings, not as constituted by mere lifeless, insentient matter" (PCH 17–18). The point is not that we never attribute more to an object than what the object contains; it is, rather, that objects are never given to us in experience as completely lacking affective tone. Hartshorne never strayed from the conviction that *matter devoid of feeling* is an abstraction from experience and not a datum of experience.

Hartshorne's theory is organized around the defense of five theses: (1) the sensory modalities exhibit quantitative continuity, exhibiting no absolute difference of kind; (2) sensory qualia are essentially affective (a theme echoed in the early Heidegger with whom Hartshorne studied); (3) all experience is analyzable as essentially social in the Whiteheadian sense of "feeling of feeling"; (4) sensation is essentially "adaptive" in the evolutionary biological sense; and (5) sensory qualia have a common origin in evolutionary history. The whole doctrine might be conveniently labeled as the "affective continuum hypothesis." The third item is central to the thesis of panexperientialism, which Hartshorne defended throughout his career. In view of its importance to his metaphysics, it requires separate discussion (see Chapter Four). Here the focus is on an exposition of the other mentioned theses.

Hartshorne remarked that "perhaps the most brilliant of those [conceptions] we owe to the fertile brain of Charles Peirce" (PPS 208) is the idea of particular qualities emerging from a continuum. Hartshorne, like Peirce, conceived the qualitative continuum as without definite qualities; however, unlike Peirce, Hartshorne conceived it as having definite dimensions. Otherwise, Hartshorne argued, the qualitative continuum would coincide with Aristotle's prime matter and would be equally unintelligible. Hartshorne proposed that three qualitative pairs of variables characterize experience as a social-affective continuum. He names the pairs as activity-passivity, positive-negative (or joy-sorrow), and intensity-faintness (PPS 196, 224). According to Hartshorne, pairs of sensory qualities correspond to these dimensions. In the color spectrum, the corresponding pairs are red-green (for active-passive), yellow-violet (for positive-negative), and white-black (for intense-faint). In Hartshorne's evolutionary account of sensory qualities, this means, for example, that the very redness of red is its character of exciting activity, as in activating nerve endings, sweating, and aggressive behavior.

In his summary of Hartshorne's theory, Lawrence E. Marks refers to this aspect of the theory as "remarkable." Marks explains:

> That designation [i.e. remarkable] stems largely from subsequent empirical evidence, which accords with the idea that three common, bipolar dimensions underlie all sensory experience. For it turns out that the same three dimensions that Hartshorne derived have been established, it appears totally independently, from studies on the connotative meanings of verbal concepts.[2]

Marks cites a 1957 study by Osgood, Suci, and Tannenbaum that attempted to map all important dimensions of meaning by means of an experiment that presented subjects with fifty bipolar dimensions, many of which were sensory quality pairs.[3] The subjects then rated each of the pairs on a graph so as to fix their perceived meaning. The researchers' analysis of the results distilled three major factors which they called *activity*, *evaluation*, and *potency*. As Marks summarizes, "The three factors derived through the semantic differentiation of concepts correspond exactly, or almost exactly, to the bipolar dimensions that Hartshorne proposed underlie sensory quality."[4]

Despite this striking consilience, Marks points out that not all of the results of the study confirmed Hartshorne's one-to-one correspondence of specific sensory qualities to three basic pairs of contrasts. In a word, peoples' semantic evaluations of sensory adjectives did not always match "the specific affective representations that Hartshorne proposed."[5] The agreement with Hartshorne was greatest on the pairing of active-passive with red-green. However, the study also revealed evaluative connections such as red-bad and green-good. The results were furthest from Hartshorne's predictions in the failure to find any correlation between evaluation (joy-sorrow) and the yellow-violet pair. Marks points out that the results of the study are not a simple disconfirmation of specific correlations projected by Hartshorne, for the subjects were assessing the *conception* of the sensory qualities through verbal names. In addition, it must be noted that one would have to take care in separating the strictly biological factors from the cultural factors in the valuation of sensory qualities, a problem of which Hartshorne was well aware, as we shall shortly see. What seems clear is that Hartshorne was on the right track in positing and searching out the intrinsic hedonic dimensions of sensory qualities and in correctly surmising the triad of bipolar pairs as the broad outlines of the dimensions of sensory experience.

Hartshorne rejected the "classical" doctrine of Hermann von Helmholtz that the various sensory modalities (visual, olfactory, tactile, gustatory, and auditory experiences) are tightly compartmentalized, allowing no degrees of lesser or greater similarity, and no transition from one modality to another. According to the classical doctrine, while degrees of qualitative similarity or analogy might be permissible within a given sensory modality (e.g., dark magenta and royal purple are qualitatively "closer" to one another than are, say, candy red and canary yellow), no intermodal sensory analogies are permissible such that we could intelligibly say that, for instance, certain odors are more or less similar to certain colors. Moreover, the classical theory of sensation held that sensations are not inherently emotional or affective in character; any affective properties found to be associated with sensations are culturally conditioned "additions" to the sensations; in effect, sensations are essentially pure "registrations" of cognitive data. For classical theory, emotions and sensations are entirely separate functions of consciousness. To the contrary, Hartshorne argues that (1) the classical theory does not fit the phenomenological and empirical evidence, (2) it is out of touch with the intersensory analogies provided in all manner of ordinary language metaphors, and (3) it does not cohere with the concept of an evolutionary history of sensory systems.

While experimentation on intersensory phenomena is a complex affair and interpretation of some results is disputable, it is fair to say that a body of evidence has emerged which bodes well for the thesis of intersensory connection. Indeed, it is now a commonplace of contemporary psychology texts to discuss evidence for intersensory analogies, for instance, the establishment of connections between visual and auditory neural systems as well as evidence of visual-auditory correlations in the cognitive development of infants. It is also particularly telling that neuroscientists have developed sensory substitution systems that can allow the blind to construct images, objects, and words from tactile stimulation. Moreover, Hartshorne points to abundant metaphors of common parlance which make inter-sensory connections: some colors are said to be "warm" or "loud," some sounds are said to be "sweet" or "sour," some affective states or moods are said to be "blue" or "dark," or some smells are said to be "delicious" or "distasteful." The practice of employing intersensory metaphors occurs widely across cultures, and is broadly communicative or publicly accessible, pointing (at the very least) to the possibility of intersensory continuity and to an underlying objective affect-quality in sensation, thus grounding the communicability of the intersensory metaphors. If the sensory modes are as rigidly separated and analogical connection is as unintelligible as classical theory maintains, it is difficult to explain that language is so saturated with inter-sensory metaphors. Hartshorne does not deny that there are strong qualitative differences between the qualia of various sensory modes (indeed his theory posits qualitative difference in terms of a geometric notion of "distance on a continuum"); nor does he deny that cultural conditioning can play an important role in constructing affective associations with sensations. Rather, his theory rejects the *rigid* discontinuity of the sensory modes and the *separation* of sensation from affectivity.

While Hartshorne is cognizant of cultural conditioning of sensory experience, he argues that such conditioning can be shown to presuppose an underlying affect in the "conditioned" sensation. Consider a *locus classicus* case of culturally constructed associations of affectivity in classical theory: the preference for white dress in traditional Chinese funerals as opposed to black or dark dress in traditional Spanish or Italian funerals is said to show that there are fundamentally different emotional qualities attached to white in Chinese as opposed to European cultures. Hartshorne argues that this misconstrues the situation. The cultural difference is found in different attitudes toward death and funeral rites, not in different feelings concerning the colors white or black—the Chinese think of funerals as positive celebrations of past life (CS 299). Hartshorne also applies this reasoning to variations in individual sensory-qualitative preferences. He remarks on the fact that some persons prefer a certain bitter quality of strong dark chocolate does not show that such individuals "fail to sense the contrast, sweet-bitter, as essentially positive-negative" (CS 301). It means rather that they do not want *mere* sweetness or pleasantness; they want a more complex sensory experience. Hartshorne's point is that an adequate phenomenology of sensation must include the appropriate "layered" complexity of sensory experience and thus accommodate the fact that we have "feelings *about* our sensory feelings" (CS 301). It is the duality of this, so to speak, "meta-feeling/object-feeling" situation which is the source of what Hartshorne calls the "pseudo-duality" of affectivity and mere sensation posited by the classical theory of sensation.

Added to these considerations is the fact that Helmholtz's theory of sensory mode discontinuities leaves unanswered a number of questions about how it can be squared with any plausible construction of the evolutionary development of sensory modes. If the sensory modes are as separate as classical theory supposes, then how could new sensory modes which evolve have meaningful connections to older modes? Were the transitions from one mode to another simply *de novo* additions abruptly occurring all-at-once, contrary to standard neo-Darwinian assumptions of gradualism? We grant, however, that this is not a clear defeater of the classical doctrine, since there appear to be at least some abrupt changes in the biosphere, the so-called "saltations," such as the abrupt appearance of the amniotic egg, which challenge incrementalism as a universal characteristic of evolution.[6] Nevertheless, if one sensory mode evolved from another, then how could it be *impossible* for the new sensory mode to have analogical connections with its modal parent? How could information from the different sensory modes be coordinated during early moments of evolutionary transition if there is no meaningful analogical connection between them? Would not an organism that possessed the capacity to integrate information from different sensory modes be better adapted to its environment? Hartshorne's theory, on the other hand, supposes that sensory modes are intrinsically connected by their common evolutionary origins (with tactile capacities as the earliest), that sensation is a form of affectivity that serves the purpose of enhancing the prospects of an organism's survival, and that this underlying physiological connection of sensation and affectivity is what is primal—it is the "object-feeling" pole of the "meta-feeling/object-feeling" duality found in our complex emotional life. Hartshorne's judgment was that, "No more evolutionary theory of sensation has been proposed to my knowledge."[7]

The affective properties of sensation are most immediately evident in the case of pain; indeed, intense haptic sensations of pain are ineluctably described in strongly affective terms such as "horrific" or "torturous" or "excruciating." While there may be cases in which, paradoxically, pain is experienced as pleasure, such cases by definition posit a hedonic property to the experience inimical to the notion of a thoroughly "disinterested" pain. The affective *aversion* that is part and parcel of the experience of pain also clearly coheres with the biological or adaptive value of affectivity that Hartshorne's theory asserts. Organisms that are not warned of injury by virtue of pain, and that do not seek to avoid such injury by virtue of visceral, emotional aversion to pain, are insofar vulnerable to their environments. Other tactile qualia such as sensual touch are obviously inseparable from hedonic content. Gustatory qualia are also affective as enjoyment of delicious foods and strong aversion to extremely sour or spoiled foods attest. New born infants react with aversion to sour, bitter, or fetid substances, and so it is difficult to "argue away" gustatory affect as culturally conditioned. Here again there are obvious biological or adaptive advantages for organisms capable of being affectively reinforced by and motivated to seek nutritious foods and avoid fetid substances or spoilage. Sounds, especially in the form of music, are readily seen to evoke emotions in immediate ways. Minor chords, for instance, have an immediate "sad" or "melancholy" tonality which explains their use in ballads evocative of such moods.

Hartshorne understood that the more difficult case for his theory is visual phenomena. For this reason, he discusses at length the affective nature of visual experience with a particular emphasis on color sensation. Careful attention to our experience of color reveals that strong primary colors exhibit affective qualities, as in the paradigm cases that "gaiety" is part and parcel of yellow and "warmth" of red (PPS 7). While Hartshorne admits that there seem to be dull color sensations to which we may seem affectively indifferent, that such sensations possess some slight degree of affect could be shown by imagining blindness with respect to such colors; in addition, such colors have a valuable contextual role to play in providing certain nuances of contrast. In his treatment of Hartshorne's theory, psychologist Wayne Viney notes that some previously blind persons who are successfully re-sighted attach much significance even to the visually trivial.[8] Importantly, Hartshorne argues that without such an affective account of color, it is extremely difficult to give a coherent account of the visual arts. If affective qualia are *always* merely accidently "associated" with color by virtue of idiosyncrasies of personal experience, how could artists communicate or express intelligibly? For instance, the dulled grayish-brownish tones of an Edward Hopper painting convey the depressive *atmosphere* of life during the Great Depression far better than would the alternative use of bright yellows or Kelly greens or Titian reds. Indeed, certain projects of modern art, such as found in the work of Kandinsky, depend on the notion that color expression can in and by itself evoke emotion without mediation through well-defined objects, whether in surreal juxtaposition or otherwise.

Adaptive values for color sensation are not difficult to conceive. The greater discriminatory information provided by color sensation at least enhances, say, human abilities to demarcate and map out their immediate environments. Moreover, at least one affective property of color can be correlated with experimental neuro-physical evidence; the inherent "aggressiveness" of red correlates with the empirically discerned increase in cortical stimulation when compared to exposure to blue. While this may be explained by cultural conditioning (e.g., our learned response to red stop signs), such an explanation may also beg the question as to why red is so often selected as a color of warning. On Hartshorne's theory, the selection of red occurs precisely because it has the stimulating or aggressive affect it does. In general, Hartshorne sides with Julius Pikler in connecting all affectivity of sensation at its most fundamental level with excitations to act or with behavioral avoidances, and these in turn have an evolutionary "cash value" or utility. Nonetheless, empirical study of the affectivity of color sensation is by no means settled, and results are unclear, for one reason because it is difficult to separate out learned from universal emotional responses to color. Hartshorne's theory, however, points in the direction of an overall evolutionary account of sensation. Even if Hartshorne has some of the details mishandled, the *general thesis* of color affect brings color vision in line with other sense modalities and best explains why it was strongly "naturally selected."

There are other aspects of the classical doctrine of color sensation that are deeply problematic in ways that Hartshorne's affective continuum hypothesis avoids. Hartshorne's account of color sensation is in the final analysis superior irrespective of the above subtleties of color affectivity. As an important example, consider the geometry of the color-relation spectrum (PPS 40–49). The classical theory posits compartmentalization not only between different sensory modalities but also between classes of sensory qualia within the same sensory modality. For instance, the classical theory posits that colors reside on a continuum of transition such that some colors are similar to each other while others are not. Red and orange share resemblance to one another while other colors such as red and yellow do not. This presents a continuum of graduated difference wherein three qualitative items or "points" X, Y, Z are related in such a way that X is a finite distance from Y and Y is a finite distance from Z while X and Z are separated by an infinite distance. Yet this is unintelligible: "How could continuously graduated difference become at some point not simply more but absolute difference?" (PPS 41). What makes intelligible sense is rather a model of the continuum of graduated color relation that presupposes no absolute difference of one color from another. What fits the observed facts well is a geometry of color where red-yellow are polar extremes (forming a Cartesian x axis) and yellow-blue are polar extremes (forming a Cartesian y axis): "Yellow and blue, red and green, are opposites such that both extremes of one pair are intermediate or neutral with respect to the extremes of the other pair" (PPS 44, Plate I, Cartesian Coordinates for Color). The classical Helmholtzian system is impossible as it pairs red-yellow and blue-green as the polar extremes. These are not phenomenologically evident as the polar opposites, nor does it fit the observed facts to hold that in transitioning from yellow to red "is it necessary to pass through blue or green intermediaries; [nor] to reach green from blue to pass through red or yellow" (PPS 44). The classical theory's notion of a color continuum as constituted partly by similarity and partly by dissimilarity is thus incoherent. An alternative continuum wherein transitions between colors are all characterized by *some* degree of similarity is free of such incoherence.

Hartshorne's first book could be seen, in one respect, as a systematic attack against the form of materialism that finds inspiration in the theory of sense data. From the times of John Locke and David Hume, some empirically minded philosophers and psychologists analyzed experience in terms of "sensory impressions." Emotions were conceived as annexed onto bare impressions; Hartshorne characterizes this as "the annex view of value" (PPS 94). As already noted, this view of emotion is at odds with evolutionary thinking, since a sensation-minus-affect would be lacking in adaptive value. Equally, it is not clearly a deliverance of experience.

The analysis of experience into sensory impressions is, Hartshorne held, bad phenomenology; it is an intellectualized reconstruction of experience. The mistake was, in part, due to the excessive attention paid to visual experience, which as we have noted, is where affect is least apparent. Visual experience exhibits less felt relevance of the body than one finds in the other sensory modalities. This may account for the prevalence of visual metaphors for a supposedly immaterial process of intellection. It is easier to forget that one *sees with the eyes* than it is to forget, for example, that one *touches with the skin*.

In light of Hartshorne's conviction concerning the data of experience, it is not difficult to understand why he resonated to the expression "feeling of feeling," an idea (if not the exact wording) that he found in Whitehead's *Process and Reality*.[9] The clearest instance of a feeling of feeling, for both Whitehead and Hartshorne, is memory, for it is at a minimum the record of a past experience in a present experience. The example of memory also supports Hartshorne's contention that, while every sensation is a feeling, not every feeling is a sensation. Hartshorne would later refer to the difference between introspection and perception as the difference between personal and impersonal memory (WP 3; CE 42).

When Hartshorne came to the business of ontology, he could find nothing more consonant with his psychology of sensation, nothing more in keeping with evolutionary thinking, and nothing more coherent philosophically than panexperientialism, the view that the basic constituents of reality are momentary flashes of experience. Whitehead called these actual entities or actual occasions; Hartshorne sometimes called them dynamic or active singulars. Panexperientialism implies that there must be nonhuman and nonconscious forms of experience. Leibniz had argued this case before evolutionary theory, but evolution made the case even more convincing. Humans are different from the creatures from which they evolved by matters of degree. Mind-like qualities, Hartshorne argued, are susceptible to an infinitely flexible number of forms. Hartshorne and Whitehead held that every concrete particular is an experient occasion; they did not, however, believe that every whole made of such occasions can be said, *as a whole*, to feel the world. Whitehead spoke of a tree as a democracy, the cells making up its members—there can be cellular feelings even if the tree as a whole does not feel.[10] Hartshorne used the analogy of a flock of birds: there are feelings in each bird but the flock itself does not feel (CS 142).

If Hartshorne followed Whitehead on the ontology of actual occasions, he parted ways with him on how best to construe the nature of possibility. The young Hartshorne recorded in his notes of Whitehead's lectures the idea of the "patience of [the] ideal world for actuality."[11] Whitehead construed the ideal world of possibility as an array of eternal objects, which included particular sensory qualities. As is evident in his first book, Hartshorne preferred to think of sensory qualities as existing along an affective continuum. Whitehead, it seems, was not dogmatic in rejecting this view. Hartshorne reports that he presented Whitehead with the following reasoning, which can be found in Hartshorne's first book: if points are constructed from the extensive continuum and not vice versa, as Whitehead held, perhaps, by parity of reasoning, particular sensory qualities are extracted from an affective continuum and not vice versa (for basically the same argument see PPS 207). According to Hartshorne, Whitehead called the argument "subtle" requiring "further reflection."[12] It is also worth remarking that Hartshorne's view is more radically processive than Whitehead's since it implies that sensory qualities are *emergent* as the affective continuum is sliced in various ways through the evolutionary process within and between species.

Hartshorne's study of birdsong neatly coheres with his concept of the affective continuum. He was convinced that oscines have a primitive aesthetic sense.[13] He accepted the theory that birds sing to mark territory, to warn, and to woo a mate. He noted, however, that birds often sing beyond what is necessary to these biological needs. Birdsongs are not cries, yelps, or growls, nor merely mechanical; they are learned by imitation. Moreover, when judged by criteria appropriate to music, the songs are indeed musical; there are themes with variations, melodies, rhythm, and even harmony (some birds can sing contrasting notes simultaneously). Birds make music in the only ways that creatures of their limited attention span and vocal ability could be expected to make it. Most importantly, Hartshorne found that birds with more varied repertoires have shorter pauses between their songs than birds with less varied repertoires. Hartshorne's hypothesis is that simpler repertoires invoke more boredom, which a pause relieves, whereas varied repertoires are more interesting. This is Hartshorne's theory of a "monotony threshold" in songbirds. The theory correctly predicts that it would be rare to find birds with varied repertoires that have lengthy pauses between songs, or to find birds that repeat the same song without significant pauses.

Finally, he noted that birds with varied repertoires vary the order and the number of their songs unpredictably, a practice that Hartshorne calls "juggling with numbers."[14] In sum, Hartshorne says, "Bird song is a fine symbol of what I believe is the meaning of all nature, the development of varied forms of free and beautiful experience."[15]

If Hartshorne's findings concerning the aesthetics of birdsong cohere nicely with his evolutionary view of sensation and affective tone, it is equally true that they are in keeping with his more comprehensive theory of beauty. He characterizes beauty—which could also be called *intense satisfactory experience*—as a mean between two extremes: absolute order vs. absolute disorder and ultra-complexity vs. ultra-triviality. According to Hartshorne:

> Experienced harmony in experienced contrasts, the more varied and intense the contrasts that can be harmonized the better, is the most fundamental meaning of "beauty," and it is beauty in this sense, or something more or less closely related to it, that we seek.[16]

Aesthetic experience, like all sensory experience, must have, on Hartshorne's account, both a subjective and an objective side. Hartshorne denies that the quality of beauty is "merely in the eye of the beholder," or to generalize, "merely in the perception of the perceiver." Of course, one must take into account the capacity of the perceiver to appreciate beauty. A symphony, for example, would be hopelessly complicated for a bird to appreciate.

Finally, it should be noted that Hartshorne's emphases on the primacy of feeling in perception and of aesthetic experience are evident in his form of theism. God, he held, has the eminent form of "feeling of the feelings" of others. In the first instance, this means that God's knowledge is suffused with affect and is not simply an intellectual awareness of the world, for example, a knowing of the truth value of propositions. According to Hartshorne, divine cognition is a form of what William James called "knowledge of acquaintance" rather than simply a "knowledge-about." This idea yields a view of omniscience that is decidedly more intimate than one that is couched in terms of the metaphor of an "all-seeing" deity. Since, for Hartshorne, the relation of "feeling of feelings" has a temporal structure, every instance of awareness in the present must be nothing other than an awareness of the past. It stands to reason that, if God is the eminent embodiment of "feeling of feelings," God must also have the eminent form of memory. This is indeed Hartshorne's view, which he calls "contributionism." Every experience of a non-divine being is felt and retained in perfect memory by God, thereby contributing to the richness of the divine immortal life. In Hartshorne's words, God's possession of us, not our possession of God, is our final achievement (WM 90).

✣ THREE ✣

Metaphysics:
Its Nature and Methods

A FTER HIS FIRST BOOK, and with the notable exception of his book on birdsong, Hartshorne focused mostly on the questions of metaphysics. In *Creative Synthesis and Philosophic Method*, he provides no fewer than a dozen definitions of "metaphysics" which, he argued, differ only as a matter of emphasis (CS 19, 24). Central to all of Hartshorne's definitions is that genuinely metaphysical propositions are unconditionally necessary and nonrestrictive of existential possibilities. If metaphysical propositions are true at all, they hold true of all possible world-states or state-descriptions. This means that they are propositions which are illustrated or exemplified by any *conceivable* observations or experiences when such observations or experiences are properly understood or reflected upon. Hartshorne is careful not to identify experience with human experience, and, indeed, he argues that human experience is only one type of experience as such. In Hartshorne's view, metaphysical propositions stand in contrast to both the propositions of mathematics and of empirical science. Mathematics deals in unconditionally necessary, but (in a qualified sense) nonexistential possibilities.[1] Empirical science deals in restrictive existential possibilities that is, possibilities that admit of counter-instances.

51

Like Whitehead and Peirce, Hartshorne rejected the idea that the propositions of metaphysics are self-evident axioms from which metaphysical theorems could be deduced. Only a mind ideally wise, knowledgeable, and lucid could perceive the network of metaphysical truths as a coherent whole. Human experience, however, is shot through with error and proneness to error, subject to all of the vicissitudes of history, culture, and language. Hartshorne argues that intellectual history suggests that metaphysics is "that part of a priori knowledge in which clarity and certainty are least readily attained" (CS 32). Perspicuous verbalization, far from being a natural endowment of human beings, is an art that can be developed only through much training, education, and effort. Hartshorne considered himself and some others to have achieved a measure of clarity about metaphysics—and he often expressed himself with a confidence that some found excessive— but he was quick to acknowledge when his own thinking seemed to reach an impasse (e.g., PCH 721). He asked of philosophers, and those interested in philosophical questions, not to block the road of inquiry, to argue for their views, and to honestly face the difficulties confronting them. Philosophy, he held, is a rational discipline involving a willingness to be changed by argument and not the "self-defense of one's own castle of ideas" (HB 62). For Hartshorne the history of ideas is itself a testing ground of metaphysical hypotheses which it behooves anyone interested in metaphysics not to ignore (PCH 582–83).

That Hartshorne thought at length about questions of philosophical method can be inferred from what Paul Weiss called the systematic "machinery" at work in his metaphysics, and from the very title of one of his most important mature philosophical works, the above-mentioned *Creative Synthesis and Philosophic Method*. Hartshorne's method for neoclassical metaphysics results from both original insights and critical reflection on a wide swath of influences. These range from the work of American pragmatists, especially Peirce, to phenomenology and existentialism, to the speculative thought of Whitehead, to the work of analytic philosophers—with particular attention given to Popper and the logical investigations of his Harvard teachers Lewis and Sheffer as well as his University of Chicago colleague Carnap. The section titled "Reply to Everybody," published in *The Philosophy of Charles Hartshorne*, lists no less than twenty-one methodological principles to be used in the proper adjudication of metaphysical claims (PCH 583). Among the most important of these are what could be termed the principles of "positivity," of "dipolar contrast," of "inclusive asymmetry," and of Peirce's doctrine of "position matrices or diagrams." In what follows, we discuss each of these ideas and close with Hartshorne's reflections on the relations between metaphysics and science.

Positivity

In Hartshorne's view, a genuinely metaphysical statement is verified by any conceivable observation. "Conceivable observation" is here understood in terms of Karl Popper's notion that observation is always of the form "such and such is the case" rather than "such and such is not the case." Cognitive definiteness is gained only by noting what *is* observed, rather than what is *not* observed, which is indefinite or infinite. Plato argues that negation is parasitic upon affirmation—"that which is not" is not contrary to what exists, but something different from what exists.[2] In effect, quantificational criteria for identity can apply only to events that occur, not to events that do not occur. The question, "How many storms did *not* occur?" has no definite answer. In Hartshorne's view, there are no merely negative facts. Every negation presupposes some actually existing state of affairs. For example, to say that there are no swans in the lake is to say that every part of the lake is occupied by something other than a swan. Or, more generally, to say that swans do not exist is tantamount to saying that every location in the universe is occupied by something other than a swan. Claims purporting to state negative facts are efforts at representing an absence of positivity, and this is a key feature of metaphysical error. Properly metaphysical propositions are unique in never being *falsified* by any actual or genuinely possible states of affairs and in always being *verified* by actual or genuinely possible states of affairs. They represent, in effect, the kind of necessity defined since Leibniz and found in modern modal logic as "that which is common to all possibilities."

This distinguishes genuinely metaphysical propositions from other kinds of a priori necessary propositions, such as truths of mathematics and hypothetical necessities. Hartshorne maintains that mathematical propositions are nonexistential, for they express relations between conceivable states of affairs (CS 162). "Two apples plus two apples equals four apples" is an existential assertion containing a true mathematical relation, but "two slithy toves plus two slithy toves equals four slithy toves" is a nonexistential assertion that nonetheless contains the same true mathematical relation. The bare arithmetical truth that "2 + 2 = 4" is neutral to existential instantiation. Similarly, "The number nine is not integrally divisible by two" is necessarily the case given the conventional meanings of the vocabulary of finite arithmetic. However, although no conceivable state of affairs *falsifies* the proposition, it is not *verified* by any conceivable state of affairs. And while hypothetical necessities express necessary relationships between possibilities, Hartshorne takes them to be covert *denials* that there are any states of affairs which falsify the relation asserted by the conditional. By contrast, genuinely metaphysical propositions are unequivocally affirmative, and *their* denials can only be *sheer denials*, expressions of utter absence or privation. The denials of metaphysical propositions are impossibilities; they are failed attempts to represent that which would never be found among possibilities.

As a prime illustration of a metaphysical truth, Hartshorne used the proposition, "Something exists." This is properly metaphysical since it could not be falsified under any conceivable observational or experiential circumstances, yet it could be verified by every such circumstance; in fact, to assert both of these features is to assert something that is analytically true of the proposition, since any attempt to verify the proposition would posit, at minimum, a verification-event which would in turn falsify the counter-proposition that "nothing exists." Some philosophers suggest that it is a contingent truth that something exists, as seems to be assumed by the question, "Why is there something rather than nothing?" Henri Bergson said that one could attempt to arrive at the idea of nonbeing by imaginatively negating every true statement asserting the existence of something.[3] Hartshorne points out, following Bergson, that this thought experiment is self-defeating. It ends in one of two ways: either there is no assertion, but only a denial, or there is an assertion that is self-referentially incoherent such as, "Nonexistence exists." It is logically kindred to such "nonsense" propositions as "I was told something by nobody" or "I ate nothingness." There is literally *no possible state of affairs* that could make "Nothing exists" true. If it is impossible for "Nothing exists" to be true, then "Something exists" must be necessarily true. For this reason, Hartshorne rejects Paul Tillich's claim that "Being as the negation of possible non-being is the basic cognitive position, which precedes in logical dignity every characterization of being."[4] Hartshorne insists that the being of non-being is a conceptual impossibility; thus, the formal alternatives are the necessity of being and the impossibility of non-being. (We discuss this at further length in the appendix of Chapter Six.)

It is worth noting that no traditional theist could accept the possibility that there might have been nothing since God was thought to be a "something" that exists without the possibility of not existing. This is a reminder that in most philosophical and theological contexts, the question "Why is there something rather than nothing?" is an abbreviated way of asking, "Why is there a universe with the properties we find in it rather than no universe at all?" The physicist Lawrence M. Krauss argues that our universe arose out of relativistic quantum fields, which Krauss identifies as the nonbeing or nothingness of which philosophers have spoken. Doubtless it is useful to operationalize "nothing" so as to deal with it as a scientific idea. As David Albert notes, however, to presuppose the existence of the "something" of relativistic quantum fields is not an answer to questions raised by philosophers and theologians. Put in somewhat more technical terms, where N = Nonbeing, Q = relativistic quantum fields, and $\exists$ is the existential quantifier, $(\exists x)(Nx)$ is not logically equivalent to $(\exists x)(Qx)$.[5] Hartshorne's argument is that the first formula is incoherent since, by virtue of the meaning of N, there is literally nothing over which the variable x could possibly range. The second formula does not suffer this defect.

If Hartshorne is correct that it is impossible for "Nothing exists" to be true, then there can be no state of affairs that meaningfully contrasts with "Something exists." The lesson in this is that sheer denials represent an absence of positivity, and this is a key feature of metaphysical error in Hartshorne's view. Put somewhat differently, there are no merely negative facts (CE Ch. 3). Hartshorne accepts the notion of negative facts in the standard logical forms $(\exists x)(\sim Px)$ or $\sim(\exists x)(Px)$. But the negations grammatically attach to states of affairs as represented by the variable *x*. Sheer negation—asserting simply "it is not the case that"—is neither true nor false and is not a self-standing assertive mark in any grammatically well-formed logical system that can be used to model ordinary language. Writing a simple negation sign ("$\sim$") on the *n*th line of a proof is never acceptable.[6]

Hartshorne argues that the rejection of sheer negative facts has wide-ranging implications. For example, the total absence of mind-like qualities in a thing implies the presence of something in the thing that is incompatible with mind. This principle plays a role in Hartshorne's rejection of both mind-body dualism and materialism. In philosophical theology, the rejection of sheer negative facts implies that a purely negative or apophatic theology is mistaken. Any statement that the apophatic theologian makes about what God *is not* presupposes a positive statement or statements about what God *is* (even if what God *is* cannot be adequately expressed in human language).

To say that it is necessary that something exists does not provide any information about any existing thing; in other words, "Something exists" is too abstract to tell one about the concretely existing things (pluralism) or thing (monism) that may exist. This observation, however, presupposes the contrast between the abstract and the concrete. A further metaphysical question, therefore, is the relation that exists between the abstract and the concrete. "Something exists" does not describe an existing thing but rather presupposes the existence of entities (or an entity) more concrete than the sentence itself—this is the case even if, *per impossibile*, only the sentence existed, for "Something exists" is more abstract than "Only the sentence 'something exists' exists." In light of these kinds of considerations, Hartshorne concludes not only that "Something exists" is necessarily true but also that "Something concrete exists" is as well, where the adjective "concrete" is the contrary of "abstract." There is a hint of paradox in the fact that "concreteness" is itself abstract, but this leads to another of Hartshorne's definitions of metaphysics as the study of the abstraction "concreteness" (CS 24 and 32). Indeed, Hartshorne maintains that all metaphysical mistakes are instances of what Whitehead called "the fallacy of misplaced concreteness," that it is to say, of mistaking an abstraction for what is concrete (CS 22).[7]

Conceivable propositions involve conceivable states of affairs in order for them to count intelligibly as propositions. Natural deduction systems of modern symbolic logic seem to make this supposition as in the decision of Whitehead and Russell in *Principia Mathematica* to make "there exists something X which either does or does not have an arbitrary one-place predicate P" axiomatic: in effect, they disallow an empty universe of discourse since an empty universe produces incoherence in the system such as counter-instances to the law of Universal Instantiation. While it is to be granted that free logics can avoid this assumption, it is also true that free logics entail difficulties precisely in determining their semantical domains. Most important, free logics that are designed to formalize ordinary language presuppose "objects" in both their inner or outer domains. Despite such monikers as "null inner domains," such domains assume objects that are non-actual possibles. All free logics that have *cognitive import* for the description of "possible worlds" assume a semantical domain of objects that are conceptualized on the basis of actual objects or properties; for example, "Batman is a superhero" can be formalized in free logic, but it ultimately makes oblique reference to actualities (bat ears, masks, muscular strength, courage, etc.) that are posed in non-actual combinations or juxtapositions. In effect, free logics can be interpreted in such a way that they do not contradict basic tenets of Hartshorne's modal theory. Where cognitively meaningful, they assume objects as values for variables, and they formalize fictional scenarios that indirectly display the conceptual priority of actualities.

Dipolarity

Hartshorne's principle of dipolar contrast derives, in part, from the semantic "law of polarity" found in Morris R. Cohen's *A Preface to Logic*. Following Cohen, Hartshorne holds that genuine metaphysical concepts are semantically interdependent. In effect, such concepts have logical contraries which cannot mean anything in utter isolation from one another. In spite of the extreme generality of metaphysical concepts, each such concept entails a polar contrast to it. Even the highly general concept "reality" requires that the concept "unreality" be assigned some meaning. To use Hartshorne's illustration, the concept of "reality" ought to include the notion of having mental states, but the concept of "unreality" should include the notion of intentional objects of real mental acts which fail to designate anything extra-mental. Perhaps a more telling example could be found in the notion of necessity. A standard definition of necessity is "that which has no alternative," yet alternativeness clearly invokes contingency, since a contingent state of affairs is to be characterized as "this rather than that alternative." Hence, the semantical analysis of necessity invokes contingency. For Hartshorne, then, each metaphysical concept has a corresponding contrast: necessity requires contingency, being requires becoming, unity requires variety, and so on, for any concept that is non-restrictively general, having applicability across possible states or state-descriptions. The two interdependent contraries in each case warrant the term *dipolarity*.

Lack of recognition of dipolarity is, for Hartshorne, a chief difficulty in previous metaphysical theories that suppress expression of a polar contrast. In effect, they suffer from a certain conceptual poverty or "fallacy of monopolarity." Monopolar theories allow expression of only one pole of a pair of contrasts; stated in different terms, they completely deny one pole of a pair of contrasts. One example of denying dipolarity is monistic theories such as that of Spinoza, which allow causal necessity and internal relatedness, but which disallow contingency and external relatedness. At the opposite "monopolar" extreme are logical atomist theories like that of Russell, which allow causal contingency and external relatedness, but which disallow causal necessity or internal relatedness. Hartshorne asks if these contrary extremes make any more sense than supposing that doors must have hinges on both sides or on neither side (CS 216; IO 155–56). Hartshorne's metaphysical project is guided by the observance of dipolarity and thus conceptual inclusiveness; in his view, a neoclassical process theory of reality is structurally dipolar and offers comprehensive accommodation of *both* necessity and contingency, *both* causal determination and a degree of freedom from such determination, *both* internal and external relations, etc., throughout the range of metaphysical polar contrasts.

Inclusive Asymmetry/Concrete Inclusion

Hartshorne's principle of dipolarity is complemented and qualified by a principle of inclusive asymmetry or concrete inclusion. As Hartshorne points out, the principle of dipolarity does not justify metaphysical dualism. One should distinguish between asserting that a metaphysical concept requires a contrary polar conception in its definition, and asserting that two polar concepts have an equivalent metaphysical status. It may well be the case that one concept requires the other polar concept in its definition, while the other polar concept *both* requires the polar contrast in its definition, and yet is itself the ground or source of that polar contrast. In other words, it may be the case, as Hartshorne asserts, that dipolarity is itself grounded in a logically *asymmetrical* relation between the contraries.

The model for this relation can be seen in logical implication, which Hartshorne, following Peirce's trailblazing work on "illation" as logically fundamental or primal, takes to be the ultimate concept in formal logic and a resource for metaphysical generalization. "*p* implies *q*" means that *p* implies *both* itself and *q*. This can be formally expressed in the following tautology:

$$(p \supset q) \text{ iff } [(p \supset p) \wedge (p \supset q)]$$

This result is mirrored in Lewisian systems in which the formula—changing material implication to strict implication—is a theorem. However, given a standard material implication, $p \supset q$, (where *p* and *q* are not equivalent in meaning), we cannot say *conversely* that *q* logically implies *p*. This is reflected in the fact that the correlative formula, shown below, is *not* a tautology, for it is false where *p* and *q* have opposite truth values, and thus implicitly involves a species of "fallacy of affirming the consequent."

$$(p \supset q) \text{ iff } [(q \supset q) \wedge (q \supset p)]$$

Analogously, the similar formula using strict implication is not a theorem. Thus, entailment is *essentially* asymmetrical. Consider furthermore the defining power of variant connectives of standard systems of propositional logic. For Hartshorne, it is immensely significant that the defining power of propositional operators or functions "varies inversely with symmetry." The symmetrical function of logical equivalence, as in "*p if and only if q*," has the least defining power of the propositional functions, since, even when combined with negation, it can be used to produce only eight (including itself) out of the sixteen propositional functions. On the other hand, the directional or asymmetrical functions, which contrast with the equivalence function, are constitutive of entailment. Hartshorne points out that Peirce, followed by Sheffer, was the first to see that either the combination of negation and conjunction ("not both") or the combination of conjunction and negation ("neither/nor") are singly sufficient to define all the others.

The Sheffer functions (the "stroke" and "dagger") are the most definitive functions, but they possess a triadic asymmetry that yet *includes* dyadic symmetry. We see this, Hartshorne notes, in their truth-tabular definitions. The Sheffer stroke is false if and only if both propositional variables are true, while the Sheffer dagger (also Peirce's *ampheck*) is true if and only if both propositional variables are false. [8]

In effect, the triadic relation of the stroke, i.e., the truth-value product of the binary Sheffer construction $p|q$, which is dyadically symmetrical in terms of its propositional truth-value assignments (p is true *and* q is true), stands as an asymmetry in terms of its truth value (i.e., it is false in relation to symmetrical truth). Hartshorne finds a metaphysically ultimate pattern here, namely, symmetry *within* an all-embracing asymmetry.

Hartshorne holds that the relation between dipolar metaphysical contraries exhibits this asymmetrical structure. As an illustration, consider his argument that "becoming" logically contains its polar contrast "being," but not the converse (CS 13–14). Suppose there is a reality, X, that does not come to be, that is eternal; and another reality, Y, that does come to be. The total reality, XY, is not eternal; XY comes to be, for Y itself is not eternal. This shows that becoming is the more inclusive category, for it preserves itself (becoming) and its polar contrast (being). No comparable argument can show that being can include becoming without destroying the contrast. The concrete or definite, *the creatively cumulative*, is the inclusive element, and is the key to the abstract, not *vice versa*. The concrete and the abstract are neither sheer conjuncts as posited by varieties of dualism, nor some mysterious "third" entity, but, in consonance with both Whitehead's ontological principle and Aristotle's ontological priority of the actual, is rather, "the abstract *in* the concrete."

In his "Logic of Ultimate Contrasts" (CS ch. 6; ZF ch. 7), Hartshorne calls the concrete terms in a pair of metaphysical contraries the r-terms (correlated with Peirce's categoreal "seconds" and "thirds"), while abstract terms are called a-terms (correlated with Peirce's categoreal "firsts"). While he provides 21 r-terms and 21 a-terms in his table of metaphysical contraries, a few samples could be taken as illustrative, especially given his Rule of Proportionality; namely, as any one r-terms stands to its contextually correlated a-term, all other r-terms stand to their contextually correlated a-terms (Table 1).

r-terms	a-terms
1r. relative, dependent internally related	1a. absolute, independent, externally related
2r. experience, subject	2a. things experienced, objects
3r. whole, inclusive	3a. constituents, included
10r. contingent	10a. necessary

TABLE 1: Selected Categoreal Contrasts

Hartshorne argues that 1r *includes* 1a, but not vice versa, while 2r *includes* 2a, but not vice versa, and so on through all items in the table. Given the items above, we see that, for Hartshorne, the analysis of experience should be constructed so as to include the notions that objects or things experienced are independent of or externally related to the contingent acts of experience which include the objects as their necessary (but not sufficient) conditions. If correct, these conceptual relations all exhibit the essential *asymmetry* of entailment. Yet, there is a two-way necessity within this overall asymmetry, for while the relation of logical inclusion falls always on the r-term side of the table, a-terms nonetheless necessitate that "a class of suitable r-term correlates be non-empty." For example, the necessary can be expressed, Hartshorne contends, as "the *non-emptiness* of the class of contingent states of affairs." This particular rumination is a key feature of Hartshorne's revision of the ontological argument.

While the detailed arguments for and proper adjudication of each case of r-term/a-term relation is a complex affair, it is interesting to notice that some independent considerations of modern logic arguably shore up Hartshorne's basic principle of r-term inclusion. For example, Hartshorne pointed to the fact that an important theorem of contemporary modal logic "mirrors" the logical inclusiveness of contingent concreta or "r-terms" in juxtaposition with abstract necessity or "a-terms"; namely, the theorem that $[(\Box\ p \wedge \sim \Box\ q) \rightarrow \sim \Box\ (p \wedge q)]$ where $\Box$ is a modal operator for "necessarily" and "$\rightarrow$" is strict implication. In effect, the conjunction of necessary and contingent propositions logically entails the *modally contingent status* of the conjunction of assertoric propositions—in effect, contingency in a relevant sense "includes" necessity rather than *vice versa*.

Position Matrices

Hartshorne also holds that metaphysical theories can be tested by subjecting them to processes of rational elimination and/or comparison of cognitive costs that begin with a formal logical elaboration of theoretical possibilities. This idea has its origin in Peirce's doctrine of position matrices or diagrams. The point here is that no philosophical topic can be declared fully rationally adjudicated until the constituent fundamental aspects of that topic have been subjected to an exhaustive "mathematical analysis." Much error can occur unless and until all possibilities have been foreseen and subjected to thorough rational consideration.

Consider the issue of the God-world relationship in philosophical theology. Hartshorne argues that, where modality of existence is concerned, there are sixteen combinatorial possibilities for theological and atheological models of this relationship. God and the world can each be either ontologically necessary, ontologically contingent, can possess these modal properties in diverse aspects, or are neither ontologically necessary nor contingent (ZF 83; CE 150).[9] In the following matrix (Table 2), upper case letters (N and C) represent ontological modalities as applied to God and lower case letters (n and c) represent ontological modalities as applied to the world. The zero case (O) represents lack of modal status or impossibility.

	God in all respects necessary	God in all respects contingent	God in different respects contingent & necessary	God lacking modal status or impossible
World in all respects necessary	N.n	C.n	NC.n	O.n
World in all respects contingent	N.c	C.c	NC.c	O.c
World in different respects contingent and necessary	N.cn	C.cn	NC.cn	O.cn
World lacking modal status or impossible	N.o	C.o	NC.o	O.o

TABLE 2: 16-Fold Matrix of Ontological Modalities as Applied to God and the World

Hartshorne's matrix provides a method of making distinctions among various types of historically significant worldviews as well as highlighting the distinctiveness of his own position. For example: Parmenidean monism or classic Advaita Vedanta can be symbolized as

N.o; early Buddhist thought is O.cn; Aristotle's theism is N.cn; Aquinas's theism is N.c; Stoic and Spinozistic pantheism is N.n; LaPlacean atheism is O.n; John Stuart Mill's theism and most forms of deism are C.n; William James's theism is C.c; Lequyer's is NC.c; Bertrand Russell's atheism is O.c. Hartshorne argued that his preferred option (NC.cn) is the most formally inclusive of the theoretical options, and that no specific options are logically compossible (otherwise we would have modal incoherence or contradiction).

Hartshorne's presentation of the position matrix representing necessity and contingency as applied to God and world developed over the course of his career. He did not come to the four-row, four-column arrangement until after his ninetieth birthday, with the help of Joseph Pickle at Colorado College. A more substantive change was in the way that Hartshorne interpreted the zeros. In *Creative Synthesis*, the zeros are the atheistic and acosmic positions (CS Ch. 13). In later discussions, however, he interprets the zeros more broadly as "God is impossible (or has no modal status)" and the "World is impossible (or has no modal status)." To illustrate the difference between these interpretations, consider the position of W. V. O. Quine. He would say that God does not exist, the world *does* exist, but the world has no modal status. This option cannot be represented as O.n, O.c, or as O.cn since each presupposes modal status for the world. Nor can it be represented as O.o without serious distortion, since Quine does not deny that the world exists. Another illustration of the problem is Robert Neville's emphasis on apophatic theology. On Neville's view, the necessary/contingent contrast is a product of God's creative act; God cannot be characterized as either necessary or contingent, but only as indeterminate, at least prior to the act of creation.[10] Hartshorne's table, as presented here, finesses these issues by interpreting the zeros in a strictly formal fashion to mean "neither necessary nor contingent," leaving open the possibility of further refinement.

Whatever one's ultimate convictions about this particular topic, Hartshorne's approach arguably represents an advance in metaphysical or philosophical theology since it provides a matrix that may well suggest missed possibilities in traditional or conventional ways of thinking about the topic. Furthermore, Hartshorne's method can be extended: similar 16-fold matrices can be made for other polar contrasts such as infinite/finite, eternal/temporal, and so on. If any two matrices are combined (16 x 16) the number of formal alternatives leaps to 256. More generally, if m equals the number of contrasts one wishes to include in talking about God and the world, then 16^m is the number of formal alternatives available. There is no apparent antecedent in the history of philosophical theology for Hartshorne's doctrinal matrices. It is no wonder, therefore, that he considered them one of his original contributions to metaphysics.[11]

Kant's Antinomies as a Challenge to Metaphysics

Hartshorne admitted that, as Karl Popper has alleged, one weakness in Whitehead's philosophy is its lack of rigorous responsiveness to Kant's antinomies of reason (IO 305), which, if sound, show that the aspirations of systematic metaphysics are impossible, since reason, in the case of the antinomies, hits upon insoluble *aporias*. Despite the gravity of the antinomies, Hartshorne holds that there are more than considerable consolations in the matter. He submits that Ivor Leclerc has long provided a cogent Whiteheadian response to the Second Antinomy regarding atoms and continua.[12] Hartshorne likewise contends, correctly in our view, that all but the first of the antinomies involve highly problematic "arbitrary restrictions" imposed by Kant, especially pronounced in the Third Antinomy related to freedom and strict determinism. Kant's proof of the antithesis in the Fourth Antinomy begs the question of temporalistic process theism wherein a Necessary Being can be both a temporal agent and cause of this world (and any other cosmic epoch). Such arbitrary restrictions clearly undermine the force of the Third and Fourth antinomies.

Hartshorne confesses that the most difficult case for Whiteheadians is the First Antinomy regarding whether time and space are infinite or finite in extension, the case of time being the more problematic. In fact, the issue with time is central. For process philosophy insists that creativity is an ultimate category having no alternative. This means that God as eminent embodiment of creativity has always been creating some cosmic epoch or another. Thus, by definition, the past has no beginning. This flies directly in the face of Kant's proof of the Thesis of the First Antinomy, namely, that the world must have a beginning in time since an *infinite* past cannot be successively synthesized and is thus logically impossible. This argument and variations on it have been resurrected by the work of William Lane Craig.[13] Not only does Craig, like Kant, use *a priori* arguments to show the impossibility of the past, he also appeals to arguments for temporal finitude derived from interpretations of big bang cosmology. At this juncture, we address the *a priori* arguments and leave a discussion of the scientific arguments for Chapter Eight.

Given the centrality of the doctrine of an infinite past in process philosophy and the fact that arguments related to this doctrine have received much attention in contemporary philosophy of religion, it is imperative that we discuss these important and weighty matters in some detail. Hartshorne could be said to have given insufficient attention to this problem in relation to the challenge it poses to his metaphysics. He does, however, offer some genuine insights, so he cannot be said to have dismissed the problem, in the expression of Colin Gunton, with a "shrug of the metaphysical shoulders."[14]

Hartshorne points out that the notion of an absolute "first event" appears to be quite counterintuitive and ontologically anomalous. He argues that a first temporal entity would be, by definition of "first," unlike any other actuality, possessing no memory, actualizing no antecedent purpose, and as such could not be recognized as a "state"— like an animal without parents, a ball of cosmic gas unrelated to existing gases or other cosmic processes, a hill formed without geological forces, etc. Hartshorne describes this hypothesis as "an ontological lie, a joke of existence upon itself" (MVG 234). It is instructive to note that, even those who have argued for a first temporal moment have often tempered their claim by suggesting that it would not appear to be a first temporal moment. For example, two years before Darwin's *Origin of Species*, Philip Gosse proposed the theory of *prochronism*, that anything God creates *necessarily* appears older than it is. If God first created a chicken, it would appear to have come from an egg, and if God first created the egg, it would appear to have come from a chicken. Hence, the allusion in the title of Gosse's book to the Garden of Eden—*Omphalos*, meaning navel, reflecting Gosse's belief that the first man, would have been created fully adult, complete with a navel, making it appear that he was born of a woman.[15] Gosse's views were resurrected in the late twentieth century—apparently without knowledge of Gosse's work—by those calling themselves "scientific" creationists.[16]

Hartshorne's most important suggestion, *contra* Kant, is that the issue of the duration of the past may not be reducible to a matter of counting. Indeed, does the universe or God-and-universe *need* to start somewhere? As Hartshorne observes acutely, "that is the very question at issue" (CS 126). Many medieval philosophers, including Averroes and Thomas Aquinas, held similarly that, as far as human reason is concerned, the world *need not* have a beginning.[17] For it would be possible for God, a being possessed of inexhaustible potency, to create an infinite series of creaturely events. This suggestion regarding the circularity of counting a beginningless past is what we take to be Hartshorne's main insight on the matter, for as we will see momentarily, Kant appears to have begged the question, since he tacitly must posit a "beginning" to an infinite series of past events in order to execute his "impossible" successive count to the present.

Exactly how are we to apply successive synthesis to the series of past events in order to demonstrate its incompleteness on the infinitist hypothesis? Are we to start with the upper limit "1" of the ordinality ". . . . 4, 3, 2, 1" and then count backwards? But, as Hartshorne notes, "the universe did not start with the present [the upper limit of the series]" (MVG 234). In order to show that an "incompleteable" eternity has elapsed up to the present moment we would have to start from some indefinite point n on the left-hand side of the ordinal series "n . . . 4, 3, 2, 1" and count from that "point" on. But where in the ordinal series is n? In effect, it seems that to require that there be some point n on the left-hand side of the ordinal series is just to posit an additional limit to the series. As James Thomson comments, "it is almost as if Kant illicitly replaced the proposition that the world did not have a beginning with the proposition that it did have a beginning which is infinitely remote in time."[18] This reasoning is curiously circular as it already assumes an artificial "beginning" of a series which by definition has no beginning.

In discussing this question, it is important that we distinguish between the following two propositions:

(a) A being infinite in time could successively synthesize an infinite quantum.

(b) A being finite in time could not successively synthesize an infinite quantum.

What Kant's proof of the Thesis seems to establish, if it establishes anything, is proposition (b), not proposition (a). This leaves his proof vulnerable to the possibility that *God* could causally influence and know an infinite series of past events. As Thomas Swing points out, Kant himself admitted that counting an infinite quantum is perhaps a possibility for a divine mind (albeit, a divine mind on a classical theological model).[19] But, more importantly, Swing also points out that Kant's proof of the Thesis exacts the high price of accepting subjective idealism—the view that the world has no existence independent of the knowing subject that constructs it—a position that Kant himself sought to avoid in his "Refutation of Idealism" added to the B edition of the first *Critique*. That an infinite series cannot be completed by successive synthesis "because it is limited by its finite unit of synthesis [the individual human subject] and its finite span for apprehension, is valid when it is construed in the context of the individual subject. But this exacts a high price—the acceptance of subjective idealism."[20] In effect, the finitude of the world in time is shown if and only if the world is a *finite construction* of an individual human subject. This does not, however, disprove the possibility of a world infinite in time known or intuited by an infinite divine subject.

This theme of the relation of divine mind to an infinite series of past events surfaces again in an important paper by Julian Wolfe and in George Shields's related critique of William Craig's argument for temporal finitude as presented in *The Kalām Cosmological Argument*.[21] In this work, Craig holds that the argument shows that the universe began to exist, because an infinite series of past events cannot be completed so as to reach the present. The argument also shows, according to Craig, that a *personal* Creator of the first event in space-time (the purported big bang event) exists. Numerous philosophers of religion hold that a *personal* Creator, who by definition has thoughts and may entertain purposes, is *ipso facto* a temporal (and everlasting or sempiternal) entity, since thinking and entertaining purposes intrinsically possess temporal structure. Any philosopher wishing to assert otherwise must posit exceedingly anomalous and conceptually strange notions of either mental activity or timelessness that contradict the standardly accepted phenomenology of time that intrinsically couples temporal duration and any variation of consciousness or mental activity (from Augustine to James to Husserl and beyond).

Craig holds that the *kalām* argument he proffers is neutral to the question of whether, prior to the hypothesized act of creation, God is timeless or sempiternal. Shields objects that this issues in incoherence, since a personal Creator would be temporal, yet as sempiternal the Creator would *actualize* an infinite past, namely, at minimum *an infinite past of divine experience*. In effect, the following ensemble of propositions to which Craig seems to be committed are logically inconsistent taken *in toto*:

(1) God is personal and thus temporal.

(2) God has always existed.

(3) As personal, God has experiences or consciousness.

(4) The past cannot be infinite.

Propositions (1), (2) and (3) logically entail the rejection of (4). Craig objects to this counter-argument by holding that the *kalām* argument contends only "that an infinite number of *events* cannot elapse, not that an infinite *time* cannot elapse."[22] Shields responds that this forgets that it is not *mere* time that would elapse but divine *experience* that would elapse on the hypothesis that a personal God has existed sempiternally. The notion of actual experience and the notion of actual events cannot be decoupled as it is perfectly commonsensical to discriminate, say, "my thought that P at past time *t*" from "my thought that Q at a later time *t**" as differing events. In other words, it is perfectly intelligible to differentiate two mental events having different temporal indices: event A as "my thought that P at time *t*" and event B as "my thought that Q at time *t**." Such demarcation of mental events could be applied to the divine case such that there is actualization of an infinitude of such mental events on the hypothesis that God is sempiternal. Yet even if there were a single divine thought or experience somehow sustained sempiternally prior to creation, by definition of "sempiternal," an infinite past would be actualized. Now, either there were one or many divine experiences prior to the hypothesized act of creation, thus there seems no escape from the conclusion that a sempiternal personal Creator would actualize an infinite past.

In his more recent work Craig has taken a different approach by rejecting the alternative that God has existed sempiternally prior to creation of the hypothesized first event in space-time.[23] This move would indeed solve the problem of logical consistency pointed out by Wolfe and Shields, but, in our view, at a very high cognitive cost. The cost incurred resides in the notion that a *timeless* entity could *deliberately act*, since deliberate action posits temporality. We concur with the argument of Richard Swinburne that the notion that God acts and is *essentially* temporal is perfectly clear and coherent as it conforms with what Kant articulated as the necessary "temporal schematism of cognition," while the alternative theory that a timeless entity can engage in deliberate action is entirely outside the temporal schematism.[24] As such it is not at all clear what one even *means* by asserting the existence of timeless actions. This argument, if correct, would also undermine Quentin Smith's view that the natural universe *arose* from a *timeless* singularity.[25] The neoclassical process view, which dovetails here with Swinburne's doctrine that God is sempiternal, invites no such problems. It conforms to common sense notions of time and action. The neoclassical process model of deity is thus, on the matters of time and agency, intuitively clear and far more parsimonious than the alternative notions proffered by the later Craig or by Quentin Smith.

Hartshorne occasionally gave arguments from authority on this issue, citing such experts in mathematics and logic as Bertrand Russell and Louis Couturat and their agreement that an infinite past is logically possible (CS 126). While this is a worthy consideration, it must be admitted that *ad vericundium* arguments even of the valid sort hold limited weight, since, of course, even appropriate authorities can be wrong. But one such appeal deserves attention because it is puzzling that Hartshorne would even suggest it. More than once he approvingly cites the argument found in G. E. Moore's essay on "The Notion of Infinity" (CS 125–26; IO 374).[26] Moore contends that relativity physics assures us that space is in fact finite but unbounded (a position with which Hartshorne, we think rightly, concurs), although, *contra* Kant's proof of temporal finitism, time can be coherently conceived as infinite in past extension. The particular argument Moore gives for such coherence involves the premise that any finite volume of space is constituted by an infinite number of real infinitesimals or Zeno-points. He then adds that, as common sense insists, we do, in fact, "traverse finite volumes" and thus by implication we "traverse the infinite." Consequently, the notion of an infinite past is only a species of "traversing the infinite," and, as such, is logically coherent. Of course, the main premise regarding Zeno-points is logically incompatible with Whitehead's rejection of actual infinitesimals given in the doctrine of extensive abstraction, so it is not an argument that Hartshorne can consistently employ given his explicit acceptance of extensive abstraction.[27] In our view, a far better *a priori* case for at least the intelligibility of an infinite past—one that appears to be free from contradicting basic principles of process philosophy—is found in Quentin Smith's argument that past events can be coherently mapped on to the set of negative numbers, where 0 is an arbitrary present and the set (. . . -4, -3, -2, -1, 0) correlates with past events. Following standard doctrine in transfinite mathematics, this set taken as the transfinite ordinality-type ω* has a cardinality of aleph-zero *yet no particular member of the set* has such cardinality. This property of ω* undermines the notion that there is an "infinitely distant" point in the past from which to begin an "impossible" count through an infinite number of intermediary events to arrive at 0. We come full circle to Hartshorne's insight that an infinite past is a *beginningless* series. Applying Smith's reasoning to the First Antinomy, Kant's proof of temporal finitism assumes tacitly but illicitly that there is a "beginning" to an *ex hypothesi* beginningless past.[28]

Since we have mentioned the topic of extensive abstraction and infinitesimals, we should point out that one apparent area of weakness in Hartshorne's philosophy is its lack of sufficient attention to some deep and puzzling issues surrounding the notion of *real infinities*—a topic with which Peirce struggled in his efforts to show the comprehensive applicability of his Pragmatic Maxim (real infinities seemed to Peirce to be metaphysically required, yet they also constitute counter-examples to his Maxim). While, on the one hand, as we have argued in this section, Hartshorne does offer some genuine insights on the question of the infinitude of the past, on the other hand, he leaves untouched a problem of systematic coherence that attends the denial of infinitesimals while affirming the infinitude of the past. As pointed out in separate papers by John W. Lango and George Shields, the predicament of Georg Cantor's doctrine of infinity and the response to it found in the contemporary Non-Standard Analysis School raises some serious questions of logical consistency for the standard process scheme.[29] While Cantor famously developed his proofs for the coherence of transfinite sets that were at first very reluctantly but eventually embraced by mathematicians, Abraham Robinson explains that Cantor tried to accommodate his (at the time) more orthodox finitist critics (such as his former teacher Kronecker) by rejecting the existence of infinitesimals.[30] Cantor's position here has been widely viewed as incoherent, because the arguments he presented against infinitesimals smack of the very same question-begging circularity found in his finitist colleagues' arguments against transfinites. The Non-Standard Analysis School was born out of the conviction that logical consistency forces an acceptance of both concepts of infinitude. If transfinites are acceptable, then so are infinitesimals. Indeed, a precise definition of the infinitesimal involves reference to the transfinite; that is to say, the infinitesimal can be coherently defined as *the multiplicative inverse of transfinite quanta*; in effect, if a transfinite quantum ω is coherent and allowable, then so is $1/\omega$.

Does acceptance of this result have a pernicious effect on the doctrine of actual occasions? After all, Whitehead offers Zenonian-style arguments for the very existence of occasions. Lango and Shields both argue that it does not, although for different reasons. Lango holds that a case can be made for infinitesimal occasions, while Shields finds Lango's case to be too intuitively sketchy and underdeveloped to be plausible (specifically Lango's "honeycomb hypothesis").[31] For Shields, whether an infinitesimal could exist or even has existed at some limit situation of the cosmos such as the big bang singularity, notwithstanding, standard actual occasions will be needed in order to explicate *becoming* coherently, as well as the temporal change grounded in becoming. This is because there can be neither instantaneous nor continuous *process*, and consequently process *must* be atomized or quantized by occasions as asserted by both Whitehead and Hartshorne. For consider the following: No process of becoming can be characterized by zero duration, for it is part and parcel of our intuitive notion of becoming that it involves *somehow* a *from-to*. If it were constituted by zero duration, it would have the from-characteristic and to-characteristic *simultaneously*; in effect, it would have some characteristic and not that characteristic *simultaneously*, thus violating the law of noncontradiction. (Moreover, adding sequences of zero duration would not make for a process having duration, since $0 + 0 = 0$.) On the other hand, process also cannot be continuous. On this score, as we will see in the next chapter, Hartshorne offers the argument of G. H. von Wright that continuous process violates the logical principle that 'No S can be p and *not-p* at the same time t': "For then, in any second, for any S and some p there is both p and $\sim p$, and *the same for any other fraction of time.* So (assuming continuous [process]) either we must take S at an instant (or in zero duration) or give up the principle of noncontradiction."[32] Since neither of these options is rationally palatable, there is no alternative but to embrace non-instantaneous and non-continuous quanta of process such as the actual entities of Whitehead or Hartshorne's dynamic singulars.

Of course, even if the allowance of infinitesimals does not undermine the necessity for actual occasions, such allowance will nonetheless require some revision of Hartshorne's Logic of Ultimate Contrasts. As Hartshorne himself worried, specifically with regard to the infinitude of the past (CS 125), the neat correlations of the conceptual contrasts potential/actual and infinite/finite are compromised, and this is doubly so if the above points issued by Lango and Shields regarding infinitesimals are admitted. One suggestion would be to hold that the line of demarcation between the potential and the actual in relation to infinitude/finitude is as follows: the domain of potentiality is *never* finite, while the domain of actuality may be either finite or infinite depending upon whether the actuality in question refers to what might be regarded as the "middling" ontological regions (standard actual occasions and societies of occasions which constitute macroscopic entities such as honey bees or rocks or humans) or to the ontological extremes of maxima (the totality of the past) or minima (infinitesimal singularities). Infinitude would thus always be correlated with potentiality (given the Peirce-Hartshorne view of potentia as dense continua); on the other hand, finitude would correlate with all actualities of the middle regions, while infinitude would correlate with the maxima and minima. This surely complicates the Logic of Contrasts and leaves it less elegant, but logical and metaphysical considerations would seem to require such unique but complicating qualifications.[33]

An additional and very important point arises from consideration of Cantor's position on real infinities, a point that in this case much favors a central feature of Hartshorne's neoclassical theism, namely, the concept of deity as eminent *self*-surpasser. This concerns Cantor's argument for the Absolute Infinite or so-called Big Omega. Cantor was greatly excited by his discovery of a coherent case for transfinite sets as he believed that it also allowed for a proof of the Absolute Infinite isomorphic with the classical concept of God. This led of course to the Russian-German thinker's letter to Pope Leo XIII, announcing a new scientific argument for the existence of God.[34] For most mathematicians and philosophers of mathematics today, however, Cantor's Big

Omega suffers from special problems of coherence, problems that do not attend his "lesser" transfinites (e.g., Aleph-null). In effect, the notion of "ordinary" infinities (as in the infinity of the whole numbers or "regular" transfinite sets codified as Aleph-null or Aleph-one, etc.) is coherent and acceptable, but the purportedly all-encompassing Absolute Infinite is not. This view is tailor-fit for Hartshorne's position. One of the most important counter-arguments to the Absolute Infinite or Big Omega has been articulated by Rudolf Rucker in what might be called the "Argument from the Reflection Principle" [hereafter RP]. One version of this argument runs as follows:[35]

> That the Absolute Infinite Ω (the set of all ordinals), and the related set-theoretic concept of Everything or *V* (the set of all sets), are strictly inconceivable can be shown by appeal to the RP. The RP is the principle that, for every conceivable property *P* of *V* (or Ω), there is a set *S* constitutive of *V* (or Ω), that is non-identical to *V* (or Ω), which has *P* as a property. For example, let *P* be the proposition that "*V* is not an ordinal number." By virtue of the RP, this is at once to introduce a set *S* constitutive of *V*, namely, the *set of thoughts S** such that "*V* is not an ordinal number." But this set must be included within *V* by virtue of its conceptual intention as the set of all sets. Since this would hold of any conceivable property, it is entailed that *V* can never be described in principle, because each such property would be at a meta-step from the complete description of *V*. There would indeed be a vicious infinite regress of reflections here such that there is also the set *S*** which includes *S**, that is, *S*** defined as the set of thoughts such that that there is a set of thoughts such that "*V* is not an ordinal number," and so on and on *ad infinitum* without completion. (This is a variant on John Locke's discovery of an infinite regress attaching to awareness of any item of knowledge. If one knows that *p*, one knows that one knows *p* and knows that one knows that one knows *p*, etc., etc., *ad infinitum*.) But to take something as actual which cannot be definitely described in principle seems too close to contradiction to be plausible. For in conjecturing such a circumstance, one is asserting that something which is *intrinsically protean* in its conception is also definitive or actual, that is to say, not protean. In effect, the indefinite is the definite, the potential the actual.

Because of the RP, it seems more reasonable to think of V or Ω as vector notations for maximal possibility which never reach the status of the achieved or actual. This is tantamount to the view of Peirce and Hartshorne that *the domain of possibility is never closed in principle*. And this result yields precise analogies for theological models. The classical deity as modeled in, say, Aquinas's famous definition of God as the immutable *actus purus*—the actualization all at once of an absolute maximum of potentiality—is incoherent since, as the above argument from the RP contends, there is simply no such thing as an *absolute maximum* of potentiality to be already actualized; there is only and always a *relative maximum*, that is, the domain of potentiality as accrued so far at any arbitrary present juncture of the creative advance of God. By contrast to the classical "closed" conception, the neoclassical model holds that God's potentiality is to be characterized as *always* inexhaustibly protean, that is to say, the domain of potentiality can always be superseded.

Although Bertrand Russell for a fleeting moment found himself seduced by reflections on the ontological argument (exclaiming "Great Scott, the ontological argument is sound!"), he was a convinced atheist for the majority of his adult life.[36] This conviction was largely grounded in his view that traditional theistic arguments are unconvincing but also because, in his treatise on *The Principles of Mathematics*, he rejected the coherence of the "class of all classes" and saw this as isomorphic with the classical concept of God.[37] However, as we have just seen, neoclassical theism's concept of the creative advance of an *intrinsically protean* God is perfectly suited to handle this sort of *a priori* anti-theistic reasoning, since for neoclassical theism there is no "class of all classes" in the absolutist sense attacked by Russell.

It is also interesting to notice that Whitehead affirms the *results* of the above RP reduction to absurdity in his essay on "Indication, Classes, Numbers, Validation." There he asserts that a proper logical definition of the null class necessarily involves a denial of the assumption that every propositional function "is associated with a unit entity which in some unique way is derived from the totality of the arguments satisfying it." The significant implication of this denial is that "there is no class [V] of all entities, such that for every class a, $a \cup V = V$. Thus, the symbol (V) for the 'Universal Class' is *not* introduced. There is no such class."[38]

Metaphysics and Science

Hartshorne contrasts metaphysical propositions with empirical and contingent propositions, which are restrictive of some existential possibilities. In Hartshorne's words: "*All* truths will agree with experience, hence the difference between contingent and necessary truths can show itself only in this, that the former could while the latter could not *conflict* with *conceivable* experiences" (CS 19–20). An empirical proposition is *essentially* restrictive, always involving an actualization of a state of affairs that excludes other possible alternatives. For example, "Barack Obama resides in the White House during 2011" tells us about states of affairs obtaining in the White House during 2011, and it tacitly *excludes* the state of affairs of John McCain, his opponent in the 2008 presidential election, residing in the White House during 2011. This feature of exclusion among alternative possibilities is definitive of contingency, and, for Hartshorne, follows from Leibniz's insight that the scope of disjunctive possibilities cannot be actualized *simultaneously or conjunctively*, since there are incompossible possibilities. Thus, the selection among possibilities confronted by natural processes must involve the acceptance of one alternative and the rejection of others, and this is a signature feature of empirical propositions. Hartshorne never considered the many-worlds interpretation of quantum theory, which by virtue of quantum branching into conjunctively realized alternative space-times, denies Leibniz's principle of contingency as exclusion of alternatives. We are convinced, however, that Leibniz's principle is indeed defensible since "many worlds" ontology is deeply problematic.[39]

If empirical propositions are essentially restrictive, it follows that every empirical state of affairs is positive, but has negative implications. The denial of these negative implications is also an empirical state of affairs. For example, one alternative to Obama's having won the 2008 presidential election is Hillary Clinton's having won it. Since this alternative did not occur, the denial of this alternative, namely, "Hillary Clinton did *not* win the 2008 presidential election" is true of the actual world. However, if an empirical proposition is one which excludes alternatives, how is this true of negative empirical implications of such propositions? Is not a negative empirical proposition simply an assertion of an absence or privation? Hartshorne holds that this is clearly not the case. What is excluded from actualization in the above negative empirical statement is Hillary Clinton's winning the 2008 presidential election, and this exclusion is achieved by a *positive* state of affairs. Positivity and exclusion of possibilities are thus features of all empirical propositions having negative as well as affirmative logical quality. While this must be true of empirical, contingent assertions, it begs the very question of metaphysics simply to declare that such restrictiveness is a property of all propositions about existential possibilities.

The division between metaphysics and empirical science is, in principle, clear. Hartshorne notes that, in practice, it is not always clear which statements count as empirical and which as metaphysical. It is well to keep in mind that Hartshorne uses Popper's idea about falsifiability as *a criterion of what it means* to be an empirical statement and not as the guiding method of empirical science. Popper elevated falsification over verification as the proper method of science. Hartshorne never rejected the idea that science should aim at falsifying hypotheses, but he agreed with Popper's critics that his denial of verification and corroboration in science was too drastic (CS 19). Hartshorne does not address in a systematic way the question of the proper methods of science; even so, showing that a given statement is falsifiable is, on Hartshorne's principles, one way in which it can be discredited as a true metaphysical idea. If a true metaphysical claim is falsified by no conceivable observation it is also the case that it is verified by every conceivable observation. Hartshorne holds that verifiability fails as a criterion for empirical statements but succeeds as a criterion for true metaphysical statements (CS 22). It follows that false metaphysical ideas are falsified by every conceivable observation and verified by none.

Nuanced issues emerge, however, when one considers particular case studies of the relationship between metaphysical and empirical propositions on Hartshorne's theory. Some critics have urged that Hartshorne's neoclassical positions may sometimes conflict with apparently well-corroborated empirical scientific hypotheses. Among other hypotheses, these include (i) the beginning of physical events in space-time a finite time ago as posited in standard hot big bang cosmologies (as noted earlier, Hartshorne's metaphysics of creativity posits an infinite past of cosmic epochs, the latest of which is our actual cosmos since the purported big bang event), and (ii) the apparent empirical result from Special Relativity that there is no cosmic simultaneity and thus no privileged or divine time (Hartshorne's theory of deity posits a temporal God). We discuss both of these issues in some detail in Chapter Eight. For now we simply observe that such apparent conflicts do not actually speak to Hartshorne's *theory* of metaphysical and empirical propositions, but rather to a different issue, namely, whether or not Hartshorne has actually succeeded in articulating a set of properly metaphysical propositions that would in fact be illustrated by any conceivable state of affairs.

While Hartshorne can be described as a kind of rationalist insofar as he maintains, like classical rationalists such as Descartes and Leibniz, that metaphysics *is* a matter of consistent and adequate *meanings* of concepts, he was hardly a dogmatic "armchair" or purely speculative philosopher who desired no engagement with the special empirical sciences—his first and thirteenth books demonstrate that he was a serious psychologist and ornithologist. His rationalism is in fact "critical" and rather severely qualified. For instance, *a propos* of the above comment regarding the question of the "success" of his metaphysical project, Hartshorne speaks of metaphysics as our quite *"contingent* ways of trying to become conscious of the non-contingent ground of all contingency" (CS 32). Leemon McHenry neatly makes the same point by stressing the category of process: "[The] universe is a process of becoming and so are our accounts of it."[40] We noted at the opening of this chapter that Hartshorne insists on the qualification that the notion of the *a priori* should hardly be conflated with the epistemic notion of "certainty." David Ray Griffin is correct when he writes: "Instead of *a priori* and nonempirical, [Hartshorne's] approach could well be called 'deep empiricism,' because it seeks those universal features at the depths of every experience, beneath the fleeting superficialities."[41] With Whitehead, Hartshorne insists that philosophers should be epistemically wary by avoiding the "dogmatic fallacy" such as found in the confidence of the Continental rationalists. Hartshorne declares, "All philosophizing is risky: cognitive security is for God, not for us."[42]

Perhaps the most fundamental objection from the side of science to any process metaphysic, Hartshorne's included, is the claim made by a number of philosophers and physicists (e.g., Adolf von Grünbaum, Julian Barbour, Huw Price, and Stephen Hawking) that time itself is ultimately an illusion.[43] The most definitive doctrine of process philosophy, namely, that the temporal modes (past, present, and future) are objectively real or that temporal becoming is objectively real, is thereby directly challenged.

This anti-process perspective is grounded in a realistic ontological reading of General Relativity Theory such that all events are atemporally present on four-dimensional Einstein-Minkowski "world tubes." Our common sense notions of the passage of time are illusions created by, in Herman Weyl's famous expression, the "crawling of consciousness along world-lines [or world-tubes]."[44] Thus, every mental event simply supervenes upon a physical event which "already" exists in the sense that it is to be found somewhere on the world-tube continuum. "Antecedent" physical events can be said to be causes of other physical events picked out on the continuum in the sense that they can be understood as "reasons" for those events.

If, as Weyl says, "the objective world simply is, it does not *happen*" what accounts for the illusion of temporal experience? A profound difficulty emerges when we reflect on explanations for this supposed illusion. Consider the following counter-argument championed by philosopher of science Milič Čapek.[45] We here reconstruct the argument with some liberties taken in terminology.

1.   All partisans accept the notion of temporal experience as a phenomenological given. The words "past," "present," and "future" are communicable and intelligible, because we remember the past, experience the present, and anticipate the future.

2.   Parallelism, which denies mind-brain causal influence of any sort, is inherently mysterious and arbitrary; it is an *ad hoc* solution to the paradoxes of Cartesian interaction.

3.   All other models of the mind-brain relation posit at least *sine qua non* causal influences (at least in the direction of brain to mind).

4.   If a tenseless monistic ontology holds, then brain events are tenseless and are already present simultaneously somewhere on a continuum of being.

5.   If brain events are at least *sine qua non* causal influences upon conscious states, then conscious states should be tenseless, because brain events are.

6.   Therefore, either parallelism is to be embraced (with all its mystery) or premise 1 must be rejected, contrary to the assumption of eternalist-physicalists themselves.

Now, granted, the argument must be framed slightly differently if we adopt a supervenience approach to the mind-body relation as advocated most famously by Jaegwon Kim in his *Supervenience and Mind*. In such case we would need to replace the notion that brain events are causes of mental events with the notion that mental events supervene upon brain events, and that brain events cause other brain events to occur. Yet, if we wedded the supervenience interpretation with eternalism, the underlying philosophical difficulty would remain since there is, on the eternalist ontological assumption, no *real transition* from one physical state to another physical state and thus no real transition from one supervenient mental event to another supervenient mental event. There is only the eternal continuum of being.

The difficulty of the eternalist's view is that there seems to be no plausible way to explain the sense of "the *crawling* along" world-tubes. Whence the crawling—a notion that invokes transition or movement? Whence the "illusion" of temporal experience? Since mental events are ontologically dependent on brain events, when wedded to eternalism, we should expect our mental life to be "all at once and simultaneous," contrary to the phenomenologically evident "on-flow" of lived experience. This problem in modern dress seems to be just as rationally intractable as the classical Vedantist-eternalist philosopher Sankara admitted it to be. The source of Brahman's or Being's active dreaming that yields *maya*, the "illusion" of temporal becoming, is an unsolvable mystery. We submit that this mystery vanishes, however, if we assume with Hartshorne and the entire process tradition that temporal becoming is hardly an illusion, but is rather a fundamental, irreducible reality. We observe that such important physicists and philosophers of science as Lee Smolin and Roberto Unger are in clear agreement: current theoretical physics can and should be rethought in such a way that its abstractions are not ontologized and we avoid fallacies of misplaced concreteness; as such, in Smolin's apt phrase, we find "time reborn."[46]

An auxiliary consideration that supports the realistic view of temporal becoming is that science itself is embedded in human culture and activity, phenomena which seem to presuppose that the past is settled and that the future is, in some respects, a field of open possibilities yet to be settled. Hartshorne accepted the commonplace of both pragmatism and existentialism that we do not merely know the world (or attempt to know it); more fundamentally, we are agents who make decisions. In making decisions we are also part-makers of ourselves and, by parity of reasoning, we are part-makers of the world. Hartshorne argued further that, for theism properly understood, this entails that we are part-makers of God. Hartshorne credited the nineteenth century French philosopher Jules Lequyer with first clearly drawing out these implications from the idea of freedom (PSG 228).[47] We shall see in Chapter Five that this does not mean that any individual brings it about that God exists; rather, every individual, by his or her decisions, brings about something within God's experience (if only the knowledge that the decision was made) that would not have existed without that individual making decisions. Hartshorne insisted that this is no extraordinary use of the verb "to make," but is its ordinary meaning.

Hartshorne ventured as one criterion of sound metaphysics that its principles not contradict the conditions for the living of life conceived as a process of decision making. In Hartshorne's words, "what we have to be guided by in our decision-making, we should not pretend to reject theoretically" (PCH 624). Or again, "Metaphysics must be live-able" (PCH, 687). To be sure, we are capable of acting on false beliefs; moreover, we may live much of our lives holding a variety of false beliefs, some of which may be useful to us or simply be pragmatically irrelevant. Prior to the modern era, for example, the common belief was that the earth is stationary. From a pragmatic standpoint, and in a day without space travel, it was irrelevant whether the earth moved or was stationary. Astronomers charted the movements of the heavens, sailors navigated the seas, and more generally, people lived and died without any interference from the falsity of the belief in an immobile earth. The same can be said of many other ideas that have been clarified and corrected by the progress of science. It should also be mentioned that the progress of science brings with it not only greater assurance of the truth of certain claims but also more fruitful ways of dealing with the world. For example, Newtonian physics, unlike that of Aristotle, allowed us to connect apparently disparate phenomena, such as the trajectory of a cannon ball, the motion of the moon around the earth, and the periodic appearance of a comet. One would be hard pressed to send a rocket to Mars based on the physics of antiquity. Another dramatic example of the usefulness of science is Neo-Darwinian evolutionary theory, which combines Darwin's insights with modern genetics.

The fact that the truth of a belief is not necessarily the same as its usefulness does not mean that it is false that some beliefs should be considered true precisely because they are useful, or perhaps better, indispensable, in the sense that their denial involves a performative self-contradiction. An example is the efficacy of final causes or purposes in the practice of science. Whitehead once remarked that, "Scientists animated by the purpose of proving that they are purposeless constitute an interesting subject for study."[48] The practice of science is saturated by purposive activity, including the design of experiments, the development of theories, and the testing of hypotheses. To attempt to demonstrate or to argue, by means of science itself, that purpose plays no role in how scientists go about their work, is a self-defeating enterprise. It is on a par with a native English speaker who would say, "I have never spoken a word of English in my life." The very act of uttering the sentence refutes the truth of the sentence. At a minimum, dismissing purposes where the activity of science is concerned is an instance of what Whitehead called the fallacy of misplaced concreteness. One may ignore purposes, but what remains is a mere shadow of the practice of science.

Other examples of ideas that specifically human activities (not alone science) seem to presuppose are (1) the reality of the external world or the falsity of solipsism, (2) the existence of causal regularity or the affirmation of some internal relations amongst events, (3) the reality and inalterability of the past as opposed to its nonexistence, (4) the partial indeterminacy of the future awaiting human decisions (or the decisions of some agent) to make it fully determinate as contrasted to a future decided in advance or in eternity.[49] We shall see in the next chapter that Hartshorne develops and defends each of these ideas as substantive metaphysical claims concerning the social nature of existence and the modal structure of temporal process. It is, in any event, foreign to Hartshorne's thought to arrest philosophical speculation in the realm of truths with no practical use, as Descartes apparently did in warning against using methodical doubt as a guide to action in ordinary life.[50] Likewise, Hartshorne rejected the divorce of theory and practice suggested in Hume's remark: "Be a philosopher; but, amidst all your philosophy, be still a man."[51] If metaphysical truths are, as Hartshorne claims, unconditionally necessary and non-restrictive of existential possibilities, then a strict bifurcation of theory and practice represents the failure of the metaphysical enterprise.

Conclusion

As is evident from the foregoing, questions of method in metaphysics quickly lead one to the question of the truth or falsity of particular metaphysical claims. As Hartshorne notes, "[It] is a moot question how far one can distinguish methodological from substantive issues" (CS 71). This problem is perhaps the inevitable byproduct of aspiring, from our very limited perspective within the universe, to gain a sense of the strands of necessity that connect any possible universe (or cosmic epoch) with all others. Like Whitehead, Hartshorne denied that there is any creaturely vantage point from which something is not hidden from us. Nevertheless, we are not without resources for crafting a metaphysic that may reveal some of the necessary features of existence. There is the history of metaphysical thinking on our planet, which Hartshorne considered to provide us with a mine of suggestions, of hypotheses for consideration, of blind alleys, and sometimes of insight. In order to use the history of philosophy in this way, Hartshorne argued that one must focus less on the important figures than on important ideas (CS 86). In this way, the history of philosophy becomes integral to the metaphysical task by providing a testing ground or laboratory of ideas and theories (PCH 582–83).

As we hope to have shown in this chapter, Hartshorne's position or doctrinal matrices provides a grid for understanding the doctrinal alternatives actually available in the history of philosophy. In this way, one gains a better sense of the ideas and theories that are possible but, more importantly, to have a better perspective on those metaphysical views that have and have not been explored in the history of philosophy. Hartshorne, like Whitehead but even more than Whitehead, was expert at highlighting neglected aspects of the works of well-known philosophers (e.g., Plato and Leibniz) as well as emphasizing what he considered to be the important ideas of philosophers who are largely neglected by those who write philosophy's history (e.g., Fechner and Lequyer). Moreover, Hartshorne was never parochial in his approach to philosophy; although trained primarily in Western traditions, he was interested enough in Eastern thought to make substantive contributions to comparative philosophy, discussing a variety of Indian, Chinese, and Japanese philosophers.[52]

☙ FOUR ☙

Neoclassical Metaphysics

HARTSHORNE REFERRED to his metaphysics as "neoclassical" to emphasize its continuity with classical traditions, especially as they sprang up in antiquity from the pre-Socratic philosophers and from Plato and Aristotle. He was also keen to stress that his views are importantly different, or new ("neo"), in their substantive claims. He would eventually highlight the parallels of his metaphysics with ideas in early Buddhist thought. The family of metaphysical views to which Hartshorne's ideas belong is often called process philosophy or, following Bernard Loomer, process-relational philosophy. One finds anticipations of process-relational philosophy in Peirce's tychism, James's pluralistic universe, and Bergson's *la durée*. Hartshorne was influenced by these philosophers (with Peirce being the most dominant of the three) but his greatest debt was to Whitehead's later philosophy.

Creativity

Philosophers venture various hypotheses as to the character of the finally real constituents of existence. One remembers Parmenides's *Being*, Democritus's tiny impenetrable atoms, Aristotle's hylomorphic *ousia*, Descartes's dual substance ontology, Leibniz's monads, and Whitehead's

83

actual entities. Hartshorne adopted a Whiteheadian view, sometimes speaking of "dynamic singulars" instead of "actual entities" (IO 274; CA 174, 241, 261; CE 21, 24).[1] Dynamic singulars are instances of what Hartshorne called "creative experiencing," an expression that suggests an activity of synthesis, a bringing together of diverse elements from an entity's antecedent world into a unity of feeling. Hartshorne often used Whitehead's word "prehension" to name the feelings from which a dynamic singular weaves its own experience from the welter of data from its past. The "diverse elements" from the past that are synthesized are themselves instances of creative experiencing; for this reason, Hartshorne was fond of the expression "feeling of feeling," which is close to Whitehead's language.[2] The prime example on which both Whitehead and Hartshorne model this activity is memory. Memories are themselves experiences that may have previous experiences as component parts. Moreover, memories are *active* in the way that they highlight some items of experience but place other items in the background, sometimes almost forgotten. Memory also serves as a model of the way emotional tone suffuses experience, in accordance with Hartshorne's theory of the affective continuum. Finally, in keeping with process-relational philosophy, memory is a *process*, a coming-to-be, and not an unchanging substance; its very existence, moreover, depends upon its *relation* to past events.

Hartshorne agreed with Whitehead when the latter spoke of *creativity* as "the category of the ultimate." In Whitehead's words, "the many become one, and are increased by one."[3] For both Whitehead and Hartshorne, creativity is not itself a substance but rather the name for the activity that characterizes every concrete particular, from the lowliest puff of existence to God. Thomas Aquinas restricted creativity in the strict sense to deity alone.[4] Whitehead and Hartshorne, on the other hand, treat creativity as what medieval thinkers called a transcendental, a universal concept that is not restricted to this or that kind of real thing but which identifies a thing *as such* as real (CE Ch. 11). Another departure from traditional ideas about creativity is that, for Whitehead and Hartshorne, creativity is never *from nothing* (*ex nihilo*), whether it is God's creativity or the creativity of individuals within the cosmos. According to Hartshorne, the "nothing" in the expression "*creatio ex nihilo*" would be a purely negative fact, which as noted in the previous chapter, Hartshorne rejects. Thus, Hartshorne concluded that a creative act always presupposes an antecedent world from which the novel act arises.

Hartshorne's emphasis on creativity illustrates his commitment to the principle—summarized in the previous chapter—that that which comes-to-be (becoming) includes but is not included by that which is but does not come to be (being). Hartshorne insists on taking "becoming" in the strictest sense as a process that adds to the definiteness of reality something that was not included in the class of real things prior to the act of becoming. Nothing corresponds to the word "reality" considered as a single nontemporal or eternal fact; rather, reality *grows* with every act of becoming and is, as it were, *defined* by them. Hartshorne rejects the idea that there is literally "nothing new under the sun"; on the contrary, there was a time when even the sun was new. Hartshorne is not simply reaffirming the flux of Heraclitus where all concrete things change; he is affirming that reality is a *growing totality*, an idea that is also prominent in Peirce's evolutionary cosmology. The growth of reality, moreover, is thoroughly temporal—*time itself is the process of creation*. The past is determinate, the future is a field of relatively indeterminate *possibilia*, and the present is the process of determination. Finally, Hartshorne argues that what comes to be, once it has become fully determinate, is a permanent fixture of all subsequent becoming, guaranteed in the final analysis by God's memory of it. In Hartshorne's words, "there is no de-becoming of facts" (CE 85). This is why Hartshorne speaks of creation as a *cumulative process*.

An early reviewer of *The Divine Relativity*, Philip Phenix, characterized Hartshorne's view as "the 'cosmic snowball' view of the world, gathering the past into itself as it rolls through time." (The analogy fails, in part, because the ball's rolling isn't *in* time, the process *is* time.) Phenix maintained that Hartshorne's idea that the past is preserved in the present and that God's awareness houses the past with all its achieved value "is likely to prove as unsatisfying to the pious as it will be incredible to the critical-minded."[5] The problem Phenix raises is that Hartshorne's view seems to undermine the distinction between the past and the present. The same criticism was expressed by John Wild and revived in more recent times in a dissertation by Antony Thomas Kalathil. According to Kalathil, "To say that the past is still actual seems equivalent to the statement that it is present, and thus not past. Today's sunset does not include yesterday's sunset. It succeeds it. As past, it is not; it *once was*."[6] The first thing to notice about this criticism is that the example of sunsets succeeding one another is flawed since it is not an instance of what Hartshorne calls a dynamic singular prehending the past. To be sure, a sunset is an event, but it has no dynamic unity except as it exists in someone's experience, and as far as the "cosmic snowball" is concerned, the relevant experiencer is God.

Hartshorne realized that his view of the past is contrary to the idea that the past is on a par with the future in that neither one exists.

> That 'actual' process is past process, rather than strictly present process, will trouble or offend some readers, I fear. But I hold with Bergson that actuality is pastness, since presentness is a becoming actual rather than a being actual. (CS 117–18; cf. ZF 123)

It was the doctrine of the nonexistence of the past that Hartshorne found more paradoxical. If the past does not exist, then what distinguishes mere nonexistence from "having been"? This is why he so often objected to Whitehead's metaphor, used in the final line of *Process and Reality*, of the past perishing. As Hartshorne explained, "It is the reality of the new *as added to that of the old*, rather than the unreality of the old, that constitutes process" (WP 84, cf. PCH 650). Reality has three modes on Hartshorne's view: the past as actual, the present as the becoming of what is actual, and the future as potential for actualization. Once this is understood, the objection that Hartshorne collapses the distinction between past and present collapses. Nor will it make sense on Hartshorne's view to say simply that neither past nor future exist.[7] What answers to the concept in ordinary parlance of "what no longer is" is precisely the actual data for any particular act of becoming; what answers to the concept of "what may yet be" is the array of possibilities for actualization for any particular act of becoming.

Hartshorne's view of temporal process and what Whitehead called "the creative advance" is an attempt to avoid what he saw as the extremes of *presentism* and *eternalism*.[8] Presentism holds to the existence of a "moving" present moment—as present becomes past and the future becomes present—and the nonexistence of past and future. This idea is often associated with J. M. E. McTaggart's idea of an A-series. Eternalism, on the other hand, holds that all moments are equally present and that the "movement" of the present is an illusion. The only "direction" of time recognized by eternalism is that which is provided by McTaggart's B-series—events arrayed as being "before and after" each other, recognizing that every event is "before" some and "after" others.

Presentism and eternalism hold in common that the past and the future are on a par—equally nonexistent for the presentist or equally existent for the eternalist. Hartshorne rejects both views, and in this, his ideas bear a strong resemblance to C. D. Broad's concept of the universe as a "growing block" in which temporal change involves "fresh slices of existence [being] added to the total history of the world."[9] In order to avoid collapsing the distinction between any two of the modalities of time, Hartshorne affirms the triad: the determinate or actual past, the present process of determining what is actual, and the relatively indeterminate array of possibilities for what may become actual. We will return to these ideas in what follows to give a more complete understanding of Hartshorne's views of time and modality.

Hartshorne, like Whitehead, was a metaphysical atomist in the sense that he believed the world to be composed of discrete parts. Whitehead called atomism the "ultimate metaphysical truth."[10] Dynamic singulars or actual entities are the "building blocks" of the universe. In this belief, Hartshorne and Whitehead parted company with other process philosophers like Peirce and Bergson who held that becoming is continuous. Sandra B. Rosenthal notes that Whitehead and his followers think of time as arising from the fusing together of discrete elements into fully determinate actualities. She argues that Whitehead's popularity among process philosophers tends to eclipse the fact that there is a pragmatic strain of process thought that construes time as the emergence of essentially vague elements in an ever-expanding field of actualization.[11]

Nicholas Rescher makes a stronger claim; he argues that metaphysical atomism goes against the spirit of the very idea of process. According to Rescher, "Whitehead's theory of processes as rooted in the aggregation of atomistic 'actual occasions' is an unhappy concession to a thoroughly process-estranged point of view." Of course, the same criticism applies to Hartshorne's atomism. Rescher's argument is as follows:

> Why should the succession of subordinate processes inevitably have to come to an end? It is far more appropriate to contemplate a Chinese box-like succession of larger processes enhancing over small ones: the poet's situation of larger fleas having ever smaller ones to bite 'em—ad infinitum. After all, if nature is indeed processual, then why should not its composition be processual "all the way through"? Why should there be ultimate particles of process that are nowise resolvable into more basic

constituents? From the process point of view, it is surely only natural to see nature as a manifold of concatenated processes that admit—in principle—of decomposition into ever-smaller processual units.[12]

Rescher's use of the analogies of the Chinese boxes and the fleas biting fleas is unfortunate, for neither image is an illustration of his conclusion. Frederick Ferré makes this point in discussing a similar image: "an infinite set of Russian dolls, a smaller doll nesting inside each larger one 'all the way down.'"[13] Ferré notes that the analogy is seriously flawed. It is an analogy of one thing *containing* another, not of one thing *being made of* another. All of the dolls are made of molecules, and at some point in the regress to smaller dolls, it would be impossible to have a doll since there would be too few molecules. The same logic applies to Rescher's Chinese boxes and fleas biting fleas. Ironically, Rescher's analogies support the atomistic view.

Although Rescher's analogies are defective, the question he raises is legitimate. Is it a "thoroughly process-estranged point of view" to suppose that there exist "ultimate particles of process that are nowise resolvable into more basic constituents?" Perhaps what Rescher has in mind is something like Bergson's idea that it is absurd to suppose that, "movement is made of immobilities."[14] It would indeed be contrary to the spirit of Hartshorne's metaphysics or any version of process thought to suppose that the world's fundamental constituents are not processive, like Bergson's immobile parts of movement. Indeed, this is not only against the spirit of process thought, it is not process thought at all. Nevertheless, it is not obviously contrary to process thought to suppose that the constituents of the world are discrete processive "atoms." In other words, what is contrary to process thought is not that the world is composed of discrete parts but that those discrete parts are non-processive. Of course, it is precisely the view of Hartshorne and Whitehead that the elements of the world are processive. As Hartshorne says, recalling Whitehead, "The fully determinate units of reality are momentary actualities that 'become but do not change'" (WM 18).[15] Thus, Hartshorne and Whitehead adhere to the central claim of process philosophy that process is ontologically basic.

What reasons led Whitehead and Hartshorne to the atomistic conclusion? Whitehead rejected what he called the "baseless metaphysical doctrine of 'undifferentiated endurance'" by considering William James's discussion of Zeno's paradoxes in *Some Problems of Philosophy*.[16] According to Whitehead, when one dismisses those Zenoian paradoxes that are products of inadequate mathematical knowledge, a legitimate paradox of becoming remains. A contradiction results in accepting the following two propositions:

(1) In [an act of] becoming something (*res vera*) becomes.

(2) Every act of becoming is divisible into earlier and later acts of becoming.

Suppose an act of becoming, *B*, that is divisible into earlier and later acts of becoming, call them *B-first half* (*B-1ˢᵗ½*) and *B-second half* (*B-2ⁿᵈ½*). *B-1ˢᵗ½* must occur before *B-2ⁿᵈ½* can occur. However, the same logic applies to *B-1ˢᵗ½*, which must be divisible into earlier and later acts of becoming, *B-first fourth* (*B-1ˢᵗ¼*) and *B-second fourth* (*B-2ⁿᵈ¼*). *B-2ⁿᵈ¼* cannot occur before *B-1ˢᵗ¼* occurs. Likewise, *B-1ˢᵗ¼* is divisible into earlier and later acts of becoming, *B-first eighth* (*B-1ˢᵗ⅛*) and *B-second eighth* (*B-2ⁿᵈ⅛*) and *B-2ⁿᵈ⅛* cannot occur before *B-1ˢᵗ⅛* occurs—and so forth, *ad infinitum*. In effect, *B* cannot occur until an infinite number of smaller and smaller acts of becoming take place. Whitehead's solution to the puzzle was to deny that an *act of becoming* is divisible into earlier and later acts of becoming. An actual entity has temporal thickness, although its act of coming to be is not a process that unfolds through time, however brief. An actual entity is a packet of duration that makes its appearance all at once. Time is the process whereby actual entities succeed each other, not the process by which an actual entity comes to be. Whitehead summarizes the case by saying, "There is a becoming of continuity, but no continuity of becoming."[17]

Hartshorne accepted Whitehead's conclusion but he preferred a different argument, one derived from Georg Henrik von Wright.[18] Hartshorne writes:

> Von Wright holds that the logical principle, 'no *S* can be *p* and not-*p* at the same time' is inapplicable if change is taken as continuous. For then, in any second, for any *S* and for some *p* there is both *p* and not-*p*, and the same with any other fraction of time. So (assuming continuous change) either we must take *S* at an instant (or in zero duration) or give up the principle of

non-contradiction. With many other philosophers, von Wright rejects the notion that an actuality can have a definite character in zero time. The conclusion then follows: becoming cannot be continuous.[19]

Put somewhat differently: if becoming is continuous, then either moments of zero duration have definite characteristics or some temporally thick processes have contradictory characteristics. With von Wright, Hartshorne rejected both disjuncts of the consequent; it follows that becoming is not continuous.

We have noted that Hartshorne's acceptance of an atomistic ontology of events or dynamic singulars put him at odds with Peirce's doctrine that "all that exists is continuous," which is one aspect of what Peirce called *synechism*.[20] It is clear that, for Peirce, the essential character of a continuum is that it has no least member.[21] Peirce was most impressed by the use of continua in the progress of science, from the idea of infinitesimals in the calculus to the idea of transitional forms in evolutionary development. Hartshorne agreed with Peirce that evolutionary theory is contrary to the ancient idea of the immutability of species. But this does not in any way imply a continuum of species. Hartshorne noted that all of the animals that have lived on earth do not in any sense form a continuum since they are, in every respect, finite and no addition of finite quantities equals an infinite set. "Only all thinkable creatures, being infinite or indefinite in number, may be conceived as forming continua with respect to various properties" (CAP 84). Beyond its metaphysical meaning, synechism served, for Peirce, as a methodological principle. He argued that hypotheses positing continua leave open "the greatest field of possibility" and thereby do not block the path of inquiry.[22] Hartshorne called this argument specious. He countered that the hypothesis of a continuum excludes "any and every one of the infinite forms of possible discontinuity." Hartshorne continues:

> Our initial hypothesis should be that actuality is discrete, but with our minds open among the unlimited, mutually incompatible, possibilities for discontinuity. The totality of ways in which a continuum of possibility can be broken up into discrete actualities—what is that but the continuum over again? So I think Peirce really missed the target here. (CAP 85)

In what follows, we shall see that, for Hartshorne, the growing totality of the past is qualitatively definite, an ever-expanding selection or cutting of the infinite continuum of possibilities that is the essence of futurity.[23]

In one important respect, the appearances *do not* favor metaphysical atomism. If Hartshorne is correct (also James and Whitehead) that reality grows in discrete segments, why does it seem to our experience that it grows in an unbroken blossoming of novel forms? Phenomenology, naively taken, offers more support to Rescher's (also Peirce's and Bergson's) preference for the idea of process as a continuum than it offers the metaphysical atomist. Hartshorne argues that while phenomenology does not clearly support the atomistic view, neither does it clearly contradict it. He proposes as a general principle: "What is *positively and definitely given* in perception must be accepted as really there; but what is not so given may yet also be there" (PCH 637). The basis of the second conjunct of this principle is the logical truth that the absence of the perception of something is not equivalent to the perception of something's absence (CS 79).[24] The precedent for supposing that discreteness in the world is not mirrored in our perception of it has been set by the progress of science, especially in the last two centuries. Seventeenth century scientists were surprised to find more stars in the heavens when seen through a telescope than what was visible with their eyes alone. Or again, neither the cells and molecules of biology nor the atoms and the quantum energy packets of physics are apparent to unaided perception. It would not be surprising, therefore, if the "metaphysical atoms" of becoming, supposing they exist, were not apparent to our perception. Be that as it may, Hartshorne's argument for metaphysical atomism is *not* drawn from phenomenology. The theory that actual entities become but do not change is proposed as an account of a world in process that escapes the Zenoian paradox without contradicting the data of experience.[25]

Before leaving the subject of creativity as an ultimate metaphysical principle, we wish to address what might be called an argument from linguistic convention against thinking of the final units of reality as processual. Mario Bunge, for example, calls Whitehead's process philosophy (and this applies as well to Hartshorne's) "logically untenable" for "the notion of a process presupposes that of a thing, because a process is defined as a sequence of changes in a thing."[26] In short, if there is change, or process, then there must be something that changes or is in process; therefore, it is *things* changing and not the *changing* itself that is metaphysically basic. For example, the change in the color of a leaf in autumn is a process, but there must be a leaf underlying the change. Hartshorne responds as follows:

> Very well, suppose the weather changes from wet to dry, does this mean there is an entity, the weather, as concrete as the wet and dry states? Are these "in" the weather? Surely the weather is in them. Suppose "public opinion" changes, or "the situation" changes—is it not obvious that the "subjects of change" here are relatively abstract entities? Process philosophy generalizes this insight. It treats change as the successive becoming of events related to one another, but also differing from one another in some more or less abstract respects which interest us.[27]

Hartshorne's examples show that the principle, "where there is change there is something concrete that is changing," is not necessarily true. Even in those cases where it seems to be true that something is undergoing change, the subject of change may itself be a process. At one level of analysis, for example, the leaf is the subject of change—but what exactly is the leaf? Is it a self-identical substance that is itself without change? No merely empirical investigation could show this. On the contrary, scientific investigation, especially in the realm of subatomic phenomena, disrupts the usual categories of thinghood and may best be interpreted as a world of events.[28] At the very least, we may agree with Nicholas Rescher who says, "Clearly, storms and heat waves are every bit as real as dogs and oranges. Even on the surface of it, verb-entities have as good a claim to reality as noun-entities."[29]

Psychicalism

The fact that Hartshorne takes experience to be ontologically foundational means that his metaphysics is a type of what has traditionally been known as panpsychism, Early in his career, he used "panpsychism," but later he preferred "psychicalism" (occasionally he spoke of "psychical monism") and he said that he did not object to David Ray Griffin's word "panexperientialism" (HP 181). Ferré observed that most modern theories of reality are committed to "a kind of methodological behaviorism in which questions of 'interiority' . . . are simply ruled out from the start. The entities of physics have no insides. They are what they do."[30] Hartshorne's philosophy is one of the important exceptions to this rule, but he typically made the point somewhat differently than Ferré made it. His preferred distinction is between the more quantitative and structural features of a thing studied by physics, chemistry, and biology and its qualitative features, ignored by these sciences, which he associated with the qualities of experience, generalized to their most generic form which, following Whitehead, he called *feeling*, or as he insisted time and again, "feeling of feeling."[31]

It is by now a truism among most philosophers—but one worth repeating—that the scientist's understanding of the world involves an act of abstraction whereby certain aspects of things are ignored and others are highlighted. Stephen Hawking—surely among the world's most famous scientists and science popularizers—raises the question whether a grand unified theory in physics could account for all the complexity and apparently trivial detail we find around us. He asks, "Can one really believe that the grand unified theory has determined that Sinead O'Connor will be the top of the hit parade this week, or that Madonna will be on the cover of *Cosmopolitan*?"[32] Hawking suggests that such details might be attributable to quantum indeterminacies in the initial stages of the universe.[33] What is missing from Hawking's speculation is that the concepts and laws of physics provide no vocabulary for talking about persons (Sinead O'Connor, Madonna), popularity (being at the top of the hit parade), or words and photos on the cover of a magazine (*Cosmopolitan*). For example, the configuration of elementary particles that a particular copy of *Cosmopolitan* exhibits provides no clues as to the identity of the person depicted on the cover, the meaning of the words written there, or indeed whether this configuration of particles is a copy of a magazine. Physics is silent on such things. Physicists begin, like most of the rest of us, with the magazine in hand, knowing that it is a popular magazine and knowing how to read and understand the meaning of the images and words in it. But this is not knowledge gained from physics; it is knowledge gained in other ways; and insofar as it *is* knowledge, physics is incomplete as an account of the world.

The laws of physics—quantum or otherwise—explain a great deal about the universe that we want to know, but they are blind to other aspects of that same universe precisely because they are abstractions from our experience of it, most notably, as Hartshorne says, its qualitative and affective dimensions. Galen Strawson makes the same point by highlighting the power of physics to reveal the "quantities and relational structures" but he notes "the silence of physics" concerning "the intrinsic *nonstructural* nature of the thing or things that exemplify them."[34] On this point, Hartshorne (also G. Strawson) alludes approvingly to a discussion in Russell's *Human Knowledge: Its Scope and Limits*. Russell argues as follows:

> Names for colors were used for thousands of years before the undulatory theory of light was invented, and it was a genuine discovery that wave lengths grow shorter as we travel along the spectrum from red to violet. If we define a shade of color by its wave length, we shall have to add that sensations caused by light of the same wave length all have a recognizable similarity, and that there is a less degree of similarity when the wave lengths differ, but only by a little. Thus, we cannot express all that we know on the subject without speaking about shades of color as known directly in visual sensation, independently of any physical theory as to light waves.[35]

Machines can be constructed to detect the longer wave lengths, but in that case, the experience of red is missing.[36] As with our previous example, the physicist begins, like the rest of us, with a knowledge not gained from physics—in this case, knowledge of the qualitative character of redness.

For a self-reflective creature—one who reflects on its own experience—there is an additional piece of knowledge, which is the knowledge of the experience itself. Hartshorne summarizes the case in these words: "Since knowledge must be based in some fashion upon experience, it is axiomatic that if anything can be known to exist or occur and the fact of this knowledge can itself be known, then so can the reality of some experiences."[37] It is unavailing to respond that one may only seem to have conscious awareness of experience, for *the very seeming is itself an experience*. The ancient Chinese sage, Chuang Tzu, dreamed of being a butterfly, but upon awaking, he was unsure whether he was the man having dreamt of being a butterfly, or a butterfly dreaming he was a man.[38] Whatever else one may learn from Chuang Tzu's philosophical playfulness, it is true that he was having experiences. Again, Strawson is of one mind with Hartshorne on this point when he says, "Any such seeming or illusion is already and necessarily an instance—an actually existing example—of the thing that is being said to be an illusion."[39] The point at issue is not whether there can be a purely functional or behavioristic explanation of illusions or mistaken perceptions; rather, the point is that one's having of experience cannot itself be a mirage: there are experiences of what is real and experiences of what is not real (as in dreams), but the common element is precisely *the having of experience*.[40]

Throughout his career, Hartshorne maintained that an exclusively behavioristic science—from physics to psychology—inevitably leaves the qualitative features of experience unexplained. In his first book he wrote:

> We are often told that the question "What is it?" has been superseded by the more scientific "How does it behave?" But it is overlooked that the former question is elliptical for the colloquial "What is it like?" and that this again needs expansion into "With what groups of other things and in what logical manner does it form dimensional systems of graduated differences?" These dimensions include others besides those specifiable exclusively in terms of behavior; and the inquiry concerning these hyperphysical likenesses and differences among things is a legitimate appeal to observation and logical analysis. It can never rightfully be cut off by a priori dogmas.
> (PPS 191)

Hartshorne argued that our direct knowledge of objects outside our bodies is indeed limited to a knowledge of how those objects behave; but in our experience of ourselves, we have a "dual access to reality," for we not only observe our own behavior, but we can know what it is like to be the sort of creatures we are. In Hartshorne's words, "We know what it is like to be a person studying rocks or molecules, in a sense in which we do not know what it is like to be a rock or a molecule."[41]

We shall see that Hartshorne did not believe that a rock is an experiencing object, but he did not confine experience to human beings. Nevertheless, he found within human experience the clue to the qualitative aspects of experience in other creatures. Evolution implies a continuity of life forms and thereby suggests a continuity of feeling qualities, the idea that is the basis of Hartshorne's theory of the affective continuum. He recognized the profound gap that exists between the experiences of other creatures and the human form of experiencing, which in its developed stages involves a high capacity for symbolic interaction. He emphasized the difficulty in bridging this gap by often asking what it is like to be something besides a human being. What is it like to be a honeybee, a gorilla, a turtle, a paramecium, a dog, a porpoise, a honeybee, a whale, an amoeba, an atom, or even an inhabitant of another planet?[42] He counted among his "heroes" Donald R. Griffin, not only because of his discovery of echolocation in bats, but because of his defense of an experiential and cognitive continuity amongst humans and other animals.[43] Hartshorne certainly saw the point of Thomas Nagel's 1974 article "What Is It Like to Be a Bat?" one of the most cited articles in the philosophy of mind.[44] Of course, Hartshorne's most thorough empirical investigation of the question of animal awareness is his study of birdsong in which he asks "how the bird experiences its songs" and concludes that it is remotely analogous to what we experience in aesthetic enjoyment (BS xi, 10).

Two important consequences of Hartshorne's distinction between structural and qualitative aspects of a thing is, first, a denial of mind-body dualism, and second, a rejection of the assumption that minds are essentially nonphysical entities. Even Descartes, who argued for nonphysical minds, acknowledged that certain mental qualities are experienced as spread throughout one's body or as being in specific regions of the body. Ordinarily, for example, one satisfies an itch by scratching the irritated area (a specific *location* on the skin). To be sure, one hardly knows if it makes sense to ask how much a tickle, a sharp pain, or the taste of an orange weighs; on the other hand, tickles, pains, and tastes seem to occur in definite regions even if, as in phantom limb cases, the causal source is misidentified.[45] Mental and physical qualities are indeed distinguishable but it does not follow that they are separable, Descartes's thought experiment notwithstanding. We noted above that Hartshorne did not object to David Griffin's use of the word *panexperientialism* to characterize his own position. One may guess that he would also have little problem accepting Griffin's use of the expression *panexperientialist physicalism* to name the view that minds are *not* nonphysical and that every actuality has a physical aspect or structure.[46] For Hartshorne, mind, or more generally experience, is the more inclusive category; for this reason, he could say that any alternative to psychicalism commits the fallacy of misplaced concreteness (WP 28). This is the fallacy of mistaking the abstract for the concrete. In this instance of the fallacy, the abstract or structural features of an entity (its physical characteristics) are mistaken for its full concreteness which is the qualitative whole of which the physical is its structural aspect.

Apart from Descartes and some of his followers, few have been willing to confine experience to specifically human experience. With the rise of developmental thinking in science and the hegemony of evolutionary theory, which brings in its wake a vast array of studies on comparative animal intelligence, the denial of experience to nonhuman creatures has become wildly implausible. The question now is how far down the evolutionary scale experience reaches. As Hartshorne asked in an early article: "The question arises, at what point in the downward series of forms do we draw the line and say, here such a thing as feeling (memory, desire, etc.) absolutely ceases?"[47] Once there was a time when, by asking this question, one might have been accused of anthropomorphizing other creatures; but that is erroneous as Hartshorne clearly saw when he observed that an animal caught in a trap need not become a human in order to suffer (BH 120). Experience comes in a variety of forms, some perhaps unimaginable by us, but certainly not all human. Hartshorne writes: "We psychicalists are accused of attributing human traits to the subhuman, yes, even to the inanimate. In fact we attribute not a single specifically human trait even to apes, let alone to atoms."[48] Hartshorne concedes that the further removed from a human being a creature is, the more difficult it is for us *to imagine* the quality of its experience, but it remains possible *to conceive* that it has something analogous to what we feel. He turns the charge of anthropomorphism on the critic: "To make the limitations of our human imaginations in this regard the measure of reality . . . I regard as a subtle form of anthropomorphism."[49] Or, again, he says, "Once more I suggest that the 'pathetic fallacy' is to be balanced against the possibility of a 'prosaic fallacy': supposing the world to be as tame as our sluggish convention-ridden imaginations imply."[50]

Rather than taking experience as an exceptional or rare phenomenon relegated to certain organisms, Hartshorne believed that it provides the clue to the nature of reality, and we must begin with human experience:

> [It] would be silly to refuse to take advantage of the fact that in ourselves we have the one individual piece of nature which we

know in its individuality from two sides: externally, quantitatively, and by behavioristic observation and test, and also internally, qualitatively, by immediate intuition—whether termed
introspection or retrospection (short-run memory) is no matter.
Here is our only complete clue, not to noumena out of time, but
to concrete spatio-temporal reality. (LP 183–84)[51]

As just noted, however, Hartshorne cannot be accused of
anthropomorphism. To be sure, he begins with human experience, but
he attributes mind-like qualities (not specifically human-like qualities) to
every concrete particular (i.e., dynamic singular). He accepted Leibniz's
two-fold criticism of Descartes that self-consciousness is not the only
form of human experience, and that human experience is not the only
form of experience. His study of birdsong lends further support to this
idea. In keeping with the theory of the affective continuum, Hartshorne
conceives mind-like qualities as existing along a continuum from the
simplest feelings to the most complex thoughts. He argues that it is
precisely in its psychological characteristics that it is possible for a
nonhuman being to be infinitely other than a human being (BH Ch.
8). This is because psychological variables such as memory, feeling, and
volition are infinitely variable. Memories are conceivably of any span (a
few seconds, a million years, etc.) and of any condition of vagueness or
precision; feelings can be any degree of intensity or complexity; volitions,
which presuppose memory and feeling, are likewise infinitely variable.

Hartshorne denied the assumption of much modern philosophy that
an experience can have only itself as an object. He argued that a datum
of experience must be independent of the experience:

> The thing must be independent, for its existence or occurrence,
> from the experience. Without this assumption the escape from
> solipsism can only be a *tour de force*. It is a dismal way to begin
> an epistemological inquiry to allow even a logical possibility of
> an experience which is aware only of itself or its own creation.[52]

The errors of waking experience as well as the false impressions during
dreams provide no sure ground for a global skepticism—in the words of
Peirce, "as if doubting were 'as easy as lying.'"[53] Hartshorne maintains
that the question "What if all of our experience is a dream?" is based on
a faulty phenomenology of dreaming and he points to Henri Bergson's

essay, *Le rêve*. Bergson argued that, during dreams, perceptions are indistinct, memory is free-floating, and attention is mostly disengaged, but the connection with the world through the body is never severed (CS 77).[54] Events and concerns of the day as well as immediate stimuli from the environment regularly appear in our dreams. Hartshorne gives the example of having dreamed of a propeller airplane and, as he awoke, hearing the sound of the airplane blend imperceptibly into the sound of a fan blowing in the room (DL 338). As perception is not lacking in dreams, so more generally experience is always *of* something not itself. What philosophers call "the given" in experience are, according to Hartshorne, the independent causal conditions of the experience. Introspection, too, conforms to this model: it is a present experience having the immediately previous experience as an object.

If an experience does not have itself as an object, then it must have as its object either something that is itself an experience or something that lacks experience. In the case of short-term memory, the object of experience is indeed another experience. If A is an experience, and B is the memory that immediately succeeds it, then B is the experience of an experience, or in Hartshorne's preferred terminology, a feeling of a feeling. For example, if one sings three notes in a C-major scale, from the tonic (C), to the sixth (A), and back to the fourth (F)—as in the familiar NBC television network musical signature—the memory of the sixth lingers as the tonic fades, and the memory of the tonic and the sixth linger as the fourth completes the melody. Subsequent stages in singing include the memory of their immediate predecessors. More controversially, Hartshorne maintains that the experiences we have of our own bodies are examples of "feeling of feeling." He says:

> Cells are living individuals. Our bodily experiences involve such individuals. The mind-body relation is not a one-one but a one-many relation. It is one sentient individual relating to many such individuals. Apply this to physical pains and pleasures. Hurt my cells and I am likely to suffer. Make me unhappy and my cells are likely to suffer.[55]

There are two qualifications to this theory. First, Hartshorne does not say that we experience individual cells; rather, we experience the cells indistinctly, *en masse*, similar to the way that one experiences a field of grass as green without distinguishing each blade of grass in the field.

This idea was first clearly expressed in Leibniz's concept of the blending of *petites perceptions,* and it is incorporated by Whitehead in his concept of transmutation or transmuted feelings.[56] Second, Hartshorne maintains that: "In 'feeling of feeling' the subject of the first feeling [A] is not identical with the subject (or subjects) of the second feeling [B]. . . . A's feeling of B's feeling has its own 'how' or 'subjective form,' which is not that of B's feeling" (IO 344). A's feeling is not a mere replica or mirrored reflection of B's feeling. There is the added element of A's reaction upon the feeling of B, A's subjective form. For this reason, Hartshorne can say, "I feel *how* the other felt, I do not feel *as* the other felt. I see no contradiction here" (CAP 199).

An interesting case in relation to Hartshorne's "feeling of feeling" thesis concerns so-called "mirror touch synesthesia" and the related research topic in neurophysiology known as "mirror neuron theory." "Mirror touch synesthesia" is a condition wherein one human being "feels" another human being's physical sensations intensely and, for all practical purposes, immediately upon visual or casual tactile contact. For example, a needle puncture to the skin of one person is felt immediately as a needle puncture by the synesthetic person who is viewing the person being punctured. For the mirror touch synesthete, this experience is not felt as if it were present in the imagination, but is felt as if it were identical to being physically punctured by a needle, although the feeling is not accompanied by a physical wound or bleeding capillaries, etc. Harvard Medical School neurologist Joel Salinas has had this condition since childhood and has written about it from both subjective and neurophysical points of view.[57]

Given the suggestive subtitle of Salinas's book—*Notes from a Doctor Who Can Feel Your Pain*—it might be tempting to understand mirror touch synesthesia as a direct example of Hartshorne's notion of "feeling of feeling" as a mode of physical causation. However, mirror synesthesia is better described as a kind of mimicry rather than a direct causal relation of feeling, for the synesthete also responds to inanimate objects *as though they had feeling.* For example, Salinas describes how, when looking at the Statue of Liberty, he feels the cloth draped across his feet, the sensation of holding the torch in his hand, and "the tension of my triceps and shoulder as if I were, like Lady Liberty, extending my arm upward."[58] The Statue of Liberty is obviously not an entity that feels—it is certainly *not* on Hartshorne's metaphysical theory—and so it could not count as one terminus of a literal "feeling of feeling" relation. Nevertheless, when we look at the underlying neurophysiology of synesthesia, issues emerge which have strong potential import for Hartshorne's theory of the mind as a series of dominant occasions that at least influence neural occasions which in turn feed into the production of new dominant occasions of experience.

The current, perhaps predominant, neurophysical theory of this radical variety of synesthesia holds that persons with this condition are pointed or special examples of mirror neuron activity in humans more generally. "Mirror neurons" are widely believed to play an important role in heightened states of empathy. For example, if one person sees another touch the hot element on a stove, that person may wince and even feel a burning sensation as though he or she had actually touched the element.[59] Giacomo Rizzolatti and his research team also argue that mirror neurons explain the ability of one individual to discern the intentions of another.[60] Mirror neurons have significance for Hartshorne's claim that lower-level neurons can be profoundly affected by the data of regnant or dominant occasions, since such mirror neurons must be capable, by definition, of receiving and processing empathetic emotional tonalities. Put another way, assuming the existence of distinctive human mirror neurons,[61] what is significant is that there must be some bits of emotional quality *in* such neurons in order to *differentiate* them from other kinds while asserting that they are somehow "causally responsible" for intense experiences of empathy and perhaps even certain kinds of aesthetic experience.[62]

Mirror neuron theory is accepted by many leading neuroscientists, although there are also important skeptics and far more study is necessary to clarify the exact nature and causal role of mirror neurons (e.g., is autism a pathology of the mirror neuron system?).[63] Should mirror neuron theory be shown to be on sound footing, it would represent strong empirical evidence that the "higher" emotional tonalities are indeed present *in* the lower level or basal entities of nature, including the primal neuronal entities of the brain itself, befitting Whitehead's "Doctrine of the Conformation of Feeling."[64] In effect, mirror neuron processes would be especially clear examples of Whitehead's generic or categoreal notion of physical interaction, that is to say, emotional quality *is* "[t]he primitive form of physical experience" and, as emotional, actual occasions "feel conformally *with* another."[65] This phenomenon of a "higher" quality present at the lower level of neurons, as found in mirror neuron theory, bodes well for Hartshorne's general contention that neurons can be affected by higher-level dominant occasions of emotional experience. At the same time, Hartshorne's doctrine of "feeling of feeling" is hardly dependent upon the existence and purported empathetic nature of mirror neurons, since the relation of mirror neuron theory to Hartshorne's doctrine is entirely supplemental and at best represents a special case of social sympathy as the general character of causal efficacy.

D. S. Clarke champions elements of Hartshorne's psychicalism, but he finds the doctrine of "feeling of feeling" to be its least defensible aspect. Clarke argues as follows:

> [Supposing we can attribute mentality to the neurons of the brain as fixed cells with specialized functions], this mentality . . . seems restricted to a type specific to the level of cells, namely, sensitivity to the potential nutrients and toxic substances that may pass through cell walls. If restricted in such a way, this mentality would seem totally independent of any pains or pleasures of those persons as wholes of which the neurons are constituent parts, a view that is contrary to Hartshorne's view of interaction between ourselves and our constituent cells. This is even more obvious for our experiences of visual images. It is implausible to claim that nerve cells without sense receptors have such images. But if visual images are absent at this level, we are left with the problem of explaining the relation between processes in these cells and our visual experiences—the same mind-body problem that the "feeling of feeling" doctrine was supposed to solve.[66]

Clarke is surely correct that the object-feeling (the cell's) is not the same as the subject's feeling, and Hartshorne says as much, as we have just noted. What is essential to Hartshorne's view, however, is not that there is an exact transfer of sensory quality but that there is a transfer of affectivity that contributes to the subject's experience. The theory of the affective continuum insures that there is no absolute discontinuity between the sensory-affective modalities. The feeling of feeling doctrine is not designed to answer every puzzle about mind-to-mind interaction. However, with the affective transfer, one is not left with the mystery of how a vacuous actuality could cause any sort of experience, a problem that Clarke recognizes as detrimental to materialistic accounts of the mind.[67] Hartshorne denies any evolutionary jump from "mere matter" to feeling and thought, "but only from feeling or thought to more or less different and sometimes superior feeling or thought."[68]

An additional consideration in response to Clarke is that if neurons are as closed to affective transfer from dominant occasions as Clarke is suggesting, it is hard to explain such phenomena as neuroplastic change that posits top-down causation—for example, repeated thought exercises that eventually alter brain metabolism and thus neuronal activity in the brain circuitry correlated with certain psychiatric disorders, as found in cases of efficacious "attentional therapy" for treatment of obsessive-compulsive disorder and Tourette's Syndrome.[69] Hartshorne's view of neuron-occasions maintains that proximate prehensions of neighboring neuron-occasions and other physical entities in the neural environment are predominant, yet there is some openness to afferent input from dominant occasions which is capable of altering neuronal metabolism. We should add that there are other dramatic examples of psychosomatic changes that appear to posit or strongly suggest top-down causal agency as in cases of "split" or multiple personality where physiologies will radically change abruptly: with one personality there is no discernible diabetes, but with another diabetes is manifest.[70] It is difficult to understand how such changes are directed to their ends if *only* low-level neuron-occasions are the causal agents at play. The closed neuron explanation must be that the neuron-occasions are just somehow mysteriously "programmed" to give out the global or macro-ego results that they do and when they do. Not only does this seem implausible on the face of it, but it entangles the closed neuron perspective in determinism, a theory that, with Hartshorne, we reject.[71]

Are there experiences of things that themselves lack experience? If Clarke's criticism of Hartshorne is correct, then the answer is "yes." The answer would also seem to be "yes," as in the more ordinary case of our awareness of inanimate objects. However, Hartshorne, invites us to take note of a subtle ambiguity. If an object of experience is not an experiencing object, does it follow that there can be no experience in it? The answer to this question is "no, it does not follow." To understand Hartshorne's meaning, recall that Descartes raised the question of the criteria for the *presence* of a rational mind in a physical object (and he denied the existence of animal minds), thereby making materialism the default position for anything outside one's own consciousness. Since, however, mind-like qualities are so pervasively present in varying degrees in so much of nature, Hartshorne asked for the criteria for the *absence* of mind or more generally feeling. He proposed that complete inactivity and lack of unity indicate lack of feeling.

> A chair, for example, is an ensemble of molecules not as a whole dynamically unified, by comparison with each one of these molecules. So the chair, by two criteria is shown to be insentient. It is an inactive aggregate of entities themselves active and significantly unitary.[72]

The problem, as Hartshorne sees it, is as much with the concept of mind as with the concept of the physical or of matter. He asks whether there is anything that positively corresponds to the concept of a *merely* physical entity, that is to say, a physical entity in which mind-like qualities—not simply *human* mind-like qualities—are wholly absent, even from its most basic constituent parts.[73] To be sure, there are physical entities in which mind seems to be absent (such as the chair), but Hartshorne argues that this is no more evidence of the total absence of mind than the appearance of inactivity in a physical object is evidence that there is no activity in it (e.g., in its molecules and atoms).[74] Leibniz guessed otherwise and modern science is on his side; the microworld, even where apparently "dead matter" is concerned, is buzzing with activity. The adage, "absence of evidence is not evidence of absence" applies.[75]

As the foregoing suggests, Hartshorne found inspiration in certain aspects of Leibniz's panpsychism. With Leibniz, he distinguished parts and wholes. Hartshorne's dynamic singulars, which themselves have mind-like qualities, are constituents of wholes, some of which share the qualities of the parts, and some of which do not share these qualities. He argues by analogy that feeling can be everywhere even though not everything feels, somewhat as vibration can be everywhere but not everything vibrates (ZF 134). Another analogy that Hartshorne uses is that a flock of birds does not have feeling, but there are feelings in the individual birds (CS 142). Hartshorne also developed a modified version of Leibniz's concept of a "dominant entelechy" (*entéléchie dominante*)[76]; in Hartshornean terms, this amounts to the claim that some physical systems are organized in such a way that the experiences of the dynamic singulars (the parts) can be channeled into a single more or less unified stream of experience or even conscious experience, as in the case of animals with complex nervous systems. Some organic wholes, such as plants, do not have a structure integrated enough to allow for a dominant stream of experience. Hartshorne viewed plants as having no feeling, but he attributed feelings to their individual cells. He held that the phototropism of a flower tracking the sun is more a function of the activity of the cells than of the plant as a whole (cf. BH 178). Hartshorne generalizes this analysis along Leibnizian lines to the inorganic world. Leibniz spoke of monads in inorganic substances as being in a "stupor."[77] Hartshorne attains a similar result in his theory of the infinite variability of mind-like qualities. There is no such thing as "mere matter," only matter in which mind-like qualities are far removed from what is recognizably human-like, animal-like, or even cell-like. With Leibniz's distinctions, Hartshorne is able to theorize that there is experience in every object, but not every object of experience is an experiencing object.

Despite Hartshorne's use of Leibniz's ideas, the dissimilarities between their versions of panpsychism are as striking as their similarities. As already noted, dynamic singulars are entities that come to exist in the creative-cumulative advance of the world; Leibniz's monads do not *come to exist* within universe but are *coexistent with it*. For Leibniz, God's creation of the universe is nothing more than God's creation of the monads that make it up. Another significant difference between the two philosophers concerns relations of cause and effect. Leibniz denied causal relations among nondivine monads—*"Les Monades n'ont point de fenêtres"* (monads have no windows). He secured the appearance of relations of cause and effect by positing a divinely imposed pre-established harmony.[78] For Hartshorne, *every* dynamic singular is *both* a partial result of causal conditions that precede it *and* a partial causal condition of events that succeed it. In short, every dynamic singular is both an effect and a cause. The word "partial," especially as regards the relation from cause to effect, is important. Hartshorne rejected determinism (see below), and this represents another departure from Leibniz. For Hartshorne, causal conditions are necessary, but not entirely sufficient, for the emergence of a dynamic singular. The individual's response to its own causal past—the way it synthesizes the world given to it—provides an ineradicable aspect of the explanation for why it is the way it is. *It acts and is not merely acted upon.* According to Hartshorne, the same principle applies to God, although allowance must be made in the divine case for the modal difference between existence and actuality (as explained in the following chapter). The twin ideas that there are real relations among dynamic singulars and that each is unique by virtue of its manner of experiencing the world highlight two features of Hartshorne's metaphysics. First, reality has a *social* structure; second, every concrete particular that "makes" the world retains at least a minimal degree of freedom.

One objection to Hartshorne's theory is that mental qualities seem to require a central nervous system. In *Beyond Humanism*, Hartshorne makes several points that are crucially relevant to this objection. He notes that among animals with central nervous systems, physical and psychical qualities are correlated. Hartshorne observes, in an almost Teilhardian turn of phrase, that physical complexity is a sign of psychical complexity (BH 116). The more complex is the mental life, the more complex is the nervous system that underlies it. Can one generalize beyond creatures with a nervous system? Hartshorne points out that one-celled animals manage the functions of digestion, oxygenation, and locomotion without the organs and body parts that in creatures with nervous systems make these possible. He asks whether mental function, broadly conceived, may not be analogous. Hartshorne asks if it is any more reasonable to say that a paramecium feels nothing because it lacks a central nervous system than it is to say that it cannot swim because it has neither motor nerves nor muscle cells (BH 119). If it has primitive feelings, then it displays them behaviorally in the only way it could, by responding to stimuli. Hartshorne argues that the only conclusion that can be drawn from physiology is that mind in a one-celled creature cannot be less dissimilar to a human mind than a cell is structurally and functionally dissimilar to the human body (BH 201). Physical wholes insufficiently organized to allow a dominant stream of experience are the closest thing in Hartshorne's philosophy to what materialists call "matter."

An important objection to Hartshorne's psychicalist theory is suggested in the work of Karl Popper. In his classic treatise on the mind-body problem titled *The Self and Its Brain* (co-authored with neuroscientist John Eccles), Popper objected to "psychicalist" or "proto-mental" conceptions of the brain's elementary particles, arguing that such conceptions have no empirical explanatory power and are thus "metaphysical in the bad sense." Popper maintains that elementary particles can have no "interior states" because they are "completely identical whatever their past states." For example, any arbitrary proton selected at any time for measurement will have the same physical properties as any other proton selected at any time for measurement: its mass will be 938 MeV/c^2, its charge +1, and its spin ½.

Contrary to Popper, it does not follow from this that elementary particles are *absolutely, predicatively identical* no matter what their past states. To use Hartshorne's dipolar vocabulary, Popper is here conflating "genidentity" and "strict identity." Such properties as mass, charge, and spin are genidentical features of protons that are present in each proton-occasion. However, protons do not in fact remain static in terms of their empirically discernible *behavior* over periods of time. For example, a proton P in a tritium nucleus of hydrogen has a rate of radiation decay as compared to a distinctive proton P^* in a lead-206 nucleus, which has no such decay, as is now familiar to us through the "half-life radiation law." Notice that the behavioral differences occur precisely because of *differences in physical contexts.*[79] This is an instance of what Hartshorne meant when he said that modern science had "disclosed the elements of illusion in the idea of mere bits of stuff hurtling about in space, each being what it is simply in itself, with no necessary reference to anything else."[80] It is what Whitehead called the fallacy of simple location.[81]

That physical context matters to the behavior of protons is readily explicable on a Hartshornean interpretation of elementary particle-occasions, because such particle-occasions are "open" to their environments—in Whitehead's vocabulary, the environments are their "actual worlds"—through prehension. More recent empirically well-corroborated developments in quantum physics are likewise readily explicable on Hartshorne's psychicalist interpretation, again through the notion of prehension. One may note in this regard the phenomena that (a) "information transfer or influence" occurs between well-separated particles faster than light-cone propagation (i.e., quantum entanglement, when interpreted as information transfer) and (b) that physical states are discernibly influenced by the selection and rapidity of an observation or measurement process (i.e., quantum Zeno effect). It may well be no accident that one of the first philosopher-physicists to devise experimental tests for quantum entanglement phenomena was Abner Shimony, a student of Hartshorne's at the University of Chicago, who has remained indebted to the "Whiteheadian paradigm."[82] We noted above, in response to Clarke, that in neuroscience, the emergence of neuroplastic phenomena in which rigorously repeated thought or "attentional" exercises have an empirically discernible effect upon brain metabolism, as is shown through PET-scans. This conjures a top-down causation model which again can be readily handled by a Hartshornean interpretation of particle-occasions as prehensive. Thus, Popper's dismissive estimate of the empirical explanatory power of psychicalist or panexperientialist concepts seems to be, at the very least, seriously challenged by more recent developments in physics.

Hartshorne believed that his concept of the infinite variability of mind-like qualities provides the theoretical bridge to extend the categories of experience beyond the human, the animal, or even the organic. He does not deny that these speculations about the possibility of radically nonhuman or nonanimal minds are, for the foreseeable future, of little or no use to much of science. Physics, for example, needn't worry whether atoms or electrons have "feelings"; but this may simply be a way of saying that what is of interest to metaphysics is not necessarily of interest to physics. In an early article, Hartshorne's characterized physics as the behavioristic aspect of the lowest branch of comparative psychology, or even of comparative sociology since reality, on his view, has a social structure.[83] Hartshorne argued further that psychicalism is the metaphysic best suited to an evolutionary worldview. Psychicalism does not face the problem of the emergence of mind from what is wholly lacking in psychical qualities. Hartshorne calls this view variously "emergent dualism" or "temporal dualism"; all of the problems of mind-body dualism of how to relate nonphysical mind to nonmental matter are repeated, only in an evolutionary context.[84] For Hartshorne, on the contrary, new forms of mind emerge in the process of evolution, but not mind itself.

Hartshorne escapes one version of what David Chalmers identifies as the "hard problem" of consciousness, that is to say, the problem of showing how and why physical processes give rise to or accompany the qualitative features of experience, and in particular that quality of "what it is like" to have an experience.[85] On Hartshorne's reckoning, there is no merely physical stuff, or, in Whitehead's language, vacuous actuality. Questions remain, however, about the extent of the analogies between different forms of mentality. One may guess, for example, that the consciousness of a chimpanzee is closer to that of a human than it is to that of a bat, but there must still be a considerable leap in imagining "what it is like" to be any other species besides a human being. Even within the human group imaginative leaps are required—consider, for example, the difficulty for any person without a womb to imagine what it is like to be pregnant. Finally, to our knowledge, Hartshorne nowhere addresses the problem of why certain qualitative experiences should be associated with certain structural features, as in Russell's example of wavelengths of light growing shorter as one travels along the spectrum from red to violet. This apparently contingent pairing of quality and quantity remains a mystery.

Hartshorne's psychicalism is a metaphysical theory, not a scientific one. Thus, in listing arguments for it he speaks of "the argument from categories."

> First and above all is what might be called "the argument from categories." If feeling is the most general character of the immediately given, then we can form no more general category by which to describe existence in general than this very character. (WP 28)

Analogy is important, but it plays a subsidiary role. At one point, Hartshorne says that he agrees with Alvin Plantinga, that the argument by analogy to other minds, despite its defects, is all that we have for moving beyond the immediately given of one's own mind and body.[86] Yet, as we have hinted at here and as we shall see further on in this chapter, Hartshorne thinks that one's own mind—one's "self," if you will—escapes the so-called egocentric predicament because it is composed of successive unit events, each one in some measure transcending and feeling its predecessor events. It will not do to reason after the manner of Descartes: where there is thinking there is a thinking *substance*. Hartshorne is more in line with Buddhism and with William James who wrote: "The passing Thought then seems to be the Thinker; and though there *may* be another non-phenomenal Thinker behind that, so far we do not seem to need him to express the facts."[87] In addition, if there is anything to Hartshorne's claim that the cells of one's own body are best construed as "other minds," then already, in the awareness of one's own body, one is aware of other minds—as he says, the mind-body relation is a one-to-many, not a one-to-one relation. Perhaps Hartshorne will be accused of begging the question by appealing to cells as "other minds," but there is a legitimate *prior* question of the analysis of one's experience of one's own body, especially given what is now known about the body as a collection of cells that are themselves living. It is here that analogy can play a crucial role, but it is analogy as enhanced by the deliverances of science concerning the world as it exists below the threshold of our unaided senses.

D. S. Clarke argues that Hartshorne's most important contribution to panpsychism is the method of analogical extension. According to Clarke, the argument grows weaker the further the analogy extends, although one compensates somewhat for the weakness by making the attribution of mind more and more indefinite—"*some* qualitative aspects and *some* spontaneity."[88] Hartshorne would doubtless insist on the clarification that the indefiniteness resides in our ability to *imagine* the qualitative aspects of primitive feelings not in our ability to *conceive* that they exist. In any event, Clarke maintains that the analogical argument cannot take one to the elementary constituents of matter that do not themselves have bodies. Clarke notes that in *Beyond Humanism* Hartshorne spoke of this level as "least-minds" (BH 171), but says Hartshorne never returned to this idea in his later work. In truth, Hartshorne *did* return to this idea on at least two occasions. In the 1977 article "The Organism According to Process Philosophy," Hartshorne maintained that a body is "the set of those other subjects which a given subject most intimately experiences." In "the least parts with no subparts . . . the role of the body is taken over by neighbors."[89] In this way, Hartshorne sought to preserve the conceptual continuity of psychicalism. It must be conceded, however, that Hartshorne succeeds in preserving conceptual continuity only by an analogical extension of the meaning of *body*; with the exception of the "least-minds" a body includes, at a minimum, self-maintaining organization. In the final analysis, Hartshorne's case is metaphysical, with analogy playing a subsidiary role; in addition, as we have seen, it depends upon a critique of the idea of material substance. Hartshorne's final verdict is that experience, at every conceivable level is essentially social—dynamic singulars feeling the feelings of others.

Because of the recent work of such philosophers as Thomas Nagel, Gregg Rosenberg, and Galen Strawson, views close to or roughly in the same family as Hartshorne's psychicalism have been gaining more traction and serious consideration among analytic philosophers and

natural scientists interested in philosophical questions. This development
has also occasioned objections. For example, Amy Kind argues that
Rosenberg's version of panpsychism is incoherent because it seems to
require experiences unattached to any subject of experience. She focuses
on Rosenberg's analogy that "interactions between very simple atoms
or molecules" might produce "extraordinarily simple and brief feeling,
like fireflies quietly flickering in the night."[90] Kind notes that Rosenberg
accepts that "phenomenal properties could not exist unless some subject
was experiencing them and that experiences could not exist unless they
were experiences of phenomenal qualities, . . ."[91] Kind then asks rhetorically, "But without consciousness, how can we make sense of the notion
that there is a subject of experience?"[92] We have seen that Hartshorne
argues that most experiencing entities are, in fact, not conscious beings,
and that consciousness is a higher-order form of experience. It follows
that Kind's criticism of Rosenberg also applies to Hartshorne.

We reply to Kind that, first, she takes Rosenberg's image of the
"fireflies quietly flickering in the night" much too literally. It is an image
meant to convey the most primitive nature of experience. We are reminded
of Whitehead's poetic reference to actual entities, comparing God to "the
most trivial puff of existence in far-off space."[93] Second, Hartshorne's denial
that one must have a conscious being to speak of an experiencing subject
does not in the least seem incoherent. Indeed, it is much more congruent
with evolutionary and developmental categories than its contradictory.
We commonly attribute "life" to bacteria or starfish or protozoa, yet
we do not, and should not, attribute full-blown consciousness to such
entities; we recognize that somehow such entities receive information
from their environment and react to it, thus fulfilling Plato's criterion
for *animus* as "self-motion." A phenomenology of experience, such as
we find in Whitehead's and Hartshorne's versions of panexperientialism,
makes room for and distinguishes between different modes of experience,
from full blown *conscious* experience which is capable of higher orders of
cognition to merely *sentient* experience. This seems to us more adequate as
a description of the wide *range* of *self-reactive* phenomena in nature than
the notion that all experience must be conscious experience.[94]

An interesting application of Hartshorne's ideas, and in some
respects a test-case for them, is the field of artificial intelligence which
was gaining momentum as a serious area of study in the latter part
of Hartshorne's career. Of course, speculation about the possibility of

a merely mechanical man date to the time of Descartes[95]; but it was arguably the computer, and especially the advent of powerful computer simulations of mental processes that fueled serious and detailed speculation about the possibility of mechanical forms of intelligence. Hartshorne begins reflection on this question by noting that there is an obvious difference between behavior and experience. Each of us interprets the behavior of others as involving certain experiences, but we do not guess our own experience from our behavior, we directly feel it. Moreover, it would be irrational to suppose that experience is unique to one's own case.[96] It is equally irrational to suppose that behavior alone is sufficient to generate experience. Building on this distinction, Hartshorne argues that the nervous system is not a mere means to behavior but that behavior itself is, in part, "a means to preserving and stimulating the nervous system and its accompanying experiences."[97] It is also the case that any mechanism capable of generating or sustaining human-like experiences would have to be a system that is at least as complex and integrated as the human body. To date, nothing close to the complexity of the human organism with its countless neural connections has been constructed artificially. It may well be the case that only a living organism can generate and sustain experience; if that is true, then it will only be by wedding organic tissue to machines that a machine could ever have or enjoy experiences.

A main concern of artificial intelligence is to duplicate behavior by, in large measure, relying on sophisticated systems of information processing and data retrieval, all the while ignoring the experiences associated with them. This is true, even if it is a question of simulating emotional response. If Hartshorne is correct, then it is precisely *the lack of organic unity* within the machine that makes it impossible for it to feel, even as it is capable of powerful and elaborate calculations within seconds. In Hartshorne's words, "the difference between metal and protoplasm is not a detail."[98] Hartshorne explains: "The brain connections, in contrast to machine connections, are not merely used, they are enjoyed, and this is the happiness of the thinker while thinking. It constitutes thinking as a conscious operation."[99] Hartshorne says that one may, if one chooses, define "thinking" as a process of drawing conclusions and following rules, but that is not all that human persons do when they think. "Thinking is a mode of integrating feelings which machines do not have."[100]

It is often an experience or a type of experience that is at the heart of the buzzing activity of the central nervous system. The enjoyment of music is a perfect example of this. To be sure, it is essential that one's hands, feet, and mouth be guided in the appropriate ways in order for instruments to be played and songs to be sung. It is also vital that the brain coordinate a massive amount of information involving almost unimaginable data retrieval if the music is to be performed properly. A defect in the physical mechanisms of the brain can prevent the playing and the enjoyment of the music. The point, however, is that the behaviors and the neural mechanical and chemical operations are not the primary aim of playing the music, at least not usually. The aim is to enjoy it. In Hartshorne's words, "The brain supports a life of feeling." [101] Thus, what Hartshorne's psychicalism contributes to the debate about artificial intelligence is a robust and much needed reminder that any account of the mind that makes experience or feeling secondary is deeply flawed.

Although Hartshorne does not explicitly mention this point, we add another variation on his theme: the problem of bridging the gap between syntax and semantics. Any artificial intelligence machine that would be capable of consciousness must be a "machine" that has the capacity for semantics rather than only syntactical functions related to digital inputs and outputs.

This idea is the heart and soul (if we may pun) of John Searle's attack on the claim of "hard" artificial intelligence proponents (like Marvin Minsky) that current computers are already, quite literally thinking machines.[102] At first glance, the marvelous achievements of Watson may seem to prove that existing computing machines can think, but we contend with Searle (and Hartshorne) that this is illusory: Watson is only a much, much more complex and sophisticated example of a calculator which simulates thinking through behavioral outputs. The illusion is created by Watson's vast program of complex *relevance algorithms* that will mechanically select the right context of meaning, but ontologically no more has happened than inputs-outputs of electrons moving through switching circuits governed by the functions of propositional logic.

To make this concrete consider this example, namely, Watson's processing and "speaking" the sentence "I am blue" while conducting a "conversation." (We here provide a rough and casual model of description using notions of input signifiers *S*, selection of context *C*, and various behavioral outputs, all of which are connected to software relevance algorithms.) Without any given context, the predicate "blue" is ambig-uous. Relevance algorithms pick up on inputs which cue different con-texts of meaning so that Watson will continue the conversation in an appropriate, socially intelligent way. Input signifiers S for context C referring to color or $S1$ for context $C1$ referring to emotion (or a subset of emotions) or even $S2$ for $C2$ as a taste for erotica will select the right output and eliminate irrelevant outputs. So, if $S1$, then C, and if C, then E (where E refers to "sadness.") (If Watson is not given appropriate input signifiers, it is programmed to ask questions to determine the appropriate signifiers.) So, Watson will respond appropriately as if it "understands" that the sentence "I am blue" means that "I am sad" not that "I am a member of the Blue Man Group" precisely because, if $S1$, then $C1$ *and neither C nor C3*. But $C1$ will dictate a Boolean predicate that represents just the "right," that is, semantically appropriate output.

At the level of hardware or physical description what is occurring is that electron gates connected to C and $C3$ are thus closed while $C1$ is open. This is completely mechanical. There is no more "consciousness" or "understanding" in Watson than there would be in an automobile when gas encounters a spark plug; in that case we would not want to say that the automobile literally "understands" that it has gas. Likewise, the relevance algorithms built into the software of Watson dictate a socially appropriate output response, and this *behavior* creates the illusion that "Watson knows what we are talking about." Of course, it is only the external human programmers who "understand" anything. This is in no way to diminish the great intellectual achievement that was the Watson project, which involved a stupendous amount of work by linguists, cognitive and computer scientists, logicians, and mechanical engineers working in concert over many years. But Watson should not be misdescribed as being something it is not, namely, a genuinely thinking, conscious entity capable of grasping semantical content, rather than an "if-then" push-and-pull machine made up of electronic movements entirely directed by algorithms and digitally converted tableaux of operators of propositional logic.

Indeterminism and Freedom

The philosophy of creative becoming is inherently anti-deterministic. This is not to say that Hartshorne denied relations of cause and effect or that he rejected the laws of nature discovered through scientific investigation. It is all-too-common for philosophers to argue that the falsity of determinism implies what we shall call chaoticism, the doctrine that there exists, at most, an appearance of causal regularity in the world.[103] By way of clarification, Hartshorne noted that determinism posits *absolute modal regularity* in the sense that, for every set of causal conditions, it is not only the case that, then and there, there is only one effect that *will* occur (which may well be a truism), but that there is only one effect, then and there, that *can* occur (note that "can" is a modal concept) (LP 188). As William James argued in "The Dilemma of Determinism," if some sets of causal conditions allow for more than one possible effect, then determinism is false. Therefore, the *logical contradictory* of absolute regularity is non-absolute regularity, *not* absolute irregularity. Absolute irregularity is the *logical contrary*, not the contradictory, of determinism. For this reason, it is a recurring theme in Hartshorne's thought to contrast determinism and chaoticism as the extreme metaphysical positions, both of which may be false (e.g., WM 8; ZF 52). If both are false, then some form of indeterminism must be true.

Determinism has sometimes gone by the name of the doctrine of necessity. The meaning of "necessity" as it applies to determinism is that a specific effect could not have been otherwise given the causes that brought it about; in other words, causes *necessitate* their effects. Indeed, determinists seek to minimize the extent to which events seem contingent—that they could have been otherwise—by uncovering their causal antecedents. The deterministic theory is that all contingency in the world, which is to say, all of the variety and novelty or all deviations from absolute regularity, are apparent only. Alternate effects *seem* possible, but determinists claim that this is only because of our *ignorance* of all of the factors—the causes and the laws that link cause to effect—that explain a particular effect. Nevertheless, hidden within the seeming contingency of our ignorance is another necessity: the causal nexus of events absolutely fixes the details of our knowledge in any given situation. Of course, whether determinism or indeterminism is correct, a considerable degree of ignorance and fallibility is an inescapable aspect of the human condition. The indeterminism espoused by Hartshorne also admits of unknown causes that limit what is possible. For example, an athlete may eat breakfast with plans of competing later in the day, not realizing that the food she is eating is contaminated and will incapacitate her.

On Hartshorne's theory, however, contingency is not merely a function of ignorance; on the contrary, sometimes there are real alternatives, no one of which the concatenation of causal conditions entirely eliminates. The incapacitated athlete, for example, may nevertheless have a variety of real alternatives for how to respond to the food poisoning.

In "The Doctrine of Necessity Examined" Peirce argued, and Hartshorne agreed with him, that one cannot help but posit real alternatives: either reality as a whole could have been otherwise or contingency enters the world piecemeal or incrementally.[104] In Hartshorne's words, the problem of "objective chance" (or contingency) is unavoidable, for "in spite of Spinoza, the totality of facts cannot follow from any necessary premise, so that chance either comes into the world in a single cosmic throw of the dice, or piecemeal" (LP 181). Determinists may attempt to eliminate contingency within the universe by tracing events to their causal antecedents—to a singularity at the beginning of the universe or to an eternal decree from deity—but there remains the question of why the universe has the exact initial conditions that it has. There is no plausible modal theory that would allow one to consider the contingency of the initial conditions as a hidden form of necessity. Thus, as Hartshorne says, there is no alternative to there being alternatives (CS 29). Hartshorne, following Peirce and James, locates the contingency of the universe *not* in an absolute beginning or in the divine will but within the universe's own creative processes—in Hartshorne's words, "contingency seeping into the world bit by bit" (CAP 123). James spoke of "pluralism's additive world," and this is Hartshorne's view: the coming-to-be of each dynamic singular introduces a morsel of novelty into existence and, in so doing, *adds itself* to the universe.[105] Every subsequent dynamic singular must take account of this prior addition to the universe as a causal factor in its own emergence. In this way, there is a rhythm of the universe as each new subject of experience inevitably becomes a new object for a new experience.

As a supplement to the Peirce-Hartshorne argument against determinism, we offer the following. We submit that strong or absolute determinism is a theory that can be *shown* to involve *modal absurdity*. Indeed, such analytic philosophers as Storrs McCall and Peter van Inwagen have issued reduction to absurdity arguments against absolute determinism that are strengthened by including within their purview Hartshorne's Principle of Inclusive Contrast.[106] Discussion of this argument, in addition to bolstering Hartshorne's overall case against determinism, will bring out in a concrete way the significance of Hartshorne's methodological assumptions. If dipolar semantics is correct, then monopolar positions like strong determinism *should* issue in logical absurdities. The argument below illustrates this.

Strong determinism is a theory which contends that cause and effect relations are such that, given a complete condition of the cosmos *C* at a given juncture, a *deterministic* result *R* will be produced such that *R* is an actual state with *completely defined properties.* As such *C* is a sufficient reason for *R* and only *R*; in other words, no other result could obtain given *C*. In effect, strong deterministic theory, by definition of "deterministic," invokes a *strong* principle of sufficient reason or PSR. (It is no accident, for example, that Spinoza begins his system by verbalizing the PSR as the fundamental Axiom III in Book I of the *Ethics*.) Now, we hold that Peter van Inwagen has argued effectively that any such appeal to the PSR is modally absurd upon reflection.[107] Immediately below we present a slightly different version of his argument that is enhanced by Hartshorne's Principle of Inclusive Contrast, which invokes what can be regarded as an epistemically conservative assumption that could be labeled "logically weak contingency" (CS 89–90).[108]

The Principle of Inclusive Contrast maintains that the concept of contingency must have *some* role to play in any categoreal scheme that can merit serious consideration, since, as stated earlier, the polar conceptual contrast of necessity cannot be well defined in pure abstraction from contingency (and *vice versa*); for instance, "necessity" is that which has "no *alternative*." In standard modal logic, it is a commonplace of operator semantics that $\square = df \sim \lozenge \sim$, where $\square$ represents "necessity" and $\lozenge$ represents "possibility," that is to say, possibility (which intrinsically invokes *this* or t*hat*) enters into the definition of necessity. Now, a determinist can hold that the actual world (or current actual cosmic epoch) contains no really alternative states of affairs at any juncture, and every outcome of processes in the actual world is the only outcome that could have occurred. However, if Inclusive Contrast is allowed, then there is *at least a single possible world or cosmic epoch* in which alternative outcomes could have occurred. This is what we have in mind in speaking of "*logically weak* contingency." It seems to us that this is the most conservative assumption we could make about the existence of alternative possibilities without succumbing to "monopolarity"—that is, the notion that only "necessity" possesses conceptual viability. Indeed, the discourse of logic seems to require at a minimum the *possibility* of contingency; in effect, for the purposes of logic, one cannot think of alternativeness in *merely* epistemic terms, since well-formed formulae are perfectly allowable in natural deduction systems which are irreducibly contingent.

The assumption of weak contingency seems to us to be in fact necessary to van Inwagen's argument because a determinist could reply to it by holding that the universe-class of contingent truths assumed in the first step is empty (because in their view all truths are necessary). We think this response (of the determinist) will not do, for the reasons pointed out by Hartshorne and also found in Peirce's doctrine of the logical basicality of implication or logical inclusion as asymmetrical and contingent (notice again that conditional and negation are sufficient for expressing all *wffs* of the propositional domain whereas biconditional and negation are insufficient for this purpose) (cf. CAP 77). As demonstrated below, from this "conservative" assumption about the possibility of contingency, along with the required PSR, it can be rigorously shown that any deterministic theory is absurd because its essential principle, namely, the PSR, entails contradiction.

Let there be a complex conjunctive state of affairs X that includes all true contingent states of affairs and by virtue of Inclusive Contrast, the contingent states in X are non-empty.

1. Let X be expressed as ($\Box\, p \land \sim \Box\, q$), where q is itself the large conjunctive fact of contingent truths.

2. By the standard modal axiom that a single contingent conjunct renders contingent the larger conjunction that contains it, in effect, ($\Box\, p \land \sim \Box\, q$) $\supset$ $\sim \Box$ ($\Box\, p \land \sim \Box\, q$), X is itself contingent.

3. No contingent truth can be sufficient reason for itself (for if it were its own sufficient reason, it would be necessary, which it cannot be by virtue of the result at step 2).

4. By virtue of the PSR, all states of affairs must have sufficient reason, and thus X must have sufficient reason in some true state of affairs S.

5. If S holds, then it must be necessarily true or contingently true. (It certainly cannot be "impossible and true.")

6. However, S cannot be necessary, because if it were necessary it

would imply that X is necessary, contrary to the result in (2) that X is contingent. (The necessity of an antecedent entails the necessity of the consequent.)

7. However, S cannot be contingent, because if it were contingent, it would be a conjunct of X, and, if it were a conjunct of X, it could not be a sufficient reason for X by virtue of step 4, that is, X must have sufficient reason outside itself.

8. Thus, the PSR entails that X cannot have a sufficient reason in some state of affairs S, which contradicts the PSR.

9. By reduction to absurdity, the PSR must be rejected since it yields a contradiction: X must have a sufficient reason and yet it cannot have a sufficient reason.

We note that in a recent critical discussion of van Inwagen's argument, Alexander R. Pruss has rejected it.[109] However, his reasons boil down to the notion that there can be alternative conceptions of the PSR that are "sufficient enough" even if the Strong *PSR* fails. We have no quarrel with this in principle. Indeed, neoclassical process philosophers must be committed to some weaker version of a *PSR*, since no event occurs without past causes in Hartshorne's metaphysics. Rather, the neoclassical position is that no event is determined to occur *in all its predicative detail* by past causes, a notion which is thus not to be conflated with deterministic causation. Also, the revised version of the "van Inwagen argument" that we present above simply does not appeal to the premise that "no necessary proposition explains a contingent proposition," which is the focus of Pruss's critique.

It should now be clear that Hartshorne intended his version of indeterminism to leave ample room for the massive regularities—the order—of the world that scientists make it their business to discover, but these regularities are not absolute as determinists conceive them to be. Hartshorne turned on its head the traditional doctrine that effects are contained in their causes; for Hartshorne, it is the other way around: at the most basic metaphysical level of analysis, causes are contained in their effects (CE Ch. 7). Again, Hartshorne finds a clue in the experience of memory. One's memory-of-X includes X as an indispensable causal component, but X as partial cause of one's memory-of-X does not contain the memory itself. Hartshorne goes further and denies that memory-of-X

is contained, implicitly or virtually, in the entire set of causal conditions leading up to the memory. In short, the causal antecedents of the memory provide the necessary but not the sufficient conditions of the memory. The present memory-experience *is* an instance of creative experiencing; as such, it adds a novel element to reality. Nevertheless, the causal conditions are limiting factors in what experience may result from them; the causes define a field of possible experience activity. Not just any effect can result from a particular set of casual conditions and this principle is enough to block the inference from indeterminism to chaoticism. This principle also provides the metaphysical ground of developmental processes. For example, every adult human has a developmental history beginning with a fertilized egg, but no single-celled zygote and its genetic make-up is sufficient to make an adult. The countless intermediate steps of growth and education, as well as the person's own reactions to his or her circumstances, are required to complete the process.

Since at least the time of David Hume, philosophers have acknowledged that empirical science cannot establish the truth of determinism. There remained, however, the idea that scientific explanations presuppose or require a deterministic framework. On Hartshorne's reckoning, Peirce disposed of this claim once and for all. First, Peirce observed that measurements can be no more fine-grained than our instruments and our proneness to error will allow. There can be no empirical or scientific meaning to the concept of an absolute measurement. Second, the far-reaching regularities in nature that a reasonable indeterminism posits are enough for the purposes of scientific theorizing; saying that the regularities are absolute, as determinism does, adds nothing. The greatly diminished levels of novel experiencing that Hartshorne's psychicalist metaphysics locates in the world of inorganic beings makes that realm as deterministic in appearance as it needs to be for the purposes of discovering laws of nature. To be sure, those laws must be understood as stochastic, but this fits well enough with scientific judgments which are couched in terms of probabilities rather than certainties. It is worth noting that Hartshorne did not look to subatomic physics for his main support for indeterminism, for he believed that the case against determinism had already been made by Peirce and others.[110] As far as Hartshorne was concerned, quantum indeterminacies buttress the case against determinism by showing that physics, the supposedly most materialistic of sciences, does not require determinism. Even Einstein, who rejected indeterministic interpretations of quantum phenomena, did not deny that those interpretations were scientific.

Numerous philosophers use moral freedom as an argument—perhaps the central argument—against determinism. Hartshorne agreed that moral freedom is indispensable to a proper understanding of human life, but he was more interested in defending a more generalized idea of freedom that extends beyond moral decision-making and even into the nonhuman realm. "Moral freedom . . . is a special, high-level case of the creative leap inherent in all process, the case in which the leap is influenced by consciousness of ethical principles" (LP 169). Freedom in its most generalized sense, as a creative act, complements and completes Hartshorne's indeterminism. He speaks of causality as crystallized freedom and freedom as causality in the making (LP 233). As we have just seen, for Hartshorne, every effect is more than, and even includes, the causal conditions that make it possible. If one analyzes the effect, abstracting from its causes, one is left with the particular way in which a dynamic singular experiences its causal antecedents, which is the measure of novelty in it. The word "experience" may call to mind a merely private epiphenomenon, but as we saw above, Hartshorne insists that experience has a public aspect that cannot be eliminated as it becomes a datum for subsequent experiences—a cause for future effects. In *Creative Experiencing: A Philosophy of Freedom*, he stresses that this idea of freedom is essentially social. Every creative act is a combination of self-determination and determination by others. The creative act, once completed in a dynamic singular, becomes part-cause of subsequent dynamic singulars. In this way, cause and effect relations are explained by the more basic principle of freedom limiting freedom.

Because of his forceful rejection of determinism, Hartshorne saw no reason to dwell long on the question of the compatibility of determinism and human freedom. "Determinism is not a doctrine anyone lives by. So why worry about what is compatible with determinism?"[111] His impatience with compatibilism was a function both of his denial of determinism but also of what he saw as a coopting of and misuse of the word "freedom."

> Determinists claim that what makes us free is that our "character" as already formed, plus each new situation, determines our decisions. So then the child was determined by the character

already formed in its infant past and by the surrounding world, and this character by the preceding fetus and world, and that by the fertilized egg? What kind of freedom is that? By what magic do people miss the fact they are misusing words? Skinner is right; once accept determinism and all talk of freedom is double-talk. The word 'voluntary' (liking it) is good enough for the determinist's freedom; why not stick to it, without trying to borrow the prestige of the glorious word 'freedom'? (OO 17)

Hartshorne was aware that a large number of philosophers identify human freedom with acting (or the capacity to act) in such a way that one is neither compelled to do something against one's will nor constrained from doing what one wishes to do, even though one's decisions are the strict results of causal conditions preceding them. Hartshorne denied that any conscious decision could be deterministically caused. Equally, however, he argued that what is meant by freedom is more than what compatibilists want to emphasize in speaking of voluntary decisions. According to Hartshorne, one's character is expressed in one's acts, but "each new act creates a partly new character, and character as already formed implies only a certain range of probabilities and possibilities for action" (ZF 195). To act voluntarily (not merely in the compatibilist's restricted sense) is, in effect, to bring about a new element of one's own past, to set further conditions upon one's future. This is exactly the position that James took when he said that we are "habitually fashioning our characters." James's emphasis on the moral gravity of our decisions was not lost on Hartshorne. In James's words: "Every smallest stroke of virtue or of vice leaves its never so little scar." [112]

Some philosophers, like Hegel and Marx, contrast blind necessity and consciousness of necessity, the latter of which they identified with freedom. Hartshorne argued that this definition fails to take into account the distinction between the idea that there is consciousness of *only one possibility* and the idea of consciousness of *a limited range of possibilities*. As the range of possibilities becomes narrower, necessity is approximated, but as long as freedom is a reality, the range must not be reduced to a single possible outcome. Hartshorne likens the determinist's idea to reducing a river to its banks.

Between the banks the particles of water have options as to where they flow; bring the banks close enough together to deprive the particles of all options and there is no longer a flow or a river. This is what determinism does, unwittingly, with the idea of freedom. It tries to justify itself by pointing out what no one doubts, that without banks or limitations there is no river and no freedom. . . . Show me an argument for making this leap [to determinism] and I will show you a mind that fails to distinguish between the river having banks at all and the question: "How far apart are the banks set?"[113]

Hartshorne's analogy brings us full circle to the *pons asinorum* of the debate—a particularly apt expression in light of Hartshorne's analogy—between the determinist and the indeterminist, to wit, the failure to distinguish determinism from chaoticism, the conflation of the distinction between logical contradictories and logical contraries. Hartshorne denies the contrary extremes in favor of freedom, even if it is slight. "The rivers may be narrow; still, their banks are at finite, not zero, distances from each other."[114]

For all of Hartshorne's animadversions on determinism and his advocacy of a philosophy of creativity, he was deeply sensitive to the limits, sometimes extreme limits, on freedom in any particular situation. He illustrates the limits of freedom with a mathematical analogy:

I sometimes think of an individual's freedom as the fraction of which the numerator is the momentary experience of the individual, and the denominator is the past of the universe, so far as effectively involved. The value of this fraction is small, but still not zero. (LP 180)

It is with these limits on freedom in mind that he speaks of a present creation as adding "only its little mite" to the vast totality of the universe (LP 233). He argued that, strictly speaking, epiphenomenalism is false, but it is true nevertheless that our minds are more dependent on our bodies than our bodies are dependent on our minds. He observed:

Our cells can do a lot without us, as one can see from the fact of dreamless sleep when our experiences are in abeyance, but we can do nothing without them. We must participate in their feelings, they can dispense rather largely with ours. There is, therefore, a stronger case for our bodies influencing our minds than our minds influencing our bodies.[115]

Hartshorne speculated that the effect of the mind on the body is not due to an influence of massive proportions but resides rather in something more delicate but also more pivotal, like pushing a button to launch a missile. James argued that the question of the reality of free will comes down to whether, in any particular case, one could exert more or less effort of attention, a phenomenon so subtle and apparently insignificant that it would escape detection by science, but like a fulcrum on which a lever pivots, can make all of the difference in whether a weight is lifted.[116] Hartshorne's ideas of the mind-to-body relation do not seem far distant from this way of thinking.

Hartshorne maintained that a phrase like "creative experiencing" escapes redundancy because there are degrees of creativity (LP 166). Indeed, his indeterminism provides the metaphysical ground for developmental ideas, so the concept of freedom limiting freedom provides the ground for a meaningful concept of degrees of freedom. Freedom increases to the extent that there are more options of more complexity, allowing for greater contrasts of feeling. The development of more and more complex organisms during the course of evolution makes for new levels of organizational structure (e.g., in the convolutions of brains), more varieties of experiencing, and a widening range of possibilities for creative realization. The most dramatic example of augmented freedom occurs when organisms cross the threshold from experience to *conscious* experience. This occurred in the evolution of the human species, but it is also the natural development within each member of that species. Hartshorne remarks on how the complexities of a symphony can be appreciated by a human being, but they are hopelessly beyond the understanding of creatures with simpler brains (CS 306). Consciousness also makes possible *moral* freedom which brings with it increased opportunities for achievement and for risk of failure in the attainment of high ideals. The opportunities and the risks go hand-in-hand in such a way that one cannot be had without the other. (We discuss these ideas as they apply to deity at the close of the following chapter under the heading "panentheism.")

Personal Identity

The attribution of responsibility for acts worthy of praise or censure involves the concept of a person. With the problematic exception of a supernatural deity that exists outside of time, persons do not simply exist, they *persist*; their existence requires days, months, and years. Dynamic singulars, as momentary flashes of experience, are not persons, but in Hartshorne's view, they are the raw materials from which persons are made and they always involve at least a remote analogy to ourselves (CAP 242). One can say that a person is a whole of which dynamic singulars are the parts. Hartshorne adopts the more refined categories of Whitehead's philosophy in order to express, in neoclassical terms, the concept of personhood. Whitehead spoke of a *nexus* as any "particular fact of togetherness among actual entities."[117] A *society* is a type of nexus whose constituents prehend (feel) a common element of form.[118] Every mammal, for example, is a society of dynamic singulars, each of which inherits from its predecessors and passes along to its successors the form of "mammal." A society is more than a mere mathematical set, for the common form of the society is passed along—shared by prehensive relations—from one grouping of dynamic singulars to another.

In the philosophies of Whitehead and Hartshorne, the existence of a person requires that there be a special type of society, one that exhibits *personal order*. A personally ordered society is a sequence of dynamic singulars, no two of which are contemporaries.[119] This is the neoclassical metaphysical account of our sense of being persons that persist through time. Both Whitehead and Hartshorne emphasize, however, that personally ordered societies are *embodied*. A personally ordered society is a sub-society within the larger society that is the human body.[120] We have already noted that Leibniz spoke of a dominant entelechy or soul associated with each animal body, itself a collection of monads; a personally ordered society is a very rough equivalent of this (taking into account all of the caveats mentioned in the discussion of psychicalism). Each dynamic singular making up a personally ordered society inherits not only from its predecessor in the sequence but also from the dynamic singulars that make up the rest of the body. The body, one might say, is the immediate environment of the soul, or more colloquially, the self. Whitehead and Hartshorne believed that a personally ordered society does not survive without the body. Although neither philosopher definitively dismissed the possibility of a limited postmortem existence, they did not show the slightest interest in speculating on the details of such a possibility (RSP 143; LP 253). Hartshorne remarked, "What our awareness would be like without its ever-present relations to its bodily cells, we have only blind guesses."[121]

Of course, disembodied existence is not the only form that after-life belief has taken. In Zoroastrianism, later Judaism, and in both Christianity and Islam, there is the idea of bodily resurrection. As we mentioned in Chapter I, early in his career, Hartshorne broke with his parents on various Christian doctrines and this included abandoning belief in the resurrection of Jesus. When called upon to comment on a debate between Gary Habermas and Antony Flew on the bodily res-urrection of Jesus, Hartshorne defended the idea of a Whiteheadian objective immortality but he had very little to say about the details of the debate. He admitted, with his father, that it is "remarkable that a crucified man should have been the source of so vast a company of believers."[122] He said he was no more able to explain this than he could explain how other religions grew as they did. He suggested that the idea of bodily resurrection requires positing "bodies with no real analogy to anything we know," a remark borne out by the way Paul struggles in the first letter to the Corinthians (verses 16:36f) to characterize the resurrection body, using the unfortunate analogy of a seed dying before it comes to life—"unfortunate" because the seed, as the embryo of a plant, is dormant but *living* and therefore fails as an analogy of dying and coming back to life.[123] As to the debate itself, Hartshorne indicated that he neither believed nor disbelieved the "swoon theory" that Jesus never actually died on the cross but revived afterwards in the tomb. He added: "I can neither explain away the evidences to which Habermas appeals [of Jesus rising bodily from the dead], nor can I simply agree with Flew's or Hume's [skeptical] position."[124] Hartshorne ends with a hint of criticism by saying that because of his belief in rational inhabi-tants of some other planets, his view is not humanistic or earth-centered but "cosmic and God-centered." One may guess that he found it difficult to understand how a man rising from the dead on this planet could have cosmic significance. His final comment, however, is simply: "My metaphysical bias is against resurrections."[125]

Whitehead's and Hartshorne's lack of interest in personal survival of death has not discouraged others from venturing theories about the afterlife grounded in neoclassical principles.[126] Among the more interesting revisionary work in process metaphysics that bears directly on the question of the afterlife is Marjorie Suchocki's systematic efforts in her landmark treatise *The End of Evil: Process Eschatology in Historical Context*.[127] Suchocki is interested in revising the process scheme in a manner that would allow for affirmation of personal subjective immortality. She suggests that God experiences the very *satisfaction* of personally ordered finite processes of becoming so that God retains and continues the subjectivity of such processes even beyond the bodily death of the person. That is to say, God endows personally ordered sequences of finite actual occasions not only with objective immortality but also with subjective immortality. In her imaginative reconstruction of Whitehead, the consequent nature of God becomes enriched by a community of interactive, subjectively immortal entities that either must accept an omniscient judgment about their actual achievement of value in relation to that of other entities and, if so, will experience permanent "transformation, redemption, and peace," or they can refuse this judgment and thereby render themselves alienated from God and other creaturely occasions.[128] In this way, she believes that process theology can be made consistent with the basic tenets of traditional Christian eschatology—immortality, morally righteous judgment of free conduct, and (self-elected) status of continuance in a "Kingdom of Heaven" or alienation from such kingdom, in effect, electing a state of Hell (much like Berdyaev's concept of self-elected Metaphysical Hell or the allegory of "the great divorce" as in the book of the same title by C. S. Lewis—either of these views free the doctrine from the unjust and sadistic elements criticized by Nietzsche and others).

Suchocki suggests that her view is "closest" to the perspective of Hartshorne in that Hartshorne holds that God retains the immediacy of the satisfaction of an occasion, but she notes, of course, that Hartshorne does not hold that the immediacy of the satisfaction undergoes transformation into a subjectivity persisting in the consequent nature of God.[129] Although bold and highly original, we find Suchocki's proposal difficult to evaluate as the ontological status of this "transformed" subjectivity seems to us unclear. What plays the role of the physical pole of new post-bodily actual occasions? Is the requirement of a physical pole/mental pole distinction no longer applicable in the case of post-bodily occasions? If so, why so? Are there repetitions of each occasion such that there is a subjectively immortal transformation for each post-bodily occasion *ad infinitum* (the so-called "problem of a million Marjories")? Perhaps Suchocki can answer these queries effectively.[130] Hartshorne would presumably not agree with the infinitude of subjective experience posited in Suchocki's eschatology. As we mentioned earlier, Hartshorne leaves the door open for the possibility of postmortem existence perhaps warranted by empirical arguments from parapsychology, but he firmly rejects the notion of subjective immortality that posits an infinitely ongoing sequence of postmortem occasions of experience. For Hartshorne, God and God alone is everlasting. Thus, we do not see the possibility of a full-bodied Hartshornean concurrence with Suchocki's eschatology.

Similar considerations apply to Randall Auxier's attempt to formulate a Hartshornean concept of subjective immortality.[131] Auxier argues that, because of Hartshorne's account of God's omniscience, according to which God empathizes completely with a person's experience, there are "two loci of our subjective immediacy in life—our physical actuality, and our existence in God." According to Auxier, one's death is the point at which the limitations of one's physical being are dissolved, and one realizes oneself fully as a "self-in-God." Indeed, because God knows us even more fully than we know ourselves, "we are not even the *main* locus of our own subjective immediacy in life." For this reason, Auxier says, "I do not become less in death, I become more."[132] When Auxier originally presented these ideas at a celebration of Hartshorne's centenary, George R. Lucas raised the question we have raised in connection to Suchocki's proposal. In simplest terms, how is it possible, on Hartshornean principles, for a person to exist without a body? Persons, whether divine or creaturely, are minimally "dipolar" in having both mental and physical poles (more precisely, the occasions of which they are made have both poles); for a creature, at death, the physical pole ceases to function. If this is true, then in Lucas's words, "you cease to be able yourself, as a mode of existential personhood, to provide any new experiences in the divine life other than what your *actual* life, your physical life had to offer." Auxier responded that Lucas's question was the obvious one that needs to be addressed; he indicated, as a partial response, that he rejects the idea that embodiment is a necessary condition of personhood, whether for God or for the creatures.[133] Whatever merits this idea may have, it shows that Auxier has departed from a Hartshornean framework.

Daniel Dombrowski raises the question about Auxier's proposal from a different angle, by exploring "a defensible use of pronouns."[134] Auxier speaks of the "two loci" of one's subjective immediacy in life, one located in one's body and another in God. On Auxier's account, at death one loses the thread of experiences associated with one's body, but one retains one's subjective immediacy in God. However, according to

Hartshorne, what exists in God is *God's prehension* of one's subjective immediacy, not one's own experience of it. This is why Hartshorne can say that God experiences *how* we feel but not *as* we feel (CAP 199). When the body dies there is no more locus for the ongoing addition of one's experiences. Of course, Auxier recognizes this, but his response only serves to highlight his distance from Hartshorne. For Auxier, a creature's personhood is not to be identified with any series of actual experiences but is the *existential condition* of the creature, impressed upon it by "the special acts of God." In Auxier's words:

> Persons are existentially what they are because of their unique relation to their creator, not because of anything they do or do not do, and not because of anything that does or does not happen to them in space and time.[135]

Hartshorne maintained, on the contrary, that our personhood is indeed subject to what happens to us in space and time, that unlike God, we do not begin as persons, we *become* persons. Perhaps this was one of the things on Hartshorne's mind when he told Auxier, after the centenary conference, that Auxier was taking the analogy between personhood in God and the creatures too literally, that human beings are not related to their personhood in the same way that God is related to God's personhood.[136] This is a point that is directly relevant to the ethics of abortion (which we address in Chapter Nine).[137]

A neoclassical theist might be able to go part of the way, affirming a "limited" doctrine of life after death. The mechanism for this might be supplied by some sort of physical continuant after brain death, as in the speculations of some parapsychologists concerning an electro-biomagnetic "remnant" that could in principle serve as a physical infrastructure for continuing subjective experiences after death. Such a physical remnant might also be part and parcel of the purported "excesses of psychic energy" residing in the unconscious as posited by some neo-Jungians.[138] The existence of such a physical remnant would in principle alleviate the doctrine from having to answer the abovementioned questions concerning physical poles of occasions and repetitions of subjective transformations. Given a physical electromagnetic remnant, postmortem subjective experience would take place in a way in which the ordinary Whiteheadian conceptual scheme for actual occasions would hold, although questions arise concerning the status of phenomenal space in relation to such postmortem occasions. Perhaps this speculation is further assisted by the suggestion of neuro-scientist Eben Alexander that the loss of brain function at death in fact releases consciousness from the constraints and shackles that focus ordinary human consciousness in limited and particular ways.[139] We stress that, of course, these are speculations only, but they point to the conceivable directions a future philosophical and empirical scientific justification that a specifically Hartshornean eschatology might take. A resolute neoclassical theologian who does not agree with Hartshorne that objective immortality by itself is religiously adequate could appropriate this model of personal life after death and conjoin it with the doctrine of objective immortality and relevant moral considerations (including perhaps the notion of "judgment" as found in postmortem "life reviews") to produce a more traditional "Doctrine of the Kingdom of God" than the symbolic eschatologies of certain theologically liberal theologies.[140]

Hartshorne argued that his and Whitehead's view of personhood avoids two extremes.[141] A person is not—Hume to the contrary notwithstanding—a mere bundle of qualities existing from moment to moment, with no internal relations among its component parts. Every dynamic singular within a personally ordered society is a creative appropriation of its successors in the sequence and in the wider environment of its body. As noted in the previous section, Hartshorne denied determinism without denying the efficacy of the past and causal regularities. Certain kinds of damage to the brain, for instance, are real causal factors in seriously altering or even eliminating personality. The other extreme that Hartshorne claims to avoid is the denial of external relations among the components of the self. According to Leibniz, the identity of a monad, including a dominant entelechy, is in its "concept," which is all of the properties that ever were or will be true of it. Hartshorne maintains that a person is a product of developmental processes that are inherently open-ended, allowing for different outcomes. For this reason, Hartshorne accepted the Jamesian view that one's character as so far formed is no absolute guarantee of one's future behavior. It is true, as is said, that people "act in character," but one is also part-creator of one's character. We meet here once again, but now as applied to the problem of self-identity, the protean nature of creativity in neoclassical metaphysics. As each dynamic singular in one's personally ordered society emerges, one is a partly new self.

On Hartshorne's principles, personal identity is not a matter of strict or mathematical identity. The additive nature of creativity entails that identity through time, or genidentity, is relative only—a question of "more or less" rather than "all or none." The unity of self-identity in a person is a function of the inertia that past dynamic singulars carry into the present of a personally ordered series and the degree to which the coming-to-be of the present dynamic singular appropriates the common element of form. Hartshorne sometimes spoke of this relation as being among past and present "selves." Hartshorne would agree with James who wrote: "Each Thought is thus born an owner, and dies owned, transmitting whatever it realized as its Self to its own later proprietor."[142] For most of us, most of the time, the broad outlines of our personality remain stable, allowing us to speak of ourselves as being "the same person." Yet, dramatic changes are possible, for the better and for the worse. The annals of both brain science and of religious conversion are full of case histories of persons who undergo changes that are sufficiently global to speak of a new person being born. It is also worth noting that Hartshorne's metaphysics allows for the possibility that a single body could support more than one personally ordered society; this might provide the outlines of an account of multiple personality or even of aspects of the unconscious mind.

Hartshorne's theory of personal identity is not reductionist. Like his indeterminism and philosophy of freedom, it is inherently developmental. Consider the beginnings of a human life. In most cases, conception results in a full complement of chromosomes necessary for a human person to develop. Much more must be accomplished, even within the mother's reproductive system, to complete the process. The single-celled zygote from which we grow is genetically human, but it is arguably not the individual we associate with being a person. As Hartshorne says, "I require my gene mixture but I am certainly not identical with it."[143] Far from being one individual rather than another, the fertilized egg has the potential to divide to produce twins or triplets. Hartshorne noted that his identical twin brothers, James and Henry, were very different persons despite having the same genetic make-up (DL 57). Another argument against reducing personhood to genetic structure is that the nervous system and a functioning brain, which provide the physiological basis of human personhood, are not present from the moment of conception; they are the result of development both *in utero* and after birth. These observations do not determine the moral or legal status of the unborn, but they are relevant to those questions, for they argue against reducing personhood to genetics. To be sure, the question of abortion is complicated. When, if ever, does the unborn become a person with rights and how do these rights, assuming they exist, stand vis-à-vis a woman's manifest right to self-determination? Hartshorne was firmly on the side of allowing women to decide for themselves, apart from interference from government or religion, whether to terminate an unwanted pregnancy. His position on abortion was basically that of Roe v. Wade.[144] What Hartshorne's metaphysic of personal identity brings to the debate is a robust rejection of reducing personhood to genetics and a corresponding emphasis on *developmental categories*. To paraphrase Simone de Beauvoir, Hartshorne takes seriously the idea that one is not born, but becomes a person.[145]

Hartshorne drew interesting ethical implications from his metaphysics of personal identity. We shall explore these in some detail in Chapter Nine; for now, let us note that a metaphysics which includes such Whiteheadian notions as prehension, personally ordered societies of actual occasions, and transmutation of conformal feeling, could never countenance what Hartshorne calls the "illusions of egoism." Even (arguably) more plausible so-called "enlightened" versions of ethical egoism, which allow interest in others for the sake of welfare of self, are incoherent. Enlightened self-interest theories are based on a partially true but very misleading "common sense" conception of self-identity that fails to grasp the logical distinction between being *an individual* and being *the concrete states of an individual*. The former is an abstraction from the latter. No momentary state is strictly identical with any other but there can be enough continuity to speak of an abstract, relatively unchanging, character. As Hartshorne says, "The identity is somewhat abstract, the non-identity is concrete. Without this distinction the language of self-identity is a conceptual trap" (ZF 185). When this distinction is grasped, we see that the claim to have an interest in self cannot be simpliciter or absolute, since there must always be an "other," namely, the future concrete states of the individual self, to which the interests of the self in a concrete state now must be addressed. Moreover, the fact that (psychologically normal) individuals "enjoy the enjoyment of others" is grounded in the metaphysical structure of social selves, whose dominant occasions of experience are built up and transmuted by conformal feeling of the feeling-tone in constituent neural occasions. We are, quite literally on Hartshorne's account, "members one of another." That is to say, a "self" is precisely a creative synthesis of feelings of others through its "perceptual mode of causal efficacy" in Whitehead's language. The capacity for feeling the feelings of others—in a word, "sympathy"—is basic, and thus the capacity for altruism as well as selfishness is built into the nature of being a social organism.

Hartshorne did not fail to notice the parallels of his views on personal identity and those of Buddhist philosophers. The twin Buddhist doctrines of the unreality of a substantial self (*anatman*) and of dependent origination or dependent arising (*pratitya-samutpada*) allow for the same concept of personal or genidentity that Hartshorne advocates, which combines continuity of abstract aspects of the "self" with the concrete becomings of dynamic singulars of which it is composed. In *Philosophers Speak of God*, Hartshorne and Reese included a brief passage from the *Sabbāsava Sutta* where the Buddha speaks of the idea of a permanent and unchanging self in these terms: "This, brethren, is called the walking in delusion, the jungle of delusion, the writhing of delusion, the fetter of delusion" (PSG 412).[146] Hartshorne appropriated this thought with a slight change of wording in which he spoke of the belief in the absolute nonidentity of one person with another or the belief in the complete identity of successive moments in a single person's life as "writhing in delusion" (IO 365; ZF 190).

Time and Modality

Hartshorne's philosophy of creative experiencing is inseparable from his philosophy of time. As already explained, he posits a universe that is *forever in the making* by the dynamic singulars that come to be. What has already been made is the past, what has yet to be made is the future, and the present is the locus of activity where future possibility *becomes* past actuality. This characterization of time is in one sense circular, for the *definens* presupposes the *definiendum*; for example, "yet to be" presupposes "future." What keeps the definition from being vacuous is Hartshorne's concept of creativity, or making. Classical ideas about creation in the Christian tradition, for example, place God outside of time as its creator. According to this theory, God brings the temporal world—past, present, future—into existence, but the divine act itself is not in time. From God's eternity, what is future *for us* is as fully detailed as any moment that has *for us* become past. Hartshorne, on the other hand, finds a fundamental asymmetry in temporal relations. There is no such thing, even from a divine perspective, of a future that is as fully detailed as the past. The future, as "yet to be made," lacks details that will not exist until the making of them. The "making of them," as already noted, adds something to the universe that was not previously part of it; moreover, once the past is "made" it cannot be "unmade"—it is irrevocable.

> There are no definite '*a's* or *an's*' in mere possibility. Futurity and possibility are two aspects of one feature of reality, and both are essentially nonparticular. Only past facts are fully definite and qualitatively complete. Before I existed there was, and in pure eternity there is, no single possibility or set of possibilities duplicating my qualities. (CH 288)

The universe, and time itself, is nothing more than this *process* of accumulated and accumulating acts of becoming and all that they contain.

It is tempting to see in Hartshorne's theory of time a variation on J. M. E. McTaggart's concept of an A-series.[147] However, in his article on "Time" for Vergilius Ferm's 1945 *Encyclopedia of Religion*, Hartshorne distinguished his own ideas from those of McTaggart. McTaggart distinguished two ways of marking time: the A-series of relations of past, present, and future, and the B-series of relations of before and after. McTaggart said that if one abstracts from the A-series and B-series relations one is left with an ordered array of events, called a C-series, without temporal order of any kind.[148] If a C-series is like a film strip, with each frame representing an event, the A-series is analogous to frames passing in front of the light of the projector; as the light shines through a particular frame the photo on that frame is a present event, beforehand it is a future event and afterwards it is a past event. By contrast, Hartshorne's cumulative theory of becoming entails that there is no such thing as a C-series from which A-series relations could be abstracted. To continue the analogy, there is no film running on a projector with frames yet to be viewed. In short, there are no future events. At best, and in keeping with Hartshorne's indeterminism, there is a field of possibility that is only as detailed as the past determines it must be, all else in the field remaining *essentially* vague, awaiting full determination as novel dynamic singulars arise in the creative advance. By parity of reasoning, B-series relations are not fixed in eternity but are themselves results of temporal becoming.

For example, the fact denoted by "Socrates died before Aristotle's birth" could not exist until Aristotle was born. This is no mere limitation of human knowledge. After Socrates's death and before Aristotle's birth, there was no such relation as Socrates-having-died-before-Aristotle-was-born; what existed at the time of Socrates's death was a range of recently emergent possibilities of someone or other being born after Socrates, for example: a-great-philosopher-born-fifteen-years-after-the-death-of-Socrates. As Hartshorne says in the *Encyclopedia* article, "Time is not a mere relation of becomings but a becoming of relations."[149]

Hartshorne's theory of temporal becoming entails that time cannot, without remainder, be represented as a variable in a space-time coordinate system, with the other three variables being the dimensions of space. Of course, time can indeed be represented in this way, but Hartshorne insists that this cannot be the last word on the nature of time. Following an argument of Milič Čapek, Hartshorne maintained that spatial relations are derivative from temporal relations, or "space is a complication of time, not time of space" (CS 218). According to Hartshorne, all relations of causal inheritance are time-like relations. For instance, if occasion C prehends occasion A, then C is the temporal successor of A—no spatial relation is involved between A and C. Suppose, however, that C also inherits from B and that neither A nor B inherit from each other. In that case, A and B are strict contemporaries and there is a spatial relation between them. Conversely, occasions arrayed in space alone generate nothing in the way of temporal relations.

Hartshorne's argument shows, yet again, the primacy of asymmetrical relations in his philosophy. Symmetry is the degenerate or negative case where there is no causal or prehensive inheritance. As to space, Hartshorne distinguishes two sorts of symmetry. The simplest sort of symmetry is where two occasions are causally independent, as A and B in the diagram (Figure 1, next page).

The more complicated form of symmetry is between individuals that persist through time long enough to exchange influences, as in a conversation between two people. A simplified representation of such an exchange is shown in the diagram of Figure 2. Since the advent of Einstein's relativity theory, it has become customary to speak not of "space and time" but rather of "space-time." If Hartshorne and Čapek are correct that temporal relations are primary, it might be more accurate to speak of "time-space."[150]

Arrows represent time-like relations of inheritance.
Dotted line is simultaneity.

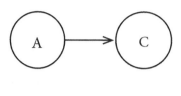 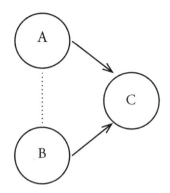

C prehends A   C prehends A and B
Time-Like Relation   A and B do not prehend each other

FIGURE 1: The Primacy of Temporal Relations

Hartshorne grounded modal concepts in the temporal structure of the world. He often quoted, with approval, Peirce's dictum that time is a particular variety of objective modality (CS 133).[151] For Hartshorne, however, time is not merely a species of objective modality; it provides the semantic anchor for *all* discourse about possibility and necessity. If this is correct, then there is no absolute division between *de re* and *de dicto* modalities, a topic to which we shall return in discussing Hartshorne's version of the ontological argument. For now, suffice it to say that, on Hartshorne's view, the past is fully determinate or actual,

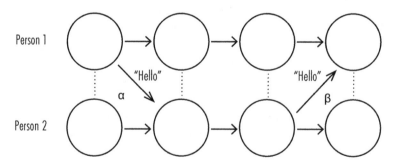

The circles represent successive occasions in a person's experience.
The arrows represent prehensive, hence asymmetrical/temporal, relations amongst the occasions.
Arrow α represents Person 1 greeting Person 2; β represents Person 2 returning the greeting.
Dotted lines represent non-prehensive or strictly symmetrical relations.
FIGURE 2: Symmetrical relations between enduring individuals

the future is relatively indeterminate or possible, and the present is the becoming of the actual as the relatively indeterminate becomes determinate. Possibility and futurity are inextricably linked. Nothing is possible that was not once, or one day will be, a possibility in the future. On Hartshorne's view, *if something is (was, or will be) possibly actual then it is (was, or will be) actually possible.* Unrestricted necessity, on this view, is what is common to all temporal possibilities. Hartshorne interprets the modal principle that a necessary proposition is implied by every proposition as an illustration of this (IO 121).

A consequence of Hartshorne's modal theory of time is that one may distinguish two concepts of necessity. Because temporal process is, on Hartshorne's view, cumulative, his theory recognizes what medieval philosophers called the accidental necessity of the past. The past, once having occurred, cannot be changed. As Thomas Aquinas said, not even God could restore virginity to a person who had lost it.[152] This is clearly a different meaning of necessity, than the unrestricted necessity that spans all possible world-states. Having lost one's virginity is not common to all temporal possibilities unless determinism is the case. Hartshorne characterizes the difference between these kinds of necessity, following von Wright, as necessity upon some contingent condition (*q* is necessary assuming *p*) and necessity upon tautological conditions (*q* is necessary on condition that *p* or not-*p*) (LP 53).

Following the lead of both Peirce and James, Hartshorne argued that determinism denies the reality of time. As noted previously, the only objective modality where determinism is concerned is necessity. Hartshorne's indeterminism, on the other hand, posits necessity in the direction from effect to cause; in the direction from cause to effect, however, there is an element of contingency, and this is the objective modality of the future (CE Ch. 7). A diagram of Jules Lequyer (Figure 3) helps to highlight the asymmetrical relation between past and future:[153]

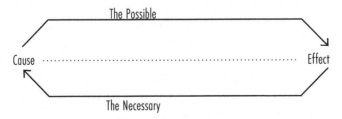

FIGURE 3: Lequyer's diagram of the relation of cause and effect in the free act

Hartshorne would doubtless modify the forward arrow of the diagram to say "a range of possibility" in order to indicate that different causal conditions allow for different degrees of openness for the future, but there is never absolute necessity from past to future. Indeed, this is precisely the revision of Peirce's category of Thirdness which Hartshorne introduces—"nondependence with respect to definite particulars, dependence with respect to more or less general outlines" (CAP 79). hen applied to time this means that "the future is what (within certain limits of probability) *may* happen" (CAP 79). Determinists emphasize our ignorance of causes and the consequent inability to clearly perceive the necessary relations among all events. For the determinist, however, the ignorance includes the systematic illusion of time's direction. From a practical point of view we cannot help but treat the illusion as reality. Aristotle remarked in the *Nichomachean Ethics* (VI, 2) that no one decides to have sacked Troy; however, the war (assuming its historicity) was once a matter of urgent decision in which the future was not something to be known but something to be made. For this reason, Hartshorne maintained that we act as though the future is relatively indeterminate even if we sometimes convince ourselves otherwise.

Hartshorne argued that the human capacity to form general conceptions and to frame principles that guide actions is another illustration that it is necessarily the case that we act as though determinism were false and time is real. The asymmetry between remembering a past event and planning for a future event is a powerful indication of the asymmetry of time. The past *as now remembered*, for example, does not include the memory one *now* has of it. Moreover, one may remember or misremember any amount of detail about a plan that has been carried out, but when the plan has yet to be executed, the only details that can be known are ones within the plan itself. As a script for future activity, the plan is abstract compared to its eventual realization. One may remember having taken one's dog for a walk, including the memory of having intended to take a particular route; however, the memory of the originally intended route cannot include everything that happened on the walk: on *this* walk, a toddler peered at you from beside a car, a fallen branch blocked your path, you stepped on two ants, a street lamp burned out, a raccoon scurried into a sewage drain—these, and countless other details were not included in the plan. Of course, what one anticipates by way of plans, intentions, or purposes, can be more or less specific. Regardless of the amount of detail, however, one's future projects leave innumerable particulars undecided. When things go "as planned" it is not because every aspect of the plan matched some detail fixed in advance, for there are many ways that plans can be successfully fulfilled. Musicians know that every musical score leaves a great deal to be decided; different performances can be equally faithful to what the composer wrote. Or, to use Hartshorne's example, "A man who goes to the theater to be amused can say that he has accomplished his purpose without implying that he knew in advance just what jokes he wished to hear!" (LP 214).

Hartshorne realized that if his theory of modality as essentially temporal is correct then there can be no such thing as merely possible worlds that are not parasitic upon the actual world. At most, there are possible world-states; that is to say, there are ways the actual world might have been. For any given past event, there was a time when something else might have occurred in its place. We can ask "What if?" about the past in order to conceive of ways the world might have been different, even though nothing can now be done to change what occurred. The future, on the other hand, is the arena of what might yet occur given the actual history of the world up to the present. Hartshorne's view contrasts neatly with Leibniz's idea that possible worlds are completely detailed descriptions of universes that God might choose to create. Possible worlds, in the Leibnizian sense, contain possible persons. As Leibniz argues in his correspondence with Arnauld, when the "concept"—the complete description of a possible person—is made actual by God, the person exists; the making actual of a different "concept" (i.e., altering the description in some way) would result in a different person.[154] Hartshorne objects that persons cannot be merely possible (MVG 308). Contrary to Leibniz, an actual person could have had properties other than what it has and the properties that it has could have been had by others. For example, Hillary Clinton could have been elected the US president in 2008 or in 2016 and someone besides Hillary could have been Bill Clinton's first lady. A fictional character, on the other hand, has no reality beyond the description of it; it has enough specificity to simulate a real person, but no feat of magic could transform it into a real person. Hartshorne's arguments clearly anticipate and dovetail with those of Saul Kripke in *Naming and Necessity*.[155] Kripke maintains that a proper name designates the same object across possible worlds (e.g., Hillary

Clinton) whereas a description designates different objects from world to world (e.g., "winner of the 2008 US presidential election"). Kripke also suggested that "counter-factual situation" or "possible state (or history) of the world" are less misleading expressions than "possible world." To speak of a "counter-factual" is to presuppose the factual. On these points, Hartshorne and Kripke are in full agreement.

On the question of the nature of possibility, Hartshorne sided closely with Peirce but parted ways with Whitehead. Peirce conceived the realm of possibilities as a continuum which, by definition, has no least member, but is infinitely divisible. There are no actual parts of a continuum, only an infinite number of ways to slice it. We have already found this idea at work in Hartshorne's concept of the affective continuum. Whitehead, on the other hand, spoke of "eternal objects" as "forms of definiteness" that identify what a thing is. The point of calling eternal objects "eternal" is that none of them are novel; the point of calling them "objects" is that they are definite; for example, a particular shade of green is *this* shade and no other. On Whitehead's view, a leaf on a tree changes colors but any particular shade of color exhibited by the leaf does not change.[156] Hartshorne maintains, by contrast, that the shades of color in question are neither eternal nor are they definite objects; put somewhat differently, they are definite only insofar as they are not eternal. The successive shades of color of the leaf are slices of the color continuum that exist as definite only when instantiated in the leaf. The color of the leaf at a particular moment is novel. On Hartshorne's account, we speak of sameness of color because the gradation between any two shades may be so infinitesimally slight as to be imperceptible. He noted that observed sameness of color is not a transitive relation. An object S may appear to be the same color as T and T the same color as U, but S may appear slightly different than U. In other words, there is a threshold defined by a degree of separation on the color continuum below which real differences are not observable for creatures like us (CS 63–64).[157]

According to Hartshorne, any quality that admits of a negative instance is not eternal. There are, in short, emergent universals. Hartshorne notes that "lover of Shakespeare" is a universal in the sense that it may be true of more than one thing but it is emergent in the sense that it could be true of nothing prior to Shakespeare (CS 58). By parity of reasoning, specific qualities in the affective continuum—particular tonal qualities, particular shades of color, etc.—emerge as the affective continuum is cut in various ways and patterns by dynamic singulars. On the other hand, the generic quality of "feeling" may be classified, on Hartshornean principles, as eternal, if not quite an "object" in the Whiteheadian sense. As previously noted, qualities that admit only of positive instances are metaphysical. A consequence of Hartshorne's view is that similarity is not simply a function of partial identity. It is true that we count two things similar when they have a sufficient number of qualities in common. But it is also the case that qualities themselves are similar to each other, as when we observe that orange is closer to red than it is to blue. Hartshorne concludes that similarity is as metaphysically ultimate as identity (CS 59).[158]

The Aesthetic Motif

One of the best and earliest interpreters of Hartshorne's philosophy, Eugene Peters, spoke of "the aesthetic motif" that runs through neoclassical theism.[159] Peters was drawing attention to the fact that, for Hartshorne, the most inclusive values are aesthetic (WM 51–52). We have seen that Hartshorne began his career proposing, *as an empirical hypothesis*, that all sensations are feelings and that all feelings exist along an aesthetic continuum. Hartshorne's metaphysics completes and complements the empirical hypothesis by considering the value-achievement and value-enrichment of dynamic singulars as the very foundations of existence. Daniel A. Dombrowski rightly says that, for Hartshorne, aesthetic experiences are not merely woven into the real, they *are* the real.[160] The poet e. e. cummings wrote, "Since feeling is first / who pays any attention / to the syntax of things . . ." Hartshorne did precisely what cummings dismissed (at least in the poem): he recognized feeling as first (i.e., as a metaphysical category) but he also paid close attention to the syntax of things (i.e., to understand the structure of feeling).

In his first book Hartshorne rejected the "annex view of value" (PPS 94). In the context of neoclassical metaphysics this means that there is no merely *valueless stuff* (what Whitehead called "vacuous actuality") onto which values are projected by human or divine purposes. Our pre-reflective experiences of our bodies, our memories, and of the world are never, Hartshorne insists, of bare valueless existence. The mother hears her baby's cries *as* irritating and the mother's songs are heard *as* soothing by the child. The values in experience, however, are not primarily ethical but aesthetic, a fact most clearly illustrated in the animal kingdom. The experiences of subhuman creatures are productive primarily—and for most creatures, exclusively—of non-moral values. When a lion fells an antelope, it is good for the lion pride and bad for the antelope, but moral judgments are out of place. One may, it is true, stress what is adaptive in behavior and useful for the survival of the species. There remain, however, the values of living for the lions and for the antelope that derive from being aware of the world around them, of breathing, eating, and the interactions with their fellows. These creatures don't think about their worlds but they *feel* them. For them, *aesthesis,* or feeling (the root of "aesthetics"), is indeed "first." Hartshorne's extensive study of songbirds supports this hypothesis; oscines have what in us would be called an aesthetic sense.

Hartshorne did not consider beauty to be the only aesthetic value, but "beauty" was his word of choice for what anchors his aesthetic theory (BS 6). One could generalize or gloss "beauty" to mean *intense satisfactory experience* without distorting Hartshorne's meaning. Much of traditional aesthetics holds that beauty is unity within diversity. Hartshorne argued, however, that another contrast is necessary to make sense of beauty, that of complexity and simplicity.[161] This concept of beauty, along with the relation of beauty to other aesthetic values, is expressed in the Dessoir-Davis-Hartshorne Circle (CS 305; BS 7; ZF 205).[162] Max Dessoir and Kay Davis helped Hartshorne with the diagram (Figure 4). If Hartshorne is correct, then beauty is a mean between two extremes, between order and disorder on the one hand (the vertical axis of the circles) and between complexity and simplicity on the other (the horizontal axis of the circles). Outside of the boundary of the outer circle is not merely aesthetic failure but also the failure of experience and therefore (because of Hartshorne's psychicalism) of existence itself.

For Hartshorne, beauty (or any aesthetic quality) is not *merely* in "the eye of the beholder" (or the perception of the perceiver). One must take into account not only the perceiving mind but what the mind perceives. A mind of sufficient complexity, cultivation, and education, is required to appreciate the elements that make for beauty in something. For example, until one knows what counterpoint is and until one is taught to listen for

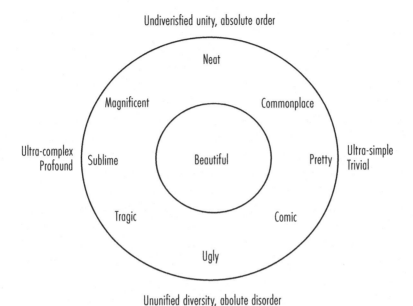

Undiverisfied unity, absolute order

Neat

Magnificent · Commonplace

Ultra-complex Profound · Sublime · Beautiful · Pretty · Ultra-simple Trivial

Tragic · Comic

Ugly

Ununified diversity, absolute disorder

FIGURE 4: The Dessoir-Davis-Hartshorne Circle

it, one is not in a position to be fully aware of it and one may not even be able *to hear* it. An adequate grasp of such things is beyond the ability of creatures with simpler nervous systems or of humans with certain kinds of brain damage. There is, in short, an intellectual component of beauty that requires a higher intellect to appreciate. This intellectual side of beauty predominates in science and mathematics, but Hartshorne argues that the twin contrasts of order / disorder and complexity / simplicity remain. He chronicles the ways in which ideals of beauty guide pure scientific inquiry and how the deliverances of science themselves are beautiful.[163] Science seeks a proper balance between imagination (e.g., theorizing) and observation. Hartshorne speaks of the "romance of science" as "the disclosure of a universe whose wild harmonies surpass the most vivid dreams of imagination not submitting itself to criticism and observational test." He reminds us that Darwin closed the *Origin* with "a prose poem on the beauty of the web of life."[164]

Prediction is one of the goals of scientific inquiry, but even here there is an aesthetic component. Too little predictability is chaotic, but too much predictability is monotonous. Good science is also heuristic, meaning that it is fruitful, leading to more discoveries. But discoveries in the strict sense are not predictable and are often quite surprising. Hartshorne accuses the determinism of traditional Newtonian science of aesthetic failure for it posited absolute regularity as the ideal to the exclusion of spontaneity, chance, and freedom: the adventure of life—at once beautiful and terrifying—reduced to mechanistic obedience to law. Hartshorne's indeterminism, as we have seen, respects the rule of laws of nature but provides a balance between regularity and irregularity. Traditional theology, Hartshorne claims, was as defective from an aesthetic point of view as the traditional philosophy of nature. Classical theologians stressed divine simplicity and unity to the exclusion of complexity and variety. According to Hartshorne, "The beauty of the world is in its partly unprogrammed spontaneities."[165] Hartshorne's neoclassical theism affirms a world of multiple creative agents in interaction with each other and with God. On Hartshorne's view, God is affected by the creatures and, consequently, the divine experience is a complex reality, full of all of the serendipity and tragedy that interactions with others routinely brings. If Hartshorne is correct, there is an ever changing beauty of the world as a whole that is fully appreciated only by deity and to contemplate this divine experience is to have something akin to what classical theologians called the beatific vision.

✤ FIVE ✤

Neoclassical or
Dipolar Theism

WE NOTED IN THE PREFACE that Hartshorne's guiding intuition in philosophy throughout his long career was the idea that "God is love." This "intuition" presupposes both that there is a divine reality and that that reality answers to some positive description of being a loving God. Hartshorne vigorously defended both propositions by clarifying what he meant by the phrase, "God is love," by defending his views against a variety of objections, and generally by arguing that his dipolar or neoclassical theism survives critical scrutiny better than its philosophical competitors. Heavily influenced by Whitehead, Hartshorne borrowed some of the Englishman's technical vocabulary, and he often promoted broadly Whiteheadian ideas. It is a mistake, however, to style him as Whitehead's disciple, for he departed from the older philosopher on a number of points, most notably where this and the next chapter (also Chapter Eight) are concerned, on questions surrounding the concept and the existence of God.

In what follows, we first examine Hartshorne's ideas about the concept of God and only in the next chapter do we turn to the question of arguments for and against the existence of God. The reason for taking the topics in this order is that Hartshorne argues that the concept of God itself determines the sorts of arguments of which theism or atheism is susceptible. The existence of God, according to Hartshorne, is the quintessential metaphysical issue and, as such, the question must be adjudicated by the methods of metaphysics. Scientific arguments for or against theism have a limited usefulness, but they are fundamentally flawed since they misconstrue the nature of the theistic question. In any event, the formulation of a coherent theism is an integral part of the rational defense of theism. This fact was at the forefront of Hartshorne's mind since he spent much of his career in a philosophical atmosphere in which the question was not so much "Does God exist?" as it was "Does 'God' name a coherent idea?" It can plausibly be claimed that Hartshorne accomplished at least two tasks: first, he introduced a sophisticated and religiously important form of theism heretofore unheard of or at least very poorly developed through philosophical argument and, second, he shifted the burden of proof onto those who claim that the concept of God is hopelessly muddled.

Divine Love and Divine Relativity

The only deity worthy of worship, Hartshorne believed, is one that could be described as "Love divine, all loves excelling," as in the title of Charles Wesley's hymn (ZF 167). Hartshorne did not identify himself as Christian, nor did he consider himself a theologian. He argued, however, that Christian thinkers had an unfortunate tendency to allow what he considered to be warped ideas about absolute power and unchanging perfection to eclipse the central teaching of their faith concerning divine love. The parables of Jesus and the personal qualities he exhibits in the Gospels reflect, for the Christian, the image of a loving God. They portray one who not only acts for the benefit of the beloved but also sympathizes with others in such a way as to rejoice in their well-being and feel sorrow in their tragedies. These ideas about God are also clearly evident in Hebrew Scripture in the concept of *chesed*, or lovingkindness, so characteristic of prophetic literature and the Psalms. These are the qualities of love that Hartshorne takes to be essential to it; at a bare minimum, love requires both the capacity to act for the welfare of others and to sympathize with their feelings. As the etymology of "compassion" suggests, it is "to suffer with" another in the desire to ameliorate the other's suffering. If this sort of love is to be attributed to the divine being, then it must be possible for God to act for the welfare of the creatures but also to be affected by their weal and woe. In short, divine love entails *the divine relativity*.

Divine relativity is precisely what much of traditional theology would not allow. As Aquinas said, God is really related to the creatures but the creatures have only a rational relation to God (i.e., a relation only in the mind).[1] In short, God is impassible or unaffected by anything external. The only doctrine of divine love consistent with the doctrine of impassibility is one in which God promotes the welfare of the creatures, but is unaffected by what happens to them. On this view, divine love, unlike human forms of love, involves neither sympathy nor empathy. John Sanders demonstrates that Christian thinkers, from as early as Justin Martyr, realized that there is a tension between the belief in the goodness of God and the denial that God somehow shares in the joys and sorrows of the creatures.[2] Anselm raised the question explicitly in *Proslogion*: How can God be all-loving without any sympathetic responsiveness?[3] Anselm answered by promoting a kind of *theological behaviorism*: in other words, we feel the effects of God's goodness, but God feels nothing. The problem, however, is that this doesn't answer the question, it only reasserts divine impassibility.

Hartshorne affirms God's love as involving both benevolence and feeling. Because God loves the creatures, what happens to them is felt also by God. As a loving parent suffers for a child who is ill or who has lost her or his way in life, so the God in whom Hartshorne believes, suffers through the misfortunes and the mischief of the creatures. Hartshorne was fond of quoting one of the final statements from *Process and Reality* that "God is the great companion—the fellow-sufferer who understands."[4] Hartshorne, following both Whitehead and Berdyaev, maintained that there can be tragedy, even for God (WP Ch. 13).[5] As Martha Nussbaum argues, tragedy can happen only to someone who cares enough about others to be disappointed by them or hurt by what happens to them.[6] God, in Hartshorne's view, is one who cares and who can therefore be disappointed or hurt by the actions of the creatures.

Hartshorne's basic argument for divine relativity is stated throughout his writings (e.g., DR 13–14; AW 12f; DL 232–33).[7] In effect, Hartshorne argues that the denial of real relations in God cannot be sustained if one affirms, as Aquinas does, that God has perfect knowledge of all contingent realities. We here reconstruct it in the weakest modal system so that its validity is more readily apparent.[8] (For a similar proof concerning Spinoza's critique of Descartes's concept of God, see the appendix to this chapter.) Let us use the following symbols:

Gx, God knows a particular worldly event x.

Wx, Worldly event x exists at t. The variable x can stand for any worldly event that exists at a given time, t; for example, a bird singing.

The proof is a *reductio*. The first two premises are accepted by all parties to the debate. The third premise, accepted only by Aquinas, is introduced as the assumption from which a contradiction is derived.

1. $\Box\,(Gx \supset Wx)$	Axiom of God's infallible knowledge
2. $\sim \Box\,Wx$	Assumption of the contingency of a worldly event
3. $\Box\,Gx$	Thomas's denial of contingency in God
4. $\Box\,Gx \supset \Box\,Wx$	From 1 by the modal principle: $\Box\,(p \supset q) \supset (\Box\,p \supset \Box\,q)$
5. $\Box\,Wx$	From 3 and 4 by *modus ponens*
6. $\Box\,Wx \wedge \sim \Box\,Wx$	From 2 and 5 by conjunction
7. $\sim \Box\,Gx$	From 3 through 6 by *reductio* argument

In effect, Hartshorne presents one with the following alternatives. Either God does not know worldly events ($\sim Gx \wedge Wx$)—Aristotle's theism or the view of anyone who denies the existence of God; or God's knowledge of worldly events and those events are equally necessary ($\Box\,Gx \wedge \Box\,Wx$)—pantheism; or God's knowledge of worldly events and the events of the world are equally not necessary ($\sim \Box\,Gx \wedge \sim \Box\,Wx$) —Hartshorne's alternative. The alternative that is not possible is Aquinas's view that God's knowledge of worldly events lacks contingency but those events are not necessary, ($\Box\,Gx \wedge \sim \Box\,Wx$).

Aquinas was aware of something like this argument. He replied that the world is indeed necessary, but only with respect to God's knowledge, and not as the world is in-itself. God knows the world *as present*, and "*for everything that is, while it is, must necessarily be.*"[9] Thus, the world is necessary only in the trivial sense that it is necessary for a thing to exist in order for propositions about it to be known, and this is the case whether the knowing is creaturely or divine. Hartshorne counters that what God knows, supposing the world to be contingent and God's knowledge to be perfect, is that a world exists but *it might have failed to exist*. The addendum, *it might have failed to exist*, is enough to introduce contingency into God's knowledge. This is true also of creaturely knowing. One's *knowledge that q is contingent* must itself be contingent if *q* is contingent.

Aquinas's counter argument is merely a restatement of the first two premises. He argues that the world's events (Wx) are given on the condition that God knows them (Gx), from which it does not follow that the world's events are necessary ($\Box Wx$). Neither Aquinas nor Hartshorne believes that the first premise, by itself, entails the conclusion of the necessity of the world's events. In other words, "$\Box (Gx \supset Wx) \supset \Box Wx$" is false. The falsity of this formula, however, is logically equivalent to the conjunction of the first two premises, as the following derivation demonstrates:

$\sim [\Box (Gx \supset Wx) \supset \Box Wx]$	Assumption: falsity of "$\Box (Gx \supset Wx) \supset \Box Wx$"
$\sim [\sim \Box (Gx \supset Wx) \vee \Box Wx]$	Definition of material conditional
$\sim \sim \Box (Gx \supset Wx) \wedge \sim \Box Wx$	DeMorgan's rule
$\Box (Gx \supset Wx) \wedge \sim \Box Wx$	Double negation

On the truth of these propositions, Hartshorne and Aquinas agree. Aquinas affirms, however, not only that God's knowing of the world's events entails that those events exist; he also affirms that there is no contingency in God, symbolically, ($\Box Gx$), and that's what leads to the contradiction.

It is open to Thomists to question whether Aquinas is committed to $\Box Gx$ in any sense that would be damaging to Aquinas's theory. The expression "$\Box Gx$" means that it is necessary that God knows a specific worldly event. However, Aquinas holds that God freely creates the universe. In Thomas's words, "The knowledge of God is the cause of things when the will is joined to it" (*scientia Dei causa rerum voluntate adjuncta*).[10] If God freely creates the singing bird, then the singing bird's existence is not necessary and therefore God's knowledge of the bird singing is not necessary. Aquinas maintains that God necessarily wills God's own goodness, but because the divine goodness can exist whether or not the things willed by it exist (e.g., the bird singing), it follows that God does not necessarily will the created order.[11]

Hartshorne's reply is that Aquinas cannot hold that God freely, or nonnecessarily, creates the universe and also maintain that there is no contingency in God. Aquinas's explanation of divine willing posits necessary and nonnecessary volitions in God. God necessarily wills divine goodness, but does not necessarily will things willed by that goodness. Hartshorne concludes:

> Yet all the being of God is held [by Aquinas] to be purely necessary. Ergo, the nonnecessary acts are not in the being of God. Still they are either in God or not in him. If in him, then he has accidents, additional to what is necessary in him. If not in him, what is meant by calling them "his" acts, and why are we assured always that "God's will is his essence"? (PSG 133)

Hartshorne's point is that the problem of contingency in God's knowledge resurfaces as the problem of contingency in God's willing the universe into existence. No self-consistent theology can *deny* all contingency in God and *affirm* God's knowing of or God's willing of contingent truths or realities.

Hartshorne's basic argument for divine relativity is expressed in terms of the idea of God's exhaustive knowledge but it could equally well be rephrased in terms of inexhaustible love, for love, like knowledge, has its objects. Of course, these are not the only qualities that theists usually ascribe to God—there are also such qualities as eminent creativity, perfect power, and infinite wisdom. Hartshorne attempts to do justice to these ideas in formulating his neoclassical concept of God, but for him divine love remained paramount. This is significant for it highlights Hartshorne's commitment to the principle that negation is parasitic upon positive attributions, that there are no merely negative facts. Many theologians, eager to affirm the transcendence of God, emphasize what cannot be known of God and argue that, in view of this ignorance, the most appropriate theological language is by way of negation (*via negativa*): God is *not* finite (infinite), *not* changeable (immutable), *not* affected by anything external (impassible), *not* contingent (necessary), *not* in time (nontemporal), and so forth. Hartshorne also emphasized what is not known of God, and he did not deny that negations play an important role in religious discourse. Hartshorne comments that our knowledge of the concrete divine reality is "negligibly small" (DR 35; NT 77). He argues, however, that as the sole or even primary approach to religious language, "the negative way" is a case of false modesty. Negative theologians are supposedly being deferential to God by stressing what cannot be known or said of God, but this masks the fact that they consider themselves privy to enough knowledge about the divine reality to know what cannot be attributed to it.

Hartshorne couples the accusation of false modesty with the charge that the negations used of deity by negative theologians almost invariably presuppose invidious contrasts: the finite is inferior to the infinite, the changeable to the unchangeable, the passible to the impassible, the temporal to the nontemporal, and so forth. Hartshorne argues that it is much too simplistic to label one side of an ultimate contrast as "better" and the other side "worse." On the contrary, there are better and worse forms of each side of each contrast (PSG 2–3). For example, there are better and worse ways of being affected by others (passibility) and better and worse ways of being unaffected by others (impassibility): to identify too much with the suffering of others is damaging to one's own well-being and may prevent one from helping others in need; to remain unaffected by the plight of others exhibits the character flaw called insensitivity. In Hartshorne's view, theologians should not chase after negations if they wish to speak of One that is worthy of worship; rather, they should explore ways of attributing to God what is best in both sides of any particular contrast. For this reason, Hartshorne maintains that, to the extent that language is adequate to theological purposes, only a properly *dipolar* concept of deity can reflect the divine perfection: God is *both* finite and infinite, *both* passible and impassible, and so forth, but in different respects and in eminent ways. Hartshorne emphasizes positive or kataphatic theology when he avers that we do not worship God because of the defects God lacks but because of God's "positive and all-encompassing love and beauty" (AD 69).

It may be tempting to find warrant for the traditional emphasis on negative theology in the experiences of mystics.[12] In the chapter on mysticism in his classic study, *The Varieties of Religious Experience*, William James identifies ineffability as the first of four characteristics of mystical experience (the other characteristics are their noetic quality, their transiency, and their passivity). According to James:

> The subject of [the experience] immediately says that it defies expression, that no adequate report of its contents can be given in words. It follows from this that its quality must be directly experienced; it cannot be imparted or transferred to others. In this peculiarity mystical states are more like states of feeling than like states of intellect.[13]

Hartshorne notes that it is a consequence of his dipolar theism—or any theism that accepts the doctrine of the omnipresence of deity—that God is directly experienced, which means directly felt, by all creatures. To claim not to experience God is, on Hartshorne's view, "no less paradoxical than the contradictory claim."[14] Following his teacher Rufus Jones—himself known as a great scholar of mysticism—Hartshorne held that the difference between mystics and others is only a matter of the degree and clarity to which they are aware of the presence of God (DL 121). Hartshorne also agreed that there is a sense in which mystical experience is ineffable, if "ineffable" means "not exhaustively describable," for every experience can be so characterized—all the more so if the experience is of "the Eminent Actuality" of God.[15]

We would emphasize that, where mystics are concerned, the adjective "ineffable" is used for *the mystic's experience of God*, not as a description of *the God that mystics experience*. Indeed, Hartshorne points out that, whatever the ineffability of mystical experience means, it *cannot* mean that one description is equally as good as any other, notwithstanding that "some Buddhists do talk almost in this way."[16] Henri Bergson, who Hartshorne often alluded to on this topic, emphasized the positive aspect of the reality of which mystics claim to be aware, "the love wherein the mystic sees the very essence of God."[17] Bergson wrote:

> As a matter of fact, the mystics unanimously bear witness that God needs us, just as we need God. Why should He need us unless it be to love us? And it is to this very conclusion that the philosopher who holds to the mystical experience must come. Creation will appear to him a God undertaking to create creators, that He may have, besides Himself, beings worthy of His love.[18]

Certainly, most mystics employ positive language in speaking of their experience. It is the *felt unity* with what is ultimately real that the mystic seeks, and it is the language of union in love that is so often employed to express this experience. To cite an example given by Evelyn Underhill: no sooner does Plotinus try to safeguard the Absolute from all categorization "by the icy method of negation" than he "breaks away into the language of ardent feeling," speaking of "the veritable love, the sharp desire which possessed him."[19] It is also worth remarking that, historically, the metaphysical trend—evident in the dominant streams of Western and Eastern thought—was to categorize time, change, and contingency as inferior modes of existence to eternity, immutability, and necessity. In Hartshorne's words:

> Historically there have been certain rather pervasive biases in metaphysical traditions, and mystics show signs of being limited by these biases. If Process Philosophers are right, it is only in the last few decades that an adequate metaphysics has been available.[20]

The preference of the mystics for the language of *Being* over the language of *Becoming* may then be not so much a deliverance of mystical experience as it is the flawed philosophical framework in which mystical ideas were expressed.[21]

We noted in Chapter One that Hartshorne reported having had a near mystical experience in 1917 as he contemplated the idea of a finite God during the voyage to France; but one does not ordinarily think of him as a mystic.[22] Nor would one so describe most of those who influenced him, including Whitehead and Peirce. The scholar working within the stream of process thought who has the most to say about mysticism is Daniel Dombrowski. He makes a compelling case that the writings of the sixteenth-century mystic, John of the Cross, are best interpreted through the lens of dipolar theism.[23] However, if there is a mystic among the modern founders of process thought, it is the French Jesuit Pierre Teilhard de Chardin.[24] Teilhard was trained as a geologist and is known in scientific circles for his role in the discovery of *Homo Erectus Pekinensis*, so-called Peking Man.[25] Teilhard's lyrical and devotional writings burn with the intensity of the greatest of mystics, but they are informed by the modern perspectives of the vastness of space, the depths of time, and the astonishing complexity of nature—in short, the entire sweep of cosmic and terrestrial evolution.[26] Teilhard argued for a mysticism that finds union with God not in isolation from the world, nor in the denial of one's distinctive personality, but in and through the world. As he wrote in an early essay, "There is a communion with God, and a communion with the earth, and a communion with God through the earth."[27] His signature expression, "union differentiates" highlights the idea that union with God in love preserves and enhances the distinctive value and personalities of those that are brought within its sphere.[28] It seems clear, therefore, that something like Hartshorne's dipolar theism allows for the expression and practice of mysticism in what are arguably its higher forms.

Much of the discussion of mysticism centers on the problem of language as it pertains to experience and as it pertains to God. Dombrowski notes that Hartshorne sought a theory of religious language that avoids two extremes: (1) language is wholly inadequate to describe God, and (2) verbal formulae may capture God without doubt or obscurity.[29] Like Duns Scotus, Hartshorne considered the formal abstractions of metaphysics to be the most nearly univocal language that is possible for deity, for they do not admit of degrees. For example, on Hartshorne's view, God is, in different respects, necessary and contingent; we shall see, however, that this does not mean that God is more or less necessary or more or less contingent. Hartshorne calls the most nearly equivocal language about God "symbolic" because it presupposes particular times, places, and situations. Metaphors such as "shepherd," "mother," "father," are examples. Analogical language holds a place between the abstract contraries of metaphysics and the concrete imagery of poetic imagination. Analogical language is a matter of degree, as when one says that love comes in many forms, but the eminent form of love belongs to God. We have already seen that Hartshorne claimed that psychical predicates such as memory, feeling, and volition admit of an infinite variability (BH ch. 8). Hartshorne sometimes says that these sorts of predicates only apply literally to God and not the creatures. As Dombrowski avers, the most parsimonious interpretation of this "negative anthropology" is that Hartshorne is emphasizing that God alone has the supreme or eminent form of these qualities.

Existence and Actuality

To say that God exhibits both sides of a metaphysical contrast would be a logical contradiction unless there was a way of showing that the polar extremes apply to God *in different respects*. When speaking of the Christian doctrine of the Incarnation, Søren Kierkegaard seemed to relish "the contradiction" (or paradox) that the eternal came to be in time. There is reason to believe that he did not intend to *assert* a contradiction.[30] Hartshorne did not mention Kierkegaard in this connection; nevertheless, he apparently saw little advantage in this way of speaking. He complained that a theological paradox seems to be what a contradiction is when applied to God (DR 1). In Hartshorne's view, in the enterprise of rational metaphysics, asserting contradictory things of God is not a sign of profundity but of confusion. If one is to make sense of God one should not speak nonsense. Hartshorne's proposal is to make a three-fold distinction of logical type, applicable to both God and the creatures, among *existence* (that a thing is), *essence* (what a thing is), and *actuality* (the particular state in which a thing is). To illustrate how this distinction can be applied to both God and the creatures, consider the case of a woman listening to a white-crowned sparrow sing and of God knowing this fact (LP 63). The woman *exists*, has the cognitive capacity to hear songbirds, which is part of her *essence* (insofar as audition is part of her natural endowment), and she is currently listening to a bird sing, which is her *actual* state. The same distinctions apply to God: God exists, has the essence of being all-knowing, and is in the actual state of knowing that the woman is listening to the bird.

The tripartite distinction of existence, essence, and actuality is one of *logical type* analogous to the logical type difference between universals and particulars. One may, for example, deduce that the woman exists if she is listening to the bird, but one may not deduce from the fact of her existence that she is listening to a bird. For this reason, Hartshorne maintains that existence (also essence) is abstract relative to actuality. Actuality is, so to speak, *information rich*, relative to existence (and essence). This is recognized in modern logic in the use of the existential quantifier which, by itself, gives no details about the existent object (LP 64–65).

Hartshorne's three-fold distinction also allows one to make a distinction *within* God between what is necessary (could not be otherwise) and what is contingent (could be otherwise) (Table 3). It is conceivable that God exists necessarily and necessarily has the quality of being all-knowing, but the actual state of God's knowing (e.g., knowing that the woman is listening to a bird sing) might be contingent. Barring determinism, the woman's listening to the bird is contingent: she might have been asleep, she might have been listening to a different bird, she might have been distracted, and so forth. If God is necessarily all-knowing, then God knows about the woman and her actual state, regardless of what it might be. Moreover, God's actual state of knowing the woman as listening to the bird sing is as contingent as the fact that she is listening to the bird sing. The diagram below summarizes how the distinctions between the concrete and the abstract and the necessary and the contingent map onto Hartshorne's three-fold distinction of existence, essence, and actuality as it applies to God and the creatures.

	Creatures	God	
Actuality	Woman listening to a bird singing (contingent)	God knowing the woman as listening to the bird (contingent)	Concrete
Essence	Human nature as including various cognitive capacities (contingent)	God as knowing whatever is knowable, as omniscient (necessary)	Abstract
Existence	The woman existing (contingent)	God existing (necessary)	Abstract

TABLE 3: Hartshorne's View of Actuality/Essence/Existence

The three-fold distinction is often referred to by means of the simpler distinction between existence and actuality, thereby anticipating the thesis of Hartshorne's ontological argument that existence belongs to the nature or essence of God. One need not accept the ontological argument, however, to appreciate the importance of the distinction. David Tracy calls the distinction "Hartshorne's Discovery" and Hartshorne himself said, "I rather hope to be remembered for this distinction" (EA 75).[31] Hartshorne notes that Aristotle anticipated the tripartite distinction of existence, essence, and actuality when he spoke of substance, essence, and accident. Hartshorne's criticism of the Stagirite is that he considered substance as ontologically basic and thus could speak of accidental compounds. For Hartshorne, actuality is ontologically basic in the sense of being most concrete. Hartshorne writes, "It is actuality of accidents, not existence of substances that is prior" (PSG 72). It is well to remember, following Hartshorne's principle of inclusive asymmetry which we discussed in Chapter Three, that divine contingency is the more inclusive category, that the contingency includes the necessity. To miss this is to miss one of the central contributions that Hartshorne made to thinking about God.[32]

Hartshorne's distinction is important because it allows, among other things, that there can be give-and-take relations between God and the creatures without reducing God to the status of a creature. Contrary to the ancient tradition of divine impassibility, God can be conceived as affected by the creatures. In the previous example, the woman listening to the bird *brings it about* that God knows that she is listening to the bird, although she does not bring it about that God is omniscient, for God would have been omniscient even had she never existed. It is in this sense that Hartshorne speaks of the creatures as "part-creator of God" (MVG 109). Aquinas argued that any contingency in God implies the possibility of God's non-existence, thereby reducing God's existence to the status of creaturely existence.[33] In view of the difference between existence and actuality, the inference is invalid. God's actual states can be contingent while God's existence and essence remain necessary. Moreover, the essence of God must now be described not merely as necessary but as *necessarily somehow actualized*.

It is of interest that, while Aquinas never achieved a dipolar conception of deity, he held a kind of dipolar conception of angels. Aquinas says that angels are not subject to decay and destruction by natural means; they are incorporeal and have no corruptible bodies and so are immortal. Like God's existence, their existence is not affected by the flow of time. Unlike the Thomistic God, however, they are susceptible to change. While their existence is immutable, they have free will, their knowledge can increase, and in a certain sense they can even move from place to place. Aquinas says that between the unqualified changelessness of God's eternity and the qualified changeableness of corporeal existence, there is the qualified immutability of angelic being. The technical expression for this is æviternity, which is the mean between the extremes of eternity and time. What neither Aquinas nor any other scholastic philosopher, nor even philosophers to the time of Kant, could conceive is an æviternal God.[34]

One often has the impression in metaphysical disagreements that philosophers are talking past each other, using common words and expressions but giving them different meanings. It was precisely this problem that John Wild raised in the course of criticizing Hartshorne's *The Divine Relativity*. Wild accused Hartshorne of characterizing *being* in a way that has little to do with its classical meaning. Wild explained that *being* should not be identified with "that fixed and determinate aspect of finite being" traditionally called "essence." According to Wild, it includes this aspect, as it includes anything that is real, be it concrete or abstract, "But being is not exhausted by the constant, changeless essences of finite things and accidents. It also includes *the act of existing* which realizes such possibilities, bringing them out of their causes, and giving them a being of their own *in rerum natura*."[35] Wild could not understand how *being*, in this sense, could be an abstract aspect of contingent happenings. Furthermore, he maintained that characterizing *being* as the "absolute," independent," and "necessary" aspect of contingent happenings is "Pickwickian."

> If the whole concrete happening is "contingent," in what sense can an abstract phase of this contingent happening, contained within it, be absolute or necessary? Surely not in its existence. If so, it would necessarily exist, and could not be called contingent. If not, then we are surely concerned with a finite entity, whose essence is distinct from its existence.[36]

Wild realized that this criticism, if correct, would undermine Hartshorne's use of the ontological argument for God's existence. It further raises the question of what reason Hartshorne might have to believe in such a God, that is, one whose essence does not include existence.

There are certainly different uses of the concept of *being* as between Wild and Hartshorne, but that is precisely because Hartshorne was at pains to argue that the classical concept of God as the pure act of existence (*actus purus*) does not survive rational scrutiny. Hartshorne offered an alternative concept of God that he believed would avoid the difficulties he found in classical theism. It is interesting that Wild congratulates Hartshorne in accepting that "Knowledge adds something real to the knowing agent, nothing whatsoever to the object known."[37] Of course, this is a central idea in Hartshorne's *reductio* argument against classical theism—which we formalized and discussed above. That argument, as we have seen, depends crucially on the insight that knowledge adds something to the knowing agent, even when that knowing agent is God. To be precise, if the object known is contingent, then God's knowledge must have a contingent aspect. This is not because—as Wild would have it—Hartshorne commits a fallacy of reasoning from a general rule about knowledge having the same modal properties as its objects.[38] This would, in any event, be self-defeating for Hartshorne since he holds that it is possible for our very contingent ways of knowing to grasp the reality of a being whose existence is necessary. The principle, rather, is that if the object of knowledge could fail to exist, then knowledge of it could fail to exist. As we have seen, this in no way prejudices the case against theism since it does not entail a denial of omniscience. As the example of the woman listening to the bird singing makes clear, had she not been listening to the bird, then God would have known that fact.

When it comes to addressing Hartshorne's *reductio* aimed at classical theism, Wild maintains that there is a confusion of the logical necessity of entailment and the "existential necessity involved in the classical concept of God."[39] However, he never explains precisely which step in the argument is mistaken. He accepts, for example, that the act whereby God exists is necessary in the sense that it cannot not be.[40] He agrees that knowing something changes something in the knower. In addition, he makes the same move as Aquinas in claiming that "there is no reason for supposing that God cannot know a contingent world by a knowledge which is hypothetically necessary."[41] As we have shown, this observation is beside the point, for it is simply a logical reformulation of the first two premises of the argument (as we have formalized it); that is, the worldly event exists on the condition that God knows it. Thus, it is not clear how Wild can avoid the conclusion that God's "act of existing," as Wild characterizes *being*, is not wholly necessary but has contingent aspects.

Fourteen years after Wild's second article in response to Hartshorne was published, the debate between the two philosophers was taken up again. Hartshorne once more presented Wild with a precise formulation of his *reductio* and challenged him to show which premise was in error. Wild found no formal fault with the argument, but he fell back on his claim that Hartshorne confused different modes of necessity. Seemingly unable to move the debate forward, he presented a caricature of Hartshorne's theism:

> So Professor Hartshorne confronts God himself with this dilemma. Is God necessary or is he contingent? To say that God is all one or all the other is one-sided and reductive. So

Professor Hartshorne concludes that God is a little bit of both, something in him (existence) being necessary and something else (his knowledge of the world) being contingent. This splits God up into parts that are not only different (which is bad enough), but absolutely contradictory.[42]

Of course, it is not God who is being presented with the dilemma but Wild and the classical tradition. We urge that this is simply a failure to take seriously Hartshorne's triad of existence, essence, and actuality. Oddly enough, Wild admits that the distinction makes sense for a non-divine being: "There is certainly a sense [he says] in which I might not have been as I am, for contingent choices played a role in my whole origin and development."[43] Thus, Wild distinguishes one's personal identity from various contingent states in which it exists or is actual. Why this same distinction cannot be applied to God—recognizing, however, that, unlike non-divine beings, God's existence, cannot not be—is not clear. It is precisely Hartshorne's contention that the divine act of existing is necessary, but the manner of its existence—its actuality—is contingent, depending in large measure on the creative advance of the universe. As though weary of argument, Wild seems to abandon the search for philosophical understanding in this case: he says that God's acts are both necessary yet contingent, but how this is so we do not know. "We are faced with a real transcendence which looms above our finite categories."[44] This was not a game Hartshorne was interested in playing.

Hartshorne's doctrine of existence and actuality represents a departure from Whitehead's form of theism. To be sure, Whitehead and Hartshorne are in firm agreement, and they insist, that the relations between God and the world are symmetrical. In addition, both philosophers regard God as supremely worshipful not only with respect to the divine absoluteness but also with respect to the divine relativity. Nevertheless, Hartshorne conceives God as an individual who endures through various actual states. In the technical language of Whitehead's philosophy, this makes God a "society," that is to say, a collection of actual entities extended in time, each member of which shares a defining characteristic, passed along from one moment to the next. All enduring objects are societies of actual entities; moreover, no actual entity endures through various states. On Whitehead's view, God is *not* an enduring object but a single nontemporal actual entity.[45] To speak of Whitehead's

God as dipolar is to indicate that God has a physical and a mental pole. This sense of "dipolar" is different from the meaning that Hartshorne commonly gives the expression. Hartshorne does not deny that actual entities are dipolar, nor does he deny that there are physical and mental aspects of deity, but his God is dipolar in having an enduring character embodied in successive states, the character being abstract compared to the concrete actual states. Hartshorne says, "Unlike Whitehead, I . . . define God as an enduring society of actualities, not a single actuality. Here I think Whitehead was just mistaken."[46]

Whitehead indicated that he considered the possibility of God being an enduring object, and thus a society, but rejected it on the grounds that God's consequent nature loses nothing of the past whereas societies are characterized by partial loss of the past.[47] This argument is curious, for it would seem to apply to actual entities as well as to societies. No non-divine actual entity preserves its entire past without distortion and loss; yet Whitehead attributes to deity—in the doctrine of objective immortality of the past in God—what no other actual entity can accomplish. Hartshorne notes that the unique excellence of retaining the past perfectly in memory must be no less true if God is an actual entity than if God is a society.[48] He argues that the consequent nature of God is itself abstract, for it is the generic property of being *somehow actual* or affected by others (WP 75–76). Thus, Hartshorne proposes that Whitehead would be more true to his own metaphysics by conceiving God as an enduring object, and thus as a society, rather than as a single actual entity. Hartshorne's theory is not without its own puzzles, not least of which is coordinating the concept of a divine temporal worldline with the relativistic view of space-time in contemporary physics, a topic we address in Chapter Eight. Suffice it to say that the question whether God is best conceived as a single actual entity or as an enduring object is a major parting of the ways between process theists.

Divine Perfection

Hartshorne's three-fold distinction allows one to appreciate the extent of his divergence from the dominant tradition in philosophical theology which he called "classical theism." We have noted that classical theists, committed to the transcendence of God, were fond of the *via negativa*: God was placed on one side only of the pairs of contrasts, absolute/

relative, infinite/finite, immutable/mutable, impassible/passible, necessary/contingent, and eternal/temporal. Hartshorne rejects this as a "monopolar prejudice," an expression that highlights not only the "monopolar" aspect of classical theism but also the invidious character of the contrasts—the "prejudice"—as applied to God and the creatures (PSG 8, 14, 81, 146). Hartshorne speaks instead of God's *dual transcendence* (CS Ch. 11; WM 133; ZF 6, 10, 125; CE Ch. 9).[49] God transcends the creatures by being the supreme instance of *both* sides of the contrasts. The distinction between existence and actuality permits a logically coherent doctrine of dual transcendence by distinguishing different aspects of God. For example, God is immutable with respect to existence and essence, but mutable with respect to actuality. That is to say, God's existence and essence are always the same, but God's actual states are constantly being added to with the creative advance of the world. Or again, God is both necessary and contingent, but in different respects. God's existence and essence are necessary (i.e., could not be otherwise) whereas God's actuality is contingent (i.e., could be otherwise). The examples of divine mutability and contingency represent God's flexibility in being able to respond to every possible change. It should now be clear why Hartshorne was making a serious point when he quipped that he believed in twice as much transcendence as was found in classical theism.

Because Hartshorne speaks of the finitude of God, one might suppose he promotes a merely finite deity such as one finds in John Stuart Mill's essay *Theism*. Hartshorne's commitment to the principle of dual transcendence entails that this parallel is mistaken. Insofar as God has actual states, God is indeed finite. Furthermore, God can be nothing other than finite *in this respect*. God's actuality is the realization of concrete value in the life of God and *every* realization of value, whether in God or in any other being, is finite in the sense that it excludes values that could have been achieved. For example, from an early age, Mozart's father set his son on the trajectory of being a musician. Apart from this education and training, Mozart might have lived a very different life, as a lawyer, a military leader, or a peasant farmer. Each path would have led to a certain value achievement, but each, to a greater or lesser extent, excludes the others. In some fashion, God incorporates Mozart's achievement into the divine life; as the values that Mozart did not achieve were not part of his life, no more are they part of God's. To say that God is not finite in this sense is to risk accepting a doctrine according to which God is *merely infinite*—that is to say, that God excludes whatever is of worth in the enjoyment of a finite realization of value. Hartshorne long maintained that the concept of the realization of all possible values is a meaningless ideal. God must, therefore, be finite, but not *merely* so. Dual transcendence means, among other things, that God must be infinite in receptive capacity; whatever comes to be, comes to be for God and becomes an everlasting component in God's memory. There must also be in God an inexhaustible or infinite capacity to appreciate the creative advance. In addition, Hartshorne allowed that God is *actually infinite* in the sense that there was never a time when God did not exist and that God is omniscient with respect to this past life (CS 126, 235). Hartshorne was quick to add that this form of infinity is *not* the realization of all possible values, for the actually infinite life of God could have been different in as many ways (an infinite number) as the creative advance itself could have been different.

Classical theologians adopted an ideal of perfection as unchanging, often using the argument from Plato's *Republic* that change for the better or worse implies an unchanging measure of perfection.[50] The argument is that if something changes for the better then it is not yet perfect, but if it changes for the worse then it is no longer perfect. In either case, change implies imperfection. God, being perfect, must be devoid of change. This argument, however, begs the question against a dipolar conception of God like Hartshorne's by assuming that there cannot be perfect forms of change. Hartshorne argues, on the contrary, that some forms of value—aesthetic qualities in particular—do not admit of a maximum. Just as it is impossible to speak of a greatest possible positive integer, so it may be impossible to speak of a greatest possible beauty (CS 38, 310). The fact that Mozart's music achieved a new level of beauty does not mean that there was nothing left for Beethoven to do. Another analogy is interpersonal relationships. It is a good thing to be flexible in one's responses to others. The ideal is not unchangeableness; it is, rather, adequate response to the needs of others. It is true that stability and reliability of character are desirable. But this means, in part, that the person can be relied upon to respond in ways appropriate to each situation, and responsiveness is a kind of change. The analogy is particularly appropriate in the divine case since there are always new creatures to which God must respond and hence there is no upper limit to the values associated with these relationships, for each is as unique as the individuals with whom God is related.

As Hartshorne distinguished existence and actuality, so he distinguished different ways in which God is perfect. Taking a clue from the work of Gustav Fechner, Hartshorne noticed an ambiguity in the concept of perfection (PSG 243–57). If one is perfect, then one is unsurpassable, but by what or by whom is one unsurpassable? The obvious answer is "by others." This leaves open the possibility that one may surpass oneself. Thus, there is a distinction between (a) being unsurpassable by all others *including* self and (b) being unsurpassable by all others *excluding* self." Hartshorne labels these two ideas respectively A-perfection (for absolute perfection) and R-perfection (for relative perfection) (MVG 7–8).[51] God is A-perfect with respect to existence and essence and R-perfect with respect to actuality. Hartshorne agrees with more traditional theists who spoke of God as infinite, immutable, impassible, necessary, and eternal, for this is God's A-perfection. Hartshorne quickly adds, however, that God is *not in all respects* infinite, immutable, impassible, necessary, and eternal. To use our previous example, if aesthetic values exhibit an unlimited possibility of increase, then God's appreciation of beauty may—indeed *must*—exhibit this possibility. Again, Beethoven's music introduces new forms of beauty that did not exist prior to his creative life. Hartshorne would also say that God, in enjoying the changing beauty of the world, is also the supremely beautiful object of contemplation, a point to which we shall return in the discussion of panentheism. Hartshorne summarized these ideas about divine perfection when he spoke of God as "the self-surpassing surpasser of all" (DR 20).[52]

Divine Power

Theologians have often commented on how difficult it is to define "omnipotence." Most of those who have thought about this, Hartshorne included, conclude that René Descartes was wrong to suppose that God could bring about logically inconsistent states of affairs.[53] Aquinas, for example, denied that God could make a circle with unequal radii, for this involves a logical inconsistency: one must *fix the angle* of the compass in order to guarantee that the arc becomes a circle, but one must at the same time *not fix the angle*, allowing it to become wider or smaller, in order to make the radii unequal.[54] Aquinas also denied that God could change the past once it has occurred. As noted in the previous chapter, Aquinas says that not even God can restore virginity to someone who has lost it. Finally, Aquinas denied that God can do what is contrary to God's nature, such as doing an unloving deed.[55] On each of these points, Hartshorne agrees.

Beyond these agreements, Hartshorne attributes both more power and less power to God than did the Angelic Doctor. For Aquinas, God can act but not be acted upon by anything external—this is the doctrine of impassibility. As we have seen, Hartshorne argues that God has the power to be acted upon by the creatures and to respond to them. In this sense, Hartshorne attributes more power to God than does Aquinas. On the other hand, Aquinas believed that God can unilaterally bring about some states of affairs in which more than one agent makes decisions. Hartshorne rejects this claim and holds instead that any state of affairs in which more than one agent makes decisions cannot be conceived as the product of one agent, even if that agent is God (WM 86). Suppose Ruth loves Naomi and Naomi loves Ruth—their mutual love can be explained only by referring to the activity of two persons, Ruth *and* Naomi. The logic of the situation does not change if one of the agents is God. The state of affairs described by God loving Ruth and Ruth loving God can only be explained by the activity of both God *and* Ruth, and not by God alone. Of course, if God is all-loving, then it is impossible that Ruth (an actual person) not be loved by God; but this does not change the fact that two agents—God *and* Ruth—are required to create the situation of their mutual love. If this is correct, then it is false that God, acting alone, can bring about any state of affairs in which more than one agent is making decisions. A corollary is that it is false that God can bring about any state of affairs the description of which is logically consistent—for there is nothing logically inconsistent about two individuals loving each other.

Classical theists, Aquinas in particular, are not without responses to Hartshorne's reasoning. Aquinas made a number of claims relevant to Hartshorne's argument. First, he maintained that the self-same result could be *wholly* attributed to two different causes; perhaps Ruth's loving God can be wholly attributed to Ruth and wholly attributed to God. Aquinas's example is that the music of a flute is wholly attributable to the instrument and to the musician.[56] Of course, the music is manifestly not attributable to either the instrument or the musician singly; both are required, which supports Hartshorne's claim. It is relevant to note that it is illicit to distribute "wholly" through a conjunction. There is no valid inference from "X is wholly the result of (A and B)" to "X is wholly the result of A and X is wholly the result of B." A second thing that Aquinas says that might undermine Hartshorne's argument is his claim that God has the power to bring about some events necessarily and to bring about other events contingently.[57] In this way, one might make headway in making sense of the idea that God creates a person's decision while yet preserving the contingency (an element of freedom) of the decision. Again, however, Hartshorne demurs. It makes sense to say that one can be the cause of a contingent event—every roll of the dice is proof of that. It is much less clear that it makes sense to say that one can guarantee the outcome of a contingent event. If one loads the dice in such a way that a particular number must appear (say, seven), then the outcome is not contingent; only if the dice are not loaded is the outcome truly contingent. Again, one should take note of an illicit distribution, but this time it is the problem of distributing "causes" or "guarantees" over a disjunction. There is no valid inference from "X causes (A or B or C)" to "X causes A or X causes B or X causes C."

Aquinas defended a strong version of creation *ex nihilo* in which God alone can be said to create.[58] Moreover, as we noted above, Aquinas maintains that God knows the world *because* God creates it. Thus, as David Burrell notes, there is, for Aquinas, a relation that God has to the creatures that is real, cognitive, and intentional.[59] In particular, Aquinas's concept of *gratia cooperans* [cooperating grace] expresses a relationship with God in which humans are said to cooperate with God in defining their destiny by either enlarging or diminishing their *moral capacity* for love and good deeds.[60] However, this intentional relation is also an eternal and timeless one that, on the divine side, is accomplished in "a single operation" (to use the language of *Summa Contra Gentiles*). This means that it is God who is at once *willing* and simultaneously knowing the human "cooperation." From an ultimate metaphysical perspective, it is God who is *causing by virtue of* willing and knowing the creature to cooperate or not to cooperate. Arguably, however, Aquinas's view contradicts our standard notions of cooperation. It is as if we were "genuinely cooperating" with a hypnotist who asked us to do some deed even though the deed had been "programmed" by the hypnotist. We seem to ourselves to be freely cooperating in such a situation, but in fact we are not, since we would not necessarily behave in the manner programmed by the hypnotist without the causal influence of the hypnotist.[61]

Various analogies, besides the concept of a divine hypnotist, have been suggested to reconcile creation *ex nihilo* with the freedom of the creatures. For example, James Ross argued that the freedom of the characters in Shakespeare's plays is in no way negated by the fact that they are Shakespeare's creation.[62] Ross denied that he was arguing by analogy in using the example of Shakespeare and his creation. Nevertheless, he clearly believed that beings whose every attribute depends upon the actions of the divine creator may nonetheless be free. In any event, Ross's claim presupposes the controversial claim that the characters in Shakespeare's plays are genuine individuals (cf. CS 242). Even granting this assumption, the only freedom the characters have is compatibilist freedom, a point that Ross seemed to concede.[63] We dealt with Hartshorne's rejection of compatibilism in the previous chapter.

William Lane Craig proposes another possibility. Perhaps the world's dependence on God is similar to a dream's dependence on the mind dreaming.[64] Again, the same objections apply. Dream people are not genuine individuals and, even if they were, they could not be said to have libertarian freedom. If we are God's thinking or dreaming, we possess at best a compatibilist form of freedom. However, Craig is at pains to stress that the dreaming analogy does not imply that the world is God's thinking. According to Craig, "God's creating and sustaining a world in being is *like* my creating and sustaining a world in thought— but this does not imply the world is God's thinking."[65] This is correct, for there are always disanalogies in any comparison between God and the creatures to be considered. But this does not address Hartshorne's criticism. According to Hartshorne, the *likeness* between God's creating and sustaining a world in being and my creating and sustaining a world in thought compromises human freedom. Alternately, if the creatures make decisions not wholly determined by God, then the relation of those decisions to God's activity is *unlike* the relation between one's mind and one's dreams. Craig's response is that analogies for creation *ex nihilo* serve only an illustrative purpose. He continues: "the philosophical concept of *creatio ex nihilo* is clear and well-understood and demonstrations of its truth or falsity may be discussed wholly without reference to human analogies."[66] Of course, Hartshorne does not concede this point. The "human analogies" that Craig thinks are optional seem, at every turn, to undermine the intelligibility of attributing power to God to unilaterally create a world of free or even partially free creatures. On the other hand, analogies drawn from real persons making decisions lend *no* support to the idea that they might be freely enacting God's will for them.

As far as classical theism is concerned, Hartshorne is at his most controversial in his denial of creation *ex nihilo*. The argument just given that some states of affairs require multiple decision makers is itself an argument against *ex nihilo* creation, at least in its classic form. God was said to create the universe, which includes the decisions that creatures make, in one nontemporal and unilateral act. Hartshorne's argument entails that no universe with multiple decision makers can be created *in its entirety* by God alone. Aquinas notwithstanding, the making of decisions is a paradigm of creative activity, for something is brought into existence if only the decision itself. For this reason, Hartshorne's example of multiple decision makers is also an example of multiple creators. Hartshorne saw in Jules Lequyer's statement that "God created me creator of myself" an anticipation of his own views on divine creativity (Epigraph to OO and CS xi).[67] A hallmark of Hartshorne's neoclassical theism is that the universe is a joint creative product of (a) the lesser creators that are the creatures, localized in space and time, and (b) the eminent creator which is God whose influence extends to every creature that ever has or that ever will exist.

We saw in a previous section that Hartshorne defends a metaphysical view that posits creativity as a transcendental, applicable to both God and the creatures (CE Ch. XI). In such a metaphysic, creativity is never "from nothing" but is relational, requiring a preexistent universe. It follows that there can be no such thing as God without a universe or, for that matter, a universe without God. A common objection to this view is that it portrays God as dependent upon the universe. Hartshorne considers the objection to be flawed in two ways. First, it assumes an invidious contrast between independence and dependence. We have seen that Hartshorne attempts to instruct philosophers and theologians to be wary of devaluing dependence (and, more generally, to be cautious of simplistic valuations of metaphysical contrasts). Second, the objection is subtly ambiguous. If Hartshorne is correct, then God and the universe are indeed necessary to each other. The proviso, however, is that no particular set of creatures (i.e., no particular universe) is necessary to

God. An analogy that Hartshorne uses is of a mathematical set that necessarily has numbers, but the numbers that it has are not necessary (CS 144)—a set with three numbers, two odd and one even, would be an example; each of the following satisfy the definition of such a set: {1, 2, 3}, {3, 4, 5}, {5, 6, 7}. God's actual states, being contingent, are dependent upon interaction with the creatures; God's existence, on the other hand, is necessary, for it depends upon no particular creatures or groups of creatures. It should also be noted that Hartshorne preserves the distinction between God and the creatures: the divine being meets with no universe that it did not have a hand in co-creating whereas the creatures, because they begin to exist, are born into a universe that they had no part in making. Of course, once the creature exists, it becomes a lesser, co-creator, with God.

Hartshorne distinguishes two forms of power involving direct and indirect causation (DR 155). Direct causal influence occurs when one entity acts on another without an intermediary as when a present experience acts upon an immediately subsequent experience in the life of a single individual; one's memory of the preceding moment, for example, is the feeling of one experience acting on its successor in direct fashion. Hartshorne avers that a similar direct action occurs between parts of the nervous system and between the nervous system and the body. Indirect causal influence, on Hartshorne's account, occurs when one body acts upon another body, which often involves modifying the inter-bodily environment in some way, such as speaking, which causes air to move and sound waves are heard by another person. Some cases of indirect causal action are examples of "brute force," whereby one body moves another body from one place to another. Barring telepathy, cases of one person acting on another are always indirect. On the other hand, Hartshorne maintains that God's action on dynamic singulars is never indirect (PCH 649). Because each entity retains its own power of creative experiencing, this direct causal influence is not deterministic. Hartshorne, following Whitehead (who was following the later Plato), refers to this mode of influence as "divine persuasion" which is, in effect, the active side of divine love. God acts as a supreme ideal, urging each dynamic singular to achieve an intensity of experience appropriate to its level of complexity. Thus, Hartshorne says, "It is the [divine] love that explains the [divine] power, not vice versa" (CE 7).

Some philosophers accept Hartshorne's critique of the traditional concept of omnipotence but argue that the neoclassical account of divine power does not endow God with the highest degree of power conceivable. One may concede that "divine persuasion" is the most admirable form of power, but insist nevertheless that God should also be conceived as having the ability to thwart human decisions by preventing them from being acted upon or by preventing their natural consequences from occurring. David Basinger notes that a parent can force an unruly child to go to bed by physically putting the child there. If God is unable to accomplish such a feat then, Basinger argues, God does not have the highest degree of power, for the parent is able to do what God cannot.[68] In response one may note that Hartshorne's metaphysical principles allow that God has the ability to persuade the child to get into bed or even to persuade the parent to force the child into bed. Hartshorne denies that God has a body with a location within the cosmos with which to move things about in the manner that localized beings do. This is also contrary to classical theism (also Basinger's "free will theism")—the idea that Jesus was God embodied involves metaphysical issues which Basinger's critique does not presuppose. In view of these qualifications, Basinger's objection seems to be that if God is to be conceived as having the highest degree of power, God must be able to accomplish *miraculously* what the parent accomplishes without a miracle through the use of his or her body.

Hartshorne responded to Basinger's critique in a letter (dated August 4, 1988) and said, among other things, that he doubted that he ever claimed that miracles never occur.[69] He was disinclined to believe that miracles have in fact occurred on grounds similar to those offered by Hume (also Montaigne): probabilities favor deceit or error over genuine miracles.[70] Hartshorne attributed the laws of nature to God's influence over *all* dynamic singulars (see the section in the following chapter on the "Global Argument") and said that he doubted our wisdom to judge how far the value of such laws "justifies the absence of notable divine intervention." Doubting, however, the quality of evidence for miracles is different from doubting the possibility of miracles. Basinger replied to Hartshorne (August 24, 1988) that he wasn't "quite sure" what it could mean in neoclassical metaphysics to suppose that miracles could occur. It is a fair question, especially in light of Hartshorne's denial that God acts indirectly. On the other hand, it is fair to ask for an account of divine power that is not merely *ad hoc* but flows naturally from general metaphysical principles such as Hartshorne was at pains to give. With the possible exception of Descartes's concept of omnipotence, every account of divine power includes propositions of the form "God cannot X." The force of the "cannot" may be in the logical impossibility of the act named (e.g., making a circle with unequal radii), in the nature of God (e.g., God cannot intend evil), in the nature of that over which divine power is exercised (e.g., God cannot create a creature's creative act), or in the particular relations that God has with the creatures (e.g., God cannot act indirectly). It is a legitimate question what it means to speak of attributing the highest degree of power to God apart from a system of metaphysical principles. It is not that a particular metaphysic is a final court of appeal for a concept of divine power; on the other hand, an appeal to divine power may be no more than a *deus ex machina* apart from a well-articulated metaphysic.

Divine Knowledge

One of the lessons to be learned from debates about divine power is that ideas about God have implications for ideas about the world and ideas about the world have implications for ideas about God. To assume that God can bring about any logically possible state of affairs presupposes that all states of affairs are such that, in principle, they require only a single being to bring them about. That presupposition, however, begs the question against a worldview like Hartshorne's in which reality has a social structure. In such a world, it is no limit on God if God cannot bring about every logically possible state of affairs. There is an analogous lesson where divine knowledge is concerned. If reality is continually in-the-making, as Hartshorne maintains, then there is a fundamental asymmetry between past and future. The past is fully determinate and the future is the realm of the partially indeterminate. If God is all-knowing, then God must know the future for what it is, as partially indeterminate. If one raises the objection that such a deity is *not* omniscient because the future is partially hidden from it, one has failed to appreciate the most elementary idea on which the debate turns. It is a defect in divine knowledge not to know a fully determinate future *only if* there is a fully determinate future to be known—this is, as it were, the *pons asinorum* of the debate. The assumption of a fully determinate future is evident in the analogy made famous by Boethius and later appropriated by Aquinas: as each point on the circumference of a circle is equidistant from the center, so God is equally present at and equally knowledgeable of every moment of time.[71] As Hartshorne noted, however, the analogy assumes that time can be represented as a completed whole, whereas time may be more like an endless line whose points are added from moment to moment.[72]

Hartshorne's criticism of the circle analogy was anticipated by the late medieval philosophers like John Duns Scotus and Luis de Molina.[73] The questions raised by the circle analogy concern not only the nature of time, but also the nature of God. Classical theists, as we have seen, were reluctant to attribute any passive potency to God; they thought that the perfection of the divine being required that God be immutable and impassible. If, however, God is not affected by anything external, then how is it that God knows the world? Aquinas answered that the cognitive relation in God is the reverse of what it is for humans. We know the world because it affects us, but God knows the world because God is its creator.[74] The Thomistic solution may preserve divine impassibility but at the expense of making human freedom problematic, as we saw in the previous section. There was, however, another very imaginative solution to the "mechanics of omniscience" given by Molina. He argued that, prior to creating, God has knowledge of what any possible free creature *would do* in any particular circumstance. Using this "middle knowledge" in combination with the knowledge of what creatures God has in fact chosen to create, God is able to know what every free creature *will do* in the circumstances where they have been placed.

New life was breathed into Molinism by analytic philosophers of religion in the late twentieth century. For his part, Hartshorne never directly addressed Molina's theory. It is easy enough, however, to reconstruct a Hartshornean response to Molinism. Above all, it is important to appreciate that, *of necessity*, the logical subjects of God's middle knowledge are *possible persons*. God's knowledge of what would be the case for any free creature is pre-volitional; that is to say, God knows, *prior to creating*, what any creature, *whether it is eventually created or not*, would do under any given circumstance. Middle knowledge cannot serve to guide God's providential decisions about which world to create if it depends upon which world God creates. For this reason, the usual characterization of middle knowledge as "counterfactuals of freedom" is seriously misleading. Prior to God's decision to create a world, there are no creatures and, hence, no fact of the matter about any *actual creature*. There are only *possible creatures*. We have already explained, in our discussion of time and possibility, Hartshorne's reasons for denying that there are merely possible persons. Given these views, it is clear that Hartshorne would reject Molinism.[75]

There is a hint of irony in claiming to know what Hartshorne *would* say about middle knowledge. Does this not presuppose a kind of middle knowledge of Hartshorne? In view of what was just said about the logical subjects of middle knowledge, the answer to this question should be obvious. Hartshorne was not a possible person; he was a real person whose views on various philosophical topics were clearly stated. The argument is this: Molinism entails belief in possible persons; Hartshorne denied the existence of possible persons; therefore, Hartshorne would deny Molinism. This argument points to one of the most puzzling features of Molinism, to wit, that middle knowledge is not grounded in fact. Hartshorne's developmental and cumulative view of process permits speculation about what a given actual person would or might do under various sets of circumstances. These "would be" and "might be" statements are grounded in the world-historical process itself, including a person's character as so far formed or (as in Hartshorne's case) as it *was* formed. Hartshorne made precisely this point in another context (PCH 662). For Hartshorne, God's knowledge of the world is similar to our knowledge in at least this respect, that it requires a real relation from the object of knowledge to the knower. The difference, in God's case, is that divine knowledge is eminent—God perfectly knows the extent to which the future is open or closed at any particular juncture of the creative advance.

A subtle objection to Hartshorne's theory of omniscience is that it represents God as ignorant of certain truths. To be sure, the neoclassical God perfectly knows the past—what did or did not happen—but does God, as so conceived, know everything that will or will not happen? Consider a person, P, at time $T1$ as yet undecided about a difficult choice: will P choose B or not-B? Let us suppose that at $T2$ the person decides B. On Hartshorne's account, God knows at $T2$ that P chooses B, but God does not know at $T1$ that P will choose B. The argument can be further refined: an omniscient being knows all truths; at $T1$, either "P will choose B" or "P will choose not-B" is true; the neoclassical God does not know at $T1$ which of the statements is true; therefore, this God is not omniscient.

Hartshorne's initial response to this objection was to argue, in effect, that there are three truth values: true, false, and indeterminate. According to this view—which may have been Aristotle's—future tense statements have an indeterminate truth value.[76] Hartshorne says that before the paper was published, he saw the error of this view.[77] He was unhappy with this idea because it requires abandoning the law of excluded middle; if p concerns a future event, then "p or not-p" is best construed as indeterminate rather than (as in traditional logic) a tautology. In *Man's Vision of God and the Logic of Theism* (100–01), Hartshorne hit upon a different response to the argument, one which he would develop more fully in an article in *Mind* in 1965 (reprinted in CE Ch. XIII). Hartshorne's mature position was to argue that "P will choose B" and "P will choose not-B" are best construed as contraries rather than contradictories, as in the following diagram (Figure 5):

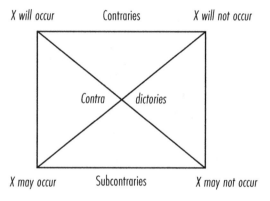

FIGURE 5: Hartshorne's Square of Opposition for Future-Tense Statements

The strict contradictory of "P will choose B" is "P may not choose B" and the strict contradictory of "P will not choose B" is "P may choose B." The statement forms in the triad—"P will choose B" "P will not choose B" and "P may or may not choose B"—are mutually exclusive: if one is true the other two are false. In this way, Hartshorne preserves the law of excluded middle as to truth values while allowing for the openness of the future.

Since, on Hartshorne's view, "will" and "will not" statements are contraries, it is incorrect to represent them in the sentential metalanguage as, respectively, p and *not-p*. Rather, "X will occur" and "X will not occur" should be represented as p and q, where ~ $(p \wedge q)$ (i.e., "not-$(p$

and q)"). A similar mapping of object language expressions onto sentential meta-language is needed in other domains as when one represents the pairs of contraries, "commands X" vs. "forbids X" or "legally requires X" vs. "legally requires not-X": the remaining alternative in each case, respectively, is "makes no command with respect to X" and "there is no legal requirement with respect to X." The metaphysical underpinning of Hartshorne's proposed semantics of future tense statements is his indeterminism, according to which past causal conditions require (X will occur), exclude (X will not occur), or permit (X may or may not occur) various effects in the future.

Anticipating an objection, Hartshorne admits that it seems paradoxical to say that "X will occur," as a prediction, is false even when X in fact occurs. Hartshorne replies that the "paradox" may be no more problematic than the familiar fact that a false scientific law can be verified (or corroborated). This is simply one more instance of the so-called paradox of material implication. We accept that "if p then q" is true when p is false, even if this seems counterintuitive. The paradox dissolves upon the realization that any other truth functional definition of the conditional besides the standard one—"if p then q" df. "not-p or q"—yields manifestly invalid inferences.[78] Hartshorne takes a clue from Popper and says that the decisive operation where "will be" statements are concerned is falsification (CE 83). "X will occur" is shown to be false when X does not occur, but it is not shown to have been true when X occurs. Hartshorne's view requires that, in the strictest philosophical sense, "will be" statements are disguised "must be" statements. Intuitions among competent speakers of the language differ on this point so it is reasonable not to expect the issue to be decided by ordinary language. When Scrooge, in Dickens's *A Christmas Carol*, asks the Ghost of Christmas Future whether he is seeing the shadows of the things that "will be" or the shadows of the things that "may be only," he is expressing in a precise way Hartshorne's analysis of future tense statements.[79] If the shadows are of the things that "will be," then all hope is lost, but if they are the shadows of the things that "may be only" then Scrooge can change his ways and make for himself a different future.

William J. Wainwright appreciates a number of Hartshorne's arguments and positions— especially the critique of divine immutability and impassibility—but he issues an interesting objection to Hartshorne's view that a God who does not know all the details of the future can yet be said to be "maximally perfect." Wainwright notes that Hartshorne and others consider the future to be partially unsettled and therefore not knowing all of the details of the future must be a limitation on any knower.[80] But Wainwright replies:

> This is doubtful, for the restriction does seem to involve imperfection. Most facts about persons depend upon facts about person's volitions. For example, my birth depended upon the volitions of my parents, and these in turn depended upon the volitions of countless others. Thus, if God doesn't know future choices, then God knows little about humanity's future.[81]

To be sure, says Wainwright, such God will not be totally ignorant of the future, and like human beings, such God can "make estimates of the relative likelihood of alternative futures."[82] But these are estimates only and thus God is subject to error regarding the future. As a consequence, such a God would be "constantly changing his mind and intentions . . . forming new schemes and projections" and presumably many of these would have to be revised.[83] All of this inconstancy seems to stand in stark tension with the notion of God as a "maximally perfect being."

We believe that Wainwright's ascription of inconstancy and cognitive error to the neoclassical concept of God's activity is strongly exaggerated, and in two fundamental respects. First, on Hartshorne's theory, God's ability to respond to creaturely events is supra-discriminational and eminently rapid (especially given the preferred "temporally thin" model of God's responses to the creative advance vis-à-vis relativity theory as we present it in Chapter Eight). Alterations in creaturely decision could never in principle "outpace" the responses of deity. Second, there is no reason to think that Hartshorne's God would not have extensive knowledge of *imminent* future choices or in fact any future choices in which the generic properties of the choices were antecedently determined. Indeed, this is the basis for Hartshorne's nuanced response to critics of the sixteenth-century theologian Fausto Socinus concerning prophecy. In an arresting passage, Hartshorne clarifies:

> The Socinians worried particularly over [Christ's prophecy to Peter—"Thou shalt deny me thrice"] It is not smoothly to be fitted in, one must admit. (Perhaps it was meant as a statement of probability, not meant as sheer fact or certainty. Perhaps it

meant that in that respect the act was *not* free. It would not follow that there was no sin in it, for that Peter was not free to do better might have resulted from acts that *were* free, so that there might have been a time when even divinity could have made the prophecy. The Socinians seemed to have missed this way out.) (MVG 139)[84]

In effect, there is a distinction between, on the one hand, the distant or non-imminent future which is dependent for its characteristics upon many decisions yet to be made by purportedly libertarian agents and, on the other hand, the imminent future in which, as the example of Peter illustrates, in some particular respect (such as firm denials to authorities) were in fact determined to occur.

Hartshorne argues that a religiously tenable concept of omniscience is one that would require "perfect knowledge of past and present, and *sufficient* knowledge of the future to constitute a providential plan, but with enough uncertainty in details of execution to allow for human free choice" (MVG 140, our emphasis). These two factors, taken together, seem to us to qualify profoundly Wainwright's attribution of inconstancy to the neoclassical God. Hartshorne has every intellectual right to claim that his concept of God properly represents that which is maximally perfect in all logically possible respects. It is the concept of a God who knows reality just as it is: in all respects in which the creative advance is determinate (including imminent future events), God knows it as such, and all respects in which it is indeterminate, God knows it as such in all its propensity and possibility. This allows God to have genuine give-and-take interactions with the creatures without logically excluding providential planning and guidance.

Our discussion to this point has followed philosophical orthodoxy by focusing on whether God knows the truth values of propositions. For Hartshorne, however, this question is secondary, for there is more to knowledge than knowledge that a proposition is true. In *The Principles of Psychology*, William James, following John Grote, distinguished "knowledge of acquaintance" and "knowledge-about," a distinction later made famous by Bertrand Russell who spoke of "knowledge by acquaintance" and "knowledge by description."[85] To have information *about* something or someone is not the same as having first-hand awareness of them. The two sorts of knowledge are related as more abstract to more concrete. It is one thing to read about a battle, quite another to have experienced it for oneself. Moreover, as a general rule, the more abstract the knowledge, the more emotionally detached it can be. The basic form of knowledge that Hartshorne attributes to deity is direct acquaintance through the affective bonds of feeling (MVG 241)[86]; as previously noted, Hartshorne adopts Whitehead's term "prehension" for the most concrete facts of relatedness among dynamic singulars. If God's knowledge is prehensive, it is perhaps easier to understand why Hartshorne resists the idea that God knows the future as determinate: no one is acquainted with the future; at best one has knowledge of acquaintance of the future as an array of tendencies towards actualization or as possibilities entertained. Moreover, conceiving God's relations with the creatures as prehensive places emphasis on the affective dimension of divine knowing. God's knowing, as feelings of the feelings of others, can then be conceived as a form of *caring*.[87]

Hartshorne's theory posits God's perfect knowledge of the future as relatively indeterminate and of the past as determinate. Yet, the past, even if it is determinate as Hartshorne claims, *is* no longer. Does this mean that God also lacks knowledge of acquaintance with the past? Hartshorne answers in the negative and it is important to understand his reasons. A creature, having specific spatio-temporal location, has acquaintance with at most a vanishingly small segment of events in space and time, and even that knowledge is shot through with fallibility. Most of our knowledge of the past is through inference and by description. We know by acquaintance the past we have lived, but most of our knowledge of the past is *about* the past. God's knowledge is both quantitatively and qualitatively different. Divine experience encompasses everything that has ever come to pass. As a localized individual has acquaintance with *its* past, God, in an analogous fashion, has acquaintance with *all* that is past. Divine knowledge, moreover, not only knows all of the past but knows it with perfect adequacy. God's is the eminent form of prehension. On Hartshorne's principles, the distant past must be as vivid for God as the recent past. In other words, the past does not "fade" for God. The difference, for God, between distant past events and recent ones is in the knowledge that recent events were preceded by the distant ones whereas there was a time when the recent events were, at best, outlines of what could be relative to distant past events.

The extent of God's knowledge of the past is a point of contention between Whitehead (or Whiteheadians) and Hartshorne. In the concluding lines of *Process and Reality*, Whitehead speaks of how creaturely achievements, though transient, are everlastingly remembered by God, making them objectively immortal. The "unfading importance of our immediate actions" are said to "perish and yet live for evermore."[88] Lewis Ford interprets Whitehead to mean that each actual occasion (Hartshorne's dynamic singulars) undergoes a two-stage process, its coming-to-be (during which it is a subject of experience) and its objectification (in which it ceases to be a subject of experience) in the coming-to-be of subsequent occasions. According to Ford, it was Whitehead's "momentous discovery" in metaphysics that the subject/object distinction is a difference in temporal modality; that is to say, an occasion's status in the present, as it comes to be, is to be a subject, but as past it is an object (PCH 325). Hartshorne agrees with much of this analysis, but he objects to Whitehead's metaphor of perishing. Hartshorne contends that the objects that are prehended by subsequent occasions are *past subjects* (PCH 650). If the *being* of an actual entity is constituted by its *becoming*, as Whitehead says (and Hartshorne agrees), then God's prehension of an occasion is precisely God's feeling of that occasion's feelings.[89] What exists everlastingly in the divine memory is not merely a *knowledge that* a dynamic singular felt in a particular way, but *an acquaintance with how it felt*. Hartshorne likens God's memory of a person's experiences to the person's own vivid recollection of their past experiences.

Panentheism

A distinctive feature of Hartshorne's theism, and one that sets it apart from Whitehead's theism, is that God includes the universe in a way that bears a distant analogy with the way that a person includes his or her body. Until 1941 Hartshorne spoke of a "new pantheism," but afterwards he spoke of panentheism, meaning that all (*pan*) is in (*en*) God (*theos*) (MVG 347f).[90] Hartshorne cited Plato's World-Soul analogy in some of the later dialogues as an anticipation of panentheism. Hartshorne, however, divests the doctrine of any vestige of mind-body dualism. God is not an immaterial entity haunting the universe; rather, Hartshorne maintains that God is "the *individual integrity* of 'the world,' which otherwise is just the myriad creatures" (OO 59). Hartshorne relies on modern cell theory for an analogy which, of course, was unavailable to Plato. Every localized dynamic singular is, as it were, a cell, in the body of God. An important disanalogy is that the universe, unlike a body within the universe, has no environment external to itself (PCH 649). Thus, in the divine case, the "body" of God and the "environment" in which God operates are one and the same. Hartshorne expresses this idea by saying that God's "environment" is wholly internal. He adds that the disanalogy explains why there are no specialized organs—such as liver, heart, and brain—in the divine body as there must be in a localized body. Specialized organs allow a localized body to monitor itself in its relation to its environment, but there is no other environment for God to negotiate except the universe. Dombrowski rightly says that, for Hartshorne, it is as true to say that the cosmos is ensouled as to say that God is embodied.[91]

Hartshorne also used analogies of persons related to persons as symbolic language for the relationship between God and the creatures. He was deeply critical, however, of the male bias of traditional theology. The few female metaphors used for God in the Bible, for example, were overshadowed by the dominance of male images—Lord of Hosts, Father, King—which reinforced patriarchal attitudes. Hartshorne considered himself a feminist and when, sometime in the late 1970s or early 1980s, he was alerted to the problem of sexism in language, he began using inclusive language as one can see in *Omnipotence and Other Theological Mistakes* and elsewhere.[92] He said that, in retrospect, it would have been better had his early book *Man's Vision of God* been titled *Our Vision of God* (HB 159, note 62). Hartshorne's feminism is also apparent in a variation he gives to panentheism. He argued that the relationship between mother and fetus is decidedly more intimate than the relation between father and fetus (OO 60; cf. PSG 479). Thus, for some purposes, the analogy of a pregnant mother for the relation between God and the creatures is preferable to any male counterpart. Of course, the pregnancy analogy, like all symbolic language for deity, has a restricted use. Nevertheless, re-imagining God as a woman is a useful reminder of the male bias of traditional theology and it highlights aspects of the God/World relationship that were obscured by that bias.

Analogies like World-Soul, person-cell, or pregnancy, are at best distant approximations for the relationship of God to the world. As metaphors they are literally false, but they are aids in understanding what Hartshorne has in mind when he says that God includes the world. (In Chapter Eight we return to a discussion of the limitations of the World-Soul metaphor.) Hartshorne's argument for panentheism is disarmingly simple: If God is the greatest conceivable reality, then God must include all that is valuable in the universe (DR 19). Otherwise, there would be a reality greater than God, namely, the universe-plus-God. Could God include what is valuable in the universe without including the universe? Hartshorne does not think so. Each dynamic singular that comes to be is not simply an additional fact; it is, by virtue of Hartshorne's panexperientialist physicalism also a value-achievement, and that value-achievement is greater in more complex organisms. We have previously used the examples of Mozart and Beethoven as introducing new values into the universe, but other examples are legion. The sum total of value in the universe, which is inseparable from the dynamic singulars that comprise it, is ever increasing according to Hartshorne's process-relational metaphysic. It must therefore be included within God if God is to be conceived as the reality than which none is greater.

W. Norris Clarke maintained that medieval philosophers anticipated Hartshorne's argument and replied to it. According to Clarke, the medievals said that the reality described by "God plus the universe" involves more beings in a quantitative sense, but not greater perfection of being in a qualitative sense. More precisely, says Clarke, "God plus the universe" means that there are more *sharers in being*. All value is in God, and the creatures merely share or participate in that value. By way of analogy, Clarke says that a mathematician may impart her knowledge to her students. Once the students learn what the teacher has to teach there is not more knowledge in the class, there is only more of those sharing in the knowledge.[93] A different analogy, however, could be used to bring out the distinctiveness of Hartshorne's view (cf. CH 271). A music teacher may provide her class with the basics of theory and composition, but the students can create new musical pieces, each with a value of its own. In this example, there are not simply more *sharers of being*, but more *creators of value*. The medieval response that Clarke gives is defective, on Hartshorne's reckoning, at precisely the point that process-relational theology departs from classical theism: the universe is not simply a product of divine creativity but of multiple creative agents. Classical theism had the unhappy consequence of divesting the creatures of any value that is their own, except for what is on loan from God. The sum-total value or perfection of existence is the same *whether or not the creatures exist*. For this reason, Hartshorne considered his panentheism to give a better account than classical theism of what it means to serve God. If the value in a creature is wholly borrowed from God, then the individual can offer God nothing that did not already belong to God by natural endowment. For Hartshorne, on the other hand, the creatures may be imperfect, but they are not mere conduits for values that God already possesses. On the contrary, their value contributes to that of God—hence, Hartshorne's expression, contributionism (LP 242; CAP 153).

A question that Hartshorne raised in *Man's Vision of God and the Logic of Theism* and that he discussed with E. S. Brightman in their correspondence was whether it is possible for God to include individuals that hold erroneous beliefs without also holding those beliefs. Put somewhat differently, if different individuals hold contradictory beliefs and God "includes" those individuals and their beliefs, does God hold contradictory beliefs? Similar puzzles can be raised about God's inclusion of individuals who commit terrible crimes—is the evil of the criminal deed a property of God? Or again, can God include creatures who are anxious about their death without also being anxious about death? Hartshorne commented that he was "inclined to think that this paradox is not so very severe."[94] His reply to the apparent paradox is that the logic of parts and wholes is such that they do not necessarily share properties—for example, a sand dune is not the size of a grain of sand even though it is made of grains of sand. Each part of the universe, Hartshorne holds, is a dynamic singular with an activity of its own that is not simply the activity of the universe as a whole (this is another way of expressing indeterminism). By parity of reasoning, these centers of individual activity, or the organisms of which they are parts, can have properties (such as false beliefs, evil deeds, or anxiety about death) that are not shared by the whole. A person can remember formerly holding a false belief or doing something wrong; God, by analogous extension, can prehend—that is, make part of the divine life—the errors and sins of the creatures without thereby being in error or sinning. It is important to add that while Hartshorne denies that God is the author of creaturely lack of wisdom and virtue, God nevertheless suffers their negative effects. According to Hartshorne, God feels *how* others feel without feeling *as* they feel (CAP 199).[95]

Three advantages of panentheism, as Hartshorne argues for it, are (a) it provides a ready argument in support of monotheism, (b) it addresses the empiricist challenge of how to identify the referent of the word God, and (c) it shows not only that God is integral to the good of the creatures but also that the good of the creatures is integral to the divine good. Together, these advantages provide the key to understanding the *in-principle superiority* between God and other individuals that is a desideratum of monotheism. As Hartshorne says, "There must be about God a *superiority in principle* when compared with any other individual."[96] The argument for monotheism in Hartshorne is that God is all-inclusive. If God is an all-inclusive reality, then there can be only one God because there can be only one all-inclusive reality. Hartshorne defines inclusion in these terms: if X includes Y, then $X + Y = X$.[97] If X denotes God and Y denotes the universe, then God, plus the universe is God. The argument that there could not be two all-inclusive deities is this: suppose W and X are two all-inclusive deities; this means that each must include the other. That is to say, $W + X = X$ and $W + X = W$, but in that case, $W = X$.

As for the empiricist challenge, the conditions for the identification of the panentheistic God are not the same as would be required to identify a localized being. Individuals within the cosmos occupy a tiny portion of the universe for a vanishingly brief period. Their influence is felt locally but not universally. God, on the other hand, is affected by all and affects all. As Hartshorne says, God is the one individual with strictly universal functions. From this, he infers that God is the one individual identifiable, or picked out, by concepts alone (DR 31; NT 76). Other individuals have properties that might have been had by others (e.g., Obama was the Democratic candidate for president in 2008, but he need not have been) and the properties they actually have might have been different (e.g., Hillary Clinton was born in Chicago, but she could have been born elsewhere). The formal properties of God as all-inclusive are unique to God: no other individual has universal functions. One might search the earth for Obama or Clinton, but it would be profoundly misguided to search the earth, or the cosmos, for God. The description of God attributed to St. Paul in Acts is applicable to Hartshorne's panentheism: God is the one "in whom we live, move, and have our being."

We shall see in the next two chapters that Hartshorne's distinction between the universality of God and the locality of the creatures plays an important role in his cumulative argument for God, particularly in the teleological argument. However, he also highlights the importance of this distinction as a way of understanding the specific difference between God and the creatures and how it bears on the role of religion in human life. We are so accustomed to hearing that God is infinite, and the creatures are finite that, even when Hartshorne's idea of dual transcendence is explained, it is tempting to fall back on old habits and accuse Hartshorne of destroying the distinction between the infinite God and the finite creatures. Hartshorne's response is to insist that all value realization is finite, whether in God or in the creatures; what distinguishes God and the creatures is not finitude but fragmentariness. *"Fragmentariness, not simply finitude, distinguishes us from deity"* (OT 131, cf. ZF 71). The creatures are fragmentary in three senses, by being located in space (rather than encompassing all of space), by being temporally limited (by birth and death), and by the various ways they fall short in the realization of value (in contrast to optimal realization of value in deity). Dombrowski neatly expresses the third sense of fragmentariness when he says that we are "fragmented fragments," for "in our fragmentary state we could do better jobs of managing our lives than we do."[98] Hartshorne stresses the existential dimension of fragmentariness when he says that it is the role of religion to bring us to a realistic acceptance of our fragmentariness; among other things, this acceptance is a check against making an idol of anything within the cosmos, including ourselves (WM Ch. 6).

Finally, Hartshorne argues that the possibility of having ill-will or destructive tendencies towards another is related to the fact that, for localized beings, other beings or persons are part of one's external environment. Insofar as no creature is external to God and all creatures comprise the divine body, there can be no basis for God to envy them or have competitive conflict with them (RSP 137–38). In the case of the relation of God to the creatures, there must be a perfect coincidence between self-interest and interest in others. As the well-being of the members of one's own body contributes to the well-being of the person whose body it is, so the enjoyment of the creatures contributes to the enjoyment of God. We have noted that there is also the possibility of tragedy in God as when the creatures suffer in avoidable ways or treat each other in ways that are wicked, but Hartshorne made clear in his correspondence with Brightman why he believed that this can in no way reflect on the goodness of God. A possible criticism of Hartshorne's position is that, in the creaturely case, one's own body can be plagued by disease as when the growth of a cancer threatens one's well-being and even one's existence. Once again, however, the categorical difference between God and the creatures makes all the difference. The cancer affects our well-being in large measure because it threatens our ability to survive, which is related to the fact that we have an external environment. Having no external environment, God's existence cannot be threatened for there is literally nothing that could threaten it.

Paul Tillich is famous for saying that "God is being-itself, not *a* being."[99] Hartshorne agrees with Tillich that God is not one being among others within the universe, sharing all of their limitations in space, time, and quality. In this sense, God is "not *a* being." On the other hand, on Hartshorne's reckoning, God is indeed a being in the sense of being an individual distinguishable from other individuals. In Hartshorne's words, "individual self-identity is a kind of low-level universal."[100] One may remain the same individual through various changes even though no two moments of one's existence are numerically identical. The woman listening to the bird singing would have remained the same individual had she only been listening to the wind in the trees. As we have seen, Hartshorne argues that the same is true of God. The three-fold distinction between essence, existence, and actuality, allows that one's defining characteristics (essence-existence) can be realized in multiple contingent ways. Nevertheless, God has the characteristic of Tillich's "being-itself" in having unlimited power to exist—God's existence is a necessary existence, unlike the contingent existence of the creatures.

Conclusion

Hartshorne's development of a philosophical theology according to which God is transcendent yet inseparable from temporal processes is arguably one of his lasting achievements. He considered the deity of classical theism as at once too active and too passive. It is too active in the sense that nothing falls outside its control; the creatures are left to unwittingly play roles decided for them in eternity—"imitations of life" as Lequyer called them.[101] It is too static in the sense that it cannot change or be affected by the triumphs and tragedies of the creatures. In short, it is a deity that acts but is never acted upon and can therefore never interact. This is captured in the Aristotelian formula that was borrowed and reinterpreted by medieval thinkers to denote the God of the Abrahamic traditions: God as the "unmoved mover." In a public discussion of Mortimer Adler's use of this formula, Hartshorne once called it a half-truth parading as the full truth.[102] We noted in the Preface that Hartshorne distilled the essence of neoclassical theism by amending Abraham Heschel's expression of God as the "most moved mover" to say that God is the most *and best* moved mover (ZF 6, 39).

Chapter Five Appendix: Spinoza's Argument Against the Coherence of Descartes's Concept of God[103]

Spinoza's argument against the coherence of Descartes's concept of God is found at *Ethics* I, prop. 33, scholium 2. The argument is relevant to our inquiry since Descartes and Aquinas agree on the assumptions on which Spinoza bases his argument and therefore presents an interesting parallel to Hartshorne's reasoning. The reasoning given here is framed in terms of C. I. Lewis's S5. The semantics of S5, where possibilities are construed atemporally and as all "on an equal footing," is the logically appropriate modal framework for presentation of Spinoza's argument, since as Spinoza scholar Edwin Curley insists, "eternity is assimilated to necessity" in seventeenth century rationalist philosophy.[104] Let us assume the following definitions:

W = the actual world within the set of possible worlds[105]

p = "God knows that W exists"
q = "W exists"

1. $\Box \sim (p \wedge \sim q)$	Cartesian assumption of divine infallibility. This is equivalent to "$\sim \Diamond (p \wedge \sim q)$" by modal definition of "$\Box \sim$" and is to be read "It is not possible that both God knows that W exists and it is not the case that W exists.
2. $\Box p$	Cartesian assumption: God's knowledge is timelessly eternal.
3. $p \rightarrow q$	From 1 by Lewis's definition of strict implication, i. e., "$\Box \sim (p \wedge \sim q)$ *iff* $(p \rightarrow q)$"
4. $\Box q$	From 2 and 3 by Modal *Modus Ponens*
5. $\Box q \rightarrow \Box \Box q$	From 4 by axiom of S5: The modal status of a proposition is itself necessary.

6. $\Diamond q \wedge \Diamond \sim q$ Cartesian assumption: The created or actual world is contingent; both the existence and non-existence of W are possible. This follows from Descartes's acceptance of *creatio ex nihilo* as well as his distinction between necessary and contingent existents in his version of the ontological argument (See his *Principles of Philosophy*, Part I, Art. 15.)

7. $\Diamond \sim q$ From 6 by Simplification.

8. $\Diamond \sim q \rightarrow \Box \Diamond \sim q$ From 7: Modal status of a proposition is necessary.

9. $\Box \Diamond \sim q$ From 7 and 8 by Modal *Modus Ponens*.

10. $\Diamond q$ From 6 by Simplification.

11. $\Diamond q \rightarrow \Box \Diamond q$ From 10: Modal status of a proposition is necessary.

12. $\Box \Diamond q$ From 10 and 11 by Modal *Modus Ponens*.

13. $\Box \Diamond q \wedge \Box \Diamond \sim q$ From 9 and 12 by Adjunction.

14. $\Box \Box q$ From 4 and 5 by Modal *Modus Ponens*.

15. $[\Box \Box q \wedge (\Box \Diamond q \wedge \Box \Diamond \sim q)]$ From 13 and 14 by Adjunction.

16. $[\Box \Box q \wedge \Box \Diamond \sim q]$ From 15 by Simplification.

Step 16 expresses the severe modal contradiction that "in all possible worlds 'W exists' is necessarily the case while simultaneously in all possible worlds it is possibly the case that 'W does *not* exist'." Since "possibly not" is the contradictory of "necessarily," as brought out explicitly by the logically deduced result at 16, Descartes's assumption that the actual world is a contingent product of the divine will while yet God's knowledge is both infallible and timelessly eternal collapses into absurdity. This is a rationally intolerable set of assumptions. Spinoza got rid of this absurdity by denying that the actual world is contingent. As we have noted in this chapter, another way out is to follow Hartshorne in rejecting Step 2, that is to say, God's timelessly eternal knowledge of the actual world. We hold, with Hartshorne, that the rejection of the contingency of the actual world is also modally absurd. For this reason, Hartshorne's dipolar route of holding that God's knowledge is subject to the temporal "schematism of cognition" appears to us to be the only possible way of escaping the absurdity in question.

❧ SIX ❧

Theistic and Anti-Theistic Arguments

$\mathbf{F}$ ROM THE BEGINNING of his career Hartshorne was interested in arguments for God's existence. His first attempt at making the case for theism was in his dissertation. In some respects, this early work anticipates his later ideas, but as we have already noted he never published any part of it. From the time of the dissertation, however, Hartshorne continued to refine his ideas about the nature and the limits of theistic arguments. His answers to these questions are, in many respects, as novel and imaginative as his defense of the coherence of neoclassical theism. Of course, the project of defending the coherence of dipolar theism is necessary if one is to make a case that such God exists. No argument for God's existence can be successful if the very concept of God is hopelessly confused. We have already mentioned the fact that Hartshorne spent much of his career in an intellectual environment where philosophers as diverse as logical positivists and existentialists (Jean-Paul Sartre in particular) questioned the coherence of the concept of God. Hartshorne agreed that classical theism fails the test of coherence, but he was vigorous in defense of dipolar theism. The question remains whether there is reason to think that God, conceived in dipolar terms, exists.

Hartshorne is well-known for his rehabilitation of the ontological argument, but he consistently, clearly, and explicitly denied that it was his

191

reason for being a theist.[1] The importance of the ontological argument, as far as Hartshorne was concerned, is that it reveals the logical status of the theistic question. Just as arguments for God's existence presuppose a coherent concept of God, so anti-theistic arguments presuppose ideas about the concept of God which, if not sufficiently clear, will lead to a mishandling of the theistic question. Hartshorne argues that this is what happens when the existence of God is treated as a question that can be settled by empirical or scientific means. If Hartshorne is correct, the ontological argument reveals the folly of this approach to God's existence: one is left with the options that God exists and cannot fail to exist (i.e., the divine existence is necessary) or that God does not exist and cannot fail not to exist (i.e., the divine existence is impossible).

If the ontological argument does not establish God's existence, it is nevertheless one strand in a fabric of reasoning which Hartshorne sometimes called *the global argument* (CS 276; NT 45, 49). He followed Peirce's recommendation that philosophy—or in this case, natural theology—should rely on a variety of interrelated pieces of evidence rather than trusting to the conclusiveness of a single argument. Peirce used the analogy of a cable, the strength of which is in the combined strength of its numerous slender fibers. Peirce specifically mentioned that this way of arguing is typical of science, but it is also evident in other areas such as law, history, and literary criticism.[2] Hartshorne's global argument self-consciously applies the Peircean strategy to metaphysics. Nowadays, philosophers use Basil Mitchell's terminology and call the multiple argument strategy a "cumulative case."[3] Probably the most well-known cumulative case argument for theism in recent philosophy is that of Richard Swinburne.[4] Also of note is that some philosophers employ cumulative case arguments for atheism, most notably J. L. Mackie and Michael Martin.[5] Three years before Mitchell's book and nine years before Swinburne's, Hartshorne published his most systematic presentation of the cumulative case for dipolar theism, titled "Six Theistic Proofs" (CS Ch. 14).[6]

Not long after this essay appeared, Hartshorne stopped calling the arguments proofs, for he recognized that it is often the case that equally rational and informed philosophers disagree on fundamental issues. In Hartshorne's words, "It seems unlikely that we can ever have arguments about important matters in philosophy that would coerce everybody to agree."[7] For this reason, he presented the global argument in a way that emphasizes both the rational basis of neoclassical theism and the rational cost of rejecting it. What Hartshorne claimed for his theistic arguments was less than what some theists would wish but more than what some atheists believe is possible.

> In the sense in which the reality of God is indemonstrable, everything philosophical is so, for all that I can see. As philosophical arguments go, I hold that the theistic proofs, properly formulated (and thereby hangs a tale of a hundred misses for one bull's eye) are sound and cogent.[8]

Hartshorne remarked on the attention philosophers have paid to traditional arguments for God as classically conceived and their corresponding failure to attend to arguments for deity conforming to the formal structure of the idea "surpassing itself and all others" (RSP 124–25). Hartshorne's global argument is a beginning to redressing that imbalance.

Anselm's Discovery and the Ontological Argument

It used to be customary to speak in the singular of "Anselm's ontological argument." Hartshorne was the first to argue that this is mistaken. Setting aside the question of Anselm's intentions, Hartshorne found that two arguments are suggested in Anselm's *Proslogion,* one in Chapter II, another in cChapter III. Hartshorne made this point in 1944 in an article published in *The Philosophical Review* and again in 1953 in *Philosophers Speak of God* (96f).[9] The philosophical world did not take notice until 1960 when Norman's Malcolm made the distinction between the two arguments famous.[10] Hartshorne, like Malcolm, agreed with Anselm's critics that the first argument (in Chapter II) is fallacious, but he judged the second argument (in Chapter III), which has a modal structure, to be valid. The difficulty in showing that the argument is sound is an important reason that Hartshorne did not consider the argument as a demonstration of God's existence as he made clear in a 1961 comment on Malcolm's paper, which included a partially formalized version of the argument using Lewis's S5 system.[11] In 1962, Hartshorne presented a fully formalized version of the argument using S5, the first such formalization to be published (LP 50–51). In *Anselm's Discovery* (1965), he again defended a version of the argument and canvassed the various treatments of Anselm's reasoning in the history of philosophy, including an anticipation of the argument in Plato.[12]

In the Foreword to George L. Goodwin's *The Ontological Argument of Charles Hartshorne,* and again in *Creative Experiencing* (CE 107), Hartshorne reduced the modal ontological argument to what he considered to be its essentials.[13] In the argument as presented here, the arrow is strict implication (as noted in our key to logical symbols); p^* stands for "God exists," where 'God' is defined as 'a being unsurpassable by any other conceivable being.'

1. $\Diamond \, p^*$

2. $\Diamond \, p^* \rightarrow \, \sim \Diamond \sim p^*$
3. Therefore, $\sim \Diamond \sim p^*$

If unrestricted necessity ($\sim \Diamond \sim$) is what is common to all possibilities—a common definition—and if any state of affairs that is actual is also possible—a standard modal principle—then the conclusion to be drawn is that God exists (p^*). Hartshorne was under no illusions that this mode of reasoning would convince the skeptic that God exists. Nor did he use it as his reason for believing in God. Nevertheless, the argument is not, in the hyperbole of Graham Oppy, "completely worthless."[14] Hartshorne credited George Mavrodes with the insight that it is unreasonable to suppose that because all doubts about theism cannot be removed by an argument that no doubts can be removed (NT 30). Moreover, the simple deductive structure of the argument clarifies what is at stake in the theistic question. If one denies the conclusion, one must deny one or more of the premises or what their denials entail. Hartshorne follows Leibniz in urging that, in questions of metaphysics, philosophers are more apt to err in what they deny than in what they affirm. Highlighting the rational cost of rejecting theism can, for this reason, be a fruitful method in metaphysics.

If one rejects the conclusion of Hartshorne's modal argument one of two alternatives is possible. First, it may be that God's existence is impossible ($\sim \Diamond \, p^*$), which is the denial of the first premise. This is the view that J. N. Findlay took in his famous 1948 article, "Can God's Existence Be Disproved?"[15] In effect, Findlay's argument turns Hartshorne's modal *modus ponens* upside down to make a modal *modus tollens* disproof: If $\Diamond \sim p^*$ and $\Diamond \, p^* \rightarrow \sim \Diamond \sim p^*$, it follows that $\sim \Diamond \, p^*$. Hartshorne referred to this as the *a priori* atheist or positivist position. The second alternative is that the second premise is false. One may deduce from the second premise that it is not the case that God's existence and nonexistence are equally possible. The deduction is as follows:

1.	$\Diamond p^* \to \sim \Diamond \sim p^*$	Second premise of the ontological argument
2.	$\sim \Diamond \sim (\Diamond p^* \supset \sim \Diamond \sim p^*)$	Meaning of Strict Implication
3.	$\sim \Diamond \sim (\sim \Diamond p^* \vee \sim \Diamond \sim p^*)$	From 2 by Conditional Equivalence
4.	$\sim \Diamond (\sim \sim \Diamond p^* \wedge \sim \sim \Diamond \sim p^*)$	From 3 by DeMorgan's Rule
5.	$\sim \Diamond (\Diamond p^* \wedge \Diamond \sim p^*)$	From 4 by Double Negation

If the conclusion of this deduction is false, then it is possible that God's existence and nonexistence are equally possible: $\Diamond p^*$ and $\Diamond \sim p^*$. This was the view of David Hume for whom every proposition asserting (or denying) existence, including "God exists," is logically contingent. Hartshorne calls this the empiricist position, or sometimes empirical theism or empirical atheism depending on whether or not the empiricist thinks that God exists (NT 87).

Hartshorne considered the empiricist position vis-à-vis the ontological argument the least tenable. The second premise says, colloquially, if God is so much as logically possible, then it must be the case that God exists. Hartshorne calls this "Anselm's principle," or more forcefully, "Anselm's discovery," as in the title of his eighth book. The discovery is that God, as unsurpassable, cannot exist with the possibility of not existing. Put somewhat differently, *contingency of existence* is incompatible with deity. Anselm's formula that God is "that than which nothing greater can be conceived" means, among other things, that any abstract characteristic for which a greater can be conceived cannot properly be attributed to deity. For example, if there is something greater than being partially ignorant, then God cannot be conceived as partially ignorant. Or again, if there is something greater than interacting with some but not all others, then God cannot be conceived as a merely localized being. Applied to the question of modality of existence, Anselm's principle means that a deity that can fail to exist is not the greatest conceivable. If this is correct then it is a mistake to suppose it is possible to conceive God as possibly existing and as possibly not existing.

Hartshorne emphasized that the empiricist's view that he considers

Anselm to have refuted is shared by, among others, those who consider the existence of God as a hypothesis to be established or refuted by science. We have already noted that Hartshorne accepts the Popperian idea that empirical statements must be falsifiable by some conceivable experience. If "conceivable experience" means that one is conceiving something to be the case in a possible world-state, then Anselm's principle entails that *if* God exists, there could be *no disconfirming empirical evidence* of God's existence. On the other hand, if God does not exist, then by parity of reasoning, there could be *no confirming empirical evidence* of God's existence. If premise 2 of the modal argument is correct, the remaining options are that God exists necessarily ($\sim \Diamond \sim p^*$) or God's existence is impossible ($\sim \Diamond p^*$). This removes the question of God's existence from the domain of science. Of course, this is not the same as removing the question from rational justification, unless metaphysics is impossible; we have already explained Hartshorne's case against this view. In effect, treating the existence of God as a scientific hypothesis is a failure to conceive God as an unsurpassable being and therefore begs the theistic question or changes the subject.

Hartshorne's presentation of the ontological argument highlights a feature of traditional thinking about God. Arguably, the concept of God in the high theistic religions is most properly understood as a subject of metaphysics rather than science. This fact is reflected in the arguments that have been offered in support of the reality of God, including the so-called *a posteriori* arguments—various versions of cosmological and teleological arguments. The classical arguments conclude to a deity that is not located within the universe but that is, in some way, uniquely required by the very conditions of existence. Hume, who was no friend of theistic arguments, remarked on the fundamental conceptual difference between beings (supernatural or otherwise) that are products of nature's powers and a supreme creator that is responsible, in some fashion, for nature's powers. He notes as an example that the writings of Homer and Hesiod characterized gods and men as having "sprung equally from the unknown powers of nature."[16] The ancient Greeks framed their mythologies—including stories about the origin of the universe—in terms of the concept of generation rather than creation. The famous book of Hesiod is titled *Theogeny*, "the origin of the gods." Hume also notes that the Greek gods were subject to necessity and he goes so far as to call polytheism *superstitious atheism*.[17]

On the subject of the uniqueness of God, Hume and Hartshorne are in near agreement. Where Hartshorne parts company with "le bon David" is in denying that all propositions about existence are logically contingent and in denying that God's existence is an empirical question. This two-fold denial places Hartshorne in contrast to those who look to science to settle the theistic question:

> Astronomy, physics, chemistry and biology will never settle it, will never even throw any great light on it. The theistic question simply is not asking what particular world exists. I think you have to say that, given the meaning of "God," any universe would need him. The scientist's job is to tell us which of the possible universes we have got. That is neutral to the question of God's existence. I think most of the best scientists know this. If they had found a different world that would have shown that God has made a different world—that is all.[18]

Empirical versions of theism and atheism understand God's existence to be contingent. In itself, this does not entail that God's existence is a question that science can settle, for there may be contingent truths beyond the competence of science to adjudicate.[19] On the other hand, the advocates of a scientific approach to the question of God's existence are empirical theists or empirical atheists to the extent that they accept the doctrine of the logical contingency of the divine existence—they claim that God may or may not exist as a matter of contingent fact. This is the view of the new atheists, a group we examine in detail in the next chapter. Hartshorne's ontological argument is a direct challenge to these ideas.

We can gain a deeper insight into how Hartshorne understands the modality of God's existence by looking at his response to the criticisms of John Hick. Hick, a theist who held that "God exists" is logically contingent, pressed the objection that Hartshorne's ontological argument confuses two kinds of necessity, necessity as it pertains to propositions (*logical necessity*) and necessity as it pertains to a being (*ontological necessity*).[20] (We discussed a similar charge by John Wild in the previous chapter.) To say that God exists of necessity is to say no more, according to Hick, than that God exists *a se* or has the property of aseity. That is to say, God's existence, unlike all creaturely existence, depends upon nothing outside of itself. This does not mean, Hick claims, that "God exists" is a necessary truth. To speak of God's existence as logically necessary is, in Hick's view, a category mistake, applying to a *being* a predicate that is properly a predicate of *sentences*. Hartshorne agrees with Hick that, *excluding the case of God*, all propositions asserting the existence or nonexistence of this or that individual are logically contingent.[21] However, in *all* of these cases, there is a causal explanation for the possibility of the individual's existence which neatly explains why the proposition asserting or denying existence is not necessarily true. For example, the nonexistence of X's monozygotic twin is explained by the fact that the fertilized egg from which X came did not split; X's existence also has a causal explanation in the union of a particular sperm and egg. Hartshorne notes that there is no analogous explanation, on Hick's empiricist account, for why "God exists" is logically contingent. Hartshorne, however, has a ready explanation for why the proposition is not logically contingent, an explanation moreover that Hick uses in explaining the meaning of divine necessity: neither God's existence nor nonexistence could have a causal explanation.[22] In both *The Logic of Perfection* (73–84) and *Creative Experiencing* (107–08), Hartshorne discusses other characteristics of logically contingent propositions that "God exists" lacks. For example, God's existence excludes no positive form of existence whereas the existence of any creature within the universe excludes certain positive states of affairs. Hartshorne says that God's existence is not competitive. Hartshorne's conclusion is that, on Hick's account, "God exists" breaks the usual semantic criteria for a proposition to count as logically contingent.

Hartshorne's response to Hick is that the meanings of modal terms must be anchored in the causal-temporal matrix. In Hartshorne's words, "contingency has its ontological basis in the creativity of becoming as productive of noneternal things."[23] If this is true, then not just any noun-adjective combination is logically conceivable. Numerous parodies of the modal argument—beginning with Gaunilo's "Lost Island"—consist in joining the concept of necessary existence to real or imagined localized beings.[24] On Hartshorne's account, these ideas are stillborn—or one might say, "improperly conceived"—for they cannot withstand the application of semantic criteria that distinguish contingent and necessary truths.

> Clearly ... an island is not in essence unproducible and self-sufficient. ... But it is not apparent what would make such a world

an island, if the "waters" which "washed" it never wore its shores, and if it were not a part of the surface of a body in space surrounded by other bodies capable of smashing it to pieces, and were not composed of particles capable of ultimately separating, etc. The question is if such a conception would in the end be distinguishable from the idea of the cosmos as the perpetually renewed body of God, that is, not an island in the least, but an aspect of the very idea of God whose self-existence is upheld by the argument. (MVG 303-304; cf. IO 101)

Michael Martin counters Hartshorne's reasoning by conceding that Gaunilo's island would be a miracle defying the laws of nature, but it would not for that reason be conceptually incoherent.[25] Exactly how this might work is not clear. Does Martin mean to deny that it is part of the concept of an island that it is dependent on sea level? Or does he conceive the miraculous island to have the power to keep the sea at bay and thus have powers that ordinary islands do not have? The more power it has to withstand the forces of nature, the less it seems to be anything that resembles an island. Martin does not address Hartshorne's contention that, considering all that is necessary to conceive such a miraculous island, one approximates the very concept of God for which it is meant to be a counter-example.[26]

Attaching necessary existence to a being that is properly conceived as contingent is the reverse of the error of attaching contingent existence to a being that is properly conceived as necessary. Hartshorne counts both extremes as errors. It is no accident that it was J. S. Mill, an empiricist, who, in recalling in his autobiography his father's influence, made the question, "Who made God?" famous. The question, as used by Mill, and later by Russell (followed as well by the new atheists), is designed to short-circuit the cosmological argument by highlighting the absurdity of assuming "Everything has a cause" as a premise.[27] Aside from the fact that no defender of the cosmological argument reasoned from the premise that everything has a cause, Mill's question betrays a misunderstanding of the concept of God.[28] Hartshorne correctly observes:

> But this never was the premise of the argument, but rather that everything whose nonexistence is possible (as shown by its not having always existed, or in some other way) depends for its existence upon something whose nonexistence is impossible, or

again, that everything which exists through another involves
something which exists through itself. (RSP 188)

If "God" signifies a being unsurpassable by all others excluding God's self,
then asking for the cause of God's existence is a *petitio* against theism.
An analogy may help. If one lives on a spinning spheroid like the earth,
it makes sense to ask, "What is north of X?" provided that X is not the
North Pole. To ask what is north of the North Pole is to misunderstand
the geometry of a spinning sphere. Analogously, if one is considering
monotheism, it makes sense to ask, "What is the cause of X's existence?"
provided X is not God. To ask "What is the cause of God's existence?"
is to misunderstand the metaphysics of monotheism. Of course, on
Hick's account of divine aseity, no less than on Hartshorne's account,
it is a mistake to ask for the cause of God's existence. Hartshorne has
the advantage, however, of having a theory of the semantic grounding
of modal terms in temporal process that provides the reason why it is
a mistake.

William Rowe put forth a widely discussed criticism of the
argument, contending that modal versions of the argument fail by
virtue of question-begging fiat.[29] According to Rowe, modal versions
which assume, like Malcolm's and Hartshorne's, that "the possibility
of God" is the crucial philosophical premise are mistaken, since they
fail to distinguish between "actualized possibilities" and "unactualized
possibilities." To illustrate this point Rowe uses the linguistic device of
a "Magican," which is to be *defined*, analogous to Anselm's definition of
God, as an "existing magician" whereby the notion of a "non-existing
Magican" is rendered incoherent by fiat. Douglas Walton agrees and
argues explicitly that Hartshorne's version of the argument in *The Logic of
Perfection* is both "trivial" and "absurdly circuitous."[30] Applying Rowe's
argument, Walton takes Hartshorne's reduced argument structure to be
trivial and circuitous because the affirmation of the possibility of God
simply means that God, like all other possibly existent things, is either
an actualized possibility or an unactualized possibility, yet Anselm's
Principle defines God such that "no non-existent thing can be God," and
this decides by definition that God is an actually existing thing, which
of course is the very question at issue. Walton goes further to present
an alternative first-order quantificational revision of the argument that
attempts to avoid this circularity and triviality.

George Shields has presented a detailed analysis of Walton's quantificational revision and argued that Hartshorne's original argument is neither trivial nor incompatible with the circularity avoiding revision of Walton's argument.[31] Shields argues that Rowe and Walton both miss the full significance of the *uniqueness* of the divine possibility in relation to other possibilities. The divine possibility is not to be simply equated with Rowe's "possible thing" defined as anything on the positive side of our "imaginary line," or which logically belongs on that side, as contrasted with verbally conjectured possibilities such as "a thing which is both round and square in the same respect." Unlike magicans or magicians, categorically no descriptive predicate (or "meaning postulate") which is required in the definition of "God" can have a contingent modal status as in, say, the notion that "God *became* omniscient" implies the possibility that at some time t God lacked knowledge of some *knowable* state of affairs S, but at a later time t^* God acquires knowledge of S. By contrast, the notion that "some person P learned a first trick of illusion and thereby assumed the mantle of 'magician' at a time t which P did not possess at an earlier time $t - n$" is perfectly intelligible and illustrates a properly contingent characteristic of being a magican or magician.[32] The fact that the concept of a magican is infected with all manner of contingencies while the concept of God ramified into its many meaning postulates, all of which are devoid of contingency upon close semantical analysis, makes the concept of a magican profoundly disanalogous to the concept of God. In effect, we see nothing in the efforts of Rowe or Walton to establish that Hartshorne's version of the ontological argument is either trivial or circuitous.

Besides these criticisms of Hartshorne's reasoning concerning the ontological argument, three other criticisms stand out as deserving special treatment, one from Findlay, one that grows out of Willard Quine's reflections on modal logic, and one from H. G. Hubbeling. Hartshorne praised Findlay for giving the clearest statement of the objection that the concrete cannot be deduced from the abstract and that this is what the ontological argument purports to do (AD 255–61).[33] Definitions are abstract, but God's existence must be concrete; from the logically weak definition of 'God' one may not deduce the logically stronger conclusion that God exists. Put somewhat differently, if the deduction succeeds, then God's existence must be as abstract as God's essence. Hartshorne's response to Findlay is to accept the principle but to appeal to the distinction between existence and actuality. To be sure, the ontological argument concludes to the *existence* of God, which is abstract, but more explicitly, it concludes to God's *existence as somehow actualized.* No actual state of God—which is the concreteness of God—can be deduced by a metaphysical argument. The structure of this reasoning is analogous to the argument touched on in Chapter Three that nonbeing is impossible. The statement "Something exists" may be necessarily true, as Hartshorne urges, although it gives no information as to what actually exists. It says that the set of existing things is not empty. By parity of reasoning, the conclusion of Hartshorne's modal argument can be rephrased to say that the set of actual divine states is never empty. With good reason, Hartshorne insisted that he knew very little about God.[34] At most, his metaphysics yields only the most abstract truths about deity, although he stressed that it is no small achievement to advance the subject of metaphysics when so few attend to its reasoning.

Another important objection to Hartshorne's modal ontological argument, especially as presented in *The Logic of Perfection,* arises from Quine's attack on the intelligibility of *de re* modality. While Hick criticized Hartshorne's modal argument for moving illicitly from *de dicto* (linguistic) to *de re* (ontological) conceptions of modality, another strategy for a resolute critic of the argument would be to reject the very intelligibility of *de re* modality. If successful, such a critique would surely devastate the modal version of the argument in *The Logic of Perfection,* since Hartshorne claims, in his reply to Hick, that *de re* modality permeates the argument, because at the appropriately abstract level of the argument logical modality mirrors objective modality. Quine's challenge to the intelligibility of *de re* modality has been taken up in great detail by George L. Goodwin, an approach to the problem that Hartshorne endorses in his "Foreword" to the work.[35] The arguments could be summarized as follows.

Quine objected to the idea of *de re* modality, since it involves quantification across modal operators; for example, the formulation "$(\exists x)$ (necessarily, x is greater than seven)" is logically illicit, claims Quine, because the modal operator "necessarily" is inserted within a quantifier-bound variable-predicate expression. Quine points out that we cannot legitimately existentially generalize from the licit *de dicto* formulation:

(a) necessarily, nine is greater than seven;

to the illicit

(b) $(\exists x)$ (necessarily, x is greater than seven).

This is because "nine" in (a) is referentially opaque; it fails to denote in a singular way, and thus opens the door to counterexamples in the generalized sentence (b). For instance, Quine says that "nine" can name "the number of planets" (since Pluto's demotion, we would say "eight"); it is not a property of "the number of planets," however, that it is *necessarily* greater than seven. Hartshorne, given his theory of contingent states of affairs, would not object to the notion that "the number of planets," presumably in our solar system, is indeed a contingency. The thrust of this is that, because of referential opacity in quantified modal logic, we do not know what it *means* to introduce propositions of the existentially generalized form (b). However, Goodwin notes that Hartshorne is indeed committed in his modal version of the argument to such forms as:

(c) $(\exists x)$ (necessarily, x is perfect).

Consequently, an effective Hartshornean response to Quine's critique requires an intelligible semantics for modal logic.

Goodwin argues that Kripke supplies such a semantics in his essay, "Semantical Considerations on Modal Logic."[36] According to Kripke, we *can* give an intelligible account of sentences involving quantification into modal contexts. A sentence having the form of (b) can be interpreted to say: there is an object, x, in this world which has the property 'greater-than-seven' and x has this property in every possible world in which x exists. In other words, x exists in this world and at least some possible worlds accessible from this world, and x falls under the extension of the predicate, 'greater-than-seven', in every world in which it exists. However, this only takes one so far as the provision of an (arguably) intelligible formal semantics for sentences involving quantification into modal contexts. Quine replies that the very terms of this *formal* semantical solution to the problem of opacity raises the further question of what it means for an individual or object to exist in various possible worlds. This problem has come to be known as the problem of trans-world identity. Quine challenges any response to his critique of *de re* modality based on Kripke's semantics by arguing that Kripke's solution to referential opacity issues in a semantics involving the notoriously difficult idea of "essential properties." For instance, let the value for x be C. S. Peirce, while the predicate attributed to x is "being a speculative philosopher." Must Peirce be a speculative philosopher in any possible world in which he exists in order to be Peirce in such worlds?

Could Peirce be a "seventeenth-century sea captain" in some possible worlds and still intelligibly remain Peirce in such possible worlds?

It is precisely here, argues Goodwin, that Hartshorne's ontology of temporal process can be employed, providing Kripke with intelligible criteria for making "trans-world" identifications. The problem of trans-world identity seems perplexing and insolvable when assuming, to use Quine's phrase, "Aristotelian essentialism," in which essential properties belong to substances that make no inherent reference to temporality. By contrast, Hartshorne's process or event ontology positions the search for an intelligible criterion for trans-world identity in the much wider matrix of successive and causally efficacious temporal units of becoming. This is one reason why, as noted in Chapter Four, Hartshorne prefers to speak of "possible world-states" rather than "possible worlds." Temporal inheritance becomes the *essential* factor in determining identity, and thus more readily settles the above questions: Peirce might well exist as, say, a professional painter in some possible world-state, since he might have been one in the history of *this* actual world, that is, since there may have been a juncture in Peirce's development in which he was not particularly taken with questions of speculative philosophy, but was exposed to an environment of intense interest in artistic expression. But surely he could not be, in any possible world-state, a seventeenth-century sea captain, since this would bear *nothing* in common with his succession of temporal events. Thus, to conclude the issue cautiously, perhaps we should say that, even if Hartshorne's event ontological criterion of temporal inheritance does not fully resolve the issue of trans-world identity, it seems clear that it profoundly simplifies it. More pointedly, such criterion answers directly to Quine's charge of the unintelligibility of any solution based on an Aristotelian essentialism that appeals to temporally decontexualized substances in its discourse concerning essential properties.[37]

A technically sophisticated objection to Hartshorne's modal argument, especially as expressed in *The Logic of Perfection,* comes from H. G. Hubbeling.[38] Hubbeling presents Hartshorne with a dilemma: the modal argument is valid if and only if the theory of temporal modalities is false. The problem is that Hartshorne's *Logic of Perfection* version of the argument is expressed in Lewis's S5 system in which modal status is necessary. Symbolically: "If $\square\, p^*$ then $\square\,\square\, p^*$" and "If $\Diamond\, p^*$ then $\square\, \Diamond\, p^*$". Temporal modalities, however, are best expressed in the weaker Lewis S4 system which includes the first of these formulae as an axiom, but in which the second formula is neither an axiom nor a theorem. Without "If $\Diamond\, p^*$ then $\Box\, \Diamond\, p^*$" Hartshorne's argument isn't valid, for then it could be the case that God's existence is possible but not necessarily so. On the other hand, Hartshorne wants to ground the meaning of modal terms in temporal process. The most plausible semantics for S5, however, leaves modal concepts untethered to time.

Hubbeling's dilemma is directed at the argument as it is formalized in *The Logic of Perfection* which relies on S5. It is to be noted, however, that Hartshorne gave other versions, both informal and formal (such as the version used above) which do not depend on S5. Hartshorne was convinced that an element of intuitive judgment that goes beyond the logical formalism is involved in assessing the argument. However, to grant the element of intuitive judgment does not directly answer Hubbeling's dilemma. What remains to be explored is whether Hubbeling's challenge can be met from within Hartshorne's particular form of dipolar theism. It is true that S5 seems to be the appropriate modal system for expressing the abstract point of the argument relating to God's unique characteristic of universal existential tolerance, that is to say, God's existence in every possible state of affairs. S5's property of complete "world accessibility" symmetry is exactly what is needed. On the other hand, S4 is applicable to the description of what Hartshorne calls God's actuality or God's concrete states. So, Hartshorne's existence/actuality distinction maps onto the S5/S4 distinction.

The Global Argument

If Hartshorne is correct, the ontological argument reveals the logical status of the theistic question as metaphysical rather than empirical. The argument falls short of a proof of theism, in large measure, because it depends on the premise that the existence of God is logically possible. Hartshorne's own arguments against classical theism show that this is not a premise that can be taken for granted. Hartshorne once commented that John Duns Scotus also concluded that the question of God's existence is not empirical. Hartshorne added, "My quarrel with him is that I regard his form of theism as either self-inconsistent or meaningless."[39] Hartshorne believed that the weak premise in the modal argument is the first one, that 'God' names a possible reality. He said in his reply to Hick that all of his misgivings about believing in God rested on the suspicion, difficult to remove, that every form of theism masks an absurdity.[40] This explains, at least in part, the efforts that Hartshorne made to defend the project of metaphysics as the search for necessary truths about existence and to develop a coherent version of dipolar theism. One can think of the global argument as the completion of this process. Discounting the modal argument, each element of Hartshorne's cumulative case is designed to buttress the claim that the existence of God is logically possible.

Richard Purtill, a theist who argued for the validity of Hartshorne's argument, raised the interesting question whether the ontological argument is "sound but superfluous."[41] An obvious way to argue against the impossibility of God's existence ($\sim \Diamond\, p^*$) is to give an argument directly *for* God's existence. If God exists then, clearly, God's existence is not impossible. By parity of reasoning, an atheist could argue (say, from the existence of evil) that the universe is incompatible with God's existence, and thus, agreeing with Anselm that God could only exist non-contingently, conclude that God is impossible. Hartshorne agreed with Purtill that any proof which establishes the conceivability of God can as well or better be so formulated that it directly establishes God's existence. Hartshorne insisted, however, that the theist should accept the ontological argument's validity and realize that "blanket empiricism begs the theistic question."[42]

A different objection was raised by Martin. Like Purtill, Martin concedes the validity of Hartshorne's ontological argument, but he maintains that arguing against "($\sim \Diamond\, p^*$)" by giving another theistic argument is to have things backwards. "The theistic proofs *presume* that the concept of God is coherent; they cannot demonstrate it."[43] We contend, however, that the form that Hartshorne gives to the global argument escapes this problem. None of the elements of the global argument make the presumption that dipolar theism is coherent. In keeping with Hartshorne's use of position matrixes, each argument is presented as a logically exhaustive set of options. We have already hinted at this style of reasoning in the modal argument where one has the choice that God's existence is a necessity ($\sim \Diamond \sim p^*$), an impossibility ($\sim \Diamond\, p^*$), or a contingency ($\Diamond\, p^*$ and $\Diamond \sim p^*$). Other strands of the global argument are also presented in this way: to affirm one alternative is to deny all of the others, and alternately, to deny one is to affirm that one and only one of the others is true. Beginning from highly general concepts (e.g., existence, order, knowledge, the good, the beautiful), the various strands of the global argument, bring into relief what Hartshorne considered to be the theistic implications of neoclassical metaphysics. The coherence of dipolar or neoclassical theism takes shape in the mosaic of these arguments as a conclusion, not as a hidden presupposition or even a procedural presumption.

Each argument in Hartshorne's global argument is given a familiar name that suggests precursors in the history of philosophy, but none of them has an exact equivalent in the world's philosophical literature. In addition to the ontological argument, Hartshorne develops his own versions of the cosmological, teleological, epistemic, moral, and aesthetic arguments. The array of alternatives for each argument are designed to be mutually exclusive and formally exhaustive. However, there is no question of providing a strict demonstration of dipolar theism. In each case, Hartshorne employs what he calls "the principle of least paradox" to conclude that the rational cost of rejecting neoclassical theism is greater than the cost of accepting it (CS 88–89). Time and again, Hartshorne acknowledged the difficulties in the way of an unqualified verdict in favor of neoclassical theism, but he also believed that his view better answered the questions of metaphysics than did its rivals. Hartshorne was epistemically cautious in recognizing that his method would not yield a decisive victory for his own views. As with the modal argument, Hartshorne believed that no degree of logical rigor can eliminate the need for an element of intuitive judgment. The "essential element in rational procedure in metaphysics" is to honestly face the logically possible alternatives and to weigh up the cost of accepting or rejecting them.[44]

Much of the global argument is anticipated in Hartshorne's explanation and defense of neoclassical metaphysics. Consider Hartshorne's cosmological argument. He presented a unique version of the argument which is especially clearly stated in Chapter Eight of *Man's Vision of God and the Logic of Theism*. This version has received little specific critical attention, despite the fact that, in our estimation at least, it remains a tightly reasoned systematic presentation of important essentials of neoclassical process theism refracted through the lens of a single argument. Also of interest is the fact that one can hear discernible echoes in this chapter of the position Hartshorne once deemed "teleological monism" in the Harvard dissertation on "The Unity of Being." Thus, for both substantive philosophical and historical reasons, the argument is worthy of consideration.

The overall argument or argument schema can be stated as follows. Hartshorne presents the argument casually in "outline" without reference to the formal inferences involved (MVG 255f). We have made the logical principles of valid inference explicit in the following presentation:

1. Temporal existence implies everlasting existence, that is, $(T \supset E)$.

2. Everlasting existence can belong to but one individual, which can only be conceived as "God," that is, $(E \supset G)$.

3. Therefore, Temporal existence implies that there is an everlasting individual that can only be conceived as "God," that is, $(T \supset G)$. [Derived from 1 and 2 by Hypothetical Syllogism.]

4. There is temporal existence, i.e., something temporal exists. (T)

5. Therefore, God exists. (G) [Derived from 3 and 4 by *Modus Ponens.*]

In effect, this argument represents the fleshed-out phenomenological and logical analysis of the proposition that "something exists"—again, Hartshorne's primary example of a metaphysical truth.

The argument could be broadly explicated as follows: We begin with the proposition that "something exists" which can be "experientially established only in the form 'something exists in space and time'" (MVG 255).[45] It is also a phenomenological fact that the experientially evident spatio-temporal data exhibit locomotion and qualitative change. To illustrate with an arbitrary example where any would suffice: you move your book from the table and notice a coffee stain on the title page that was not there, say, an hour ago. Note that in this mundane example, that which exhibits change is, of course, *something* which changes. But that there is a unified something which changes is tantamount to saying that the changes "belong" to an identity which endures change (although the identity must be in its abstract characteristics, as in Hartshorne's example of a weather pattern, mentioned in Chapter Four). That there are subjects of temporal change is thus a necessary feature of temporal change; in effect, there are no "subject-less" temporal changes. Moreover, this something which changes cannot be something in abstraction from its changes, but is instead, *the thing which changes*—"it is that which alters and in altering remains itself" (MVG 256). In other words, temporal change is not to be attributed to the "unchanging" aspect of a series of temporal changes, that is, the aspect or aspects held in common by the series, but is rather to be attributed to, so to speak, the final cumulative and enduring term of the series. Logically, the something which endures the change from state X at t to state Y at t^* (where $t \neq t^*$) is the thing as an inclusive change, as XY at t^*, or stated in a way which better reflects physically prehensive relationships, as X-in-Y at t^*, not the thing taken in its unchanging aspect, i.e., the X common to state X at t and X-in-Y at t^*.

What is critical to notice is that this changing something cannot be identified with a generative and corruptive series or sequence of changes. That is to say, the sufficient or ultimate subject of change cannot be identified with *finite* temporal entities. For generative change is causally grounded in preceding actuality and corruptive change "belongs" to a preceding actuality (as, for instance, when we speak of a deceased person as bearing the identity of one who underwent particular changes of disease). Something preceded, say, one's body prior to its emergence—in fact, all of its matter-energy preceded it if we grant natural science's sacrosanct principle of conservation, a principle affirmed by Whitehead in his notion of the continuous transference of energy from one actual occasion to another.[46] Likewise, something endures after the death of my body—in fact, again, all of its matter-energy, albeit, not in its previously vivified form of organization. Properly speaking, the emergence of a new entity is not a change to be attributed to the just-emerged-entity, for the entity is simply not there to receive such attribution—but rather, as we are wont to say, is to be attributed to "the world" or "the cosmos" or "reality" or "being" or some other catch-all expression. The logically proper, *sufficient* subject of change is thus the inclusive *enduring* subject which functions as a preexistent subject of generative change and the post-existent subject of corruptive change. Generated and corrupted entities are thus only included, subordinate subjects of change. They are subjects of change relative to their own careers, and as such they are not "universes" unto themselves. Rather they are genuine parts of the universe, genuine parts of the whole-that-changes.[47] To say otherwise—to say that we and other spatio-temporal natural entities are not *integral* parts of a whole-that-changes—is simply to deny the real or *de re* applicability of the categories of relationality and causality, at the very least eccentric positions surely not recognized in either the *practice* of natural science or the unshakeable presuppositions of deep common sense.

Numerous philosophers have recognized the cogency of this line of reasoning. That is, they have recognized the need to supply some notion of an enduring, ultimate subject of change. When we eliminate positions that deny either the extra-mental reality of temporal process and an open future (e.g., Spinoza's One Substance, Bradley's Absolute) or real causal agency as exercised by finite entities upon other finite entities (e.g., Leibniz's windowless monads deterministically programmed by God)—positions outside the realistic processual framework of the argument—the remaining proposals in the history of metaphysics range from atomistic materialism (Epicurus, Lucretius, contemporary materialists)[48] to hylomorphism (Aristotle and various Aristotelians) to notions of a primordial space-time (Samuel Alexander). Could any of these candidates adequately and coherently represent the cosmic identity, the enduring, ultimate subject of change? Hartshorne argues that each of these alternatives fails in one of two basic ways: either it mistakes arbitrary and contingent characteristics for modally necessary ones or it postulates something so abstract and empty that it cannot provide a positive identity for that which endures change.

Consider the eternal material atoms of Epicurus. They are constituted by contingent features of vibration and speed of locomotion, yet these features cannot be eternal or necessary, for such quantitative-structural properties are, by definition, peculiar and arbitrary. (This holds even more clearly in the modern theory of atomic elements with its mathematically precise characterizations of atoms. Nothing in the nature of things *requires* that there be an atomic particle with an isotope mass of 1.007825 u [a characteristic of hydrogen]. To conceive an alternative we merely have to alter the numbers.) On the other hand, Aristotle's prime matter escapes the modal paradox of atomism because it does not bear the peculiar characteristics of Epicurean atoms, but it possesses no phenomenologically accessible identity, and thus, as Aristotle says, it cannot be found as distinguishable in nature but is distinguishable only "in thought"; it offers no positive identity for the subject of temporal change. It is, in effect, a mere potential for change which endures all change. As Hartshorne says it has the property of being flexible to a unique or maximal extent, but the "identity [of the subject of change] is presupposed not clarified" (MVG 259). Finally, Samuel Alexander's primordial pure space-time (out of which actualities are said eventually to emerge) provides an eternal, enduring subject of change which bears no logically contingent features, but it fares no better than Aristotle's prime matter in terms of providing a positive conception of the identity of that which endures. As a concept of metaphysically *pure* space-time it possesses no aesthetic nor quantitative-structural properties as it contains no objects or determinations which would have such properties; rather it represents only the pure potential for such determinations (MVG 263–64). Again, a maximally flexible identity is only presupposed and not clarified.

With these alternatives rendered highly problematic, the question remains: *What* then is the "eternal something" which endures temporal change? One immediate response to this query is negative: The cosmic identity we are seeking cannot be fundamentally quantitative-structural. Indeed, the still unscathed phenomenological insight of the idealist tradition from Bishop Berkeley to F. H. Bradley is that measurable or actual quantitative-structural characteristics are "dependent upon" aesthetic qualities. For instance, there are no *mere* actual shapes, but only shapes that can be determined as outlines and contours of actual aesthetic content. The *content* of that which changes is thus primarily aesthetic and secondarily (and dependently) quantitative-structural. It is also only with reference to aesthetic content that *any* qualitative determinations of similarity and dissimilarity can be made.

Granted that the essential character of the sufficient subject of change must be aesthetic-qualitative, what is the *something* which can hold the vast variety of aesthetic qualities in unity? Experience suggests to us one and only one candidate, namely, mind and its capacity for preservation of the past, that is, memory (MVG 264f). The analogical focal point here is not the *human* mind with its peculiar characteristics and traits, but rather the most general features of mind common to our acts of experience, namely, the unified retention over time of widely varied and spatially spread aesthetic qualia. In effect, the general phenomenology of experience analogically yields a general positive conception of the cosmic identity as the continuant of temporal change: To experience something is to experience qualitative contrasts that are spatio-temporally extended and held in unity through a temporally related schema of perception (or immediate retrospection) and memory (as Husserl would similarly have it in *The Phenomenology of Internal Time Consciousness* "through noetic-noematic schemata"). Consequently, the notion of mind as the continuant of change seems to fit all the requirements: by definition it is experientially accessible and thus "positively identifiable" and exhibits unity, retention or preservation, relationality, causal influence, endurance through change, entertainment of aesthetic qualia, and flexibility. As argued earlier, all other alternatives to this analogical projection seem much too high in cognitive cost. Again, they either do not conform to realist convictions of deep common sense (and thus issue in performative self-contradiction) or they commit us to modal paradox or they fail to offer any positive conception of identity through temporal change.[49]

Hartshorne's conclusion is that the only positive, analogically and experientially accessible conception of the sufficient subject of temporal change is an all-enduring, all-inclusive cosmic mind, a mind which entertains in unity all manner of aesthetic qualities with maximal flexibility. Such characteristics could belong to one and only one individual as notions of plural yet all-inclusive and sufficient eternal subjects of change commit us to all manner of absurdities, including the absurdity that they arguably would have less unity than finite temporal subjects, which would contradict what it means to be a sufficient subject of change (MVG 269–74).

If Hartshorne's argument succeeds—thus an all-inclusive cosmic mind exists—the result is intrinsically and properly *theological*. This is evident from the fact that the word "God" has been associated with historical doctrines claiming cosmic or consummate mind as world-inclusive, for example, as in the concept of God as Holy Spirit in the more immanentist-organic strands of Eastern Orthodox Christian theology or God as the World-Soul in the theology of Plato and Plotinus and certain later Christian Neo-Platonists or the omniscient world-inclusive Deity of the Hindu sage Ramanuja or even the Unborn and Undying (*dharmakaya*) Buddha-Mind of certain theistic (perhaps more exactly panentheistic) strands of Buddhism. More specifically, if successful, the argument establishes a personalistic form of theism, since we would concur with Richard Swinburne that the possession of at least one so-called higher-order P-predicate (knowing, willing, desiring, thinking, hoping, etc., with or without associated embodiment) is sufficient for attribution of personal character to the entity possessing the P-predicate.[50] This would apply *a fortiori* to the case of an omniscient mind. But while the argument has obvious theological significance, it is equally clear that it is insufficient in the sense that it does not do all the work wanted of a systematic natural theology. For instance, what is the exact relation between the cosmic mind and good or evil intention? The Moral Argument and direct considerations of philosophical theodicy are far more appropriate for adjudicating this issue. Nor, of course, does Hartshorne make an exaggerated claim for the efficacy of the argument. Hartshorne's concept of the global argument for theism is precisely the notion that multiple strands of argument, theoretical and pragmatic, work together reinforcing and enhancing one another and emphasizing different aspects of a comprehensive theistic philosophy. Hartshorne's Cosmological Argument—especially in its more sustained version summarized here—has its appropriate role to play, namely, reinforcing the metaphysical unity and cognitive-aesthetic aspects of divinity.

Casual principles enter Hartshorne's cumulative case in his argument from cosmic order (RSP 191–92; NT 49–50, 53, 57–65; CS 281, 284–85).[51] Recall that Hartshorne defends a metaphysic according to which the cosmos is a theater of interactions among dynamic singulars, all of which act and are acted upon. The existence of many real beings, thus defined, raises the problem of cosmic order. The question is not why there is order rather than mere chaos. For Hartshorne, chaos presupposes order as much as non-existence presupposes existence; he agrees with Bergson that mere chaos is indistinguishable from nonbeing.[52] The question, rather, is how there can be *order on a cosmic scale* if there is only an uncoordinated set of centers of creative activity. Localized order or order within the cosmos can be explained by localized activity of entities *within* the cosmos. The order *of* the cosmos, however, cannot be the outcome of a coordinated effort by the many entities since their very existence, severally scattered throughout the cosmos, presupposes the cosmos as a field of activity. If there is a cosmic ordering power that itself falls under the metaphysical principle of acting and being acted upon, then cosmic order can be explained. Moreover, the explanation is not *ad hoc* since all real beings, localized ones and the cosmic ordering power, fall under the same metaphysical principle. The cosmic ordering power is not, in the words of Whitehead, an exception to metaphysical principles, invoked to save their collapse, but is their chief exemplification.[53]

Hartshorne allows that the expression "cosmic order" permits different values; the laws of nature must include constants as well as variables, and the values of the constants (for example, the speed of light), are not logical necessities. In this way, one may speak, with Whitehead, of different "cosmic epochs" in which the laws of nature beyond the singularities of our universe are not identical with our own. Hartshorne insists, however, that the problem of cosmic order remains. This is because our conceptions of the fundamental laws of nature are contingent and mathematically peculiar in character. For instance, an epoch such as our own with a law of gravitation specified by "mass x mass proportioned to the radius squared" is a particular nomological condition to be conceptually contrasted with, say, gravitation specified as "mass x mass proportioned to the radius cubed." Basic laws of nature appear to have the logical earmarks of "contingent decrees," and as such it is legitimate to ask for a causal explanation of them. Recent thought experiments in cosmology such as "bubble inflation" models also seem to posit background assumptions of *contingent* cosmic conditions, including the operation of laws of quantum mechanics which necessarily involve quite specific quantitative values (e.g., as in the use of Planck's Constant).

Thought experiments which assert that basic laws of nature could be entirely instituted by chance mechanisms beg the question of basic order. An example is Hume's suggestion of an Epicurean universe of swerving atoms that happen to arrange themselves into the cosmic "regularities" we observe. As Hartshorne says, talk of atoms with a definite character persisting through time is "already a tremendous order" (NT 57). The idea which has more recently gained wide recognition of non-Darwinian self-ordering systems faces the same problem if construed as an answer to the problem of cosmic order. In self-ordering scenarios, the "chaos" from which new forms of order emerge is never absolute but is ringed about by a world already in existence, with an order all of its own.

On Hartshorne's neoclassical theistic alternative, one arguably need not settle for any metaphysically inexplicable contingent cosmic order nor a freedom-suppressing necessitarian universe. It is also well to remember that Hartshorne vigorously defends indeterminism. If determinism is false, then neither the order within the cosmos nor the order of the cosmos is absolute. Multiple real beings with varying degrees of creative power are a recipe for conflict. To be sure, the existence of multiple real beings also opens the possibility for cooperative endeavors, whether it is cooperation among localized beings or between them and the cosmic "designer"; but multiple creativity guarantees a mixture of disharmony and harmony. The cosmic ordering power can guarantee a *cosmic order,* but because of the existence of a plurality of real beings that act, and are not simply acted upon, not everything that happens can be chosen by a single individual, even a divine one. This is relevant to the problem of theodicy, for it shows that, in neoclassical metaphysics, the conflict of decisions among the creatures, and between the creatures and God, are possible, opening the way to tragedies that not even God can avoid.

A possible criticism of Hartshorne's argument comes from Joseph Bracken who takes seriously Jacques Derrida's criticism of traditional metaphysics as logocentric and sees in Hartshorne's solution to the problem of the one and the many a residual element of logocentrism. *Logocentrism* is the tendency of classical metaphysics "to locate the order and intelligibility for a given set of terms (or 'signifiers') in a 'transcendent signified,' i.e., in an object of thought which stands outside the system of terms to be thus defined as their 'Logos' or objective principle of intelligibility."[54] According to Bracken, Whitehead was not clear whether the world has an order independently of God's consequent nature (an objective order) or if the order of the world is nothing more than God's consequent nature (a subjective order). The problem was solved, says Bracken, for many Whiteheadians by distinguishing, with Hartshorne, *compound* individuals and *composite* individuals.[55] Compound individuals are unified by a dominant society, a personally ordered society, whereas composite individuals are more democratic. In Hartshorne's view, the universe is a compound individual that derives its order from the divine society—which society Hartshorne characterizes as "monarchical" (RSP 37–39). As noted in our previous chapter, the God-World relationship for Hartshorne is analogous to the soul-body relation, or more precisely, "a person as soul or conscious individual [related] to the physical body of the individual" (OO 54). Bracken finds Hartshorne's view too logocentric and suggests as a revision that no society is monarchical in Hartshorne's sense. In Bracken's revision, some subsocieties within a society have greater influence than others, but none, by itself, determines the order of the whole.[56]

Bracken's revision should be considered separately from the charge that Hartshorne's metaphysics is, or tends to be, logocentric. We maintain that the charge of logocentrism is simply *not* applicable to Hartshorne's metaphysics. Hartshorne's God, it is true, lays down the conditions of *cosmic order* and is therefore the necessary element in any cosmos. However, it is false that God stands outside the system of terms to be defined—which is characteristic of logocentric thinking. On the contrary, Hartshorne's God, perhaps even more than Whitehead's, is no exception to metaphysical principles. Hartshorne maintains that reasoning about God must meet four conditions and that his metaphysics meets those conditions (NT 37–41). We have explained these conditions in the previous chapter, but it will help to clarify issues to summarize them here (Table 4).

Conditions for reasoning about God	How Hartshorne's system meets the conditions
1. There must be rules applicable universally, to both God and the creatures.	1. All individuals interact (i.e., they act and are acted upon).
2. There must be rules applicable to all individuals, save God.	2. All non-divine individuals have limited (local) scope of interaction.
3. There must be a rule or criteria for distinguishing the rules as applicable to all beings and the rules as applicable only to God.	3. Rule: Distinguish interaction generally (applies to God and creatures) and scope of interaction (God alone acts on an unlimited scale).
4. There must be reasons why the distinction is made.	4. Limited scope of interaction is unintelligible without unlimited scope of interaction.

TABLE 4: Hartshorne on Conditions for Reasoning About God

The transcendence of God, on Hartshorne's view, is not a transcendence outside the system to be defined; transcendence here signifies unlimited scope of interaction. God is the only individual for whom it is possible to act and to be acted upon by every other individual. However, God's influence is exerted over creatures that retain, to greater and lesser degrees, the power of self-determination; that is to say, they retain the power to act. God provides the framework of physical laws within which meaningful activity is possible. The framework is only the outline or the most abstract aspects of creaturely activity. To deny that the creatures contribute to this outline does not entail that the creatures contribute no forms of order to the universe. On the contrary, there are virtually unlimited examples of forms of creaturely order (e.g., social structure, economic structure, sporting activities, artistic creation, etc.)

Hartshorne would argue that Bracken's revision leaves unexplained order on a cosmic scale. The interaction of "the many" presupposes an antecedent order in terms of which interaction can occur. It is not clear, however, that Bracken is entirely consistent on this point, for he maintains that the dynamic interrelation of the three divine persons— Bracken *assumes* the Trinity as a starting point—"give a necessary order and structure to the cosmic community, but the *Logos* or ontological principle of unity is distributed among all its members, both divine and creaturely, in terms of their dynamic interrelation to one another and their collective contribution to the order and well-being of the whole."[57] Bracken asks, what is the "necessary order and structure of the cosmic community" if not cosmic order provided by the Trinitarian God?

Hartshorne's God, no less than Bracken's, provides the "necessary order and structure of the cosmic community." Note too that the ontological principle of unity—what Bracken refers to as *Logos*—is no less distributed in the universe among God and the creatures in Hartshorne's scheme than it is in Bracken's scheme, provided that the principle refers to the ability to contribute to an ordered whole. Where Hartshorne parts company with Bracken is not on the question of logocentrism. Rather, they seem to part company over the question whether the creatures can contribute anything to the *cosmic* order. What, after all, can any creature or group of creatures do to contribute to or detract from the gravitational constant?

Bracken is critical of what he sees as the tendency among Whiteheadians to follow Hartshorne in privileging monarchically organized societies—societies possessing a dominant or ruling monad. This ignores the fact, says Bracken, that the vast majority of societies are not organized in this way.[58] One may agree with Bracken that most societies are not monarchical in Hartshorne's sense. However, it should be noted that Hartshorne follows Whitehead in speaking of a tree as a democracy (i.e., as non-monarchical). Hartshorne also notes that Gestaltists were right to deny that the plant is the mere sum of its parts (RSP 58). In any event, Hartshorne's chief concern in talking about societies was the extent to which it is legitimate to attribute to them psychological properties, as opposed to only biological or physical properties. This is possible, on Hartshorne's view, only for monarchical societies. We do not believe that Bracken would dispute this.

Despite these differences, Bracken's view of the God-World relation is surprisingly close to Hartshorne's panentheism. According to Bracken, "the field proper to God as a personally-ordered society of actual occasions thus coincides with the extensive continuum as the all-encompassing field of activity for the societies of actual occasions in the world, both past, present, and future."[59] Bracken sees that Hartshorne preserves God's independence of the world in the sense that God is the "soul" of any possible world. Bracken believes, however, that he can assure God's independence even more clearly by his own Trinitarian understanding of God. The three divine persons preside over a common field of activity that is nothing other than the divine nature. Moreover, this divine field of activity has no necessary connection to any world, possible or actual. "The world is necessarily emergent out of the field of activity proper to the three divine persons in their dynamic interrelation."[60] Bracken preserves the *possibility* of God's existence as independent of a universe. In other words, it is possible for God to exist without a universe but it is not possible for the universe to exist without God. In these views, Bracken is not so much neo-Whiteheadian as non-Whiteheadian. It is a fair question whether Bracken can avoid a spirit/matter dualism. God—even a triune God—existing without a universe seems to fit perfectly the description of a being of pure spirit.

While we disagree with Bracken on whether Hartshorne makes a tacit commitment to logocentrism, we find Bracken's interpretation of Jacques Derrida's central notion of *différance* and its correlation with Whitehead's concept of creativity to be insightful.[61] Since Hartshorne likewise affirms creativity, it appears to us that Bracken's correlation with Derrida's *différance* would apply to Hartshorne's philosophy as well. Moreover, Bracken himself suggests that his "field-oriented approach to the God-World relationship can still be fruitfully employed if one conceives God in strictly monotheistic terms," and he uses Hartshorne's example of God as a personally ordered society of divine actual occasions as his model of God conceived in "strictly monotheistic terms."[62] Despite this, a complicating factor in interpreting Hartshorne's relation to Bracken's revisionary field-oriented view is that one can discern a three-fold structure in Hartshorne's neoclassical theism. There are three distinctive but noncontingent "aspects" of divinity required for a comprehensive description of God on Hartshorne's theory: (1) God's "primordial" aspect as the "eternal plenum" of the most abstract potentialities (DL 238), that is, God's abstract essence and all that it contains; (2) God's "consequent" aspect, that is, God as universal, omniscient prehender and appreciator of the cosmos; and (3) God's "outgoing" or "superjective" aspect, that is, God as evaluator and responder to the prehended cosmos with desiderata embedded in each response (DR 142). Bracken does not seem to notice this three-fold structure in Hartshorne's doctrine. But given the importance Bracken places upon the doctrine of the Trinity as containing an inherent reply to Derrida's concerns with logocentrism, it is at least an open question as to how Hartshorne's three-fold analysis of God relates to Derrida's concerns. We are not suggesting that Hartshorne's three-fold analysis is isomorphic with Trinitarian thinking.[63] However, Hartshorne's concept of divinity is certainly not unidimensional—a hallmark of logocentric perspectives—but rather complex and polysemic.

Let us return to Hartshorne's argument from cosmic order, the idea that order on a cosmic scale requires a cosmic ordering power, and that the power is divine. A skeptic may embrace any of the options in the argument that Hartshorne denies, but at a cost. Hartshorne argues that each of the nontheistic options has dubious metaphysical credentials and that his solution to the problem of cosmic order is the most parsimonious. If there is no cosmic order one must explain the apparent success of science in discovering that order. If there is no cosmic ordering power, then either localized beings are being used to explain an order that their activity presupposes or there is no explanation of the order. Another atheistic option is to accept that there is a cosmic ordering power but deny that it is divine. Hartshorne considered panentheism to provide a superior analogy to anything atheism can propose for the cosmic "designer"; however, the remaining three strands of the global argument can also be used to support this idea. The cosmic ordering power is not only an agent causally affecting the world but is also affected by it and incorporates it into the divine life, as one that perfectly knows the world (epistemic argument), perfectly preserves its achievements (moral argument), and fully appreciates it (aesthetic argument).

In the epistemic argument, Hartshorne raises the question of the relation between reality and knowledge.[64] In one respect, knowledge depends upon the real, for one cannot know what is not real. On the other hand, it is difficult to give an account of the real apart from some form of knowledge. As Hartshorne notes, Immanuel Kant suggested that appearance differs from reality because "the content of our sensory intuition differs from the content of a non-sensory intuition."[65] The object of the non-sensory intuition is the "noumenon." (Hartshorne parts company with Kant in conceiving God's knowledge as partly passive rather than as wholly active). Taking up Kant's point, no merely partial or fallible knowing can circumscribe the real, for the extent of errors in knowing are measured by the real—if one is mistaken about *x*, then something about *x* escapes one's knowledge. In view of these conundrums, it is tempting to say that reality is the potential content of infallible knowledge—what an epistemically unsurpassable being would know if it existed. The problem with this solution, as far as atheism is concerned, is that an infallible knower, by definition, could not possibly be mistaken. However, it would know its own existence, so one is led to posit not simply the possible existence of an infallible knower, but also its actual existence. Hartshorne drew precisely this conclusion, that reality is the actual content of infallible knowledge. He argued further, following Josiah Royce, that defects in cognitive experience are internal to experience. Hartshorne mentions confusion, inconsistency, doubt, inconstancy of beliefs, and "above all, a lack of concepts adequate to interpret our percepts and of percepts adequate to distinguish between false and true concepts" (CS 288).

We have already discussed Hartshorne's claims that perfect knowledge requires both cognitive and affective components. God must be conceived not only as knowing all true propositions but also as knowing the creatures themselves, which is to say as feeling their feelings. Whatever one has been and however one has felt become transformed thereafter as an everlasting memory in God's consciousness. This applies also to the collective life of the creatures. There is no mere *numerical sum* of value in God—as if value were simply a question of set membership—for the experiences of the creatures become woven into the fabric of God's own undying experience. This is what Hartshorne means by *contributionism*, that the creatures enrich the divine life in a way that would not have been possible apart from their activity. Hartshorne asked, "If people can live or die for country, or other human groups, why can they not live and die for that which embraces all groups and their intrinsic values—the divine life?"[66] Hartshorne was fond of quoting the Jewish prayer: "Help us to become co-workers with You, and endow our fleeting days with abiding worth" (AD vii; NT vii; AW 48; OO 118; WM 30; ZF 6).[67] The moral argument brings out the attractiveness of this ideal as the supreme aim of creaturely existence.

There are a number of ways to reject contributionism. One may deny that there is any supreme aim, theistic or nontheistic. Hartshorne argues that this robs comparative value judgments of a standard of comparison; if, as most reflective people would accept, it is possible to squander one's life on trivial, unimportant, or immoral pursuits, then there must be a measure of the good life that is being used as a comparison. Another option is that self-interest is the supreme aim. We have already mentioned, in Chapter Four, Hartshorne's reasons for rejecting this. Hartshorne agreed with the Buddhists that living solely for self is delusional, in Hartshorne's words, "writhing in delusion" (IO 365; ZF 190; cf. PSG 412). More plausible is the idea that the aim of life is to live for self and for others either during this life or in a postmortem existence. Hartshorne considered this laudable, but finally unsatisfactory as the *supreme aim* of life. First, he argued that there is at best a numerical meaning of "general welfare," whereas neoclassical theism provides an experiential meaning in God's experience. Second, there is the problem of mortality. Russell stated the problem clearly when he proposed to build a philosophy of life upon a foundation of "unyielding despair." The despair stems from the recognition that "the noonday brightness of human genius" and "the whole temple of man's achievement" is destined to perish.[68] There is, to be sure, apparent nobility in such Sisyphian labor, except that "nobility" and "tragedy" become, on this account, as if they had never been. Dipolar theism, on the other hand, accounts for the value of past achievement as an enduring aspect of the unending process of God's life and memory. Moreover, the value of living for self and others is included in Hartshorne's account, for the supreme "other" is God. The extent and nature of value that one contributes to God is precisely the extent and quality of value that one has contributed to others. Hartshorne argued that contributionism captures the inclusive nature of love that one finds expressed in biblical ethics: one cannot love God if one does not love others and one is to love God with everything one is and to love one's neighbor as oneself. We will delve more deeply into Hartshorne's ethical philosophy and its theological implications in Chapter Nine.

An argument from the beauty of the world as a *de facto* whole rounds out Hartshorne's cumulative case and ties it to the aesthetic motif of his philosophy. It is quite natural, and *prima facie* rational, to speak of enjoying the beauty of the cosmos. Most people consider it appropriate to include aesthetic predicates in descriptions of the universe: it is endlessly interesting, mysterious, and awe inspiring. We have noted in Chapter Four Hartshorne's description of science as the search for the hidden beauty of the world. Hartshorne expresses the idea in these terms:

> [The faith of great scientists] is that nature is more beautiful than our self-indulged imaginative creations can be. And looking back, one sees a confirmation of their faith. The real world keeps turning out to be more thrillingly beautiful, in a vastly greater variety and intricacy of ways, than our previous dreams. How dull and unaesthetic the Newtonian picture seems now; how messy the notion of special creation in biology, or of the movements of heavenly bodies in Ptolemaic astronomy; how tame the tight little universe, and its four thousand years of development, which was all that the Middle Ages in Europe contemplated by way of the "material sublime." One could go on and on. The romance of science is its disclosure of a universe whose wild harmonies surpass the most vivid dreams of imagination not submitting itself to criticism and observational test.[69]

Many great scientists would agree, even those who have little or no use for philosophy or religion, like Steven Weinberg who avers that the universe is sometimes beautiful beyond what seems necessary.[70]

An aesthetically displeasing universe, says Hartshorne, would be either chaotic or monotonous. What we find, on the contrary, is *order* in the laws of nature and *variety* in the evolution of new arrangements of matter and levels of mind. Hartshorne speaks of the world as a *de facto* whole, for he means to stress its open-ended and dynamic character. If atheism is true, then it is non-divine individuals alone that enjoy the beauty of the universe as a whole, catching a glimpse of it in the slice of time that is available to them and to the species. The peek that we have of the beauty of the cosmos, moreover, reveals horizons suggestive of aesthetic riches forever beyond our grasp. Hartshorne argues that this would represent an irremediable aesthetic defect in the universe, for beauty should be enjoyed and only God could adequately enjoy the beauty of the world as a whole. Of course, *what should be* is not necessarily *what is*. Hartshorne insists, however, that unlike merely *contingent defects*, the lack of a divine spectator would be a *necessary defect*, "an eternally necessary yet ugly aspect of things" (CS 290). It is a thought without intrinsic reward or pragmatic value, best conceived as a thought experiment whose purpose is to bring us to the realization of a divine mind that can appreciate the beauty that escapes us.

The conclusions of the design and epistemic arguments, together with Hartshorne's psychicalism, lend support to his aesthetic argument. As the supreme cosmic ordering power, affecting all and affected by all, whose knowledge is the ultimate measure of reality, the divine, in any particular state of its life, must find within itself the entire wealth of all creative experiencing that has ever existed. This experience of a universe in process is, as Whitehead says, "beyond our imagination to conceive"; it includes the (to us) soundless abyss of the past as well as the infinite possibilities of a future yet to be created.[71] It is here that these lines of inference dovetail with the moral argument. God must be conceived not only as the supreme spectator appreciating the beauty of the world as a *de facto* whole, but also as the supremely beautiful (or sublime) object of contemplation, adoration, and worship—an endlessly unfolding cosmic experience to which we contribute. Also implicit in Hartshorne's theology is that God is the supreme actor, the main character, as it were in the play of existence. The various roles of the deity, as Hartshorne conceives it, are neatly summarized in the title of one of his articles: "God as Composer-Director, Enjoyer, and, in a Sense, Player of the Cosmic Drama."[72]

The Problem of Evil and Theodicy

As long as there have been theists, there has been a problem of evil, whether as a believer's lament (as in Job), as a theologian's conundrum (as in Augustine), or as a skeptic's argument (as in Hume). Contemporary philosophers of religion speak of two forms of the problem of evil, the logical and the evidential. The logical problem of evil raises the question whether the existence of evil, conceived as gratuitous suffering, is logically consistent with the existence of a God that is perfect in power, knowledge, and goodness. The evidential problem of evil raises the question whether the existence of evil renders the existence of a perfect God improbable. Hartshorne found neither version of the problem especially troublesome for his form of theism. He held that the problem with both versions of the problem of evil, as they are usually stated, is that they pose a loaded question, presupposing a concept of divine power that, in Hartshorne's words, "is not even coherent enough to be false."[73] We have seen that Hartshorne's is a metaphysic of shared creativity in which no individual, not even a divine one, can have a monopoly of power. He was fond of disagreeing with Einstein who said that God does not play dice (BH x; LP 206; NT 92; IO x; WM 115; OO 71; ZF 66). On the contrary, chance is an inevitable result of multiple decision makers; it is no accident, said Hartshorne, that there are accidents.[74] Although God has the eminent form of creative power, it is not enough to guarantee a world without accidents, wrongdoing, and tragedy. Hartshorne would say that the evidential problem of evil suffers from the additional defect that it assumes that God's existence is an empirical question. We have seen that, according to Hartshorne, this represents a failure to appreciate the logical consequences of "Anselm's discovery."

Much of the appeal of traditional religion is that it offers the hope that the gulf between *what is* and *what ought to be* can be bridged in a future existence. It promises that the cosmic scales of justice are finally balanced either through the mysterious operations of karma in the process of reincarnation or through the omnipotence of God in a heavenly or hellish afterlife. Hartshorne considered these to be false hopes and false fears. As noted in Chapter Five, he did not definitively reject the possibility of a postmortem existence, but he showed no interest in speculating about it or defending the idea. He argued that it is the divine prerogative alone to persist through infinite variations; the self-identity (i.e., the genetic identity) of a non-divine individual cannot sustain itself indefinitely. Even if there were an afterlife, there could be no guarantee that the individual would survive long enough for every injustice, or even the greatest of injustices, in that person's life to be rectified. Moreover, an afterlife could not eliminate the risk inherent in multiple or shared creativity. Traditional accounts of the afterlife are plausible only to the extent that creaturely freedom bends to a higher moral law (karma) or will (God's) imposed on it. The heavens, hells, and purgatories of religion are elaborately orchestrated so as to place all lesser freedoms in perfect harmony with justice. In Hartshorne's neoclassical metaphysics, God has the power to insure order on a cosmic scale, a power that is tantamount to insuring a field of activity for localized individuals. Divine power does not, however, extend to insuring what decisions the creatures will make. No particular outcome can be guaranteed.

Hartshorne maintained that the ancient Jews—or at least the author or authors of the book of Job—"soared far above" most of the theological thinking of earlier and later times concerning the problem evil. According to Hartshorne, there are important lessons to be learned from what he called "the sublime book of Job" (NT 116; OO 32), the biblical book he mentioned more than any other in his writings.[75] First, the distribution of human suffering (also animal suffering) is not divinely arranged. In Hartshorne's words, "The cosmos cannot be a legal system . . . Job's comforters, but not the voice from the Whirlwind, try to apply legal ideas cosmically" (CH 306). Second, God's rhetorical questions remind Job of his creaturely status. The awesome power of the Whirlwind is not, however, a mere show of brute force, or a threat that Job will be punished. Hartshorne interprets God's speech to mean that the mystery is divine power, not divine justice. Job is shown that he has little to no understanding of what it is to wield power over the cosmos. Finally, there is no hint of appeal to a heavenly afterlife as compensation for Job's suffering. "Job worships and serves God because God is worthy of worship and service, not because of any future rewards, on earth or in heaven" (IO 73). In Hartshorne's view, what modern philosophy can add to the solution of Job's problem is the idea that power, even divine power, is necessarily power over other beings that retain some power of their own (CS 271).

The prologue to the book of Job mentions the Adversary (*ha-satan*) who is permitted by God to cause all manner of suffering to his servant Job. As far as the argument of the book is concerned, this character is a mere literary device, for Job is *never* made privy to the argument in the heavenly courts. Moreover, the evils that befall Job befall a great many people, and it is implausible to argue—especially based on the book of Job—that a single being is behind all of this mischief; the idea of the devil as a cosmic rival to God is from a later era, given further emphasis by the imagination of some Christians. The point of the book of Job is not to explain evil by the Adversary's activity but, in large part, to deny that suffering is punishment for sin.[76] Arguably, this is also the message of Jesus when discussing Pilate's murder of some Galileans and the people on whom the Tower of Siloam fell (Lk 13:1–5). It is worth mentioning that Hartshorne made no appeal in his own answer to the problem of evil to supernatural entities within the universe such as angels or demons. He showed as much interest in them as he did in fairies—to wit, none. Thus, his only references to Satan are as a literary figure, not as a real person.[77] In any event, the existence of angels or demons would not alter Hartshorne's claim that suffering is the inevitable result of multiple freedom. A supernatural realm of spirits would only add an additional layer—hard to justify—of free beings with which to contend.

To grant the insights of the book of Job (as Hartshorne interprets it) or to grant that the two versions of the problem of evil do not undermine neoclassical metaphysics, still leaves the question of God's role vis-à-vis suffering and injustice. The facts that generate the problem of evil do not go away because one successfully rebuts a philosophical argument. Hartshorne claims that his theology makes better sense of "God is love" than its competitors, yet, there is a great deal of suffering that is undeserved, pointless, and widespread. Evolutionary theory adds another dimension. Entire ecosystems and countless species have come and gone in the course of geologic time. Throughout this history, creatures compete for the goods that will insure their survival and very often live at each other's expense. Nature seems entirely indifferent to comparative values; as John B. Cobb Jr. notes, "lower" species thrive at the expense of "higher" species as when malarial mosquitoes feed on human beings.[78] Finally, there is what Marilyn McCord Adams calls *horrendous evils,* evils that are so pernicious that they give reason to doubt that the person's life could be a great good to him or her on the whole.[79] Hartshorne claims that a loving God is a necessary and indispensable character in this drama. One may ask whether this is plausible, but one must also take care not to permit the presuppositions of classical theism to color one's judgment. Hartshorne counsels to be suspicious of the question whether our world is the sort that one would expect from an almighty and all-loving creator. In the context of dipolar theism, and remembering the lessons of Job, the question must be rephrased: Is this the sort of world that one would expect of a deity that is perfect in power and love that *presides over a world composed of beings, each of which exercises some degree of creativity?*

If Hartshorne is correct, God accounts for order on a cosmic scale. There must be, however, two aspects to this activity which are distinguishable but not separable. On the one hand, there is the ordering activity that establishes the cosmic order *per se,* making possible all non-divine forms of freedom in dynamic singulars. On the other hand, there is the ordering activity that lures each localized being towards greater intensity of experience. Hartshorne holds that both aspects of God's creative ordering of the world follow aesthetic principles. According to these principles, as expressed in Hartshorne's circle diagram, the double extremes between which the divine ordering power operates are (1) unqualified unity and unqualified diversity (or chaos) and (2) ultra-complexity and ultra-simplicity (or triviality). The mere fact of an ordered cosmos does not automatically avoid the aesthetic defects of being overly chaotic or trivial. Avoidance of these extremes requires a *cumulative developmental process,* which requirement is implicit in Hartshorne's cumulative view of process. According to Hartshorne, "the explanation for the contingent must be a genetic one" (IO 82). It could not be everlastingly true that there have been elephants or seahorses. Because the process is cumulative, it must also be developmental. For example, an elephant is not created *de novo* from a mixture of atoms and molecules; it requires a lengthy process of species development. This is why Hartshorne claimed that the general idea of evolution is derivable from his metaphysical principles (OO 83).

God's role in the economy of nature is not simply maintaining cosmic order, but also eliciting higher forms of order, making possible forms of experience with greater levels of unity in diversity. A law of axiology as firm as any law of nature discovered by science is that varying levels of creative experiencing are necessarily correlated with varying levels of what can be achieved in the way of value. For example, as complex and emotionally rich as a dog's interior life may be, it is not sufficient to produce scientific theorizing or high artistic accomplishment. A corollary of the foregoing is that varying levels of creativity exhibit varying levels of opportunity and risk. For instance, one cannot be ironic with a dog. Irony may amuse or offend only if one's audience is equipped to understand it. As goes creative experiencing, so goes freedom. The cost of actual or possible achievement is the risk of failure. This analysis is evident in the few comments that Hartshorne made about sin. In a 1944 symposium on world peace, Hartshorne said that much can be learned from Reinhold Niebuhr that sin is not a struggle between "lower" (bodily) and "higher" (spiritual) aspects of personality; rather it is a perversion of what is highest in a person, one's sense of the divine: it is the claim *to be divine,* "a rebellion against our humble station in the universe."[80] This idolatry comes in many forms, religious and nonreligious, in the pernicious claims to infallibility or any attempt to place ultimate worth in something less than deity. As far as our experience goes, these are the highest and most tragic manifestations of the general principle that greater degrees of freedom are necessarily accompanied by greater possibilities of its abuse.

Hartshorne agrees that the world is better to the extent that sin, and the suffering it brings in its wake, is not part of it. It does not follow, however, that the world is better to the extent that the *possibility of sin* is excluded from it. The conditions for the possibility of good or evil are the same: freedom. Indeed, Hartshorne maintained that some degree of evil is inevitable if good is to be possible. It is true that the particular evils that occur are not inevitable. Knowing this, we imagine that the cosmos could be altogether free of the blemish of evil, but this is to imagine an ideal that no single individual could bring about; alternately, it is to imagine a cosmos with slight to minimal opportunity for value achievement, where the evolutionary ascent to higher order freedom never occurs. The latter alternative is an example of aesthetic failure, a decidedly "boring" universe. One might agree with these points but ask, with Hartshorne, whether there is more possibility of evil than might be expected from an all-loving cosmic designer. Hartshorne spoke of human beings as the "bullies of the planet," heedless of the welfare of other creatures, cruel to our own kind, and too often lacking the will to prevent such cruelty (ZF 222). He asked whether the seemingly unbridgeable distances between the earth and other solar systems might be a providential arrangement (ZF 214). He allows himself an expression of doubt as to whether the "perilous experiment" of creatures free of instinctive guidance was too dangerous. He said that if he played at criticizing God, it would be at this point, but he also said that he accepted on faith the infallible wisdom and ideal power of God (OO 126). Hartshorne denies that limited intellects are in a position to know whether there is too much risk of evil in the world, for such a judgment must include a potentially infinite future (WM 86–87). He also stressed that the justification of the world is in the world, that is to say, in the open-ended adventure of life itself that God's creativity insures.

The issue of God's decision to engage in the "perilous experiment" of aiming the natural universe toward a biosphere that contains complex creatures like human animals endowed with immense destructive as well as constructive power is indeed a difficult aspect of the problem of evil from a process perspective. There are, however, some considerations that, as far as the authors are aware, have been little discussed and certainly little emphasized, which make an enormous difference to the question of "indicting" God. It should be recalled that, assuming Hartshorne's psychicalism and theory of God's attributes, God possesses an omniscience to be defined in terms of eminent feeling, and this entails that God eminently enjoys any and all aesthetic achievement but also *eminently feels any and all suffering*. Thus, perhaps paradoxically, *God suffers most*. Now, in making the decision to bring forth a complex biosphere of cognitively developed organisms, God well knew the high order propensities for and thus high order probability of holocausts that not only the creatures, but also *God*, would experience, as no other individual could experience, in all their horrific detail. In an important sense, then, the choice of the perilous experiment was a choice for self-sacrifice (albeit, not existential self-sacrifice). This self-sacrifice would be part and parcel of the cost of producing the stupendous beauty and value of the cosmos.

Now, it occurs to us that there are analogies to be drawn from human experience that involve moral intuitions that shed light on this perilous aspect of the theodicy issue. We are thinking of situations where, say, a strong warrior-leader, who is well aware of impending dangers probably to be suffered by many, will knowingly go to the very front of the battle, ferociously throwing himself/herself into the heaviest fighting and conceivably will suffer more than the other men or warrior women. Also suppose that much is at stake in the battle: engaging the fight and winning will mean freedom from tyranny and an era of peace and great prosperity. We are reminded concretely of such a situation in Jeff Shaara's gripping historical novel about the American Revolution. Shaara depicts the arguments between, on the one hand, the loyalists who wished to avoid war at virtually any cost and constantly admonish about the great horrors of war and, on the other hand, the radical "sons of liberty" and later framers of independence and a new constitution who are willing to pay the cost of rebellion to make a free nation ripe with adventurous promise.[81] These arguments are somewhat analogous to the decision landscape of God's "perilous experiment." In Shaara's follow-up history George Washington is portrayed as a leader largely without ego who suffers the very vicissitudes of his comrades at arms and charges into the midst of British fire (sometimes to the shock of his own troops—an apparent historical fact rather than mere hagiography), all done with an iron-fisted determination to bring the possibilities of a great nation into being.[82] This is weakly analogous to the God of neoclassical process theism in the divine decision to risk "building the Kingdom of God" along with the sometimes halting cooperation of partially free creatures.

Of course, there are disanalogies here as well. Washington, as a human being, could not suffer literally *all* of the vicissitudes of his troops in the metaphysical sense imputed of God, nor was Washington solely responsible for making the decision to engage in war. Yet there are aspects of the cosmic situation on Hartshorne's account—its risk and inevitable tragedy and knowing self-sacrifice—that are echoed in the original American historical drama. The analogy strongly suggests to us that the question of the moral indictment of the neoclassical God is *radically different* from the case of any deity who, as unilaterally omnipotent, purportedly could avoid all risks of horror and who would be, under any condition, *apathos*, beyond suffering, in patristic theologian Origen's famous expression. We ask then: Should John Adams, Benjamin Franklin, George Washington and others on their side of the debate—all of them knowingly and willingly placed in harm's way—be indicted for the great pain of the Revolutionary War, a war that also made possible the greatness of America (in so far as it has achieved greatness alongside its enormous failings and injuries)? At the very least an affirmative answer to this question is by no means obvious, and seems to us to be negative, although we can certainly fathom disagreement. The question of a moral indictment for God's decision to undertake the perilous experiment is analogous.

We noted in the previous chapter that Hartshorne characterizes religion as the acceptance of our fragmentariness (WM Ch. VI). We are fragmentary both in the sense that we are limited in space and time (i.e., we are localized) and in the sense that our capacities for knowledge and goodness are limited (i.e., we are imperfect). If panentheism is correct, we are also fragmentary in the sense that we are part of the divine being-in-becoming. In Hartshorne's panentheism, as we have seen, God includes all but does not determine all, somewhat as a person includes the cells of his or her body without being able to decide the details of their activity. Thus, what we do makes a difference in and to God in the sense that we can enhance or diminish in admittedly limited ways the divine enjoyment of the world—hence, the concept of tragedy in

God mentioned previously and God's own involvement in the "perilous experiment." We have also seen, in the moral argument, that Hartshorne regarded the aim of consciously contributing to the divine life as the highest purpose to which we can aspire. He says, "God's possession of us is our final achievement, not our possession of God" (WM 90). Every creature that has ever existed—all that it has been or accomplished— became part of the inexhaustible memory of God and every creature that ever will exist is destined to be so remembered. In Plato's *Symposium,* Socrates, reporting the views of Diotima, speaks of immortality as the achievement of doing acts worthy of being remembered by future generations. Hartshorne offers a similar kind of immortality except that the fallible and mortal memory of future generations is replaced by the infallible and unending memory of God.[83]

A Hartshornean theodicy does not allow one to say that everything, or every evil, happens for a reason. There is no cure for the fact that the "lower" sometimes lives at the expense of the "higher" and that horrendous evils are part of this universe. On the other hand, a Hartshornean theodicy allows one to say that anything that happens, or any evil that occurs, can become part of a reason for striving to overcome evil with good thereby depriving evil of its capacity to dishearten us. The true depth of divine power, on Hartshorne's view, is not God's ability to manipulate events to the best possible outcome, but to be able to bear the suffering of the creatures without being overcome by it. God is forever seeking ways to bring good from the world no matter how bad things may get. The world weariness that sometimes overcomes the creatures never overcomes deity. In the language of William James, Hartshorne's God is neither a pessimist (thinking that things cannot get better) nor an optimist (thinking that things are for the best), but a kind of *cosmic meliorist* (thinking that things can get better). This theology may console in at least two ways. To those who are helpless and who suffer, Hartshorne claims that there is a divine co-sufferer. To those who are not helpless and who work for the welfare of others, Hartshorne maintains that they are indeed working on the side of the cosmos itself, as co-workers *with* God. This is what Pierre Teilhard de Chardin called "building the earth."[84] In this way, Hartshorne's theism promotes a resilient spirit in the face of defeat, hope that may conquer despair, and love that holds the promise of harnessing evil.

Conclusion

Hartshorne clearly rejected rigidly nonrational acceptance or rejection of God's existence. The theistic question, he said, "should not be answered dogmatically" (CH 244). However, where theistic arguments are concerned, he attempted to navigate between the extremes of a simple fideism and traditional foundationalism. According to the former, all argument for or against the existence of God is unavailing and what is called for is a leap of faith. According to the latter, the existence of God can be rationally accepted if and only if the divine existence is self-evident or if there is a compelling argument that God exists. Hartshorne wrote:

> I have no quarrel with those who believe in God without making use of arguments to do so. I do hope, however, they will examine carefully just what notion of God they entertain. I also think it important that there be reasonable grounds for religious belief since the fact, if it could be a fact, that all possible arguments for belief are fallacious would be, for some, a cogent argument *against* belief. (CH 288)

Hartshorne apparently saw nothing epistemically suspect or morally pernicious in simple faith in God. But even simple faith may be confronted with what Alvin Plantinga calls *defeaters*, reasons to question one's faith. Hartshorne found these defeaters in the concept of a non-relational God that so many philosophers and theologians of the past advocated, and he considered this idea of God as *defeated*. Simple lack of faith in God may also be challenged by the concept of God. As we shall see in the following chapter, failure to take note of the most sophisticated concepts of God can be a source of atheism.

The role played in Hartshorne's global argument by the concept of God is central and is best brought out by the ontological or modal argument: if it is possible for God to exist, God cannot fail to exist and if it is possible for God not to exist, God cannot possibly exist. The issue is not one of empirical investigation but of the very architecture of existence. The various elements of the global argument are meant to highlight the advantages of Hartshorne's neoclassical understanding of that widest structure of existence. Because the "proofs" are presented as lists of options in a matrix, there is no question of arm-twisting logic in favor of dipolar theism, but only of the rational cost of denying it, which Hartshorne viewed as excessive. In no case, however, did Hartshorne advocate that belief in God is no more than a question of rational argument. His own metaphysics implies that there is a nondiscursive relation to deity, two-way prehensions between God and the creatures. He spoke of "the challenge of mysticism," which is to say, the challenge to be open to *feeling the divine* and not merely *thinking* it. But, after all, Hartshorne's project was metaphysics—though it is not the whole of life, it is not to be ignored. We conclude with Hartshorne's own concluding statement on the question of mysticism and reason: "Possibly we need to devote more time to meditation and less (though at present it is no vast amount) to rationalistic metaphysics."[85]

Chapter Six Appendix: Hartshorne's Ontological Argument and Continental Doctrines of "Nothingness"

The topics of non-being and negation have been a central concern to philosophers since the time of Parmenides and Plato's *The Sophist*. Likewise, Jewish and Christian theologians learned in Greek philosophical literature were most occupied by such topics, especially as they related to the concept of God; Augustine's meditations on non-being and evil come to mind immediately as an example. This preoccupation has continued in the discourse of certain contemporary Continental thinkers, in particular, theologians Karl Barth, Nicholas Berdyaev, Paul Tillich, and Jurgen Moltmann. Martin Heidegger, who in varying degrees influenced all these theologians, also had much to say about "the Nothing," non-being, and negation. And Jean-Paul Sartre famously made striking claims about the status of non-being and its relation to imagination and human freedom. Indeed, Sartre's concept of "neantizing" has prompted one reviewer of Hartshorne's ontological argument (as presented in *The Logic of Perfection*) to notice that a mere logical possibility unmoored in real possibility would be like a Sartrean "hole," a neantizing realization of absolute non-being, that would deconstruct Hartshorne's thoroughly positive universe, and thus defeat Hartshorne's argument.[86] This observation appears to us to be correct. Indeed, the deepest implication of Hartshorne's principle of positivity discussed in Chapter Three is that the notion of absolute non-being is incoherent and its very *possibility* is precluded; this implies that "necessarily, something exists." As Kant saw with clarity in the Transcendental Dialectic, it is this proposition, purportedly to be established by the ontological argument for a Necessary Being, that the other theistic arguments logically require; thus, like a "domino effect," if this proposition is to be rejected, the other arguments fall.

All of this raises the question about the exact status of contemporary Continental doctrines of "nothingness" that have played such a pronounced role in the resultant ontologies of such thinkers. Are these doctrines intelligible, and do they accomplish legitimate intellectual work? In effect, is Hartshorne's ontological argument threatened by any Continental conceptions of nonbeing? While Hartshorne discussed some of these doctrines as found in Berdyaev, Tillich, Heidegger and Sartre, he did not touch upon Moltmann or this aspect of Barthian thought. The discussions he did provide are scattered throughout his corpus, and to our knowledge no account in the critical Hartshorne literature has brought all these matters together in a unified and systematic way as we attempt to do here.

In order to make discussion of the issues clear, we should first introduce some important terminology concerning nonbeing as presented by Paul Tillich. Tillich writes the following:

> The mystery of nonbeing demands a dialectical approach. The genius of the Greek language has provided a possibility of distinguishing the dialectical concept of nonbeing from the non-dialectical by calling the first *me on* and the second *ouk on. Ouk on* is the "nothing" which has no relation at all to being; *me on* is the "nothing" which has a dialectical relation to being.[87]

After attempting to sketch how the dialectical concept of nonbeing is inevitable in the history of Christian thought, Tillich then writes these incisive sentences: "Being, limited by nonbeing, is finitude. Nonbeing [as *me on*] appears as the 'not yet' of being and as the 'no more' of being."[88] The dialectical conception of non-being thus exhibits what we might call two ontological poles or aspects—the aspect of the "not yet" and the aspect of the "no more." Tillich's distinction between the notion of dialectical *meontic* nonbeing and non-dialectical *oukontic* nonbeing seems to have a direct correspondence in what Hartshorne calls "relative non-being" and "absolute non-being" respectively (see IO, Chs. 27 and 28). What Hartshorne's "necessarily, something exists" seems to preclude is non-dialectical *oukontic* nonbeing as a "state" of the universe at any juncture in its history. On the other hand, relative non-being is acceptable to Hartshorne. Most famously perhaps, *meontic* nonbeing as a fundamental ontological concept is embraced in the philosophy of Russian Christian "existentialist" philosopher Nicholas Berdyaev, whom Hartshorne often applauded as insightful. As Hartshorne notes, Berdyaev's key concept of metaphysical "freedom" is described as "'not-being', which is yet distinguished from sheer nothing" (WP 186f). Hartshorne also claims that the "interchangeability" of Berdyaev's concept of freedom and Whitehead's concept of creativity "is not difficult to establish" for both thinkers (WP 185). Thus, Berdyaev's meontic nonbeing is to be correlated with Hartshorne's concept of creativity.[89]

Now, as mentioned earlier, the concept of nothingness plays an important role in the theology of Jurgen Moltmann. He appears to assert that "nothingness" is a condition created by God in a willful act of "withdrawing the divine presence." (In a somewhat related way, Berdyaev speaks of Metaphysical Hell as the absence of the divine presence, but this is a condition willed by finite creatures rather than deity.) This "withdrawing" creates a sort of void that is a *potency*, in fact a demonic potency, which is ultimately "overcome" by God.[90] Conceptualized as a potency, it would seem that Moltmann's "nothingness" is in fact *meontic* in character and does not invoke the concept of absolute nonbeing as it has "nothing to do with the beings." While *meontic* in character, this concept differs from Berdyaev's in that, as a source of the demonic, nothingness stands in stark opposition to God and figures importantly into God's salvific activity (Berdyaev's *me on* is ground for creative good and evil). In the aspect of demonic potency at least, Moltmann's nothingness more resembles Barth's conceptions.

Karl Barth, on the other hand, presents a most complex, conceptually difficult and challenging discourse on "nothingness" (*das Nichtige*) in his weighty *Church Dogmatics*.[91] His position is difficult to interpret precisely because, in the interest of respecting the radical otherness of God, he quite consciously rejects standard criteria for consistency and rationality. Thus, Barth rejects not only the concept of natural theology (recall his famous protest to natural theologians—"Nein!"), but even the concept of systematic theology, as he holds that our reason is profoundly corrupt, and theology itself is necessarily "broken." Rational consistency fails us, and theological discourse breaks down precisely where it must take seriously the concept of *das Nichtige*. Authentic theological thinking can only take place, then, in a piecemeal fashion as directed by an encounter with the Word in Scripture that is accessible only to "the theologian under grace." Not surprisingly, there appear to be multiple strands to Barth's doctrine of nothingness that are not consistent with one another, and he unabashedly affirms the modal contradiction that "nothingness" is an "impossible possibility" (III/3, 351).[92] Despite this ontological contradiction, he insists that nothingness is real, and it is so *sui generis* (III/3, 352). It was not properly created or willed by God, because God properly creates and wills only beings. Nothingness thus has the "impossible" being of non-being, "the existence of that which does not exist" (III/3, 77). Since only God and finite creatures created by God properly exist, nothingness "exists" in an absurd way; Barth refers to this ontological condition of nonbeing as a mysterious and alien "third way" of being (III/3, 349).

Although this is not the whole story, *these* qualifications of non-being appear to amount to a radical affirmation, *contra* Hartshorne, of the reality of non-being in the absolute *oukontic* sense. Moreover, standing in tension with Tillich's declaration that *ouk on* can have no relation to the beings, Barth nonetheless sees *das Nichtige*, with Heidegger, as a source of human angst and dread, but also as taking the forms of absolute chaos, real sin, real death, real evil, the demonic, and hell, but chiefly the form of human sin (III/3, 74, 300, 305, 310). All of these forms in which *das Nichtige* can be expressed are united by the leitmotif that they are the anti-thesis of God's grace (III/3, 331f). Sounding almost Leibnizian, Barth sometimes speaks of "nothingness" as the infinite number of rejected possibilities that God passes over as they had no good reason to be willed by God (III/3, 77). Thus, despite Barth's characterizations of nothingess as *oukontic*, "as that which does not exist," he also seems to treat nothingness as a demonic potency as does Moltmann, and thus as *meontic*. To make matters more confusing, at least from the standpoint of a rational philosophical perspective, unlike Moltmann, Barth rejects the notion that God creates nothingness, and yet nonetheless, for Barth, God is the ontological source of nothingness in the indirect sense that God's very rejection or "non-willing" of non-being somehow mysteriously actualizes non-being; this act of non-willing actualization ultimately subsumes *das Nichtige* under the Lordship of deity and thus dismisses Barth from any charge of Manicheanism.

The above broad description of Barth's ontology of nothingness does not represent the whole of his doctrine, however, as this is the narrative only in abstraction from the Christ event. Given the saving activity of Jesus Christ—the Incarnation, Crucifixion and Resurrection—the grace of God that worked through this activity has completely "overcome" *das Nichtige* so that it "no longer exists"! "Evil" in *all* its forms has now been completely "overcome" by God's gracious activity in Jesus Christ (see the discussion of God's "alien work," III/3, 359–67). Everything, just as it is, is now exactly right in the light of Christ. In direct opposition to the bleak cynicism of modern secular culture, the optimism of certain seventeenth and eighteenth- century philosophers and poets—Leibniz, Wolff, and Alexander Pope—is ultimately, and perhaps shockingly, correct. In the final analysis, the "theologian under grace" must deliver the deepest meaning of Scripture, the radical meaning of the Christian "good news," namely, that there is no theoretical "problem of evil" because after Christ there is now no genuine evil.

Adjudicating all that has been said above regarding Barth from a neoclassical perspective is a very complex matter that, of course, we simply cannot accomplish here, but some matters are to us clear enough.[93] While Hartshorne appreciates certain aspects of Barth's thought—in particular, his concept of a unique "divine time" (NT 126) and the insightful discussion of Anselm in Barth's operculum *Fides Quarens Intellectum* (AD 11, 13, 238, 261, 283)— Hartshorne's critical rationalist/ deep empiricist perspective and Barth's notions of the perversity of reason, his "theological positivism" and closed perspective of the "theologian under grace" are irreconcilable epistemological orientations. From Hartshorne's perspective, Barth's discourse on nothingness is thoroughly ambiguous, tacitly shifting as it does between *oukontic* and *meontic* characterizations of non-being. More importantly, Barth's view is simply absurd (as Barth openly admits) in its embrace of bald contradictions and unintelligible notions of "non-willing as actualization of non-being" and of an ontological shift from "non-being as existent" to "non-being as non-existent." One wonders if this discourse is to be taken literally at all, but Barth claims not to be inventing some sort of theological allegory or delivering a religious poetics, but is rather describing "objective reality" as it is addressed in Scripture. Ironically in Barth's case, however, it is hard to see this ontology of nothingness as anything other than the product of a very active speculative theological imagination; importantly, the biblical grounding for such notions hardly seems obvious or clear. Indeed, a number of biblical scholars reject Barth's claims that these views have Scriptural credentials.[94]

Heidegger's talk about "the Nothing" in such works as *Was ist Metaphysik?* has also been interpreted as invoking the reality of absolute nothingness; in fact, Hartshorne seems to have read Heidegger in just this way (IO 328–29). However, despite some passages that, on the surface at least, seem to lend support to this interpretation, it is unlikely that this is Heidegger's meaning.[95] For Heidegger was moved to correct the "nihilistic impressions" created by his talk about "the Nothing" by making it clear, in a Preface expressly written for the 4th edition of *Was ist Metaphysik?,* that his talk about Nothing and negation is not to be equated with the "facile" notion of *das Wesenlose* or what is translated as "the merely nugatory" (*Existence and Being,* 46). Literally parsed, *das*

Wesenlose means "the essence-less" which, given Heidegger's equation of essence and potency, thus means the "potency-less." The clear obverse implication is that "the No-thing is potency." If this is correct, then it would make perfect sense for Heidegger to equate Being and the Nothing, as he does in fact.[96] What he seems to have in mind is that Being is No-thing, that is to say, as it were tautologically, Being is not a thing, an ontic entity in space and time alongside other ontic entities; yet as Heidegger also says repeatedly, "Being is always in the beings." In the light of this interpretation, Heidegger's otherwise strange and syntactically awkward expression that "the Nothing is being-er (*seinender*) than the beings" makes complete sense. Given this reading, Heidegger's view of nonbeing can be coherently accommodated by Whitehead and Hartshorne's notion of creativity, which is also ontological potency or appetition to being that is not an ontic entity in space and time, and yet is always in the beings, *in* the actualities.

Heidegger's talk of nothingness invites comparisons with Buddhist ontologies, especially the key Buddhist conception of *sunyatta* or "emptiness." Reportedly, Heidegger once said after reading Japanese thinker D. T. Suzuki, well-known for his "ontology of zero," that if he understood Suzuki correctly, then such Buddhist views express "everything I have been trying to say." But some may well wonder whether *sunyatta* should be considered the chief and perhaps most obvious example of positing the reality of *oukontic* non-being. While interpretation of this central concept of Buddhism has a long and vexed history, it is certainly arguable, and many Buddhist thinkers themselves appear to hold, that *sunyatta* ought not to be given an absolutist, nihilistic interpretation. A case in point is the position argued by Japanese Buddhist philosopher Takeo Tanaka in a now classic essay.[97] Tanaka focuses attention on the work of Nishida Kitaro, founder of the so-called Kyoto School, who is often regarded as the most important Zen Buddhist philosopher of the twentieth century. Tanaka insists that Nishida's philosophy, although it employs the explicit terminology of *sunyatta* as "absolute nothingness," is not "nihilistic," adding immediately in this context that Buddhists "want to share the Whiteheadian 'principle of relativity'" (the principle that every being is potential for every becoming).[98] If this is so, it is hard to see how Nishida's nothingness is *oukontic* if "it" has relationality to all entities, that is, since non-dialectical *ouk on* in the primal Greek sense "has no relation to beings." Rather, Nishida's nothingness is identified as the "All in One," an "infinite sphere," a standpoint that is nowhere and yet everywhere, the "absolute present" through which all entities are mediated. Tanaka even correlates this concept of nothingness with God. "In a sense, God is Nothing. God is not a thing that belongs to this or that."[99] However, what Whitehead calls the Ontological Principle is required for Nishida's conceptuality; further Tanaka contends that, for Nishida, Whitehead's categories of creativity, the one and the many, are also accorded ultimate ontological status. Importantly, given his advocacy of *meontic* nonbeing as ground, Nicholas Berdyaev is referenced explicitly by Nishida as a most congenial Western thinker even if, according to Nishida, Berdyaev "does not get beyond the limits of [Jacob] Boehme's mysticism."[100]

In his reply to Tanaka, John Cobb makes the interesting suggestion that Nishida's absolute nothingness probably best correlates with (although it is not identical to) Whitehead's extensive continuum rather than with the concept of God.[101] Yet even if this is so, nothingness taken as characterizable by the extensive continuum cannot exist untethered from actuality and real potency given Tanaka's description of Nishida as invoking the Ontological Principle; that is to say, the continuum (like Nishida's absolute nothingness) as that which "lacking any standpoint of its own, both provides all standpoints and establishes the relativity of all that actualizes those standpoints" cannot exist in abstraction from the demands of the Principle; as such nothingness must always "mediate" *something* actual. In the light of all the above characterizations, it would seem to make more sense to understand the qualification "absolute" in the terminology "absolute nothingness" as signifying more precisely "that which is absolutely empty of ontic content." We conclude that whether correlated with God or with the extensive continuum, Tanaka's account of Nishida's absolute nothingness seems very difficult to square with a non-dialectical *oukontic* interpretation. Thus, a deeper reading of both Heidegger and Nishida strongly suggests that, in neither case is their talk of nothingness truly nihilistic, concerned with "merely the nuggatory."

Lastly, we consider the case of Jean-Paul Sartre's thought-experiments with neantizing as analogical significations of absolute nonbeing. Sartre's doctrine of negation is central to the existentialist-phenomenological ontology of his classic *L'être et le néant*. Sartre also attempts to "signify" absolute nonbeing in his study of aesthetic objects in *L'imaginaire*. We will examine both sources.

Sartre maintains that consciousness is necessarily self-constituting, and it is this feature which distinguishes it from the physical world, the domain of *l'être en-soi*. This doctrine of self-constitution stems in part from Sartre's thinking through the implications of Husserl's doctrine of *Intentionalitat* or "intentionality." In Husserl, intentionality is an absolute in the sense that it is something that refers to nothing outside itself. Moreover, Sartre contends, such self-constitution is required in order to defend a thoroughly libertarian and radical "Kierkegaardian" existential freedom, for which there is (purported) warrant in his (Sartre's) phenomenological descriptions of the quirky, contingent, random, and even "monstrous" character of consciousness. Sartre thus resists all efforts at causal theories of consciousness such as those found in Freud's account of unconscious motivations (for Sartre, Freud's account involves the incoherent idea of an "unconscious conscious state"), and neuro-physical accounts (for Sartre, such accounts only succeed in correlating "locations for subjectivity" with subjectivity, and can never be ontological reductions). Our interest here is not whether these notions regarding causal independence are defensible (with Hartshorne and other process philosophers, we do not think they are for a host of reasons); our interest, rather, is in another central feature of Sartre's insistence on the self-constitution of consciousness—the inherent capacity of the "not" in reflexive self-consciousness.

The ontological domain of *l'être en-soi* conforms straightforwardly to the canons of classical logic: physical being-in-the-world simply and tautologically "is what it is," while the ontological domain of *l'être pour-soi* conforms to a different logic, since there are appropriate senses in which entities of the *pour-soi* type, "are what they are not and are not what they are." [102] On the surface, this seems to be a bold violation of non-contradiction, which if allowed to stand as contradictory would deconstruct Sartre's own numerous *reductio ad absurdum* arguments which appeal to non-contradiction (e.g., his argument against Freud, his "phenomenological-ontological disproof" of the existence of God, his arguments on the incoherence of the traditional psychology of imagery, etc.). A more careful reading, however, shows that this is not Sartre's intention, for he makes appropriate distinctions that relieve the appearance of contradiction. In fact, his phenomenological point has a certain structural parallel with Whitehead's notion of the "fallacy of simple location." For the self-conscious *pour-soi* there is an object of consciousness that *as object* is non-identical to the self, and a self which is non-identical *as self* to the object of consciousness. Hartshorne agrees as he says explicitly that consciousness is always consciousness of an object that is not identical to the act of consciousness (IO 275). Thus, negation is integral to the very definition of *l'être pour soi*. Negations, then, are not properties of things-in-themselves, but come into the picture as involving an almost Kantian category whose justification resides in the fact that the self-conscious structure of consciousness necessarily involves negation.

Sartre states his position in language that approaches the *oukontic,* especially in its capitalization of nothingness: *"... the being by which nothingness comes to the world must be its own nothingness."*[103] Thus, negation goes to the very core of Sartre's idea of self-consciousness, which logically involves at once a notion of self-nihilation, an idea that is intimately connected to Sartre's phenomenology of imagination. Indeed, imagination is a privileged aspect of consciousness in Sartre's theory as it is so closely tied to his notion of human freedom. If I am truly self-reflexively conscious, I can always imagine a "not" with respect to any choices I may confront in an existential situation. To use Sartre's dramatic example, one is just as free in a concentration camp as one is outside the camp, because one can always say "no" to the choices presented in the "factical situation": I can say "no" to the Nazis and simply charge the gates risking my death. Or I can refuse this choice and take responsibility for living inside the camp.

Hartshorne notices that Sartre's doctrine of nothingness is not Heidegger's; indeed, it lacks such Heideggerian characterizations of nothingness as "identity with Being" or with *meontic* potency, as found in the previous interpretation. Instead, Sartre wants to suggest a radical notion of neantizing that *intends* absolute nonbeing. Phenomenological thought-experiments with neantizing acts of imagination can, in Hartshorne's description, "somehow [help] us to grasp the idea of absolute non-being," although falling short (IO 328). But on close analysis, Sartre's sample thought-experiments either (1) tacitly re-confirm Henri Bergson's demonstrations of the dissolution of neantizing into cases of relative non-being or "othering," or (2) deconstruct themselves as they involve tacit reference to existence, while at the same time verbally denying existence.

Consider, for instance, Sartre's famous scenario of a feigned visit to a restaurant. I have an expectation of meeting my friend at the restaurant, and thus, my imagination projects "the world with my friend at the restaurant." When I arrive at the restaurant, my imaginative act is broken by the absence of my friend. My friend is *not* there. Sartre claims that this is purely vacuous as "my friend of the imagined scenario" is purely absent. My friend is not partly there or sortally there, but completely absent, *nihil absolutum*. This imaginative act is taken to signify the concept of absolute nonbeing. How does it so signify? Presumably, the signification would be achieved by means of the generalization of the neantizing through a plenitude of "imaginative variations" (to use Husserl's vocabulary). But this simply and precisely falls back into Bergson's "false problem of non-being." For it is hard to see phenomenologically how this in any way involves more than comparisons of content-filled possible worlds, and issues only in what Gilles Deleuze has characterized as *différence* or as what Hartshorne envisions as "positive incompossibilities," that is, a selection of one contingent alternative among others as they cannot be actualized conjunctively. The imaginative variations involve only the comparison of, say, possible scenario A—my expected friend Marsha at Rue Descartes Café occupying spatial sortal S during times t through t^*, and a *class* of possible scenarios B—Rue Descartes Café during time t through t^* with my friend Joseph or with the presence of the waiter or with air molecules occupying spatial sortal S, etc. As Hartshorne again observes, we think correctly, this backhanded or tacit appeal to an essentially Bergsonian thought-experiment, which really reaches "the opposite conclusion" from what Sartre wants, is simply an "oddity" (10 328).

In *L'imaginaire*, Sartre goes into detailed examinations of works of art, and argues that they are "unreal" in what is verbally presented as a very strong sense of unreality (an English translation reproduced in a reader on Contemporary Aesthetics appropriately gives it the title "The Unreality of the Esthetic Object").[104] Sartre suggests that, while I listen to a symphony, the symphony as aesthetic object is "utterly absent," as it cannot be found in its dative performances or any of its properties as represented at a place in space and time. It is not even correct to say that there is any *analogia entis* with respect to the aesthetic object and its performances. In a startling passage, Sartre writes that to say that the symphony is heard through its dative analogues already assumes what he calls the "imaginative reduction" and that the symphony occurs as a "perpetual elsewhere, a perpetual absence."[105] He says that he is not suggesting that the art work is to be understood platonistically as if it existed outside of space and time: "It is not only outside of time and space—as are essences, for instance—it is outside of the real, outside of existence. I do not hear it actually, I listen to it in the imaginary."[106]

If we interpret this idea in the most starkly anti-realist terms, and Sartre may well have intended this to convey the *oukontic* or the *nihil absolutum*, it is internally incoherent. For, if the *nihil absolutum* is what is intended, there simply cannot be an "it" in the imaginary. This is radically unintelligible as a conceptual intention, since there could be no distinctions provided through Sartre's examples; there would be no criterion for determining whether he was actually discussing Beethoven's Seventh Symphony (his actual example) or Wagner's Valkyrie, for taken as *nihil absolutum* there can be no directed intentional "it" of the discourse. What Sartre succeeds in saying in fact is something quite different from this. He conceptually intends a radical break between the real as lived actuality and the domain of the imaginary, which is tied not to a Platonic heaven of essences, but to *the acts* of a temporalizing ego which access the imaginary. This conceptual intention conveys something quite different from the stark anti-realist interpretation, and as such does not suffer from the bewildering unintelligibility of any oblique references to *oukontic* nonbeing.

The underlying theory of the imagination in *L'imaginaire* perfectly fits the non-causal absoluteness of Sartre's conception of self-consciousness in *L'être et le néant*. His central argument is that the contents of the imagination go beyond the actual domain, as we just stated. He goes on to assert that a causal theory of the imagination would be unwarranted, because any actual causes would render actual effects, while the imaginary is precisely the domain of the non-actual. This argument is unconvincing, however, since it confuses the modal status of the contents of the imagination as non-actual with the notion that the capacity for imagination is *itself* non-actual, which Sartre, of course, does not presume. This is quite analogous in logical structure to saying that, because I am thinking *of* my dreams, I am therefore dreaming. So far as we can see, then, there is nothing in Sartre's phenomenological thought-experiments throughout his corpus which establishes any warranted analogies or clear significations of *oukontic* non-being.

As we see it, contemporary Continental doctrines of nonbeing either (1) invoke Berdyaev's intelligible notion of nonbeing as *meontic* potency coeval with process philosophy's notion of creativity (as in

Heidegger's case, or, as in Moltmann's case, *oukontic* nonbeing is not invoked), or (2) they have engaged in ambiguous, inconsistent, and unintelligible speculation (as in Barth's case), or (3) they have tacitly engaged in "othering," that is, while intending signification of absolute emptiness, they have engaged in comparisons of differently *content-filled* imaginative variations of possible worlds (as in Sartre's case). We conclude that nothing that is philosophically intelligible in this tradition countermands Hartshorne's central intuition about the unintelligibility of *sheer or absolute* nothingness in the primal Greek sense of *ouk on*.

SEVEN

Hartshorne and the
New Atheism

CHARLES HARTSHORNE died in 2000, just a few years before the new atheism became a cultural phenomenon. Arguably, Sam Harris's *The End of Faith*, published in 2004, launched the movement with its no-holds-barred attack on religion. Richard Dawkins's *The God Delusion*, published two years later, took the same strident tone as Harris, and lent the new atheism the star power of a famous scientist. Also at the forefront of the new atheism are Daniel Dennett and the late Christopher Hitchens. In an ironic inversion of biblical imagery, Harris, Dawkins, Dennett, and Hitchens gained notoriety as "the four horsemen" of the new atheism.[1] The new atheism gained momentum as others joined their ranks.[2] Hartshorne, for his part, was never one to ignore critics or those who held views contrary to his own, so it is of interest to know how he might have responded to the new atheists. It is not very difficult to guess at his possible responses for, in his day, he confronted skepticism about theism in a variety of thinkers: Carneades, Hume, Nietzsche, Schopenhauer, Russell, the Logical Positivists, Dewey, Freud, and Sartre. It is of interest that Hartshorne gave positive notice of an early article by Dawkins, but he never discussed Dawkins's views on religion in his publications (WM 147; ZF 135, 137).[3]

There is nothing particularly new in the works of the new atheists by way of arguments against theism and for atheism. They have, however, breathed new life into the critique of religion as being untrue and harmful. Of course, these were the themes running through much of Bertrand Russell's views on religion, and the new atheists are fond of repeating some of his examples and arguments. Many of the new atheists are inspired by an almost missionary zeal. They aspire to convert the world away from what they regard as the puerilities and barbarisms of religion—especially theistic religion—and to the sane judgment and moral balance that they believe science promotes. Dawkins says that he hopes that religious readers of *The God Delusion* follow the examples of Douglas Adams (author of *The Hitchhiker's Guide to the Galaxy*) and others who became atheists after reading Dawkins's earlier books.[4] All of the new atheists look to science as the best hope for a more civilized world. Some of them embrace the philosophy of *scientism,* the idea that science is the sole path to knowledge. They characterize religion as built on unreasoned faith, a faith that is the enemy of reason. Because of the vitriol with which many of the new atheists attack religion, it might be more accurate to call them *the new anti-theists.* It is no accident that the new atheism arose in the wake of the events of September 11, 2001. Dawkins ended one of his public addresses by explaining that the events of 9/11 had changed him; he said: "Let's stop being so damned respectful."[5] The new atheism also strikes a responsive chord in those who harbor serious misgivings about the value of religion and who have grown weary of being vilified by militant monotheists.

Hartshorne did not live to see 9/11, but he shared the new atheists's abhorrence of putting religion in the service of brutality, cruelty, and tribalism. He characterized the problem, however, as one of deeds rather than beliefs. In 1990 or 1991, Hartshorne wrote:

> We should, in serving God, not forget how much murder and torture have been committed and are now being committed by those employing the word "God" (or "Allah," or "Isvara," or "Brahma"). By their deeds, not their assertions or denials of theistic belief, we must primarily judge our human fellows.[6]

Hartshorne was sympathetic to some elements of Judaism, Christianity, and Buddhism, although he did not fully identify with any religion. The only church he supported in his adult life was Unitarian-Universalist.[7] He held that, "every religious tradition is shot through with human—all too human—error."[8] He believed that an element of intuitive judgment is inevitable in philosophy, but he was unwavering in his commitment to the sort of reasoned argument that seeks out the best in any position, including those with which one eventually disagrees. Hartshorne was critical of Russell, especially his popular writings on religion, for what he perceived to be a failure to engage with the best that theistic philosophers had to offer (BH 60-62 and ch. 13; RSP, ch. 13). In his last book he remarked, "Russell's attempts to poke fun at theologies are on the level not much above some 'village atheist,' and scarcely need refuting" (ZF 171).[9]

As to science, one would be hard pressed to find anyone more enthusiastic about it than Hartshorne. His professional work was often closely informed by science, as we have seen in his early work on sensation. We have also mentioned his contribution to the scientific study of birdsong. Hartshorne's admiration for great scientists, especially Darwin, is evident, and he was an ardent evolutionist throughout his life.[10] When Hartshorne was critical of scientists it was usually not for what he perceived as shortcomings in their scientific theories but in the philosophical opinions they sometimes venture.[11] Thus, he criticized both Darwin and Einstein for what he judged to be their adherence to a freedom-suppressing determinism. Like Whitehead, Peirce, and Bergson (but also Darwin and Einstein), he denied that science is equipped to answer every question of what is and is not true. In Hartshorne's words, "The prestige of science is misused if it is taken as establishing the universal competence of empirical methods" (CS xviii). In his last decade, Hartshorne wrote articles that were critical of the ideas about philosophical and religious topics espoused by Carl Sagan, Steven Weinberg, and E. O. Wilson, scientists whose specifically scientific accomplishments he praised.[12] He took a generally charitable view towards the nontheistic scientists he criticized: "I do not scorn nontheists (though I may find some of their arguments unimpressive) but I am glad that their special problems are not mine."[13]

Hartshorne's effort may well be the most sustained and informed of the twentieth century at constructing a philosophical theology closely attuned to the deliverances of science but whose guiding intuition was that God is love. While he did not gain the notoriety of the new atheists, his name is well-known in philosophy and some public intellectuals (like Carl Sagan and Martin Gardner) have been aware of his work. Also, he received modest public exposure, as in Greg Easterbrook's 1998 two-page interview for *U. S. News and World Report*.[14] Thus, it is unfortunate that the new atheists have heretofore ignored his work. One looks in vain for mention of Hartshorne in the works of Dawkins, Dennett, Harris, and Hitchens, and in most of the new atheist literature. This oversight is particularly ironic since the new atheists generally consider themselves to have surveyed the theological landscape with sufficient clarity and thoroughness to declare theism false beyond a reasonable doubt. Of course, theists disagree; indeed, some of the more philosophically informed atheists object to the strident tone of the new atheists.[15] For example, in his review of *The God Delusion,* James McBain says that the recurring problems in Dawkins's book are "raging bluster and bad arguments."[16] This is not to say that the new atheists are guilty of every philosophical failing of which they are accused, or that their arguments could not be buttressed by supplementary considerations and a more charitable exegesis.[17] There is no question, however, that Hartshorne would have been unimpressed with their rhetorical excesses and that he would have found their arguments a long way from convincing. It remains only to put Hartshorne in dialogue with the new atheists, if only retrospectively.

Fundamentalism

The form of theistic religion on which new atheists most often focus, and which they take as normative for theistic belief is fundamentalism, particularly fundamentalism in its most radical forms. Dennett is refreshingly free of this assumption, but too many of the new atheists have not learned from him.[18] They often take any divergence from fundamentalism as a dodge by more liberal theologians to avoid the consequences of their own system of beliefs. For example, Harris says, "Religious moderation is the product of secular *knowledge* and scriptural *ignorance*—it has no bona fides, in religious terms, to put it on a par with fundamentalism."[19] A. C. Grayling is equally strident:

> 'True' versions of these religions [Judaism, Christianity, Islam] are by their nature fundamentalist, while 'moderate' versions of religions are temporizations, the path from the latter to the former is short for anyone on whom the enthusiasms of faith take a grip.[20]

If Harris and Grayling are right, only fundamentalists truly understand their religion. To his credit, Dawkins can speak of "non-fundamentalist 'sensible' religion," but it is fundamentalist forms of belief that he usually targets; in addition, like Harris, he accuses moderate religious believers of "making the world safe for fundamentalism" by advocating "unquestioning faith" as a virtue.[21] Dawkins does not provide evidence for this claim, but in any case, it is easy to find evidence against it. The history of theology and philosophy is a treasure trove of examples of religious people who encourage the questioning of one's faith. What must be admitted is that moderate religious believers wish to keep the world safe *for the freedom to adopt what religious beliefs one chooses.* This Enlightenment ideal is included in the list of freedoms in the French Declaration of the Rights of Man and it heads the list in the American Bill of Rights. Among the new atheists, Harris is farthest removed from these ideals when he declares that "we can no more tolerate a diversity of religious beliefs than a diversity of beliefs about epidemiology and basic hygiene" and that lack of toleration may include killing people for their beliefs to defend their own lives.[22]

In one rather obvious sense, the dominant new atheist view of authentic religion turns history upside down. The word, "fundamentalism," as is well-known, had its origin in late nineteenth-century America when a group of Protestant Christians defined the "fundamentals" of Christian faith in terms of belief in the inerrancy of the Bible, the Virgin Birth of Jesus, the atoning death of Christ, Jesus's bodily resurrection, and the historical reality of the miracles of Jesus. Kathleen C. Boone notes that fundamentalist creeds, contrary to Christendom's classical creeds, place belief in biblical inerrancy before belief in God.[23] In Christian circles, fundamentalism retains its original meaning, but the word has come to signify any group, Christian or non-Christian, that privileges literal readings of writings considered sacred by that group and that is nervous about the encroachments of modernity. Fundamentalism in the twentieth century was often associated with outright opposition to the teaching of evolution or to calls for teaching an alternate theory in which God tweaks the evolutionary process.[24] The legal battles over evolution have lasted for eighty years, beginning with the Scopes trial of 1925 in Dayton, Tennessee, and extending at least to the Dover, Pennsylvania, trial of 2005.

Modern fundamentalism was not what most fathers of the Church, medieval theologians, and early modern religious thinkers taught. It is true that there is some continuity of doctrine—although doctrine often also changed—but their approaches to the Bible are quite different. First, as Boone notes, the classical creeds of Christendom do not mention belief in the Bible. Harris, in agreement with fundamentalist Christianity but against the traditional creeds, places belief in the Bible as *first* among Christian beliefs.[25] Second, from at least the time of Plato, many ancient thinkers were keenly attuned to the nuances of language, including its limitations in dealing with theological topics. Ancient Christian authors, though they accepted the scientific views of their day, were not dogmatically wedded to literalistic views of Scripture. For example, they usually accepted that the earth is spherical.[26] Origen and Augustine stressed the intention of the author as the key to understanding the meaning of a text.[27] Augustine's consistent pattern of reasoning in his mature work, *The Literal Meaning of Genesis* (completed in 415 CE) is to abstain from inferring scientific views from Genesis and to focus on its spiritual message. Repeatedly, when it comes to theories in astronomy, he tries to accommodate varying views. Those who quote chapter and verse to settle disputes in science he called "reckless and incompetent expounders of Holy Scripture."[28] In the modern period, Galileo appealed to Augustinian principles that are summed up in the pithy words of Cardinal Cesare Baronio: the Scriptures tell us how to go to heaven, not how the heavens go.[29] The fundamental irony of what Descartes called the Galileo Affair is that, historically, theologians prior to Galileo's time had adopted the very principles of exegesis that Galileo outlined, and they would do so again long after Galileo. However, in the words of Jerome Langford, "an amazing number of theologians" [in Galileo's day] made the mistake of inferring scientific conclusions from their analysis of the Bible.[30]

The new atheists' penchant for focusing on radical fundamentalist forms of religion may account for the fact that they invariably see religion as dangerous, in part because they believe it opposes science and reason, but also because they believe it fosters violence. These are the recurring themes in Harris's *End of Faith* and in Hitchens's *god is Not Great*. One of the clearest statements of the supposed moral inferiority of religion comes from Steven Weinberg. According to Weinberg, "With or without religion, good people can behave well and bad people can do evil; but for good people to do evil, that takes religion."[31] E. O. Wilson makes a similar claim. In the context of a discussion of religion, Wilson asserts: "Faith is the one thing that makes otherwise good people do bad things."[32] Weinberg and Wilson are weighty authorities in their respective areas of scientific expertise, but the fact is that these pronouncements are no more plausible than the claims that one requires religion to be exceptionally good or that atheists are naturally prone to be immoral. Poverty, hunger, fear, and social insecurity can also lead otherwise good people to do evil things or at least not to oppose evil. Hartshorne gave a more measured judgment: "[There are] hateful as well as superstitious and no longer reasonably believable forms of religion. This is only too true. But there is also no scarcity of hateful and not reasonably believable forms of atheism and quasi-deifications of the planetary species to which we belong" (DL 393). In a similar vein he observed, "Religious fanatics have often brought ill upon mankind; so have atheistic fanatics. Without a better religion than either of these extremes has to offer, what hope is there?" (WM 139). The "atheistic fanatics" Hartshorne mentions are communists in Southeast Asia, presumably the Khmer Rouge in Cambodia, site of the numerous "killing fields" of Pol Pot. Of course, he knew of other examples: Hitler's death camps, Stalin's gulags, Mao's Cultural Revolution (cf. BH 30).[33] There is evidence aplenty of irreligion's sins.[34] Nor will it do to say that these were "bad people." Grant that they were bad people—or at least not very good people—but many good people participated in the atrocities. *Prima facie,* theists are not particularly prone to vice, and atheists have no corner on virtue.

When presented with evidence that there are nonreligious sources of inhumanity, such as certain political regimes, one might reply that such regimes are, after all, religious, or in Wilson's words "dogmatic religionlike ideologies."[35] Harris refers to Nazism and Communism as "political religions."[36] If asked what makes Nazism and Communism religious, Harris's response is that they immunize themselves against evidence and encourage blind faith in an ideology; according to Harris this is the essential character of religion. This raises the question whether religion is necessarily based on a willful ignoring of evidence. Harris claims that faith is "unjustified belief in matters of ultimate concern."[37] He speaks of one who *"really* believes" religious creeds.[38] Such a believer is one who holds nonnegotiable ethical views and who, in the name of metaphysical absurdities, is willing to die, but more importantly, to kill others and send others to be killed. But is this accurate or even plausible?

Moderates in religion deny that faith is wholly blind and they eschew cruelty in the name of a God of love and compassion. They maintain that torture, violence, and injustice done in the name of a God of love is an offence to that God; many theists have understood this and lived by it. By lumping all faith claims together, Harris fails to take into account *the content of faith,* which includes the value commitments that are normative for the religious life (e.g., in Judaism and Christianity, to love others as oneself and to love God). Harris replies that moderates in religion "don't know what it is like to *really* believe in God."[39] The clue that Harris's reasoning has run its course is in the italicized *"really."* His argument by italics is breathtakingly circular: Religious moderates do not know what it is like to *really* believe because people who know what it is like to *really* believe aren't moderates.

Harris's view of religious moderation ignores the normative structure of faith, and his argument is question-begging. Perhaps worst of all, his idea of what it means to live in faith as a moderate is a caricature. In a word, his argument fails not only at the level of ideals, but also at the level of facts. The life stories of religious liberals and moderates reveal individuals who are fully aware of their beliefs and their consequences. Hartshorne saw religion at its "best and wisest" in the lives of Abraham Heschel and Reinhold Niebuhr. "Both men were not just theoretically good, they were activists [in the causes of justice and peace]" (ZF 77). Other examples abound from the twentieth century: Albert Schweitzer at Lambaréné in tropical Africa caring for the sick; Pierre Teilhard de Chardin risking his life as a stretcher bearer in the First World War; Dietrich Bonhoeffer at Flossenbürg awaiting execution at the hands of his Nazi captors; Gandhi's nonviolent resistance to British rule in India; Dorothy Day's constant advocacy of pacifism and care for the poor; Heschel walking side by side with Martin Luther King Jr. during the Selma Civil Rights March. The idea of lecturing such people of faith on what it means to *really* believe is more properly a subject of ridicule than refutation. Of course, Schweitzer, Teilhard, Bonhoeffer, Gandhi, Day, Niebuhr, Heschel, and King are dramatic counterexamples to Harris's claims, but there are plenty of examples of moderates with great breadth of learning who admirably lived by their principles.[40] To be clear, the point is not that people outside the circles of faith cannot live admirable and inspiring lives. The point, rather, is that Harris's view of the meaning of moderate faith is tendentious and cartoonish.

Hartshorne spent his last forty-five years in what is often called "America's Bible Belt" (seven years in Atlanta, Georgia, and thirty-eight years in Austin, Texas), so he was fully aware of fundamentalism's popular appeal. In his many letters to the editors of newspapers, he often criticized fundamentalist ideas such as severely limiting a woman's access to abortions and the promotion of anti-evolutionary theology as in so-called "Creation Science."[41] Both of these ideas come under fire in the book he wrote for a wider audience, *Omnipotence and Other Theological Mistakes.* He did not mince words when it came to creation-science; he considered it "bad philosophy, bad science, bad theology, and bad hermeneutics (textual interpretation), and no good thing at all" (OO 67). For Hartshorne, the idea of an inerrant revelation—such as the Bible or the Qur'an are said to be by certain believers—is not rationally defensible.

> From an infallible God to an infallible book (to an infallible reader of the book?) is a gigantic step. For many of us it is a step from rational faith to idolatry. No book in a human language written by human hands, translated by human brains into another language, can literally be divine, "the word of God." What we know is that it is the word of human beings about God. The beings may be divinely inspired but they are still human (OO 41).

Hartshorne did not deny the possibility that some individuals might be gifted with more religious insight than others (OO 37); indeed, as we saw in Chapter Five, his theology requires that God influences all creatures and is thus, in some fashion, "felt" by all creatures. These ideas, however, do not entail that there are infallible revelations. God may be without error, but every reception of divine revelation must be sifted through the fallible filter of the human mind as well as the vagaries of language and culture. Moreover, Hartshorne denied the ability of any individual, *including God,* to unilaterally determine the mind or the behavior of another; hence, the idea of a human being as a mere tool for God's revelation is erroneous—this is one of the reasons Hartshorne called the concept of omnipotence a mistake.[42]

Hartshorne's denial of any infallible access to the divine notwithstanding, his approach to revelation was decidedly pluralistic and open-ended. For Hartshorne, the Jewish and Christian Scriptures contain expressions of *genuine* experiential encounters with God, with holiness, and with all the wisdom of an ethics of love, but these encounters must be understood as profoundly qualified by the finitude, fallibility, and historical-cultural conditioning of the human "receiver" of revelation. In addition, Jewish and Christian Scriptures cannot be taken as the sole repository of experiential encounters with deity. On Hartshorne's theory, human beings prehend God unconsciously at every occasion of experience, and this explains the potential for the eruption into consciousness of spiritual/religious genius at any time and in any culture. Deep theological insight, psychological wisdom, and moral guidance can be found in literary/scriptural traditions ranging from the *Upanishads* to the spiritual poetry of Sufi *faylasufs* to the Buddhist sutras and beyond.

The fact that religions can and do outgrow the beliefs and practices in which they formerly expressed themselves is something one finds in any religion that lasts for more than a few generations. Consider, for example, the dramatic changes in Judaism from the Levitical laws with their instructions on animal sacrifice, to the rise of Rabbinic Judaism and the gradual composition of the Talmud, to modern-day Judaism with its many varieties. The idea of change in religion is strikingly captured in the teachings of Jesus in the image of trying to fill old wineskins with new wine (Mk 2:22; Mt 9:17; Lk 5:37–38). Any number of recent thinkers have made this idea integral to their theories of religion, none more clearly than Henri Bergson in the book Hartshorne so often cites as Bergson's best, *The Two Sources of Morality and Religion* (e.g., LP 15; IO 6; DL 393; ZF 14, 57, 67, 75). Bergson famously distinguished static religion and dynamic religion; he attempted to explain the movement by which religion is transformed from tribal loyalties and mythmaking—telling stories "on a par with those with which we lull children to sleep"—to advocating identity with humanity as such and indeed "with the creative effort which life itself manifests."[43] One need not accept every aspect of Bergson's theory to recognize the truth in the idea of the creative transformation that occurs in the course of a religion's development. We will return to this idea in the following section.

Changing "God"

Hartshorne never dwelt very long on what he considered the falsehoods of fundamentalism, for he viewed it as among the least satisfactory forms of religion. He assumed, as matters of sound procedure in intellectual discourse, that one should seek the best arguments and theories that are available and fairly represent opposing views. Where questions of the concept of God are concerned, these aims are well-illustrated in *Philosophers Speak of God,* the anthology that he edited with his student William L. Reese.[44] The book includes excerpts—fifty-five selections—from the writings of the *world's great philosophers,* East and West, theistic and atheistic; in addition, Hartshorne and Reese included excerpts from what they considered some of *the greatest writings* (sometimes not by well-known philosophers) on the question of God. One may quibble with the selections, but by any reckoning it is impressive, for it is more varied than any other vaguely comparable anthology. Each selection is followed by Hartshorne's response; the book is essentially Hartshorne in dialogue with the global history of philosophical theology.[45] For any major thinker whose writings are not included in *Philosophers Speak of God,* it is a fair bet that Hartshorne addresses their views in one of his other books or articles.[46]

One way to sidestep Hartshorne's project is to claim that any move away from traditional ideas of God is a move in the direction from *more definite* to *less definite* ideas of God. Victor Stenger, for example, complains of "highly abstracted concepts of a god" developed by sophisticated theologians that would be unrecognizable to typical believers.[47] Stenger is surely correct that some ideas about God developed by philosophers and theologians would be unrecognizable as the meaning of "God" as many believers understand it. Blaise Pascal famously called attention in his Memorial to the difference between the God of Abraham, Isaac, and Jacob and the God of the philosophers.[48] Hartshorne uses the example of one of Pascal's famous contemporaries to make the point:

> Spinoza has been called 'God-intoxicated' and also 'atheist'. There is a fairly strong case for both descriptions. . . . It seems odd to think that an idea so essentially religious should be so mistakenly conceived by all the great religions concerned with it as the religious idea must be if Spinoza is correct. (NT 2)

Of course, Spinoza was labeled an atheist precisely because his concept of God was *not* a version of the supernaturalism that dominates the religious imagination. Hartshorne had a different, and, we argue, far more profound focus than Stenger. He asked whether *traditional* philosophers and theologians had not effectively distorted the essential meaning of "God" as it is expressed in practice and in the literature of the great theistic religions. He remarked that Pascal's "God of the philosophers" was "the God of philosophy at [Pascal's] time. . . . They are not necessarily so different, the God of philosophy and the God of religion."[49] Hartshorne posed the question: "In what kind of philosophy is the religious idea of God most at home?" (NT 25). For Hartshorne, as we saw in Chapter Five, no philosophy that does not insist on the divine relativity can provide an adequate account of the theistic religious idea. "The Divine Relativity" refers, among other things, to a genuine give-and-take relationship between the creatures and God; as a consequence, God is the supreme, but not the only, decision maker and God is affected by creaturely decisions. There is indeed a spectrum of such philosophies, but only a philosophy of this type can best express the idea that "love is the key to life's riddles" (RSP 109).

Philosophers Speak of God not only places the varieties of theism on display, it is also a testimony to Hartshorne's belief that theological ideas may change, and even advance. He recognized that not all concepts of God are equally attractive, and this he regarded as one source of atheism:

> Examine unbelievers and you will often find them focusing on some more or less antiquated, discredited form of theism, not theism simply as such. Often they are rightly rebelling against some tyrant view of deity that insults or belittles human capacities and makes God far from the most lovable of conceivable beings. (CH 244)

Hartshorne's observation correctly describes much of the new atheist literature. Dawkins, for example, is happy to be rid of the one that he characterizes as a "cruel ogre."[50] But Hartshorne went further. In a 1990 letter to the editor, he wrote:

> Like Thomas Jefferson, the great spokesman for democracy, I believe in God, but defend the right of others not to do so. Far too many professed believers have ugly notions of God and of human values for me to deny this right. So long as there are poor forms of theism, and that may be a long time, I hope there will be atheists.[51]

If Hartshorne saw some value in atheism in helping to rid the world of "ugly notions of God," he also appreciated the fact that nontheistic humanism could serve as "an effective protest against intellectual dishonesty and laziness in religion" as when the facts of history or science are distorted in the name of faith in a putative revelation (RSP 180–81). At the same time, he was critical of both atheists and theists who are unwilling to explore alternative forms of belief and disbelief than what is most familiar to them (WM 77). Hartshorne spent much of his life exploring and mapping the varieties of theism and (by implication) atheism.[52]

John Loftus, an Evangelical Christian turned atheist, goes so far as to call for an end to teaching philosophy of religion in secular institutions. According to Loftus, a course in philosophy of religion is analogous to a course that would explore the existence and attributes of fairies. No self-respecting atheist should teach such a subject so it should be left to the seminaries and private schools where there are enough supposedly self-deluded theists who want to teach it or students who want to take it.[53] It seems to escape Loftus's notice that philosophy of religion, at least as normally practiced by professional philosophers, is not an apologetic religious undertaking (even when taught by persons with religious convictions), but is rather rational-philosophical thinking *about* religion on the model of philosophy of art, philosophy of history, or philosophy of law. Philosophical atheists such as Antony Flew (before his turn to a minimal theism),[54] J. L. Mackie, William Rowe, Kai Nielsen, Michael Martin, and Graham Oppy can be properly understood as specializing in philosophy of religion. Should their work no longer have a place in academe despite their high standards of scholarship? We believe, with Hartshorne, that the answer to this question is an obvious "No."

Loftus also severely underestimates the possibilities for religious opinions that are enormously plastic, wide-ranging, and hardly to be conflated with personal theistic options. One has only to think of Einstein's God, Buddhist worldviews, and various nontheistic yet religious interpretations of reality, as in J. L. Schellenberg's ultimism, the cosmic mysticism of Milton Munitz, C. J. Ducasse's belief in an afterlife based on parapsychology, or Donald Crosby's religious naturalism that is so carefully and imaginatively articulated in his numerous books. We wonder if Loftus believes that distinguished astrophysicists, mathematicians, and other natural scientists such as John Barrow, George Boole, Francis Collins, Arthur Compton, Paul Davies, Arthur Eddington, Arthur Peacocke, Arthur Pinsent, John Polkinghorne, and Frank Tipler, should keep quiet because they hold that there is considerable evidence for the existence of God but none for fairies. Finally, whose attitudes about religion and human well-being are most plausible and psychologically adequate—Bergson's, Buber's, Dewey's, Freud's, James's, Jung's, Kristiva's, Nietzsche's, Ricoeur's? An adequate answer to this question is intrinsically entangled with properly philosophical and conceptual issues. Where in academe should this legitimate question be pursued if not philosophy of religion? Loftus's perspective seems absurdly simplistic and wrongheaded in the light of these considerations. Worse, it is an unsophisticated and unlearned call to break what Peirce identified as the preeminent and first rule of reason: "Do not block the road of inquiry."[55]

New atheists are curiously estranged from evolutionary or developmental categories in their view of theistic ideas. It is as though the entire world, with the exception of theology, undergoes a process of development and that theology alone is incapable of progress. Consider Dawkins's very colorful and adjective-laden rejection of what he calls "the God of the Old Testament":

> The God of the Old Testament is arguably the most unpleasant character in all fiction: jealous and proud of it; a petty, unjust, unforgiving control-freak; a vindictive, bloodthirsty ethnic cleanser; a misogynistic, homophobic, racist, infanticidal, genocidal, filicidal, pestilential, megalomaniacal, sadomasochistic, capriciously malevolent bully.[56]

In Dawkins's defense, some ideas about God in the Hebrew Bible are at odds with finer moral sensitivities and some of them are quite naïve. Nevertheless, Dawkins's critique misfires on the questionable assumption, *made without argument,* that the various images of God in the Bible form *a single literary entity* identifiable as "*the* God of the Old Testament." The Bible is a library of books written over many centuries by people of widely divergent backgrounds and interests. Dawkins acknowledges this.[57] Yet, he never considers the view of someone like Rabbi Heschel who said, "In the hands of many people [the Bible] becomes a *book;* in the life of Israel it remained a *voice,* a Torah within the heart (Isaiah

51:7)."[58] Dawkins might respond that he is an atheist and so he does not believe that there is a divine "voice" to be heard. This, however, simply returns us to the original question. Why would Dawkins assume, *against all evidence to the contrary,* that there is a single *concept of God* running through its pages?

Not only is Dawkins's assumption questionable, it is almost certainly false. What Harry Emerson Fosdick said of the New Testament is true of the Bible as a whole: *there is no such thing as biblical theology, only biblical theologies.*[59] Indeed, it is a commonplace of contemporary biblical scholarship—also, the history of religion—that there exists a continual dialectic between continuity and change in the very concept of God and, correspondingly, in what it means to serve God. Dawkins speaks as though there is a single concept of God in the Old Testament, but in the Hebrew Bible the savagery of "God" is set side by side with talk of caring for foreigners, orphans, widows, and strangers, themes that are virtually definitive of the prophetic tradition which places God on the side of the powerless against those who abuse worldly power. The constant theme of the Psalter is the centrality of *chesed* (or *hesed*), meaning "lovingkindness" which identifies both the character of God and the call for human life to be characterized by the ideal of care for others. Rabbinic tradition, preserved in the Talmud, expresses the same ideal: For the sake of three things the world was created, Torah, prayer, and *chesed*.[60]

Jews and Christians, it is true, speak of "*the* God of the Bible." This is most charitably understood as an expression of faith that there is a God who is revealed in the Bible or who inspired it in some fashion. However, to speak of *the* God of the Bible should not be taken to mean that it contains a single *concept of God*. Even if one supposes that God is revealed in the Bible or that it is divinely inspired, it does not follow that every concept of God found in the Bible is an accurate reflection of that deity. Jonathan Sacks, quoting the Talmud, characterizes Judaism as "a conversation scored for many voices. It is, in fact, a sustained 'argument for the sake of heaven.'"[61] One finds a lively conversation during the time of Jesus with debates among Pharisees, Sadducees, Zealots, Essenes, and Jesus's own followers, and it is amply illustrated in Rabbinic Judaism in the centuries that followed. All of these facts would lead one to expect a gallery of perspectives, some of which are critical of others, sometimes even within a single book of the Bible. Building on the idea of "an argument for the sake of heaven," one must seriously entertain the idea that the new atheists ignore, to wit, that *the Bible, and the theological tradition more generally, preserve a centuries long argument about the nature and activity of God with a trajectory towards conceiving God as a just and merciful creator.*

By considering the Bible in all its diversity—historical, geographical, linguistic, and theological—and by situating it as an integral part of religious traditions which themselves present different points of view—specifically, Judaism and Christianity—one avoids the oft-cited worry of "cherry picking" one's favorite quotes to support a particular theological position. One biblical author may critique another, and each believer can join the ongoing conversation, using what literary, historical, and philosophical tools are at his or her disposal. The charge of cherry picking only makes sense if the Bible is treated as a kind of oracle—or as Timothy Beal says, an "icon"—as though all of its statements expressed the self-consistent viewpoint of a single author.[62] Fundamentalists do this when they treat it as "the inerrant word of God," and the new atheists do this when they criticize biblical religion as though the fundamentalist approach to the Bible represents the best that religion can offer. Hartshorne rejected the basic assumption of both the fundamentalists and the new atheists. Against the fundamentalists he wrote: "'The Word of God' is a neat little phrase, but what does it express if not one of the many species of idolatry, worshiping as divine what is not worshipful, but human, all-too-human?" Contrary to the new atheists, he claimed that the Bible contains both human fallibility "writ large" but also "religious truth," as in the great commandments to love God with all one's capacities and to love one's neighbor as oneself (CAP 132).

The overarching hermeneutical principle that ought to be used in constructing an enlightened and morally adequate Jewish or Christian theology which holds the Bible to be in some way normative is to reject as fallible, as human culturally conditioned "chaff," anything that is logically inconsistent with the Great Commandments. Thus, the militant, proslavery, and anti-biophilic characterizations of God are chaff, while the *chesedic* characterizations are not. In this way, the Bible "deconstructs" itself.[63] Whatever qualms one may have about the various portrayals of God in the Bible and in theological literature, the outlines of a sophisticated theology begin to emerge and lend support to what is arguably the most refined message of theistic religion. A common way of summarizing this message is to cite Micah 6:6–9:

> He has told you, O man, what is good,
> And what the Lord requires of you:
> Only to do justice
> And to love goodness,
> And to walk humbly with your God;
> Then will your name achieve wisdom.[64]

The Jewish Publication Society translation highlights the centrality of this verse: "This didactic saying is one of the most influential and often quoted sayings in prophetic literature. It was considered as a possible compendium of all the Mitzvot [Commands]." Hartshorne understood this more nuanced approach to Scripture. On the one hand, he was horrified by the militarism of some parts of the Old Testament and the merciless treatment of enemies (CH 302). On the other hand, in his second book he cited the work of Duncan Black MacDonald to show that *some* biblical ideas about God are superior to the supposedly more refined ideas of the philosophers and theologians (BH 42, 57)[65]; specifically, Hartshorne argues that the idea often found in the Bible of a God genuinely open to interactions with the creatures is far superior to the idea of a God that realizes all possible positive values.

The best ethic of philosophical argument has always rested on a principle of charity. Philosophers are usually taught to seek the most fully developed ideas and the best arguments for them. Charity comes in when one's interlocutors fail in this task and one is obliged to explore ways of strengthening their views. The Talmud is more succinct. It teaches to judge persons with the scales weighted in their favor.[66] And, one could add, the person's *arguments*. In far too many cases, the new atheists do not adopt these values where religion is concerned. What is more, there is little, if anything, in the new atheist critique of fundamentalist religion that is not also in Hartshorne's rejection of fundamentalism. What is missing from new atheist critiques, however, is precisely what Hartshorne's treatment of the theistic question provides, to wit, a careful consideration of what the most sophisticated philosophers and theologians have said about God. This is no mere question of philosophical etiquette, but a question of how best to serve a larger public which, increasingly, is theologically uneducated. Hartshorne explains:

> Again, how many have been atheists because of arguments which, according to many theologians and philosophers, misconceive the nature of the theistic question! People should not be forced to deny or neglect their own intuitions by clever sophistries, or intellectual fashions resting on no thorough, careful survey of the speculative possibilities and the thereto relevant evidence. This is a vicious narrowing of a valuable form of freedom in an advanced society. (CS xvi)

Hartshorne would have applauded the new atheist campaign against unreasoned faith and violent religion. But he would most certainly have accused them of presenting a seriously impoverished view of the live options available for theistic religious belief. An effective corrective to the new atheists' myopic view of theism is the position matrices developed by Hartshorne that we discussed in Chapter Three.

God and Science

A dramatic illustration of narrowing the options of theistic belief is the new atheists' insistence that the question of God's existence is a matter for science to settle. The title of one of Stenger's books provides a good example: *God, the Failed Hypothesis: How Science Shows that God Does Not Exist*. Dawkins agrees. God, he claims, is *best* considered as a scientific hypothesis.[67] Hartshorne, on the other hand, was in agreement with the philosophical tradition stretching from Plato to Leibniz, and beyond, that God's existence is not a matter for science to settle. One might expect from the new atheists a serious engagement with that tradition. But there is none. That God's existence is a scientific question is not a conclusion for which new atheists argue so much as it is a presupposition of their critique. We have seen that Hartshorne argued that Anselm's ontological argument, though inconclusive as a theistic proof, shows the futility of framing God's existence as an empirical question; this directly challenges Dawkins's (also Stenger's) assumptions. Hartshorne says that those who treat the existence of God as a scientific hypothesis are "intoxicated with the (very real) glory of 'empirical inquiry'" but that this represents a "sheer misunderstanding of the theistic problem, and indeed of all metaphysical problems."[68] Dawkins (also Stenger) tends to treat science as providing a royal road around philosophy. Thus,

Dawkins attempts to dispose of the ontological argument by means of an anecdote. He tells of piquing some philosophers and theologians by his adaptation of Anselm's (first) argument to prove that pigs could fly. He adds this enticing morsel: "They felt the need to resort to Modal Logic to prove that I was wrong."[69] Yet, modalities are precisely what one needs to deal intelligently with Anselm, and with the question of God's existence.

Dawkins argues that there is *almost* certainly no God, as the title of one of his chapters asserts. Stenger agrees when he says that "we can be pretty sure" that no such being as God exists.[70] For Dawkins, the argument against God's existence turns on what he takes to be the extreme improbability of God's existence. "God, or any intelligent, decision-taking, calculating agent, would have to be highly improbable in the very same statistical sense as the entities he is supposed to explain."[71] Dawkins rightly dwells on the baffling complexity of nature as revealed by science, from the intricate interrelations of cosmological constants that make life possible, to the web of life that stretches around our planet, to the countless connections within the human brain that make our thinking possible. According to Dawkins, anything capable of explaining this sort of complexity would have to be at least as complex (and hence, improbable) as the phenomena it is invoked to explain. Dawkins uses Dennett's concept of cranes (explanations not involving mind) and skyhooks (mind-first explanations) to express his view:

> But the very least that any honest quest for truth must have in setting out to explain such monstrosities of improbability as a rainforest, a coral reef, or a universe is a crane and not a sky-hook. The crane doesn't have to be natural selection. Admittedly, nobody has ever thought of a better one. But there could be others yet to be discovered.[72]

Dawkins goes further and says that any deity capable of bringing order to the universe would itself be the product of a cumulative process—perhaps in a prior universe—that produces complex objects. If a designer existed, it would have to be "the end product of some kind of cumulative escalator or crane, perhaps a version of Darwinism in another universe."[73]

Dawkins has cleverly changed the subject from philosophy (or natural theology) to science. In the previous chapter we noted the distinction made explicit by Hume, but affirmed by all modern theists, of (a) beings that are products of the processes of the universe and (b) the universe as, in some sense, a product of God. Any being whose existence is the "end product of some kind of cumulative escalator or crane" would simply not fit the description of God and would be contrary to the meaning of "God" as used in theistic religion. In a word, to concede that "any honest quest for truth" to explain the universe is a search for cranes is already to concede Dawkins's form of atheism. Conversely, Dawkins's assumption that this is the case begs the question against theism. Dawkins's assertion is in the same general class of sentences as Mill's question, "Who caused God?" To be sure, Dawkins changes the question by insisting on a crane rather than a skyhook: "*What* caused God?" To raise such questions is not a refutation of theism or even an intimation of its failure. At best it is a misunderstanding of the meaning of "God," and at worst it is an unwillingness to engage in reasoned discourse about God.

There is more. Classical theism insists upon the simplicity of God, meaning that God is n*ot complex*. Hartshorne agrees that there is a sense in which God is not complex, but he *insists* that there is another sense in which God is supremely complex. He wrote: "To take God as exclusively simple is to make deity an empty abstraction. Concreteness means complexity. To love all actualities is to be the most complex yet singular reality, not the simplest" (CH 308). Here, at least, Dawkins is in the neighborhood of a critique that would apply to Hartshorne's theism since, unlike classical theism, it affirms the complexity of God. The critique, however, misfires by failing to take into account one of the things that makes dipolar theism so distinctive, to wit, the logical difference between existence and actuality. As we saw in Chapter Five, Hartshorne maintains that God's *existence* is simple but God's *actuality* is complex; moreover, the relation of existence to actuality is the relation of the abstract to the concrete. In a 1992 talk to Unitarians, Hartshorne worded the question of God's nature carefully: "Must not God be the *most complex* of actualities?"[74] Hartshorne's greatest theological innovation is to recognize and argue for the coherence of a divine relativity according to which God is related to, and affected by, all that has been or will come to be. For this reason, Hartshorne can say that there are certain statements about God that are "in a sense scientific or historical."

For example, does God know that Washington crossed the Delaware? Well, if Washington did cross the Delaware then, yes,

God knows this. But God only knows it because Washington did cross the Delaware. So every historical truth and every scientific truth can be stated theologically by saying: "God knows that . . ." All such statements about God are in a sense scientific or historical questions. That is, you could not settle them without first settling an historical or scientific question.[75]

Hartshorne's point is that the doctrine of divine relativity and complexity entails that *some* truths about God are contingent. In no way does it follow that *all* truths about God are contingent. God's *existence* requires no explanation, whether by cranes or skyhooks.

What, then, to say about Dawkins's claim that God's existence is supremely improbable? Hartshorne would say that God's existence is not subject to probabilities in any sense in which science can shed light. In one of Dawkins's lists of complex things are included "a rainforest, a coral reef, and a universe." Rainforests and coral reefs are objects within this universe; their existence and development *presuppose* its laws. They are, Hartshorne would agree, proper phenomena for science to explain; in addition, the explanations must be genetic or developmental. The question of the explanation of a universe is more subtle: it doesn't presuppose its laws so much as it is coextensive with them. Hartshorne follows Whitehead in accepting various cosmic epochs, of which our universe (presumably beginning with the Big Bang) is one. There may be other universes preceding or succeeding ours, and therefore it is proper to use an indefinite article and speak of "a universe." One may also speak of laws pertaining to the development of such universes. However, if we speak of *the* universe (note the definite article) as the widest context of existence, then it makes no sense to speak of its probability. There is nothing outside of existence itself by means of which one could gauge statistical frequencies or mathematical probabilities. If Hartshorne is correct, it also does not make sense to speak of mere nonexistence. We have already discussed Hartshorne's reasons for thinking that the question "Why is there something rather than nothing?" is wrongheaded. The universe must exist.

If one speaks of "the universe" as the widest context of existence, then Hartshorne says that this is simply another name for God. We have seen that this does not make Hartshorne a pantheist, but it does make him a panentheist and he uses the metaphor of the universe as the body of God. This "body," presupposed by all others, is that within which we "live, move, and have our being."

> The world as an integrated individual is not a 'world' as this term is normally and properly used, but 'God.' God, the World Soul, is the individual integrity of 'the world,' which otherwise is just the myriad creatures. (OO 59)

On this account, nature's laws are the self-ordering of the divine body which makes possible, though not inevitable, the various forms of order within the universe (such as rain forests and coral reefs). Panentheism— as with any theism worth the name—entails that *some,* though certainly *not all,* skyhook explanations are ontologically foundational. For the new atheists, this may be enough to discredit a philosophy. But now we are clearly in the thick of the debate amongst psychicalism, reductionistic materialism, and dualism. This debate is decidedly metaphysical, not scientific. Certainly, nothing in the theories or practice of science dictates that cranes are the only true explanations of things. At the very least, Hartshorne's distinction between order *within* the universe and the order *of* the universe is a reminder that explaining rainforests and coral reefs must be a fundamentally different enterprise than explaining the universe itself.

Stenger believes that current cosmology holds the key to answering the problem of cosmic order. He recounts the results of modern astrophysics according to which the galaxies are moving away from each other at speeds approximately proportional to their distances—in a word, the universe is expanding. The second law of thermodynamics predicts that as the universe expands, its total entropy increases. Because the total *possible* entropy increases faster than the total *actual* entropy, there is room for immense localized order. When the curves for possible and actual entropy are traced backwards in time, they converge "to the smallest possible region of space that can be operationally defined, a *Planck sphere.*"[76] At this time, the universe had as much entropy as an object of that size could have; this is in contrast to the present state of the universe which has less actual entropy than an object of its size could have. Stenger says that at the initial moment of maximal entropy "the disorder [of the universe] was complete and no structure could have been present." He goes on to characterize this as "a state of chaos."[77]

Stenger is usually careful to couch scientific results in terms of what can and cannot be measured by current instruments or what is and is not allowed by current theories. We have just seen, for example, that when speaking of a Planck sphere as "the smallest possible region of space," he adds "that can operationally be defined." Likewise, he says that "the earliest definable moment" is *the Planck time*"—Stenger would have been even more precise had he written "definable by current physics."[78] A bit later, he says:

> Basically, by definition time is counted off as an integral number of units where one unit equals the Planck time. We can get away with treating time as a continuous variable in our mathematical physics, such as we do when we use calculus, because the units are so small compared to anything we measure in practice. We essentially extrapolate our equations through the Planck intervals within which time is unmeasurable and thus indefinable.[79]

Again, greater precision demands that "indefinable" be changed to "indefinable by current physics." No mere philosophical fussiness requires these clarifications. Stenger says that in physics, "time is simply the count of ticks on a clock."[80] Granted that judgments in physics are tied to what can be measured, it would be intellectually reckless to conclude that time is nothing more than what physics can measure. The question remains whether or not the unmeasurable "intervals" that Stenger mentions exist. Or again, one should not conclude that time really is continuous simply because "we can get away with" treating it as such for the purposes of doing physics.

What holds for Stenger's explanations of time holds *mutatis mutandis* for his explanations of the disorder of the universe at the earliest measurable time. The "disorder" or "chaos" that Stenger identifies within the Planck sphere should not be described as "complete" but as "complete *as known to physics.*" All that Stenger is justified in saying is the latter, not the former. To put the point somewhat differently, there is no meaningful difference between "complete disorder" or "complete chaos" and nonbeing. On the other hand, "complete disorder as known to physics" does contrast with nonbeing since there may be a deeper order beneath the order detectable by physics. (If Hartshorne is correct, the order would have to be of an indeterministic sort.) It seems clear, at any rate, that Stenger does not identify the disorder or chaos of the initial Planck sphere with nonbeing. Stenger is skeptical that the big bang represents an absolute beginning and he speculates that our universe "'tunneled' through the chaos at the Planck time from a prior universe that existed for all previous time."[81] Presumably, our universe could not "tunnel through" something that did not exist. "Tunneling through" is a metaphor, but one must suppose that it describes some *ordered or nomological relation*. If there is indeed an ordered relation between our side and the far side (so to speak) of the big bang singularity, then Hartshorne's problem of cosmic order resurfaces. By as much as Stenger's scientific reconstruction of the cosmic past falls short of a metaphysical account, so does it fail to answer the question that Hartshorne raises about cosmic order. Hartshorne would ask how any scientific account could bootstrap its way outside of the very laws of physics it is trying to explain. At the widest level, these laws are presupposed, not explained, by science.

This critique of Stenger does not entail that Hartshorne's answer to cosmic order is shown to be true. It provides, however, another example that there are questions concerning the character of the real that are simply not within the realm of empirical science. For their part, the new atheists reject or are deeply suspicious of metaphysical claims, and so they press scientific explanations as far as they can go. Hartshorne had no objection to this but he was no champion of *scientism,* the belief that science alone is the arbiter of what we can reasonably judge to be true or false. Of course, scientism is not itself a deliverance of science or of scientific investigation but a thesis about the competencies of science. It follows that scientism, by the very standards it sets up for judging what is true and false (i.e., scientific ones) cannot be judged as true or false. It is, at best, a proposal for thinking about science, a proposal that Hartshorne rejected.[82] Moreover, because scientism is not a product of science, denying scientism in no way commits one to any sort of backward thinking about science. In a Hartshornean spirit, one might add that the denial of scientism can save one from backward thinking about both science and metaphysics.

Conclusion

One of the glories of science is that its methods often lead reasonable people to agreement on difficult empirical questions. Metaphysics does not have this advantage. Its methods are more controversial, its theories are more removed (and if Hartshorne is right, completely removed, if true) from empirical disconfirmation, and its practitioners are in continual disagreement. To be sure, metaphysics is *logically rigorous* in the minimal senses that contrary views cannot be true and that it employs rational methods of inquiry. As it is practiced by Hartshorne and other philosophers of his ilk, it guards against replacing scientific theories with metaphysical ones. Moreover, Hartshornean metaphysics is *epistemically cautious* in eschewing dogmatic claims to self-evidence and absolutist certainty. Finally, metaphysics is *cognitively messy* in the sense that equally informed and reasonable people can come to contrary conclusions. We remind the reader of Hartshorne's remark that cognitive security is for God, not for us.[83] Despite the difficulty of metaphysics and the apparently intractable disagreements that characterize competing viewpoints, its questions are legitimate, its problems are genuine, and its speculations deserve serious response. Leemon McHenry speaks of metaphysics, in its Whiteheadian form, as arising from "the fatigue of methodology and the need for refreshing novelty in answering fundamental questions." He argues that "metaphysical daring is required to break the spell of custom and conjure fresh perspectives."[84] Hartshorne would doubtless agree. Hartshorne's call to intellectual humility is a reminder that theologians and religious people informed by neoclassical perspectives are neither anti-scientific nor rabid zealots. Of course, they have not been silent on biblical hermeneutics, but they also have an extremely good track record of promoting scientific curiosity, responsible moral thinking, and high ideals about economic development, ecological management, and social justice.[85]

Religious belief is easier to dismiss to the extent that it is saddled with defending fundamentalism, made immune to intellectual development and progress, or characterized as a primitive substitute for science. The crude anthropomorphisms of various tutelary spirits and of ancient deities who control the forces of nature and even our destinies, lend themselves to these interpretations of religious belief. One may grant an element of truth in these views, but there are dimensions of religious belief and practice not clearly amenable to these forms of reductionism. To name a few of the obvious: there are the needs that religion fills (psychology), the roles it plays in society (sociology), and the symbolism of its narratives (literature), all of which are incorporated into Bergson's nuanced approach to religion which Hartshorne endorsed. What most interested Hartshorne, however, is that religious belief is never far from philosophical concerns—metaphysical, epistemic, and axiological. In the contemporary world, those who reflectively participate in religious ceremonies and adopt religious views are generally aware of religion's history, its lingering atavisms, and its uneven progress. A reflective religious believer is generally aware, painfully aware, that not everyone is as reflective about their faith as they should be. Like Jacob wrestling with the angel, they feel the pain of the struggle even when they have reached a better understanding of things. These same people, like Hartshorne, are also aware of the perennial importance of religion in addressing the meaning of being human and the question of our relation to what is ultimate. Religion, like science, does not stand still. To anyone energized by neoclassical perspectives, Hitchens's declaration that religion spoke "its last intelligible or noble or inspiring words a long time ago" rings hollow.[86]

EIGHT

Dipolar Theism and Cosmology

Hartshorne maintains that a properly metaphysical understanding of God cannot come into conflict with any theory in science. As we have seen, on Hartshorne's view, metaphysical propositions are unrestrictedly necessary statements about existence whereas scientific propositions are empirical in the Popperian sense of being open to falsification by some conceivable experience. Hartshorne was aware, however, that in certain respects, his neoclassical metaphysics, and particularly his dipolar concept of God, seem to be in tension with the deliverances of modern science. One problem concerns the comparison Hartshorne sometimes makes between God's relation to the universe and the mind's relation to the brain. One may ask, given this comparison, whether the extreme conditions of a big bang singularity, or of the exhausting of energy available for work in projected endings of our universe, are compatible with the idea of a divine memory. In addition, in Chapter Three, we mentioned two problems raised by prevalent interpretations of current scientific theories. First, big bang cosmology has seemed to some commentators to require that Hartshorne's (also Whitehead's) idea of our universe as one in a series of countless many universes (cosmic epochs) is incorrect. Second, Einstein's special theory of relativity posits the relativity of inertial reference frames. From one frame of reference, two events may appear simultaneous, but, from another, they may appear successive, and there is no fact of the matter that would dictate that either frame of reference is the true one. It seems difficult to explain how this idea can be reconciled with Hartshorne's conception of God as coextensive with the cosmos, but also as having a definite past and a future.

These apparent tensions between Hartshorne's metaphysics and scientific theories raise a larger concern. Metaphysical concepts, on Hartshorne's view, are true in *every possible world-state*. If it is possible for science to show that the universe existed for a finite time or that there can be no meaning given to an absolute past, present, and future, then those aspects of Hartshorne's metaphysics that require the falsity of these propositions must themselves be considered as false. The problem can be stated in even more general terms: if it is so much as logically possible that a particular scientific theory can be incompatible with Hartshorne's metaphysical claims, then those claims, by Hartshorne's own theory of what constitutes a true metaphysical proposition, must be false, and necessarily so. In that case, one must conclude either that Hartshorne has not correctly identified the genuine metaphysical principles or that his view of what constitutes a metaphysical statement must be revised.

Big Bang, Heat Death, and Divine Memory

Two important critics of Hartshorne's neoclassical theism in the light of contemporary cosmology are David Haugen and L. Bryant Keeling.[1] They argue that Hartshorne faces a dilemma: If neoclassical theism is compatible with the findings of contemporary cosmology, then it must embrace both the big bang event and the likely "heat death" of the cosmos. However, if Hartshorne affirms these events, then he cannot hold that the divine memory can be sustained since only a complex and well-ordered universe can encode physical information that God could prehend and thus remember. For given Hartshorne's fundamental analogy that God is related to the world just as mind or soul is related to the brain, then there must in all instances be a physical component, a body, in any divine awareness. But such a physical component would be destroyed in the case of the big bang or possibly at this cosmic epoch's demise in extreme thermodynamic dissipation or a "big crunch." The only escape from this, they suggest, would be for Hartshorne to affirm something like Cartesian dualism, in which case God is a disembodied spirit, a view that conflicts with his fundamental commitment to panexperientialism and its concomitant idea that God must have a body. So, either Hartshorne must admit that his concept of God is incompatible with important deliverances of contemporary natural science, or he must embrace dualism. Both horns of this dilemma are ruinous for Hartshorne's metaphysical project.

Hartshorne's response to Haugen and Keeling is disappointingly brief, but he makes two points worth exploring in more detail. First, he avers that "the mind-brain analogy need not be as 'close' in the divine instance as Haugen and Keeling require for their argument."[2] A significant limitation of the analogy that Hartshorne notes is that actual brains are filters that are as important for forgetting as they are for remembering, yet God cannot forget anything. The second point is that, in neoclassical metaphysics, it is the most abstract contrasts that are most literally applicable to God. Hartshorne has in mind contrasts like relative/absolute, contingent/necessary, and dependent/independent; the mind-matter distinction is not metaphysically ultimate since (as we explained in Chapter Four) material objects always have components that are fundamentally psychical by nature.

Theodore Walker, Jr. built on Hartshorne's response by claiming that Haugen and Keeling fundamentally misunderstand the nature of Hartshorne's "psychicalism," for, according to Walker, Hartshorne's analogy is more accurately understood as a generalized soul-body relation rather than a soul-brain relation. Moreover, Walker submitted that the Hawking "no boundaries" proposal renders the reference to a big bang singularity in Haugen and Keeling's argument obsolete (since there is no original singularity in Hawking's new theory).[3]

These responses did not convince Haugen and Keeling who published a rebuttal of Walker's arguments. Again, they make very strong critical claims: Until some neoclassical process thinker can coherently explain the compatibility of divine memory and cosmic mind with a big bang event and, more importantly, a forever dissipating and expanding cosmos (what they call the "heat death" but which is more accurately labeled the cosmic "cold death"), the conclusion must be that, "Hartshorne's entire metaphysical system seems untenable."[4]

Our response to this exchange is that, while granting there is mystery here (as Hartshorne himself admits) since we are dealing with identifying God's concrete interactions with creatures, Haugen and Keeling are mistaken in thinking that the divine memory, as construed neoclassically, must be utterly destroyed in either a big bang or cold death event. This is because such extreme cosmic events are not fundamentally different from "ordinary" events in the cosmos from the standpoint of the divine memory and its relation to such events. To be sure, Haugen and Keeling are correct that Hartshorne draws a comparison between the mind-brain relation and the God-universe relation, and that he did so throughout his career (MVG 185f; DR 155; NT 97–99; LP 197–98; AD 294; OO 55–56; WM 89; ZF 91). But Hartshorne was on the right track, in our view, in pointing to the limitations of the analogy. He spoke of the nervous system as "a sort of body within the body" (OO 55) that mediates incoming stimuli and helps guide behavior, in part by *filtering out* much information (CAP 50). The brain's immediate environment is the body itself, and outside of that is the external world. In the case of an all-inclusive God, there can only be the "internal environment" of the beings that make up the universe. In principle, God could have no need of specialized organs (such as the brain) to adjust to an external environment—thus, Hartshorne, following Plato, speaks of a World Soul. He sometimes brings the two analogies together: "[Every] physical individual in the [World] Body becomes as a nerve or brain cell to the [World] Soul" (OO 135). The World Soul analogy is best for expressing the omnipresence of God, whereas the analogy of the mind to brain cells is best for expressing the immediacy and intimacy of God's relation to the creatures (ZF 71). Thus, Hartshorne is careful to stress the strengths and weaknesses of each analogy.

David Ray Griffin has emphasized the limitations of the panentheistic analogy in the following lucid and succinct way: "As with any analogy, there are features of the soul-body relation that do not apply to the God-world relation, such as the fact that the soul *emerges* out of the body and is thereby *dependent upon* it for its very existence."[5] Hartshorne's God is not identical to the cosmos, and thus is not an emergent entity dependent for existence upon the particular kind or kinds of entities which do emerge (through divine influence). A body within the cosmos must have a beginning, but Hartshorne argues that the divine body must include not only our cosmic epoch, but all past epochs.[6] In consonance with this suggestion of partial disanalogy, what is missing on Hartshorne's behalf is a reminder of the metaphysical argument for objective immortality and a concomitant emphasis on the *transcendent and unique* nature of divine occasions which always eminently embody Whitehead's Creativity, or equivalently in Tillich's expressive vocabulary, the infinite power of Being. In effect, if there is any such thing at all as objective immortality, and *if there is any such thing at all as God's abstract essence with its "eternal plenum" of potency,* then such metaphysical conditions *always* obtain as descriptions of God whether we are speaking of a divine prehension of a single neuronal event or a momentary occasion of a far-future, extremely dissipated remnant-photon in a "cold death" state of this cosmic epoch. Such entities provide *whatever particular and contingent additions* there may be to the divine cognition. No matter what their nature, they have no special metaphysical privilege in terms of somehow ontologically deleting the past. A remnant-photon occasion, for example, would offer God an extremely trivial aesthetic content for prehension, but it would "destroy" nothing.

It is true that, on Hartshorne's theory, God's experience requires a quantitatively structured physical pole of *some* kind, but this would be satisfied on *any* coherent cosmic-epochal origin or cosmic-epochal death scenario: On the one hand, as advocated by Neil Turok and the Cambridge Relativity group, the new "P-instaton" event that replaces the Hawking-Penrose singularity has some magnitude (that is to say, P-instaton $\neq 0$). On the other hand, if a big bang or big crunch singularity has occurred or will occur, then by definition of "singularity," it is infinitely dense and should be construed as an infinitesimal. However, *as coherently interpreted in Non-Standard Analysis,* even an infinitesimal has some magnitude, that is to say, $1/\omega \neq 0$. If, as the currently reigning narrative has it, the far-future destiny of this cosmic epoch is a "cold death" of trillions upon trillions of super-dissipated remnant-photons each separated by voids larger than the apparent size of the existing cosmos, then there would simply be trillions upon trillions of remnant-photons available for God's physical prehension. In effect, the most plausible and workable cosmological narratives posit a "physical something with magnitude" to be physically prehended by God even at the extreme points of cosmic-epochal origin or demise. But that is what is metaphysically required—a physical component in the necessarily social structure of all experience. Moreover, Haugen and Keeling fail to notice that the current "cold death" narrative with its dissipated remnants represents precisely what is presumed to exist by process philosophers prior to the emergence of this cosmic epoch. So, the argument can be turned on its head: Current cold death cosmology predicts the kind of cosmic destiny that process philosophers expect if the idea of an ongoing series of cosmic epochs is correct. Epochs born out of earlier relative chaos are then sustained so as to produce the evolution of life, then slowly dissipate, eventually being reinformed and recharged as a new epoch is born.

It is as if Haugen and Keeling are tacitly contending that, for Hartshorne, the physical component of divine experience is not just an influence, but somehow *determinative* of God's very existence; this would require Hartshorne to affirm some version of pantheism rather than pan*en*theism. To the contrary, a panentheist holds that God "includes" the natural universe (and any other universes there may be or may have been) but also infinitely transcends it and is inexhaustible by virtue of essential possession of Creativity. Once again, our point is that the neoclassical process theist has the *intellectual right* to assert this given the metaphysical probity of Creativity—an ultimate urge or appetition to becoming which has metaphysical primacy and is thus never emergent or subject to decision.[7] The process theist may also rightly insist on the epistemic argument for omniscience. In effect, *that* God continues and *that* God remembers no matter what the condition of the cosmos is independently supported by Whitehead's case for the metaphysical ultimacy of Creativity and by Hartshorne's arguments concerning the cognitive costs incurred in denying omniscience, as in the intolerable paradox of the loss of past truths.

It is important to notice that, in the above reasoning, there is one cosmic origin scenario that has been famously proposed that we are not accepting within the domain of plausible origin scenarios. This is the original Hawking-Penrose singularity theorem wherein the so-called *Lamda* or magnitude value is 0. Our objection to this theorem is based on *a priori* logico-metaphysical grounds. If the proposed singularity is said to exist somehow as an infinitely dense physical "something" that is yet also described as "zero," we submit that the proposal is conceptually absurd. Absolute zero cannot constitute an intelligible *physical* referent. Note that this proposal can be described as the notion of a transition from being to sheer nonbeing, a reverse violation of the ancient and hallowed logical dictum that *ex nihilo nihil fit*. Of course, Einstein was also disturbed, likewise for *conceptual* reasons, by the suggestion of a singularity as a solution to the field equations of general relativity, thus prompting him to stipulate his famous cosmological constant (the principle that matter-energy has an intrinsic property of resistance to complete shrinkage or compression). The new P-instaton device represents a return to the cosmological constant idea, at least in principle. Since a P-instaton possesses some physical magnitude, we submit that it is at least an intelligible concept, although of course it may not in fact correctly describe the origin of our current epoch.

Hartshorne was most astute in warning about the illicit employment of the concept of zero in contexts where empirical meaning is involved. His invention of the terminology "the zero fallacy"—the title of one of his books—has application in this instance. The fallacy can be put this way: In order for a concept to be empirically meaningful it must somehow involve *a least positive quantum as a unit for conceivable observation* (cf. ZF 166). Only under such an assumption can there be an intelligible notion of the empirical *absence* of a thing or property. To use Hartshorne's example, from this criterion of empirical meaning we can deduce that, for instance, the hypothesis of absolutely continuous radiation is empirically meaningless; accordingly, Planck's determination of his famous value h (where the joules per second measure is $6.626070040(81) \times 10^{-34}$) establishes *a least positive quantum* of radiation. From this it is empirically meaningful to postulate least units of light, i.e., photons. "No light in a spatial region S" can then be defined as the absence of least units or photons in region S—more exactly, it can be defined as the state-description such that "not a *single* photon can be detected within the confines of S." But a zero-magnitude event, by definition, is not a *positive* quantum of anything, and thus is not conceivably observable. In effect, the hypothesis of a zero "physical something" commits the zero fallacy and fails to be empirically meaningful.

Another issue which Haugen and Keeling urge against Hartshorne is that they cannot determine what he is referring to when he speaks of a "deeper qualitative identity" that persists during transitions from one cosmic epoch to another.[8] They cite the following from Hartshorne:

> I do not doubt that the present quantitative system of the cosmos is doomed. But this is compatible with there being a deeper qualitative identity through change whereby the universe as "the living garment of deity" retains this status forever. (LP 215)

We contend that Hartshorne is here referring simply to the fact that, whatever quantitative-nomological conditions God might induce in a new cosmic epoch, the new epoch will involve new participants in the affective continuum, will build entities that become participants in "the eternal ideal of love, of the social enjoyment of aesthetic feeling" (BH 88). The deeper qualitative identity *is* the social enjoyment of aesthetic feeling that persists between cosmic epochs. While we agree with Haugen and Keeling that the explanation for *how* this can occur must be metaphysical (they complain that it is "too metaphysical"), and of course this admittedly involves by the nature of the case some mystery and speculation. Nonetheless, the explanation is hardly blind or vacuous as there are some clear components to it derivable from Whitehead: The process theistic theory of epochal origin posits input of information by God which influences early and nearly-chaotic denizens of the new epoch who are least resistant to such influence. As Hartshorne suggests, the fundamental or grounding information—the contingent fundamental laws of nature—may well be "put in" at the big bang event assuming such an event (CS 125). Early fleeting or "non-enduring" individuals then become more persistent "enduring" entities—the nucleo-synthesis of new elements—and these engrain ordered habits which allow for more complex modes of organization. A new cosmic epoch is thus born.[9]

In addition to the argument above, consider that, as many contemporary physical cosmologists assume, there may well be a plurality of worlds existing in parallel, but non-contiguously, with the current cosmic epoch. In such case, God would have opportunities for physical prehension of the denizens of such worlds even while our own epoch undergoes a death by cosmic crunch or by cold hyper-dissipation. This is precisely the view of Rem Edwards: God is bringing about alternative epochs which coexist within a Divine Super-Space-Time (see our discussion of Edwards below). Surely this is a logical and thus metaphysical possibility. Observe also that the alternative epochs model would resolve any problem of "extreme aesthetic dissipation" in divine experience that would occur during the far-future cold death era of our epoch: While cold death remnants of our epoch would indeed be extremely trivial objects of divine prehension (and by process criteria such extreme triviality counts as a kind of evil), nonetheless through divine influence interesting, vibrant biospheres could become available for divine prehension in alternative epochs. In such case, life would always prevail in the universe.

Whitehead did in fact speculate about a coexistent plurality of worlds, as he held that it would be logically possible because of the conceivability of plural dream spaces.[10] A more rigorous argument for the possibility of alternative spatial epochs is provided by Anthony Quinton.[11] Quinton reflects upon Kant's arguments in the Transcendental Aesthetic of the first *Critique,* where Kant argues for the metaphysical unity of both space and time as held by common sense. In a thought experiment where the unity of space is denied, Quinton shows the intelligibility of plural spatial domains (because intercalated communications across domains can be imagined), although the denial of the unity of time, as process philosophers would expect, does produce absurdity (reinforcing Kant's idea of time as the *a priori* necessary "schematism of cognition"). If this is correct, then speculation about alternative spaces seems to be logically coherent. Consequently, the currently popular cosmological narrative that includes alternative worlds coexisting in a super-space is at least insofar a live possibility and would countermand Haugen and Keeling's hypothesized scenario of total information destruction in a far-future state of cosmic dissipation. So, the Haugen-Keeling critique, even when provisionally granting destruction of this cosmic epoch, surely would not hold *necessarily.*

We close this section with the following further considerations. First, we stress that the cosmic cold death and big crunch scenarios are, at this point and properly speaking, *speculative,* despite the apparent finding of recent astronomy that the cosmos is expanding at increasingly faster rates, thus currently favoring a cosmic "cold death." We cannot say that either scenario constitutes an empirically well-corroborated theory that reaches the mantle of a virtual "scientific fact" that a philosopher or natural theologian is *forced to accept.* This is because our empirical vantage point is the relative present, not the far distant future. For all we know, it may well turn out that the cosmos makes a reversal due to mechanisms of which we are not aware, in the same way we were not aware of the increasingly rapid expansion of supernovae only some two decades ago. The mechanism for this reversal could turn out to be some intrinsic property of cold death states of matter-energy themselves. Moreover, it is possible that the phenomenal "universe" is only an island universe separated by unimaginably vast distances from other island universes that will eventually interact in the far future so as to provide a sufficient field for the emergence of a new or renewed cosmic epoch. Neil Turok's Cambridge Relativity Group has developed computer simulations presupposing cosmic membranes which randomly "crash" with our own projected dissipated membrane in such a way that a big bang event results. This suggests a scenario of ongoing cosmic activity despite "cold death." Such speculations are within the vanguard of current cosmological thinking.

We also stress that there are some properly metaphysical considerations that move us to hold that the natural universe, taken as God's body or "sensorium," would end forevermore *ad infinitum* in a state of absolute thermodynamic dissipation is not possible. There are two arguments. First, since (we take it with Whitehead and Hartshorne) absolute creation out of nothing is not possible—there are cosmological goings-on prior to our and every other past epoch. Why then would this current epoch be the "final" one in which all nontrivial aesthetic achievement would end forevermore? Our epoch would in that case be an absolute metaphysical anomaly. Second, connected with the conjectured end of nontrivial aesthetic achievement would be the idea of a cosmic epoch that is deeply, despairingly, and intrinsically ugly. Hartshorne's aesthetic argument surveyed in Chapter Four stands directly against any such scenario. Since there is reason to hold that there must be a beauty of the cosmos as a whole, this is *ipso facto* reason to hold that the divine cannot be the "last word" on cosmic activity. In short, the divine enjoyment of any single cosmic epoch, including ours, is not "the last word" on cosmic activity. According to this reasoning, the annihilation of our own cosmic epoch would not be the end of aesthetic achievement, and thus would not be the end of non-divine existence.

Big Bang Cosmology and the Finitude of the Past

In Chapter Three, we addressed Kant's antinomies, focusing especially on the First Antinomy and, in particular, on Kant's claim that pure reason, left to its own devices, can prove that the world had a beginning in time. Kant's argument is entirely *a priori*, appealing to no empirical factor whatsoever, and our reply to Kant was at the level of conceptual analysis. We now turn to a more properly scientific argument for the beginning of the universe and for the idea that time does not stretch infinitely into the past.

As early as 1927, the Belgian priest-astronomer George Lemaître theorized, based on the radial velocities of "extra galactic nebulae" (later known as galaxies outside our own), that the universe is expanding at a constant rate. A few years later, he theorized that the universe had expanded from what he characterized as a "singularity," where the known laws of physics break down. These ideas were prescient, for, within the century, this theory would receive dramatic confirmation and sway the scientific community to its acceptance. The first important piece of evidence had come in 1924, when Edwin Hubble discovered that the light coming from other galaxies is uniformly shifted to the red end of the spectrum, suggesting that the galaxies are moving away from us (or alternately, that we are moving away from them) at a uniform rate. Turning the clock backwards yields the result that the universe had a smaller diameter in the past than it has now; following this progression backwards leads to Lemaître's singularity, the infinitely hot and infinitely small point of origin of our universe where the known laws of physics break down. The singularity is not a point *in space* or *in time;* rather, it is the point from which all matter and all the space and time that make up our universe emerged.

Fred Hoyle proposed an alternate "steady state" model for the universe and ridiculed the idea of the initial singularity, calling it a "big bang." Of course, it could be neither "big" nor an actual explosion or "bang." It would have to be infinitely small and there would be no material for an explosion, nor known laws according to which the "material" could blow up. Nevertheless, the expression stuck as the new popular name for Lemaître's singularity—more precisely, "big bang" refers to the brief time after the singularity began to expand. There was much support for Hoyle's steady state model until 1964. In that year, Arno Penzias and Robert Wilson accidently discovered a remarkably uniform microwave background radiation in the universe whose source, they concluded, could not be objects within the universe but which must have emanated from its origin. This cosmic microwave background (CMB) was the telltale signature of the oldest light in the universe, dating to just after the big bang occurred, and it served as the crucial factor in deciding between Hoyle's model and the big bang. For these and a variety of other supporting reasons, the dominant view in science is that our universe has existed for a finite time, not for an infinite time.[12]

We saw in the previous chapter that acceptance of the big bang does not necessarily lead to the conclusion that all existence is contained within our universe. Victor Stenger proposes that there was a "tunnel" at the Planck time connecting our universe and a prior universe. Somewhat as we discovered that the limits of our galaxy are not the limits of the universe, so may we discover, or at least speculate, that the big bang does not define the limits of existence. Indeed, this observation is connected with an argument derived from philosopher of science W. H. Newton-Smith. Newton-Smith argues that, even if we accept the standard big bang narrative with an initial singularity, this in no way constitutes an empirical argument for an absolute first event. This is because such an event does not escape inquiry about antecedent "causal goings-on" in precisely the same way that we do not regard the hypothesis of singularities existing in black holes as somehow utterly free from causal explanation.[13]

Stephen Hawking is famous for his quip that asking what is prior to the big bang singularity is like asking "What is North of the North Pole?" We point out that: (i) contemporary cosmologists (including the later Hawking himself) are very much engaged in asking about causal explanations for a big bang event (as well as rejecting the notion of a singularity as defined by the Hawking-Penrose theorem where the magnitude value Lamda = 0), and that (ii) Hawking's quip has a clever commonsensical response: Hawking's analogy simply does not hold necessarily. One can imagine a globe B being attached to the North Pole of an original globe A, and thus globe B would constitute territory where one could move in a direction that is analogous to north of "the North Pole" of globe A from the perspective of a larger space that includes both globes. This spatial analogue fits the case of big bang cosmology exactly. For the question at issue for many cosmologists today is, "What might be behind the current cosmic epoch that may have begun in a big bang event?" This speculation in effect "adds a globe" behind the origin point of this cosmic epoch. Current M-Theory (M for cosmic "membrane," a theory we neither affirm nor deny) speculates about just such a possibility (see discussion below). The point is that, strictly speaking, the current big bang model leaves the question of events prior to this cosmic epoch *open or neutral.* The theory, if correct or largely correct, tells us about the earliest behavior of the matter-energy of *this* cosmic epoch with an empirical threshold at the cusp of the first Planck time after the purported singularity. As such, the appropriate and epistemically conservative thing to say about the question, "What does the standard account of the big bang event imply about the question of a metaphysically absolute beginning of events?" is that, in and by itself, it implies nothing about such beginning. For all we know the big bang event could have arisen from prior cosmological goings-on (and again as Newton-Smith reminds us, this is the more reasonable expectation). As such the mere existence of a big bang event with singularity does not prove the existence of an absolute first event.[14]

Since our topic is empirical cosmology, it should be pointed out that there is certainly much more skepticism about the standard big bang model than was evident in 1979, when Craig published his book on the *kalām* argument.[15] There are numerous alternatives to the standard model that are being taken seriously in various scientific circles. It is now quite common to speak of the conditions that may have eventuated in the big bang, as in the title of Brian Clegg's popular presentation, *Before the Big Bang*.[16] Below we briefly sketch three models that all hold that the universe did not begin with an absolute first event:

(1) Neil Turok and Paul J. Steinhardt of Princeton have developed an alternative cyclic theory of the universe—deemed ekpyrotic theory after the Stoic concept of cosmic *ekpyrosis* or expansion and contraction—in which so-called space-time membranes or "branes" existing prior to the big bang (or big bang-like event, one absent the initial singularity of the standard model) collide to produce our current universe. This cyclic model would provide a solution to a major nagging difficulty in the big bang model-with-inflation, namely, an account of the energy involved in the inflation action that supposedly occurred in exceedingly small fractions of a second after big bang. As one science writer explains:

> The only way that [inflation] could have happened is if there had been some incredible energy source pervading the newborn cosmos and blowing it apart. We don't see anything like that in the universe today, however, so cosmologists had to assume the potent energy field existed for only a fraction of a second after the big bang and then vanished. [But] conjuring up new, unknown energy fields goes against both common sense and one of the most cherished scientific doctrines [namely, Occam's Razor—do not multiply entities beyond necessity].[17]

While the Steinhardt-Turok cyclic theory does seem to accommodate critical cosmic observational data (e.g., the cosmic microwave background radiation), its postulation of branes and their collisions nonetheless remains highly speculative. The theory fits with the process model in so far as a cyclic theory coalesces with the general idea of cosmic epochs, but it is far from clear how the mechanics of brane-collision coheres with process notions. We will have to await much observational testing in the coming years—such as the proposed LISA space probe project designed to test for clues of inflation—in order to have much confidence in the ekpyrotic theory.

(2) Another alternative is the attempt at appealing to David Bohm's quantum potential theory and Bohm's geodesic trajectories to correct equations of general relativity from which a big bang singularity was first predicted. This effort eliminates the big bang singularity (in fact, all singularities since Bohm geodesics do not cross at "points"), and also predicts against the existence of dark matter, while postulating a universe that exists indefinitely in the past and continues indefinitely into the future. Ahmed Ali and Saurya Das are confident about the ability of this theory to accommodate forthcoming developments of a quantum theory of gravity.[18]

(3) Cosmologist Eric Lerner has propounded a theory that focuses on the behavior of plasma and electromagnetism and posits an infinitely old universe without a big bang event. As he puts it summarily in his "Open Letter to the Scientific Community":

> These [the Plasma Cosmology] and other alternative approaches can . . . explain the basic phenomena of the cosmos, including the abundances of light elements, the generation of large-scale structure, the cosmic background radiation, and how the redshift of far-away galaxies increases with distance. They have even predicted new phenomena that were subsequently observed, something the big bang has failed to do.[19]

While this point of view has received strong criticism, it is also the case (to our knowledge) that such alternatives as Lerner's have not been *definitively* disconfirmed by observational evidence.[20]

The overall point we wish to make is that, in the light of such alternative models, the state of large-scale cosmological physics is very much in play, and nothing like strong epistemic confidence should be attached to the standard big bang cosmic narrative. Profound empirical questions remain regarding the standard model which the above alternatives seek to address.[21] Whether or not we should put stock in any of the above alternatives, we are convinced that the questions outstanding with respect to the standard big bang-with-inflation scenario make it abundantly clear that current big bang cosmology does not possess the epistemic credentials either to make probable or *a fortiori* to "prove" the existence of an absolute first event.

One other empirical argument for a first event should be mentioned that depends on no particular cosmological model but rather appeals to a fundamental law of physics. This is the argument from the law of entropy or second law of thermodynamics. Paul Davies summarizes this argument succinctly. Given the second law of thermodynamics, "The universe cannot have existed forever, otherwise it would have reached its equilibrium state an infinite time ago. Conclusion: the universe did not always exist."[22] Since the second law of thermodynamics holds only for a closed system, this argument for a temporally finite universe assumes that the universe is a closed system. Such result would hold in a closed nontheistic universe, although there would be the problem of why, in the first place, there should be a fund of energy available for work. On the other hand, on a theistic model—be it classical or neoclassical—God could simply add the appropriate information (which can be regarded as energy à la information-theoretic physics) or other mechanism which would "wind up" the universe at various junctures. This becomes more plausible metaphysically if there are independent arguments for the existence of God as an inexhaustible entity.

Rem B. Edwards, a philosopher friendly to Hartshorne's ideas, has suggested various emendations that he believes are true to the spirit of Hartshorne but also accommodate current cosmological thinking. Inspired by recent developments in speculative cosmology among astrophysicists—which he insists is really metaphysics—Edwards asks whether our universe may not be one of many actual universes existing within an infinite superspacetime. This super matrix of coexisting but independent universes could be interpreted by process theism as the divine body, much as Hartshorne views our universe as God's body. Edwards goes further and maintains that these ideas allow for a concept of creation *ex nihilo*. Within the divine superspacetime, God can create universes from no preexisting material. On this view, it is not necessary to conceive our own universe as created from the dying embers of a previous cosmic epoch. The initial singularity of our universe could represent an absolute beginning. This does not mean that one must jettison the claims of process theism that God is necessarily social, embodied, and creative. In Edwards's words:

> Within infinite Divine Superspacetime, God could be infinitely loving, social, embodied, and creative without being tied to a single temporal strand of spatially finite antecedent-and-successive universes. Within infinite Superspace and throughout infinite Supertime, God could create many co-existing universes out of nothing.[23]

Edwards notes that his suggestions are not as far removed from the metaphysics of Whitehead and Hartshorne as one might suppose. Whitehead speaks of cosmic epochs, and Hartshorne argues that this involves a time beyond what is available to physics that connects various cosmic epochs (CS 53–54).[24] Edwards views himself as amending Hartshorne's idea to include superspace as well as supertime.

Edwards's treatment of creation *ex nihilo* retains the essential meaning of the idea—creation from no preexisting material—but it also suggests both less and more than the concept as it was expressed in classical theism. It suggests less in the sense that God's creative act in traditional theism takes place in eternity. Superspacetime differs from the Boethian idea of eternity in at least this much: it is complex whereas eternity has no parts. Edwards also wishes to avoid the deterministic connotations of the traditional idea of creation. To create another creator is not to create that creator's decisions; this is one reason Aquinas denies that God creates other creators, for he regards God as creating, with us, the decisions we make in such a way that God's activity is a sufficient explanation of our decisions (although he denies, contrary to the charge of process theists, that this deprives us of our freedom). Finally, Edwards imports more into the idea of creation *ex nihilo* than was traditionally in the doctrine. The idea that the universe had a first temporal moment is not to be identified with creation *ex nihilo* since, according to traditional theism, God could have created a temporally infinite universe *ex nihilo*.

Edwards's revisions of process theism are made largely, though not exclusively, in light of criticisms from those who do not share his commitment to process metaphysics. The extent to which they are in the spirit of Hartshorne's neoclassical theism is a fair question.

Certainly, Hartshorne found nothing of value in the doctrine of creation *ex nihilo*. While Edwards's revision of *ex nihilo* creation avoids one of the thornier problems with it—the problem of creating the supposedly free decisions of every creature—it attributes to God an ability that is contrary to the spirit of Whitehead and Hartshornean ideas of creativity. On Hartshorne's view of causation, as we saw in Chapter Four, past actual entities provide the necessary *(but not sufficient)* conditions for the emergence of every entity. Edwards's view seems to require that *in some cases*—in particular at the initiation of a cosmic epoch within superspacetime—God in fact does create from no preexisting material and would thus be the sufficient condition of the existence of those entities thus created. The occasions emergent from this process would, by the nature of the case, lack all novelty of their own, for they would be totally the product of a divine decision. They would represent an arbitrary exception to otherwise necessary and universally applicable metaphysical conditions. Thus, whatever advantages the Edwards's proposals may have for rendering Hartshorne's ideas consistent with current cosmological thinking, the metaphysical cost seems excessively high.

Divine Temporality and Special Relativity

Albert Einstein's special theory of relativity, or perhaps more carefully stated, implied philosophical interpretations of that theory, pose a peculiar challenge to Hartshorne's neoclassical theism. The challenge is that Einstein's theory apparently denies any privileged frame of reference from which one could speak of a cosmic simultaneity, whereas Hartshorne's theism posits a deity whose life is coextensive with the cosmos and which has a definite past and a definite future. As James F. Ross once put it starkly, special relativity theory makes any process theistic description of divine experience as a personally ordered sequence of actual occasions "cosmologically incoherent."[25] Hartshorne understood the objection and offered a number of conciliatory suggestions throughout his career as to how to handle it. However, as late as 1991, he confessed himself ultimately "incapable" of giving a truly intellectually satisfying resolution to the issue (PCH 616 and 642). More recently, Griffin mounted a defense of the compatibility of relativity theory and divine experience construed in terms of a personally ordered sequence of actual occasions.[26] In light of both Hartshorne's own sense of the gravity of this problem and persistent disagreements about it, the question is raised acutely, *is* there a successful defense of compatibility? What *should* be said about this problem?

At the outset, it is worth pointing out that the problem of compatibility is generated by the notion that divine experience is to be understood in terms of a personally ordered sequence of occasions of experience, isomorphic with a personally ordered sequence of human occasions of experience. We noted in Chapter Five that Whitehead conceives God as a single actual entity. It is to the advantage of Whitehead's theology that the problem of incompatibility with relativity theory does not arise. For, on the single actual entity model, prehended data of finite actual occasions can come into divine experience at any "moment" and will be continuously incorporated into God's everlasting concrescence, with divine aims for finite or creaturely occasions targeted variably and appropriately to actual world conditions as lures for best outcomes.[27] On the single actual entity model, by definition, there is no requirement that there be a linear temporal structure to divine experience where a whole cosmic object is prehended as the initial physical pole of a new divine occasion, which upon satisfaction is, in turn, prehended by new finite occasions of experience as their "total object of prehension," as Hartshorne puts it (DR 134). *Prima facie,* this represents an Occam's razor consideration in favor of Whitehead's theory. Perhaps what this means is that process theology *as such* need not be undermined by any charge of cosmological incoherence on grounds of relativity theory, since only Hartshorne's specific version of such theology would be so undermined (if such incoherence in fact holds), and provided, of course, that the single actual entity theory is itself otherwise coherent and philosophically adequate. This latter provision is precisely the rub of the problem for advocates of the personally ordered society theory of deity. Their contention is that Whitehead's theory of God as a single actual entity does not logically cohere with other elements of his own metaphysical theory. The theory requires correction by holding a consistent, metaphysically uniform analysis of higher-grade experience in terms of the personally ordered society model as held by Hartshorne.

The problem for the Whiteheadean theory is at least three-fold. First, by holding that initial subjective aims derive only from the primordial nature of God, Whitehead's ontological principle, according to which only actualities can be explanatory reasons, is directly violated. Whitehead famously characterizes the primordial nature as an abstraction and as "deficient in actuality."[28] Whitehead here commits a "fallacy of misplaced concreteness" by tacitly treating an abstraction as an *actuality* that could in principle act in a way that provides aims for finite occasions. As he confessed to A. H. Johnson, this was indeed a spurious line of thinking, a "great carelessness on my part."[29]

A second problem with conceiving God as a single actual entity is this: since the primordial nature is eternal and unchanging as well as the purported active source of initial aims, it seems that God would be unable to provide finite occasions with initial subjective aims that are *contextually appropriate to the actual historical condition* of such occasions. In order for there to be provision of aims which are contextually appropriate, there must be temporal knowledge of the actual conditions of occasions. This requirement immediately invites a reinterpretation of the "consequent nature" of God in Hartshornean terms as the abstract characteristic of successively being in different actual states, broadly analogous to human regnant or dominant occasions that prehend subordinate (neuronal) occasions which in turn prehend subsequent dominant occasions—in effect, a linear series of personally ordered occasions. By definition such a series attributes to God temporal acts of prehending actual occasions. As Griffin puts the point:

> [I]n each moment God prehends all the actual occasions that have just occurred, then unifies all these prehensions into a divine satisfaction, which includes initial aims for the next moment of the universe. These initial aims are based on God's primordial aims *combined with God's sympathetic knowledge of the present situation.*[30]

The temporally structured serial account of the consequent nature is thus consistent with the ontological principle (since the reinterpreted consequent nature necessarily involves the idea of God's concrete actual states) and it makes possible knowledge of the actual conditions of occasions for provision of relevant initial aims.

A third issue with Whitehead's theology concerns how an entity can prehend another entity that has not reached satisfaction and is thus not a determinate object for prehension. On the one hand, Whitehead insists that finite occasions prehend God, but, on the other hand, he maintains that only determinate entities can be prehended.[31] Yet, if God is an eternally concrescing actual entity, God never reaches determinate satisfaction. So, either finite occasions never prehend God (contrary to Whitehead's explicit statements) or the doctrine of prehension itself is rendered problematic; Whitehead contended that contemporary occasions cannot prehend each other, for no occasion can prehend another in its subjective immediacy. Hartshorne's personally ordered society model allows determinate divine satisfaction and thus makes prehension of God metaphysically possible. There are numerous other problems of coherence that accompany Whitehead's single actual entity model, but these three issues taken together constitute a very strong case for the Hartshornean model of the consequent nature. To be sure, Whitehead's view has a number of able defenders.[32] However, not without reason did Griffin refer to the idea of God as a single everlasting actual entity as Whitehead's "greatest blunder."[33]

In addition to these arguments against the coherence of the single actual entity model, we observe that there is a distinct advantage to Hartshorne's view for anyone concerned to employ the resources of process philosophy for constructing a properly Jewish or Christian theology of creation. For those theologians who criticize process theology for being too often "heterodox" in its positions, it may come as a surprise to realize that Hartshorne's temporal-social model of divine action arguably accommodates *both* of the traditional modalities of creation: *creatio originans* and *creatio continuans*. On the one hand, Hartshorne's deity "initiates" the cosmos (that is, *this* cosmic epoch) by dominantly influencing whatever extremely passive or chaotic cosmic remnant there may have been (correlative to the Genesis notion of "the waters"), while providing our emerging cosmos with its fundamental nomological conditions or dispositions at the big bang event (assuming the occurrence of such event). Thus, we have *creatio originans*. Moreover, because each finite creaturely occasion prehends God as its "total object of prehension"—a kind of prehension that by definition is not available in Whitehead's eternally concrescing single actual entity· model—the divine occasion *ontologically constitutes* the finite occasion as the necessary condition for its very concrescence. In addition, within this total object of prehension are the divine aims or desiderata for subsequent finite occasions. In effect, literally for Hartshorne, *no physical prehension of God means no finite occasion*. Thus, we have *creatio continuans*. It must not be forgotten that, for Hartshorne, the existence of God itself *is the ground of* the existence of finite occasions. Hartshorne was persistently anxious to correct classical theism in its monopolar position that God is not genuinely affected by finite creatures, and this perhaps overshadowed or de-emphasized the "active" side of his model of deity. Keeping in mind the full scope of Hartshorne's view, however, we can see that there are appropriate senses in which we can say that the neoclassical God acts by creating nature (the "initiating" component), by aiming or calling nature forward (the "desiderata" component), and by literally sustaining it.

We suggest that the foregoing is a more robust doctrine of creation than some theological critics have surmised. While Christopher Dawson was certainly wise to suggest that "one person's orthodoxy is another person's heterodoxy," it is worth pointing out amidst the chorus of disdain for Hartshorne's position in certain conservative theological circles that his view of divine creativity is more within the historical mainstream of Jewish and Christian theology than has been realized, certainly at least from a structural point of view (meaning that it provides for both traditional modalities of creation). Being "orthodox" was never at the center of Hartshorne's concerns, and he always insisted (correctly in our view) that orthodoxy does not necessarily mean "correct doctrine" but rather "historically accepted doctrine." We hold nonetheless that a balanced appraisal of his position shows that facile dismissive attitudes about Hartshornean "heterodoxy" are misinformed, at least on the score of creation. Reasonably "orthodox" Jews and Christians, it seems to us, can hold a neoclassical doctrine of creation as broadly described here.

If all of this renders Whitehead's single actual entity model unpalatable, then we are pushed back into the problem of showing the compatibility of God's social-temporal consequent nature and relativity theory. Again, the notion of a "cosmic now" is an ineluctable part of the Hartshornean position, as the cited language from Griffin clearly attests. There are at least six maneuvers of varying degrees of plausibility that can be made in an effort to resolve this problem:

1. Based on Bell's Inequalities phenomena, H. P. Stapp argued for a revised model of space-time involving an ontology of a rigorously asymmetrical sequence of quantum events. In 1977 Hartshorne endorsed this proposal but dropped it from his later discussions without explanation.[34]

2. Hartshorne also suggested that the analogy of God with human persons may need radical qualification in light of special relativity. Perhaps one must speak of "God here-now" for every inertial reference frame. This is what Paul Fitzgerald called the hypothesis of "God as Infinitely Interlaced Personalities."[35]

3. Frank Tipler and John Barrow argue that an unambiguous notion of past, present, and future resides in the cosmic microwave background radiation.[36] This would provide a "cosmically privileged" time frame in terms of which divine time could be understood.

4. David Griffin ventured the proposal of an extended temporal duration for divine occasions of experience such that God's duration includes all others, but that God only directly prehends certain occasions.[37]

5. In 1941 Hartshorne averred that God's present might be as brief as the briefest specious present of any non-divine occasion. He conceded that "this involves problems of synchronization that inevitably baffle my lay mind" (WP 87). However, John Cobb later took up the proposal in his advocacy of a more Hartshornean understanding of deity.[38]

6. Following Henri Bergson and Dewitt Parker, Hartshorne noted that the denial of simultaneity in special relativity is predicated on the notion of *localized* observers dependent upon light-signals which are necessarily productive of "time lags" over distances, a situation which may tell us nothing about "the deep truth about time," time as experienced by an omniscient *non-localized* prehender (WP 86–87; CS 125; NT 93–97).

In view of the problems inherent in the idea of God as a single actual entity, each of these proposals deserves serious consideration. We believe that the last two alternatives provide the most promising solutions to the problem, but we shall consider each in turn.

H. P. Stapp, noted senior quantum physicist at UC-Berkeley and the Lawrence National Laboratory, argued for an ultimate, linear, asymmetrical sequence of quantum events that perfectly conserves momentum energy and is ontologically prior to space-time location. Developed in the light of experimental tests of Bell's Inequality

phenomena, wherein the classical relativistic principle of local causality—
that is to say, the principle that information transfer remains strictly
within the confines of light-cone propagation—is given up; on Stapp's
model the universe is a strict creative advance of quantum events.
Relativistic effects such as temporal measurement differences in different
spatiotemporal frameworks are entirely phenomenological effects
attaching to localized observers bound to light signals. Relativity has
no fundamental ontological status that tells us anything about the order
of events coming into existence. Stapp's ultimate quantum series, by
contrast, stipulates that there is a strict temporal order to the occurrence
of events wherein each new quantum event is conditioned by an
ontologically definite past. Postulating this temporally ordered advance
solves the basic conceptual problems of quantum physics. Writes Stapp:

> The basic conceptual problems of quantum theory disappear
> once it is admitted that the potentia for each event is con-
> ditioned *by the entire preexisting world* [our emphasis]. For
> example, interference effects in optical experiments pose no
> problem in principle if the event of photon absorption by a
> particular grain in the photographic plate has the potentia to
> occur that is conditioned by the entire experimental setup.[39]

While Stapp does not address the issue of divine cognition or agency,
it is easy to see how his model would apply to the case of neoclassical
theism. God would prehend each event as it occurs in the ultimate series
and then respond to it with a desideratum embodied in the completed
divine occasion which in turn would be prehended by the next quantum
occasion in the ultimate series. This would entirely bypass the problem
of relativity and any denial of simultaneity.

Of course, Stapp's model posits an enormously complex view of
events, and divine interactions with such events, as it would involve
literally trillions of quantum events occurring within a given second.
While this view is indeed fantastic in its complexity, this does not mean
that it is logically or metaphysically impossible or even metaphysically
implausible. By any standard, contemporary science reveals workings of
nature that are jaw-dropping in terms of their rapidity—one only has to
think of the flow of electrons involved in supercomputing where millions
of bits of information are processed in a second. Although the empirical
status of Stapp's theory seems unclear at present—to our knowledge, it

has not been experimentally disconfirmed—we concur with Stapp that it provides a considerable measure of coherence to the interpretation of quantum phenomena. It is a possible solution to Hartshorne's problem of simultaneity.

We should note, however, that Hartshorne misconstrued Stapp's theory. Hartshorne wanted to assimilate Stapp's ontology to the formal model of entailment in such a way that it solves the problem of "contemporary relations." According to Hartshorne's reading of Stapp's ontology, contemporary events are neither mutually independent of one another nor mutually dependent upon one another. Applying this idea to the interpretation of Bell's entanglement phenomena, a change in spin vector at experimental setup A means supra-luminal change in events occurring at well-separated experimental setup B (an impossibility on the relativistic principle of local causality). Hartshorne writes:

> Events at place A and those at place B cannot be independent [as the experiments on Bell's Theorem empirically confirm]. Not that they must be interdependent. But either an influence goes from A to B or from B to A. The analogue in formal logic is that of P and Q being neither equivalent nor simply independent, though we do not know which is the entailing and which the entailed proposition.[40]

The problem is that on Stapp's ontology *there are no contemporaries;* instead there are unique "metaphysically present" events following in strict rapid sequence. Hartshorne apparently came to realize this—as he said in 1984, on Stapp's model, "In the absolute sense of contemporaries, there would be none" (CAP 108).[41] His understanding this consequence of Stapp's idea would explain why, after his initial enthusiasm for Stapp's idea, he ceased making reference to it, for Hartshorne had no reason or desire to deny contemporary events—indeed, his account of spatial relations requires them (CS 218; CE 52–53).

The second idea for avoiding the apparent incompatibility of special relativity and neoclassical theism is to question the sequential ordering of divine occasions. One of Hartshorne's suggestions had been to urge that, rather than speak of "God" *simpliciter,* we should instead speak of "God *here-now,*" so that God has multiple frames of reference. This would solve the problem of relativity by asserting that there is no privileged or unique frame of reference for God. While this would indeed be consistent with the denial of simultaneity in standard interpretations of special relativity, this move creates havoc for Hartshorne's concept of God as a *unified* experiential entity as well as the concept of the God-World relation as analogous to the temporally sequential mind-body relation. Hartshorne worried over this implication since the "simple analogy with human consciousness as a linear succession of states collapses" (CS 124). Given Hartshorne's early insistence that we *begin* with the unity of human experience and abstract from or develop analogies with it in order to grasp any concrete unity (WP 117), the multiplicity proposal stands in stark tension with this principle of metaphysical method. While Paul Fitzgerald has argued that what he calls Hartshorne's hypothesis of God as "Infinitely Interlaced Personalities" is the least problematic proposal for harmonizing process philosophy and special relativity, we regard this hypothesis as a drastic measure which is ultimately unnecessary in the light of other considerations we present below.

The third way of addressing the problem of special relativity is outlined by Barrow and Tipler in *The Anthropic Cosmological Principle.* They argue that Hartshorne's quest for a uniform philosophy of time with real separation between the temporal modalities is well-founded in theoretical physics. General relativity, unlike special relativity, includes a privileged global time coordinate framework; Barrow and Tipler connect this privileged framework with the cosmically isomorphic microwave background radiation. At first glance, this would seem to resolve neoclassical theism's apparent need for a cosmic "now" in terms of which God's experience could be understood. The Barrow-Tipler proposal, however, has one chief difficulty from the standpoint of neoclassical process philosophy. Since the proposal is predicated on the basis of general relativity it carries with it the strong deterministic implications of that theory. Such implications are logically incompatible with Hartshorne's (and Whitehead's) relative indeterminism.

When all the implications of Barrow-Tipler's anthropic cosmology are understood, it is evident that its view of the universe is strongly deterministic in precisely the same manner that the metaphysics of classical theism is deterministic; that is to say, the universe is strongly determined to be just as it is by virtue of God's eternal knowledge of all things. This is made explicitly clear in Chapter Five of Tipler's book *The Physics of Immortality.*[42] We, and our cosmos, at this juncture of evolutionary process, exist precisely because we are being observed by

God (Tipler's "Omega Point") *at the end of physical "conformal" time.* Moreover, since general relativity has not been fully synthesized with quantum theory and consequently we do not yet have a complete or unified physical theory of space-time, our current physics is inherently theoretically undetermined or incomplete. This incompleteness is, by itself, an important reason for taking seriously Hartshorne's suggestion that physics does not give us the "deep truth about time." Moreover, even if it is the case that the cosmic microwave background radiation provides a global time coordinate framework and thus allows for an unambiguous past, present, and future, this would not resolve the problem of compatibility. The problem of compatibility resides in the fact that God must prehend *objectified* occasions, that is to say, using Whitehead's technical vocabulary, superjective occasions that are capable of being prehended. Since these objectifications occur at different rates, irrespective of any cosmic "now," questions still arise as to how to describe God's "simultaneity" with objectified events.

The fourth proposal is based on an intriguing suggestion from Griffin. Suppose that Whitehead can be read in a way that does not commit him to the notion that God must prehend occasions that are contiguous to one another in a strict sequence. If free of any necessary contiguity requirement (which Griffin apparently thinks is the correct interpretation of Whitehead), then why not assume the following, analogous to the temporal order of the mind-body relation: just as God's prehensions are spatially extensive, they are also temporally extensive. For the sake of illustration, suppose that God prehends my experience at a time interval S (representing a second), and that each of my regnant or dominant occasions of consciousness is one-tenth of a second. In that case, God would directly prehend one of my dominant occasions, label it D, at an interval S. This divine prehension of D would indirectly "include" the just previous dominant occasions and other subordinate compounding occasions (including, say, billions of electronic occasions) *as prehended by* D. God then provides a response, an initial aim based on the prehension of D, to occasions in the next second that is subsequent to D, and this process would be repeated continuously (and would be applied to other occasions throughout the cosmos available for prehension at S). Although God would not thereby prehend every occasion directly, this would not entail, Griffin argues, that God's ability to guide the cosmos would be rendered impossible.

This is because an analogous situation arguably holds with the mind-body relation. "If every second there are, say, ten dominant occasions of experience and, say, one hundred living occasions in a brain cell, there would be ten cellular occasions between every dominant occasion. And yet the mind is able to provide tolerable guidance to the body."[43]

While this view seems logically possible, and Griffin's reply to the "no guidance" objection is plausible, at least one element of this proposal is less than ideal from the standpoint of Hartshorne's project of developing a concept of God as "the greatest *conceivable* being." This is an objection of which Griffin is aware, but which we think is underemphasized in his discussion. Griffin's proposal entails a certain loss of richness in the divine experience since the "included" actual occasions are not prehended in their immediate freshness but are mediated through the occasions which God happens to prehend directly. Moreover, every finite occasion has at least some negative prehensions of other actual occasions, and this entails a certain limited contextualization or emphasis in perspective for every finite occasion. This limitation, endemic to the condition of negative prehension, would infect the divine experience, even if only in some negligible way. For this reason, Griffin's "delayed" divine prehension theory falls short of the requirements of omniscience. On the basis of Griffin's proposal, God would have great and perhaps even cosmically sufficient knowledge, but God would not have knowledge arguably commensurate with what is logically possible to be known, namely, *all* the finite occasions in their states of immediate satisfaction, which would eliminate any negative prehensions in God.

We regard the two remaining proposals as the most promising for demonstrating a deep compatibility between special relativity and Hartshorne's neoclassical theism. If actual occasions differ in temporal extent, and if God is truly omniscient, then God must be capable of knowing all of them. John Robert Baker pointed out that this entails, on Hartshorne's model according to which God prehends and responds to every finite occasion, that divine occasions must be as temporally thin as the thinnest occasions in nature.[44] This is supposed to show that Hartshorne's view is intrinsically suspect and we have already seen that Hartshorne himself was baffled by the problem of how occasions of various temporal extent could be synchronized in the experience of God. Marjorie Suchocki complained that the model defies "probability."[45] We respond that these judgments seem to be based on certain limited psychological standards of human imagination, but they have no properly logical force. Yet, the human imagination itself can expand to at least conceive, if not strictly imagine, ever briefer spans of time. For example, we can now conceive information processing provided by a quantum computer. In any event, the Hartshorne-Cobb proposal exhibits a clear metaphysical principle for determining the duration of God's occasions: *God's prehensions will be as temporally thin as the temporally thinnest occasions that can occur within a cosmic epoch according to that epoch's nomological conditions and constraints (or most ingrained physical habits).*

We are not claiming that omniscience should be defined as knowledge of anything that can be expressed in a grammatically correct sentence. We believe that Hartshorne (and indeed, the tradition of classical theism) was correct to deny this. For example, the idea that a properly omniscient being should know all of the details of the future is incorrect if, as Hartshorne argues, certain details about the future have yet to be decided and are therefore not "there" (in the future) to be known. Or again, the idea that a properly omniscient being should know an actual occasion *during* its process of concrescence cannot be correct if, as Hartshorne came to believe, actual occasions cannot be prehended until their processes of becoming have reached satisfaction or objectification.[46] Only then are such occasions *actually there* to be known. There is no comparable logical or metaphysical limitation involving God's knowledge of the temporally thinnest occasions. On the contrary, such occasions are, by definition, *actually there* to be prehended and known. We may also ask, following Griffin, what reason there is to think that the God of neoclassical theism would be intrinsically limited to any specific "delay" in divine prehensions. To set such limits is to inject arbitrary, contingent restrictions into our conception of God's knowledge. If an omniscient being, defined as a being who knows all actuality as actuality and all possibility as possibility, exists, then such a being knows reality just as it is and this includes knowing all of its finest grained truths.

Griffin points out that temporal extension for an occasion expands as the extension of proximate prehended data expands. For instance, an electronic occasion will be temporally thinner than a neuronic occasion that includes the data of the electron and will be far thinner still than that of a regnant occasion of human conscious experience that includes the data of the neuron. By this logic a divine occasion should be the most temporally extensive of occasions. It occurs to us, however, that a divine occasion would be categorically different from any non-divine occasions for the reason that God is ubiquitous and thus non-localized. Localized or finite actual occasions will be dependent upon light-cone propagation for at least much of their prehended data (granting there may be quantum entanglement influences free of such light-cone limitations that are also part of the occasion's data). Thus, there is a categorical difference between divine and non-divine occasions that correlates with the difference in temporal extensions.

We submit that the most plausible approach to the problem is to embrace both Hartshorne's observation about God as a *non-localized* prehender and the earlier Hartshorne-Cobb proposal regarding divine synchronization through prehension of all objectified occasions from the temporally thinnest to the most temporally extensive. The purported problem about variant "phases" of the satisfaction of occasions that this proposal raises does *not* make a rigorous linear sequence of divine occasions logically impossible or incoherent, although it does make the divine "now" exceedingly short. But we hold that what has not been seen with sufficient clarity or emphasis is that such durational brevity of divine occasions is not a deleterious consequence for the doctrine of God. On the contrary, such prehensive discrimination amplifies the neoclassical concept of *divine power*. That is to say, the ability to have the kind of supra-discriminational prehensions and responsiveness required by the synchronization proposal is just the sort of agency that only God, the *eminently* capacious entity in the neoclassical view, could appropriately possess. Indeed, as Cobb suggests, such brevity of experience is quite psychologically unimaginable by us, and yes, this is a view of divine experience that displays staggering complexity, *but not inappropriately so for God*. We often do not ask this question in the context of considerations of the concept of omniscience, so often focusing instead on the range or completeness of God's propositional knowledge, but "how *fast* can an entity process data or information?" is a legitimate question (indeed, this is an issue of great importance for quantum computer engineering). If Hartshorne is correct in accepting that God is the greatest *conceivable* being, our intuitive expectation should be that God has a maximal capacity for prehending and processing physical data. There should be no limit *in* God for prehensive discrimination, only limits to the duration of finite actual occasions as grounded in the physical conditions of particular cosmic epochs, such as the apparent limits or constraints given in the Planck constant or the Compton action limit for our present cosmic epoch.

Let us clarify what we are asserting. Each divine "now" is defined by the *cosmic or global intersection of objectifications* of actual occasions. Such an intersection is *not* phenomenologically accessible to finite observers tied to localized space-time frameworks and conditioned by the time lags of light-cone propagation.[47] As a consequence nothing about what we are proposing conflicts with the results of observational tests of special relativity such as we find, for instance, in the recent OPERA experiments which confirm relativity effects up to gamma factors of 10 to the 12th power.[48] However, *ex hypothesi,* such a global intersection for prehensions would be available to a *non-localized* prehender, since, in such case, by definition, there would be no light-signal time lags to prohibit the immediacy of prehensions of objectified occasions. These intersections might be as durationally short as the durationally shortest actual occasion (e.g., a virtual particle occasion on a realist interpretation of virtual particles or even some other "micro" occasion whose duration is above the Compton limit), but in principle could be even shorter if there are objectifications of longer durational occasions that occur in the midst of some "bottom level" micro-occasion's concrescence.

Nothing about this picture seems to us to be either logically or metaphysically impossible. At a bare minimum, we believe we have shown that the alleged incompatibility of neoclassical theism and special relativity is *very* far from obvious. The field of cosmological physics has rapidly changed since the early 1980s with the experimental confirmation of quantum nonlocality. The old apothem that "relativity shows that there is no cosmic simultaneity" is now widely viewed as problematic when taken as an ontological rather than merely phenomenological judgment.[49] If the neoclassical deity exists, it is plausible that one of the proposals we have discussed provides a resolution to the *prima facie* conflict between special relativity and neoclassical theism. We submit that the *directives* of Hartshorne's theory of metaphysics have been met in this case. Again, as Hartshorne demands of a rational metaphysical theory, "there must be an at least *possible* way of harmonizing what physicists say is true of our epoch and what metaphysicians say is true of all possible epochs" (CS 54).

Metaphysics and Science Redux

There are at least three considerations which make it clear that, at the very least, it is not obvious that Hartshorne's neoclassical metaphysics conflicts with the above-mentioned empirical hypotheses, or that he is "cavalier" about empirical challenges. Following Popperian distinctions, Hartshorne never claimed that his proposed metaphysics is in principle exempt from empirical *disconfirmation,* although it is exempt from the quite distinct notion of empirical *confirmation.* If a "metaphysical" proposal really does conflict with an empirical fact, then it is disconfirmed and fails to be a genuinely metaphysical proposition. No genuinely metaphysical proposition, however, could be "empirically confirmed" in the standard sense that some restrictive state of affairs *as opposed to another* illustrates the proposition, because this would deny the universality of the candidate metaphysical proposition's requirement that it be illustrative of any conceivable state of affairs. This requirement does not prevent it from being the case that some states of affairs are phenomenologically "privileged" in the sense that certain metaphysical truths may be more readily apparent in special cases of phenomena. Hartshorne agrees with the early Heidegger that metaphysics can be about profoundly general concepts, yet such concepts are neither phenomenologically vacuous, nor inexplicable, nor utterly without discernible structure. For instance, the process metaphysical theory of the necessarily "social structure of all experience" might be seen with particular clarity via the special phenomenon of the "active concern" (Heidegger's *sorge*) of human being.[50]

Our discussion of big bang cosmology and the special theory of relativity indicates that the determination of the relevant "empirical facts" (or interpretations of them) which a philosopher is forced to accept is a subtle, highly theory-dependent and much-disputed matter. For example, we have seen that it is not clear or agreed upon by philosophers of science that relativity physics establishes that time is "relative" even in Newton's sense, or that special relativity robs us of any objective, uniform notion of temporal modes of past, present, or future; nor is it clear that the standard big bang model, even if sound, "proves" the absolute finitude of either time or creative process as such. We repeat here what was said in Chapter Three: Hartshorne's line of demarcation between metaphysics and science does not entail that, *in practice,* the line is easily seen or understood. All that is required is that the line

304 THE MIND OF CHARLES HARTSHORNE

exists, not that we have divine-like knowledge of its exact boundaries. Edwards, as we saw, considers current astrophysics to be a form of metaphysics. That assertion is understandable in light of the line, so often unclear in practice, that exists between metaphysics and science. In this context, Hartshorne's dictum bears repeating, that metaphysics is "that part of a priori knowledge in which clarity and certainty are least readily attained" (CS 32).

NINE

Hartshorne's Applied Philosophy I

Moral Philosophy, Abortion, and Environmental Ethics

THOSE WHO KNOW Charles Hartshorne primarily as a metaphysician, a philosopher of religion, or a scholar of Whitehead's work, may be surprised to learn that he wrote a great deal on matters related to ethics and applied philosophy. He left no systematic treatise on ethics, but he often spoke on questions of moral philosophy, and he was especially vocal on issues that he considered to be of pressing concern for the times in which he lived—war and pacifism, environmental destruction, overpopulation, racism and sexism, the rights of nonhuman animals, the effects of modern technology, and abortion. (We have already seen his commitment to feminism in the theological sphere.) He insisted that the treatment of such questions is impoverished or ill-formed when utterly divorced from properly metaphysical considerations. This insistence (if correct) is, in and by itself, an argument of some force for the indispensability of metaphysical inquiry. In effect, such inquiry has implications for the living of life and conversely the living of life has implications for metaphysics. Hartshorne was critical of any philosopher who he believed to be deficient in ethical insight. For example, he referred to Schopenhauer, Wagner, and Nietzsche as "a somewhat sinister trio," to which he added Freud "in some of his least attractive aspects" and Heidegger, "that mystic without an ethics."[1]

Acknowledging the genius of these five men, he nevertheless found in all of them "ideas or attitudes capable of obscuring the ideals and beliefs with which human life tends to lose its bearings, its hope and its nobility" (IO 239). Hartshorne knew Heidegger "before his ghastly Nazi period" and shared more in common with him than with the other four just mentioned, but he was bothered, like Emmanuel Levinas and Hans Jonas, by what he saw as Heidegger's "lack of any convincing ethics" (DL 20–21).[2]

Had Hartshorne attended to moral philosophy in the way that he attended to metaphysics, we would have a much better idea of how he would have responded to the great ethical systems such as those of the Buddha, Aristotle, Aquinas, Kant, or Mill. Of course, he mentioned such thinkers rather frequently, but only as the points that they made were relevant to some point that he wished to make. Hartshorne was clearly not a cultural relativist, for he believed in the possibility of a rational critique of the prevalent moral values of society. He accepted pragmatism in the basic sense that "ideas must be expressible in living and behavior or they are merely verbal" (CS xvi). What he called the "pragmatic principle"—the second of the twenty-one principles of metaphysics listed in his "Reply to Everyone"—is an important test of the adequacy of metaphysical proposals (PCH 572–73). For Hartshorne, any philosophy that has little ability to illuminate concrete problems inherent in the living of life, or worse, undermines the ability to live life amounts to intellectual failure. He considered nihilism to fail the fundamental pragmatic test for there is no way to live as though all is in vain (IO 334). The high importance of praxis in doing philosophy for Hartshorne is nowhere better exhibited than in the rebuke of his famous former student Richard Rorty. Says Hartshorne, Rorty is "over concerned about problems invented by philosophers and too little concerned about problems of human beings" (CAP 257).

In addition to the connection with pragmatism, Hartshorne's philosophy accommodates a kind of existentialism. In his own distinctive ways, Hartshorne embraces eight criteria which allow his work to be classified as what Jean Wahl called a "philosophy of existence."[3] To be specific: (1) philosophy must be considered an existential engagement (Hartshorne's Pragmatic Principle; Sartre's notion of the philosopher as *engagé*); (2) there is a primacy of the "felt life-world" or *Lebenswelt* as an "existential" correction of phenomenological method; (3) there is a primacy of concrete existence (or "actuality" as in Heidegger's specific use of the term *Existenz*) over abstract essence; (4) both temporality and contingency have an ontological or *de re* status; (5) the concrete is the key to the essential or the abstract rather than the converse; (6) human freedom is affirmed as (at least partial) self-determination; (7) special experiences (e.g., love or anxiety or intense religious feeling) are privileged phenomenological apertures for ontological insights; and (8) there is a humanistic critique of technocracy or the cultural predominance of a reductive means-to-end mentality. In addition, Hartshorne holds, with numerous existential thinkers from Berdyaev to Unamuno, that tragedy is an ineradicable element of existence. In correspondence with Shields (December 1975), Hartshorne affirmed this comparison, writing that Shields had shown "correctly enough I think" that "I am an existentialist of a sort [also a pragmatist]."[4]

There remains, however, the problem of situating Hartshorne vis-à-vis the major ethical systems that often inform contemporary ethical discussion; in particular, virtue ethics, deontology, and consequentialism. In this chapter we begin with an overview of Hartshorne's moral philosophy so as to clarify its relation to his metaphysics and to gain at least a rudimentary understanding of the ways it relates to the classifications of ethical systems one finds in the philosophical literature. Afterwards, we turn to Hartshorne's thoughts on abortion, environmental ethics, technology, politics/economics, and war and peace. In each case, we seek to highlight Hartshorne's contributions to these topics as well as to address salient criticisms. We also hope to demonstrate the truth in George Allan's judgment on Hartshorne's moral philosophy: "Here is an ethic of tenderness and valor, the ennobling blend of a respect for past achievements and an attraction toward fresh adventures. It is an ethic able to wed optimism and uncertainty."[5]

Hartshorne's Moral Philosophy

While Hartshorne rejected atheism in favor of neoclassical theism, he did not draw a direct correlation between "lack of any convincing ethics" and atheism. As we have seen in the previous chapters, he was critical of theologians and philosophers who defend "ugly" concepts of God that make atheism more attractive; but the ugly theologies are not the only theologies. For Hartshorne, skeptical attacks on religious ideas are a useful corrective to idolatrous theologies—i.e., theologies that place something less than the perfection or eminence of God at the center of worship. In two early articles published four years apart in the *International Journal of Ethics,* Hartshorne endeavored to make love the central organizing idea of his moral philosophy. He maintained that theologians had never taken seriously or never developed adequately the proposition that "God is love," and he characterized love as "that sympathetic sharing of experience which to a spiritual philosophy is the very atmosphere of being."[6] He asked, "[W]here then has the conception of love, or any practical equivalent, been provided with its intellectual credentials?"[7] One of Hartshorne's aims in philosophy was to provide love with these credentials by emphasizing "sympathetic sharing of experience"—Whitehead's feeling of feeling—as ontologically foundational for all relations between dynamic singulars and to develop and defend the idea that God has feelings of love and acts in the most loving ways possible for one whose very existence is coextensive with the cosmos.

The dipolar theistic cast of Hartshorne's philosophy does not mean that he took a sectarian approach to the questions of ethics. As we have seen throughout this study, Hartshorne never showed an interest in defending doctrines unique to any religion nor did he appeal to supposedly revealed or sacred writings as *privileged* avenues to truth, theological or otherwise (although, as we saw in Chapter Seven, he respected such writings as being capable of much wisdom and moral insight). It is also clear that he had no use for an exclusively *a priori* morality. His reflections on human obligations remained firmly grounded in a biological understanding of human life and values. In a 1978 article he noted that the discovery of cells was three centuries old and that "cell theory" had been developed more than 140 years prior to his writing.[8] However, he did not think that the theory had been adequately assimilated into the general culture. Hartshorne noted that humans, like all higher animals, are multicellular creatures with specialized organs, and the cells themselves are tiny living organisms. As the geneticist Sewell Wright observed, "The concept that organisms are composed of suborganisms has become one of the most significant principles of biology."[9] Each animal and each plant is a marvel of cellular organization in which the basic principle is "life serving life"—the cellular parts serve the whole organism. According to Hartshorne:

> Since ethics is concerned with social relations, the fact that our very bodies are cases of social organization and cooperation is not to be brushed aside as a mere detail; rather, it is an illustration of a basic principle on which all ethics must rest [i.e., "life serving life"].[10]

Hartshorne did not deduce specific moral obligations from this observation, but he did find in the cellular biological basis of life important clues concerning the obligations that we have to others, including others that are non-human.

The bodies of multicellular organisms are not alone in exhibiting an essentially social organization; individual organisms reproducing and living in groups are also forms of social organization, with human societies being the most complex of which we are aware. In such groups, Hartshorne observed, one finds an interdependent mixture of instinctual drives for self-preservation and for species-preservation. "[Warder Clyde] Allee was right, *all* animals are in some degree 'social.'"[11] Indeed, whatever might be called "self-identity" in any particular animal is inextricably tied to the identity of the larger group of which it is a member. As much as Western ethics sometimes prizes individuals as standing apart from the herd, a "lone wolf" is precisely a beast whose survival is most in jeopardy. It is true that in human personality, individual differentiation reaches its greatest level; this is so much the case that the differences (psychological and intellectual) between so called races and even between the sexes is less various than what one finds in individuals *within* these groups—in a word, racial and sexual differences are nothing as compared to the differences among persons generally. Great as individual differences may be, and however much an adult human may achieve a relatively independent existence, one *never* ceases to be dependent on others for survival and well-being. Survivalists must be extremely well-trained, and then only the most hardy and lucky among them could escape disease, accident or attack from other creatures for any length of time. In any event, the ideals of the survivalist are hardly a recipe for the long-term prospects of human flourishing, for cooperative effort is essential for that goal. The social nature of human beings would be considered a truism were it not for the often-exaggerated claims to individual uniqueness and independence.

Hartshorne took several lessons from these observations. First, the idea that self-preservation is the first law of nature is "a vicious half-truth." It is a half-truth because it ignores the drive for species-preservation. Hartshorne maintains that it is "bad biology" to omit the aim of species-preservation or to try to reduce it to the drive for self-preservation, or to mere self-interest.[12] The fact that self-preservation and species-preservation are so intimately intertwined means that the concept of a self as something that could use all others as means to its own ends is deeply problematic. The needs and ends of the "self"—conceived in social terms—are inseparable from the needs and ends of the species. A possible counterargument is that taking satisfaction in acting for others is a sign that one necessarily acts from a motive of self-interest. Hartshorne calls this "an old sophism."[13] He recognized that this counterargument illicitly identifies "the enjoyment inherent in the act itself with its intended result or product." In short, if one finds enjoyment in acting for others, it does not follow that one acted for others in order to find enjoyment. Hartshorne points out that, in the abstract, there is a clear distinction between (a) present enjoyment taken in acting for one's own future advantage and (b) present enjoyment in acting for the future advantage of others. "As to the present enjoyment, it is simply not the point at issue." What differentiates (a) and (b) is not present enjoyment but future aim. Moreover, as Hartshorne notes, it is precisely a mark of good persons that they find enjoyment in the enjoyment of others.[14]

Hartshorne also calls the idea of the primacy of self-preservation "pernicious." This is because it is sometimes expressed as the foundation of an ethical philosophy. In Hartshorne's view, the idea that the *sole aim* for which one should act is to satisfy the needs or desires of oneself is "unenlightened superstition."[15] He marshals two arguments in favor of this conclusion. First, he notes that, as a matter of fact, those who we consider to be "well-balanced men and women" find fulfilment not only in how others may benefit them, but in how they may benefit others.[16] In Hartshorne's words, "So far from our valuing others only for their usefulness to ourselves it is in no small part for our usefulness to others that we value ourselves" (ZF 190). Hartshorne goes so far as to claim that one is "subnormal, "irrational" and perhaps "sick" to the extent that one denies that, all else being equal, it is best that others (including animals) should be happy, even if one cannot share in their happiness (ZF 190). Hartshorne's point seems to be that ethics is as much a matter of mental health as it is of philosophical argument. Certainly, in most quarters, one does not openly confess an ethic of mere self-interest if one expects to be taken as an ethically sensitive person. Mere self-interest as a basis for ethical behavior might be the best that one could hope for in a society composed only of psychopaths, but fortunately, the genuine psychopath is a rare aberration from the norm of human feeling.

There is, however, another argument against strict ethical egoism and that is that it *arbitrarily* elevates the good of an individual person above the good of others. The same mode of reasoning that condemns racism, sexism, and homophobia also condemns egoism, to wit, it divides people in a morally arbitrary way. The color of a person's skin, the sex of a person, and the sexual orientation of a person do not mark differences that justify treating people differently. But equally, the fact that one is the person one is does not distinguish any individual from any other. As Hartshorne notes:

> The self is one among others. It exists for a limited span and then dies, whereupon (barring some dreadful catastrophe) others of our species take over, inheriting results, good or bad, from our activities. To me there is something marvelously irrational in the notion that justification for my concern for human life generally and as such must come from assuming, as my absolute good, to which all else for me is merely instrumental, a desirable sequence of my bodily and mental experiences, a sequence which could end at any time, and in any case will end within some years.[17]

As we noted in Chapter Four, Hartshorne appealed to Buddhism to buttress his argument. To live only for self, Hartshorne said, is writhing in delusion (ZF 190).

We should observe that the Freudian doctrines that narcissistic self-preservation and autoerotic relief of bodily tensions predominate in the very first experiences of infants have long been challenged by empirical research in the field of developmental psychology. In particular, Ian Suttie, the Scottish psychiatrist, argues in his classic treatise on *The Origins of Love and Hate* that the basic orientation of the child to the mother is one of social give-and-take. Suttie speaks of a "symbiotic communion," where play seeking a loving or approving response from the mother is primal.[18] As a specific example, consider that infants are often observed gazing into the mother's eyes during breast-feeding and then pausing to gurgle and smile upon noticing a response from the mother. The comparative religions scholar, Huston Smith, deftly describes Suttie's relationship to Freudian thinking this way:

> In the Freudian view the infant believes itself to be omnipotent, able to summon the mother magically with its cries. It cathects to the mother because she relieves its bodily tensions. To Suttie this was as preposterous as saying that the mother loves the baby because it is a breast-reliever who drains her swollen mammary glands.[19]

For Suttie, the eventual separation and differentiation from the mother and the prospect of abandonment is the real root of the pronounced human potential for anxiety and rage. Correlatively, any society that represses tenderness and creative play in children is a society rife with potential for all manner of psychic pathology, ranging from self-medication through overuse of psychoactive drugs and alcohol to emotionally unsatisfying sexual promiscuity. Consonant with Hartshorne's emphasis on love, Suttie insists that the *empirically well-grounded* view is that our deepest longings are for emotional intimacy with others. Above all other psychodynamic factors, love matters most.

Hartshorne's denial of the primacy of self-interest should not be taken to imply that self-interest is not an important dimension of the ethical life. He praises Kant for his "wonderful shrewdness" in deriving an indirect duty to be happy. Hartshorne considers this shrewd because "the unhappy person is bound to be a nuisance or worse to others."[20] Kant's position is not quite as Hartshorne describes it, although both philosophers accept that there is a connection between self-love and love of others and that one should not be a stumbling block to others.[21] Hartshorne argues for a direct duty of happiness to oneself and to others. More precisely, "one's present self has duties to one's future self as truly as it has duties to other human beings" (ZF 198). The very consideration mentioned in the previous paragraph that counts *against* ethical egoism, counts *for* the idea that we have obligations to ourselves as well as others. In Hartshorne's words:

> Otherwise expressed, a truly enlightened interest in self will adopt the ideal of seeing that self as one among others, valuable by the same criteria as the others, which are no more means for it as end than it is means for their ends.[22]

If one has obligations to others, and if others are not relevantly different than oneself, then one has obligations to oneself.

> To value oneself rationally is to value oneself for the same reasons, and by the same criteria, as are used in valuing others. In short, "love others as oneself" is a command of reason, not just a requirement or gift of grace. (ZF 188)

Hartshorne shows his own shrewdness in the observation that, "Too pedantic an insistence upon altruistic considerations may, by destroying spontaneity and zest, make one a less valuable person, both to oneself and to others" (ZF 199).

An important difference between human beings and other creatures is the high degree to which humans are symbol using creatures. Hartshorne emphasizes this time and again:

> Symbolic capacity is our human advantage and superiority. Is it a difference in kind from other animals or only one in degree? I answer: it is a difference in degree so vast that for many purposes one can safely forget that it is one of degree. However, recent experiences in teaching what seem to be primitive visual languages to chimpanzees show that for some purposes the difference may be relative. My guess is that the chimpanzee will turn out to be capable only of what a quite small child can accomplish semantically.[23]

The extent of the ability to use and manipulate symbols not only distinguishes humans from all other creatures on the planet, it is also this ability that makes ethical reasoning possible. As Hartshorne notes, when a predatory animal kills it is gathering food and cannot be accused of murder. The animal is guided by instinct, not by principle. But the human murderer knows about death, knows that life is valuable to the victim, knows that the act of murder affects the meaning of life for the individual and those who care about that person, knows that murder "conflicts with principles without the observance of which by most people he himself would never have existed" (WM 125).

If the ability to use symbols makes it possible to be ethical it also makes it possible to be unethical. Hartshorne goes so far as to say that an animal that thinks and speaks, as humans do, cannot be merely non-ethical—it must be ethical or unethical (ZF 197). As Hartshorne says, "To speak is to be at home with universals" (ZF 198). The animal capable of reflecting on universals is one that envisions alternate futures and can, under most circumstances, decide between them. One envisions one's future existence, for example, and decides whether to care about oneself only or whether to generalize this care to one's family, one's friends, one's tribe, one's nation, to humanity at large, or even to other creatures. Rationality demands consistency in one's choices and the principles on which one decides to act. Here, the parallel with Kant's reasoning is very close, for Kant maintained that the rational creature is aware of the maxims upon which it acts and decides for itself whether the maxim can be universalized. Hartshorne puts a biological twist to this perspective. We have seen that he finds the basis of ethics in the twin instincts of self-preservation and species-preservation; it is the generalization of these concerns through the power of thought that yields ethical thinking. According to Hartshorne:

> Ethics is the *generalization of instinctive concern,* which in principle transcends the immediate state of the self and even the long-run career of the self, and embraces the ongoing communal process of life as such. (ZF 198)

This comes close to addressing the famous is/ought problem in ethical theory. At a minimum, Hartshorne assumes that consistency in one's reasoning is binding on a rational being, so his argument does assume an imperative, if only an epistemic one.

Hartshorne does not think that the difference between humans and other creatures entails that the other creatures are valueless or that they exist merely to be used for human purposes. He holds, rather, that "No form of life should be thought a mere means, a mere utility. All forms are beautiful and good in themselves."[24] This idea is illustrated in a touching story about Leibniz that, ironically enough, Kant tells. After observing a tiny worm, Leibniz carefully replaced it on the tree so that it should come to no harm through any act of his.[25] Kant realized that those who are cruel to animals tend to behave badly towards their fellow humans, and so he argued against cruelty to animals, except when it serves what he considered to be a praiseworthy purpose such as vivisecting animals to help understand human anatomy and illness.[26] For Kant, humans have no direct duties to animals, they exist to be used for human purposes. Hartshorne rejects the Kantian view.

The question is: In what sense does the nonhuman have rights? According to Kant, only rational beings have rights. The sole reason he sees for being kind to animals is that being unkind to them tends to carry over into unkindness to persons. I agree with [Albert] Schweitzer and almost the entire Eastern world that this will not do. A better reason for treating animals kindly is that their lives, too, have intrinsic value.[27]

Hartshorne maintains that Kant took an untenable position by claiming that human beings alone are ends in themselves because they alone are rational beings. As Hartshorne argues, Kant recognized that human beings can never be sure of their complete rationality.[28] This prerogative belongs to God alone (WM 118–19). On this basis, Kant should have said that God is the only true end in itself.

The intrinsic value that Hartshorne finds in all creatures is based on his psychicalism, or panexperientialism, and in what Eugene Peters called the aesthetic motif of Hartshorne's thought, subjects we discussed in Chapter Four. According to Hartshorne, "where there is feeling there is value in a more than instrumental sense" (WM 122). One might say that every creature, in virtue of its experiences, has a claim on existence. But "experience" should be understood in this context primarily as an aesthetic category, not an ethical one. As we saw in Chapter Four, for Hartshorne, aesthetic categories have a universal application since the basic units of reality are dynamic singulars. The foundations of reality are *processes* whereby the "many" antecedent data (which are themselves experiences) of a nascent singular are woven into a new experiential "one" in the creative activity of the present moment, and this relatively novel experience, becomes, in turn, an element in subsequent dynamic singulars. No unchanging substance underlies the process: "The action itself is the actor."[29] Moreover, the process is inherently selective and valuational as the relatively novel entity defines itself. In Hartshorne's metaphysics, as in process thought generally, there is no ontologically neutral stuff, no supposedly "primary qualities," onto which "secondary" or "tertiary" values are annexed. We have used the expression "relatively novel" to emphasize that novelty comes in gradations, some of them so fine as to appear to be, for ordinary purposes, completely nonexistent.

We have also seen that the logic of parts and wholes plays a decisive role in Hartshorne's metaphysics. While every whole is made of parts that are dynamic singulars and hence are "drops of experience," many wholes lack the organizational unity to funnel the "many" experiences into a dynamic singular that is inclusive of the whole itself that could constitute a new "one." The marvelous complexity of the human body with its specialized organs and nervous system, can support, in most cases, a "personally ordered society" of dynamic singulars that is commonly referred to as a self or a person. More generally, creatures with a central nervous system have sufficient organizational complexity to be understood as individuals and not merely as collections of cells. The botanical world is in many respects still a mystery where consciousness is concerned. To what extent can any particular plant be thought of as an experiencing individual? Or are its movements and growth simply a function of the cells of which it is made? Hartshorne took the latter view, but some in the process camp such as Frederick Ferré and Carol Christ are open to the idea of a form of responsive awareness in some plants that stands between a mere collective and the organizational unity of an animal.[30] This is a question of detail rather than principle, so it need not detain us. It is interesting to note, however, that Hartshorne argued that, in dreamless sleep (supposing there is such a thing), we come nearest to reverting to a colony of cells with no central nervous system. "Thus, I take [dreamless] sleep to put us on both sides of a great divide, between two profoundly different levels of reality."[31]

While Hartshorne holds that every creature with feeling has value in a more than instrumental sense, he recognizes the need to make comparative value judgments about the relative importance of the creatures. Subrational organisms make decisions instinctively; only human beings, as far as we know, attempt to decide such matters on principles. The crucial pair of distinctions for Hartshorne are, first, intrinsic value and instrumental value and, second, greater value and lesser value. We routinely employ such distinctions when judging human works of art, thinking that some are more valuable than others without supposing that any are wholly without value. By parity of reasoning, two sentient individuals may have intrinsic value, but it does not follow that they are entirely equal in value or that one cannot rationally prefer one over the other. Schweitzer's ethic of reverence for life did not prevent him from understanding the necessity of killing microorganisms in order to save his patients. Schweitzer (and Hartshorne) recognize that this is not enough to say that the microorganisms are simply valueless or have no value for themselves. The question is whether such preferences can be rationally justified, and if so, how. Hartshorne appealed to aesthetic principles to resolve the issue.

> An ethically good act is good in two senses: it contributes to harmony and intensity of experience both in agent and in spectators. A good will enjoys a sense of harmony between self and others (insofar, virtue is indeed its own reward); and its consequences, if it is wise and fortunate as well as good, will be to enhance the possibilities in the community for intense and harmonious experiences. Obviously cruelty produces ugliness in the experiences of many; genuine kindness produces beauty, directly in itself, and indirectly in many ways. (ZF 199)

In this way, for Hartshorne, "the intrinsic content of good is, broadly speaking, to be judged aesthetically."[32]

Hartshorne found it useful to distinguish between the value we place on an individual *qua* individual and an individual *qua* specimen of a species.

> John Cobb makes a helpful suggestion. We tend to think that humanity is important because of the values in each individual person; but we tend to think that one nightingale or one hermit thrush is significant chiefly as a specimen of its species. (WM 124–25)

We often view members of the human species as valuable in their own right whereas we tend to view members of other species primarily as specimens that exemplify the species. This is, in large measure, because each human being, from an early age, is so clearly a distinct personality (even in the case of monozygotic twins) whereas we are less likely to notice the distinctness of personality in other species, although this becomes easier with pets and with chimpanzees and gorillas. Hartshorne was less confident in judging the value of entire nonhuman species:

> Our intuitions seem less responsive to this question. There are not far from nine thousand species of birds. Which would be a greater loss to the universe, the disappearance of all birds, or premature deaths of nine thousand human beings? I could

perhaps seriously consider giving up the remainder of my life if it would definitely save a threatened species for millennia. But it would be merely silly to risk one's life for a single individual bird, whose life expectancy anyway is probably less than three years. Perhaps the best we can do with this question of the relative values of ourselves compared to the other animals is the following. We can try to view man and the rest of nature as one ecosystem in which our species is, so far as possible, complementary, rather than competitive, with the other creatures in the system. (WM 126–27)[33]

In order to balance human interest and interest in other species, Hartshorne makes consequentialist arguments for, among other things, rethinking human population growth (because of the burden to ourselves and nature of an overpopulated world), transportation by car (because of the acres of concrete covering arable land), consumption of meat (because of the inefficiency of cycling essential nutrients through animals), and birth control for pets (so as to limit the slaughter of other animals to feed them) (WM 127f).[34]

Ethics and Dipolar Theism

Before turning to a discussion of specific applications of these ideas to ethical problems, let us look once more at the relevance of neoclassical theism for Hartshorne's ethics. Time and again, Hartshorne says, "Reason should universalize our ends as well as our means" (ZF 188, cf. ZF 190).[35] We have seen that he rejected egoism (psychological and ethical) and advocated expanding the circle of moral concern beyond what George Eliot called the "miserable aims that end with self." He was also sensitive to how male privilege had disfigured human relationships; in later years, he often expressed solidarity with feminism and regret at the historic sexism of men (e.g., OO 56–57; DL 62–63; ZF x). His attitude towards homosexuality was similarly nonprejudicial. He considered those who crusade against homosexuality and who are under the impression that gays and lesbians are out to recruit people to be homosexual to be "public nuisances" (DL 209). We noted in the first chapter how Hartshorne opposed racism, but he also said that he dealt poorly with it, because he tended "to turn aggressive and intolerant against the aggressive and intolerant" (DL 37–38). He spoke of the "folly of racism" (CS 313) and called it "one of America's greatest national shames" (DL 401). The moral concern that stops at the borders of a country was also foreign to him, both in his temperament and in his philosophy. He wrote, "We have to inculcate the sense of world citizenship and of membership in all humanity, not just in some part of humanity" (ZF 200). However, for Hartshorne, the universalization of ends should not stop at humanity. From the time of his first book, he never abandoned the ideal that one should be, in Stoic fashion (though without Stoicism's determinism), a "citizen of the universe" (BH 1). He wrote: "The power of living consciously as a citizen of the cosmos is the basic human prerogative, and the more fully this power is realized, the more clearly it reveals itself as the vision of God" (BH 72).

The ever-expanding circle of identity represented in this movement of thought ends in "the vision of God." In this, Hartshorne's philosophy has profound affinities with other theistic (and even atheistic) systems, a point to which Hartshorne called attention:

> To me it seems clear that the ultimate and inclusive obliga-
> tion is neither to self nor to other human beings nor to both
> together, but to the cosmic and everlasting Something (call it
> God, Nirvana, or The Universe) so far as we can contribute
> permanently to the whole of this Something. Anything short
> of this is childish, considering the long history of the high
> religions, every one of which has (however inconsistently and
> ambiguously) transcended any merely partial, local, or tempo-
> rary object of endeavor, or referent of obligation.[36]

Hartshorne's qualification—"however inconsistently and ambiguously"—
is significant, for he saw himself as clarifying the nature of the "Something" to which our ultimate loyalty is due, and thereby explaining what it means to serve it. As discussed in Chapter Five, Hartshorne's God is not only supremely absolute but, more importantly, supremely relative: the *existence* and *essence* of God are unaffected by the world, but the *actuality* of God is affected by all that occurs in the world.

Hartshorne considered it blatantly biased towards humanity to suppose that God does not cherish nonhuman creatures.

Is it likely that God takes no delight whatever in the more than

> a million other living forms on this planet, yet does delight in, derive value from contemplating, the one human species lately emergent on the planet? If such an idea is not sheer anthropomorphic [anthropocentric?] bias, what would be such bias? (WM 118)

Every creature, not alone the human ones, makes some contribution, however humble it may be, to the *Summum Bonum* (WM 119). For this reason, Hartshorne could say, "To the extent that we fail to love life in its myriad forms, to that extent is our being outside our love for God."[37]

Classical theistic perspectives, both East and West, most often portrayed the ultimate as immutable and incapable of increase; but this made the idea of service to God problematic, for it is impossible to contribute to a complete and immutable being. Neoclassical theism introduces a genuinely novel and useful idea: If the divine is supremely relative then not only can God be an *infallible spectator* of cosmic events, God can be the *eminent form of compassionate understanding* of the feelings of the creatures, and the *ideal participant* in their weal and woe. The title of one of Hartshorne's articles expresses this idea: "God as Composer-Director, Enjoyer, and, in a Sense, Player of the Cosmic Drama."[38] As Hartshorne summarizes in another article: "love's supreme and inclusive object is also its supreme and inclusive subject . . . [and] . . . God the supremely lovable is also the supreme love."[39]

Hartshorne's theology entails that God is no mere spectator of the cosmic drama but is its ideal participant. With John Wilson, Hartshorne accepts that, through interaction with others—which Wilson calls "external lines of communication"—one may gain insight into the shortcomings of one's awareness of oneself—which Wilson labels, "internal lines of communication." In this way, one has an interest in strengthening the external lines of communication—"[one identifies oneself] emotionally with others and [shares] their experience and aims, so far as possible."[40] While self-knowledge and knowledge of others are thus intimately related, the perfect coincidence of these forms of knowledge are possible, according to Hartshorne, only for God. "[God's] valuations, without self-deception, indifference, sadism, or possibility of error, take all other valuations fully into account. Only [God's] lines of internal and external communication are always and fully open."[41] If the rational ideal is the full and equitable balancing of the good of all individuals affected by a decision or a policy, then that ideal must be embodied in deity. If, as Hartshorne holds, God exists necessarily, then the rational ideal also exists necessarily. Moreover, Hartshorne argues, nothing that could not have been otherwise—that is, nothing that is without qualification necessary—can be objectionable. It follows that there is no alternative to the rational ideal as it is embodied in God.

It must be emphasized that the rational ideal is itself abstract, although there must be concrete realizations of it at any given moment. There can be no question of the mechanical application of an algorithm to every situation. God, as the ideal participant in the creative advance of the universe, taking into account the total actual world at any given moment, must customize and evaluate the range of possible futures for every dynamic singular, or every genuine individual; then, according to the rhythm of becoming, there is a divine memory of accomplished fact and a continual give-and-take between God and the creatures. Hartshorne emphasizes that, by the very fact that willing the good of the creatures is at the same time willing its own good (because of its participation in their weal and woe), deity must be immune to selfish desires.

> God alone inherits all the harvest for which he, or anyone, sows the seed. To forbid him to enjoy the harvest, since that would make him selfish, is one of the oddest confusions into which sentimentalists have ever fallen. 'Selfishness' has meaning only in application to a partially ignorant, more or less apathetic (or perhaps malicious), and mortal creature whose usefulness to others cannot be guaranteed to bring proportionate future benefits to itself. (CS 309)

In Hartshorne's panentheism, self-interest and other-interest coincide in God. If God is inclusive of every being that comes to be as it comes to be—which Hartshorne calls "all-inclusive"—then every divine action boomerangs upon God, and necessarily so.[42] On the other hand, selfishness, in the sense of depriving another of a possible good that one keeps for oneself, is impossible for God, for every good experienced by the creature is necessarily experienced by God.

We have seen in the discussion of Hartshorne's aesthetics that aesthetic values are metaphysically basic, being more widely applicable than ethical values. One may speak, for example, of the good of nonrational creatures, but this in no way involves questions of duties or virtues between those creatures. Of course, ethical value judgments come into play when we ask about specifically human obligations towards other creatures, but this is not the same as imposing a moral framework on *their* lives and experiences. Nevertheless, it is worth noting that the dipolar God is in the categorically unique situation of embodying a perfect coincidence of "is" and "ought." There can be no discrepancy for an ideal agent—and God is nothing if not the ideal agent—between what it does and what it ought to do. This allows Hartshorne to provide a solution to the ancient problem that was first formulated in Plato's *Euthyphro,* of whether something is good because God commands it or if God commands it because it is good. The very substance of the divine life, its warp and weft, is its ideal participation in the lives of the creatures, a participation that in its abstract aspects could not be otherwise. Understanding that, for Hartshorne, "it is [divine] love that explains the [divine] power, not vice versa" (CE 7), to speak of a possible discrepancy of the "will of God" and the *Summum Bonum* can have no meaning.[43]

According to Hartshorne's moral philosophy, the imitation of God is, in part, the striving to perceive others (aesthetically and cognitively) as they are perceived by the love of God. It is also a striving to create in a manner analogous to God's own creative activity. Hartshorne was fond of summarizing Nicholas Berdyaev's moral imperative as: "Be creative and foster creativity in others" (IO 185; OT 58; DL 244; ZF 73, 200; CE 130).[44] We have seen that Hartshorne's metaphysics is a system in which creativity is a *descriptive category,* what the medieval philosophers called a transcendental, a concept that applies to every concrete particular which Hartshorne identifies as dynamic singulars. Here, however, "creativity" is used as a *normative category,* conceiving God's activity as the norm against which all lesser forms are compared. One is creative in the laudatory sense when one produces rich experiences and tends to increase the capacities of others for being creative in this optimal sense in the degree to which their nature allows (CE 131). At this juncture, moral philosophy and aesthetics dovetail for the creation of nobility, justice, and harmonious relationships is at the same time to create beauty.[45]

Abortion

Let us now turn to Hartshorne's positions on specific ethical issues and consider some of the important criticisms that have been given of them, beginning with the subject of abortion. Hartshorne first waded into these turbulent waters with his January 1981 article for *The Christian Century,* "Concerning Abortion: An Attempt at a Rational View."[46] In early April of the same year, *The Christianity Century* published ten letters in response to Hartshorne; one of the letters was supportive, but the rest were highly critical of his views.[47] In the same year, Hartshorne accepted an invitation from Dartmouth College to debate the question whether selective abortion should be made illegal. He wrote:

> I find this a monstrous proposal and do not greatly enjoy the idea of a formal debate about it. But I think I am well loaded for the fray. Debating is a political activity, not a search for truth. But it has some relation to such a search.[48]

Hartshorne's opponent in the debate was Dr. Mildred Jefferson (1926–2010) who had served as the President of the National Right to Life Committee. Hartshorne later reported that he lost the debate, with his side getting 47 votes compared to 87 votes for Dr. Jefferson. He added, "I have written an effective reply I think to letters to the *Christian Century* on my essay. That way I may win."[49] Hartshorne's reply to the letters were published in the closing pages of a 1985 article.[50]

We have seen that Hartshorne finds breadth enough within human experience to include both sides of the divide between animal and plant. When we fall into dreamless sleep, it is only or primarily the cells of the body that continue to feel. Another "great divide," on which humans stand on both sides, is that between the subhuman and the human. In this case, however, "human" is not to be understood in a genetic sense but in the sense of an animal with the ability to manipulate symbols, as in the expression "rational animal." Hartshorne argues: "The line between the human and the subhuman is crossed in the life of each one of us, if by *human* one means actually rational" (WM 119). Each human individual can trace its origin to the union of a sperm and egg, from a single-celled zygote. Very rapidly, through cell division, there is a multi-celled zygote. In most cases, in the earliest stages of the human embryo, there is genetic information necessary for the development of a fully human individual. Even so, precision demands that we prescind from speaking of *a single individual* since multiple individuals may arise from a single fertilized egg, as in the case of monozygotic twins or triplets. There is also the rare case of a chimera, when two fertilized eggs fuse to make one individual.[51] The individual (or individuals) in the early stages still lacks a brain that could coordinate its (their) experiences. Finally, the individual with a brain, once it develops, is not sufficient of itself to realize its potential for a consciously rational approach to relationships. The infant must be cared for, interact with other persons, and be exposed to human language and culture before it can function at a minimally human level. In view of these facts, Hartshorne was unwilling to reduce personality to genetic inheritance or to environmental influences. Nor does the dichotomy "nature versus nurture" exhaust what Hartshorne believed to be necessary for the development of personality. There is, in the final analysis, the individual's own continuing creative appropriation of its genetic and environmental influences. In Hartshorne's words, "Personality is partly made, partly self-made; it is not inborn."[52]

Hartshorne would agree with David Hume's remark that, in view of the high infant mortality rate in the 18th century, "the half of mankind die before they are rational creatures."[53] Almost every fertilized egg has the potential to become the biological basis of a fully functioning rational individual, but no fertilized egg can reasonably be described as such. Hartshorne considered it indefensible to finesse the distinction between the actual and the potential or between the actual and the possible:

> The difference between possible and actual is either important or unimportant. If it is important, then respect for a human adult is different from respect for a human fetus. If the difference is not important, then it must be taken as a terrible tragedy that millions of fertilizable human egg cells never are fertilized.[54]

The fact that no one, including the most ardent critic of abortion rights, considers it a "terrible tragedy" that so many human eggs are never fertilized indicates that the distinction of the actual and the possible is indeed important. There is, however, a genuine distinction between a potential being and a being with potential, and critics of abortion rights frequently emphasize that a fertilized human egg is indeed a being with potential. Hartshorne agrees, but he draws a conclusion that does not deny a woman the right to an abortion:

> The 'beginning of a human life' is not, by any evidence, the actuality of a being on the human level of value. It is the possibility of such a being, and therefore an important and

marvelous creature, but the mother is also marvelous and far more important.[55]

In addition to distinguishing actual humanity in the mother and potential humanity in the fetus, Hartshorne added a consequentialist argument. He called abortion "a nasty thing," but added that children growing up unwanted or neglected is even nastier and "truly horrible."[56]

According to Hartshorne, the most substantive argument from the pro-life side of the debate is that respect for the humanity of the fetus cannot be easily separated from respect for the humanity of an infant.[57] This point is neatly made by Jane English in her classic article "Abortion and the Concept of a Person." According to English:

> A fetus one week before birth is so much like a newborn baby in our psychological space that we cannot allow any cavalier treatment of the former while expecting full sympathy and nurturative support for the latter.[58]

Hartshorne agrees that the difference between a fetus and an infant is a matter of degree, but matters of degree are important, for it does not take much development for the infant to be much closer to full humanity than is the fetus.

> [The infant] is beginning to have primitive social relations not open to a fetus; and since there is no sharp line anywhere between an infant and a child able to speak a few words, or between the latter and a child able to speak very many words, we have to regard the infant as significantly different from a three-month or four-month fetus.[59]

This difference in degree between a fetus and an infant corresponds, in Hartshorne's view, to a difference in degree of importance, and, in any case, the mother's importance outstrips the importance of either fetus or infant. He considered infanticide wrong without equating it with murder. "Infanticide can be wrong without being fully comparable to the killing of persons in the full sense."[60] From a legal and practical standpoint, however, he considered it unwise to tamper with received wisdom.

> Our society has somehow made the decision to extend the connotations of 'murder' or utterly wrong homicide to infants that

have by natural forces been freed from the womb. To tamper with this decision is to weaken the support of tradition for our moral and legal structures.[61]

Again, English helps to clarify the question:

[The] alleged "slippery slope" between conception and birth is not so very slippery. In the early stages of pregnancy, abortion can hardly be compared to murder psychologically, but in the latest stages it is psychologically akin to murder.[62]

Given the competing perspectives and differing intuitions of the value of the unborn and of the newborn, Hartshorne considered the decision of the United States Supreme Court in Roe v. Wade as "a reasonable compromise."[63]

Without challenging Hartshorne's stance on the legal status of abortion, Anita Miller Chancey questions whether he was true to his best insights of elevating love as the principal ethical value. She observes that we sympathize more with a woman who chooses to have an abortion only after agonizing about what is most caring for all concerned (e.g., the unborn, other children, herself as a mother to the child), than a woman who is casual in having an abortion. The same action is taken in both cases, but the difference is that one decision is made from love and the other is not, or it is merely a case of self-love. Chancey also notes that, very often, the lack of rationality in the unborn in no way diminishes the mother's love for it. Mothers often willingly sacrifice a great deal out of love for the fetus in order to ensure that the person it becomes has the best chances in life that are possible. In short, rationality is not the sole determining factor in an organism's value; rather, it is its capacity to enhance loving relationships. According to Chancey:

Only when discussing abortion does Hartshorne fail to account for synergy in our relationships. Synergy between two creatures creates a value beyond what either of them can create independently, even when some creatures are non-rational.[64]

Chancey maintains that Hartshorne's stress on the criterion of rationality leads him to forget that rationality is value-neutral in a way that love is not. "Without love, rationality has the capacity to remain inhuman and immoral, which contributes little to God."[65]

What Hartshorne would add to Chancey's observation about rationality is that, without rationality, love cannot achieve its genuinely ethical character of *consciously directed care for the welfare of others,* be they subhuman or human. If at times Hartshorne overemphasizes the subrational status of the fetus, he does not deny the capacity of a mother to care for it and to sacrifice a great deal for it. He goes so far as to say that, in some respects, the mother-fetus relation provides a better symbol for the God-creature relation than does the father-fetus, for it is decidedly more intimate (OO 60). In any event, Hartshorne reminds us that "the moral question of abortion is one thing and the legal question quite another" (WM 126). Many in the pro-life movement have consistently argued that a mother should be *coerced under penalty of law* to carry the unborn to full term, even when the pregnancy is the result of rape or when it threatens the health of the mother or the livelihood of her family. The assumption of this position is that the unborn, at every stage of its development, is a person worthy of the same moral consideration as any adult human being. This is a contentious moral judgment that the many advocates of pro-life wish to enshrine in law. Hartshorne's arguments are a direct challenge to the specifically moral claim that a fetus should be afforded such a status. Hartshorne also vociferously challenged the more extreme view put forward by many pro-life advocates, that the rights of the fetus *override* the rights of the mother to make decisions about her own life and health—as he says, "a monstrous proposal."

Many proponents of making abortion illegal or unavailable argue for the inviolable right to life of every genetically human life, from the fertilized egg to the fully-grown adult. Hartshorne invites us to take a more developmental perspective and to consider that a genetically human being's claim on life, and our obligations towards it, increase as it becomes more developed and more capable of a rich emotional-cognitive life. Here again, the category of potentiality is central. Hartshorne argues:

> [Even] the potentiality of a functioning rational animal has its value. But this has to be weighed against the values of the numerous actually functioning ones and the harm that allowing this potentiality to mature may do to these actual values. (WM 125)

The most important "other actually functioning" values are those of the mother, and of her right to self-determination. To make the issue of abortion turn solely on whether the unborn has rights is to ignore the one individual who is manifestly a person and who is most dramatically affected by whatever laws or moral injunctions are in place. Inasmuch as the unborn is dependent upon a living uterus—which at the present stage of technology the mother alone can provide—it is, in Hartshorne's view and in ours, morally abhorrent to dismiss the mother's interests as irrelevant to the moral and legal status of abortion. Roe v. Wade identified viability as the line beyond which the state has a compelling interest in protecting the child. Hartshorne considered this a good compromise as it balances the protection of the child against the protection of the rights of the mother, which should not be compromised.[66]

Environmental Ethics

Hartshorne's emphasis on the social structure of reality lends itself quite naturally to a sensitivity to the values inherent in the ecological web of life. Hartshorne himself believed this, as does one of his most prolific students, John B. Cobb, Jr. Cobb has been especially interested in developing the insights of Whitehead and Hartshorne for the articulation of an ecological outlook that takes seriously the moral responsibility of humanity for stewardship of the environment and for progress toward a sustainable future that meets human needs while promoting a rich biodiversity.[67] Hartshorne, in turn, strongly endorsed Cobb's ecological focus based on process principles.[68]

At the risk of repeating ourselves, it is well to be reminded that Hartshorne's neoclassical metaphysics, like all of process philosophy, rejects the mechanistic-materialistic interpretation of nature residing in the notion that atomic particles are inert, dead, purely externally related entities that make up substances which persist through time. In addition, as we have seen, Hartshorne rejects an ontological dualism between mind and matter, or indeed any view that would characterize nonhuman creatures as *insentient automata*. In line with process philosophy's most basic convictions, Hartshorne and Cobb understand reality to be, always and everywhere, a creative social-relational process, wherein dynamic unit-events of experience inherit from past events or occasions, synthesizing the past occasions into new units of experience which in turn become fabric for future syntheses of experience. All finite entities in nature are thus quite literally "members one of another" (in

St. Paul's memorable expression). As Cobb and co-author David Griffin put the point crisply, "The whole of nature participates in us and we in it."[69] Thus, in the process view, there is no such thing as an isolated action absent of social consequence. Our metaphysical situation is such that no human actions can escape the web of ecological connectivity.

It is also a basic process conviction that value and sentience are part and parcel of one another; if this is correct, then there are objective or intrinsic values *in* the natural environment that make a claim upon our moral sensibilities. Moreover, as Hartshorne stresses, value as experiential is "aesthetic" in broad characterization, and aesthetic value is always enhanced by seeking a balance of unity and variety or diversity. Put another way, aesthetic value is always enhanced by seeking a middle way between the extremes of, on the one hand, sameness and order and, on the other hand, diversity and disorder. In the words of Eugene Peters "Without unity, there is chaos and confusion; without variety, deadly order and monotony."[70] The God of dipolar process theology accordingly seeks the promotion of aesthetically valuable experiences by luring or guiding natural processes through the dangerous extremes of total discord and total monotony. As an appropriated principle for human conduct, this aesthetic ideal entails the promotion of species diversity *coordinated with* human flourishing, which should in turn be achieved by avoiding extremes of species-overpopulation and over-consumption (over-consumption by both human and nonhuman animals) with its resulting environmental habitat taxation or even (eventual) habitat decimation. This ecological picture is complicated not only by the requirement of coordination with human needs, but by the broader consideration that Hartshorne rejects strong versions of bio-egalitarianism wherein all creatures are of equal importance. As we have seen, for Hartshorne, there is a hierarchy of natural values which lays a claim upon our moral sensibilities.

Palmer's Critique of Process Thought

While such ecological sensitivity has seemed an obvious implication of process thought, at least one major environmental ethicist disagrees. Clare Palmer's *Environmental Ethics and Process Thinking* provides a multifaceted and entangled challenge to the claim that process philosophy is an intellectually credible underpinning for a robust, morally adequate environmental ethic.[71] She maintains that (a) process thought involves elements of historically conditioned "colonial" thinking (as in Whitehead's notion of the "advance of civilization" vis-à-vis indigenous cultures), (b) process thought is unwary of its ahistorical "totalizing" metaphysical tendencies, and (c) its doctrine of actual occasions will not sustain a properly environmental outlook. Given such pointed criticisms, it is no wonder that the journal *Process Studies* invited Palmer to engage in a critical forum with process thinkers John Cobb and Timothy Menta, both of whom offered counter-challenges to her critique.[72] Given our interest here in Hartshorne's philosophy, we are particularly interested in Palmer's assessment of Menta's "Hartshornean response." This is an excellent foil in terms of which we can further articulate Hartshorne's environmental ethic but also clarify aspects of his overall ethical theory, including the place of deontological considerations, a topic which has been little explored in the critical literature.

We call attention first to Palmer's claim that neoclassical process philosophy may well advocate the ethical treatment of nonhuman animals on the basis of their value, but they do not so advocate it as a matter of proper deontic rights. "Proper deontic rights" can in this context be regarded as "rights to life" which induce a moral obligation to preserve such rights irrespective of consequences for the whims and desires of human beings. According to Palmer, when Hartshorne and his critical expositors such as Daniel Dombrowski or Menta speak of "animal rights," what they in fact mean is that nonhuman animals have "value" that must be respected. However, says Palmer, this is not what "animal rights" advocates are talking about (at least sometimes) when they speak of "animal rights." Most important, the core conviction of neoclassical process ethics seems to be the teleological notion that the aim of all morally right action is to optimize the richness of experience (abbreviated by Palmer as ROE) for deity. According to Palmer, this focus on ROE entails that a neoclassical process ethics is merely consequentialist, meaning that it is concerned with the ends of an action primarily. If that is indeed the case, a number of philosophers are prepared to argue (we think quite rightly) that a neoclassical process environmental ethic such as Hartshorne's is thereby rendered morally deficient, for all of the commonplace reasons that have been leveled against ethical positions that are based entirely upon consequentialist criteria.

Palmer describes Menta's perspective, saying "where the natural world (excluding humans and animals) is concerned, Hartshorne is consequentialist; where humans and animals are concerned Hartshorne is both consequentialist and deontological."[73] Palmer then states that, while she can grasp the consequentialist portion of Menta's analysis, she does not "see the evidence for" any deontology, or duty-based obligation, in Hartshorne's perspective. While Menta makes much of a purported distinction between moral and aesthetic value in Hartshorne's philosophy—a distinction that is central to his critique of Palmer—Palmer argues that she does not see sufficient evidence in the sources Menta cites to support his interpretation of Hartshorne on this score. Specifically, she discusses three of Hartshorne's essays that are relevant, all of which we have cited above.[74] Admittedly, Menta's critical distinction between moral and aesthetic value in Hartshorne is made difficult (at least at first glance) by the fact that Hartshorne is so often insistent upon the ultimacy of the aesthetic and consequently the enfolding of moral values within the aesthetic domain. While Menta may well be able to maintain this distinction successfully for the purposes of his argument against Palmer, we shall bypass these interpretive difficulties by taking a very different approach to the question of deontology in Hartshorne.

Our argument is that, considering the totality of Hartshorne's corpus, we find texts that explicitly address the deontic concepts of justice and rights-bearing in a way that is logically consistent with his core conviction that experience and value can never be divorced from one another. Whatever else we should say about the adequacy and coherence of Hartshorne's views, we argue that, in the final analysis, Menta is correct in holding that Hartshorne does, in fact, offer an ethics that contains *both* consequentialist and deontological elements. In the vocabulary of moral philosopher William Frankena, Hartshorne could be said to offer appeals to both a Principle of Beneficence (where beneficence is defined in terms of Peirce's broad notion of aesthetic value as "satisfactory experience") and a Principle of Justice (where justice is a properly deontic notion that can trump narrow and comparatively trivial consequentialist appeals to Beneficence).

The key to the above thesis is to be found in Hartshorne's conception of omniscience and its implications for the optimization of ROE. We noted above that, for Hartshorne, God is the eminent form of compassionate understanding of the feelings of the creatures as well as the ideal participant in their weal and woe. Hartshorne says:

> God is the perfection of action-and-passion, who escapes the
> defectiveness of our passivity not by impassivity but by the
> all-inclusiveness, the catholicity, of his sensitiveness, which
> give him the balance, the all-sidedness, the fairness, the jus-
> tice, which are precisely what our passivity lacks and the only
> ground for its appearing to us as a defect. (MVG 273)

On Hartshorne's view, it is not only that God wills the enhancement of
future creaturely experiences; God also *experiences this intention* and this
adds to the divine ROE.[75] Hartshorne says, "[T]he good will, the will to
enhance the value of future experiences generally, is itself, as experienced,
an element of present harmony, just as hatred is a kind of discord" (CS
308). The self-reflective experience of the divine will for enhancement
of the value of future experiences has an implication for the issue of
deontology: Unfair and unjust distributions of risks, goods, and harms
(translatable into broadly aesthetic notions related to the having or not
having of satisfactory experiences) are surely patterns of disharmony or
discord. Given the intention to enhance the value of future experiences,
this rather clearly entails that Hartshorne's God could never concretely
will or be satisfied with unfair distributions of value, for to so will
would be tantamount to diminishing the mentioned "element of present
harmony." This provides Hartshorne with a ready reply to the standard "Sweat Shop Scenario" objection to utilitarianism, (i.e., a relative
minority who suffer for the greater good of mass cheap clothing). Such
detrimental distributions themselves would affect the divine ROE in not
just one but two respects: First, a profound disharmony is experienced
by virtue of the maximal divine sensitivity to creaturely experience; and
second, any intention to continue this element of disharmony would
be, by virtue of the self-reflective factor mentioned above, an additional
element of diminishment to the divine ROE.

Given Hartshorne's theory of omniscience, there would be an
inherent element of discord or ugliness in God's experience of a situation
where, even though no difference would be made to the total happiness of
finite individuals involved, there is nonetheless a component of "injustice"
which would be experienced by God as discordant. This general aesthetic
result can also occur in novels where there is an "omniscient narrator"
who sees all sides of what is happening. To take just one example to
better explain what we mean, consider a variation on a counter-example

to consequentialist theory posed by A. C. Ewing. Suppose someone is being made the butt of vicious jokes, but knowledge of the vicious jokes is kept from the object of the jokes. On a strict value calculus, there is no pain caused the person who is the object of the jokes, but great jocularity and glee is experienced by those who engage in the jokes. There is an element of both "deceit" and "degradation" here that is principled and has nothing to do with any hedonic calculation (as required by consequentialist theory). But on Hartshorne's theory, God, like the omniscient narrator of a story, would know the whole and would see the deceit and degradation, and could judge it as morally unacceptable despite its consequences for creaturely happiness.

Our stress on the word "creaturely" points to an important point about the mereology (or relation between parts and wholes) of experience in neoclassical process theory. Any divine experience E, like every other experience in general, is not a mere sum of its constituent physically prehended parts, that is to say, the actual occasions ingredient to the becoming of and satisfaction of E. Rather, E is the result of, not merely the physical prehension of constituent occasions, but also a "subjective form" of feeling the constituent occasions that involves an evaluation in the act of creative synthesis that becomes E. Thus, any properly neoclassical process account of divine ROE must include the evaluative aspect of divine experience as well as the self-reflective feeling of the divine will, all in addition to the feeling of creaturely aesthetic constellations. We submit that, in principle, this mereological perspective shows how there must be non-consequentialist aspects in Hartshorne's theory, without which, we grant, his theory fails as morally inadequate.

Here we return to the sweat shop scenario because this scenario is related to Palmer's discussion of Derek Parfit's so-called "Impersonal Total Principle" that leads to the "repugnant conclusion" that an increase in total happiness could result through the diminished experiences of a smaller population that supports the larger segment of the population—as very probably was in fact the case with the antebellum southern United States. Would the divine ROE be increased by having a relatively small group of persons working long hours for poverty wages in hot conditions with few breaks and under physical threat, if, as a result, a much larger population, gained the quality of life provided by very affordable clothing? Given Hartshorne's stress on God's all-sided sensitivity, on the balance of perspective and sense of justice entailed by this sensitivity and balance, would not God so described greatly pity the smaller population, sense the profound unfairness, and thus negatively evaluate this constellation of creaturely aesthetic experience? Moreover, it seems to us that, since we feel such pity for sweatshop populations when we are brought face to face with such populations (as when watching an exposé on television), and when we rank or evaluate this bleakness, unfairness, and piteousness as greater than the very largely distributed but individually almost trivial good of possessing relatively cheap clothing, *a fortiori* this evaluation would hold of an all-sensitive omniscient being as posited in Hartshorne's theory. In fact, we observe, it is precisely this sense of moral repugnance at the unfairness of sweatshops that undergirds the various human legal prohibitions of such activities. Simply put, it seems that Hartshorne's God would not find sweatshops—as here described—morally acceptable, because such scenarios arguably do not create an increase in the divine ROE when the factors of all-sidedness and evaluation of the totality of prehended data are kept in mind.

We can put this point in another way by considering another analogy given by Parfit that Palmer mentions.[76] When discussing the so-called "Impersonal Total Principle" of utilitarian thought, Parfit likens the Principle to the following: "The greatest mass of milk might be found in a heap of bottles each containing a single drop."[77] Quantitatively the general principle can be differently illustrated by consider the following two sets:

Set A: 3 Bottle Milk Set: [(1 quart) + (1 quart) + (1 quart)] = 3 quarts

Set B: 8 Bottle Milk Set: [(1 pint) + (1 pint) + (1 pint) + (1 pint) + (1 pint) + (1 pint) + (1 pint) + (1 pint)] = 1 gallon

This illustrates Parfit's point about the composition of wholes such that the properties of each member of a set do not necessarily apply to the properties of the set as a whole, which can result in comparative differences between whole sets. Set A gives is a lesser total volume of milk although each member of the set has a greater volume than each member of set B. But the logical point we want to make is that Parfit's compositional example represents a *disanalogy* to the process notion of divine ROE when we consider factors of disharmony that would need to be brought to bear in order to account for the process mereology of experience. To make the Parfit analogy more relevant, not mere milk, but, say, mixtures containing toxicity (analogous to the unfairness and pain of sweat shops, for example), would have to be brought into the picture such that, analogously, God would find the composed mixture repugnant. On the other hand, this observation does not quite sufficiently tighten the analogy, for it is the unfairness of the hedonic distribution itself that factors into the element of disharmony in the divine experience. Perhaps this is just another way of putting Cobb's point made in his response to Palmer that process thought cannot accept the hedonic calculus as part of its moral outlook. We might qualify this by saying more provisionally that, if a hedonic calculus approach were taken to the construction of a process concept of divine ROE, it would have to be an enormously complex calculus with causal, qualitative, evaluative, mereological and organizational aspects built into it that would make it radically unlike any historical models of utilitarian-consequentialist thinking.

While we have so far considered only human beings, the general point that Hartshorne's ethics involves both consequentialist and deontological elements can be readily applied to the case of treatment of nonhuman animals. If the above interpretation of Hartshorne's basic ethical theory is correct, it follows that, on neoclassical grounds, practices regarding nonhuman animals lack moral justification whenever such practices (1) clearly violate standard beneficence criteria where a substantial quantity of animal suffering is involved in exchange for trivial human satisfactions or satisfactions that could be achieved by other means, or (2) disregard a basic right to life and quality of life because of trivial human satisfactions or satisfactions that could be achieved by other means. These two criteria entail that a large swath of agribusiness practices are patently unethical. For example, confining thousands of chickens into very small spaces or physically constraining young calves so that they will overfeed (as in the production of veal) are clear violations of such moral criteria. Nonhuman animals have a basic right to movement and reasonable use of space, and no gain in profits (when open range chicken farms can be profitable) or taste of veal (when there are many other delicious food choices) can hedonically override such basic rights. We have not here addressed the question whether the two criteria above commit us to vegetarianism as Dombrowski argues or whether they allow some ethically constrained consumption of animals for purposes of human nourishment as Cobb argues. While our discussion is not exhaustive, it should be clear that Hartshorne's ethical theory as stated so far provides tolerably sufficient criteria for a large domain of environmental and nonhuman animal policies.

Morris's Objection

Randall C. Morris takes a quite different view of Hartshorne's theory than what we have proffered so far. He states explicitly that Hartshorne's God is concerned "to maximize the total welfare, or beauty, in the universe . . . [but is] not concerned with the distribution of goods among finite creatures."[78] While he grants that Hartshorne's God does not "will that some individuals be forced to suffer in order to promote the greatest happiness for the greatest number," the Hartshornean God is willing, according to Morris, that some individual or another suffer although not any particular individual.[79] In Hartshorne's metaphysical system, God's aim is to maximize the ratio of opportunity to risk and to allow creaturely interaction or the "whip of competition" among creatures to decide particular creaturely fates.

We hold that Morris's interpretation, especially its notion that the neoclassical God is unconcerned about the distribution of goods, neglects certain aspects of Hartshorne's metaphysics. Specifically, it neglects not only the divine experience of discord or disharmony arising from the maldistribution of goods that we argued for above, but also the "outgoing" or "active" aspect that Hartshorne attributes to God. Notice that Hartshorne argues that God not only prehends creaturely actualities universally, but also "ideally" evaluates and responds to such prehensive data in such a way that creatures are presented with desiderata for behavior. Hartshorne says explicitly that our momentary "cues" for behavior are inspired by "what God as of this moment desiderates" (DR 142). He thus posits a divine "lure" for rectification of unjust distributions of goods. However, given the libertarian freedom that is always in some degree available to finite entities and especially higher-order finite entities such as human beings, there is no guarantee of actualization of divine aims. As we have emphasized in Chapters Five and Six, the universal metaphysical condition of freedom guarantees that the universe is always haunted by the potential for social conflict and tragedy.

While Morris is correct that Hartshorne views competition between creatures as a mechanism that pushes forward an increase in overall aesthetic value, it would not be true to say that Hartshorne thinks that there is no "check or balance" on creaturely competition. According to Hartshorne, it is not that God wills that there be creaturely competition as if some alternative noncompetitive condition were available for socially constituted possible worlds capable of actualizing significant value. This is not metaphysically possible, for Hartshorne, since divine power always has social constraints, constraints found in the various degrees of creaturely freedom which are part and parcel of their very ontological integrity as individuals separate from God. Contra Morris, as a matter of the accurate, comprehensive description of Hartshorne's theoretical intentions and explicit published statements, we cannot see the case for saying that, while Hartshorne's God is intimately affected by maldistributions of goods by virtue of omniscience, such God can be described as intending to do nothing to redirect creaturely impulses against such maldistributions. The latter seems to be explicitly denied by Hartshorne's conception of the desiderata embodied in God as "the essential or total object" of creaturely prehension.

An Ethics of Broader Sympathy for Life

We want to take another route toward deontology in Hartshorne's thought that builds on comments that we have seen he makes on Kant's doctrine of nonhuman animals. Hartshorne makes the points contra Kant that: (1) nonhuman animals are not merely instrumental to our good, nor are they like "parts of an intricate and useful machine of [an] engineer's own designing" (WM 118). Rather, they have a good in and by themselves by virtue of the fact that they have experiences and thus contribute value to God; (2) human infants do not possess the "rational freedom" that for Kant makes adult humans properly rights-bearing persons, but in the course of our lives, we all (normally) cross the line between the nonhuman as sentient but not reason-possessing and the human as reason-possessing; and (3) mere possession of rational freedom is inadequate as a criterion for moral consideration, an "ethics of sympathy broader than sympathy for life on the rational level alone" is required (WM 119). We think a coherent case can be made for saying that, on Hartshorne's theory and on the basis of the above claims, non-human animals do have a proper deontic right to life, although this is not an absolutely inviolable right but is nonetheless a *prima facie* one (as is the case for human animals).

In context, the direction we think Hartshorne is taking by comparing infants and nonhuman animals is to say that, just as infants have a right to life because they are sentient, so nonhuman animals have a right to life because they are sentient. While he does not say so explicitly, we think a fair and reasonable account of the context compels us to hold that Hartshorne is asserting a necessary link between the possession of sentience and some degree of possession of rights. This is a straightforward attribution of a principle of rights-bearing that puts pressure against the notion that his ethical theory reduces to consequentialist considerations. To explain through an example: a comb is an insentient object or instrument; it does not in any properly moral sense have a "right to existence." Were we to break the comb in a pique of anger, we would not have committed a moral error. Moreover, if we needed to break the comb into smaller pieces so that we could accomplish some perhaps urgent task such as opening a locked door, we would not be struck (in any obvious way) with a moral dilemma regarding the existence of the comb. However, if we were to shake an infant to death in a pique of rage or choke a nonhuman animal to death (in a situation where no contravening issue of self-defense is present), there is a properly moral factor involved in violating its right to life and its right to its future, because in both cases the infant and the nonhuman animal properly have lives and futures. It seems to us that the normal case would be such that, whatever the consequences for personal whims or desires, we do not have grounds to disregard the life of an infant or nonhuman animal in the way we might disregard an insentient object. In effect, a "broader ethics of sympathy for life" includes a moral regard for the right to life. We see no clear reason why possession of sentience cannot be, as Hartshorne is suggesting, a rights-bearing property in a rather straightforward manner that conforms to at least widely shared moral intuitions: Insentient objects are not ends in themselves, but animals, including humans, are ends-in-themselves.

Above we stated that Hartshorne's theory can be interpreted as involving a rights-bearing approach to our relation to nonhuman animals, but we also mentioned that such rights are not inviolable and as such must be taken as *prima facie* rights. This is because Hartshorne also addresses the question of the comparative value of species and suggests that there are rationales both for and against subordination of the needs of other species to our own (WM 126–27). Given Hartshorne's stress on aesthetic criteria, including consideration of the connected cluster of values bound up with diversity, contrast, intensity, and triviality, we think that his theory is committed to a highly contextualized answer to practical questions about our relations to nonhuman animals. Here we concur with Cobb's response to Palmer where he argues that her bio-egalitarian perspective—which simply recognizes that species are different but equal for consideration—gives no clear guidance for how we are to treat nonhuman animals.[80] Violent interference between members of species is unavoidable as a practical matter. For instance, we kill dust mites when we shower, and we kill bacteria when we wash our hands. Notwithstanding, as Hartshorne suggests, violent action on the part of rational deliberative animals should never be undertaken wantonly, or driven by entirely selfish interests, or indeed by trivial interests (WM 126–30). Rights to life in the biotic community ought to be inviolate *prima facie* unless and until there are extenuating circumstances of self-defense, disease contagion, habitat decimation, etc.

Distinctively *neoclassical* process environmental policies ought to be driven by highly context-dependent situations, and no flat bio-egalitarianism is feasible or warranted. The criteria for environmental policy decisions, on a process philosophical basis, concern (among other factors) cases regarding variables of aggregations of plant/animal values, including instrumental values related to habitat vitality, compared against the profundity or triviality of distinctively human values. *Environmental policy as directed by process thinking is a matter of figuring out balances and scales of value.* The point can be concretely illustrated through a brief case study related by Holmes Rolston.[81] Rolston is not a proponent of process approaches as such, but his example perfectly illustrates the kind of decision that process thinkers inspired by Hartshornean principles ought to embrace.

Consider the question of human interests in various kinds of logging activities and the values of certain plants and their habitats. Rolston points to the case of Chapman's rhododendron, an endangered evergreen of great beauty. It is repressed by logging, by draining its habitat in order to replant other pines, and by digging up clumps for nursery commerce. The species now exists in only three locales in the southern United States. Would attacking these locales for the production of a few more patches of Christmas pines and a few more rolls of newsprint be worth it? In this case, we submit that the neoclassical process environmentalist argues emphatically "no," because the Chapman (certainly at the very least the Chapman's cellular constituents) has its own claim to "live and blossom," but the human interests in conflict with it are trivial. The human interests are trivial in part because there are alternative ways of decorating for holiday celebrations such as the use of non-threatened tree species or artificial trees that may last for a decade or longer. And there are certainly alternative ways of producing quality newsprint such as using recycled materials. Attacking the endangered Chapman rhododendron is unnecessary, for the human interests related to it can be satisfied in other ways. The insistence upon use of the Chapman would be a mere whim or preference as weighed against both the right and instrumental value of the Chapman species. Moreover, as just mentioned, the Chapman has its own instrumental value to contribute to the local ecosystem, and that is an additional ethical consideration that compounds the case for the dismissal of logging activities. Again, from the standpoint of process philosophy's ecological outlook, the Chapman is not an "isolated" entity; the destruction of it has biological consequences for the thriving of other species in its habitat.

We conclude that Hartshorne's environmental ethic does not suffer from a morally debilitating lack of deontic principle. This is fundamentally because, on Hartshorne's metaphysics and theory of divinity, (1) the divine ROE is affected by unjust distributions of hedonic value, and (2) the possession of sentience posits a *prima facie* right to existence for nonhuman and human animals as well as other living forms. Moreover, neoclassical process applications of aesthetic criteria for decisions about our treatment of nonhuman animals and the environment seem to provide at least some practical guidance as contrasted with bio-egalitarian perspectives.

Conclusion

Hartshorne viewed it as a shortcoming for a philosopher not to have thought through ethical questions with care. We hope to have shown that Hartshorne was not guilty of this failing. He developed well-reasoned positions concerning both the foundations of ethics and its applications, despite the fact that he never produced a systematic treatment of these subjects. In addition, one finds in Hartshorne a philosopher whose ethical ideas are informed by what he considered to be the best in the way of the deliverances of science and of metaphysics. Hartshorne's neoclassical metaphysics supplies the resources for understanding every sentient creature as having intrinsic value, but not in such a way as to render comparative judgments of value impossible.

In the controversy over reproductive rights, Hartshorne denied the genetic reductionism that identifies full-fledged personhood with having the usual full complement of chromosomes; nor did he accept that this genetic endowment is sufficient to give the organism moral standing that is equivalent to a fully developed human being. He emphasized, rather, the concept of development by noting that a pregnant woman is a fully developed person whereas the organism growing inside of her is still in the process of becoming a person. While it is reasonable, on Hartshornean principles, to accept that the moral gravity of abortion increases as the fetus develops, the unborn only gradually acquires the necessary conditions for full-fledged personhood in the process of its development. In the earliest stages it lacks all internal organs while in its final stages it is hardly distinguishable from a newborn infant. Given these dramatic changes, Hartshorne denies that a single moral category, such as murder, can be indiscriminately applied to the termination of its life regardless of the stage it has reached. In any event, whereas doubts can be raised about the personhood of the unborn, no such doubts can be raised about the girls and the women who, for many and varied reasons, face the decision whether to continue a pregnancy. In these ways, Hartshorne's ethical views are consistent with and lend support to the compromise reached in the legal decision of Roe v. Wade.

Hartshorne's thoughts on environmental ethics are a direct consequence of his belief in the interrelated and social structure of all existence, where each creature is in nature and nature is in it. He accepted Whitehead's critique of scientific materialism, the doctrine that nature is composed of simply located particles devoid of subjectivity or feeling. While the materialistic perspective is useful for some purposes, it commits the fallacy of misplaced concreteness when viewed as a metaphysical generalization. Rather, feeling is a pervasive and efficacious feature of reality and is not an anomalous epiphenomenon relegated to certain higher organisms. Moreover, having intrinsic worth is not the unique privilege of those creatures with the brain capacity sufficient to manipulate symbols and to use language. Every creature and every species makes its own legitimate claim on life and cannot be thought of as *mere* means to an end, or the human purposes to which they are often put. Hartshorne avoids the anthropocentric bias of so many previous ethical systems. At the same time, Hartshorne rejects the contrary extreme of bio-egalitarianism that recognizes no value differences between types of organisms.

Finally, the neoclassical theistic cast of Hartshorne's philosophy provides the resources for addressing the concern that Hartshorne can give no meaning to deontology's talk of rights. The richness of divine awareness of the universe is no mere sum of the feelings of the creatures; it includes God's own self-reflective awareness of and reaction to creaturely feelings. Just as we feel the discordance at the very idea of many individuals flourishing at the expense of others—as in classic sweatshop scenarios—so God must experience dissonance at unjust distribution of goods, all the more so in view of God's deep sympathy with every creature, not alone the human ones.

Having examined Hartshorne's views on reproductive rights and on environmental ethics, we round out our tour of Hartshorne's applied philosophy in the following chapter by looking at his views on technology, politics, and questions of war and peace.

TEN

Hartshorne's Applied Philosophy II
Technology, Politics, and War

IN THIS CHAPTER we continue our reflections on Hartshorne's applied philosophy, looking more carefully at issues surrounding the value of technology, some of the problems of politics and economics, and the subject of peace and war and the legitimate use of military force. Apart from one article specifically addressed to the question of whether technology makes religion otiose, Hartshorne made no systematic statement on these issues, but we shall see that there exists, nevertheless, a considerable body of information about his views in articles devoted directly to these topics and in various comments he made in other articles and writings. He brought to these issues the same principles that are central to his metaphysical enterprise: the value of shared creativity and the search for a middle way between extremes.

Technology and the Human Condition

Closely related to Hartshorne's considerations concerning environmental ethics are his reflections on the nature of technology and on moral issues related to the use of technology. At least three essays, in addition to scattered comments throughout his literary corpus, are related to what we today call "the philosophy of technology"—namely, "Science, Security, and the Abiding Treasure" (LP, Ch. 9), "The Environmental Results of Technology," and "Cobb's Theology of Ecology."[1] Other process thinkers such as John Cobb and Ian Barbour have contributed extensively to discussing the nature of technology in ways that are obviously congenial to Hartshorne's basic social-relational process convictions. Of particular importance is Barbour's systematic and almost encyclopedic treatise *Ethics in an Age of Technology,* which treats the topic in much greater depth than Hartshorne's penetrating but focused and comparatively sparse contributions.[2]

In addition to Hartshorne's essays specifically addressing the meaning of science and technology and their relation to religion, we should again mention his frequent praise of Henri Bergson's book, *The Two Sources of Morality and Religion,* which we mentioned in Chapter Seven. Characterizing Bergson's treatment of religion as sociobiology before its time, Hartshorne considered Bergson to have explained why the human animal, with its relative transcendence of instinct and its reflective intelligence, would create myths that result in religion. Such myths have three functions:

> They must reconcile the animal to the knowledge, not attributable to other animals, of the inevitability of eventual death for the individual. They must provide motivations for making the sacrifices required for the care of offspring, companions in need, and the general social welfare. They must reconcile individuals to the knowledge of the uncertainties and risks of the future and the high probability that many of our goals will not be attained.[3]

Hartshorne did not believe that any of these functions could be filled by either the advance of science or developments in technology. If this is correct, then there is good reason to believe that some form of religion is inevitable, although the precise form religion takes remains an open question. The "mythmaking" of what Bergson called "static religion" may be transcended in "dynamic religion," but religion remains as "that element which, in beings endowed with reason, is called upon to make good any deficiency of attachment to life."[4] Hartshorne's thoughts on religion and its relation to science and technology are largely parallel to those of Bergson; whether it is a question of influence or parallel development we do not know, but certainly his own natural theology is one way of expressing a type of dynamic religion to which the Frenchman believed religion in its most developed forms inclines.

Hartshorne's essay "Science, Insecurity, and the Abiding Treasure" is one of his most sustained and programmatic meditations on the relation of science and technology to the human condition, written in a way that is a natural extension of Bergson's ideas.[5] This meditation might be viewed as essentially an effort to respond to the argument, presented most famously in one of its variations by Ludwig Feuerbach, that religion, including so-called "higher" monotheistic religion, is no longer necessary given the advances of modern technology. According to this argument, God and the gods were once necessary as psychological, vicarious security mechanisms against the threats of hunger, disease, physical pain, and mental anguish. Increasingly, however, technology has mitigated these threats. Even death, for many, has been held at bay in the sense that life expectancy has increased. As the argument goes, no vicarious security mechanisms are required, for we now have tangible and quite powerful technological mechanisms for addressing these problems. An essential part of the manifesto of atheistic humanism is to move humanity toward awareness of the "real" efficacy of strictly human capacities to solve problems and away from passive reliance upon unreliable, unempirical appeals to supra-human remedies found in religious practice. Feuerbach insisted that religion is a form of self-alienation on the grounds that its practices (allegedly) alienate humanity from its true sources of power.

Hartshorne dismantles this sort of argument effectively by illustrating the inherent insecurity and uncertainty of human existence. Elements of insecurity are ineradicable, perennial, existential constants of the human predicament which have their root in our very finitude and fragmentariness rather than in contingent environmental circumstances. One of his main points is that our ontological situation—particularly, our relation to an open, indeterminate future—is such that scientific technology can never *in principle* satisfy our deepest needs or provide an abiding peace. Hartshorne writes:

> My answer is the old one: security is found more in *principles* than in conditions. It consists, not in the absence of danger or in banishing the unsettled status of the future, but in the ideas and ideals whereby danger and the ambiguities of the future can be faced with courage and joy. (LP 239)

What are these principles? Hartshorne delineates three, all cast in the shape of his neoclassical theistic vision: (1) Human well-being depends as much upon creative internal or attitudinal responses to our circumstances as upon the circumstances themselves, whereas techno-science is geared toward the ideal of altering the circumstances. (2) The present moment is a "creation" which has value in and by itself and is not merely a means to some future end. There is something profoundly disadvantageous about the human cognitive faculties if their only practical virtue is the production of technologies which help mitigate dangers, but in the long run simply prolong an anxious existence. The faculty of understanding has an adequate pragmatic justification only if it allows us to produce philosophical and religious principles which enable us to transcend our ordinary orientation toward the future, and thus to experience the full value of the present. If the understanding can produce such principles, then life can be experienced as meaningful in spite of the imminent future dangers. Finally, (3) all human experience retains some value and meaning; experience is never "lost" or "for naught," for it is retained everlastingly in omniscience. Each "present" is thus redeemed from oblivion.

In contrast to Hartshorne, Feuerbach's atheistic humanism presents us with a metaphysics of sheer oblivion in which our hopes and aspirations are utterly for naught. In pragmatic terms, this amounts to nihilism, as Nietzsche saw with such clarity, contrary to our deep inclinations to affirmation of a moral "ought" and quests for aesthetic satisfaction. Albert Camus depicted the situation rightly in *L'Étranger,* where his anti-hero protagonist is mute and unresponsive to the moral outrage of the courtroom during his trial for murder, as a nihilist should be mute. Yet, as some literary critics have suggested, the entire novel is abruptly deconstructed in the closing poetic reverie on the awe-inspiring beauty of the Algerian coast and an apparent expression of solidarity with all people.[6] As Camus later confessed in 1950 in accordance with this reverie, "[a] literature of despair is a contradiction in terms."[7]

In a process theistic vision, the despair evaporates since the beauty is forevermore at least somewhere in the universe. Insofar as the theistic vision implies principles such as Hartshorne outlines, the Feuerbachian-Marxist analysis is wrong in this respect: a comprehensive theistic metaphysics has practical implications for the living of life which thwarts the thesis of the uselessness of religion, no matter what the condition of techno-science. However, it does not follow from the denial of nihilism that one ought to find no value in techno-science. Nor does Hartshorne reject techno-science *in toto*. While Hartshorne does not explicitly address positive uses of technology in "Science, Insecurity and the Abiding Treasure," a more positive attitude toward technology can be found elsewhere and can also be logically inferred from certain aspects of his philosophy: first, his systematic methodological preference for the "middle way" of avoiding extremes, including and especially in application to value theory, and second, the fundamental "aesthetic motif" of neoclassical metaphysics. In addition, Hartshorne explicitly holds that technology has at least the positive effect of multiplying "participation in the chief values" of living; in other words, it makes possible more individuals who have the possibility of living a good life, the living of which does not in and by itself require advanced technology. Moreover, "technology allows a great number of people at least a marginal existence."[8]

Let us amplify the implications of the first two items. To use Frederick Ferré's vocabulary, neoclassical process philosophers promote neither extremely "bright" nor extremely "somber" visions of technologies.[9] They advocate a "middle way" in the domain of technologies. On the one hand, Hartshorne enthusiastically endorses Cobb's chapter in *Is It Too Late?*, rhetorically titled "Let the Engineers Handle It." In the estimation of Cobb and Hartshorne, Buckminster Fuller could not be more mistaken in suggesting that more and better trained engineers would be the progressive and anti-entropic force for "God's ever swifter word." This is so, among other reasons, because there are always some deleterious as well as some good effects of large-scale engineering (for that matter any technological) projects and, thus, "we shall have to change our way of life as well as our gadgets."[10] On the other hand, while criticism of modern technology is the predominant theme, Hartshorne and Cobb never speak in a manner that calls for the utter rejection of technologies. Indeed, their discussions of technological *preferences* makes it clear that advanced technology as such is not to be rejected. For example, Charles Birch and John Cobb argue for solar as opposed to fossil fuel technologies (although they also maintain that even solar technologies will not support a "continuous growth" model of the economy).[11] Despite their critique of technology, neither Cobb nor Hartshorne could be regarded as "technophobes," the opposite extreme of the "somber" visionary in Ferré's taxonomy.

In process perspective, technologies should serve the needs of meaningful human creativity, including artistic creativity. In his essay, "Process Theology and Technology," Shields was poised to make this particular point because of a speech given on a nationally televised awards ceremony by a theatre lighting technician. The technician spoke of the new excitement in her artistic field made possible by computer technologies, technologies which had opened up novel worlds of aesthetic possibilities for theatre productions. In Shields's words:

> It occurred to me immediately that she was a living embodiment of the neoclassical or process aesthetic sensibility: the human artist, like the song bird (assuming Hartshorne's monotony threshold principle), must press for novelty within a certain parameter of order, as it were, a *cantus firmus;* in effect, technologies can be put into the service of artistic novelty and the achievement of aesthetic intensity.[12]

The authors of this book have observed in their extracurricular work as musicians that developments in musical technologies (e.g., the twelve-string guitar, the computer midi, the guitorgan, vocal double tracking, the electric guitar, etc.), when skillfully employed, can make for profound and novel differences in the quality of musical performance.

We by no means advocate that more use or any use of advanced technology for artistic purposes is *necessarily* a good thing. For example, the use of a harsh electric drum on a soft Nat King Cole ballad would be absurdly incongruent, perhaps humorous, but not to be taken as a genuine musical enhancement. Excessive reliance upon technology is not necessarily conducive to high aesthetic value. We agree with Hartshorne's point that high technology is hardly a necessary condition for living a good life, including the good life of aesthetes:

> Aristotle lived a life satisfying on a high level. What professor today does much better? Think of the quality of Shakespeare's experience as poet and dramatist, exploring imaginatively the heights and depths of human possibility.[13]

Our point about art-related technology is connected with Hartshorne's (and Whitehead's) metaphysics of aesthetic progression. Writes Hartshorne: "All definite patterns lose their appeal after sufficient reiteration. The history of art and all aesthetic experience show this"

(LP 215). Technologies can provide artists with means of exploding the boundaries of patterns of artistic reiteration. For example, Shakespeare could indeed lead a good life and enrich us immeasurably without use of a computer; nonetheless, the world left with *only* Shakespeare and his modes of expression and no historical progression of any sort in artistic exploration, including that which would eventually employ cybernetic technologies, would be insofar profoundly devoid of adventure. Artists cannot tolerate endless contentment with existing forms of artistic expression. Novelty is imperative. Just as Hartshorne has explicitly suggested that "thinking animals" can hardly altogether refuse technological possibilities in the biomedical context—the central question here being, when is there a *judicious* technological interference in the natural balance of births and deaths (WM 59)—it follows, by parity of reasoning, that artists can hardly altogether refuse technological possibilities in the quest for artistic freshness.

Perhaps this is a comparatively minor point, but its usefulness resides in showing at least one class of possible applications of technology, sanctioned by Hartshorne's system, which would accomplish the good end of aesthetic enrichment in a comparatively innocuous way. (We take it that, say, Stratocasters have killed far fewer people and even in their making have incurred far less pollution than, say, automobiles.) Thus, this is one way of demonstrating that, process thinkers cannot and do not reject any and every application of advanced technology.

The larger point, however, is as follows. The "core" neoclassical characterization of *techné* is that *all technologies are fundamentally ambiguous as they are embedded in human freedom,* which brings in its train risks and opportunities that necessarily accompany such freedom. In Hartshorne's words:

> On humble levels, actuality implies trifling forms of freedom, hence trifling forms of risk; on high levels, nontrifling forms. Man is the freest creature, hence the most dangerous to himself and others. This is what it is to be human. The great opportunities of the human kind or degree of freedom mean also great risks. Technology magnifies both opportunities and risks because it magnifies the scope of the choices inherent in freedom.[14]

In the light of this core notion of the "magnification" feature of technologies, as will be again observed in the subsequent sections, the key expression for Hartshorne is judicious technological interference and use in the course of living.

Borgmann and Ellul Contra Hartshorne

In order to clarify and illuminate further Hartshorne's fundamental approach to technology in terms of his philosophy of the middle way, we now briefly discuss his and some other compatriot process thinkers' relation to two prominent contemporary philosophers of technology who offer positions that stand in some contrast to the necoclassical process vision, namely, Albert Borgmann and Jacques Ellul.

Response to Borgmann

Albert Borgmann, a neo-Heideggerian philosopher of technology, speaks of Hartshorne's position as "debilitating" and as an all-too-common "unwarranted optimism of the pessimists" (he also associates this perspective with that of Bernard Lonergan). This is a debilitating perspective, he charges, because, on his interpretation, it accepts technology on its own terms and purportedly does not question the direction or overall character of technology. We cite his own words at some length:

> The positions of Lonergan, Hartshorne, and their spokespersons are so common and so debilitating to a principled critique of technology that it deserves a name of its own. I will call it the "unwarranted optimism of the pessimists." People like Lonergan and Hartshorne intuitively find something profoundly distressing in technology, and consequently they see an urgent need for its reform. Their distress is expressed as a deep pessimism about the prospects of technology; but their apprehension fails to break through the commonplace view of what constitutes success. They adopt the technological standards and see technology failing by its own criteria. And this allows them to be optimistic about the necessity, the likelihood, and the nature of a reform of technology. Technology will have to reform itself. The alternative is an overt and imminent technological failure or catastrophe. Moreover, technology having come to the end of its rope must turn elsewhere for

security and progress, viz. to Christianity or theism. But the pessimism is unwarranted—and so ultimately is the optimism.[15]

We want to respond to this in three ways. Our first comment is that apparently Borgmann is basing his perception of Hartshorne solely on the basis of the very focused exposition in Shields's essay "Process Theology and Technology" which was limited to the single issue of the relation between technology and religion. Unfortunately, this led him to an inadequate understanding. Indeed, it is ironic that Hartshorne the person was, in so many ways, a living embodiment of the Borgmannian ideal of "the simpler life," that is to say, someone more absorbed in meaningful work, contact with nature, and hearth and home than in devices.[16] Hartshorne was a bicyclist and rider of mass transit and owned an automobile only briefly; his favorite activities outside of philosophizing were the pleasures of bird-watching or listening to his wife Dorothy sing superb renditions of Mozart; he thrived on a simple and uniform, virtually vegetarian diet; until very late in his life he did not own a computer (we believe the University of Texas at Austin eventually provided him with one); his small home was furnished sparsely; he ridiculed the omnipresence of ice cubes for drinks and the over-use of air conditioning and electric heating. Among a long list of calls for lifestyle simplification that could be adduced, consider this Borgmann-like statement which Hartshorne uttered in an interview with Gregg Easterbrook:

> The world has too many automobiles and televisions. Now the standard is that there should be one car and TV for every person. This is not healthy for the environment or our souls.[17]

Of course, Hartshorne could not avoid certain aspects of modern life and use of technology. As one who traveled the world, he made a lot of use (as he himself noted) of taxis and airplanes. He remarked, "How far this cancels out my contribution to the ecosystem by not owning a car I do not know. At any rate these are among the questions that lovers of nature who know what the ecological score is will take into account" (WM 129). Very much in the spirit of Borgmann, Hartshorne as both person and philosophical thinker stood against the grain of techno-consumerist culture.

Secondly, we are not sure Borgmann read "Process Theology and Technology" closely, for he might well have detected observations about and prescriptions for the overall direction of technology that are in accord with suggestions of Cobb as well as of Hartshorne. For instance, the essay in question provides at least one specific criterion for selecting technologies, namely, that we should move from technologies requiring short-term energy supply or potentially hazardous fission energy supplies to the long-term supply of solar energy. While this may seem to be an obvious suggestion, its implementation against strong political headwinds has proven stubbornly difficult. More importantly, looking beyond Hartshorne to the whole purview of process thought, we find an embarrassment of riches with respect to careful, detailed, sustained reflection on the overall direction and character of technology. In particular, there are three major sources of analysis of technology from the hand of Cobb, including work with collaborators, the biologist Charles Birch and the economist Herman Daley.[18] As previously mentioned, there is also the monumental work of Ian Barbour in *Ethics in an Age of Technology*. In addition, Frederick Ferré, surely one of the deans of American philosophy of technology, wrote on technology from a distinctively Whiteheadian point of view.[19] Add to this list Hartshorne's review of Cobb's *Is It Too Late?*; his 1974 University of Georgia symposium paper on "The Environmental Results of Technology"; his numerous published comments on technology, the environment, and lifestyle that are interspersed throughout his enormous literary corpus; and we are confronted with a formidable contemporary process literature on technologies.

Thirdly, and perhaps most important, we reject the very vocabulary of "pessimism" and "optimism" as characterizations of the process position on technology, however cleverly juxtaposed. "Pessimism," in the context used, wrongly suggests that Hartshorne and other process thinkers hold that technology simply doesn't go far enough in satisfying our deepest needs. For, again, Hartshorne's position is that technology, *no matter what its condition,* could never achieve this in principle. It is not so much that technologies are "limited," as Borgmann says (although they are in fact that), as it is that they are *categorically inappropriate* to our deepest longings for peace, meaning, and security. Contrary to Borgmann's assertion, Hartshorne's view precisely contradicts "adopting the technological standards for success." On the other hand, "optimism," in the context used, wrongly suggests that Hartshorne and other process thinkers hold that "technology has come to the end of its rope" and somehow it must look to monotheistic religion ("it" here is surely an odd reifying use of language). To begin with, Hartshorne and Cobb nowhere assert or imply that technology is somehow "finished" or "at the end of its rope," as if technology will no longer need to be encountered or we will no longer need to deal with it. Hartshorne makes it clear that techno-science is too dangerous for this to be permissible—for example, the case of nuclear weapons possessed by political enemies (IO 220). On the other hand, it is not desirable that all advanced technologies be dismissed. Moreover, Hartshorne and Cobb are not merely "optimistic" about the prospects of technological reform. This is especially so given Cobb's insistence on the importance of radical shifts in whole societal attitudes toward the continuous growth model that is part and parcel of modern techno-scientific Western society.[20] Neither do Hartshorne and Cobb despair about the grip of contemporary economic and associated technological imperatives in such fashion that would align them with the genuinely pessimistic "technological determinism" of Jacques Ellul.

Ian Barbour, who holds process philosophical commitments, is, we think, helpful at this point. He upholds a qualified "contextualistic interactionist" view of technologies.[21] This view is coupled with the fundamental concept of technology as socially constructed Instrument, rather than as either essentially Liberator or Threat (notions which Barbour correlates with "optimism" and "pessimism," respectively). "Contextualistic interactionism" seems to us to be language that more appropriately describes the process position when taking into account the full extent of Hartshorne's and Cobb's closely related writings on science, technology, and cognate concerns with the environment. "Contextualism," as defined by Barbour, seems to posit views that can be readily found in Cobb's writings on technology (and in Hartshorne's endorsement of Cobb's views): (1) social, political, and worldview commitments affect the design and development of technologies; (2) there is a diversity of science-technology interactions; (3) technologies are an "ambiguous instrument of social power"; and, (4) technology policy decisions should give prominence to issues of social justice (because technologies are ineluctably social) as well as to environmental protection (because technologies always operate in natural as well as social contexts).

We also find Alan Drengson's seminal paper on "Four Philosophies of Technology" helpful in providing categories which could be invoked to situate a process philosophy of technology in a general way vis-à-vis Borgmann's imputation of "pessimism" and "optimism."[22] Drengson speaks of four basic attitudinal postures toward technology: (1) technological anarchy (an extreme laissez-faire attitude toward technology predominant in the nineteenth century); (2) technophilia (a love for or infatuation with technical objects such that they become extensions of the human person, as exemplified in outbursts such as "don't ever touch my car!"); (3) technophobia (a fear of the threat of technology to overcome human autonomy); and (4) appropriate technology. Appropriate technology involves conscious deliberation over when, to what extent, and how technologies are to be implemented and designed. Appropriate technology involves deliberation over how we are to work with nature, rather than dominate it. Appropriate technology is deeply ecosystemic in outlook. So characterized, it seems clear to us that a process philosophy of technology is to be associated with appropriate technology in Drengson's sense. This is evident from Hartshorne's concern with the question of "judicious" interference of technology into the natural balance and the strong emphasis on ecological thinking in Cobb's work.

Quite in agreement with Borgmann's call for the challenging of technology, process thinkers, employing the resources of Hartshorne, Cobb, and Barbour, will want to issue profound constraints on technologies, constraints which collectively constitute a thoroughgoing policy of reform. Consider Barbour's three-fold principles of environmental constraint on technologies; i.e., technologies should be selected or rejected by virtue of three "environmental value" criteria or tests:[23]

1.   Does the technology promote or rely upon a *sustainable* energy resource?

2.   Is the technology compatible with broad environmental protection?

3.   Is the technology compatible with respect for all forms of life? (Implicit in this criterion is concern with social justice or equitable distribution of goods and energies.)[24]

We add that each of these principles looms large in Cobb's work as well and have been touched upon in various ways throughout Hartshorne's corpus, but especially in his "Cobb's Theology of Ecology."

These are difficult tests to satisfy. Many technologies today fail to meet them. Most importantly for the present context, these criteria suggest clear directions for transition and reform. For example, hydroelectric and coal burning power plants, prolific in North America, seem to violate all three criteria. Dams for hydroelectric use incur huge environmental costs, especially deforestation and harsh ramifications for fish migration and aquatic life generally, while coal burning is clearly non-sustainable (because of the obvious finitude of coal supplies) and contributes to greenhouse gas accumulation. Neither hydroelectric nor coal burning technologies—even if they were free of deleterious effects on the environment—are feasible for developing Third World nations because such technologies are so capital intensive. Accordingly, African nations collectively use a mere 5% of their water potential for hydroelectric conversion, compared to 59% of potential usage in the United States by itself. In effect, even if hydro and carbon-conducing electricity technologies were acceptable on issues of sustainability or environmental protection (which they are not), there would still be considerations of social justice. Thus, North America and Europe would (and do) enjoy cheap and ready sources of energy, while much of Africa and Asia would (and does) not, even though "technology transfer" would be (and is) readily available.

Barbour argues that the energy technology that seems to pass all three tests and "has the most potential for the future" is specifically photovoltaic solar energy technology.[25] It is estimated that such technology would require a mere 2% of existing desert landmass (approximately 150,000 square miles) to produce the equivalent of the total aggregate energy output of current fossil fuel technologies. The chief disadvantage of photovoltaics (or PVS) is their seasonal operation and affinity for sunny climates, and thus the need for a system of storage. However, this problem currently has at least a general theoretical solution, although much research, design, and planning would be needed in order to make the solution feasible:

> Photovoltaic-generated electricity passing through water releases hydrogen that can be stored and used for transportation or residential heating. Hydrogen produced from PVS in sunny desert areas could be compressed and distributed inexpensively in a pipeline system like that now used for natural gas. Hydrogen could also be burned in fuel cells on electric-powered cars, with twice the efficiency of internal combustion motors. Hydrogen

appears very promising in the long run, since it burns so cleanly; it emits no carbon dioxide, sulfur dioxide, or particulates.[26]

Considered from the point of view of politically and economically realistic scenarios, Barbour expects that reduction of fossil fuel consumption will take place only through a transitional phase in which a combination of energy resource technologies will be employed. Citing a study by Michael Brower, published by the Union of Concerned Scientists as *Cool Energy,* the following seems plausible:

> If total energy consumption remains constant, the U.S. supply in 2020 could be 7 percent nuclear, 4 percent hydro, 6 percent wind, 18 percent biomass, 24 percent solar, and 42 percent fossil fuels (as compared to 86 percent today).[27]

The point in offering this vignette on energy technology is to show that, contrary to Borgmann's suggested criticism, a principled critique of technologies and suggestions for some clear and concrete prescriptions for the direction of technological change follow from a process orientation. Notice that such principles for the critique of technology are grounded in process philosophy's social-relational ontology and its fundamentally biophilic and holistic orientations. In effect, such principles, we submit, are properly process principles for the direction of technology.

In spite of the above critique of Borgmann's specific reactions to Hartshorne's thought, we need to make it clear that we regard Borgmann's philosophy of technology as insightful on its own terms. Specifically, the particular way in which he has seized upon the psychology of the "device paradigm."[28] Going beyond any considerations found in the process literature, Borgmann has drawn our attention to the seductive ways in which modern devices separate us from deeper fulfillments and engagements. While we find his observations to be at least compatible with a process perspective, we regard them nonetheless as important contributions in their own right.

Response to Ellul

Jacques Ellul, eminent French social thinker and theologian, has developed an influential position on technology. Ellul represents the extreme of somber visions of technology, and he stands as an interesting comparative foil for Hartshorne and compatriot process thinkers. Ellul argues that what he calls *la technique* (the whole ensemble of methods employed in modern industrial societies as contrasted with *technologie* or the study of such methods) is (1) inherently and universally sinful, (2) autonomous or independently existent, and (3) completely outside the control of human beings. In effect, for Ellul, there exists an inherently evil technological system which has its own relentless agenda of exponential growth and domination. This self-perpetuation of *la technique* can be understood in terms of two laws of technological progress: The first law is that technologies are irreversible. Once a technology has been invented, it cannot be uninvented; it will continue to be used until ousted by a new technology serving the same purpose. The second law is that technological growth is exponential, not linear or arithmetical. Technologies always give rise to new families of related technologies.

Arguing from a self-consciously Calvinist or Reformed Christian theological perspective, Ellul insists that a properly Christian and biblically grounded view of *la technique* is that it is "necessarily fallen." There is absolutely no possibility of a religiously motivated sanction for any species of technology whatsoever. For Ellul, the very essence of modern techno-science is domination, which stands in direct and radical opposition to the central Judeo-Christian value of love. Ellul clearly admits the influence of Marxist historical dialectic on his thought. Thus, Larry A. Hickman's description of Ellul's thought as "very much like a scientific [i.e., 'deterministic'] Marxist gone grim" is apt.[29] Ellul sees the historical evolution of *la technique* in staunchly necessitarian or deterministic terms:

> Our experience could not have been other than what we made it. The exploration of the world in the 15th century, for example, directed by the will to power and exploitation, could not have produced any result other than the one that has been lived (colonialism) that is to say, it could not have been directed toward the peaceful admiration of creation and the adoration of the creator. This was not a live option.[30]

In the Foreword to the American edition of *The Technological Society,* Ellul clarified that he "[does] not deny the existence of individual action or of some inner sphere of freedom." He goes on to say, however, that the individual's acts and ideas exert no influence on "social, political, economic mechanisms."[31] His conclusion was that the only escape from

the historical dialectic of *la technique,* from relentless, ever deeper envel-
opment in the techno-sphere is cataclysmic change either in the form of
super-destructive global warfare, or a cataclysmic act of God, or a radical
massive turn to spiritual values which would call for ousting the whole
of techno-scientific civilization.[32] From a purely sociological perspective,
he found none of these possibilities to be within the realm of probability.

Without mentioning Ellul, Hartshorne rejected the Ellulian two level
theory of an inner sphere of freedom and sociological determinism.[33] We
hold, in consonance with Hartshorne's view, that the Ellulian theory
is simply not supported by detailed studies of particular technological
innovations. For example, a quintessential American invention is the
apple parer, a device for peeling and coring apples, both for use in cider
and for eating. The United States granted the first patent for an apple
parer on Valentine's day 1803 to the farmer and postmaster Moses Coates.
Throughout the nineteenth century, a variety of ingenious devices for
paring apples were invented and patented. Originally conceived as a
labor-saving household tool, it was eventually modified for industrial use
as America exported more and more apples. The appearance of industrial
apple parers with interchangeable parts seems to have driven an increase
in innovation of apple parers for household use, with each manufacturer
trying to outdo others in mechanistic cleverness. These little devices are
marvels of engineering, a testimony to human ingenuity and creative
freedom. The story of their creation, use, and manufacture shows a complex interplay of individual initiative and sociological pressures, just as
one would expect from a Hartshornean analysis.[34]

It is interesting in this regard that historian of technology Arnold
Pacey offers some telling case studies which run against both the
autonomy and determinist theses of Ellul, whose position Pacey describes
as "machine mysticism." Pacey points to a more complex relationship
between human beings and technical objects. Such case studies seem
to us to offer support both for the process philosopher's concern with
the concreteness of human agency in the technological situation and
with the "contextualistic interactionism" suggested by Barbour, which
is, we have urged, a view of technology strongly congenial to Cobb and
Hartshorne's various discourses on technology. In studies of nineteenth
century high farming for grain products, lathe design, and steam engine
design, Pacey shows a pattern of "fitful evolution," where efficiency is
dependent largely on the human beings who use these technologies,

rather than on the inherent properties of the technologies. The empirical historical record is in fact replete with measurable "downturns" in technological efficiency. For instance, use of Watt engines in the early 1800s, Cornish engines in the 1850s and 60s, and British steam turbines in the 1930s and 40s, were all movements away from previous plateaus of efficiency. This is not the historical picture of technological development we should expect if Ellul's assumptions about deterministic, one-way causal influence of technical objects upon humanity, and the relentless flow of technological efficiency, are correct.

Process thinkers will reject, of course, Ellul's implied metaphysics of determinism (especially clear in his more Marxist moods). We need not rehearse the many arguments against determinism issued by Hartshorne to illustrate this point. However, a deeper issue, raised by Ferré, concerns how far human autonomy ranges against "the wheels of the advancing technological juggernaut," once the rigorous determinism of the Ellulian or "scientific" Marxist variety is eschewed.[35] In other words, perhaps determinism is false, and there are pockets of free resistance to modern technological machines here and there, but the overall, macro-level picture is that of "the momentum of technological society [which] seems unresponsive to human protest and even to basic human needs."[36] Consider, as just one example, the "mighty technologies of centralization" which force "nuclear or chemical plants—or waste storage dumps—on protesting local inhabitants in order to spread marginal benefits to distant, anonymous multitudes."[37]

Clearly, in response, for process thinkers, there must be some plausible prospect for the hope of change in basic societal attitudes. Contrary to Ellul's deterministic perspective, the theoretical possibility for change is indeed built into the relative indeterminism of process ontology. But the issue at hand is whether or not this possibility can be raised to the level of a real social tendency or propensity. In effect, are there any signs in the current human landscape which suggest grounds for real, even if cautious, hope for significant social change to a more balanced, techno-critical situation?

We submit that there are general signals of hope for social change. The various international, federal, and state efforts at controlling the environmental impact of technologies and at engaging in ongoing technological assessment is one sign of hope. Viewed from a long-range historical perspective, it is clear that awareness of environmental issues as well as environmental legislation has dramatically increased on a global scale, especially since the 1970s which saw the convergence of both landmark environmental legislation (1970 Clean Air Act, 1972 Clean Water Act, etc.) and the emergence of the environmental movement. As Barbour had pointed out, there is strong support for environmental concern across all socioeconomic sectors, and the U.S. Office of Technology Assessment has at least "built up a reputation for comprehensive and balanced assessments," even if its concerns have been too focused on short term risks due perhaps in part to the nature of its congressional reporting mandate.[38] Also, such entities as the various world congresses or summits on environmental issues and political organizations such as the Green Party, the Sierra Club, and Green Peace are bright spots on the sociopolitical landscape in terms of the prospects for critical constraint on technology. While all the above provide some evidence for the view that the overall, long range vector is toward increasing global sensitivity to the environmental consequences of technology, this must be tempered by awareness of the powerful coupling of corporate profit motives, corporate political influence, and populist movements that turn a blind eye to global environmental concerns, encourage national insularity, and trade on fear. Moreover, new technologies create new consumer appetites, and this in part drives corporate interest in technology research and development. Nonetheless, forces for constraint and assessment do exist and show no sign of abating.

A recent public television documentary/advocacy program on lifestyle simplification has convinced us that there is hope for gradual and partial, but environmentally significant, change toward a more balanced, moderated, sustainable future. We were particularly struck by the case of contemporary Holland, where so-called "postmaterialist culture" has become notably widespread and somewhat fashionable. According to the program, lifestyle simplification is being practiced in Holland on a large enough scale such that the country has been viewed as an empirical test case for steady state economics by some Harvard economists. If such change is possible for at least one free market, advanced technological country, then why not others?

A final consideration concerns a rather personal experiential disconfirmation of Ellul's view that technologies are "inherently evil." In his Special Focus essay, Shields reports the following situation:

My daughter, Kirstin Lorraine, who is now a robustly healthy, happy twelve-year-old, was born prematurely. Despite state of the art prenatal care and strict compliance with physician's orders, my wife Marsha developed preeclampsia and then blood toxemia during the seventh or eighth month of pregnancy (a condition suffered by Marsha's mother and thus quite possibly genetically inherited). Consequently, after the standard-treatment steroid injections, Kirstin was brought into the world by an urgent caesarian section. The situation was further complicated by the fact that Kirstin needed surgical repair of a "T-E fistula" condition (a procedure developed by the famous former surgeon general C. Everett Koop). A tense two-week period of "touch and go" recovery from the surgery followed. Each two hours or so of reports on essential blood gases, and two crucial emergencies, put us on a maddening emotional roller coaster ride my wife and I will never forget. However, a neonatologist gave me great comfort during those trying days when he explained that Kirstin's chances for survival and normal development were greatly enhanced because of new advances made in micro-IV technology for the delivery of lipids to the tiniest premature veins. (Lipid reserves are in short supply for premature infants, who will quickly turn to use of brain tissue in order to secure normal functioning of cellular processes.) I most probably owe a world of love and beauty—Kirstin's "very good life" (as she wrote recently in her school journal), Marsha's and my deeply joyful experiences of seemingly her every move—to a group of chemists or chemical engineers specializing in materials plasticity! Ellul's invective against *la technique* simply rings existentially hollow in the light of this profound life experience.

No doubt there is also moral ambiguity here. The very use of micro-IV technology, which had a positive result in the case of Kirstin Lorraine, also makes possible the survival of premature infants with far more serious afflictions or debilitating deformities. Such technology makes possible a severely limited human existence which otherwise would not be. But we think this only underscores the correctness of Hartshorne's basic view that technology is fundamentally ambiguous, rather than necessarily evil. Here the question of "judicious" use of technology asserts itself. And here we enter the hard terrain of bioethics—a topic beyond the scope of the present chapter.

Political and Economic Affairs

Hartshorne once wrote that political matters are, "[F]or me . . . the most difficult, baffling puzzles of all" (WM 44). Yet he took such matters seriously and did not refrain from making comments and informed observations about them, perhaps as early as a 1923 speech on the "superstitions of modernism" delivered to the Harvard Liberal Club, an organization of which he was an early and active student member (DL 324).[39] As with ethical theory, Hartshorne never wrote a systematic treatise on political ideas, but he often addressed political matters in his essays. In historical order, one may cite the following: substantial essays on "Russia and Marxian Humanism" (1937) (BH Ch. 5); a twenty-six page length "A Philosophy of Democratic Defense" (which is followed by an eleven-page essay titled "Metaphysical Foundations of Democracy" (1942) and a four-page reply to comments from several philosophers)[40]; "Politics and the Metaphysics of Freedom" (1953) (reprinted in CE Ch. 13); and two essays in The *Zero Fallacy* (1997), "Democracy and Religion" (ZF Ch. 4) and "Individual Differences and the Ideal of Equality" (ZF Ch. 14). In addition to whole essays, his numerous books and articles contain wide ranging, interspersed comments on political and economic issues.

Considering Hartshorne's essays and comments as an aggregate, at least two leitmotifs stand out as unifying themes. First, political and economic affairs, like all other aspects of human existence, are best decided by seeking a reasoned moderation, a "middle way," an avoidance of extreme tendencies. This avoidance of extremes is encapsulated in Hartshorne's dictum that "Blanket socialistic and antisocialistic dogmas are pseudo-absolutes" which miss the target of "chance and love in correct mutual adjustment" (RSP 108). Second, there is an ineluctably tragic aspect to existence—there is an undeniable truth in the "tragic vision" of existentialist thinkers and in Reinhold Niebuhr's "Christian realism," that is, recognition of a propensity to sin or moral error as part and parcel of the human condition. In Hartshorne's words, "If there is no original sin, there is something not obviously less awful."[41] Awareness of the tragic is grounds for suspicion of all programs of utopia, be they religious, pacifist, Marxist, Fascist, capitalist, technocratic or otherwise. Yet, matters are never hopeless, for theism (at least neoclassically reformed theism) grounds hope in numerous ways. Rather than follow impossible plans for "pie in the sky" utopia or be paralyzed by "all is vanity" pessimism, we should adopt the attitude of William James's meliorism—make the world *as we find it* a better place. This attitude mirrors the very *modus operandi* of the process deity—aim at the best possible route, so often the *via media* route, given the actual temporal situation.

Democracy, Equality, and Inequality

Quite logically, Hartshorne sees political and human social being and behavior as specifications of his metaphysical principles (if it were somehow otherwise the principles claimed to be metaphysical would not in fact be genuinely metaphysical by Hartshorne's criteria). In particular, the metaphysics of relative indeterminism will be reflected in the fact that human beings always have some degree of both political and social freedom (however minute) no matter how determinative the political and social circumstances. To employ two of Hartshorne's examples, even slaves have some small degree of personal freedom as do young adults who are pathologically over-dependent on parents. *Exactly* how slaves respond to their ill-treatment or children follow through on parental guidance, down to the smallest detail, is not determined by the political or social circumstances of the situation. Given this, the practical question becomes what degree of human freedom should be fostered by the most ethical political and social arrangements. Where should the boundaries to political and social freedom be drawn? The basic political question thus becomes "are there recognized limits to governmental interference, *guaranteed* 'rights' to make one's own decisions?" (CE 137).

Hartshorne answers the question of guaranteed rights by arguing for the basic political and economic liberties affirmed by the classical liberal democratic theory of Jefferson—the "inalienable" rights of human persons to life, liberty, and the pursuit of happiness—on the grounds that human persons have basic political equality. They have this equality, not because humans are equal in ability, outcome, or even value to God (e.g., an omniscient being will surely not evaluate a Lincoln as equivalent in value to the life of a vicious and sadistic slave-master), but because no human being or group of human beings can competently evaluate the complex and multifarious ways in which human beings are capable of contributing, and do, in fact, contribute value over the course of their lifetimes. In short, human beings simply are not God. For all practical purposes, although there is no literal ontological equality when comparing individual human beings, all human beings are to be presumed essentially equal in their capacities. *A fortiori,* this judgment is contrary to "groupthink"—a manner of political and social thinking in which human beings are to be treated differently based on certain physical characteristics associated with sex and race or ethnicity. Such traits "have no known relation to inborn mental or moral capacities"; all members of the human race are thus bound "to be presumed virtually equal in such capacities, and therefore in essential human worth."[42] On this basis Hartshorne denounces all forms of racism and sexism as well as denial of opportunities for the poor. We submit that this list could be consistently expanded to include sexual orientation as it is widely agreed in learned and humane circles that such orientation also has no intrinsic connection to "inborn mental or moral capacities" (we take it to be question-begging to declare that same-sex activity between consenting adults is by definition immoral).[43]

This last consideration leads to Hartshorne's affirmation of a fundamental directive for government. Government should assist in providing equal opportunities for individual self-development as determined by individual preferences (IO 226). He thus affirms the liberal notions of both tolerance of other persons' preferences and individual self-reliance for making such choices. The affirmation of self-reliance is defended largely on the grounds that persons know their own preferences, needs, and circumstances better than others (IO 226). This is not an absolute, however, as one's personal preferences cannot be decided in a way that interferes with the ability of others to pursue their own preferences. For instance, while Hartshorne raised no objection to the right to private property, such right should not be taken to such an extent that, say, one could purchase all lands containing regional water wells thereby drying up the water resources for communities beyond private property boundaries. This example must apply since Hartshorne holds that monopolies are without question social evils, and further that, in particular, utilities such as dispensation of water resources and electrical power, which intrinsically lend themselves to (at least regionally) noncompetitive distribution, ought to be subject to government regulation. Because of this example we hold that Randall Morris is incorrect to say that "it is difficult to see how Hartshorne could allow the state the right to limit an individual's accumulation of the means for self-development" is incorrect.[44] Contrary to Randall, this is not difficult to see, given Hartshorne's explicit policy regarding anti-monopoly/anti-oligarchy. Morris himself admits that Hartshorne makes qualifications here citing CAP 235, where Hartshorne expresses a need for the "substantial measure of economic equality" necessary for the achievement of "political equality."[45] Again, we see the motif of the "middle way" here: We ought to have the various political liberties defended in classical liberal democratic theory, but these cannot be absolutes any more than state interferences into such liberties can be absolutes. All must be balanced, and all must be properly contextualized.

Political Economy

The middle way in political-economic arrangements is that of moderated genuinely free enterprise and social planning that avoids, on the one hand, the extreme of communist-socialist oppression of individual expression and economic activity, and, on the other hand, the extreme of unfettered laissez-faire capitalism, which sees profit and sheer growth of GDP as the only goals worth pursuing, blind to the social and environmental consequences of such pursuit. History clearly shows that free enterprise models of economic activity are superior in wealth creation to centralized communist models (WM, 35); two examples are China prior to and after its allowance of individual enterprise and the differences between North and South Korea in diffusion of material goods. On the other hand, the unfettered interest in growth, where "more" is always better, and the pathological appetite for consumerism (Marx's "fetishism of commodities" emphasized by the neo-Marxist Frankfurt school) endemic to modern industrial-capitalist societies like the U.S. is deleterious, rife with propensity to economic inequalities, and dangerous to the environment. While capitalism as such, as an expression of the basic right to freedom of vocation, is to be embraced, "Capitalism *in its present-day form* is ugly—and doomed" (RSP 47)— these words were penned originally in 1935, but they are as relevant now as they were then. Reform of our current capitalist system, especially in the light of our dire ecological situation, is imperative, nay, existentially imperative.

One way forward toward the desired middle, Hartshorne suggests, is through more emphasis on cooperative or so-called share economies. One such "cooperativist" economic model that Hartshorne refers to early on (1937) was proposed in a more or less socialistic fashion, and explicitly as a meditation upon Christian moral principles, by evangelical activist Toyohiko Kagawa in his *Brotherhood Economics,* a series of Walter Rauschenbusch Lectures presented originally at Colgate-Rochester Divinity School. Hartshorne refers to it as a counter-example to claims of Marxist theorists that Western religious ideas must be tied intrinsically to the economic and social status quo (BH 83, n. 3). Kagawa's argument is that regional, national, and even international cooperatives in matters of credit, insurance, health care, consumer, and producer activities are "the best hope for reform today" (BH 83). Cooperativism has an obvious and direct connection to "religious ethics"—as straightforward as simply "love thy neighbor"—and may well be the religious idealist's best option that finds "its chief escape from the terrible dilemma: predatory capitalism or dictatorship" (BH 83). Hartshorne notes that Kagawa allows some private capitalism in both the short and long runs, but also distrusts the notion of ownership by the state or by municipalities when money comes from "ordinary banks" rather than banks tied to cooperatives. The latter idea points to an important element in Hartshorne's ideas about political economy: monopolies or concentrations of ownership and power are a chief economic evil—whether in the form of large banks, centralized governments, or huge corporations—where appropriate checks and balances are rendered unavailable or ineffective .

A more recent defense of share economics, about which Hartshorne expresses positive interest, is offered by Harvard environmental econ-omist Martin L. Weitzman in his now classic 1984 treatise *The Share Economy.* Among a number of monetary policy recommendations made by Weitzman is a proposal that includes a remuneration system in which workers would:

> receive a substantial part of their pay as a negotiated share of company profits or revenues (per employee). For bearing this risk, which is entirely voluntary, even though it is in the national interest, they will be rewarded by substantially lowered tax rates." (cited at WM 36)

This model (at least in theory) would stymie periodic "stagflation," help mitigate the "psychology of alienation" endemic to capitalist economies (as astutely charged by Marx in his *Economic and Philosophical Manuscripts*), and would also incentivize both individual and team performance. It would likewise help close the current enormous gap in pay between regular employees and company executives, a gap which has spiraled out of all control in the past few decades. This is profoundly fairer than our current business practices. Although Weitzman has received criticism from some economists given to an emphasis on micro-analytic dynamics of free markets (a point Hartshorne does not note), Hartshorne agrees with a number of other economists that Weitzman makes a reasonable case for these ideas. Indeed something like a share economy (the so-called bonus system) was practiced in Japan with considerable success (prior to Japan's long recessionary dip in the 1990s and beyond, a dip which had a number of complex causes unrelated to bonuses). Moreover, some progressive companies in the U.S. are also adopting profit sharing with success. There is therefore some real world evidence that share economics is workable.

The economic ideal for the mature Hartshorne (as of the publication of *Wisdom as Moderation* in 1987) seems to be a voluntary, share, free-enterprise system—where to a substantial degree the employees are the company—a system that rewards initiative and performance but that is "socially checked," especially along the lines of environmental responsibility. The ideal is to have reasonable prosperity that fulfills human needs but that unequivocally respects individual *and* national *and* global interests, a prosperity won without engaging in profiteering or in damaging the environment. In contrast to Hartshorne's ideal, we currently have an economy based on rapine profiteering as well as a concomitant emphasis on growth such that "more" is always axiomatic and unquestioned from Main Street to the White House. Today, especially true of publicly owned companies that are entangled in market speculation, we are constantly "pressing the envelope" to the limits of the law, attempting to alter or influence the law (via the omnipresent "K Street" lobbying of Congress, an institution which is itself an incubator for K Street's lobbyists), and doing virtually *anything* that will maximize profits irrespective of the fates of individuals and their families and the environment. For example, a company may move to Mexico or India in order to exploit nearly slave wages or it may continue unabated with fracking activities regardless of water-table toxicity or even possible geophysical disturbance to the point of increasing regional earthquakes. While there are some socially and environmentally responsible exceptions, the *norm* for the contemporary large multinational or not-so-large corporation is that no loyalties to individual, community, nation, or planet are part of the business "decision tree." Our current capitalist ethos thus suffers from an extreme egocentricity undergirded by "the extreme individualism of Western metaphysics" (WM 46). For numerous reasons, existential as well as ethical, this model of economic practice cannot be sustained in the long run.

Randall Morris, in his richly detailed examination of Whitehead's and Hartshorne's social and political thought, rightly emphasizes Hartshorne's concern with monopolistic concentrations of power (although, as noted above, he seems to have forgotten the implications of this when discussing Hartshorne's doctrine of state intervention).[46] He is also correct to contend that this "mirrors," in the domain of political economy, Hartshorne's metaphysics and theology in which divine power is necessarily tempered by God's social relations with finite creatures that always have some power.[47] Nothing could be clearer, given Hartshorne's use of the term "monopolistic fallacy" to describe the classical metaphysics of unilateral omnipotence. It is not without good reason then that Hartshorne would be enthusiastic about University of Chicago economist Henry C. Simons's arguments in his "positive program" for the reform of modern capitalism. Although presented in 1934 in the midst of the Great Depression, interest in Simons in recent economic circles has been revived because his model of anti-monopolistic and financial oversight predicts calamities like the Great Recession financial collapse of 2008. Unfettered, unrestricted market speculation in real estate, short-term profit interest in unsupportable mortgage procurements, and concentration of wealth in "too big to fail" banking, stock, and insurance entities are, on the terms of Simons's theory, recipes for eventual disaster. Indeed, like a diabetes drug designed to mitigate blood sugar highs and lows, Simons wants to insulate the financial system from cycles of boom and bust. Argues Simons:

> Eliminate all forms of monopolistic market power, to include
> the breakup of large oligopolistic corporations and application
> of anti-trust laws to labor unions. A Federal incorporation law

could be used to limit corporation size and where technology required giant firms for reasons of low cost production the Federal government should own and operate them . . . Promote economic stability by reform of the monetary system and establishment of stable rules for monetary policy . . . Reform the tax system and promote equity through income tax . . . Limit waste by restricting advertising and other wasteful merchandising practices.

While not every recommendation in Simons's model may be warranted (e.g., do we want to prohibit tariffs under *all* circumstances?; while granting that surely some advertising is wasteful and even harmful, exactly who is to say how advertising restrictions should be implemented and by exactly what criteria?), Hartshorne was no doubt strongly attracted to the anti-monopolistic and anti-oligarchic provisions of Simons's theory. Like Simons, Hartshorne sees monopoly and oligarchy as the enemies of both political liberty and genuinely free competition. As Simons puts it starkly and succinctly, "Political liberty can survive only within an effectively competitive economic system. Thus, *the great enemy of democracy is monopoly in all its forms.*"[48] In a review essay on Simons, Hartshorne affirms this statement, pointing to the exploitation of individuals when monopolies control pay structures and prevent competitive alternatives for the labor force.[49] In addition, he argues that inherently noncompetitive activities such as utilities should be left largely for government regulation but not without public oversight. Just as free market activities must be socially checked, socialization of public utilities must also be checked since over-socialization of commerce can lead to totalitarianism. Again, the theme here is achieving balance between extreme countervailing tendencies.

As a closing observation, we submit that, there is no clear or obvious reason why Hartshorne's political economic ideas as sketched here would be inconsonant with proposals now being proffered in process circles under the banner of "Organic Marxism," although detailed comparison would be required in order for this claim to be fully substantiated. To be sure, this organic theory is a strongly revisionary form of Marxism, since it rejects the tenets that are the objects of Hartshorne's persistent criticisms of Marxism, namely, its Dialectical Materialism, its reductionist anti-religionism, and its reduction of all cultural supra-structure to support of material infrastructure. In light of this list of rejections of Marxist theory, we wonder if it is properly Marxist at all; perhaps it should be called Organic Socially Responsible Free Enterprise Theory. Be that as it may, we note that the following summary statement of Organic Marxism by Philip Clayton and Justin Heinzekehr is very much in the spirit of Hartshorne's emphases on economic hybridity (another term for "balance") and anti-oligarchy: Organic Marxism affirms

> hybrid [economic] systems that combine profitmaking activities with regulations that are designed to prevent corruption, environmental abuse, and the inordinate acquisition of wealth by a small number of citizens.[50]

As we see it, this sentence could have been written by Hartshorne himself.[51]

Warfare and Pacifism

Another practical political question to which Hartshorne gave considerable attention is, "When, if ever, is a state justified in waging war against another state or territory?" Given Hartshorne's views about divine persuasive causal agency and his decrying the worship of the "tyrant conception of power," we might expect him to embrace pacifism, since the allowance of warfare would seem to morally countenance coercion. However, in *Beyond Humanism*, in *Man's Vision of God*, in a substantive paper entitled "A Philosophy of Democratic Defense," and in considerable correspondence on the matter with Boston personalist philosopher Edgar S. Brightman, Hartshorne argues that *absolute* pacifism is unwarranted. There are circumstances—in particular, the situation after the rise of European fascism and the onset of World War II—that morally justify state-sponsored warfare. While Hartshorne holds that declared war should always be a last resort after every other attempt to resolve conflict has been reasonably tried, and he could never be described as consciously "hawkish" in overall war policy (especially regarding the use and proliferation of nuclear weapons), some may find his criteria for the justification of war to have hawkish implications. Despite all of Hartshorne's objections, Brightman remained stout in his defense of pacifism throughout the correspondence. On the subject of war, as on the subject of monopolistic economics, we see the particular importance of Hartshorne's convictions regarding the tragic view of existence: While war is a great evil to be strongly resisted, there may be situations in which the alternative to war—likely to result in a total loss of liberty on an international scale—is morally unacceptable, and this is ineluctably tragic.

The argument with Brightman begins when Hartshorne responds to a review essay that Brightman published on *Man's Vision of God* in which Brightman rejects Hartshorne's anti-pacifism on the grounds that it makes an abstract *a priori* appeal to social awareness and that it does not consider the long-run consequences of warfare. The main historical context is Hitler and the rise of aggressive imperial aspirations in Europe and Asia in the 1930s and 1940s. The historical context should be emphasized in order to understand adequately Hartshorne's position, for he is almost entirely concerned with Hitler's totalitarian fascism and World War II as presenting the clear exception to "absolute" pacifism, a position he regards, in response to Brightman, as itself *a priori* since its claims are absolute or categorical. (So far as we are aware, the World Wars are the only wars which Hartshorne explicitly endorses as *jus bellum*.)

Hartshorne argues against "doctrinaire pacifism" on the grounds that, paradoxically, it exhibits a lack of love, a lack of social awareness (MVG 165–68). An ethics of love requires an adequate social awareness of humanity that prompts coercive action, on certain rather extreme occasions: "Freedom must not be free to destroy freedom" (MVG 173). Moreover, Hartshorne insists that, while war is indeed an evil, in the special situations where war is justified, it is a tragically necessary evil. The world does contain those who are deeply sinful in their egocentricity and extreme lack of social awareness. As a tragic consequence of this egocentricity, when a political party or dictator threatens to coerce the entire planet and engages in genocide, other states are morally justified in fighting back. This is so, even though, again quite tragically, lives will be sacrificed. This does not necessarily mean that we love the sacrificed lives less, but rather may well mean that we love the lives of others who are saved more (MVG 168). Tragically, there are times when lethal armed resistance is simply the lesser of evil choices. The empirical evidence regarding the ruthless behavior and extreme lack of ethical sensitivity to ethnic "others" on the part of Axis powers, argued strongly for American involvement in World War II as one of those rare moments in which human liberty on *a global scale* was at stake.

Brightman's most formidable objection to Hartshorne's view is his charge that one has to consider *long-run* consequences of conducting war. Peace has to be given every chance to take root; it is too easy to find reasons for pulling the trigger during fits of nationalistic passion without thinking through the aftermath and the "exit strategy." In particular, Brightman points to the overall bad results of World War I in which the vanquished greatly suffered and were severely penalized by the Allied victors. In return, they eventually sponsored yet more war. History shows that war often begets more war, violence begets more violence.

There is much to be said for this perspective as witness the results of the Iraq War. After all the blood and treasure have been spent, there is little unity or prosperity in Iraq and extremist groups such as ISIL have arisen, in part, as a remedy to the suppressed Sunni Bath party. Nonetheless, Hartshorne argues that the empirical case in relation *specifically* to World War II stacks readily on the side of preferring an Allied victory as opposed to an Axis one. For instance, he notes, one could hardly envision a United Nations if the Axis powers had prevailed, not to mention horrific fates awaiting "non-Aryan," disabled, and homosexual populations as based on the actual behavior of the Third Reich. Indeed, it should be noted that in the long run the aftermath of war seems to have so much more to do with how the conquered are treated than to factors inherent in warfare itself, especially if military actions were directed as much as possible at combatants. Hartshorne acknowledges that the behavior of the Allies after the Great War—in particular, the Treaty of Versailles, American tariffs, and lending programs that made debts unpayable—contributed greatly to the rise of Nazism (MVG 167; HP 36).

Brightman makes the important point that the prevention of World War II may well have been achieved if all parties to the treaties of World War I had kept to strict observance of the pacifist and armament provisions of the treaties (HB 56). Fortunately, we learned the lesson of punishing Germanic powers after their defeat in World War I, and thus the Marshall Plan for European reconstruction was a model of preserving the peace. The result has been the end of centuries of intra-Western European conflict. In an unpublished notice titled "Recollections of Leo Szilard" Hartshorne tells of collaborating with a church historian to pen a letter to President Harry Truman concerning the treatment of the Japanese after their surrender. Hartshorne writes:

> We did not roundly condemn the president's decision [to drop the bomb] but put the emphasis on what the country should

do, now that Japan had surrendered. The war was over; but the world was left, much of it, in misery, poverty, and hunger, with the principal exception of U.S.A. We advocated generosity. Fifty-some signatures were assembled and the document was sent to the White House. It received some publicity. I have often wondered if the Marshall Plan for the recovery of Europe was not, to some extent, occasioned by our proposal. It may have helped.[52]

While Hartshorne disagreed with Brightman about pacifism, he clearly agreed with him that helping to rebuild rather than exacting retribution was the best way to treat the vanquished in war.

There are other historical examples. One can cite Lincoln's policy of attempting to reconcile with and reconstruct rather than punish the South after the Civil War. The Truth and Reconciliation movement in South Africa after the downfall of the apartheid regime very probably prevented continuous rounds of vengeful killing. By contrast, the American treatment of disaffected Bath and other Sunni parties in Iraq both lengthened the conflict in Iraq and did much to spur on the so-called "Islamic extremist" elements with which we are currently dealing. And the arbitrary way in which the Middle East territories were partitioned after World War II has likewise been at the root of continuing conflict, including the seemingly never-ending quagmire of the Palestinian-Israeli conflict.

In his "Philosophy of Democratic Defense," Hartshorne spells out five factors that should be considered in determining when a conflict rises above the level of the local to the scale of the global war that signals serious consideration of state-sponsored military intervention.[53] Hartshorne allows that local tyrants may be tolerated within limits (thus apparently regime change would not be a preferred item of "Hartshornean" foreign policy). However, nations ought seriously to entertain the prospect of military intervention when:

1. The control of seas is threatened on a massive scale;
2. The war is calculated to achieve a worldwide precedent of successful aggression;
3. The world economy is interdependent;
4. The affairs of war will influence the political conceptions of neutral nations;

5.　One party is more likely than another to promote self-gover-
nance and preservation of basic human rights.

Hartshorne warns that such criteria are tentative, and the satisfaction
of one or more of them would not be sufficient for the judgment that
war ought to be declared. Rather, these are thresholds at which a nation
rightfully considers whether war would secure the best outcome on
balance. We note that this list was compiled during 1941 when the
question of American isolation was still viable and *was suggested prior
to the use of atomic weapons.* The prospect of nuclear warfare changes
the entire outlook, and Hartshorne rightfully warns that American
international cooperation and promotion of understanding between
nations is paramount in light of such a prospect (WM 45). Moreover,
it does not bode well for international peace that American attitudes
toward other nations are much too provincial, isolated, monolingual,
and culturally disengaged (WM 45).

Hartshorne acknowledges the possibility of nonviolent resistance
as an alternative to the use of armed force, but he does not see that this
method would produce a significant effect at the point of entrenched
Nazi and other fascist aggression. On the other hand, Mark Y. A.
Davies is probably correct in contending that Hartshorne did not give
nonviolent resistance enough consideration as a general alternative to
the use of violence, as witness the successes of Gandhi's campaign for
Indian independence, the solidarity movement in 1980s Poland, and
the U.S. Civil Rights movement under the leadership of Martin Luther
King, Jr. (HP 130–31). On the other hand, it is a fair question how
successful nonviolent resistance can be in the face of a regime that
accepts a fascist "might makes right" philosophy. Notwithstanding,
Hartshorne is, in our view, morally correct in his main contention
that armed resistance in the case of World War II stands as a sufficient
counterexample to "*absolute* pacifism." Of course, this is largely a victory
of philosophical principle, and it leaves open an enormous set of questions
which Hartshorne does not address. How *exactly* should a just war be
conducted? Granted America should have engaged militarily in World
War II, but the fiery, cruel destruction of Dresden during the Allied
invasion was surely morally indefensible and unnecessary. In the light
of more recent historical research, Nagasaki and Hiroshima appear to
have been directed at pacifying Soviet aggression rather than the official
narrative of "more readily ending the war with Japan." How should use

of drones be conducted? Are head of regime assassinations ever morally permissible? Should local genocides trigger military intervention? Given the tens of thousands of deaths and millions of refugees, should the current situation in Syria require direct American military intervention? On such important questions a systematic philosophy of military ethics seems required and this is not a topic that Hartshorne pursued.[54]

Conclusion

For one usually classified as a metaphysician, Hartshorne had a surprising number of things to say about technology, politics, and the use of military force, all of it worthy of serious consideration. In agreement with Bergson, but contrary to the Feuerbachian critique of religion, Hartshorne argued that technological advancement cannot—*in principle* cannot—address human insecurities about life arising from accident, moral failure, and death. These are problems inherent in the human condition for which only a properly metaphysical response will suffice, and Hartshorne proposes neoclassical theism as the balm.

While technology can never take the place of metaphysics, it has the potential to raise the general quality of life for more people than ever before in history. However, with high technology comes the likelihood of its abuse apart from the constraints of sound governmental and social policies that emphasize and provide an equilibrium among equality of opportunity, social justice, and responsible use of environmental resources. Following Hartshorne's commitment to the middle way, advanced technologies are to be neither enthusiastically embraced nor phobically shunned. Rather, they should be appropriately used in contexts which support life and meaningful creative activity. A process philosophy of technology consistent with Hartshorne's ideas holds that technologies are morally ambiguous, socially constructed instruments. Their value and moral permissibility depends on appropriateness and social contexts of use. As such they are subject to the constraints of resource sustainability, environmental protection, and social justice.

Hartshorne claimed no special wisdom or insight concerning politics and economics, once remarking that metaphysics is easy by comparison. There is, nevertheless, a deep harmony between his views on these subjects. In agreement with his metaphysical stance of shared creativity, where reality is a product of multiple strands of creative activity, Hartshorne's political philosophy and the economic policies he favored would take political and economic power out of the hands of a single individual (a monarch, a tyrant, a CEO) or of a few (an oligarchy or a monopoly) and ensure a just distribution of goods and opportunities. There is no natural superiority of any single race, sex, or class of people which would justify affording them special privileges beyond those that are available to all. Hartshorne would find a middle ground between unbridled free markets and a regulated economy, with the hope of preventing inordinate acquisition of wealth in the hands of a few and with an eye to preventing environmental abuse.

Concerning the use of military force, Hartshorne was, for a time, a pacifist under the influence of Tolstoy (DL 120), but he rejected doctrinaire pacifism in his mature thinking. His ideas took shape in the face of the two world wars through which he lived. He agreed with Brightman that the victors in war only invite more warfare when they exact retribution and impose unusually onerous penalties on the vanquished. But he argued that strategies of nonviolence meet their limits in the face of aggressors like the fascists of the second world war, with their jingoistic foreign policy, and their explicit racism and governmental policies of mass murder. Nevertheless, Hartshorne did not believe that the victors can hold the moral high ground with force. The greatest of leaders recognize in their enemies a common humanity, and they keep that in mind when it is time to settle accounts at the war's end. With this in mind, Hartshorne supported Allied financing for rebuilding Axis war-torn countries, as in the Marshall plan. In this way, he was true to the ethical injunction he borrowed from Berdyaev: Be creative and foster creativity in others.

ELEVEN

Hartshorne's Legacy

W E NOTED IN THE INTRODUCTORY CHAPTER that, at an early age, after reading Emerson, Hartshorne resolved "to trust reason to the end" (LP viii). He left ample evidence that he was true to this purpose, most notably in his study of the psychology of sensation, in his defense of metaphysics, and in his work on birdsong. The amount of energy that he devoted to questions surrounding the nature and existence of God might lead one to classify him as a theologian; however, as we noted in the first chapter, he self-identified as a philosopher. To be sure, he was deeply interested in questions relevant to religion, but he rejected the idea that he was a theologian. His defense of dipolar theism presupposes no sectarian dogma, makes no appeals to "revealed" truths or books, and privileges no mystical experience. There can be no question that he was, first and foremost, a philosopher who used reason to investigate questions of religious belief and practice. He was, moreover, sensitive to the many ways in which philosophy is a frail and fallible enterprise. Communication must take place across centuries and across cultural and linguistic boundaries. There is the snobbery and inertia of traditions and what Hartshorne called "cultural lag" in the recognition of genuine insights.[1] There is the tendency to forget, ignore, or marginalize objections to one's views. Hartshorne also considered it

mistaken to suppose that meeting objections is sufficient for securing
the rationality of one's ideas, or, as he wrote in his correspondence
with Brightman, to merely defend one's own "castle of ideas" (HB 62).
As Carnap said, it is one thing to ask what your metaphysical position
commits you to, but it is something else again to ask what commits
you to your metaphysical position. Despite their knowledge of formal
logic, philosophers are also susceptible to the fallacy of affirming
the consequent, looking only for confirmation of their views or for
arguments favorable to them. There is, finally, the failure to exhaust the
logically possible alternatives in considering the solutions for particular
philosophical problems. Hartshorne discussed all of these obstacles, and
more, to making progress in philosophy, and he took measures to remedy
them in his own attempt to trust reason.

Few others have been as well positioned to benefit from personal
exposure to such a variety of great philosophers for such a lengthy period.
As noted in the Preface, he called his longevity his "secret weapon." It
was, in any case, contrary to Hartshorne's upbringing, and perhaps to
his personality, to take an overly narrow view of the nature and aims
of philosophy. His mother once told him, "Charles, life is big" (DL 39);
he, in turn, took a big view of life and of philosophy. His wide-ranging
interests included non-Western philosophy. Although this topic was not
his primary focus, he was no stranger to the traditions of India, China,
and Japan. As we noted at the close of Chapter Three, Hartshorne never
took a parochial approach to philosophy, and he often addressed issues
in Eastern thought. In addition, he read Western philosophy with fresh
eyes, emphasizing what others considered minor points of major philosophers and highlighting major points of what most have considered minor
philosophers (cf. CS 86). His assessments of Western philosophy, especially in the companion volumes *Insights and Oversights: An Evaluation
of Western Philosophy* (1983) and *Creativity in American Philosophy* (1984),
provide many examples.[2] We have seen that his reading of Anselm shed
new light on an old argument which had grown stale through textbook
refutations that did not attend to the difference between Chapters Two
and Three of *Proslogion*, as well as the points Anselm made in his *Reply
to Gaunilo*. One may also note that he brought attention to Jules Lequyer
(or Lequier) who philosophers had almost forgotten but who William
James had referred to as "a French philosopher of genius."[3]

With Edith Wharton, Hartshorne distinguished those who light new candles and those who are like mirrors reflecting the candles that are lit by others. He remarked that Peirce and Whitehead had done both, and he dared to hope that he had done both (DL 402). His own "candle" has perhaps often been missed because he expended so much energy reflecting the lights of these great philosophers. His monumental contribution to Peirce scholarship (with Paul Weiss), taking on the arduous task of editing six volumes of Peirce's papers, was seminal. The Hartshorne-Weiss edition of the Peirce papers remains an important scholarly resource for the entire philosophical community while it awaits a comprehensive chronological edition of Peirce's oeuvres. As to Whitehead, an entire generation explored his later work by crossing over the bridge provided by Hartshorne's scholarship and his defense of Whitehead's metaphysics. Barry Woodbridge's 1977 primary-secondary Whitehead bibliography lists seventy-seven items by Hartshorne, considerably more than any other of the great first-generation interpreters of Whitehead's thought—Henry Nelson Wieman (thirteen entries), William Christian (eleven entries), Dorothy Emmet (nine entries), A. H. Johnson (thirty entries), Nathanial Lawrence (nine entries), Ivor Leclerc (eighteen entries), Victor Lowe (twenty-one entries), F. S. C. Northrop (ten entries), and Norman Pittenger (fifty entries). The index has one-hundred and thirty-nine listings for "Hartshorne" (discounting articles by Hartshorne himself) compared to a combined total of sixty-seven for the nine other scholars just named.[4] The point is not that "more is better," for Hartshorne did not write what are often regarded as the best introductory works on Whitehead from this period.[5] However, the numbers reflect a consensus about the preeminent place of Hartshorne among Whitehead's interpreters.

Hartshorne saw anticipations of neoclassical metaphysics in a variety of thinkers, beginning with the Buddhists in the East and, in the West, Plato. He found in Plato a nascent metaphysic that bears only a rather tangential relation to what is central to textbook treatments of "Platonism" (e.g., the theory of Forms and the immortality of an immaterial soul). According to Hartshorne, as Plato struggled with questions of self-movement, cosmology, and theism (especially in the later dialogues), he came close to neoclassical metaphysics (IO ch. 3).[6] However, philosophy had to wait for Whitehead—with near or nearly exact anticipations in Peirce, James, and Bergson—before creativity was explicitly considered as the universal of universals that describes every concrete particular.

Those who write on the history of philosophy generally acknowledge the importance of Whitehead's earlier work as co-author with Russell of *Principia Mathematica,* but many philosophers outside the circle of explicitly process thinkers bypass Whitehead's speculative philosophy of nature foreshadowed in work predating *Principia* and more fully articulated in his later works.[7] A rough equivalent to this attitude would be touting the importance of Wittgenstein's *Tractatus* while ignoring the *Philosophical Investigations.* (The equivalence is only partial since Whitehead's later work continues an interest in the philosophy of nature that began before his arrival in America.) One may surmise that the split-brain treatment of Whitehead results from the project of creating a narrative about the rise of modern logic and the supposed demise of grand theorizing in metaphysics. Hartshorne's work provides a different model. He was at Harvard during Whitehead's most intensively creative years in America and saw in the later work a way past the scientism of the positivists and the way ahead for metaphysics. As Hartshorne says in his autobiography, British culture and academic life produced Whitehead, then largely ignored him (DL 22). Hartshorne knew better than to ignore genius. Happily, there are countervailing currents of contemporary thinking that highlight Whitehead's continuing relevance.[8]

Quite a number of philosophers have known better than to ignore Hartshorne. This is especially so among some distinguished philosophers, logicians, and philosophers of science who were his students at Chicago or Emory. At a minimum, a select few should be mentioned. The late William P. Alston, in part because of Hartshorne's influence, wrote his dissertation at Chicago on the topic of Whitehead and internal relations, and in his later years he took some measure of both critical and constructive interest in Hartshorne's philosophical theology in several essays (see especially EA 78–98). Bowman L. Clarke, Lucio Chiaraviglio, and Norman M. Martin—all distinguished logicians or specialists in informatics (Chiaraviglio)—have published work on or related to Hartshorne's philosophy. Clark's excellent treatise on *Language and Natural Theology* belongs in the latter category.[9] The important philosopher of science Abner Shimony, mentioned earlier, has remained indebted to Whiteheadian thought throughout his career, an indebtedness which began with Hartshorne's instigation at Chicago. Lewis Ford, who studied with Hartshorne at Emory, founded the journal *Process Studies* which expressly mentions scholarly inquiry into

Hartshorne's philosophy as well as Whitehead's as part of its mission. From 1971 to the present, this forum has continually published articles by, on, and related to Hartshorne. Many other celebrated philosophers have been influenced by Hartshorne in some significant manner or another through their exposure to his thought while serving as his colleague at Harvard, Chicago, Emory, or Texas-Austin. The list of colleagues is long and includes Paul Weiss, Richard M. Martin, Robert Kane, and Rudolf Carnap. The last mentioned philosopher may seem surprising, for he is regarded as an "arch anti-metaphysician." In fact, Hartshorne was influenced by Carnap, especially by his insistence on high standards of logical rigor. Carnap, in turn, constructively engaged Hartshorne's work. He was reportedly intrigued by Hartshorne's formal reduction to absurdity of the coherence of classical attributes of deity as developed in *The Divine Relativity;* he worked with Hartshorne closely on the technical appendix to Chapter Two on "Relativity and Logical Entailment" (DR 95–115); he was especially intrigued by Hartshorne's Chicago colloquium paper on the notion that every contingent proposition requires an empirical concept in its formation (DL 231–32).

Certainly, Hartshorne's work has attracted the attention of theologians and philosophers of religion. The first book-length treatment of the theological implications of Hartshorne's thought was Ralph E. James's *The Concrete God* (1967)—James studied with Hartshorne at Emory, 1959–61. In 1973, a volume devoted to Hartshorne's thought was published in a series titled, "Makers of the Modern Theological Mind" written by Alan Gragg. Many theologians and theologically minded philosophers have critically appropriated Hartshorne's philosophical theology; these include, for example, Schubert Ogden, David A. Pailin, David Ray Griffin, Edgar A. Towne, Santiago Sia, Paul S. Fiddes, Marjorie Suchocki, Sheila Devaney, Anna Case-Winters, Douglas Pratt, Kurian Kachappilly, and Theodore Walker, Jr. Julia Enxing, an extremely capable young theologian, introduced Hartshorne's theological thinking to a German audience in *Perfect Changes* (2012), a book she edited with Klaus Müller, and in a major contribution of her own, *Gott im Werden* (2013). Hartshorne's student and one-time colleague at Emory, John Cobb (himself a theologian), once commented that it is often the case that a philosopher who gains a following among theologians is "handicapped among philosophers."[10] This tendency may be less prominent since the resurgence of interest in philosophy of religion in the closing decades of the twentieth century. On the other hand, at the opening of the twenty-first century, the new atheists are, for the most part, tone-deaf when it comes to philosophy of religion, and their popularity may have contributed to a diminishing of respect for the discipline. As we saw in Chapter Seven, one even advocates the elimination of the philosophy of religion from secular institutions.

Our study has amply documented that Hartshorne was active throughout the century, vigorously defending the rationality of dipolar theism in the heyday of the Vienna Circle. At a time when religious discourse was often regarded as nonsensical, Hartshorne met and challenged the positivists on their own terms. For example, his technically astute "Logical Positivism and the Method of Philosophy" (the penultimate chapter of *Beyond Humanism*), parts of which appeared in the second issue of the journal *Philosophy of Science* under the provocative title "Metaphysics for Positivists," presciently anticipated quite a number of the arguments against the soundness of positivism that have now become commonplace. As Huston Smith observed, Hartshorne "was among the first to see that the positivists were metaphysical with a vengeance."[11] The counterattack against positivism was coupled with rigorous constructive proposals for how to engage in metaphysical reasoning and an energetic defense of his own version of process metaphysics.

Metaphysician though he was, Hartshorne was attentive to the deliverances of science, ever alert to a dialogue that promises to challenge and transform both our understanding of philosophy and of science. His early work on sensation and his empirical studies on birdsong never left him far removed from psychology or biology. The great geneticist, Sewell Wright, was a colleague and friend who he met on a regular basis by virtue of Hartshorne's membership in the University of Chicago's "X club" (DL 227–30). Hartshorne was fond of reminding his readers that Wright, like him, was a psychicalist (Wright preferred the expression "dual-aspect panpsychism").[12] In later years, Hartshorne continued the practice of seeking intellectual exchange with well-known scientists. We noted in Chapter Seven that in his ninth decade Hartshorne published two articles in the *Journal of Speculative Philosophy* expressing appreciation for the contributions of the celebrity scientists Carl Sagan, Steven Weinberg, and Edward O. Wilson, but also challenging their views on mind, matter, and the metaphysics of religion. Hartshorne's articles on Charles Darwin exhibit the same unusual combination of awe in the presence of scientific accomplishment and confident assessment of what Hartshorne considered the scientist's philosophical shortcomings (in Darwin's case, his commitment to determinism).[13] Always an evolutionist, Hartshorne had very little patience with what is called "creation science." It is a good example of cultural lag, or perhaps "refutation by neglect," that the scientists among the new atheists (e.g., Richard Dawkins and Victor Stenger) ignore Hartshorne, especially his case against a merely empirical approach to the question of God's existence.

If some scientists are ignorant of Hartshorne's importance, countless contemporary philosophers of religion, not only process philosophers of religion but analytic philosophers of religion, have taken significant aspects of his philosophy quite seriously—among this group: Robert M. Adams, Richard Creel, William Hasker, James F. Ross, William Wainwright, and Nicholas Wolterstorff. In a number of cases they have yielded to his arguments or adopted his positions (or close variants of them), especially his development of a modal ontological argument and/or his critique of divine immutability and impassibility. Daniel Dombrowski points out that Ross, in his earlier work, contended that the classical concept of God is consistent but the neoclassical concept is inconsistent; however, he later conceded the consistency of neoclassical theism and spoke rather of "an impasse on competing descriptions of God."[14] One may also mention Hartshorne as a pioneer who contributed to the recent widespread interest among philosophers of religion in panentheism. Carol Christ, long at the forefront of feminist theology, sees in Hartshorne's work philosophically sophisticated ways of "re-imagining the divine in the world."[15]

Albert William Levi, one of Hartshorne's students at Chicago in the early 1930s, said that much of what Hartshorne taught "was less a vaccination than a time bomb. It took years for some of the insights to explode. But explode they finally did."[16] This is nowhere more evident than in Hartshorne's defense of divine relativity, perhaps the single most important factor in dissolving the near consensus that once prevailed that an entirely unchanging, impassible, and eternal deity should be considered normative for theology. Barry Whitney points out that Hartshorne's arguments have nudged not a few Thomists to revise their views on whether the activity and decisions of the creatures make any difference to God.[17] This is not to say that Thomists have adopted neoclassical theism, but some of them have come to recognize that some revision is in order, if only as a strategy for talking about God that would bring Aquinas closer to this aspect of Hartshorne's thinking. At one point, the Jesuit philosopher W. Norris Clarke could even speak of God as the "*Supreme Receiver* gathering in His consciousness all that creatures do" and responding accordingly and appropriately to it.[18] Clarke reported a conversation in which Hartshorne expressed delight with his [Clarke's] revision of Thomism since he considered the denial of real relations in God to be "the single greatest obstacle blocking further dialogue with Thomists."[19]

Some contemporary Catholic intellectuals, such as Chicago's celebrated public theologian David Tracy, have gone further by, in effect, converting full-scale to a neoclassical theistic model of divine attributes, although Tracy has long argued that process philosophy requires supplementation by hermeneutical philosophy.[20] Tracy has strongly emphasized the notion that Hartshorne's "existence/ actuality" distinction was his (Hartshorne's) unassailable and signal theoretical achievement, the "big breakthrough" in philosophical theology that logically corrects the overly abstract monopolar prejudice of the classical metaphysics of divinity and allows one to attribute, without contradiction, contingency, passivity, and change into the very heart of the divine reality. The distinction is central to Hartshorne's claim that coherent metaphysical sense can be made of the idea that God is love. As we noted in Chapter Five, Tracy referred to the existence/actuality distinction as "Hartshorne's Discovery."[21]

Another group that Hartshorne has influenced is Evangelical Christians who speak of "the openness of God" and "the open view of God." This is Hartshornean language. He spoke explicitly of "the openness of God" fully thirty years before the Evangelicals coopted the expression to describe a deity open to creaturely influence and that faces a relatively open future (WM 92).[22] Some of the major figures in that movement—William Hasker, Richard Rice, and Gregory Boyd— acknowledge a debt to Hartshorne's arguments for conceiving God in relational terms. Hasker reports that Hartshorne's *The Divine Relativity* convinced him that the relation from God to the creatures is as real as the relation of the creatures to God.[23] Hartshorne wrote a foreword to Richard Rice's dissertation, *Charles Hartshorne's Concept of Natural Theology*, a work that unhappily was never published; Rice's 1980 book,

The Openness of God (later titled *God's Foreknowledge & Man's Free Will*) shows clear evidence of Hartshorne's influence.[24] Boyd says that, despite his many disagreements with Hartshorne, "he has influenced my own thinking more than any other single philosopher, living or dead."[25] A prominent younger proponent of open theism, Thomas Jay Oord, told one of the authors of this text (Viney) that his movement towards open theism was, in part, occasioned by happening upon a copy in the library of Hartshorne's *A Natural Theology for Our Time;* Oord went on to study philosophy and theology at Claremont, writing a dissertation under the direction of David Ray Griffin. Like Hartshorne, he emphasizes the centrality of the concept of love in understanding God, and he has become known for his work on this subject, exploring it from multiple angles.[26]

We saw in the last two chapters that Hartshorne spoke to numerous practical, ethical, and political issues. While he was not especially well-known for his work on ethics, his published writings on the subject show a keen awareness of the biological—which is to say the evolutionary—origins of high moral principles. Moreover, he was interested in applied ethics. Indeed, John Cobb has remarked that Hartshorne was writing on ecological issues long before it was fashionable to do so, a fact that cannot be unrelated to his love of birds and his extensive knowledge of oscines.[27] He also tried to bring clarity to the abortion debate, defending a woman's right to an elective abortion consistent with Roe v. Wade, a position that fits naturally with his explicit avowal of feminist principles in political life, but also as these principles relate to issues in philosophical theology. We have also discussed in some detail the "middle way" he took on the questions of the values and uses of technology, the problems of justice and political economy, and the issue of pacifism versus state-sponsored warfare. He sought a comprehensive understanding of the human condition in its natural milieu, and a way forward, through reason and compassion, to promote the flourishing of all living forms on the planet.

Whatever one holds regarding the soundness of Hartshorne's views, it is indisputable that he made indelible contributions to philosophical and scientific research. Hartshorne's psychology of sensation continues to be within the vanguard of contemporary scientific research on sensory affectivity and evolutionary psychology. We have already noted that Hartshorne's Monotony Threshold Principle in ornithology—although not one of the subjects of this monograph—has received sympathetic interest among biologists. He substantially contributed to the scholarly interpretation of the philosophies of both Peirce and Whitehead. He presented challenging and forceful ways of thinking about the logic of the theistic issue, especially through his reformulation of the ontological argument (thereby inviting a reassessment of Anselm) and his work on the logic and metaphysics of divine attributes. Without question he was a sage expositor of a highly interdisciplinary, pluralist (and surely at least in that sense "postmodern") process vision of reality with wide ramifications for fresh thinking about religious, ethical, aesthetic, political, and scientific values. In many ways, he went against the fashions of philosophy of his day but he gained acceptance from fellow philosophers as one of the greatest philosophers of the twentieth century. In John Cobb's memorable words, Hartshorne was "a strange and alien greatness."[28] His is the legacy of a brilliantly original and highly productive thinker who worked at the fraught intersection of epistemic caution and audacious aspiration.

NOTES

Preface

1   The key to the citations and references to Hartshorne's books precede this preface. References to Hartshorne's articles are in the footnotes and also listed separately in the bibliography.

2   We borrow the expression "disciplined objectivity" from Donald A. Crosby's *A Religion of Nature* (Albany: SUNY Press, 2002), ch. 3.

3   Hartshorne said that he was affirming and amending Abraham Heschel's view of God as "the most moved mover." See Heschel's *Between God and Man*, ed. Fritz A. Rothschild (New York: Free Press, 1959), 24.

4   In addition to writing the online *Stanford Encyclopedia of Philosophy* article on Hartshorne, Dombrowski has written five books and numerous articles on various dimensions of Hartshorne's work.

5   Eugene H. Peters, *Hartshorne and Neoclassical Metaphysics: An Interpretation* (Lincoln: University of Nebraska Press, 1970). See also Peters's book *The Creative Advance: An Introduction to Process Philosophy as a Context for Christian Faith* (St. Louis, MO: Bethany Press, 1966); this book closes with a ten-page "comment" by Hartshorne.

6   George Nordgulen and George W. Shields, eds., *Faith & Creativity: Essays in Honor of Eugene H. Peters* (St. Louis, MO: CBP Press, 1987).

7   Donald W. Viney, ed., *Charles Hartshorne's Letters to a Young Philosopher: 1979–1995*, in *Logos Sophia* Vol. 11 (Fall 2001): 23 [Letter dated Sept. 8, 1984].

8   Hartshorne's work on birdsong has been favorably received by ornithologists. Maura C. Flannery, Department Editor for *The American Biology Teacher*, often mentions Hartshorne's work. See Flannery's "The Biology of Aesthetics," ABT 55/8 (Nov.-Dec. 1993): 497–500; "Birdmen," ABT 59/3 (March 1997): 180–83; and "Birds: Old Questions & New," ABT 64/4 (April 2002): 302–07. In the last article she calls Hartshorne's *Born to Sing* "a wonderful book on birdsong" (304); see also David Rothenberg, "You Make My Heart Sing," *Ethics and the Environment* 8/1 (2003): 112–25 and Rothenberg's *Why Birds Sing: A Journey into the Mystery of Bird Song* (New York: Basic Books, 2005), see especially 108f.

9   George W. Shields, *The Semantics of Perfection: An Investigation of Theistic Meaning Postulates and Their Justification in the Philosophy of Charles Hartshorne*, Ph.D. Dissertation, The University of Chicago, June 1981, 335 pp., published on microfilm at the Joseph Regenstein Library of the University of Chicago; Donald W. Viney, *Charles Hartshorne's Global Argument for God's Existence: An Analysis and Assessment*, Ph.D. Dissertation, The University of Oklahoma, 1982, 250 pp., revised by the author and published as *Charles Hartshorne and the Existence of God* (Albany: SUNY Press, 1985).

Chapter One

1   In addition to EA ix–xvii, DL, and PCH 4–45, the main auto-biographical sources for Hartshorne are: Hartshorne's "Comment" in Eugene H. Peters, *The Creative Advance* (St. Louis, MO: Bethany Press, 1966), 133–43; "The Development of My Philosophy" in *Contemporary American Philosophy: Second Series*, ed. John E. Smith (London: Allen & Unwin, 1970), 211–28; "Charles Hartshorne's Recollections of Editing the Peirce Papers," *Transactions of the Charles S. Peirce Society* 6/3–4 (Summer 1970): 149–59; "Pensées sur ma vie": 26–32/ "Thoughts on My Life": 60–66, *Bilingual Journal, Lecomte du Noüy Association* 5 (1973); "The Books That Shape Lives: Book Choices of Charles Hartshorne," *Christian Century* 44/30 (1977):

860; "Communication from Charles Hartshorne," *Proceedings and Addresses of the American Philosophical Association* 65/3 (1991): 69–70; "Reminiscences of Charles Hartshorne (member since 1942)," *Journal of Aesthetics and Art Criticism* 51 (1993): 286–89; and "Thoughts on the Development of my Concept of God," *The Personalist Forum* 14/2 (Fall 1998): 77–82 [written in May 1993]. Obituary notices for Hartshorne were written by Ralph K. M. Haurwitz for *The Austin-American Statesman* (October 11, 2000), Julie Nolen for *The Daily Texan* (October 12, 2000), Douglas Martin for *The New York Times* (October 13, 2000), and Elaine Woo for *The Los Angeles Times* (October 14, 2000). The most thorough and accurate notice was coauthored by G. Douglas Browning, Robert Kane, Donald Viney, and Stephen Phillips and published in *Proceedings and Addresses of the American Philosophical Association*, 74/5 (May 2001): 229–33.

2 Donald Wayne Viney, "Charles Hartshorne," in *American Philosophers Before 1950. Dictionary of Literary Biography*, vol. 270, ed. Philip B. Dematteis and Leemon B. McHenry (Detroit: Thomson Gale, 2003): 129–51. For the letters between Viney and Hartshorne concerning this article, see Donald Wayne Viney, ed., *Charles Hartshorne's Letters to a Young Philosopher: 1979–1995, Logos-Sophia*, vol. 11 (Fall 2001), letters of April 10, 1992, April 21, 1992, and December 10, 1992, on pp. 48–51. This work is available online at: http://digitalcommons.pittstate.edu/phil_faculty/40/. See also Viney's "Charles Hartshorne," *Dictionary of Unitarian Universalist Biography*, 1999–2004. Online at: http://www.uua.org/uuhs/duub/articles/ charleshartshorne.html (2004).

3 Viney details his own experiences knowing Hartshorne in "A Slice of Immortality: Remembering Charles Hartshorne" (Illustrated), 2016, available through Pittsburg State University Digital Commons: http://digitalcommons.pittstate.edu/phil_faculty/43/ and in "Talks and Meetings with Charles Hartshorne" (Illustrated) Pittsburg State University Digital Commons, http://digitalcommons.pittstate.edu/phil_faculty/41/.

4 For an excellent introduction to Rufus Jones see *Rufus Jones Speaks to Our Time: An Anthology*, ed. Harry Emerson Fosdick (New York: Macmillan, 1951).

5 "An Interview with Charles Hartshorne" conducted by Santiago Sia, *Miltown Studies* 4 (1979): 4.

6 H. G. Wells, *Mr. Britling Sees It Through* (New York: Macmillan, 1916), 406.

7 Wells, *Mr. Britling*, 409.

8 According to Willis Glover, in Wells's later thought, "mankind took the place of the finite God, and his humanism emerged in a more familiar form." Willis B. Glover, "Religious Orientations of H. G. Wells: A Case Study in Scientific Humanism," *The Harvard Theological Review* 65/1 (January 1972): 117–35, esp. 133.

9 For some of Hartshorne's most notable contributions to aesthetics and literary criticism see his brilliant analysis of Melville's *Mardi* (BH 102–06); the lengthy "In Defense of Wordsworth's View of Nature," *Philosophy and Literature* 4/1 (Spring 1980): 60–91; also "Some Theological Mistakes and Their Effects on Modern Literature" and "The Kinds and Levels of Aesthetic Value," chaps. 3 and 13, respectively, of ZF; finally, see, "Thomas Aquinas and Three Poets Who Do Not Agree With Him," *Process Studies* 30, 2 (2001): 261–75. For a summary of Hartshorne's aesthetic theory and some applications to modern poetry, see April Fallon and George Shields, "Toward Process Poetics: On Balancing Novelty and the *Cantus Firmus*," *The Journal of Kentucky Studies: Literary Annual of Northern Kentucky University* 28 (Sept. 2011): 89–97. (The original draft of this essay was the 2003 Kentucky Philological Association Award Winner for Literary Theory, and was translated into Modern Greek by Dr. K. P. Papadoupolos, appearing in *Celestia Nova: The Athens Olympic Center Journal for Philosophy, Art, and Culture* 4, no. 2 (2013): 323–38.) We also recommend Robert J. Valenza's articulate and substantive essay, "Aesthetic Priority in Science and Religion," *Process Studies* 31/1 (Spring-Summer 2002): 49–76.

10 In his earlier work Hartshorne made suggestions about how his philosophical theology might be used to illuminate certain specifically Christian beliefs. See the Epilogue of MVG (347–52) titled "Panentheism, Transcendental Relativity, and the Trinity." Although not a Trinitarian in a traditional sense, he applauded the idea of social relations among the persons of the Trinity but considered the idea to be spoiled by the denial of social relativity between God and the world (RSP 24).

11 Hartshorne, "The Development of My Philosophy," 225.

12 See also Hartshorne's response to the debate in *Did Jesus Rise from the*

Dead: The Resurrection Debate, ed. Terry L. Miethe (San Francisco: Harper & Row, 1987), 140.

13 Charles Hartshorne, "The Organism According to Process Philosophy" in *Organism, Medicine, and Metaphysics: Essays in Honor of Hans Jonas on His 75th Birthday May 10, 1978,* ed. Stuart F. Spicker, (Dordrecht, NL: D. Reidel Publishing Company, 1978), 153.

14 Hartshorne's response in *Did Jesus Rise from the Dead,* 142.

15 For a very readable account of the exchange between Gladstone and Huxley see Stephen Jay Gould's essay, "Genesis and Geology" in his anthology *Bully For Brontosaurus: Reflections in Natural History* (New York: W. W. Norton, 1992), 402–15. See also, Thomas H. Huxley, *Science and Hebrew Tradition: Essays* (New York: D. Appleton and Company, 1898): "Mr. Gladstone and Genesis" [1886]: 164–200.

16 According Frederick C. Grant, "[It] was probably Jesus who first combined the two 'great commandments' of Deut. 6:5 and Lev. 19:18b into a summary of the law; there is no trace of any earlier teacher's having done so, though Philo comes close to it." See *The Interpreter's Bible,* Vol. 7 (Nashville: Abingdon Press, 1979), 847. The relevant passage in Philo is from *Of Special Laws* II, 63, which reads: "And there are, as we may say, two most especially important heads of all the innumerable particular lessons and doctrines; the regulating of one's conduct towards God by the rules of piety and holiness, and of one's conduct towards men by the rules of humanity and justice" *The Works of Philo, Complete and Unabridged,* New Updated Version, trans. C. D. Yonge, foreword by David M. Scholer (Peabody, MA: Hendrickson, 1993), 574.

17 This anecdote and quotes from Emily Hartshorne Schwartz are taken from the eulogy that she presented at her father's memorial service held on December 9, 2000, at the First Unitarian Church of Austin, Texas. Emily sent a photocopy of the eulogy to Don Viney.

18 Hartshorne, "Thoughts on the Development of my Concept of God," 77.

19 Whitehead's exact phrasings are "the feeling of derived feelings," "feelings felt," and "a feeling of a complex of feelings." See Alfred North Whitehead, *Process and Reality: An Essay in Cosmology,* Corrected Edition, ed. David Ray Griffin and Donald W. Sherburne (New York: Free Press, 1978), 81 and 211.

20 Hartshorne, "The Development of My Philosophy," 213.

21 For the earliest acknowledgement of Hocking's influence on Hartshorne on this point see Charles Hartshorne, "Redefining God," *New Humanist* 7/4 (1934): 8–15, reprinted in *The American Journal of Theology and Philosophy* 22/2 (2001): 107–13.

22 For an account of the dissertation see William Lad Sessions, "Hartshorne's Early Philosophy" in *Two Process Philosophers: Hartshorne's Encounter with Whitehead*, ed. Lewis S. Ford (Tallahassee, FL: American Academy of Religion, 1973), 10–34. Randy Auxier and Hyatt Carter edited the dissertation under the title *The Unity of Being* and prepared it for publication with Open Court. The book has yet to be published.

23 Charles Hartshorne, *An Outline and Defense of the Argument for the Unity of Being in the Absolute or Divine Good* (Harvard University, May 1923), 29.

24 Hartshorne recalled writing a paper for one class titled "The Self Its Own Maker," before he knew of Lequyer, Whitehead, or Sartre, all of whom said much the same thing (PCH 21).

25 Hartshorne, "The Self Its Own Maker."

26 Hartshorne, "Thoughts on the Development of my Concept of God," 78.

27 See: "The Method of Imaginative Variations," *Journal of Philosophy* 36/9 (1939): 233–34; "Husserl and the Social Structure of Immediacy" in *Philosophical Essays in Memory of Edmund Husserl,* ed. Marvin Farber (Cambridge: Harvard University Press, 1940), 219–30; and IO chapter 23.

28 Hartshorne, "The Development of My Philosophy," 214.

29 Hartshorne, "The Development of My Philosophy," 214.

30 "Charles Hartshorne's Recollections of Editing the Peirce Papers," 159. Hartshorne speaks of the dream as vivid in the Dedication to DL.

31 Charles Hartshorne, "Notes on A. N. Whitehead's Harvard Lectures 1925–26," transcribed by Roland Faber, *Process Studies* 30/2 (2001): 301–73.

32 Charles Hartshorne, "On Some Criticisms of Whitehead's Philosophy," *The Philosophical Review* 44/4 (July 1935): 323.

33 Hartshorne, "The Development of My Philosophy," 216.

34 Hartshorne, "The Development of My Philosophy," 222.

35 Hartshorne, "The Development of My Philosophy," 216.

36 "Comment by Professor Charles Hartshorne" in Peters, *The Creative Advance*, 138.

37 For a similar assessment of the concept of prehension see Leemon McHenry, *The Event Universe: The Revisionary Metaphysics of Alfred North Whitehead* (Edinburgh: Edinburgh University Press, 2015), 114f.

38 John B. Cobb, Jr., *Theological Reminiscences* (Anoka, MN: Process Century Press, 2014), 42.

39 Cobb, *Theological Reminiscences*, 215.

40 Hartshorne, "Thoughts on the Development of my Concept of God," 79.

41 We here summarize the evidence cited in Donald Wayne Viney, "Charles Hartshorne (1897–2000)," in *Handbook of Whiteheadian Process Thought*, vol. 2, ed. Michel Weber and Will Desmond (Frankfurt: Ontos Verlag, 2008), 589–96, see especially page 590.

42 Review of *Symbolism: Its Meaning and Effect*, in *Hound and Horn* 1 (1927): 148–52.

43 Whitehead, *Process and Reality*, 162–63.

44 See Whitehead's letter to Hartshorne in Victor Lowe, *Alfred North Whitehead: The Man and His Work, Vol. II: 1910–1947*, ed. J. B. Schneewind (Baltimore: John Hopkins University Press, 1990), 345–47.

45 For example, "Interview with Charles Hartshorne," *Miltown Studies* 4 (1979): 22.

46 See, for example, Charles Goodman, *Consequences of Compassion: An Interpretation and Defense of Buddhist Ethics* (New York: Oxford University Press, 2009).

47 The files are titled "Innominates/X-Club Notes: 1917–1982" and the library description reveals that these were two informal discussion groups with limited membership ranging from 20 to 40 faculty members; eventually they shared members and occasionally interacted with one another. The Innominates were organized first in February 1917 and the parallel X-Club began when Hartshorne arrived at Chicago in 1928. Both clubs were organized on the

model of the Harvard "shop clubs" and were restricted to faculty in physical sciences, mathematics, biological sciences, and social sciences (psychology and sociology, later anthropology). One could not join the club voluntarily, but had to be nominated and selected by vote. Both clubs were quite active as they met monthly. Members often presented papers representing their latest research after dinner. Mainly they met at the Quadrangle Club, a faculty lounge and dining facility. The X-Club became inactive in 1996.

48   Papers from the Chicago conference are published in John B. Cobb, Jr. and Franklin I. Gamwell, *Existence and Actuality: Conversations with Charles Hartshorne* (Chicago: University of Chicago Press, 1984). Martin presented a paper at that conference. George Shields was, at the time, a student at Chicago and he heard Martin's extemporaneous comments honoring Hartshorne.

49   Charles Hartshorne, "Sense Quality and Feeling Tone," published in Gilbert Ryle, ed., *Proceedings of the Seventh International Congress of Philosophy Held at Oxford, England September 106, 1930* (London: Oxford University Press, 1931), 168–72.

50   Charles Hartshorne, "Redefining God." *New Humanist* 7/4 (1934): 8–15. Reprinted in *Contemporary American Protestant Thought: 1900–1970*, ed. William R. Miller (Indianapolis: Bobbs-Merrill, 1973), 315–22. Also reprinted in *American Journal of Theology and Philosophy* 22, 2 (2001): 107–13.

51   For an overview of developments at Chicago as they relate to process thought, see Gene Reeves and Delwin Brown, "The Development of Process Theology" in *Process Philosophy and Christian Thought*, ed. Delwin Brown, Ralph E. James, Jr., and Gene Reeves (Indianapolis: Bobbs-Merrill, 1971): 21–64. See especially pp. 24–35. Wieman became increasingly dissatisfied with Whitehead's speculative bent. See Cobb, *Theological Reminiscences*: 42.

52   Published as "Le Principe de Relativité de Whitehead" in *Revue de Métaphysique et de Morale* 55 (1950): 16–29. Donald W. Viney translated the article for *Process Studies* 40/1 (2011): 91–103.

53   Email communication from Robert Kane to Donald Viney, March 19, 2019.

54   David A. Pailin, "Neville's Critique of Hartshorne," *Process Studies* 4/3 (Fall 1974): 191.

55 Shields heard this story from a student colleague who sat close to Shields in Ricoeur's 1977 Seminar on "Temporality and Historicity." Paul Ricoeur, it should be noted, would later occupy a joint position in the University of Chicago Department of Philosophy and the Divinity School as the John Nuveen Professor of Philosophical Theology, the chair held previously by Paul Tillich.

56 Ralph K. M. Haurwitz, "UT Philosopher Explored the Nature of God," *Austin-American Statesman*, Wednesday, October 11, 2000): A7.

57 "Audience Discussion of 'God as Composer-Director, Enjoyer, and in a Sense, Player of the Cosmic Drama'—April 7, 1987, Central State University, Edmond, OK (transcript from the videotape by Donald Wayne Viney)," *Process Studies* 30/2 (Fall-Winter 2001): 259.

58 See also Robert A. Gillies, "The Brightman-Hartshorne Correspondence, 1933–1944," *Process Studies* 17/1 (Spring 1988): 9–18.

59 Peters was not the first to summarize Hartshorne's philosophy. See Andrew J. Reck, "The Philosophy of Charles Hartshorne," *Tulane Studies in Philosophy* 10 (May 1961): 89–108. See also: Ralph E. James, *The Concrete God: A New Beginning for Theology—The Thought of Charles Hartshorne* (Indianapolis: Bobbs-Merrill, 1967).

60 Hartshorne devoted no article to Smith's work. For a lively exchange on the perennial philosophy between Smith and a well-known process thinker see David Ray Griffin and Huston Smith, *Primordial Truth and Postmodern Theology* (Albany: SUNY Press, 1989).

61 "Response to Charles Hartshorne" in *Rorty & Pragmatism: The Philosopher Responds to His Critic,* ed. Herman J. Saatkamp, Jr., (Nashville: Vanderbilt University Press, 1995): 29–36. The article to which Rorty responded is on pages 16–28 of this book, and it is reprinted as chapter 24 of CAP.

62 Cobb, *Theological Reminiscences*, 73.

63 http://www.georgiaencyclopedia.org/articles/history-archaeology /desegregation-higher-education, accessed June 20, 2017.

64 "The Development of Process Philosophy" in *Philosophers of Process,* ed. Douglas Browning and William T. Myers (New York: Fordham University Press, 1998), 393.

65 Hartshorne, "The Development of My Philosophy," 219.

66 Email communication from Jorge Nobo to Don Viney, May 8, 2017.

67 Email communication from Jorge Nobo to Don Viney, May 8, 2017.

68 Email communication from Jorge Nobo to Don Viney, May 8, 2017.

69 Email communication from Jorge Nobo to Don Viney, June 16, 2017. Nobo says that the dinner for students was discontinued when the number of students multiplied by a significant factor.

70 Norman Pittenger, *Catholic Faith in a Process Perspective* (Maryknoll, New York: Orbis Books, 1981): x. Pittenger dedicates this book to Dorothy Hartshorne. He dedicated an earlier book, *Process Thought and Christian Faith* (New York: Macmillan, 1968) to Charles Hartshorne.

71 Letter from Hartshorne to Corrington, July 10, 1992 in Corrington's *An Appraisal and Critique*, https://users.drew.edu /rcorring/downloads/APPRAISAL%20&%20CRITIQUE%20 COPYRIGHT.pdf, 39. Accessed June 13, 2017.

72 Email from Robert Kane to Don Viney, March 19, 2019.

73 Email from Robert Kane to Don Viney, March 19, 2019.

74 "Interview with Charles Hartshorne," 19.

75 It is of interest that after Hartshorne left Chicago he published only twelve book reviews, a mere trickle compared to the flood of reviews, seventy-nine, at Chicago. After 1955, his focus was clearly on developing his own views rather than reporting and critiquing the views of others.

76 Viney, "Talks and Meetings with Charles Hartshorne," 9. Hartshorne made it clear in this same conversation that he wasn't trying to be greater than Whitehead. Of course, Whitehead lived to be 86, but his major works were composed before he reached his 80s.

77 "Audience Discussion of 'God as Composer-Director, Enjoyer,'" 258.

78 Email from Robert Kane to Don Viney, March 19, 2019.

79 *Charles Hartshorne's Letters to a Young Philosopher: 1979-1995*, ed. Donald Wayne Viney, *Logos-Sophia: The Journal of the Pittsburg State University Philosophical Society* 11 (Fall 2001): 53, http:// digitalcommons.pittstate.edu/phil_faculty/40/. Hartshorne was apparently not using the word processor for letters. His usual habit was to use a typewriter and to make corrections by inserting handwritten comments or by placing white tape over things he wished to delete.

80 Also of note is that Hartshorne contributed articles to eight volumes of the *Library of Living Philosophers:* George Santayana (vol. 2), A.N. Whitehead (vol. 3), Sarvepalli Radhakrishan (vol. 8), Martin Buber (vol. 12), C.I. Lewis (vol. 13), Brand Blanshard (vol. 15), Gabriel Marcel (vol. 17), and George Henrik von Wright (vol. 19). Hartshorne wrote reviews of the volumes on Dewey and Russell, which later became chapters 12 and 13 of RSP.

81 Quote from Emily's eulogy for Charles Hartshorne (see note 17).

82 Steven Vita, "A Philosopher at 99, Austinite Charles Hartshorne Still Searches for 'Necessary Truths'," *Austin American Statesman*, Sunday, April 13, 1997, pp. D1 and D7. Dayna Finet, "Philosophy (at) 101, Centenarian Charles Hartshorne is Austin's Preeminent Man of Ideas," cover story for *The Good Life* (after title: Life, Liberty and the Pursuit of Happiness after 40) 13 (October 1998): 15–18. The magazine, measuring 10.5 by 14 inches, was a publication offered for free to the public.

83 Hank Stuever, "A Metaphysician and his Maker, At 100 Charles Hartshorne Still Studies God; Others Study Him," *Austin-American Statesman*, Monday, October 13, 1997: pp. A1 and A6. The papers from the symposium were published in *The Personalist Forum* 14/2 (Fall 1998).

84 The report of Hartshorne's death was made by Charles Richey on the process philosophy listserv. The *New York Times* obituary was written by Douglas Martin and titled "Charles Hartshorne, Theologian, Is Dead; Proponent of an Activist God Was 103" (Friday, October 13, 1997, p. C15). The date of Hartshorne's death is not the only mistake in the article. Beginning with the title—Hartshorne did not consider himself a theologian, and his God was active but not activist (at least not in a political sense)—the article mischaracterizes Hartshorne's philosophy as one in which God is not omnipotent or omniscient, not being able to "see the future." We shall see more clearly in Chapter V how Hartshorne treats the subjects of omnipotence and omniscience.

85 The speaker was too young to have had the story at anything better than second or thirdhand.

86 Viney, "Talks and Meetings with Charles Hartshorne," 32.

87 George Shields heard this anecdote from Alan Gewirth.

88 The proceedings of the conference were published as *Rationality, Religious Belief and Moral Commitment: New Essays in Philosophy of Religion,* ed. Robert Audi and William J. Wainwright (Ithaca, NY: Cornell University Press, 1986). Ross's paper, published in the book, is "God, Creator of Kinds and Possibilities: *Requiescant universalia ante res,*" 315–35. Viney, "A Slice of Immortality: Remembering Charles Hartshorne."

89 Viney, "Talks and Meetings with Charles Hartshorne," 25.

90 Charles Hartshorne, "Pensées sur ma vie"/"Thoughts on My Life," 26/60.

91 *Process Studies* 5/4 (Winter 1975): 304.

92 Hartshorne, "Thoughts on the Development of my Concept of God," 82.

93 Nicholas Rescher, "American Philosophy Today," *The Review of Metaphysics* 46/4 (June 1993): 717–45. See Appendix 4, p. 743, where Hartshorne is listed 28th of 36 most-cited American philosophers.

94 George R. Lucas, Jr., "Charles Hartshorne: The Last or the First?" *The Personalist Forum* 14/2 (Fall 1998): 83–108. See p. 86.

95 See also "Interview with Charles Hartshorne," 20. It is worth noting that there is a volume devoted to Hartshorne in the Makers of the Modern Theological Mind series. See Alan Gragg, *Charles Hartshorne* (Waco, TX: Word Books, Publisher, 1973).

96 Hartshorne, "The Development of My Philosophy," 225.

97 Hartshorne, "The Development of My Philosophy," 218.

98 Hartshorne, "The Development of My Philosophy," 227.

99 John Wild, "Devotion and Fanaticism" in *Process and Divinity, The Hartshorne Festschrift,* ed. William L. Reese and Eugene Freeman, (La Salle, IL: Open Court, 1964), 445.

100 Jean Wahl, *Philosophies of Existence,* trans. by F. M. Lory, 1954 (NY: Schocken Books, 1969.).

Chapter Two

1 Lawrence E. Marks, *The Unity of the Senses: Interrelations among the Modalities* (New York: Academic, 1978), see especially 69–75.

2   Marks, *The Unity of the Senses,* 72.

3   C. E. Osgood, G. J. Suci, and P. H. Tannenbaum, *The Measurement of Meaning* (Urbana, IL: University of Illinois Press, 1957).

4   Marks, *The Unity of the Senses,* 72.

5   Marks, *The Unity of the Senses,* 73.

6   On saltational phenomena and their importance for qualifications of "modern synthesis" neo-Darwinism, see David Ray Griffin, *Religion and Scientific Naturalism* (Albany: SUNY Press, 2000): 277–85.

7   "Reminiscences of Charles Hartshorne (member since 1942)," 288.

8   Wayne Viney, "Charles Hartshorne's Philosophy and Psychology of Sensation," in PCH 100.

9   *Process and Reality,* 211.

10 Alfred North Whitehead, *Adventures of Ideas* (New York: Free Press, 1967), 206; also Ch. XIII, Sec. IV.

11 "Notes on A. N. Whitehead's Harvard Lectures 1925–26," 331.

12 Anon., report on Hartshorne's "My Enthusiastic but Partial Agreement with Whitehead," presented at the 11th Congresso Ineramericano de Filosophia, Guadalajara, Mexico, Nov. 15, 1985, *Center for Process Studies Newsletter* 9/4:7.

13 For Hartshorne' study of oscines and its relation to philosophy, see WM chap. 8 and ZF chap. 2. See also, "Freedom, Individuality, and Beauty in Nature," *Snowy Egret* 24/2 (Autumn 1960): 5–14, reprinted as Chap. 9 of *Hartshorne: A New World View: Essays by Charles Hartshorne,* ed. Herbert F. Vetter, (Cambridge: Harvard Square Library, 2007) but marred, unhappily, by numerous typographical errors; "The Aesthetics of Birdsong," *Journal of Aesthetics and Art Criticism* 26, 3 (1968): 311–15; "Why Study Birds?" *Virginia Quarterly Review* 46, 1 (1970): 133–40. In PCH see Alexander F. Skutch, "Bird Song and Philosophy" (65–76) and Lucio Chiaraviglio, "Hartshorne's Aesthetic Theory of Intelligence" (77–90). Finally, see Daniel A. Dombrowski, *Divine Beauty: The Aesthetics of Charles Hartshorne* (Nashville: Vanderbilt University Press, 2004), Chap. 4. For some of the critical reception of Hartshorne's work on birdsong see Maura C. Flannery's articles in *The American Biology Teacher,* "The Biology of Aesthetics," ABT 55/8 (Nov.-Dec. 1993): 497–500; "Birdmen," ABT 59/3 (March 1997): 180–83; and "Birds: Old Questions &

New," ABT 64/4 (April 2002): 302–07. In the last article she calls Hartshorne's *Born to Sing* "a wonderful book on birdsong" (304); see also David Rothenberg, "You Make My Heart Sing," *Ethics and the Environment* 8/1 (2003): 112–25 and Rothenberg's *Why Birds Sing: A Journey into the Mystery of Bird Song* (New York: Basic Books, 2005), see especially 108f.

14 "Freedom, Individuality, and Beauty in Nature," 10 [Vetter: 91]; "The Aesthetics of Birdsong": 313.

15 "Freedom, Individuality, and Beauty in Nature," 10 [Vetter: 91].

16 Charles Hartshorne, "Ethics and the Process of Living" in *Man and His Conduct: Philosophical Essays in Honor of Risieri Frondizi,* ed. Jorge J. E. Garcia (Rio Piedras, Puerto Rico: Editorial Universitaria, 1980), 199.

Chapter Three

1 The qualification is that Hartshorne is a moderate set-theoretic realist who holds that abstract entities or generic eternal objects do, in fact, exist, as do possibilities.

2 *Plato: the Collected Dialogues,* ed. Edith Hamilton and Huntington Cairns (Princeton, NJ: Princeton University Press, 1973), 1003 [*Sophist* 257b].

3 Henri Bergson, *Creative Evolution,* trans. Arthur Mitchell (New York: Modern Library, 1944), 304–05, and[Ch. IV.

4 Paul Tillich, "Reply to Interpretation and Criticism" in *The Theology of Paul Tillich,* ed. Charles W. Kegley and Robert W. Bretall (New York: Macmillan, 1952), 339.

5 See, Lawrence M. Krauss, *A Universe From Nothing: Why There is Something Rather Than Nothing* (New York: Free Press, 2012). David Albert's review of Krauss's book is in *The New York Times* (March 23, 2012).

6 In his dissertation, Shields noted that this holds in Boolean algebra. The null set or class is not logically primitive but must be constructed *in relation to* assertions about the interface or disconnection between classes.

7 Alfred North Whitehead, *Science and the Modern World* (New York:

Free Press, 1967), 51; also Chapter 3.

8   As early as 1880 Peirce recognized that "neither/nor" would suffice
     to express all truth functions. In 1902 he introduced a sign which
     he called the *ampheck* (from a Greek word, meaning cutting both
     ways), for the neither/nor function. The *ampheck* resembles a J and
     a backward J joined at the stem. Let us use $\perp$ for Peirce's *ampheck*.
     Thus, "$p \perp q$" is the same as "$\sim p \wedge \sim q$." The negation of "p" is written
     "$p \perp p$" (neither p nor p); "$p \wedge q$" is written: "$(p \perp p) \perp (q \perp q)$."
     Peirce also realized that all functions could be expressed by "not
     both," the disjunction of two negatives. In 1913 H. M. Sheffer
     rediscovered these ideas. He called the "not both" function rejection
     and wrote it with a single stroke, now called the Sheffer stroke.
     Peirce's ampheck, or "neither/nor" function, is equivalent to what is
     now called the Sheffer dagger. See *Collected Papers of Charles Sanders
     Peirce,* Volume IV, edited by Charles Hartshorne and Paul Weiss
     (Cambridge: Harvard University Press, 1933), 13–18 [sections 12–20];
     see also 212–16 [sections 260–64]. Sheffer's work is found in Henry
     Maurice Sheffer, "A Set of Five Independent Postulates for Boolean
     Algebras, with Application to Logical Constants," *Transactions of the
     American Mathematical Society* XIV (October 1913): 481–88.

9   See also, "Reminiscences of Charles Hartshorne (member since
     1942)," 288; Hartshorne, "The Aesthetic Dimensions of Religious
     Experience," in *Logic, God and Metaphysics,* ed. J. F. Harris
     (Dordrecht, NL: Kluwer Academic Publishers, 1992), 17; Hartshorne,
     "Can Philosophers Cooperate Intellectually: Metaphysics as Applied
     Mathematics," *The Midwest Quarterly* 35/1 (1993): 17; Hartshorne,
     "God, Necessary and Contingent: World, Contingent and
     Necessary; and the Fifteen Other Options for Thinking About God:
     Necessity and Contingency as Applied to God and the World"
     in *Metaphysics as Foundation: Essays in Honor of Ivor Leclerc,* ed.
     Paul A. Bogaard and Gordan Treash (Albany: SUNY Press, 1993),
     296; Hartshorne, "Peirce, Whitehead, and the Sixteen Views About
     God," *Process Studies* 40/1 (2011): 112.

10   Robert C. Neville, *Creativity and God: A Challenge to Process
     Theology* (Albany: SUNY Press, 1995). See also Neville's *Realism in
     Religion: A Pragmatist's Perspective* (Albany: SUNY Press, 2009),
     Chapter 13.

11   For a fuller account of the history of Hartshorne's matrices
     concerning the concept of God and an extension of those matrices

to deal with apophatic theology, see Donald W. Viney, "Relativizing the Classical Tradition: Hartshorne's History of God," in *Models of God and Alternative Ultimate Realities*, ed. Jeanine Diller and Asa Kasher (Dordrecht, NL: Springer 2013), 63–79.

12 Ivor Leclerc, "Kant's Second Antinomy, Leibniz and Whitehead," *The Review of Metaphysics* 20/1 (September 1966): 25–41.

13 William Lane Craig, *The Kalām Cosmological Argument* (New York: Macmillan, 1979), and, with Quentin Smith, *Theism, Atheism, and Big Bang Cosmology* (New York: Oxford University Press, 1995). See also William Lane Craig and James D. Sinclair, "The *Kalām* Cosmological Argument" in *The Blackwell Companion to Natural Theology* (Oxford: Wiley-Blackwell, 2012), 101–201.

14 Colin E. Gunton, *Becoming and Being: The Doctrine of God in Charles Hartshorne and Karl Barth* (Oxford: Oxford University Press, 1978), 104.

15 Philip Henry Gosse, *Omphalos: An Attempt to Untie the Geological Knot* (Woodbridge, CT: Ox Bow Press, 1998 reprint [1857]). Interestingly, Gosse does not address the question whether God would have given Adam apparent memories of a past he never lived. See especially chap. 10 of Gosse's book.

16 The twentieth-century version of Gosse's prochronism goes by the name of "functioning completeness." Henry Morris and Gary Parker explain the concept in these terms: "[The] 'apparent age' of the world has no necessary correlation with its 'true age.' Real creation obviously requires creation with an 'appearance of age.' Thus, Adam was made as a full grown man, the newly formed trees had fruit on them, the light from the stars could be seen on earth at the moment of their creation, and so on. If anything is ever truly *created*, it necessarily must look initially as though it had a prior existence, and therefore it has an appearance of some 'age,' if that 'age' is conceived in terms of present processes." Morris and Parker, *What is Creation Science?* Rev. and Expanded (El Cajon, CA: Master Books, 1987), 62–63.

17 For an excellent treatment of this question see Francis J. Kovach, "The Question of the Eternity of the World in St. Bonaventure and St. Thomas—A Critical Analysis," in *Bonaventure and Aquinas: Enduring Philosophers*, ed. Robert W. Shahan and Francis J. Kovach (Norman, OK: University of Oklahoma Press, 1976), 155–86.

18 James Thomson, "Infinity in Logic and Mathematics" in *The Encyclopedia of* Philosophy, vol. 4, ed. Paul Edwards (New York: Macmillan, 1964), 190.

19 Thomas Swing, *Kant's Transcendental Logic* (New Haven, CT: Yale University Press, 1969), 312.

20 Swing, *Kant's Transcendental Logic*, 273.

21 Julian Wolfe, "Infinite Regress and the Cosmological Argument," *International Journal for Philosophy of Religion* 2/4 (1971): 246–49; George Shields, "Is the Past Finite? On Craig's *Kalām* Cosmological Argument," *Process Studies* 14/1 (1984): 31–40.

22 William Lane Craig, *The Kalām Cosmological Argument* (London: Macmillan, 1979), 172.

23 William Lane Craig, *Time and Eternity: Exploring God's Relationship to Time* (Wheaton, IL: Crossway Books, 2001).

24 Richard Swinburne, *The Coherence of Theism* (Oxford: Clarendon Press, 1977), 221. For further development of Swinburne's argument against objections, see George Shields, "Davies, Eternity, and the Cosmological Argument," *International Journal for Philosophy of Religion* 21/1 (1987): 21–37.

25 Quentin Smith, "Time Was Created by a Timeless Point: An Atheist Explanation of Space-Time" in *God and Time: Essays on the Divine Nature,* ed. G. Ganssle and D. Woodruff, (Oxford: Oxford University Press, 2002). For further comments on Smith's position, see George Shields, "Review of Ganssle and Woodruff, eds., *God and Time,*" *The Journal of Religion* 83/1 (Jan. 2003): 149–51.

26 G. E. Moore, *Some Main Problems of Philosophy* (New York: Colliers, 1953), ch. 10.

27 George Shields, "Hartshorne and the Analytic Philosophical Tradition" in *Faith and Creativity: Essays in Honor of Eugene H. Peters,* ed. George Nordgulen and George Shields (St. Louis, MO: CBP Press, 1987), 206–07.

28 Quentin Smith, "Infinity and the Past," *Philosophy of Science* 54/1 (1987): 63–75. An interesting and complex dialectical exchange on this argument occurs in William Lane Craig and Quentin Smith, *Theism, Atheism, and Big Bang Cosmology.* (Oxford: Clarendon Press, 1993). Here, we will simply register our view that, in the final analysis, Smith's argument for coherence of an infinite past is

the more plausible.

29 John W. Lango, "Whitehead's Actual Occasions and the New Infinitesimals," *Transactions of the C. S. Peirce Society* 25 (Winter 1989): 29–39 and George W. Shields, "Infinitesimals and Hartshorne's Set-Theoretic Platonism," *The Modern Schoolman* 69/2 (January 1992): 123–34. See the related discussion in George W. Shields, "Process and Universals" in *After Whitehead: Rescher on Process Metaphysics*, ed. M. Weber (Frankfurt: Ontos Verlag, 2004), 135–45, and Rescher's appreciative response, "Shields on Universals," 298–302.

30 A. Robinson, "The Metaphysics of the Calculus" in *The Philosophy of Mathematics*, ed. J. Hintikka (Oxford: Oxford University Press, 1969).

31 Shields, "Infinitesimals and Hartshorne's Set-Theoretic Platonism," 132–33.

32 Charles Hartshorne, "Von Wright and Hume's Axiom" in *The Philosophy of G. H. von Wright*, ed. Lewis Hahn (LaSalle, IL: Open Court, 1989), 74, our emphasis.

33 These qualifications of the Logic of Ultimate Contrasts are first suggested in rudimentary form in George W. Shields, *The Semantics of Perfection: An Investigation of Theistic Meaning Postulates and Their Justification in the Philosophy of Charles Hartshorne*, Ph.D. Dissertation, The University of Chicago, June 1981, Section 5.6.2, "An Infinite Past Actuality and the Logic of Ultimate Contrasts," 259–63, esp. 263.

34 J. W. Dauben, "Georg Cantor and Pope Leo XIII: Mathematics, Theology, and the Infinite," *Journal of the History of Ideas* 38/1 (Jan.-Mar., 1977): 85–108.

36 Bertrand Russell, "My Mental Development" in *The Philosophy of Bertrand Russell*, ed. Paul Arthur Schilpp, 3rd edition (New York: Tudor Publishing Company, 1951), 10.

37 Of Russell's many discussions of theistic arguments, the best may be in his debate with the Jesuit priest-philosopher Frederick Copleston. The transcript of the debate is widely available and is reprinted in John Hick, ed., *The Existence of God* (New York: Macmillan, 1964), 167–91 and in *Bertrand Russell on God and Religion*, ed. Al Seckel (Buffalo, NY: Prometheus Books, 1986), 123–46.

38 Alfred North Whitehead, *Essays in Science and Philosophy* (New

York: Greenwood Press, 1968), 319.

39 For a defense of the compatibility of process philosophy and quantum theory see George W. Shields, "MWI Quantum Theory: Some Logical and Philosophical Issues," paper presented at the Center for Philosophy and Natural Sciences, California State University-Sacramento, 2008. See also, George W. Shields, "A Logical Analysis of Relational Realism" in *Physics and Speculative Philosophy: Potentiality in Modern Science*, ed. Timothy Eastman, Michael Epperson, and David Griffin (Berlin: DeGruyter, 2016). Roughly, Shields argues that the modal-actualist interpretation of Many Worlds, according to which every possible choice at a given juncture of process becomes actualized in an ontologically separate and distinctive world: (1) suffers from logical problems similar to those afflicting Davis Lewis's counterpart theory (and that despite some who hold that there are disanalogies between Many Worlds and counterpart theory); but more importantly (2) an actualist interpretation is not necessary since the superposition alternatives that accompany a quantum event can be viewed as simply displaying various probabilities for *alternative histories* after the collapse of the wave function (a view promoted by such luminaries as Roland Omnes and Murray Gell-Mann); and (3) as David Albert points out, MWI is semantically opaque when we consider its application to more complex superposition scenarios; on MWI, measurement results are arbitrary and can be manipulated according to the kind of question we pose for the quantum measurement situation. Given the combination of all these problems in addition to the embarrassments that an actualist MWI ontology creates for issues of personal identity and libertarian freedom, it is more reasonable, on balance, strongly to reject actualist MWI theory. As such Hartshorne's theory of contingent states of affairs as involving both real and distinctive decisions remains insofar unscathed. See David Z. Albert, *Quantum Mechanics and Experience* (Cambridge: Harvard University Press, 1992), esp. 113–15. See also Michael Epperson, *Quantum Mechanics and the Philosophy of Alfred North Whitehead* (Oxford: Oxford University Press, 2012).

40 Leemon B. McHenry, *The Event Universe: The Revisionary Metaphysics of Alfred North Whitehead* (Edinburgh: Edinburgh University Press, 2015), 86.

41   Griffin, "Charles Hartshorne," in David Ray Griffin, John B. Cobb, Jr., Marcus P. Ford, Pete A. Y. Gunter and Peter Ochs, *Founders of Constructive Postmodern Philosophy: Peirce, James, Bergson, Whitehead, and Hartshorne* (Albany: State University of New York Press, 1993), 219. Derek Malone-France uses the expression "deep empiricism" to characterize Whitehead's project. See his *Deep Empiricism: Kant, Whitehead, and the Necessity of Philosophical Theism* (Lanham, MD: Lexington Books, 2007). These considerations are enough to show that it is misleading to classify Hartshorne's thought as rationalistic in its methodology and to say, as Roland Faber does, that "Hartshorne began with the rational rather than the empirical side of Whitehead's cosmology." See Faber, *God as Poet of the World: Exploring Process Theologies*, trans. Douglas W. Stott (Louisville, KY: Westminster John Knox Press, 2004), 29.

42   Hartshorne, "The Development of My Philosophy," 215.

43   Adolf Grünbaum, *Philosophical Problems of Space and Time*, 2nd ed. (Dordrecht, NL: D. Reidl, 1973); Julian Barbour, *The End of Time: The Next Revolution in Physics* (Oxford: Oxford University Press, 2001); Huw Price, *Time's Arrow and Archimedes' Point* (Oxford: Oxford University Press, 1997); and Stephen Hawking, *A Brief History of Time* (New York: Bantam, 1988).

44   Hermann Weyl, *Philosophy of Mathematics* (Princeton, NJ: Princeton University Press, 1949), 166.

45   Milič Čapek, "Temporal Order and Spatial Order: Their Differences and Relations" in *Mind in Nature: Essays on the Interface of Science and Philosophy*, ed. John B. Cobb, Jr. and David Ray Griffin (Washington, DC: University Press of America, 1977), 57–58.

46   Lee Smolin, *Time Reborn: From the Crisis in Physics to the Future of the Universe* (New York: Houghton Mifflin Harcourt, 2013). See also Roberto Mangabeira Unger and Lee Smolin, *The Singular Universe and the Reality of Time* (Cambridge: Cambridge University Press, 2015).

47   See also "Comments by Charles Hartshorne" in Eugene H. Peters, *The Creative Advance* (St. Louis, MO: Bethany Press, 1966), 135–36; Donald W. Viney, ed., *Charles Hartshorne's Letters to a Young Philosopher, 1979-1995*, special issue of *Logos-Sophia* 11 (Fall 2001): 43 [letter postmarked April 25, 1991]. For more on this topic see Donald W. Viney, "The American Reception of Jules Lequyer: From James

to Hartshorne," *American Journal of Theology and Philosophy* 36/3 (September 2015): 260–77.

48 Alfred North Whitehead, *The Function of Reason* (Boston: Beacon Press, 1971 [1929]), 16.

49 George Shields argues at some length that each of these items are "deep protocols of common sense" that, when denied, issue in "pragmatic absurdity." Only a process ontology that embraces *both* real internal and external relations can avoid such absurdity. Monistic and logically atomistic ontologies fail in this respect, and as a result they yield violent paradoxes. See his "Physicalist Panexperientialism and the Mind-Body Problem," *American Journal of Theology and Philosophy* 22/2 (May 2001): 133–54.

50 René Descartes, *The Philosophical Writings of Descartes, Volume I*, trans. John Cottingham, Robert Stoothoff, and Dugald Myrdoch (New York: Cambridge University Press, 1985), 193 [*Principles of Philosophy*, Part One, number 3].

51 David Hume, *Enquiries Concerning Human Understanding and Concerning the Principles of Morals*, 3rd ed., ed. L. A. Selby-Bigge and rev. by P. H. Nidditch (Oxford: Clarendon Press, 1975), 9 [*Enquiry Concerning Human Understanding*, sec. I, part 4].

52 Hartshorne notes that the subtitle of WM, "A Philosophy of the Middle Way," calls to mind Buddhism. He says, "[T]he time has gone past when it was altogether sufficient to ignore the efforts of the Orientals to achieve wisdom" (WM x). Hartshorne's own engagement with Eastern philosophical perspectives is scattered throughout his writings. PSG includes comments and associated readings on Hinduism (30–32), Lao-Tzu (32–34), Asvaghosha (165–69), Sankara (169–77), Ramanuja (177–89), Radhakrishnan (306–10), and Buddhism (411–15). In HP see his response to Stephen H. Phillips (on Indian Theism) (188–90). In CH see his replies to Arabinda Basu (on Indian thought) (263–65), and John S. Ishihara (on Buddhism) (294–98). In PCH, see his responses to Sallie B. King (on Buddhism) (624–27), John G. Arapura (on Vedanta) (627–30) and Keiji Matsunobu (on the Kyoto School) (726–31). Hartshorne's articles that directly relate to Eastern philosophy are: "Radhakrishnan on Mind, Matter, and God" in *The Philosophy of Saevepalli Radhakrishnan*, ed. Paul Arthur Schilpp (New York: Tudor, 1952): 315–22; "The Buddhist-Whiteheadian View of the Self and the Religious Traditions,"

Proceedings of the Ninth International Congress for the History of Religions (Tokyo: Maruzen, 1960 [1958]): 298–302; Review of N. S. Srivastava, *Contemporary Indian Philosophy* (Delhi: M. R. M. Lal, 1965) in *Research Journal of Philosophy* (Ranchi University [India]) 1/1 (1966): 110–11; "Whitehead's Differences from Buddhism," *Philosophy East and West* 25, 4 (1975): 407–13; "Theism in Asian and Western Thought," *Philosophy East and West* 28, 4 (1978): 401–11; "Process Themes in Chinese Thought," *Journal of Chinese Philosophy* 6 (1979): 323–36; "'Emptiness' and Fullness in Asiatic and Western Thought," *Journal of Chinese Philosophy* 6 (1979): 411–20; "Toward a Buddhist-Christian Religion" in *Buddhism and American Thinkers,* ed. Kenneth K. Inada and Nolan P. Jacobson (Albany: State University of New York Press, 1984), 1–13; "Some Perspectives on Chinese Philosophy," *Journal of Chinese Philosophy* 13 (1986): 267–70; "Sankara, Nagarjuna, and Fa Tsang, with some Western Analogues" in *Interpreting Across Boundaries: New Essays in Comparative Philosophy,* ed. G. J. Larson and Eliot Deutsch (Princeton, NJ: Princeton University Press, 1988): 98–115; "Buddhism and the Theistic Question" in *Buddhism and the Emerging World Civilization: Essays in Honor of Nolan Pliny Jacobson,* ed. Puligandla Ramakrishna and David Lee Miller (Carbondale, IL: Southern Illinois University Press, 1994): 62–72.

Chapter Four

1 In earlier writings, Hartshorne spoke of "dynamic individuality," (MVG 205, 206), "dynamic unitary agents" (MVG (207), and "dynamic unit" (RSP 57, 58).

2 Whitehead speaks of "feelings felt" and "a feeling of a complex of feelings." See Alfred North Whitehead, *Process and Reality, An Essay in Cosmology,* Corrected Edition, ed. David Ray Griffin and Donald Sherburne (New York: Free Press, 1978), 211. Hartshorne's fondness for the expression "feeling of feeling" is evident in the fact that he uses it in all but five of his books, AD, AW, NT, PSG, and RSP. For his use of the expression see: PPS ix, 38, 134, 193, 194, 198, 208, and 241; BH 183; MVG 151, 152, 154; DR 29, 155; CS 241; LP 127; IO 112, 209, 320, 327, 344, 377; CAP 127, 128, 150, 199, 237, 242; OO 27, 62, 135; WM 25, 58, 59; DL 376; ZF 15, 24, 157; CE 14, 16, 39.

3 Whitehead, *Process and Reality,* 21. Hartshorne commented. "This is among the most powerful of all short sayings in the history of

philosophy." Hartshorne, "God and the Meaning of Life" in *On Nature*, ed. Leroy S. Rouner (Notre Dame, IN: University of Notre Dame Press, 1984), 161.

4 *Basic Writings of Saint Thomas Aquinas*, Vol. I, ed. Anton C. Pegis (New York: Random House, 1945), 439 [ST I, Q45, a5]; *On the Truth of the Catholic Faith, Summa Contra Gentiles Book Two: Creation*, trans. James F. Anderson (Garden City, NY: Hanover House, 1956), 60f [SCG II, ch. 21, para. 1].

5 Philip H. Phenix, Review of *The Divine Relativity: A Social Conception of God* in *The Journal of Philosophy* 46/18 (September 1, 1949): 596, 597.

6 Antony Thomas Kalathil, *The Theory of Evil in a Metaphysics of Freedom and The Concept of God in a Metaphysics of Love: An Exploration into the Thought of Charles Hartshorne* (Rome: Pontificia Studiorum Universitas a S. Thoma Aq. in Urbe, 2006), 77. Kalathil has here borrowed the example of the sunset from John Wild. See Wild's Review of "The Divine Relativity a Social Conception of God," *The Review of Metaphysics* 2/6 (December 1948): 72–73.

7 Hartshorne once spoke of "the unreality of the future" as in the title of his article "The Reality of the Past, the Unreality of the Future," *Hibbert Journal* 37, 2 (1939): 246–57. In the same article he even spoke of the future as "non-existent" (p. 249). However, he also characterized the future as "unsettled, and in some slight degree at least up to us to settle it" (p. 251). It seems clear to us that it is the complete determinateness of the future that Hartshorne intended to deny in this article, *not* it's complete unreality or nonexistence. In subsequent discussions, Hartshorne took more care not to use "unreal" and "nonexistent" to describe the future.

8 For Whitehead's mention of the "creative advance" see *Process and Reality*, 21. For a superb discussion of Whitehead's ideas as they relate to presentism and eternalism see Leemon B. McHenry, *The Event Universe: The Revisionary Metaphysics of Alfred North Whitehead* (Edinburgh: Edinburgh University Press, 2015), 102–07.

9 C. D. Broad, *Scientific Thought* (London: Routledge and Kegan Paul, 1923), 66.

10 Whitehead, *Process and Reality*, 35.

11 Sandra B. Rosenthal, "Contemporary Process Metaphysics and

Diverse Intuitions of Time: Can the Gap Be Bridged?" *The Journal of Speculative Philosophy* 12 (1998): 271–88.

12 Nicholas Rescher, *Process Metaphysics: An Introduction to Process Philosophy* (Albany: SUNY Press, 1996), 89–90.

13 Frederick Ferré, *Being and Value: Towards a Constructive Postmodern Metaphysics* (Albany: SUNY Press, 1996), 340.

14 Henri Bergson, *Creative Evolution*, trans. Arthur Mitchell. (New York: Modern Library 1944 [1911]), 335.

15 The exact quote from Whitehead is "Actual entities perish, but they do not change; they are what they are" (*Process and Reality*, 35). Of course, Whitehead also says over and over that actual entities "become." Thus, Hartshorne's quotation is inexact but accurate as far as Whitehead's philosophy is concerned. As noted in the previous section of this chapter, Hartshorne never liked Whitehead's metaphor of perishing for actual entities since this seems to contradict the claim that every occasion is remembered everlastingly by God.

16 Whitehead, *Process and Reality*, 68.

17 Whitehead, *Process and Reality*, 35.

18 Hartshorne refers to von Wright's *Time, Change and Contradiction* (London: Cambridge University Press, 1968). See also Charles Hartshorne, "The Organism According to Process Philosophy" in *Organism, Medicine, and Metaphysics: Essays in Honor of Hans Jonas on His 75th Birthday May 10, 1978*, ed. Stuart F. Spicker (Dordrecht, NL: D. Reidel Publishing Company, 1978), 148; the same essay is published in *Process in Context: Essays in Post-Whiteheadian Perspectives*, ed. Ernest Wolf-Gazo (New York: Peter Lang, 1988), 85.

19 Hartshorne, "Von Wright and Hume's Axiom," in *The Philosophy of G. H. von Wright*, ed. Paul Arthur Schilpp and Lewis Edwin Hahn (La Salle, IL: Open Court, 1989), 74. In his reply to Hartshorne, von Wright neither corrects nor in any way qualifies Hartshorne's interpretation of the argument against continuity and thus we may assume that it faithfully captures von Wright's position. Hartshorne holds that von Wright's argument for quanta of process is in fact superior to Whitehead's own.

20 Hartshorne and Weiss, eds., *Collected Papers of Charles Sanders Peirce*, Vol. I, 70 [CP 1.172].

21 Peirce defines a perfect continuum as one in which "first, every part has its parts; and second, that every sufficiently small part has the same mode of immediate connection with others as every other has." In *Collected Papers of Charles Sanders Peirce*, Vol. IV, ed. Hartshorne and Weiss, 541 [CP 4.642].

22 *Collected Papers*, Vol. I: 69 [CP 1.170].

23 Hartshorne notes that Peirce expressed some ambivalence about the discreteness of experience. In a discussion of James's advocacy of atomism, Peirce said that he agreed with James that there could be "no actually existent points in an existent continuum, and that if a point were placed in a continuum it would constitute a breach of the continuity." See *Collected Papers of Charles Sanders Peirce*, Vol. VI, 128–29 [CP 6.182].

24 It is worth noting that Peirce was aware of the problem that that which is not continuous may seem to be continuous. His reply, which he did not develop, was that "it could not *seem* so, if there were not *some* consciousness that *is* so." (*Collected Papers*, Vol. VI, [CP 6.182]). Peirce's claim is that conscious experience could not seem to be continuous unless there were some continuous conscious experience.

25 For a most discerning recent defense of processual atoms (the author often prefers James's "temporal buds") as coherently integrated with the lived "onflow" of experience, carefully correlated with Gerald Edelman's neurophysiology, see Ralph Pred, *Onflow: Dynamics of Consciousness and Experience* (Cambridge, MA: MIT Press, 2005). For an overview of Pred's arguments, see George W. Shields, "Whitehead and Analytic Philosophy of Mind," *Process Studies* 41/2 (Fall/Winter 2012): 310–13.

26 Mario Bunge *Philosophy in Crisis: The Need for Reconstruction* (Amherst, NY: Prometheus, 2001), 32.

27 Charles Hartshorne, in "The Development of Process Philosophy" *Philosophers of Process*, ed. Douglas Browning and William T. Myers (New York: Fordham University Press, 1998), 398.

28 McHenry makes this case in *The Event Universe*, chap. 4.

29 Rescher, *Process Metaphysics*, 29.

30 Ferré, *Being and Value*, 263.

31 Perhaps most clearly at Hartshorne, "The Organism According to

Process Philosophy," 77–78.

32   Stephen Hawking, *Black Holes and Baby Universes and Other Essays* (New York: Bantam, 1993), 128.

33   Hawking, *Black Holes,* 130.

34   Galen Strawson, *Things That Bother Me: Death, Freedom, The Self, Etc.* (New York: The New York Review of Books, 2018), 145.

35   Bertrand Russell, *Human Knowledge: Its Scope and Limits* (New York: Simon and Schuster, 1948), 261–62; cf. Hartshorne, "The Organism According to Process Philosophy," 141 [Wolf-Gazo volume, 75].

36   Charles Hartshorne gives this example in his article "Physics and Psychics: The Place of Mind in Nature" in *Mind in Nature: Essays on the Interface of Science and Philosophy* edited by John B. Cobb, Jr. and David Ray Griffin (Washington, D.C.: University Press of America, 1977), 89.

37   Charles Hartshorne, "Panpsychism: Mind as Sole Reality," *Ultimate Reality and Meaning* 1 (1978), 115.

38   *Chuang Tzu: Basic Writings,* trans. Burton Watson (New York: Columbia University Press, 1964), 45.

39   Strawson, *Things That Bother Me,* 132.

40   Strawson speaks of the denial of experience as "the Great Silliness," the origins of which he traces to the early twentieth century with the advent of philosophical behaviorism, followed by mind-brain identity theory, functionalism, and eliminative materialism. See chapter 6 of Strawson, *Things That Bother Me.* David J. Chalmers replies to Daniel Dennett's attempt to deny any form of consciousness that can't be fleshed out in terms of functional explanations in *The Character of Consciousness* (New York: Oxford University Press, 2010), 28–34.

41   Hartshorne, "Physics and Psychics," 90.

42   These are all Hartshorne's examples. See PSG 301; WM 100; DL 396; "Professor Hall on Perception," *Philosophy and Phenomenological Research* 21/4 (1961): 570; "Psychology and the Unity of Knowledge" *Southern Journal of Philosophy* 5/2 (1967): 83; "Physics and Psychics," 90.

43   Donald Wayne Viney, ed., *Charles Hartshorne's Letters to a Young Philosopher: 1979-1995, Logos-Sophia,* volume 11 (Fall 2001): 53. For

Donald R. Griffin's work, see his *The Question of Animal Awareness: Evolutionary Continuity of Mental Experience*, rev. ed. (New York: The Rockefeller University Press, 1981) and his *Animal Minds: Beyond Cognition to Consciousness*, rev. ed. (Chicago University Press, 2001).

44 Thomas Nagel, "What Is It Like to Be a Bat?" first published in *Philosophical Review* 83 (1974) and republished in Nagel's *Mortal Questions* (London: Cambridge University Press, 1979).

45 Hartshorne discusses the phantom limb case in "Mind as Memory and Creative Love" in *Theories of Mind*, ed. Jordan M. Scher (New York: The Free Press of Glencoe, 1962), 445.

46 David Ray Griffin, *Unsnarling the World-Knot: Consciousness, Freedom, and the Mind-Body Problem* (Berkeley: University of California Press, 1998), esp. chapter 10.

47 Charles Hartshorne, "Metaphysics for Positivists," *Philosophy of Science* 2/3 (July 1935): 296.

48 Hartshorne, "Physics and Psychics," 94.

49 Hartshorne, "Panpsychism: Mind as Sole Reality," 120.

50 Hartshorne, "Physics and Psychics," 95.

51 Put somewhat differently: "One can see, hear, and touch one's body, as one can other bodies; but in addition one can feel, enjoy, suffer it by physical pleasures, pains kinesthetic, and other bodily sensations in a manner not open to us with the rest of the material world." Hartshorne, "The Organism According to Process Philosophy," 137 [Wolf-Gazo volume: 70].

52 Hartshorne, "The Organism According to Process Theology," 139 [Wolf-Gazo volume, 72].

53 *Collected Papers of Charles Sanders Peirce*, Vol. V, ed. Hartshorne and Weiss, 278 [CP 5.416].

54 Bergson wrote: "Dans le sommeil naturel, nos sens ne sont nullement fermés aux impressions extérieur." That is, "In natural sleep, our senses are not at all shut off from external impressions." Henri Bergson, *Le Rêve suivi de Fantômes de vivants*, Édition critique dirigée par Frédéric Worms (Paris: Presses Universitaires de France, 2013), 8. Bergson's essay on dreams was originally published in the *Revue Scientifique* of June 8, 1901.

55 Charles Hartshorne, "Mind and Body: A Special Case of Mind and

Mind" in *A Process Theory of Medicine: Interdisciplinary Essays*, ed. Marcus P. Ford (Lewiston, NY: Edwin Mellen Press, 1987), 84. See also ZF 157 and CE 39.

56 Gottfried Leibniz, *Essais de Théodicée suivi de La Monadologie* (Aubier : Éditions Montaigne, 1962), 494. [*Monadology*, para. 21]; Whitehead, *Process and Reality*, 251.

57 Joel Salinas, *Mirror Touch: Notes from a Doctor Who Can Feel Your Pain* (New York: HarperOne, 2017). Dr. Salinas says that persons who have mirror touch synesthesia appear in aggregate to have smaller areas of the brain that are believed to be correlated with cognition of separation, and that, while this capacity comes in various degrees, it is not an isolated phenomenon but occurs in as much as two percent of the population.

58 Salinas, *Mirror Touch*, 7.

59 Jay Lombard, *The Mind of God: Neuroscience, Faith, and a Search for the Soul* (New York: Harmony Books, 2017), 38.

60 Giacomo Rizzolatti, Leonardo Fogassi, Vittorio Gallese, and Luciano Fadiga, at the University of Parma, first identified mirror neurons in their research on macaque monkeys. See Rizzolatti, Fogassi, and Gallese, "Mirrors in the Mind," *Scientific American* (Nov. 2006), http://oepf.org/sites/default/files/Mirrors%20in%20the%20Mind.pdf. Mirror neurons were later identified in humans. See Christian Keysers and Valeria Gazzola, "Social Neuroscience Mirror Neurons Recorded in Humans," *Current Biology* 20/8 (August 2010): R353–54.

61 Mohammedreza Hojat, et al., "Empathy and Medical Quality," *American Journal of Medical Quality* 28/1 (February 2013): 6–7.

62 See Keysers and Gazzola, "Social Neuroscience Mirror Neurons Recorded in Humans."

63 P. B. Pascolo et al, "The Mirror-Neuron System and Its Consistency," *Gait & Posture* 30/Supplement 1 (October 2009): 67.

64 Alfred North Whitehead, *Adventures of Ideas* (New York: Free Press, 1967), 183 [Ch. XI, sec. 14].

65 Whitehead, *Process and Reality*, 162 [Part II, Ch. VI, sec. III].

66 D. S. Clarke, "Panpsychism and the Philosophy of Charles Hartshorne," *The Journal of Speculative Philosophy*, New Series 16/3 (2002): 158.

67 Clarke argues for the conclusion that "the laws of physics, chemistry, and biology can perhaps explain the evolution of a complexity of organization required for the capacity for differential responses to environmental conditions. But in themselves, these laws do not explain how anything similar to the sensations and feelings that we ourselves are aware of and that we attribute to other species came into existence" (Clarke, "Panpsychism," 162).

68 Hartshorne, "Panpsychism: Mind as Sole Reality," 126.

69 See Jeffrey Schwartz and Sharon Begley, *The Mind and the Brain: Neuroplasticity and the Power of Mental Force* (New York: HarperCollins, 2002) for an extensive discussion of such neuroplastic effects occurring as the result of attentional therapy and the PET-scan confirmation of metabolic alterations in OCD and other patients. Schwartz and Begley are explicitly sympathetic to Whitehead's process perspective (see p. 45). See also George W. Shields, "Panexperientialism, Quantum Theory, and Neuroplasticity" in *Process Approaches to Consciousness in Psychology, Neuroscience, and Philosophy of Mind,* ed. Michel Weber and Anderson Weekes (Albany: SUNY Press, 2009): 235–60.

70 For a discussion of this and other strange psychosomatic cases such as stigmata, see David R. Griffin, *Parapsychology, Philosophy, and Spirituality: A Postmodern Exploration* (Albany: SUNY Press, 1997), 11, 67, 144, 201, and 273. For a more recent detailed and sophisticated discussion of all manner of extraordinary psychosomatic phenomena, including "spontaneous" physical changes, placebo and nocebo effects, and stigmata, see Emily Kelly, "Psychophysiological Influence" in *Irreducible Mind: Toward a Psychology for the 21st Century* (New York: Rowan & Littlefield, 2010), chap. 3, 117–239. These cases are extremely difficult to "explain away" in terms of the conventional bottom-up reductionist, materialist-physicalist explanations; Kelly clearly rejects such explanations.

71 Neuroscientists Schwartz and Begley would concur in these judgments, as they strongly rebuke "materialist determinism" throughout their treatise on *The Mind and the Brain.*

72 Hartshorne, "God and the Meaning of Life," 165. Elsewhere, Hartshorne adds to more criteria for absence of mind-like qualities, lack of freedom or initiative and lack of apparent intrinsic purpose. See "Physics and Psychics," 91.

73   Hartshorne would find much to agree with in Galen Strawson's article, "Consciousness isn't a mystery. It's matter," *The New York Times*, May 16, 2016, https://www.nytimes.com/2016/05/16/opinion/consciousness-isnt-a-mystery-its-matter.html?_r=0 [Accessed March 23, 2017.] George Shields and Leemon McHenry have argued that Strawson's much-discussed article on "Realistic Monism" is an important part of a paradigm shift that can be fairly described as "analytic panexperientialism." See their paper "Analytical Critiques of Whitehead's Metaphysics," *Journal of the American Philosophical Association* 2/3 (Fall 2016); also available from Cambridge University Press online at http://journals.cambridge.org as the August 2016 issue. Strawson himself has reviewed the paper and has expressed enthusiasm for it.

74   Hartshorne, "Panpsychism: Mind as Sole Reality," 122.

75   Hartshorne, "The Organism According to Process Philosophy," 146 [Wolf-Gazo volume: 82].

76   Leibniz, *Essais de Théodicée suivi de La Monadologie*, 502 [*Monadology*, para. 70].

77   Leibniz, *Essais*, 495 [*Monadology*, para. 24].

78   Leibniz, *Essais*, 492 [*Monadology*, para. 7.] and 504 [*Monadology*, para. 78].

79   The importance of behavioral differences of subatomic particles when aligned with different physical contexts has been recently underscored in the work of Princeton physicists J. Conway and S. Kochen, "The Strong Free Will Theorem," *Notices of the American Mathematical Society* 56/2 (2009): 226–32; this is a development of their earlier paper "The Free Will Theorem," *Foundations of Physics* 36 (2006), 1441–73. We are indebted to Tim Eastman for directing us to these important papers.

80   Hartshorne, "The Organism According to Process Philosophy," 146 [Wolf-Gazo volume: 82].

81   Alfred North Whitehead, *Science and the Modern World* (New York: Macmillan, 1925), 72. Chapter III.

82   In a largely sympathetic discussion of Whitehead, psychologist Edward F. Kelly makes the suggestion that Abner Shimony's response to Roger Penrose offers perhaps the most plausible route of defense for a panexperientialist ontology via integrating quantum theory

with Whitehead's doctrine, in effect, producing a "modernized Whiteheadianism." Kelly writes: "Shimony portrays the emergence of consciousness from an ensemble of neurons, for example, as due to large-scale quantum entanglement, analogous to the demonstrated emergence in relatively small quantum systems of novel properties transcending those of their constituents. Quantum theory, that is, already encompasses a mode of composition that has no analogue in classical physics. Penrose himself subsequently endorsed these suggestions, stating that 'although I had not explicitly asserted in either *Emperor* or *Shadows* the need for mentality to be 'ontologically fundamental in the universe', I think that something of this nature is indeed necessary' [Penrose, *The Large the Small, and the Human Mind* (Cambridge: Cambridge U Press: 175–76)]," Edward F. Kelly, "Toward a Psychology for the 21st Century" in *Irreducible Mind* (New York: Rowan & Littlefield, 2010), 636, n. 46. The books to which Penrose alludes are his *The Emperor's New Mind: Concerning Computers, Minds, and the Laws of Physics* (1989) and *Shadows of the Mind: A Search for the Missing Science of Consciousness* (1994), both from Oxford University Press. Hartshorne can thus apparently add the prestigious name of physicist Roger Penrose to his "small but distinguished list" of proponents of psychicalism.

83   Hartshorne, "The New Metaphysics and Current Problems II," *The New Frontier* 1/5 (1934): 9.

84   Hartshorne, "The New Metaphysics and Current Problems II," 13; see also, "Panpsychism: Mind as Sole Reality," 119.

85   David J. Chalmers, *The Conscious Mind: In Search of a Fundamental Theory* (New York: Oxford University Press, 1996), xiii. See also his *The Character of Consciousness*, 104–05.

86   Charles Hartshorne, "Why Psychicalism? Comments on Keeling's and Shepherd's Criticisms," *Process Studies* 6/1 (Spring 1976): 72. Plantinga's argument is in his first book, *God and Other Minds: A Study of the Rational Justification of Belief in God* (Ithaca, NY: Cornell University Press, 1967).

87   William James, *The Principles of Psychology*, Vol. I (New York: Dover, 1950 [1890]), 342. [Chapter X, "The Consciousness of Self," subsection, "The Sense of Personal Identity".]

88   D. S. Clarke, "Panpsychism and the Philosophy of Charles Hartshorne," 156. See also Clarke's two books, *Panpsychism and the*

Religious Attitude (Albany: SUNY Press, 2003) and *Panpsychism: Past and Recent Selected Readings* (Albany: SUNY Press, 2004). Although we cannot agree with all of Clarke's conclusions, especially concerning atheism, his work is marked by clarity of exposition and cogency of argument.

89 Hartshorne, "The Organism According to Process Philosophy," 146 [Wolf-Gazo volume: 82]. Another place where Hartshorne returned to the problem of "least minds" was in his article "Thinking About Thinking Machines," *Texas Quarterly* 7/1 (1964): 131–40, see especially page 137.

90 Gregg Rosenberg, *A Place for Consciousness* (New York: Oxford University Press, 2004), 96.

91 Rosenberg, *A Place for Consciousness,* 243.

92 Amy Kind, "Panexperientialism, Cognition, and the Nature of Experience," *Psyche* 12/5 (December 2006): 10.

93 Whitehead, *Process and Reality,* 18.

94 Kind's objection might usefully be compared to Sartre's critique of Freud's doctrine of the unconscious and its influences on everyday conscious experience, provoking Sartre's radically different form of existentialist psychoanalysis.

95 See Part V of Descartes's *Discourse on Method* in *The Philosophical Writings of Descartes*, Volume I, trans. John Cottingham, Robert Stoothoff, and Dugald Murdoch (New York: Cambridge University Press, 1985), 139–40.

96 Hartshorne, "Thinking About Thinking Machines," 132.

97 Hartshorne, "The Organism According to Process Philosophy," 151 [Wolf-Gazo volume: 89].

98 Hartshorne, "Thinking About Thinking Machines," 135.

99 Hartshorne, "Thinking About Thinking Machines," 136.

100 Hartshorne, "Thinking About Thinking Machines," 140.

101 Hartshorne, "Thinking About Thinking Machines," 136.

102 The classic source for Searle's critique of hard AI and his famous "Chinese Room" Argument is found in his BBC lectures published as *Minds, Brains, and Science* (Cambridge, MA: Harvard University Press, 1984).

103 For example, in the course of arguing for a compatibilist view of freedom, Moritz Schlick claimed that "[the] opposite of the universal validity of a formula, of the existence of a law, is the nonexistence of a law, indeterminism, acausality." Moritz Schlick, *Problems of Ethics* (New York: Prentice-Hall, 1939), 149. William James, like Hartshorne, did not confuse the denial of determinism with complete indeterminism or acausality. See Donald Wayne Viney, "William James on Free Will and Determinism," *The Journal of Mind and Behavior* 7/4 (Autumn 1986): 555–65. See also Donald Wayne Viney and Donald A. Crosby, "Free Will in Process Perspective," *New Ideas in Psychology* 12/4 (July 1994): 129–41.

104 *Collected Papers of Charles Sanders Peirce*, Vol. VI, ed. Hartshorne and Weiss, 28–45 [para., 35-64]; in the same volume, see Peirce's reply to Paul Carus: 390-435 [para., 588–618]. See also Hartshorne, "Panpsychism: Mind as Sole Reality," 124.

105 William James, *Some Problems of Philosophy: A Beginning of an Introduction to Philosophy* (New York: Longmans, Green, and Co., 1911), 205.

106 Storrs McCall, "Time and the Physical Modalities," *The Monist* 53/3 (1969); see especially "Section 6. A Calculus of Necessary and Sufficient Conditions," 437–46.

107 Peter van Inwagen, *An Essay on Free Will* (Oxford University Press, 1983), 202–04.

108 This is a slightly revised version of the modal argument first published by George Shields as "A Logical Analysis of Relational Realism" in *Physics and Speculative Philosophy: Potentiality in Modern Science*, ed. Timothy Eastman, David Ray Griffin, and Michael Epperson (Berlin: DeGruyter, 2016).

109 Alexander Pruss, "The Leibnitzian Cosmological Argument" in *The Blackwell Companion to Natural Theology*, ed. William L. Craig and J. P. Moreland (Oxford: Wiley-Blackwell, 2012), 50–58.

110 Some argue that quantum indeterminacies cancel out at a macro-level, making large-scale processes deterministic. Hartshorne replied that the argument begs the question in the assumption that only quantum processes can be indeterministic. See Charles Hartshorne, "Order and Chaos" *The Concept of Order*, ed. Paul G. Kuntz (Seattle: University of Washington Press, 1968), 262.

111 Hartshorne, "God and the Meaning of Life," 157.

112 Both quotes from James are from *The Principles of Psychology*, Vol. I (New York: Dover, 1950 [1890]), 127. Also the final paragraph in the chapter titled "Habit."

113 Charles Hartshorne, "Foundations for a Humane Ethics: What Human Beings Have in Common with Other Higher Animals," in *On the Fifth Day: Animal Rights and Human Ethics*, ed. Richard K. Morris and Michael W. Fox (Washington, D. C.: Acropolis Books, 1978), 161–62.

114 Hartshorne, "Foundations for a Humane Ethics," 162.

115 Hartshorne, "The Organism According to Process Philosophy," 150 [Wolf-Gazo volume: 88].

116 For an account of James's views on free will and determinism see Viney, "William James on Free Will and Determinism" cited above.

117 Whitehead, *Process and Reality*, 20.

118 Whitehead, *Process and Reality*, 34.

119 Whitehead, *Process and Reality*, 34.

120 Donald W. Sherburne, "Whitehead's Psychological Physiology," *Southern Journal of Philosophy* 7 (1969): 401–07.

121 Hartshorne's response in *Did Jesus Rise from the Dead: The Resurrection Debate,* ed. Terry L. Miethe (San Francisco: Harper & Row, 1987), 140.

122 Hartshorne's response in *Did Jesus Rise from the Dead,* 137

123 Hartshorne's response in *Did Jesus Rise from the Dead,* 140.

124 Hartshorne's response in *Did Jesus Rise from the Dead,* 142.

125 Hartshorne's response in *Did Jesus Rise from the Dead.* For the most part, Christian theologians inspired by Whiteheadian or neoclassical metaphysical perspectives follow Hartshorne in *not* dwelling on the historical details of the biblical resurrection narratives or in downplaying the stories that suggest that Jesus's body exited the tomb (i.e., the empty tomb narratives and the stories of Thomas and of Jesus eating with the disciples by the sea of Galilee). Schubert Ogden, for example, following Rudolf Bultmann, resists the idea that the "'the act of God' which the faith of Easter signifies is yet another historical happening in space

and time, subsequent to the events of Jesus's life and death." He continues: "The New Testament representations of it as though it were such a happening are undeniably mythological and demand to be critically interpreted—and that, primarily for the sake of expressing more appropriately its own distinctive reality as an act of *God*." Ogden, *The Reality of God and Other Essays* (New York: Harper & Row, 1963), 217–18. Ogden interprets the resurrection as a chief "eschatological symbol" which can be interpreted in two ways, (1) existentially as a warrant for the possibilities of authentic existence, the promise of a renewal of authentic life after death of an egoistic, sinful, and inauthentic existence, and, (2) more importantly, as the symbol which reflects the final conquest of both death and sin through the assurance of "God's unbounded love" which is *objectively immortal* (here connecting this position to the beautiful, poetic language of Romans 8:31, cf. Ogden, 229). Interpreting Jesus's resurrection as also "our" resurrection, this *immortal* bond of love answers to the serious existential question related to our transience, our "perpetual perishing," a question that remains even if we were to affirm subjective immortality. Ogden says that the question of personal immortality is an "open question" and one that he does not answer in the negative—on the contrary, he "hopes" the evidence can be construed in the affirmative (228)—but he also firmly asserts that subjective immortality is not a "necessary article of Christian belief" (228–29). As a symbolic, existential interpretation which claims only objective immortality, none of this is in contradiction to Hartshorne's doctrine; indeed, it represents an eloquent theological gloss upon his central motif that "God is love."

John B. Cobb, Jr., while more friendly to the approach of Wolfhart Pannenberg than of Bultmann, also seems uninterested in historical details. He considers the possibility that the appearances of Jesus to the disciples were "nonhallucinatory visions" (i.e., Jesus was their cause, but their sensory content was contributed by the mental activity of the recipient); but Cobb notes that this would give no support for the idea of a bodily resurrection of Jesus (*Christ in a Pluralistic Age* [Philadelphia: Westminster Press, 1975], 252–53).

Lewis S. Ford, takes "I Corinthians 15 to be our most reliable testimony to resurrection appearances, as being the only eyewitness report we have." Ford makes essentially the same move as Cobb in suggesting that the report is of visions (veridical but subjective), which stand between hallucinations (nonverdical and subjective) and ordinary sensory experience (veridical and objective) (*The Lure of God: A Biblical Background for Process Theism* [Philadelphia: Fortress Press, 1978], 72). In a nuanced discussion of the meaning of "body" Ford interprets Paul's talk of "the body of Christ" (i.e., the Christian community) as something beyond mere metaphor.

David Ray Griffin interprets the post-resurrection appearances in terms of the deliverances of parapsychology as veridical visions. However, precisely because such visions are not unique to Christianity, he gives up "every pretense, even with regard to the resurrection of Jesus, that its originating events prove its uniquely divine origin" (*Parapsychology, Philosophy, and Spirituality: A Postmodern Exploration* [Albany: SUNY Press, 1997], 282). See also the discussion of the resurrection appearances in Griffin's *God Exists but Gawd Does Not: From Evil to New Atheism to Fine-Tuning* (Anoka, MN: Process Century Press, 2016), 106–13.

For one of this book's author's views on the subject see Donald Wayne Viney, "Grave Doubts About the Resurrection," *Encounter* 50/2 (Spring 1989): 125–40. See also Viney's reviews of *Did Jesus Rise From the Dead? The Resurrection Debate*, ed. Terry L. Miethe, in *The Midwest Quarterly* 30/3 (Spring 1989): 392–95, and of *Risen Indeed: Making Sense of the Resurrection*, by Stephen Davis, in *International Journal for the Philosophy of Religion* 37/2 (April 1995): 120–22.

126 See for example: Lewis Ford and Marjorie Suchocki, "A Whiteheadian Reflection on Subjective Immortality," *Process Studies* 7/1 (1977): 1–13; Marjorie Suchocki, "Charles Hartshorne and Subjective Immortality," *Process Studies* 21/2 (Summer 1992): 118–22; Randall Auxier, "Why One Hundred Years is Forever: Hartshorne's Theory of Immortality," *The Personalist Forum* 14/2 (Fall 1998): 109–32; Santiago Sia, *Religion, Reason and God: Essays in the Philosophies of Charles Hartshorne and A. N. Whitehead* (Frankfurt am Main: Peter Lang, 2004), ch. 6, 83–100; David Ray Griffin, *Reenchantment without Supernaturalism: A Process Philosophy of Religion* (Ithaca, NY: Cornell University Press, 2001), 230–46.

127 Marjorie Hewitt Suchocki, *The End of Evil: Process Eschatology in Historical Context* (Albany: SUNY Press, 1988).

128 Suchocki, *The End of Evil*, 109 and 111.

129 Suchocki, *The End of Evil*, 166.

130 In our view, Suchocki is formidable in her reply to the arguments of Lewis S. Ford, who contends that it is impossible for God to prehend the satisfaction of an actual occasion in its immediacy since, according to Ford, the final phase of satisfaction has become static and objective. To the contrary, Suchocki contends that there is activity in the final phase of satisfaction; it is a "holding," a "culmination" rather than demise of an occasion's concrescence such that the occasion becomes a "subject-superject" urging on new occasions in coordination with God's initial aims. See Suchocki's exchange with Ford in *World Without End: Christian Eschatology from a Process Perspective,* ed. Joseph A. Bracken (Grand Rapids, MI: William B. Eerdmans, 2005), 113–27 and 211f. For Suchocki, finite occasions—Hartshorne would say non-divine or fragmentary occasions—cannot prehend other finite occasions in their subjective immediacy because, by their very nature as finite they are largely engaged in negative prehensions. Suchocki argues that a doctrine which takes seriously the notion that there are no negative prehensions in God is a doctrine which consistently holds that God prehends the entirety of actual occasions including their subjectivity. Perhaps this is what Hartshorne should have contended given his view that God prehends the satisfaction of occasions in their immediacy and that there are no negative prehensions in God.

131 Auxier endeavors to present an account of personal creaturely immortality that is consistent with Hartshornean metaphysics. He writes, "I want to claim that Hartshorne's remarkable metaphysics is actually capable of supporting a richer, more profound, and more satisfying account of immortality than he himself puts forward." Auxier, "Why One Hundred Years is Forever," 111.

132 Quotes from Auxier, "Why One Hundred Years is Forever," 117–18.

133 Audience discussion of Auxier, "Why One Hundred Years is Forever," 135–36.

134 Daniel A. Dombrowski, *Divine Beauty: The Aesthetics of Charles Hartshorne* (Nashville: Vanderbilt University Press, 2004), 186.

135 Auxier, "Why One Hundred Years is Forever," 126.

136 Auxier, "Why One Hundred Years is Forever," 130, n.26.

137 In Auxier's response to a question from Tim Eastman, Auxier suggested that the most elegant view is one that identifies being a creature with being a person (presumably, apart from the divine

case). According to Auxier, "In a very real sense, the world is a person; that desk is a person: everything is a person in a sense. Anything that's a creature is going to be a person" (134). Of course, this is far afield from anything Hartshorne would have said.

138 See David Ray Griffin's discussion of John Cobb's reading of neo-Jungian cultural historian Eric Neumann in Griffin's *Religion and Scientific Naturalism* (Albany: SUNY Press, 2000), 226–27. Neumann's classic tome is *The Origins and History of Consciousness* (Princeton, NJ: Princeton University Press, 1954). For an extremely interesting and important attempt at *rapprochement* between Whiteheadian process thought and both the archetypal psychology of Jung and that of his revisionary interpreter James Hillman, see *Archetypal Process: Self and Divine in Whitehead, Jung and Hillman,* ed. David Ray Griffin, (Evanston, IL: Northwestern University Press, 1989). In our view, this work has not received the critical attention it deserves. Apropos of Griffin's work, we add to the earlier discussion of Hartshorne's view of the resurrection that it would be possible for a neoclassical Christian theologian to supplement profoundly Ogden's point that the resurrection of Jesus is also "our" resurrection by marshalling Jung's fascinating interpretation of the resurrection narrative. The passion, crucifixion, and resurrection of Jesus closely correlate with all the general tropes of the archetypal shamanic spiritual journey: The shaman's spirit leaves on a pilgrimage in which there is sickness and torture, followed by death, followed by rebirth into a new integrated and whole self—the very point of "salvation." This correlates with Jesus's passion and tortured *via crucis,* death, descension into Hell (where symbolically there is contention with the shadow self), and finally rebirth or resurrection into a new self. From Jung's perspective, the New Testament resurrection narrative thus symbolically represents important objective truths about the dynamics of the human soul in its quest for deep and integrated wholeness. If correct, this is a most profound existential-anthropological narrative whatever the disposition of the historical details surrounding the resurrection event.

139 Eben Alexander, "Appendix B: Neuro-Scientific Hypotheses" in his *Proof of Heaven: A Neuro-Surgeon's Journey into the Afterlife* (New York: Simon and Schuster, 2012), 185–88.

140 In his dissertation, Donald Viney suggested another possible concept of a limited afterlife experience: "May not God isolate some of

those who died prematurely or suffered unjustly and allow them
to enjoy a little more happiness without thereby eliminating the
risks that were involved in bringing about the injustices? It would
remain eternally true that risks had been taken and that tragedy
occurred. God's redeeming action might be interpreted simply as a
more complete revelation of [God's] own love before the final (not
the earthly) death of the individual. This view has the advantage of
permitting more good to come to those who have suffered unjustly
without denying that a greater amount of good could have been
achieved had the suffering never occurred. Such a view of the
afterlife differs from traditional views in that the individual is not
born into another social world [except insofar as relation to God
is a social relation]. The individual is related only to God after
death, who reveals [Godself] in more fullness to the survivor. But
this view is like the traditional view in that a final chapter is, so
to speak, added to the individual's life. The individual's life then
resembles more a completed work than a half written text" (*Charles
Hartshorne's Global Argument for God's Existence: An Analysis and
Assessment* [Norman, OK: University of Oklahoma, 1982], 184–85).
See also Viney's *Charles Hartshorne and the Existence of God* (Albany:
SUNY Press, 1985), 116. Viney would stress today that the possibility
of an afterlife is, at best, a matter of hope rather than of belief.

141 Hartshorne, "Personal Identity from A to Z," *Process Studies* 2/3
(1972): 209–15.

142 William James, *The Principles of Psychology*, Vol. I (New York: Dover,
1950 [1890]), 339 [Ch. 10, in the section on "The Sense of Personal
Identity."]

143 Charles Hartshorne, "Some Not Ungrateful But Perhaps Inadequate
Comments About Comments on My Writings and Ideas," *Process
Studies* 21/2 (Summer 1992): 128.

144 Hartshorne, "Concerning Abortion: An Attempt at a Rational
View," *The Christian Century* 98/2 (1981): 42-45; reprinted in Vetter,
Hartshorne: A New World View: Essays by Charles Hartshorne, Ch.
II,.

145 Simone de Beauvoir famously wrote, "On ne nait pas femme : on
le devient." *Le deuxième sexe II l'expérience vécue* (Paris: Gallimard,
1976 [1949]), 13.

146 Elizabeth Armstrong Reed, *Primitive Buddhism* (Chicago: Scott,

Foresman & Co., 1896), 106–07.

147 Jay Wesley Richards, *The Untamed God: A Philosophical Exploration of Divine Perfection, Simplicity and Immutability* (Downers Grove, IL: InterVarsity Press, 2003), 184.

148 J. M. E. McTaggart, *Philosophical Studies* (New York: Longmans, Green & Company, 1934), 116.

149 Hartshorne, "Time" in *An Encyclopedia of Religion,* ed. Vergilius Ferm (New York: Philosophical Library, 1945), 788.

150 We borrow this expression from Leemon McHenry in his discussion of Whitehead's metaphysics. See McHenry's *The Event Universe: The Revisionary Metaphysics of Alfred North Whitehead* (Edinburgh: Edinburgh University Press, 2015), 96.

151 *Collected Papers of Charles Sanders Peirce,* Vol V, ed. Hartshorne and Weiss, 310–11 [para. 459].

152 *Basic Writings of Saint Thomas Aquinas,* Vol. I, 266 [ST I, Q25, a4, Reply to Obj. 3].

153 *Jules Lequier, Œuvres complètes,* ed. Jean Grenier (Neuchatel, Switzerland: Éditions de la Baconnière. 1952), 473. Lequyer, unlike Hartshorne, confined creaturely creativity to human beings whereas, as we have seen, for Hartshorne, creativity is a transcendental. The article in which Hartshorne most fully discusses "Creativity and the Deductive Logic of Causality" was first published in 1973, well after 1948 when he first learned of Lequyer's thought from Jean Wahl. Hartshorne recognized in Lequyer a fellow traveler, coming to some of the same conclusions as he himself had come as the result of the influences of James, Peirce, Bergson, and Whitehead. See Hartshorne's letter of July 9, 1988 to Viney in *Charles Hartshorne's Letters to a Young Philosopher: 1979-1995,* 33–34.

154 For Leibniz, any change in the individual concept of a person also involves a change in the universe itself. Leibniz writes in the correspondence with Arnauld, "this is the nature of an individual substance, namely, to have so complete a concept that from it may be deduced all that can be attributed to it, and even the whole universe, because of the inter-connection between things." Gottfried Leibniz, *Discourse on Metaphysics/Correspondence with Arnauld / Monadology,* trans. George R. Montgomery (La Salle, IL: Open Court, 1973): 110.

155 George L. Goodwin's discussion of the relations between Hartshorne

and Kripke is particularly insightful. See Chapter 4 of his book *The Ontological Argument of Charles Hartshorne* (Missoula, MT: Scholars Press, 1978).

156 Whitehead, *Science and the Modern World*, 87, Ch. V.

157 See also, Hartshorne, "Are There Absolutely Specific Universals?" *Journal of Philosophy* 68/3 (1971): 76–78.

158 For a defense of Hartshorne's theory of possibility in relation to some criticisms see George W. Shields, "Hartshorne and Creel on Impassibility," *Process Studies* 21/1 (Spring 1992): 44–59. For more on Hartshorne's views on possibility with reference to the idea of possible worlds, see the articles by Jay Wesley Richards, Donald Wayne Viney, and Daniel A. Dombrowski in *Metaphysics, Analysis, and the Grammar of God*, ed. Randy Ramal (Tübingen, Germany: Mohr Siebeck, 2010), Part 2: 107–72.

159 Eugene H. Peters, *Hartshorne and Neoclassical Metaphysics: An Interpretation* (Lincoln: University of Nebraska Press, 1970), Ch. 7.

160 Dombrowski, *Divine Beauty*: 25.

161 A wise Irish lady, Dolores Lyons (Jan. 6, 1933–Feb. 15, 2018), described beauty as "consistency without boredom and variation without chaos." Though unfamiliar with Hartshorne's thoughts on aesthetic value, Ms. Lyons nevertheless captured its essence in her pithy statement.

162 Hartshorne discusses the origin of the circle diagram in "Reminiscences of Charles Hartshorne (member since 1942)" *Journal of Aesthetics and Art Criticism* 51 (1993): 286–89. See also Hartshorne's "The Aesthetic Dimension of Religious Experience," 11, as well as his "Science as the Search for the Hidden Beauty of the World" in *The Aesthetic Dimension of Science*, ed. Deane W. Curtin (New York: Philosophical Library, 1982), 86.

163 Hartshorne, "Science as the Search for the Hidden Beauty," 95.

164 Hartshorne, "Science as the Search for the Hidden Beauty," 89.

165 Hartshorne, "The Aesthetic Dimension of Religious Experience," 14.

Chapter Five

1 *Basic Writings of Saint Thomas Aquinas*, Vol I, ed. Anton C. Pegis

(New York: Random House, 1945), 124 [ST I, Q13, a7].

2 John Sanders, *The God Who Risks: A Theology of Divine Providence*, rev. ed. (Downers Grove, IL: IVP Academic, 2007), ch. 5.

3 *St. Anselm: Basic Writings*, trans. S. N. Deane (La Salle, IL: Open Court, 1966), 13 [*Proslogion*, chap. 8].

4 Whitehead, *Process and Reality*, 351.

5 See also "Berdyaev as a Philosopher," Hartshorne's preface to David Bonner Richardson, *Berdyaev's Philosophy of History: An Existentialist Theory of Social Creativity and Eschatology* (The Hague: Martinus Nijhoff, 1968), ix-xiii.

6 See Bill Moyers's interview with Martha Nussbaum on Bill Moyer's Journal, available online: http://www.pbs.org/moyers/journal /archives/nussbaumwoi_flash.html.

7 See also Hartshorne's questions to John Wild in *Philosophical Interrogations*, ed. Sydney and Beatrice Rome (New York: Holt, Rinehart and Winston, 1964), 158–60. William P. Alston discusses, and approves of, this argument and this aspect of Hartshorne's theism (EA 83–84).

8 The system used here, commonly known as T, was set out in 1937 by Robert Feys. Its modal axioms are "$\Box p \rightarrow p$" and "$\Box (p \rightarrow q) \rightarrow (\Box p \rightarrow \Box q)$". See G. E. Hughes and M. J. Cresswell, *An Introduction to Modal Logic* (New York: Routledge, 1991), 30–31. The formalization given here follows Viney, "Hartshorne's Dipolar Theism and the Mystery of God" in *Models of God and Alternative Ultimate Realities*, ed. Jeanine Diller and Asa Kasher (Dordrecht, NL: Springer, 2013), 331-340.

9 *Basic Writings of Saint Thomas Aquinas*, vol. I, 156 [ST I, Q14, a13, Obj. 2].

10 *Basic Writings of Saint Thomas Aquinas*, vol. I, 149 [ST I, Q14, a9, Reply Obj. 3].

11 *Basic Writings of Saint Thomas Aquinas*, vol. I, 198–99 [ST I, Q19, a3]. See also, Aquinas, *On the Truth of the Catholic Faith*, Book Two, trans. James F. Anderson (Garden City, NY: Hanover House, 1955): 68 [SCG II, chapter 23].

12 Robert C. Neville thinks that the world's mystical traditions "give experiential support" to the identification of Being and nothingness

in God, when God is considered "without the creation." See Neville's "Responding to my Critics" in *Interpreting Neville,* ed. J. Harley Chapman and Nancy K. Frankenberry (Albany: SUNY Press, 1999), 309–10. Hartshorne could agree that God apart from the creation is indeed nothing (as the creation apart from God is nothing), but the "nothing" in this case is equivalent to unrestricted impossibility and inconceivability. What Hartshorne never accepted was Neville's penchant for apophatic theology and his talk of the divine *indeterminate* ground of the determinate connections among past, present, and future. See Hartshorne's contribution to "Three Responses to Neville's Creativity and God," *Process Studies* 10/3-4 (1980): 93–97 and PCH 669–72.

13 William James, *The Varieties of Religious Experience: A Study in Human Nature* (New York: Modern Library, 1929), 371.

14 Charles Hartshorne, "Mysticism and Rationalistic Metaphysics," *The Monist* 59/4 (1976): 463.

15 Hartshorne, "Mysticism and Rationalistic Metaphysics," 468.

16 Hartshorne, "Mysticism and Rationalistic Metaphysics," 468.

17 Henri Bergson, *The Two Sources of Morality and Religion*, trans. R. Ashley Audra and Cloudesley Brereton, with the assistance of W. Horsfall Carter (Garden City, NY: Doubleday Anchor Books, 1954), 254. Bergson, *Les Deux Sources de la morale et de la religion* (Édition Flammarion Paris, 2012), 325.

18 Bergson, *The Two Sources of Morality and Religion*, 255; Bergson, *Les Deux Sources de la morale et de la religion*, 325.

19 Evelyn Underhill, *The Essentials of Mysticism* (New York: E. P. Dutton, 1960), 4.

20 Hartshorne, "Mysticism and Rationalistic Metaphysics," 468.

21 Daniel Dombrowski makes points similar to those we highlight in this paragraph. Following a distinction of John Smith, Dombrowski argues that mystical experience is best understood as *direct but mediated* by the body, language, culture, and logic. See Dombrowski, "Rival Concepts of God and Rival Versions of Mysticism," *International Journal for Philosophy of Religion* 68 (2010): 153–65.

22 George Shields recalls that David Tracy mentioned in his Hartshorne Seminar at Chicago that he considered Hartshorne to be a "nature

mystic," close to those in the Catholic tradition who feel the sacred in nature, such as St. Francis of Assisi. St. Francis saw divinity especially in birds.

23 Daniel A. Dombrowski, *St. John of the Cross: An Appreciation* (Albany: SUNY Press, 1992).

24 Don Viney makes the case for including Teilhard as a founder of modern process thought in Donald Wayne Viney, "Teilhard and Process Philosophy Redux," *Process Studies* 35/1 (2006): 12–42. See also Viney's "Teilhard: Le philosophe malgré l'Église" in *Rediscovering Teilhard's Fire,* ed. Kathleen Duffy, S.S.J (Philadelphia: Saint Joseph's University Press, 2010), 69–88; and Viney's "Teilhard, Medawar, and the New Atheism" in *From Teilhard to Omega: Co-creating an Unfinished Universe,* ed. Ilia Delio (Maryknoll, NY: Orbis Books, 2014), 127–48.

25 See the lucid account of this discovery and Teilhard's role in it in Amir D. Aczel, *The Jesuit & the Skull: Teilhard de Chardin, Evolution, and the Search for Peking Man* (New York: Riverhead Books, 2007).

26 An excellent collection of Teilhard's lyrical and devotional work is *Hymne de l'Univers* (Paris: Éditions de Seuil, 1961) translated as *Hymn of the Universe* (New York: Harper & Row, 1965).

27 This statement is at the beginning of his essay "La vie cosmique" [Cosmic Life] printed in *Écrits du temps de la guerre 1916-1919* [Writings in Time of War] (Paris: Bernard Grasset Éditeur, 1965), 5.

28 Pierre Teilhard de Chardin, *Le Phénomène humain* (Paris: Éditions de Seuil, 1955), 291. Translated by Sarah Appleton-Weber as *The Human Phenomenon* (Brighton: Sussex Academic Press, 1999), 186. No one is better at explaining Teilhard's mysticism and the distinctive contribution it makes to mystical literature than Ursula King. See in particular King's *Teilhard de Chardin and Eastern Religions: Spirituality and Mysticism in an Evolutionary World* (New York: Paulist Press, 2011) and her book *Christ in All Things: Exploring Spirituality with Pierre Teilhard de Chardin,* rev. ed. (Maryknoll, NY: Orbis Books, 2016).

29 Daniel A. Dombrowski, *Analytic Theism, Hartshorne, and the Concept of God* (Albany: SUNY Press, 1996), 157–64.

30 See for example, Kierkegaard, *Philosophical Fragments,* ed. and

trans. Howard V. Hong and Edna H. Hong (Princeton University Press, 1985), 87. There is reason to believe that Kierkegaard did not intend to promote a belief in *logical contradictions*. In the journals he faults Kant for failing to establish the inexplicable as a category. Kierkegaard writes, "It is specifically the task of human knowing to understand that there is something it cannot understand and to understand what that is." This is the category of paradox. See *Søren Kierkegaard's Journals and Papers*. Volume 3, L-R, ed. and trans. Howard V. Hong and Edna H. Hong, assisted by Gregor Malantschuk (Bloomington: Indiana University Press, 1975), 406.

31 David Tracy, "Analogy, Metaphor and God Language: Charles Hartshorne," *The Modern Schoolman* 62/4 (May 1985): 259. Yujin Nagasawa uses the expression "Hartshorne's Discovery" to refer to Hartshorne's observation that two different ontological arguments can be found in Anselm's *Proslogion* II and III. See Nagasawa's *The Existence of God: A Philosophical Introduction* (London: Routledge, 2011), 34. For more on this topic see our discussion below on Hartshorne's treatment of the ontological argument.

32 For this reason, it is incorrect to say that, for Hartshorne, "the a priori of experience as the *necessary structure* of the world . . . ultimately *is* God." See Roland Faber, *God as the Poet of the World: Exploring Process Theologies*, trans. Douglas W. Stott (Louisville, KY: Westminster John Knox Press, 2004), 29. Faber's mistake leads him to two other mistakes, as when he says that Hartshorne's position "prompted the rationalistic demand that God *necessarily be demonstrable*. Hartshorne made repeated attempts to prove Anselm of Canterbury's 'ontological argument'" (29). We saw in Chapter Three that Hartshorne rejects strict demonstrations in matters of metaphysics. We shall see in Chapter VI that Hartshorne repeatedly denied that Anselm's reasoning constitutes such a demonstration. Moreover, Hartshorne's own case for God's existence is a cumulative argument strategy involving a version of Anselm's reasoning as one strand only.

33 St. Thomas Aquinas, *On the Truth of the Catholic Faith, Summa Contra Gentiles Book One: God*, trans. Anton C. Pegis (Garden City, NY: Hanover House, 1955), 100 [SCG Bk 1, 16.2].

34 *Basic Writings of Saint Thomas Aquinas*, vol. I: 499 [ST I, Q10, a5].

35 John Wild, "The Divine Existence: An Answer to Mr. Hartshorne,"

The Review of Metaphysics 4/1 (September 1950): 65. This article is a reply to Hartshorne's response to Wild's article, Review of "The Divine Relativity a Social Conception of God," *The Review of Metaphysics* 2/6 (December 1948): 65–77. Hartshorne's reply to Wild's review is titled "The Divine Relativity and Absoluteness: A Reply," *The Review of Metaphysics* 4/1 (September 1950): 31–60.

36 Wild, "The Divine Existence," 66. Wild makes the same criticism in his first article, Review of "The Divine Relativity," 74.

37 Wild, Review of "The Divine Relativity," 68–69.

38 Wild, "The Divine Existence: An Answer to Mr. Hartshorne," 81.

39 Wild, "The Divine Existence: An Answer to Mr. Hartshorne," 79.

40 Wild, "The Divine Existence: An Answer to Mr. Hartshorne."

41 Wild, "The Divine Existence: An Answer to Mr. Hartshorne," 82.

42 "Interrogation of John Wild," conducted by Henry B. Veatch in *Philosophical Interrogations,* ed. Sydney and Beatrice Rome (New York: Holt, Rinehart and Winston, 1964), 160.

43 "Interrogation of John Wild," 161.

44 "Interrogation of John Wild," 162.

45 At one time, Hartshorne seems to have believed that Whitehead endorsed the societal conception of deity (PSG 274). Later he changed his thinking about this. See Replies to "Interrogation of Charles Hartshorne, conducted by William Alston." *Philosophical Interrogations,* ed. Sydney and Beatrice Rome (New York: Holt, Rinehart, and Winston, 1964), 324.

46 Charles Hartshorne, "The Dipolar Conception of Deity," *The Review of Metaphysics* 21/2 (1967): 287.

47 A. H. Johnson, "Some Conversations with Whitehead Concerning God and Creativity" in *Explorations in Whitehead's Philosophy,* ed. Lewis S. Ford and George L. Kline (New York: Fordham University Press, 1983), 9.

48 Replies to "Interrogation of Charles Hartshorne," 324.

49 See also Hartshorne, "Love and Dual Transcendence," *Union Seminary Quarterly Review* 30/2-4 (1975): 94–100.

50 *Plato: The Collected Dialogues,* ed. Edith Hamilton and Huntington Cairns (Princeton, NJ: Princeton University Press, 1973): 627–28

[*Republic*, bk 2, 380e–381c].

51 See also, "Peirce, Whitehead, and the Sixteen Views About God," 112.

52 It is worth noting that, on at least one occasion, Hartshorne despaired of divesting the concept of perfection of the connotation of static completeness and suggested instead the concept of eminence. In 1967 he wrote, "A good term for God's superiority is the word 'eminence'. It has been the least spoiled by misuse. If you say that God is 'perfect' you are employing a viciously ambiguous term. Etymologically 'perfect' means that a project has been completely executed—something has been made and finished. But God hasn't been made, supposedly, and I don't think he is finished. There are all kinds of objections to the word 'perfect'. I think it is a very misleading word to use." Hartshorne, "God and the Social Structure of Reality" in *Theology in Crisis: A Colloquium on The Credibility of 'God'* (New Concord, OH: Muskingum College, 1967), 24.

53 *The Philosophical Writings of Descartes, Volume III, The Correspondence*, trans. John Cottingham, Robert Stoothoff, Dugald Murdoch, and Anthony Kenny (New York: Cambridge University Press, 1991), 25 [Letter to Mersenne, May 27, 1630]. For a nuanced historical discussion that urges the dialectical power of Descartes's view as against Leibniz and Hartshorne, see Chapter 13, "Descartes and Leibniz on the Priority of Nature versus Will in God" in Robert Cummings Neville, *Realism in Religion: A Pragmatist's Perspective* (Albany: SUNY Press, 2009). For Hartshorne's interactions with Neville see Hartshorne's "Response to Robert Neville's *Creativity and God,*" *Process Studies* 10/3-4 (1980): 93–97 and Neville's response, "Concerning *Creativity and God*: A Response," *Process Studies* 11/1 (Spring 1981): 1–10. See also **PCH** 377–95, 669–72. Neville reviewed Hartshorne's *Creative Synthesis and Philosophic Method* in *Process Studies* 2/1 (Spring 1972): 49–67 and David A. Pailin responded to the review in "Neville's Critique of Hartshorne," *Process Studies* 4/3 (Fall 1974): 187–98. The exchanges between Griffin and Neville are relevant. See David Ray Griffin, *Whitehead's Radically Different Postmodern Philosophy: An Argument for its Contemporary Relevance* (Albany: SUNY Press, 2007), chap. 9, and Robert C. Neville, "A Letter of Grateful and Affectionate Response to David Ray Griffin's *Whitehead's Radically Different Postmodern Philosophy: An Argument for Its Contemporary Relevance,*" *Process Studies*, 37/1 (Spring-Summer 2008): 7–38.

54 *On the Truth of the Catholic Faith, Summa Contra Gentiles Book Two: Creation*, trans. James F. Anderson (Garden City, NY: Hanover House, 1956), 75 [SCG II, ch. 25, para. 14].

55 *Basic Writings of Saint Thomas Aquinas*, Vol. I, 266 [ST I, Q25, a4, Reply to Obj. 3].

56 *On the Truth of the Catholic Faith, Summa Contra Gentiles, Book Three: Providence, Part I*, trans. Vernon J. Bourke (Garden City, NY: Hanover House, 1956), 237 [SCG III, Part I, ch. 70, para. 8].

57 *Basic Writings of Saint Thomas Aquinas*, Volume I, 208 [ST I, Q19, a8].

58 *Basic Writings of Saint Thomas Aquinas*, Vol. I, 439 [ST I, Q45, a5]. Aquinas is careful to distinguish the question whether God creates *ex nihilo* from the question whether the universe had a beginning. In *Summa Theologica* I, he argues that to create is to bring something from nothing, and this is what God does in creating (Q45, a1 and a2). Only then does he address the question whether the world had a beginning. This, he claims, cannot be demonstrated but is a matter of faith (Q46, a2). He follows the same procedure in *Summa Contra Gentiles*, II (chap. 16, 31–38).

59 David B. Burrell, *Aquinas, God & Action* (Notre Dame, IN: University of Notre Dame Press, 1979), 148–49. For a review of this work that argues Burrell misunderstands neoclassical theism in subtle respects, see George W. Shields, "Critical Study: David Burrell's *Aquinas: God and Action*," *Process Studies* 11/1 (Spring 1980): 50–52.

60 *Basic Writings of Saint Thomas Aquinas*, Volume II: 1005 [ST II, Q3, a2].

61 Hartshorne briefly discusses the metaphor of a divine hypnotist in "A New Look at the Problem of Evil" in *Current Philosophical Issues: Essays in Honor of Curt John Ducasse*, ed. Frederick C. Dommeyer (Springfield, IL: Charles C. Thomas, 1966), 203.

62 James F. Ross, *Philosophical Theology*, 2nd ed. (Hackett Publishing 1980), 250–72.

63 Ross, *Philosophical Theology*, xxx and xxxvii.

64 William L. Craig, "Creation *ex nihilo*" in *Process Theology*, ed. Ronald H. Nash (Grand Rapids, MI: Baker Book House, 1987), 141–73.

65 Craig, "Creation *ex nihilo*," 154.

66 Craig, "Creation *ex nihilo*," 154–5.

67 See also *Charles Hartshorne's Letters to a Young Philosopher*, 33 [Letter of July 9, 1988]. For Lequyer's statement see, *Jules Lequier, Œuvres complètes*, ed. Jean Grenier (Neuchatel, Switzerland: Editions de la Baconnière, 1952), 70.

68 David Basinger, *Divine Power in Process Theism: A Philosophical Critique* (Albany: SUNY Press, 1988), 30.

69 David Basinger graciously shared this letter with Don Viney.

70 See Hartshorne's response to the resurrection debate in *Did Jesus Rise From the Dead? The Resurrection Debate*, ed. Terry L. Miethe (San Francisco: Harper & Row, 1987), 137.

71 Boethius, *The Consolation of Philosophy*, trans. V. E. Watts (London: Penguin, 1969), 136–37 [bk 4, prose 6]; Thomas Aquinas, *On the Truth of the Catholic Faith, Summa Contra Gentiles, Book One: God*, trans. Anton C. Pegis (Garden City, NY: Hanover House, 1955), 219 [SCG I, ch. 66, para. 7].

72 Hartshorne, "Foreknowledge, Divine" in *Encyclopedia of Religion*, ed. Vergilius Ferm (Secaucus, NJ: Popular Books, 1945), 284.

73 Douglas Langston, *God's Willing Knowledge: The Influence of Scotus' Analysis of Omniscience* (University Park, PA: Pennsylvania State University Press, 1986), 18. *Luis de Molina on Divine Foreknowledge* (Part IV of the *Concordia*), trans. Alfred J. Freddoso (Ithaca, NY: Cornell University Press, 1988), 125.

74 *Basic Writings of Saint Thomas Aquinas*, Vol. I: 142 [ST I, Q14, a8].

75 For a more complete treatment of Hartshorne and the concept of middle knowledge, see George W. Shields and Donald Wayne Viney, "The Logic of Future Contingents" in *Process and Analysis: Essays on Whitehead, Hartshorne and the Analytic Tradition*, ed. George W. Shields (Albany: SUNY Press, 2003), 209–46. See also, *Process Studies* 39/1 (2010): Special Focus Section on Eternal Objects and Future Contingents, including essays by George Shields, "Eternal Objects, Middle Knowledge, and Hartshorne: A Response to Malone-France," 149–65, and Donald W. Viney, "Objects, Eternal and Otherwise, and the Process Response to Molinism: Response to Malone-France and Shields," 174–80.

76 Hartshorne, "Are Propositions About the Future True or False?" *Proceedings of the American Philosophical Association, Western Division* (April 20–22, 1939): 26–32.

77 Hartshorne, "Determinate Truths About an Indeterminate Future," *Process Studies* 40/1 (2011): 123

78 That "$p \supset q$" is true when p = T and q = T and that it is false when p = T and q = F is not controversial. It seems counterintuitive, however, to suppose that "$p \supset q$" is true when p = F. But consider: assuming the uncontroversial aspect of the conditional, there are only three other possible truth functional definitions for it and each of them yield manifestly invalid inferences. If one defines "$p \supset q$" as TFTF then a conditional is equivalent to its consequent; if one defines "$p \supset q$" as TFFT, then the conditional is equivalent to the biconditional, "$p \equiv q$"; if one defines "$p \supset q$" as TFFF, then the conditional is equivalent to the conjunction of p and q, "$p \wedge q$".

79 Commenting on the Dickens's quote, Hartshorne wrote, "[The] Dickens quote is perfect. There was a master of language. Will and May are nicely distinguished in ordinary speech." *Charles Hartshorne's Letters to a Young Philosopher*: 39 [Letter of January 9, 1989].

80 Wainwright mistakenly supposes that the mature Hartshorne believed in indeterminate truth values for future contingents. We pass over this mistake since it is not essential to his argument against Hartshorne's view of omniscience. See William J. Wainwright, *Philosophy of Religion* (Belmont, CA: Wadsworth Publishing Company, 1988), 22.

81 Wainwright, *Philosophy of Religion*, 22.

82 Wainwright, *Philosophy of Religion*.

83 Wainwright, *Philosophy of Religion*, 23. Wainwright here cites Jonathan Edwards's *Freedom of the Will*.

84 Lequyer did not miss this way out. In the second part of his *Dialogue of the Predestinate and the Reprobate*, he discusses Christ's prophecies at the Last Supper concerning both Peter and Judas. He speaks of "the foolish words of Bergier" [quoting from the *Dictionaire Théologique* (1788) of Nicolas-Sylvain Bergier (1718–1790)] "God would continually be obliged to change his decrees and form completely contrary ones, because he would encounter obstacles

that he would not have foreseen." *Jules Lequier, Œuvres complètes,* ed. Jean Grenier (Neuchatel, Switzerland: Editions de la Baconnière, 1952), 206–13. See also, *Translation of Works of Jules Lequyer,* edited and with an introduction by Donald Wayne Viney (Lewiston, NY: Edwin Mellen Press, 1998), 135–42. As we noted in Chapter Four, Hartshorne only learned of Lequyer in 1948, which is seven years after *Man's Vision of God* had been published.

85 William James, *The Principles of Psychology,* Vol. I (New York: Dover, 1950 [1890]), 221 [the end of chapter 8, "The Relations of Minds to Other Things"]; Russell, *The Problems of Philosophy* (London: Oxford University Press, 1973 [1912]), chap. 5.

86 See also Hartshorne, "Omniscience" in *An Encyclopedia of Religion,* ed. Vergilius Ferm (New York: Philosophical Library, 1945), 547.

87 We take the presentation and arguments of the last four paragraphs to be an effective reply to William Lane Craig's critique of Hartshorne's position on divine knowledge of future contingents. See, W. L. Craig, "Process Theology's Denial of Divine Foreknowledge," *Process Studies* 16/3 (Fall 1987): 198–202; see also the initial reply to Craig by Donald Wayne Viney, "Does Omniscience Imply Foreknowledge? Craig on Hartshorne," *Process Studies* 18/1 (Spring 1989): 30–37.

88 Whitehead, *Process and Reality,* 351.

89 Whitehead, *Process and Reality,* 23.

90 Hartshorne, "The New Pantheism I," *Christian Register* 115/8 (1936): 119–20; "The New Pantheism II," *Christian Register* 115/9 (1936): 141–43. Concerning the difference between pantheism and panentheism, Hartshorne wrote, "Freed from the one-sided stress on necessity, pantheism becomes what I call panentheism, a doctrine which, in the West especially, has been ignored rather than critically evaluated." Hartshorne, "Tillich and the Nontheological Meaning of Theological Terms" in *Paul Tillich: Retrospect and Future* (Nashville, Abington Press, 1966), 21. Reprinted from *Religion in Life* (Winter 1966).

91 Dombrowski, *Analytic Theism, Hartshorne, and the Concept of God* (Albany: SUNY Press, 1996), 86.

92 "Audience Discussion of 'God as Composer-Director, Enjoyer, and, in a Sense, Player of the Cosmic Drama'," *Process Studies* 30/2 (2001): 258.

438 *Notes to pages 180–186*

93 W. Norris Clarke, "Charles Hartshorne's Philosophy of God: A Thomistic Critique" in CH 108.

94 "Questions addressed to Professor Hartshorne" in *Theology in Crisis: A Colloquium on The Credibility of 'God'* (New Concord, OH: Muskingum College, 1967), 46.

95 In a series of articles, Henry Simoni-Wastila develops a version of Brightman's objection to Hartshorne's views: "Omniscience and the Problem of Radical Particularity: Does God Know How to Ride a Bike?" *International Journal for Philosophy of Religion* 42 (1997): 1–22; "Divine Passibility and the Problem of Radical Particularity: does God Feel Your Pain?" *Religious Studies* 33 (1997): 327–47; "Is Divine Relativity Possible? Charles Hartshorne on God's Sympathy with the World," *Process Studies* 28 (1999): 98–116. For replies to Simoni-Wastila see: Donald Wayne Viney, "What is Wrong with the Mirror Image? A Brief Reply to Simoni-Wastila on the Problem of Radical Particularity," *Process Studies* 29/2 (Fall-Winter 2000): 365–67; Donald Wayne Viney, "Is the Divine Shorn of Its Heart?: Responding to Simoni-Wastila," *American Journal of Theology and Philosophy* 22/2 (May 2001): 155–72; George W. Shields, "Omniscience and Radical Particularity: Reply to Simoni," *Religious Studies* 39/2 (Oct. 2003): 225–33.

96 Charles Hartshorne, "God and the Social Structure of Reality," 24.

97 Hartshorne, "Synthesis as Polydyadic Inclusion: A Reply to Sessions' 'Charles Hartshorne and Thirdness'," *Southern Journal of Philosophy* 14/2 (Summer 1976): 247.

98 Dombrowski, *St. John of the Cross*: 205, note 5.

99 Paul Tillich, *Systematic Theology*, Three volumes in one (Chicago: University of Chicago Press, 1967), v. I, Part II, 237.

100 Hartshorne, "Tillich and the Nontheological Meaning of Theological Terms," 26.

101 Jules Lequier, *Œuvres complètes*, 212.

102 On February 22, 1981, Hartshorne spoke at the First Unitarian Church of Oklahoma City on the subject, "Taking Freedom Seriously," a talk he later presented as a Lowell Lecture in 1983 (Cambridge Forum, taped lecture # 471 (June 25, 1983), 3 Church Street, Cambridge, MA, 02138). After the Oklahoma City presentation, a man put the following question to Hartshorne: "In

How to Think About God, Mortimer Adler speaks of the idea of God as the uncaused cause. How does this relate to your own views?" Hartshorne's response was: "The idea of an uncaused cause is a perfect example of a half-truth parading as the whole truth. A God who loves and is loved by his creatures is anything but unmoved. It is true that God's existence is uncaused, but this does not mean God is *in all respects* uncaused." For Hartshorne's assessment of Adler's philosophy see CAP, chapter 20.

103 The argument given here is a revised version of the one that originally appeared in George Shields, "God, Modality and Incoherence," *Encounter* 44/1 (1983): 27–39.

104 Edwin M. Curley, *Behind the Geometrical Method: A Reading of Spinoza's Ethics* (Princeton, NJ: Princeton University Press, 1988), 41.

105 Although we are using the standard language of "possible world" here, we are not using this term in Alvin Plantinga's metaphysically loaded sense, in which a possible world possesses "bookness"—an exact set of predicates that defines the particular world as the world it is and not some other. Our "possible worlds" are interchangeable with Carnap's notion of possible states or possible state-descriptions as employed in his classic *Meaning and Necessity: A Study in Semantics and Modal Logic* (Chicago: University of Chicago Press, 1947). See also our discussion in the previous chapter under the subheading "Time and Modality."

Chapter Six

1 For example, see the Foreword to George L. Goodwin, *The Ontological Argument of Charles Hartshorne*, American Academy of Religion Dissertation Series, number 20 (Missoula, MT: Scholars Press, 1978), xi

2 *The Collected Papers of Charles Sanders Peirce*, Vol V, 157 ["Some Consequences of the Four Incapacities," para. 265]

3 Basil Mitchell, *The Justification of Religious Belief* (New York: Seabury Press, 1973).

4 Richard Swinburne, *The Existence of God*, 2nd edition (New York: Oxford University Press, 2004). Swinburne's book was originally published in 1979 but in neither of its editions does Swinburne

take notice of Hartshorne's work. Swinburne, like Hartshorne, devotes a lot of writing to the topic of the coherence of theism. See Swinburne's *The Coherence of Theism* (New York: Oxford University Press, 1977).

5	J. L. Mackie, *The Miracle of Theism: Arguments for and against the Existence of God* (New York: Oxford University Press, 1982). Michael Martin, *Atheism: A Philosophical Justification* (Philadelphia: Temple University Press, 1990).

6	The same article appeared the same year in a special issue of *The Monist* 54/2 (April 1970): 159–80. For more on the global argument see Donald Wayne Viney, *Charles Hartshorne and the Existence of God* (Albany: SUNY Press, 1985). See also Part II of Gregory A. Boyd, *Trinity and Process: A Critical Evaluation and Reconstruction of Hartshorne's Di-Polar Theism Towards a Trinitarian Metaphysics* (New York: Peter Lang, 1992). See also Viney's three articles: "How to Argue for God's Existence: Reflections on Hartshorne's Global Argument," *The Midwest Quarterly* 28/1 (Autumn 1986): 34–49; "In Defense of the Global Argument: A Reply to Professor Luft," *Process Studies* 16/4 (Winter 1987): 309–12; and "A Lamp to Our Doubts: Ferré, Hartshorne, and Theistic Arguments" in *Nature, Truth, and Value: Exploring the Thinking of Frederick Ferré,* ed. George Allan and Merle Allshouse (Lanham, MD: Lexington Books, 2005), 255–69.

7	"Questions addressed to Professor Hartshorne," in *Theology in Crisis: A Colloquium on The Credibility of 'God'* (New Concord, OH: Muskingum College, 1967), 44.

8	Charles Hartshorne, "Martin Buber's Metaphysics" in *The Philosophy of Martin Buber,* ed. Paul Arthur Schilpp and Maurice Friedman (La Salle, IL: Open Court, 1967), 64.

9	Hartshorne, "The Formal Validity and Real Significance of the Ontological Argument," *The Philosophical Review* 53/3 (May 1944): 225–45.

10	Malcolm, "Anselm's Ontological Arguments," *The Philosophical Review* 69/1 (January 1960): 41–62.

11	Charles Hartshorne, "The Logic of the Ontological Argument," *The Journal of Philosophy* 58/17 (Aug. 17, 1961): 471–73.

12	Prescott Johnson, "The Ontological Argument in Plato," *The*

Personalist 44 (1963): 24–34.

13 Goodwin, *The Ontological Argument of Charles Hartshorne*, xv.

14 Graham Oppy, *Ontological Arguments and Belief in God* (New York: Cambridge University Press, 1995), 199.

15 Reprinted in *New Essays in Philosophical Theology,* ed. Antony Flew and Alasdair MacIntyre (New York: Macmillan, 1955), 47–67. Hartshorne's criticism led Findlay to the conclusion that "my disproof rested, for its validity, on the acceptance of certain supposedly Kantian premises, which I now do not think acceptable or Kantian at all. I have accordingly become the proponent of an Absolute-theory which has many affinities with the theology of Hartshorne"; in *Studies in the Philosophy of J. N. Findlay,* ed. Robert S. Cohen, Richard M. Martin, and Merold Westphal (Albany: SUNY Press, 1985), 463.

16 David Hume, *Principal Writings on Religion including Dialogues Concerning Natural Religion and The Natural History of Religion,* ed. J. C. A. Gaskin, (London: Oxford University Press, 1993), 147. Hume's ideas are reminiscent of the great skeptical poem, "Hymn of Creation," in Hinduism's *Rig Veda* (10.129), where the gods themselves are said to be later than creation. See A. L. Basham *The Wonder That Was India: A Survey of the Culture of the Indian Sub-Continent Before the Coming of the Muslims* (New York: Grove Press, 1954), 247–48. For a more recent translation see *The Rig Veda: An Anthology,* Wendy Doniger O'Flaherty, ed. and trans. (London: Penguin Books, 1981), 25–26.

17 Hume, *Principal Writings,* 145.

18 Charles Hartshorne, "God and the Social Structure of Reality" in *Theology in Crisis: A Colloquium on The Credibility of 'God'* (New Concord, OH: Muskingum College, 1967), 28.

19 Swinburne considers the order of nature's laws as best explained by the activity of God and as "too big" for science to explain. See Swinburne, *The Existence of God,* 160, 172.

20 Hick's treatment of the argument can be found in the following: "God as Necessary Being," *Journal of Philosophy* 57/22–23 (November 1960): 725–34; Review of Hartshorne's *The Logic of Perfection* in *Theology Today* 20/2 (July 1963): 295–98; "A Critique of the 'Second Argument'" in *The Many-Faced Argument,* ed. John Hick and Arthur

C. McGill (New York: Macmillan, 1967), 341–56; *Arguments for the Existence of God* (New York: Seabury Press, 1971), ch. 6.

21 Hartshorne, "John Hick on Logical and Ontological Necessity," *Religious Studies* 13/2 (June 1977): 155-165.

22 In reply to a question from A. Campbell Garnett, Hartshorne wrote: "'If God exists, he exists noncontingently' I regard as self-contradictory; for the 'if' can only mean that something which could be lacking is required for the existence, while 'noncontingently' means that nothing required for the existence could possibly fail, or have failed to obtain. 'If' refers to a condition, but we are speaking of unconditioned existence"; in *Philosophical Interrogations,* ed. Sydney and Beatrice Rome (New York: Holt, Rinehart and Winston, 1964), 347. Graham Oppy notes that this claim is inconsistent with Hartshorne's use of "God exists strictly implies that God necessarily exists" as a premise in his presentation of the ontological argument in *The Logic of Perfection* (LP 50)—the inconsistency is in the fact that "If God exists, then God exists noncontingently" is deducible from "God exists strictly implies that God necessarily exists." See Oppy's review of Daniel Dombrowski, *Rethinking the Ontological Argument* in *Mind* 117/467 (July 2008): 690–93. We hold that Hartshorne's claim about conditioned existence is correct, but he overstates his case in this instance. First, "if" is incidental to the truth value of the sentence; the conditional in question can easily be changed to a disjunction: "If God exists, then God exists noncontingently" is logically equivalent to "Either God does not exist or God exists noncontingently." Second, Hartshorne says, in the same passage alluded to by Oppy: "The way to insert an 'if' is to say, with Leibniz: If 'God' is logically possible, he necessarily exists." Of course, this is the second premise of the argument we have been examining and was Hartshorne's preferred formal presentation of the argument.

23 Charles Hartshorne, "Grounds for Believing in God's Existence" in *Meaning, Truth, and God,* ed. Leroy S. Rouner (Notre Dame, IN: University of Notre Dame Press, 982), 26.

24 See Hick and McGill, eds., *The Many-Faced Argument,* 22–23.

25 Martin, *Atheism: A Philosophical Justification,* 90.

26 Parodies of theism often flounder and are sunk by failing to think through the implications of the parody. In response to Daniel Dennett's comparison of theism to "Supermanism," Alvin Plantinga

points out that Superman is nothing like God insofar as, despite his considerable powers, he is still a creature with certain limitations. The more powers one gives to the figure of Superman to make him analogous to God, the less he is like Superman and the more he approximates the idea of God, until the two are indistinguishable. As Plantinga notes, the problem of Supermanism is shared by other parodies of theism, as in Flying Spaghetti Monsterism and Tooth Fairyism. See Daniel C. Dennett and Alvin Plantinga, *Science and Religion: Are They Compatible?* (New York: Oxford University Press, 2011), 58. For a humorous presentation of Pastafarianism see Bobby Henderson, *The Gospel of the Flying Spaghetti Monster* (London: HarperCollins, 2006).

27 Max Lerner, ed., *Essential Works of John Stuart Mill* (New York: Bantam Books, 1961), 34 [Part II of the *Autobiography*]; Bertrand Russell, "My Mental Development," in *The Philosophy of Bertrand Russell*, ed. Paul Arthur Schilpp (New York: Tudor Publishing Company, 1944), 8; Daniel Dennett, *Breaking the Spell: Religion as a Natural Phenomenon* (New York: Viking, 2006), 242. See also the appendix to Rebecca Newberger Goldstein's novel, *36 Arguments for God's Existence: A Work of Fiction* (New York: Pantheon Books, 2010), 348.

28 W. Norris Clarke made this point many years ago in "A Curious Blindspot in the Anglo-American Tradition of Anti-Theistic Argument" *The Monist* 54/2 (April 1970): 181–200. Ten years later, William Lane Craig schematized the cosmological arguments of thirteen philosophers, from Plato to Leibniz, some of whom gave more than one version. *None* of these arguments begins from the premise that everything has or must have a cause. See Craig, *The Cosmological Argument from Plato to Leibniz* (London: Macmillan, 1980).

29 William Rowe, "The Ontological Argument" in *Reason and Responsibility*, Joel Feinberg (Encino, CA: Dickenson Publishing, 1978), 8–16.

30 Douglas Walton, "The Circle in the Ontological Argument," *International Journal for the Philosophy of Religion* 9/4 (1978): 193–218. Walton contends that Hartshorne's argument can be reduced to the "quite trivial" argument structure, where p = "God or perfection exists": "$\Box\ p \equiv p, / \sim \Box \sim p$, therefore p" (we alter Walton's modal notation to match our own) (Walton, "Circle," 203).

31 George W. Shields, *The Semantics of Perfection: An Investigation of Theistic Meaning Postulates and Their Justification in the Philosophy of Charles Hartshorne*, Ph. D. Dissertation, The University of Chicago, June 1981, 335 pp. (published on microfilm at the Joseph Regenstein Library of the University of Chicago). See, in particular, Sec. 4.1 "The Modal Formalization of the Ontological Argument," 133–39.

32 Walton's crucial "circularity avoiding" step 9 in his quantificational reconstruction of the argument, namely, $(\exists x)(Ux \wedge Ax)$ (in ordinary language "there exists something in the understanding and in actuality"), is implied by Hartshorne's "necessarily, something actual exists" which is part and parcel of his philosophical assumption of the unique possibility of deity.

33 See also Hartshorne, "Theistic Proofs and Disproofs: The Findlay Paradox" in *Studies in the Philosophy of J. N. Findlay*, ed. Cohen et al., 224–34.

34 *Charles Hartshorne's Letters to a Young Philosopher*, 46 [Letter of Nov. 12, 1991].

35 Goodwin, *The Ontological Argument of Charles Hartshorne*, xi-xviii.

36 Saul A. Kripke, "Semantical Considerations on Modal Logic" in *Reference and Modality*, ed. Leonard Linsky (London: Oxford University Press, 1971), 63–72.

37 It is of interest that Quine commented on Hartshorne's paper, "Grounds for Believing in God's Existence," which he presented at Boston University on October 17, 1979. Leroy Rouner reports that the tête-à-tête between Quine and Hartshorne was congenial. He also says that Hartshorne revised the published version of his paper in light of that conversation. See Leroy S. Rouner, ed., *Meaning, Truth, and God* (University of Notre Dame Press, 1982), 3. See also the published paper in the same volume, 18–21; in the last three pages Hartshorne outlines his differences with Quine, stressing both the reality of *de re* modality and its grounding in temporal process. Hartshorne also devoted a brief chapter in *Creativity in American Philosophy* (1984) to Quine.

38 Hubbeling, "Hartshorne and the Ontological Argument" in PCH: 355–76.

39 Foreword to Donald Wayne Viney, *Charles Hartshorne and the Existence of God* (Albany: SUNY Press, 1985), x.

40 Hartshorne, "John Hick on Logical and Ontological Necessity," 156.

41 R. L. Purtill, "Ontological Modalities," *The Review of Metaphysics* 21/2 (1967): 307.

42 Charles Hartshorne, "Rejoinder to Purtill, *The Review of Metaphysics* 21/2 (1967): 309.

43 Martin, *Atheism: A Philosophical Justification*, 89.

44 Foreword to Viney, *Charles Hartshorne and the Existence of God*, x.

45 Recall Kant's thought-experiment in the Transcendental Aesthetic where he entertains the arbitrary example of an imaginary line that immediately exhibits spatial extension and temporal duration in its imagining—thus space and time are purportedly shown to be *a priori* transcendental characteristics of objectivity, that is, they are characteristics of any object as such. This agrees with Hartshorne's assertion of the experiential establishment of "something spatio-temporal exists."

46 See Whitehead's discussion of Poynting's conservation law in Alfred North Whitehead, *Adventures of Ideas* (New York: Macmillan, 1933), 238 [Part III, Chapter XI, section 16].

47 This is contrary to eternalist views of the whole that deny the extra-mental reality of temporal change, a tacit premise of the argument that was defended earlier in Chapter Three, cf. especially the "Čapek Argument."

48 Milič Čapek has argued effectively that the atomistic materialist conceptuality has changed little from the time of its classical expressions. See his insightful "The Logic of Solid Bodies from Plato to Quine" in his *Bergson and Modern Physics* (Dordrecht: Springer, 1971), 72–82.

49 David Hume's objection in the *Dialogues* that the cosmic identity cannot be mind because the cosmos would then require its own nervous system or brain (which seems nowhere evident), we answered in the previous chapter. However, we note that an important part of the significance of what Hartshorne has called "Whitehead's *revolutionary* concept of prehension" is that mentality can be had without mediation through special organs as in any case of direct prehension.

50 Richard Swinburne, *The Coherence of Theism* (New York: Oxford

University Press, 1977), 101

51 Hartshorne's discussions of the argument from cosmic order within his articles include: "Can There Be Proofs of God's Existence," in *Religious Language and Knowledge,* ed. Robert H. Ayers and William T. Blackstone (Athens: University of Georgia Press, 1972), 62–75; "Grounds for Believing in God's Existence" cited above; "Our Knowledge of God" in *Knowing Religiously,* ed. Leroy S. Rouner (South Bend, IN: University of Notre Dame Press, 1985), 60–61; "Metaphysical and Empirical Aspects of the Idea of God" in *Witness and Existence: Essays in Honor of Schubert M. Ogden,* ed. Philip E. Devenish and George L. Goodwin (University of Chicago Press, 1989), 180–82. See also, Donald Wayne Viney, "A Lamp to Our Doubts: Ferré, Hartshorne, and Theistic Arguments" in *Nature, Truth, and Value: Exploring the Thinking of Frederick Ferré,* ed. George Allan and Merle F. Allshouse (Lanham, MD: Lexington Books, 2005), 255–69.

52 Hartshorne, "Can There Be Proofs of God's Existence," 68–69.

53 Whitehead, *Process and Reality,* 343.

54 Joseph A. Bracken, S.J., *The One in the Many: A Contemporary Reconstruction of the God-World Relationship,* foreward by Philip Clayton (Grand Rapids, MI: William B. Eerdmans, 2001), 219.

55 Bracken, *The One in the Many,* 99.

56 Bracken, *The One in the Many,* 100.

57 Bracken, *The One in the Many,* 102.

58 Bracken, *The One in the Many,* 135–36, cf. 140.

59 Bracken, *The One in the Many,* 173.

60 Bracken, *The One in the Many,* 174.

61 Joseph A. Bracken, "Whitehead and the Critique of Logocentrism" in *Process and Difference,* ed. A. Daniell and C. Keller (Albany: SUNY Press, 2002), 91–110. Bracken's arguments are enhanced by similar interpretive arguments found in Louis Pedraja's "Whitehead, Deconstruction, and Postmodernism" in the same volume.

62 Joseph A. Bracken, "Subjective Immortality in a Neo-Whiteheadian Context" in *World Without End: Christian Eschatology from a Process Perspective,* ed. Joseph A. Bracken (Grand Rapids, MI: William B. Eerdmans 2005), 84, 85.

63 For Hartshorne's thoughts on how his view of God relates to Christian Trinitarian ideas see RSP 169–70.

64 For a formalized version of the epistemic argument see: Billy Joe Lucas, "The Second Epistemic Way" in *Process and Analysis: Whitehead, Hartshorne, and the Analytic Tradition*, ed. George W. Shields, 199–207.

65 Immanuel Kant, *Critique of Pure Reason*, trans. Norman Kemp Smith (London: Macmillan, 1933), 266–70 [A249, A252].

66 Hartshorne's response to *Did Jesus Rise From the Dead?* 140.

67 Chaim Stern, ed. *Gates of Prayer: The New Union Prayerbook* (New York: Central Conference of American Rabbis, 1994), 193.

68 Russell, "A Free Man's Worship" in *Why I Am Not a Christian and Other Essays on Religion and Related Subjects* (New York: Simon and Schuster, 1957), 107.

69 Charles Hartshorne, "Science as the Search for the Hidden Beauty of the World," in *The Aesthetic Dimension of Science*, 1980 Nobel Conference, Number 16, ed. Dean W. Curtin (New York: Philosophical Library, 1982), 95.

70 Steven Weinberg, *Dreams of a Final Theory* (New York: Vintage, 1993), 250.

71 Alfred North Whitehead, "Immortality" in *Essays in Science and Philosophy* (New York: Greenwood Pub., 1968), 94 [Section XVII].

72 Hartshorne, "God as Composer," *Process Studies* 30/2 (2001): 242–53.

73 Hartshorne, "A Philosophy of Death" in *Philosophical Aspects of Thanatology*, vol. 2, ed. Florence M. Hetzler and A. H. Kutscher (New York: MSS Information Corp., 1978): 86.

74 Hartshorne, "Theistic Proofs and Disproofs," 230.

75 For two treatments of the book of Job that are consistent with Hartshorne's views see Katharine Dell, *Shaking a Fist at God: Struggling with the Mystery of Undeserved Suffering* (Liguori, MO: Triumph Books, 1997) and Harold S. Kushner, *The Book of Job: When Bad Things Happened to a Good Person* (New York: Schocken Books, 2012).

76 The one mention of Job in the New Testament is James 5:11 where he is used as an example of one who perseveres through suffering.

77   In later writings, especially in Christianity, the Adversary takes on a cosmic role as the leader of the fallen angels and as the wicked ruler of this world. The Hebrew "satan" comes to be used as a proper name, Satan. However, as *The Jewish Study Bible* explains, the Hebrew "ha," in "ha-satan," is the definite article and cannot precede a proper noun; see *The Jewish Study Bible*, ed. Adele Berlin and Marc Zvi Brettler (New York: Oxford University Press, 2004), 1506.

78   Cobb, *God and the World* (Philadelphia: Westminster Press, 1969), 94. For more on this subject see Donald Wayne Viney, "Evolution and the Goodness of God: A Hartshornean Perspective" in *Philosophical Thinking and the Religious Context*, ed. Brendan Sweetman (New York: Bloomsbury, 2013), 80–97.

79   Marilyn McCord Adams, *Horrendous Evils and the Goodness of God* (New York: Cornell University Press, 1999).

80   Hartshorne's comment on a paper by A. Campbell Garnett in *Approaches to World Peace: A Symposium*, ed. Lyman Bryson, Louis Finkelstein, and Robert M. Maciever (New York: Conference on Science, Philosophy, and Religion in their Relation to the Democratic Way of Life, 1944), 597.

81   Jeff Shaara, *Rise to Rebellion* (New York: Ballantine Books, 2001).

82   Jeff Shaara, *The Glorious Cause* (New York: Ballantine Books, 2002).

83   Donald Wayne Viney, "Process, Parturition, and Perfect Love: Diotima's Rather Non-Platonic Metaphysic of *Eros*" in *The Many Facets of Love: Philosophical Explorations*, ed. Thomas Jay Oord (New Castle, UK: Cambridge Scholars Pub., 2007), 41–49.

84   Pierre Teilhard de Chardin, *Construire la Terre : extraits d'œuvres inédites* (Paris: Editions de Seuil, 1958).

85   Charles Hartshorne, "Mysticism and Rationalistic Metaphysics," *The Monist* 59/4 (October 1976), 469.

86   Henry W. Johnston, "Review of *The Logic of Perfection*," *The Journal of Philosophy* 60/21 (1963): 471.

87   Paul Tillich, *Systematic Theology*, Vol. 1, Part II (Chicago: University of Chicago Press, 1965), 187–88. In a letter to Robert S. Corrington dated July 10, 1992, Hartshorne mentions the distinction between *me on* and *ouk on* but seems to find no key in the distinction to unlocking a deeper meaning of "nothingness" than the sort that

presupposes an already existing reality. See: https://users.drew.
edu/rcorring/downloads/APPRAISAL%20&%20CRITIQUE%20
COPYRIGHT.pdf, accessed June 13, 2017.

88 Tillich, *Systematic Theology*, Vol. 1, 189.

89 We would want to say that "by transitivity Berdyaev's *meontic*
nonbeing is to be correlated with *Whitehead* and Hartshorne's
Creativity," but there is a somewhat technical wrinkle. At WP
187, Hartshorne suggests that Berdyaev's nonbeing has its closest
correlate in Whitehead's doctrine of "pure potentials" as the
ontological intermediaries between full actuality and sheer nothing.
But Hartshorne suspects that Whitehead's infinite multiplicity
of eternal objects, complete in God's primordial envisagement,
is "too Platonic" for the Russian philosopher, since Berdyaev
complains *contra* Plato that creation results "in the production of
new images" rather than the realization of some eternal pattern
(for textual evidence Hartshorne cites Berdyaev's *The Destiny of
Man* [New York: Charles Scribner and Sons, 1939], 97). Thus,
on Hartshorne's interpretation, for Berdyaev as for Hartshorne,
creativity is *the* transcendental eternal object with everlasting and
ever-growing finite exemplifications, under which the traditional
transcendentals (being, unity, goodness, beauty, affectivity) are to
be subsumed (cf. IO 91). If these nuanced distinctions are correct,
then Berdyaev's concept of *freedom* is to be closely correlated with
Whitehead's doctrine of creativity, but *meontic* nonbeing is more
nearly equivalent to Hartshorne's concept of creativity, specifically
in its relation to the notion of eternal objects. Thus, we say more
cautiously that "Berdyaev's concept of *meontic* nonbeing is to be
correlated with Hartshorne's concept of creativity."

90 Jurgen Moltmann, *God in Creation: A New Theology of Creation
and the Spirit of God–The Gifford Lectures* (San Francisco: Harper
& Row, 1985), see esp. 14–17.

91 Karl Barth, *Church Dogmatics*, Vol. III/3. *The Doctrine of Creation*.
Trans. G. W. Bromiley and E. J. Ehrlich (Edinburgh: T & T Clark,
1960). All references in the paragraphs on Barth are to the Bromiley-
Ehrlich edition.

92 Among these multiple strands, David Ray Griffin boldly attempts
an interpretation of Barth in which he (Barth) would reject, with
process philosophers, the idea that an omnipotent being could

unilaterally prevent all evils from occurring. This is because, for Barth, God's omnipotent "alien work"—the non-willing of nothingness that paradoxically actualizes it and thus destructively seduces finite creatures—is a necessary, intrinsic feature of God's nature. At least sometimes, Barth seems to suggest, although without clearly declaring it to be so, that with respect to this alien work, "God could not help it." Griffin concludes, however, that this strand of thought stands in tension with other strands and therefore it simply is "difficult to decide what Barth's true position is" (172). (David R. Griffin, *God, Power, and Evil: A Process Theodicy* (Philadelphia: The Westminster Press, 1976), 172 [ch. 12 "Barth: Much Ado About Nothing," 150–73].

93 Of course, entire volumes have explored comparisons between Barth and Hartshorne such as Colin E. Gunton's *Becoming and Being: The Doctrine of God in Charles Hartshorne and Karl Barth,* 2nd Ed. (Eugene, OR: Wipf & Stock, 2001). (The first edition, in the Oxford Theological Monograph Series, was published by Oxford University Press in 1978.) While Gunton is rather severely critical of Hartshorne's perspective, he nonetheless finds surprising affinities between Barth and Hartshorne's doctrines of God, focused in good measure on their common approval of a dynamic, temporalistic conception—the biblical notion of "the living God." For a critique of Gunton's objections to Hartshorne, see Daniel Dombrowski's "Method and Polar Equality in Dipolar Theism" in his *Analytic Theism, Hartshorne, and the Concept of God* (Albany: SUNY Press, 1996). George Shields argues that Gunton misunderstands Hartshorne's conception of divine agency as well as the "inductive" side of Hartshorne's so-called "rationalism," and most importantly misunderstands the proper supplementary relation between Hartshorne's analogies and his direct arguments for theistic "meaning postulates." See Shields, *The Semantics of Perfection,* esp. Section 3.3.2: "An Active God," 91–110. Gunton replied to his critics in the 2001 2nd edition.

Barth's position obviously and acutely raises the question of Hartshorne's relation to the field of Christology. Hartshorne never attempted a Christology, although he remarks with a spirit of openness "nor do I wish to criticize any" ("A Philosopher's Assessment of Christianity" in *Religion and Culture: Essays in Honor of Paul Tillich,* ed. W. Leibrecht ([New York: Harper &

Row, 1959], 179). Of course, as we have mentioned previously, he has much to say about Jesus and the event of the Cross as "the supreme symbol" of God's suffering love. Given such implicit Christological material, we believe that a full-bodied Christology consistent with neoclassical philosophy is perfectly possible, and indeed has been in fact attempted by, among others, Schubert Ogden and Ralph James as well as by David Griffin and John Cobb (albeit, in the case of Griffin and Cobb, with Whiteheadian emendations related to the doctrine of eternal objects). Notwithstanding, Barth's approach to nothingness and the problem of evil involves a Christocentric triumphalism—a *final* overcoming of *all* evil that has been accomplished *now* and that makes all "tragedy" apparent only— that is foreign to Hartshorne's ultimately melioristic-pragmatic stance that embraces the ever-present and ongoing potential for tragedy in both God and the creatures, even while also embracing an everlasting, infinite beauty in the divine life. Despite this, it is arguable that Hartshorne shares the *motives and values* that inform Barth's soteriological universalism (the theological doctrine that all humanity is ultimately to be saved). Moreover, as Ogden has observed, "Hartshorne endorses the motives behind Karl Barth in urging the *analogia fides* against the *analogia entis* of traditional philosophical theology," S. M. Ogden, "Bultmann's De-mythologizing and Hartshorne's Dipolar Theism" in *Process and Divinity: The Hartshorne Festschrift*, ed. Eugene Freeman (LaSalle, IL: Open Court, 1964), 509. See Schubert Ogden, *The Reality of God and Other Essays* (New York: Harper & Row, 1963), esp. ch. 6, "What Sense Does It Make to Say, 'God Acts in History'?" and ch. 7, "What Does It Mean to Affirm 'Jesus Christ is Lord'?" and his later *The Point of Christology* (San Francisco: Harper & Row, 1982); Ralph E. James's "Jesus Christ: An Actual Occasion" in his *The Concrete God: A New Beginning for Theology—The Thought of Charles Hartshorne* (Indianapolis: Bobbs-Merrill, 1967), ch. 8; David Ray Griffin, *A Process Christology* (Philadelphia: The Westminster Press, 1973; reprinted by University Press of America, 1990); John B. Cobb, Jr., *Christ in a Pluralistic Age* (Philadelphia: Westminster Press, 1975; Wipf & Stock reprint, 1999). Hartshorne has also strongly informed the work of feminist environmental theologian Carol P. Christ. Among other works see her *She Who Changes: Re-Imagining the Divine in the World* (New York: Palgrave Macmillan, 2003). Also, Marjorie Suchocki presents a lucid yet richly poetic and detailed

Christology and ecclesiology that is well-informed by Whitehead and Hartshorne in her *God, Christ, Church: A Practical Guide to Process Theology* (New York: Crossroads Publishing, 1992). See also our discussion of Hartshorne's relation to Suchocki's eschatology in Chapter Four.

94 See, for example, John B. Cobb's careful and detailed study of Barth in *Living Options in Protestant Theology: A Survey of Methods* (Philadelphia: The Westminster Press, 1962). Cobb observes that "Barth is often wrong on matters that can be more or less settled by [biblical] scholarship" and that "most biblical scholars read these accounts differently from Barth," 191 and 193, respectively. Barth is unmoved by such criticism as he holds that most contemporary biblical scholars are bringing in presuppositions of secular modernity that are alien to the scriptural witness. We view this response as circular. It should be recognized that everyone brings a hermeneutical *fragestellung*, "a way of framing the question of the text," that is never free of presuppositions.

95 Heidegger, "What is Metaphysics?" in *Existence and Being*, ed. Werner Brock (Chicago: Henry Regnery, 1949), 330: "For Nothing is the negation (*Vereinung*) of the totality of what is: that which is absolutely not." An alternative interpretation of this passage consistent with the view that Heidegger's "the Nothing" is *meontic* rather than *oukontic* in nature runs as follows: "No-thing" is not itself a "thing" (that is, an ontic being in space and time), and further it is that which *exists* "absolutely not" in the peculiar sense of the primordial meaning of *existere* or literally "standing out," which can be said only of ontic beings. No-thing thus stands in opposition to the "totality of what is" in the sense that No-thing is categorically never ontic unlike each member of the totality or for that matter any aggregation of ontic entities. As such No-thing taken as *meontic* potency is inexhaustible, infinite. As Heidegger says in his study of Nietzsche, Being equated with No-thing is both "utterly most void and *most abundant*" (M. Heidegger, *Nietzsche*, ed. and trans. David F. Krell. [San Francisco: HaperCollins, 1979], 193, our emphasis). For more on this view of Heidegger as well as Gilles Deleuze's sympathetic account of Bergson's argument for the concept of general non-being as a "false problem," see George Shields, "The Return of Radical Theology: A Critical Examination of Peterson and Zbaraschuk, eds., *Resurrecting the Death of God*,"

Process Studies 43/2 (Fall/Winter 2014): 29–46.

96 See, for example, Martin Heidegger, *Gesamtausgabe* I: 1977 *Vier Seminare* (Frankfurt: Verlag Vittorio Klostermann, 2005), 101: "Being:Nothing:Same"

97 Takeo Tanaka, "From a Buddhist Point of View" in *John Cobb's Theology in Process,* ed. David Ray Griffin and Thomas J. J. Altizer (Philadelphia: Westminster Press, 1977), 99–111.

98 Tanaka, "From a Buddhist Point of View," 108.

99 Tanaka, "From a Buddhist Point of View," 107.

100 Tanaka, "From a Buddhist Point of View," 108.

101 John Cobb, "Response to Tanaka" in *John Cobb's Theology in Process:* 178.

102 Jean-Paul Sartre, *L'être et le néant: essai d'ontologie phénoménologique,* édition corrigé (Paris: Éditions Gallimard, 2009), 665. See also Thomas Baldwin's lucid essay "Sartre" in *The Oxford Companion to Philosophy,* ed. Ted Honderich (Oxford: Oxford University Press, 1995).

103 Jean-Paul Sartre, *L'être et le néant,* 57.

104 Jean-Paul Sartre, "The Unreality of the Esthetic Object" in *Contemporary Aesthetics,* ed. Matthew Lipman (Boston: Allyn and Bacon, 1973), 148–54. (Excerpt from the English translation of Sartre's *L'imaginaire,* entitled *The Psychology of Imagination* [New York: Philosophical Library, 1951].)

105 Sartre, "The Unreality of the Esthetic Object," 153.

106 Sartre, "The Unreality of the Esthetic Object."

Chapter Seven

1 Among the important works of the "four horsemen" of the new atheism are: Sam Harris, *The End of Faith: Religion, Terror, and the Future of Reason* (New York: W. W. Norton, 2004) and *Letter to a Christian Nation* (New York: Knopf, 2006); Richard Dawkins, *The God Delusion* (Boston: Houghton Mifflin, 2006) but see also Dawkins's, *The Blind Watchmaker: How the Evidence of Evolution Reveals a Universe Without Design* (New York: W. W. Norton, 1986); Daniel Dennett, *Breaking the Spell: Religion as a Natural Phenomenon*

Notes to pages 247–248

(New York: Viking, 2006) and his earlier book *Darwin's Dangerous Idea: Evolution and the Meanings of Life* (New York: Touchstone, 1995); Christopher Hitchens, *god is not Great: How Religion Poisons Everything* (New York: Twelve, 2007) and the book of writings he edited, *The Portable Atheist: Essential Readings for the Nonbeliever* (Philadelphia: Da Capo Press, 2007).

2   For example, Victor Stenger, *God the Failed Hypothesis: How Science Shows That God Does Not Exist* (Amherst, NY: Prometheus Books, 2007) and Stenger, *The New Atheism: Taking a Stand for Science and Reason* (Amherst, NY: Prometheus Books, 2009). See also John W. Loftus, *Why I Became an Atheist: A Former Preacher Rejects Christianity* (Amherst, NY: Prometheus Books, 2008) and his *The Outsider Test for Faith: How to Know Which Religion is True* (Amherst, NY: Prometheus Books, 2013) and finally, his *Unapologetic: Why Philosophy of Religion Must End* (Durham, NC: Pitchstone Publishing, 2016). Others that could be included in the ranks of the new atheists are Peter Atkins, Alex Rosenberg, A. C. Grayling, Michel Onfray, and Jerry A. Coyne. Lawrence M. Krauss, E. O. Wilson, Steven Weinberg, and Stephen Fry should be included, at least as sympathetic bystanders.

The fifty-two page appendix of Rebecca Goldstein's novel *36 Arguments for the Existence of God* (New York: Pantheon, 2010), which states and refutes thirty-six theistic arguments, brims with new atheist ideas about what constitute theistic arguments. The general quality of argument is illustrated in the fact that she presents Anselm's argument in its weakest (non-modal) form, and that she presents the cosmological argument as proceeding from the premise that everything has a cause which, as we saw in the previous chapter, no defender of the argument has ever used as a premise.

3   The article by Dawkins that Hartshorne mentioned is R. Dawkins and M. Dawkins, "Decisions and the Uncertainty of Behavior," *Behavior* 45 (1973): 83–103. Hartshorne also mentions this article in his article "Physics and Psychics: The Place of Mind in Nature" in *Mind in Nature: Essays on the Interface of Science and Philosophy,* ed. John B. Cobb, Jr. and David Ray Griffin (Washington, D.C.: University Press of America, 1977), 94.

4   Dawkins, *The God Delusion,* 5, 116–17, 322.

5   Richard Dawkins, "Militant Atheism" (Ted Talk, 2002), http://

www.ted.com/index.php/talks/view/id/113

6   Charles Hartshorne, "Response to Zycnski," *Process Studies* 40/1 (Spring/Summer 2011): 149.

7   Donald W. Viney, "Charles Hartshorne," *Dictionary of Unitarian Universalist Biography* (July 15, 2002), http://uudb.org/articles /charleshartshorne.html.

8   Charles Hartshorne, "The Ethics of Contributionism" in *Responsibilities to Future Generations: Environmental Ethics,* ed. Ernest Patridge (Buffalo, NY: Prometheus Books, 1981), 106.

9   Hartshorne heard a lecture by Russell at Harvard, and he had several conversations with him from October 1938 until March 1939 when Russell was at Chicago (DL 311–14).

10   Charles Hartshorne, "Darwin and Some Philosophers," *Process Studies* 30/2 (2001): 276–88.

11   Hartshorne was also quick to mention those scientists whose philosophical ideas agreed with his own. Topping the list were Peirce and Whitehead on the subjects of relations, affective qualities, indeterminism, and, to some extent, God. Others that Hartshorne mentioned who held one or more of these positions in common with him include William James, L. T. Troland, Clerk Maxwell, J. Willard Gibbs, and Sewell Wright. He credited Gustav Fechner with the idea of a self-surpassing deity.

12   Charles Hartshorne, "An Open Letter to Carl Sagan," *The Journal of Speculative Philosophy* 5/4 (1991): 227–32, and "Three Important Scientists on Mind, Matter, and the Metaphysics of Religion," *The Journal of Speculative Philosophy* 8/3 (1994): 211–27. Sagan wrote a gracious note, dated February 27, 1992, thanking Hartshorne for the first article (on file at the Claremont School of Theology at the Center for Process Studies in the Hartshorne Archives in "Professional Correspondence to Hartshorne" #1155). Hartshorne's response, dated 1/23/1995, is in "Professional Correspondence from Hartshorne," #186.

13   Hartshorne, "Three Important Scientists," 226.

14   "A Hundred Years of Thinking about God: A Philosopher Soon to be Rediscovered" [Interview by Greg Easterbrook], *U.S. News and World Report,* February 23, 1998, pp. 61 and 65. See also Easterbrook, *Beside Still Waters: Searching for Meaning in an Age of Doubt* (New

York: William Morrow and Company, Inc., 1998).

15 A sampling of the anti-new atheist literature includes Thomas Crean, *God is No Delusion: a Refutation of Richard Dawkins* (San Francisco: Ignatius Press, 2007); Gregory E. Ganssle, *A Reasonable God: Engaging the New Face of Atheism* (Waco, TX: Baylor University Press, 2009); John F. Haught, *God and the New Atheism: A Critical Response to Dawkins, Harris, and Hitchens* (Louisville, KY: Westminster John Knox Press, 2008); Eric Reitan, *Is God a Delusion? A Reply to Religion's Cultured Despisers* (Malden, MA: Wiley-Blackwell, 2009); John C. Lennox, *Gunning for God: Why the New Atheists are Missing the Target* (Oxford: Lion Books, 2011); David Bentley Hart, *Atheist Delusions: The Christian Revolution and its Fashionable Enemies* (New Haven: Yale University Press, 2009); Jonathan Sacks, *The Great Partnership: Science Religion, and the Search for Meaning* (New York: Schocken Books, 2011). For criticisms of the new atheists from an atheistic perspective, see Scott F. Aikin and Robert B. Talisse, *Reasonable Atheism: A Moral Case for Respectful Disbelief* (Amherst, NY: Prometheus, 2011), see esp. 67–94. A volume that includes criticisms from theists, atheists, and agnostics is *The New Atheism and Its Critics, Midwest Studies in Philosophy*, XXXVII, ed. Peter A. French and Howard K. Wettstein (Boston: Wiley Periodicals, 2013).

16 James McBain, Review of *The God Delusion, The Midwest Quarterly* 48/4 (Summer 2007): 611–15. In the same number of the journal see Donald Viney's review of *The God Delusion*, 602–05.

17 Andrew Johnson, "An Apology for the 'New Atheism'," *International Journal for the Philosophy of Religion* 73 (2013): 5–28.

18 We are thinking particularly of Dennett's public exchange with Alvin Plantinga in *Science and Religion: Are they Compatible?* (New York: Oxford University Press, 2011). A. C. Grayling discusses Plantinga in *The God Argument: The Case Against Religion and for Humanism* (New York: Bloomsbury, 2013), 88–93; as we note below, however, Graying privileges fundamentalism as the most authentic expression of religion.

19 Harris, *The End of Faith*, 21.

20 Grayling, *The God Argument*, 14.

21 Dawkins, *The God Delusion*, 286; see also Harris, *The End of Faith*, 20.

22 Harris, *The End of Faith*, 46, 52–53

23 Kathleen C. Boone, *The Bible Tells Them So: The Discourse of Protestant Fundamentalism* (Albany: SUNY Press, 1989), 29 and 117.

24 Opposition to evolutionary theory is not solely an American phenomenon. See the excellent article by Stefaan Blancke, Hans Henrik Hjermitslev, John Braeckman, and Peter C. Kjærgaard, "Creationism in Europe: Facts, Gaps, and Prospects," *Journal of the American Academy of Religion* 81/4 (December 2013): 996–1028.

25 Harris, *The End of Faith*, 17; See also *Letter to a Christian Nation*, viii and 3.

26 Christian authors of antiquity generally accepted that the earth is spherical, stationary, and is located at the center of the cosmos. See Francis S. Betten, "The Knowledge of the Sphericity of the Earth During the Earlier Middle Ages," *The Catholic Historical Review* 3/1 (April 1923): 74–90.

27 George Karamanolis is particularly good on this point where Origen is concerned. See his book, *The Philosophy of Early Christianity* (Bristol, CT: Acumen, 2013): 57–58.

28 Augustine, *The Literal Meaning of Genesis*, in two volumes, trans. John Hammond Taylor, S. J., (New York: Newman Press, 1982), vol. I: 43 (1.19.39). Augustine did not foresee that science might have something to say about history and about the past. Thus, he accepted the biblical saga from Adam and Eve to the Tower of Babel as genuine history. For an account of the difficulties that science poses for the concept of a literal Eden and how Christians have confronted the difficulties, see Karl W. Giberson, *Saving the Original Sinner: How Christians Have Used the Bible's First Man to Oppress, Inspire, and Make Sense of the World* (Boston: Beacon Press, 2015).

29 Maurice A. Finocchiaro, *The Galileo Affair: A Documentary History* (Berkeley: University of California Press, 1989), 96. William of Conches (1085–1154) said something very similar to Baronio: "The authors of Truth are silent on matters of natural philosophy not because these matters are against the faith, but because they have little to do with the upholding of such faith, which is what those authors were concerned with." Quoted in James Hannam, *God's Philosophers: How the Medieval World Laid the Foundations of Modern Science* (London: Icon Books, 2009), 63. For Galileo's views on the Bible and science see his 1615 letter to the Grand Duchess

Christina of Lorraine in Finocchaiaro, *The Galileo Affair*, 87–118.
In the same volume, see also pp. 49–54.

30 Jerome J. Langford, *Galileo, Science and the Church*, 3rd ed. (Ann
    Arbor: University of Michigan Press, 1992 [originally published by
    Desclée in 1966]), 53.

31 Steven Weinberg, "A Designer Universe?" http://www.physlink
    .com/Education/essay_ weinberg.cfm. Also quoted by Stenger, *The
    New Atheism*, 29.

32 Edward O. Wilson, *The Meaning of Human Existence* (New York:
    Liveright Publishing Corporation, 2014), 154.

33 Adolf Hitler could not have been more Orwellian; it was typical of
    der Führer to pander to different audiences depending on what he
    thought would most persuade them. Richard Weikart, in his study
    of Hitler's religion, is surely correct to speak of Hitler as a "religious
    chameleon" who gave no more than lip service to religious views.
    See Richard Weikart, *Hitler's Religion: The Twisted Beliefs that Drove
    the Third Reich* (Washington, DC: Regnery History, 2016).

34 Hitchens notes the grim reality of the complicity of religious people
    and organizations in secular tyranny during World War II. *See god
    is not Great*, 235–42. This does not, however, justify the conflation
    of "tyranny" and "religion" or in claiming that faith is inherently
    blind.

35 Wilson, *The Meaning of Human Existence*, 154. Wilson also speaks
    of "religionlike political ideology" (152). Hartshorne also speaks of
    communism as a religion. He does not, however, make the mistake
    of supposing that religion is necessarily dogmatic or based merely
    on unthinking adherence to a creed.

36 Harris, *The End of Faith*, 79. On the question whether Marxism is a
    religion, consider the contrasting views expressed in two editions of
    the same book. A Soviet publishing house issued *Marx and Engels
    On Religion* (Moscow: Progress Publishers, 1957). In the introduction
    (by an unknown author) one reads: "The world outlook founded by
    Marx and Engels is based on the objective laws of the development
    of nature and society. It rests on facts provided by science and
    is radically opposed to religion" (9). The same book (minus the
    Soviet editor's introduction) was published in 1964 by Schocken
    Books with an introduction by Reinhold Niebuhr. According to
    Niebuhr, "Marx, as an empiricist, would have been just another

learned man. As an apocalyptic dogmatist, he became the founder of a new religion, whose writings would be quoted as parts of a new sacred canon" (xii).

37 Harris, *The End of Faith*, 65.

38 *The End of Faith*, 13, 22.

39 *Harris, Letter to a Christian Nation*, 83.

40 The best source on liberal theologies in America is Gary Dorrien's impressive trilogy, all published by Westminster John Knox Press: *The Making of American Liberal Theology: Imagining Progressive Religion, 1805-1900* (2001); *The Making of American Liberal Theology: Idealism, Realism, and Modernity, 1900-1950* (2003); *The Making of American Liberal Theology: Crisis, Irony, and Postmodernity, 1950-2005* (2006).

41 For example, see Hartshorne's letter opposing a bill introduced in Texas to require that creation-science be taught in public schools, "Creation Science," *Austin American Statesman*, Saturday, May 23, 1981. In the same newspaper, and on the subject of creation-science, see Hartshorne's letters of February 1, 1984, and May 11, 1989. Hartshorne's views on abortion are most clearly stated in his "Concerning Abortion: An Attempt at a Rational View," *The Christian Century* 98 (1981): 42–45, reprinted in *Hartshorne, A New World View: Essays by Charles Hartshorne* ed. Herbert F. Vetter, Cambridge, MA: Harvard Square Library, 2007). His letters to the editor of the *Austin-American Statesman* concerning abortion appeared in the editions of April 26, 1971, February 6, 1973, February 15, 1973, February 26, 1973, September 17, 1990, and July 5, 1991.

42 For a more thorough treatment of revelation based on the same general perspective as that of Hartshorne, see James A. Keller, *Problems of Evil and the Power of God* (Burlington, VT: Ashgate Publishing Company, 2007), ch. 6.

43 Henri Bergson, *The Two Sources of Morality and Religion,* trans. R. Ashley Audra and Cloudesley Brereton with the assistance of W. Horsfall Carter (Garden City, NY: Doubleday, 1954 [French edition, 1932]).

44 Carl Sagan's 1992 letter to Hartshorne mentions *Philosophers Speak of God,* although he misremembers its purpose in calling it a "classification of the world's religions" (see note 12).

45 Reese makes clear that he served primarily as Hartshorne's assistant. According to Reese, the University of Chicago Press invited Hartshorne to do an anthology of philosophical theism, and Hartshorne brought Reese on board for the project. Reese, who was Hartshorne's graduate student at the time, wrote: "I have not come upon a single ringing sentence in the material I contributed. All of the ringing sentences of the book belong to Professor Hartshorne" (PCH 187).

46 Examples: John Duns Scotus (IO, ch. 9), William of Ockham (IO ch. 9), Jonathan Edwards (CAP ch. 2), G. W. F. Hegel (IO ch. 17), Søren Kierkegaard (IO ch. 18), Bertrand Russell (BH ch. 13; IO ch. 22), John Dewey (BH ch. 3; CAP 8), Paul Tillich (CAP ch. 23), Ludwig Wittgenstein (IO ch. 25), the Logical Positivists (BH ch. 16), John Wisdom (LP ch. 5), and Jean-Paul Sartre (IO ch. 28).

47 Stenger, *God: The Failed Hypothesis*, 112.

48 Pascal, *Œuvres complètes* (Paris: Éditions de Seuil, 1963), 618.

49 "An Interview with Charles Hartshorne," conducted by Santiago Sia, *Miltown Studies* 4 (1979): 2.

50 Dawkins, *The God Delusion*, 250.

51 Charles Hartshorne, "Tolerance Test," *Austin-American Statesman*, June 18, 1990.

52 For more on this see Donald Wayne Viney, "Relativizing the Classical Tradition: Hartshorne's History of God" in *Models of God and Alternative Ultimate Realities* ed. Jeanine Diller and Asa Kasher (Dordrecht: Springer 2013), 63–79.

53 Loftus, *Unapologetic: Why Philosophy of Religion Must End*. In one of the rare references to Hartshorne in new atheist literature, Loftus caricatures Hartshorne as someone who does not understand that his own theology is based on blind faith and special pleading (58). Those who have followed our exposition of Hartshorne will recognize Loftus's statement as an amateurish misrepresentation. Learning from Hartshorne would also cure Loftus of his comparison of the concept of God to the concept of fairies.

54 For more on the case of Antony Flew, see Yujin Nagasawa, *The Existence of God: A Philosophical Introduction* (London: Routledge, 2011), 46–50.

55 Charles Hartshorne and Paul Weiss, eds., *Collected Papers of Charles*

Sanders Peirce, Volume I, (Cambridge, MA: Harvard University Press), 56 [1.135].

56 Dawkins, *The God Delusion,* 31. See also Dan Barker, *God: The Most Unpleasant Character in All Fiction,* foreword by Richard Dawkins (New York: Sterling, 2016). Throughout his book, Barker uses the expression that we find problematic, "the God of the Old Testament" (e.g., 4, 7, 8). Using passages from the Gospel of John, where Jesus is strongly identified as divine, Barker concludes, "It follows that every single attribute Richard Dawkins used to describe the fictional God of the Old Testament applies equally to Jesus, because he claimed he was the God of the Old Testament. We can therefore say: the Jesus of the New Testament is arguably the most unpleasant character in all fiction . . . [etc., quoting from Dawkins's list]," 290.

57 Dawkins, *The God Delusion,* 237. It is a mainstay of modern scholarship that even a single book may have had more than one author whose theological perspectives are at odds.

58 Abraham J. Heschel, *Between God and Man: An Interpretation of Judaism,* selected and ed. Fritz Rothschild (New York: Free Press, 1959), 248.

59 Harry Emerson Fosdick, *A Guide to Understanding the Bible: The Development of Ideas within the Old and New Testaments* (New York: Harper & Brothers, 1938): 122–23. This book outlines the varieties of biblical views on various topics. Even if one questions Fosdick's thesis of a more or less progressive development of biblical ideas, he provides more than enough documentation to refute the Dawkinsian assumption of a single literary character of "God" or of ideas of "right and wrong" in the Old Testament. For a typical example of contemporary scholarship that emphasizes the development in the concept of God through an examination of the names used for God see Howard Avruhm Addison, "The God of Israel" in *Etz Hayim: Study Companion,* ed. Jacob Blumenthal and Janet L. Liss (Philadelphia: Jewish Publication Society, 2005), 75–84.

60 Judah Goldin, ed., *The Living Talmud: The Wisdom of the Fathers* (New York: New American Library, 1957), 46f (Pirkei Avot, ch. 1). The older formula would have been "Torah, temple service, and *chesed,*" but rabbinic tradition clarifies that, with the destruction of the temple, prayer is a superior service to God. The Talmud also

makes clear the rabbinic understanding of sacrifice. When Rabbi Joshua laments the destruction of the temple, Rabban Johanan replies, "Be not grieved we have another atonement as effective as this. And what is it? It is acts of lovingkindness (*gemilut hasadim*), as it is said, 'For I desire mercy not sacrifice' (Hosea 6.6)"

61   Sacks, *The Great Partnership*, 9. For the quote from the Talmud see Goldin, ed., *The Living Talmud*, 216 (Pirkei Avot, ch. 5).

62   According to Beal, "The cultural icon of the Bible represents religious faith as what closes the book on questions about the meaning and purpose of life." Beal proposes instead that "The Bible is not a book of answers but a library of questions." Timothy Beal, *The Rise and Fall of the Bible: The Unexpected History of An Accidental Book* (Boston: Mariner, 2011): quotes from pp. 5 and 175.

63   This is H. Richard Niebuhr's hermeneutic of scripture found in his classic *The Meaning of Revelation* and underpinning his *Radical Monotheism and Western Culture*. Niebuhr's approach allows one to avoid the pernicious—and subtly anti-Semitic—contrast between the angry God of the Old Testament and the loving God of the New Testament. The contrast can be traced to the early second century Marcion of Sinope, who proposed a Christian canon that omitted the specifically Jewish parts of Scripture since he thought that the God of Jesus and the God of Moses were different beings with different natures.

64   *The Jewish Study Bible*, Second Edition, eds. Adele Berlin and Marc Zvi Brettler (Oxford University Press, 2014), 1203.

65   Duncan Black MacDonald, *The Hebrew Philosophical Genius: A Vindication* (Princeton, NJ: Princeton University Press, 1936).

66   Goldin, ed., *The Living Talmud*, 57 (Pirkei Avot, ch. 1).

67   Dawkins, *The God Delusion*, 2, 50.

68   Hartshorne, "Tillich and the Nontheological Meaning of Theological Terms" in *Paul Tillich: Retrospect and Future* (Nashville: Abington Press, 1966): 28.

69   Hartshorne, "Tillich and the Nontheological Meaning," 84.

70   Stenger, *God the Failed Hypothesis*, 18.

71   Dawkins, *The God Delusion*, 147.

72   Dawkins, *The God Delusion*, 155.

73 Dawkins, *The God Delusion*, 156.

74 Charles Hartshorne, "My Religious Beliefs," *Process Studies* 40/1 (Spring/Summer 2011): 157. Much earlier, Hartshorne wrote, "There is the question of a primordial, wholly nonderivative aspect of divinity, and of a consequent or derivative aspect. The former alone is simple, the latter is the most complex of all realities." See Hartshorne's "Arthur Berndtson on Mystical Experience," *The Personalist* 32/2 (Spring 1951): 192.

75 Hartshorne, "God and the Social Structure of Reality," 27.

76 Stenger, *God the Failed Hypothesis*, 119.

77 Stenger, *God the Failed Hypothesis*, 121.

78 Stenger, *God the Failed Hypothesis*, 119.

79 Stenger, *God the Failed Hypothesis*, 120–21.

80 Stenger, *God the Failed Hypothesis*, 123.

81 Stenger, *God the Failed Hypothesis*, 125 and 126.

82 Mikael Stenmark notes that the advocate of scientism may escape the charge of incoherence by reformulating the thesis of the omnicompetence of science as a working hypothesis to be accepted until something better comes along. Stenmark calls this "soft-core scientism." Stemark argues that scientism in any of its forms faces the problem that the practice of science presupposes forms of knowledge that are not themselves grounded in science. For example, at any particular moment we know the contents of our own minds, we remember what we were thinking (or a theory we proposed), we know language and the meanings of words, we know the social and cultural world, and we have a great deal of knowledge of the intentions and purposes of other people. Of course, there are scientific tests for the extent of the reliability of these forms of knowledge, but the very practice of science presupposes that we initially know these things and that we know them in the processes of formulating and evaluating scientific findings. See Stenmark's article, "Science and the Limits of Knowledge," in *Clashes of Knowledge: Orthodoxies and Heterodoxies in Science and Religion* ed. Peter Meusburger, Michael Welker, and Edgar Wunder (Springer, 2008), 111–20. For a more extended treatment of this subject see Stenmark's earlier work, *Scientism: Science, Ethics and Religion* (Burlington VT: Ashgate, 2001).

83 Charles Hartshorne, "The Development of My Philosophy" in *Contemporary American Philosophy: Second Series,* ed. John E. Smith (London: Allen & Unwin, 1970), 215.

84 Leemon B. McHenry, *The Event Universe: The Revisionary Metaphysics of Alfred North Whitehead* (Edinburgh: Edinburgh University Press, 2015), 83 and 86.

85 Process thinkers bring fresh perspectives to the problems of the interrelations of science, religion, and ethics. See for example: Ian Barbour's Gifford Lectures, published in two volumes, *Religion in an Age of Science* (San Francisco: Harper & Row, 1990) and *Ethics in an Age of Technology* (San Francisco: HarperOne, 1993). On the topic of science and religion see also David Ray Griffin, *Religion and Scientific Naturalism: Overcoming the Conflicts* (Albany: SUNY Press, 2000) and see John B. Cobb, Jr. ed., *Back to Darwin: A Richer Account of Evolution* (Grand Rapids, MI: Eerdmans, 2008). Process thinkers have been at the forefront of discussions that concern social justice, economics, and the interface of theology and ecology. See, for example: Norman Pittenger, *Time to Consent: A Christian's Approach to Homosexuality* (London: SCM Press, 1976); Sheila Greeve Davaney, ed., *Feminism and Process Thought* (Lewiston, NY: Edwin Mellen Press, 1981); John B. Cobb, Jr., *Process Theology as Political Theology* (Philadelphia: Westminster Press, 1982); Daniel Dombrowski, *Hartshorne and the Metaphysics of Animal Rights* (Albany: SUNY Press. 1988); Herman Daly and John B. Cobb, Jr., *For the Common Good: Redirecting the Economy Towards Community, the Environment and a Sustainable Future.* 2nd ed. (Boston: Beacon Press, 1994 [1989]); and John B. Cobb, Jr., *Is it Too Late? A Theology of Ecology,* rev. ed. (Denton, TX: Environmental Ethics Books, 1995 [1972]).

On questions of biblical interpretation see, for example: Lewis S. Ford, *The Lure of God: A Biblical Background for Process Theism* (Philadelphia: Fortress Press, 1978); Robert K. Gnuse, *The Old Testament and Process Theology* (St. Louis, MO: Chalice Press, 2000); and John B. Cobb Jr. and David J. Lull, *Romans,* Chalice Commentaries for Today (St. Louis, MO: Chalice Press, 2005).

86 Hitchens, *god is not Great,* 7.

Chapter Eight

1   See David Haugen and L. Bryant Keeling, "Hartshorne's Process

Theism and Big Bang Cosmology," *Process Studies* 22/3 (Fall 1993): 163–71 and "Hartshorne's Response": 172.

2   "Hartshorne's Response": 172.

3   Theodore Walker, Jr., "Classical and Neoclassical Theology: A Neoclassical Response to the Haugen-Keeling-Hartshorne Discussion and Stephen Hawking's 'No Boundaries Proposal'," *Process Studies* 35/2 (Fall-Winter 2006): 270–90.

4   David Haugen and L. Bryant Keeling, "Hartshorne's Process Theism and Big Bang Cosmology Revisited: Reply to Walker," *Process Studies* 37/1 (2008): 92–103, quote from p. 103.

5   David Ray Griffin, *Panentheism and Scientific Naturalism: Rethinking Evil, Morality, Religious Experience, Religious Pluralism, and the Academic Study of Religion* (Claremont, CA: Process Century Press, 2014), 27–28 (our emphasis).

6   Hartshorne's Postscript to Santiago Sia, *God in Process Thought: A Study in Charles Hartshorne's Concept of God* (Dordrecht, NL: Martinus Nijhoff,, 1985), 118.

7   The French poststructuralist thinker Gilles Deleuze has famously put the religious significance of Creativity (or the immanent urge to novelty) quite poignantly for the present context: rather than speak statically by saying that "God exists," perhaps we should speak more dynamically by saying rather that "God insists." We interpret Deleuze's language here as an expressive or evocative rather than a literal speech-act. Taken literally, of course, if God insists, then God exists.

8   Haugen and Keeling, "Reply to Walker," 101.

9   For a more detailed development of these ideas that is congenial to Hartshorne's system see Griffin's clear, and in our assessment plausible, articulation of divine activity in his "Panentheism and Cosmic Design," ch. 3 of *Panentheism and Scientific Naturalism*.

10   Alfred North Whitehead, *Essays in Science and Philosophy* (New York: The Philosophical Library, 1948), 102 [chapter on "Uniformity and Contingency"].

11   Anthony Quinton, "Spaces and Times," *Philosophy: Journal of the Royal Institute* 37/140 (1962): 130–47.

12   For an excellent account of the evidence that led to the acceptance

of the Big Bang see ch. 27 of Susan Wise Bauer's *The Story of Science: From the Writings of Aristotle to the Big Bang Theory* (New York: W. W. Norton, 2015).

13 W. H. Newton-Smith, *The Structure of Time* (London: Routledge & Kegan Paul, 1984), 106–11.

14 In chapter 6 we used the question "What is north of the north pole?" as a way of explaining that it is nonsensical to ask for a cause of God's existence; as a metaphysical necessity, divine existence can have no cause. In the present context, however, we are speaking of the present cosmic epoch or this universe, since its inception, which is contingent. It makes perfectly good sense to ask for its cause or causes.

15 William Lane Craig, *The Kalām Cosmological Argument* (London: Macmillan, 1979).

16 Brian Clegg, *Before the Big Bang* (New York: St. Martin's Griffin, 2009).

17 Michael Lemonick, "Before the Big Bang," *Discover Magazine* (February 2004): 1, accessed July 1, 2017, http://discovermagazine.com/2004/feb/cover.

18 On this see, Ahmed Farag Ali and Saurya Das, "Cosmology from quantum potential," *Physics Letters B* 741. 10.1016/j.physletb.2014.12.057.

19 Eric J. Lerner, "Open Letter," *The New Scientist,* May 22, 2004. See also, Eric J. Lerner, *The Big Bang Never Happened* (New York: Vintage Books, 1992).

20 Ned Wright, "Errors in The Big Bang Never Happened," October 2003, Ned Wright website, accessed July 1, 2017, http://www.astro.ucla.edu/~wright/lerner_errors.html. Lerner vociferously disputes Wright's critique.

21 For example, consider the time required—70 billion years based on current observations of galactic motion—to produce the observed massive voids between galaxies; how can this be squared with the nearly 14 billion year estimate of the age of our epoch on the standard model? Must the best cosmic model predict such novel and difficult entities as dark matter and the strange violent action of inflation that quickly appears and then disappears?

22 Paul Davies, *God and the New Physics* (New York: Simon and Schuster, 1983), 10–11.

23 Rem B. Edwards, *What Caused the Big Bang?* (New York: Editions Rodopi, 2001), 262.

24 Leemon McHenry notes that most Whitehead commentators assume that Whiteheadian cosmic epochs occur seriatim, or one at a time, in succession. He mentions Edwards as one who does not accept this assumption and McHenry himself agrees with Edwards. See Leemon B. McHenry, *The Event Universe: The Revisionary Metaphysics of Alfred North Whitehead* (Edinburgh: Edinburgh University Press, 2015), 79 and 143n7.

25 James F. Ross, Review of *The God of the Philosophers* by Antony Kenny, *The Journal of Philosophy* 79/7 (July 1982): 410–17. See p. 413. Ross does not specifically mention process theism in his review, but his critique of Kenny's argument is applicable in the present context. Ross dismisses as "cosmologically incoherent" any view of God that would require God to know what time it is "now," as though there were, contrary to Special Relativity, a cosmically identifiable absolute present.

26 David Ray Griffin, *Whitehead's Radically Different Postmodern Philosophy* (Albany: SUNY Press, 2007), ch. 8. This chapter is a revision of his earlier "Hartshorne, God, and Relativity Physics," *Process Studies* 21/2 (1992): 85–112.

27 Alfred North Whitehead, *Process and Reality: An Essay in Cosmology*, Corrected Edition, ed. David Ray Griffin and Donald Sherburne (New York: Free Press, 1978), 84, 244.

28 Whitehead, *Process and Reality*, 34; also see 344–45.

29 A. H. Johnson, "Whitehead as Teacher and Philosopher," *Philosophy and Phenomenological Research* 29/3 (March 1969): 351–76. See p. 370.

30 David Ray Griffin, *Reenchantment Without Supernaturalism: A Process Philosophy of Religion* (Ithaca, NY: Cornell University Press, 2001), 151; Griffin's emphasis.

31 Whitehead, *Process and Reality*, 32 and 88.

32 Jorge Luis Nobo, "God as Essentially Immutable, Imperishable and Objectifiable: A Response to Ford" in *Hartshorne, Process Philosophy and Theology*, ed. Robert Kane and Stephen H. Phillips (Albany: SUNY Press, 1989): 175–80; Palmyre M. F. Oomen, "The Prehensibility of God's Consequent Nature," *Process Studies* 27/1-2 (1998): 108–33.

33 Griffin, *Reenchantment Without Supernaturalism,* 152.

34 Charles Hartshorne, "Bell's Theorem and Stapps Revised View of Space-Time," *Process Studies* 7/3 (Fall 1977): 183–91.

35 Paul Fitzgerald, "Relativity Physics and the God of Process Philosophy," *Process Studies* 2/4 (1971): 251–73.

36 John D. Barrow and Frank Tipler, *The Anthropic Cosmological Principle* (New York: Oxford University Press, 1988).

37 Griffin, *Whitehead's Radically Different Postmodern Philosophy,* 183.

38 John B. Cobb, Jr., *A Christian Natural Theology Based on the Thought of Alfred North Whitehead,* 2nd ed. (Louisville, KY: Westminster John Knox Press, 2007 [1965]).

39 Henry Pierce Stapp, "Quantum Mechanics, Local Causality, and Process Philosophy," ed. William B. Jones, *Process Studies* 7/3 (Fall 1977): 173–82. See p. 175.

40 Hartshorne, "Bell's Theorem," 185.

41 The chapter in CAP (1984) titled "Whitehead's Revolutionary Concept of Prehension" should not be confused with the article by the same title published in *International Philosophical Quarterly* 19/3 (Sept. 1979): 253–63.

42 Frank J. Tipler, *The Physics of Immortality: Modern Cosmology, God and the Resurrection of the Dead* (New York: Doubleday, 1994).

43 Griffin, *Whitehead's Radically Different Postmodern Philosophy,* 183–84.

44 John Robert Baker, "Omniscience and Divine Synchronization," *Process Studies* 2/3 (Fall 1972): 201–02.

45 Marjorie Suchocki, *The End of Evil* (Albany: SUNY Press, 1988): 171.

46 Hartshorne changed his mind about this. Earlier in his career he disputed Whitehead's view of the mutual independence of contemporary actualities, but he came to accept this doctrine (WP 3).

47 Our interpretation, if correct, exposes the mistake in one of Royce Gordon Gruenler's expressed doubts about process theology. According to Gruenler, "If God is limited to our time, that means he's constrained to move at 186,000 miles per second—the speed of light." Guenler here construes the Hartshornean God as a localized

entity, contrary to Hartshorne's explicit statements otherwise. See "God at Risk: A Former Process Theologian Says a 30-Percent God is Not Worth Worshipping," an interview with Wendy Murray Zoba, *Christianity Today* (March 5, 2001), accessed June 26, 2017, http://www.christianitytoday.com/ct/2001/march5/3.56.html?start=1.

48 Roberto Mangabeira Unger and Lee Smolin, *The Singular Universe and the Reality of Time: A Proposal in Natural Philosophy* (New York: Cambridge University Press, 2015), 419.

49 For a lively and informed account of the origins of the problem of fitting Einstein's relativity theory with the phenomenology of experienced time, see Jimena Canales, *The Physicist and the Philosopher: Einstein, Bergson, and the Debate that Changed Our Understanding of Time* (Princeton: Princeton University Press, 2015).

50 Schubert Ogden calls attention to Heidegger's own suggestion for a philosophical construction of God's eternity, but "only as a more primordial temporality which is 'infinite'," rather than the "eternal now"—Heidegger speaks of "the 'standing now' (*nunc sans*)" of the classical tradition (see Heidegger, *Sein und Zeit*, Halle: Niemeyer Verlag, 1927: 499,n.xiii). As Ogden develops this suggestion "by drawing out its several implications in its larger context in *Sein und Zeit* as a whole," there emerge pronounced affinities between Heidegger's phenomenological analysis of time and temporality and the process conceptuality. See Ogden, *The Reality of God and Other Essays* (New York: Harper & Row, 1963), 147. There is in fact a considerable literature on the relationship between Heidegger and process philosophy. For instance, see Calvin O. Schrag's substantive essay, "Whitehead and Heidegger: Process Philosophy and Existential Philosophy," *Dialectica* 13/1 (March 1959): 42–56; Daniel Dombrowski, "Hartshorne on Heidegger," *Process Studies* 25 (1996): 19–33 and James A. Bradley, "Whitehead, Heidegger, and the Paradoxes of the New," *Process Studies* 20/3 (1991): 127–50. See also Ron L. Cooper, *Heidegger and Whitehead* (Athens, OH: Ohio University Press, 1993). In any event, Heidegger's strong identification of "the metaphysical tradition" with just those atemporalist aspects of Post-Socratic Greek metaphysics which process philosophers also typically reject seems to entail that process "metaphysics" is hardly what Heidegger had in mind as the aim of his programmatic "Destruktion" of the tradition.

Chapter Nine

1   In *Insights and Oversights,* Hartshorne devotes a chapter each to Schopenhauer (IO ch. 16) and Nietzsche (IO ch. 20). There is also a brief discussion of Nietzsche in PSG 467–68. For Hartshorne's main discussions of Freud see BH, ch. 6 and PSG 468–85. Hartshorne reflects on Heidegger in BH ch. 17, IO ch. 27 and CE ch. 2. For more on the relation of Hartshorne and Heidegger see Daniel Dombrowski, "Hartshorne on Heidegger," *Process Studies* 25 (1996): 19–33.

2   Hartshorne thought it was important that mystics who speak of going "beyond good and evil" very often have been raised in "an intensive ethical tradition" and have assimilated it; in Heidegger's case, Hartshorne mused, he had been brought up as a Roman Catholic but "how far he assimilated it is not especially clear" (DL 265). For a first step in beginning to assess the importance of Heidegger's recently published *Black Notebooks* for the philosopher's views on Judaism, see Peter Trawny, *Heidegger and the Myth of a Jewish World Conspiracy,* trans. Andrew J. Mitchell (Chicago: University of Chicago Press, 2015).

3   We here summarize points made in Shields's M. A. Thesis, *Neoclassical Metaphysics and the Philosophies of Existence* (Louisville, KY: University of Louisville, 1975). The reference to Wahl alludes to Jean Wahl, *Philosophies of Existence,* tran. F. M. Lory (NY: Schocken Books, 1969 [1954]).

4   Shields further argues that a broader view of Hartshorne's thought shows it to be an integrative synthesis of critical rationalist and existential motifs—a synthesis to which the horizon of 1970s existential phenomenology was then signaling. Precipitated by some arguments of Schubert Ogden (regarding Bultmann and Heidegger) and Thomas Hanna (cf. "The Living Body: Nexus Between Process Philosophy and Existential Phenomenology," *Soundings* 52/3 (1969): 323–33), Shields gives close exegetical attention to Hartshorne's own article-length studies of Berdyaev, Buber, Husserl, Heidegger, and Marcel, as well as various comments on other existential and phenomenological thinkers (especially Ortega, Sartre, and Merleau-Ponty) throughout Hartshorne's corpus, to make the above comparative case. This examination also reveals considerable differences between Hartshorne and individual existential thinkers,

particularly their penchant for unnecessary obscurity and their often myopic blindness to similar insights developed by American pragmatists and/or Whitehead.

5 George Allan, "The Metaphysical Axioms and Ethics of Charles Hartshorne," *Review of Metaphysics* 40 (December 1986): 293.

6 Charles Hartshorne, "Ethics and the New Theology," *International Journal of Ethics* 45/1 (1934): 97.

7 Charles Hartshorne, "Ethics and the Assumption of Purely Private Pleasures," *International Journal of Ethics* 40/4 (1930): 498.

8 Antoinie van Leeuwenhoek reported seeing "animalcules" through his microscope in 1676 (we now know that he was seeing protozoa). Mattias Jackob Schleiden and Theodor Schwann developed cell theory in the late 1830s. Schleiden published "Contributions to Phytogenesis" in 1837 in which he argued for the cellular structure of all plants; a year later, his colleague Schwann published *Microscopical Researches into the Accordance in the Structure and Growth of Animals and Plants* (1839) in which he defended the cellular structure of all lifeforms. An English translation of Schwann's book and Schleiden's article (both translated by Henry Smith) was published in a single volume in 1847 by the London based Sydenham Society. Cell theory was further refined by Rudolf Virchow in *Die Celluarpathologie* (1858). Vichow is well-known for the Latin motto: *Omnis cellula e cellula,* or all cells develop from existing cells.

9 Sewall Wright, "Biology and the Philosophy of Science" in *Process and Divinity, The Hartshorne Festschrift,* ed. William L. Reese and Eugene Freeman (La Salle, IL: Open Court, 1964), 104.

10 Charles Hartshorne, "Foundations for a Humane Ethics: What Human Beings Have in Common with Other Higher Animals" in *On the Fifth Day: Animal Rights and Human Ethics,* ed. Richard K. Morris and Michael W. Fox (Washington, DC: Acropolis Books, 1978), 154.

11 Charles Hartshorne, "Ethics and the Process of Living" in *Man and His Conduct: Philosophical Essays in Honor of Risieri Frondizi,* ed. Jorge J. E. Garcia (Rio Piedras, Puerto Rico: Editorial Universitaria, 1980), 192. Hartshorne is here referring to Warder Clyde Allee (1885–1955), the great pioneer of American ecology.

12 Hartshorne, "Foundations for a Humane Ethics," 156.

13 Charles Hartshorne, "Mind as Memory and Creative Love" in *Theories of the Mind,* ed. Jordan M. Scher (New York: The Free Press of Glencoe, 1962), 448.

14 Hartshorne, "Ethics and the Process of Living," 192

15 Hartshorne, "Foundations for a Humane Ethics," 166.

16 Hartshorne, "Ethics and the Assumption of Purely Private Pleasures," 499.

17 Hartshorne, "Ethics and the Process of Living," 194.

18 Originally published in 1935, interest in Dr. Suttie's work was resurrected by developmental psychologists in the 80s and 90s resulting in re-publication in 1999. See Ian Suttie, *The Origins of Love and Hate* (London: Rutledge Press, 1999).

19 Huston Smith, *Why Religion Matters: The Fate of the Human Spirit in an Age of Disbelief* (New York: HarperCollins, 2001), 171.

20 Smith, *Why Religion Matters,* 198.

21 Kant says "our self-love cannot be separated from our need to be loved." Immanuel Kant, *The Metaphysics of Morals,* trans. and ed. Mary Gregor (New York: Cambridge University Press, 1996), 156 [*Doctrine of Virtue,* 6.393]. Kant explicitly denies, however, that there is a duty to will one's own happiness since we unavoidably do this anyway and nothing willed unavoidably is a duty (150; 6.386). For Kant, the duty to oneself is to cultivate one's finer faculties and to preserve one's moral integrity; unhappiness in the form of "adversity, pain, and want" are temptations to violate this duty and so, one indirectly has a duty to ward off these temptations to vice (152; 6.388). Kant speaks of the happiness of others that is an end that is also a duty. What this means, for Kant, is that one should refrain from doing anything that would tempt another person to compromise their own moral integrity (155–56; 6.393–94).

22 Hartshorne, "Ethics and the Process of Living," 196.

23 Hartshorne, "Foundations for a Humane Ethics," 160.

24 Charles Hartshorne, "The Environmental Results of Technology" in *Philosophy and Environmental Crisis,* ed. William T. Blackstone (Athens: University of Georgia Press, 1974), 72.

25 Immanuel Kant, *Lectures on Ethics,* trans. Louis Infield (New York: Harper Torchbooks, 1963), 240.

26 Kant says, "Vivisectionists, who use living animals for their experiments, certainly act cruelly, although their aim is praiseworthy, and they can justify their cruelty, since animals must be regarded as man's instruments; but any such cruelty for sport cannot be justified," *Lectures on Ethics*, 240–41.

27 Hartshorne, "Foundations for a Humane Ethics," 170.

28 Kant is almost Freudian when he writes, "For a human being cannot see into the depths of his own heart so as to be quite certain, in even a single action, of the purity of his moral intention and the sincerity of his disposition, . . . how many people who have lived long and guiltless lives may not be merely fortunate in having escaped so many temptations?" Kant, *The Metaphysics of Morals*, 155 [*Doctrine of Virtue*, 6.392–94].

29 Hartshorne, "Foundations for a Humane Ethics," 158.

30 Frederick Ferré, *Being and Value: Toward a Constructive Postmodern Metaphysics* (Albany: SUNY Press, 1996), 332–33. Carol P. Christ, *She Who Changes: Re-Imagining the Divine in the World* (New York: Palgrave Macmillan, 2003), 58–59.

31 Hartshorne, "Foundations for a Humane Ethics," 155.

32 Hartshorne, "Ethics and the Process of Living," 199.

33 See also, Hartshorne, "Foundations for a Humane Ethics, 171.

34 For more on the subject of Hartshorne and animal rights, see especially, Daniel A. Dombrowski, *Hartshorne and the Metaphysics of Animal Rights* (Albany: SUNY Press, 1988).

35 Hartshorne, "Foundations for a Humane Ethics," 168.

36 Hartshorne, "Ethics and the Process of Living," 198–99.

37 Hartshorne, "Foundations for a Humane Ethics," 169.

38 Charles Hartshorne, "God as Composer-Director, Enjoyer, and, in a Sense, Player of the Cosmic Drama," *Process Studies* 30/2 (Fall-Winter 2001): 242–53.

39 Hartshorne, "Ethics and the Process of Living," 201.

40 Charles Hartshorne, "Equality, Freedom, and the Insufficiency of Empiricism," *Southern Journal of Philosophy* 1/3 (1970): 23. John Wilson's views are in his book *Equality* (Hutchinson of London, 1966).

41 Hartshorne, "Equality, Freedom, and the Insufficiency of Empiricism," 23.

42 As should be clear from our discussion of Hartshorne's modal theory of time, "all-inclusive" should not be taken to mean "inclusive of future actualities." For Hartshorne, the future is relatively indeterminate, a combination of what will be and what may be only, so that God's inclusion of the future is not of the actualization of possibilities but of the possibilities for actualization.

43 Hartshorne, "Equality, Freedom, and the Insufficiency of Empiricism," 25.

44 See Nicholas Berdyaev, *The Destiny of Man* (New York: Harper and Row, 1960), especially chs. 3 and 4.

45 Hartshorne would surely have been sympathetic to Linda Zagzebski's divine motivation theory according to which God is the final exemplar of the moral life. See Zagzebski's *Divine Motivation Theory* (New York: Cambridge University Press, 2004).

46 Charles Hartshorne, "Concerning Abortion: An Attempt at a Rational View." *The Christian Century* 98/2 (1981): 42–45.

47 *The Christian Century*, April 1, 1981: 356–60. In the May 6, 1981, issue of *The Christian Century* (p. 525) there was a brief letter from Mildred Eychaner, of Dekalb, Illinois, remarking that all of the letters in response to Hartshorne were written by men, a fact that the editor confirmed. Eychaner wrote, "The more I read of some male theology, the more I tend to agree with a great woman who said a number of years ago, 'If men could become pregnant, abortion would soon become a sacrament.' Then we could end the argument." The letters were, in fact, very uneven. Several attempted to make an end-run around Hartshorne's secular arguments by appealing to specifically Christian principles of personhood or an "unidentifiable soul." One letter claimed that Hartshorne's argument was a slippery slope that would end in goose-stepping Nazis. Another letter compared Hartshorne's denial of full rights to the fetus to nineteenth-century racist ideas about slaves. And there was the depressingly inevitable *ad hominem:* Hartshorne "writes as if he has a chip on his shoulder." The one letter in support of Hartshorne argued that, as lack of brain activity marks the end of life, so it may mark the beginning of life in the womb.

48 Letter to Donald Wayne Viney, April 12, 1981. *Charles Hartshorne's*

Letters to a Young Philosopher: 1979-1995, ed. Donald Wayne Viney, *Logos-Sophia: The Journal of the Pittsburg State University Philosophical Society,* Volume 11 (Fall 2001): 9.

49 Letter to Donald Wayne Viney, May 4, 1981, 11.

50 Charles Hartshorne, "Scientific and Religious Aspects of Bioethics" in *Theology and Bioethics,* ed. E. E. Schelp (Dordrecht: D. Reidel Publishing Co., 1985), 39–44.

51 These points about the problem of a strict identity between fertilized eggs and persons are aptly made in the article by Wayne Viney and William Douglas Woody, "Psychogeny: A Neglected Dimension in Teaching the Mind-Brain Problem," *Teaching of Psychology* 22/3 (October 1995): 173–77.

52 Hartshorne, "Scientific and Religious Aspects of Bioethics," 39.

53 David Hume, "Of the Immortality of the Soul" in *Body, Mind, and Death,* ed. Antony Flew (New York: Macmillan, 1964): 185.

54 Hartshorne, "Scientific and Religious Aspects of Bioethics," 33.

55 Hartshorne, "Scientific and Religious Aspects of Bioethics," 32.

56 Hartshorne, "Concerning Abortion: An Attempt at a Rational View," 45. One can make the same argument for birth control. For an account of the struggle in the United States to make birth control information available and to develop a birth control pill see Wayne Viney and William Douglas Woody, *Neglected Perspectives on Science and Religion: Historical and Contemporary Relations* (New York: Routledge, 2017), 142–48.

57 Hartshorne, "Scientific and Religious Aspects of Bioethics," 33.

58 Jane English, "Abortion and the Concept of a Person" in *Feminism and Philosophy,* ed. Mary Vetterling-Braggin, Frederick A. Elliston, and Jane English (Totowa, NJ: Littlefield, Adams & Co., 1981), 426. Originally published in *Canadian Journal of Philosophy* 5 (October 1975): 233–43.

59 Hartshorne, "Concerning Abortion: An Attempt at a Rational View," 44.

60 Hartshorne, "Concerning Abortion," 44.

61 Hartshorne, "Scientific and Religious Aspects of Bioethics,"43.

62 English, "Abortion and the Concept of a Person," 426.

63 English, "Abortion and the Concept of a Person," 40.

64 Anita Miller Chancey, "Rationality, Contributionism, and the Value of Love: Hartshorne on Abortion," *Process Studies* 28/1-2 (Spring-Summer 1999): 94.

65 Anita Chancey, "Rationality, Contributionism, and the Value of Love," 95.

66 There is no universal agreement among process philosophers about the moral and legal status of abortion. For example, as the authors well know from many personal conversations with him, the late George Nordgulen, former University Chaplain and philosophy professor at Eastern Kentucky University, was a tenacious defender of Hartshorne's doctrines in metaphysics and philosophical theology, but he was equally adamant about defending the view that abortions are morally impermissible except under the rarest circumstances.

67 John B. Cobb, Jr., *Is It Too Late? A Theology of Ecology*, rev. ed. (Denton, TX: Environmental Ethics Books, 1995 [1972]); Charles Birch and John B. Cobb, Jr., *The Liberation of Life: From Cell to Community* (Cambridge: Cambridge University Press, 1981); Herman E. Daly and John B. Cobb, Jr., *For the Common Good: Redirecting the Economy Toward Community, the Environment, and a Sustainable Future.* 2nd ed. (Boston: Beacon Press, 1994 [1989]).

68 Charles Hartshorne, "Cobb's Theology of Ecology" in *John Cobb's Theology in Process*, ed. David Ray Griffin and Thomas J. J. Altizer (Philadelphia: Westminster Press, 1977): 112–15.

69 John B. Cobb, Jr. and David Ray Griffin, *Process Theology: An Introductory Exposition* (Louisville, KY: Westminster John Knox Press, 1976), 155.

70 Eugene H. Peters, *Hartshorne and Neoclassical Metaphysics: An Interpretation* (Lincoln: University of Nebraska Press, 1979), 93.

71 Clare Palmer, *Environmental Ethics and Process Thinking* (Oxford: Oxford University Press, 1998).

72 John B. Cobb, Jr., "Palmer on Whitehead: A Critical Evaluation," *Process Studies* 33/1 (2004): 4–23; Timothy Menta, "Clare Palmer's Environmental Ethics and Process Thinking: A Hartshornean Response," *Process Studies* 33/1 (2004): 24–45; Clare Palmer, "Response to Cobb and Menta," *Process Studies* 33/1 (2004): 46–70.

73 Palmer, "Response to Cobb and Mentam," 60.

74 Palmer cites Hartshorne's "Aesthetic Matrix of Value" (CS 303–21), "Beyond Enlightened Self-Interest" (ZF 185–202), and "Ethical Rights of Non-Human Animals" (WM 117–30). The latter paper originally appeared in German in 1978 with the title "Rechte—nicht nur fur Menschen" ("Rights—Not Just for Humanity"). The paper was republished in 1979 in English in the inaugural issue of *Environmental Ethics* under the title, "The Rights of the Sub-Human World" and later appeared in WM as above. Palmer objects to Hartshorne's use of "sub-human," but this was not the original title of the paper, nor was it the title Hartshorne chose when he republished the paper in English. So, Hartshorne himself seems to have anticipated this particular objection.

75 George W. Shields, *The Semantics of Perfection: An Investigation of Theistic Meaning Postulates and Their Justification in the Philosophy of Charles Hartshorne,* Ph.D. Dissertation, The University of Chicago, June 1981, 307.

76 Palmer, "Response to Cobb and Menta," 65.

77 Derek Parfit, *Reasons and Persons* (Oxford: Oxford University Press, 1984), 388.

78 Randall C. Morris, *Process Philosophy and Political Ideology: The Social and Political Thought of Alfred North Whitehead and Charles Hartshorne* (Albany: SUNY Press, 1991), 146.

79 Thomas Nairn, "Hartshorne and Utilitarianism: A Response to Moskop," *Process Studies* 17/3 (1988): 173.

80 John B. Cobb, Jr., "Palmer on Whitehead," 15.

81 Holmes Rolston, III, *Environmental Ethics* (Philadelphia: Temple University Press, 1988): 121.

Chapter Ten

1 Charles Hartshorne, "The Environmental Results of Technology" in *Philosophy and Environmental Crisis,* ed. William T. Blackstone (Athens: University of Georgia Press, 1974), 69–78; Charles Hartshorne, "Cobb's Theology of Ecology" in *John Cobb's Theology in Process,* ed. David Ray Griffin and Thomas J. J. Altizer (Philadelphia: Westminster Press, 1977), 112–15.

2 Ian Barbour, *Ethics in an Age of Technology* (San Fransisco:

HarperCollins, 1992).

3   Charles Hartshorne, "Bergson's Aesthetic Creationism Compared to Whitehead's" in *Bergson and Modern Thought: Towards a Unified Science,* ed. Andrew C. Papanicolaou and Pete A. Y. Gunter (Chur, Switzerland: Harwood Academic Publishers, 1987), 379. Bergson's discussion is in ch. 2 of *The Two Sources of Morality and Religion,* trans. R. Ashley Audra and Cloudesley Brereton with the assistance of W. Horsfall Carter (Garden City, NY: Doubleday Anchor Books, 1954).

4   Bergson, *Two Sources of Morality and Religion,* 210.

5   George Shields provided an outline of a process theology of technology as found in the writings of Hartshorne, with a particular focus of this essay. See "Process Theology and Technology" in *Theology and Technology: Essays in Christian Analysis and Exegesis,* ed. Carl Mitcham and Jim Grote (Lanham, MD: University Press of America, 1984), 279–90. Shields essentially made an addendum to his earlier essay in the special focus issue of *Process Studies* that he edited, devoted to process thought and the philosophy of technology. See George Shields, ed., Special Focus on Process Philosophy and Technology, *Process Studies* 31/1 (Spring-Summer 2002): 93–163.

6   Frederick A. Olafson, "Camus, Albert" in *The Encyclopedia of Philosophy,* Vol. II, ed. Paul Edwards (New York: Macmillan, 1967), 16.

7   Albert Camus, "The Enigma" in *Lyrical and Critical Essays,* ed. Philip Thody, trans. Ellen Conroy Kennedy (New York: Vintage), 160. James Goss provides an illuminating analysis of Camus's thought vis-à-vis Whiteheadian theism. He argues that Whitehead's God—and the argument could be modified for Hartshorne's God—meets the requirements of a "rebel-artist" who makes for the "living transcendence" for which Camus longed in his philosophy. See Goss's "Camus, God, and Process Thought," *Process Studies* 4/2 (Summer 1974): 114–28.

8   Hartshorne, "The Environmental Results of Technology," 69.

9   Frederick Ferré, *Philosophy of Technology* (Englewood Cliffs, NJ: Prentice-Hall, 1988), see especially ch. 5.

10   Hartshorne, "Cobb's Theology of Ecology," 114.

11   Charles Birch and John B. Cobb, Jr., *The Liberation of Life: From*

the Cell to the Community (London: Cambridge University Press, 1981), 260, 319–20. It is of interest that this book is dedicated to Hartshorne.

12 Shields, "Process Theology and Technology," 150.

13 Hartshorne, "The Environmental Results of Technology," 69.

14 Hartshorne, "The Environmental Results of Technology," 78.

15 Albert Borgmann, "Prospects for the Theology of Technology" in *Theology and Technology: Essays in Christian Analysis and Exegesis* ed. Carl Mitcham and Jim Grote (Lanham, MD: University Press of America, 1984), 308.

16 Albert Borgmann, *Technology and the Character of Contemporary Life: A Philosophical Inquiry* (Chicago: University of Chicago Press, 1987).

17 Gregg Easterbrook, "A Hundred Years of Thinking About God: A Philosopher Soon to be Rediscovered," *U.S. News & World Report* (February 23, 1998): 65.

18 John B. Cobb, Jr., *Is It Too Late? A Theology of Ecology*, rev. ed. (Denton, TX: Environmental Ethics Books, 1995 [1972]); Birch and Cobb, *The Liberation of Life* (1981); and Herman E. Daly and John Cobb, *For the Common Good*, updated and expanded (Boston: Beacon Press, 1994 [1989]).

19 Frederick Ferré, "Whitehead and Technology" in *Whitehead's Philosophy: Points of Connection*, ed. Donald Sherburne and J. Polanowski (Albany: SUNY Press, 2004): ch. 10. See also Ferré's *Hellfire and Lightning Rods: Liberating Science, Technology, and Religion* (Maryknoll, NY: Orbis Books, 1993).

20 See especially chapter 10 of Birch and Cobb, *The Liberation of Life*, "Rural and Urban Development in Ecological Perspective."

21 Barbour, *Ethics in an Age of Technology*, 21–24.

22 Alan Drengson, "Four Philosophies of Technology" in *Technology as a Human Affair*, ed. Larry A. Hickman (New York: McGraw-Hill, 1990), 368–86.

23 Barbour, *Ethics in an Age of Technology*, ch. 3.

24 Barbour explicitly connects this third criterion with process philosophy. He finds process thought helpful in offering a rationale "for respecting all human and nonhuman creatures,

along with a principle for assigning priorities" (Barbour, *Ethics in an Age of Technology*, 70). On the latter, see Susan Armstrong-Buck, "Whitehead's Metaphysical System as a Foundation for Environmental Ethics." *Environmental Ethics* 8 (1986): 241–59. We add that Hartshorne found "modern technology" to be particularly problematic in the effect it has had on biodiversity. This has ramifications of cosmic proportions: "before the rise of modern technology, the total number of species has usually been increased rather than reduced. Variety is an aesthetic good, not only for human observers, but for all forms of mind, including cosmic mind" (IO 224).

25 Barbour, *Ethics in an Age of Technology*, 133.

26 *Ethics in an Age of Technology*, 133–34.

27 *Ethics in an Age of Technology*, 134.

28 For a discussion see Peter Limper, "Process and (Virtual) Reality: Thoughts on Technology and Value," *Process Studies* 31/1 (Spring-Summer 2002): 130–45.

29 Larry A. Hickman, ed., *Technology as a Human Affair* (New York: McGraw-Hill, 1990), 148.

30 Jacques Ellul, "The Relation of Man to Technology in the Bible" in *Theology and Technology: Essays in Christian Analysis and Exegesis,* ed. Carl Mitcham and Jim Grote, (Lanham, MD: University Press of America, 1984), 143.

31 Jacques Ellul, *The Technological Society,* trans. John Wilkinson, Introduction by Robert K. Merton (New York: Vintage Books, 1964), xxviii.

32 Ellul, *The Technological Society,* xxx.

33 Charles Hartshorne, "A Metaphysics of Individualism" in *Innocence and Power: Individualism in Twentieth Century America,* ed. Gordon Mills (Austin: University of Texas Press, 1965), 131–46. See especially 132–34.

34 Mike Viney gives a fascinating and detailed account of apple parers and their relations to apple orchards, apple types, and the growth of the apple industry in nineteenth and twentieth century United States in his article "Appeal to American Apple Parers: Historical Perspectives on Orchards and Yankee Ingenuity," *The Midwest Quarterly* 58/1 (Autumn 2016): 9-27.

35 Ferré, *Philosophy of Technology*, 130.

36 Ferré, *Philosophy of Technology*, 130.

37 Ferré, *Philosophy of Technology*, 130.

38 Barbour, *Ethics in an Age of Technology*, 230.

39 Charles Hartshorne, "Barriers to Progress: Or Some Superstitions of Modernism," *The Gad-Fly* [Student Liberal Club of Harvard University] (1923): 1–15.

40 Charles Hartshorne, "A Philosophy of Democratic Defense" in *Science, Philosophy, and Religion: Second Symposium,* ed. Lyman Bryson and Louis Finkelstein (New York: Conference on Science, Philosophy and Religion in Their Relation to the Democratic Way of Life, Inc., 1942), 130–172.

41 Hartshorne, "A Metaphysics of Individualism," 144–45 (cf. WM 103).

42 Charles Hartshorne, "Equality, Freedom, and the Insufficiency of Empiricism," *Southern Journal of Philosophy* 1/3 (1970): 21.

43 It is noteworthy that Norman Pittenger (1905–1997), one of the pioneers in calling for equitable treatment of homosexuals and for the acceptance of gay marriage, was also one of the first-generation scholars of Whitehead and process theology. His book *Process Thought and Christian Faith* (New York: Macmillan, 1968) is dedicated to Charles Hartshorne and his book *Catholic Faith in a Process Perspective* (New York: Maryknoll, 1981) is dedicated to Dorothy Hartshorne "with great affection." Pittenger was an American who spent the last thirty years of his life in Great Britain. His book *Time for Consent: A Christian's Approach to Homosexuality* (London: SCM Press, 1976) was based on an earlier work by the same title that Pittenger published in 1967. Both works were a call for a more accepting attitude towards homosexuals and same-sex marriage. The idea was so shocking that the *Church Times* refused to review the book. To the end of his days he advocated for an inclusive understanding of Christianity and was a founding member of the Gay Christian Movement (later to become LGCM). Barry Woodbridge's 1977 primary-secondary Whitehead bibliography lists fifty entries for Pittenger.

44 Randall C. Morris, *Process Philosophy and Political Ideology: The Social and Political Thought of Alfred North Whitehead and Charles*

Hartshorne (Albany: SUNY Press, 1991), 111.

45 Morris, *Process Philosophy and Political Ideology,* 247, n.27.

46 Morris, *Process Philosophy and Political Ideology,* 122–24.

47 While there is much insight in Morris's work, we nonetheless challenge implications that some might draw from his establishing (if he does so establish), a properly ideological context for the construction of process theory and not merely a limiting social locale for the construction of such theory. Morris's main thesis is that Whitehead and Hartshorne develop their social and political philosophies, whether wittingly or not, within a distinctive modern Anglo-American ideologically liberal tradition (close in spirit to the thought of T. H. Green and L. T. Hobhouse). While this may well be so, that cannot be taken as criticism in and by itself of process social and political philosophy. The arguments for process positions stand or fall on their own merits and on the criteria of logical coherence, provision of evidence, and philosophical adequacy. While such ideological analysis may be helpful as a heuristic measure encouraging us to be on the look for certain limitations of perspective, no such establishment of ideological context should be taken as an *a priori* dismissal (nor, we point out, does Morris say it should be so taken).

48 Henry C. Simons, "A Positive Program for Laissez Faire" in *Economic Policy for a Free Society* (Chicago: University of Chicago Press, 1948): 43.

49 Charles Hartshorne, "An Economic Program for Liberal Religion," *The Christian Century* 52/23 (June 5, 1935): 761-762.

50 Philip Clayton and Justin Heinzekehr, *Organic Marxism* (Claremont, CA: Process Century Press, 2015), 236.

51 Perhaps the thinker who has most systematically and profoundly developed the implications of Hartshorne's neoclassical metaphysics for the fields of moral philosophy and political theory is Franklin I. Gamwell, the Shailer Matthews Distinguished Service Professor Emeritus of Religious Ethics and the Philosophy of Religions at the University of Chicago. See his major theoretical work, *The Divine Good: Modern Moral Theory and the Necessity of God* (HarperSanFrancisco, 1990). This was followed by a number of books devoted to reflections on political theory including his *Democracy on Purpose: Justice and the Reality of God* (Washington,

DC: Georgetown University Press, 2002); *Politics as a Christian Vocation: Faith and Democracy Today* (Cambridge University Press, 2005); *By the People, For the People: A Political Vision for Progressive Christians* (Eugene, OR: Wipf & Stock, 2010); and *Existence and the Good: Metaphysical Necessity in Morals and Politics* (Albany: SUNY Press, 2011).

52 "Recollections of Leo Szilard by Charles Hartshorne," 2. On January 10, 1986, Hartshorne sent this six-page document to William Lanouette who was then writing his biography of Leo Szilard, *Genius in the Shadows, A Biography of Leo Szilard, The Man Behind the Bomb* (New York: Skyhorse Publishing, 2013). The authors thank Chase Kirham at the Center for Process Studies for locating this document. The only anecdote from Hartshorne's document that Lanouette used was an account of an audience that Hartshorne and Szilard had with Chicago's Roman Catholic Cardinal to discuss the uses that America had made of the atomic bomb. In Hartshorne's telling, "When we had been ushered into the presence of the Most Reverend, Szilard set forth his view about the importance and dangers of nuclear energy. The Cardinal made a brief reply, saying that God had locked up the energy in question so securely that only after thousands of years had it been unlocked. He assured us that, 'The church would consider the matter, and in due time make a statement about it.' We came away remarking to each other that we were tempted to wish the energy had been still more securely locked up." Recollections of Leo Szilard," 5. See also Lanouette's biography, 285–86.

53 Hartshorne, "A Philosophy of Democratic Defense," 151–52.

54 Given the need for a full-bodied military ethics, we recommend the work of process philosopher John W. Lango, *The Ethics of Armed Conflict: A Cosmopolitan Just War Theory* (Edinburgh: Edinburgh University Press, 2014). Here is a systematic development of a non-pacifist just war theory informed by UN peace principles that emphasizes prevention of armed conflict, the concept of last resort, and proportionality by a scholar sympathetic to a process-relational worldview.

Chapter Eleven

1 Hartshorne, "Analysis and Cultural Lag in Philosophy," *Southern*

Journal of Philosophy 11/1-2 (1973): 105–12. Hartshorne's earliest use of this expression is in "Ethics and the New Theology," *International Journal of Ethics* 45/1 (1934): 100.

2   An anonymous reader's report of *Insights and Oversights* (shared with Viney by Emily Schwartz after Hartshorne's death) criticized the book for not paying more attention to historical context and detailed exegesis of the ideas of each philosopher in the manner of Copleston's multi-volume *A History of Philosophy*. The report likened Hartshorne's criticisms to a beginning student of philosophy who "raises all of the obvious objections and acts as if the philosopher had never (despite having devoted perhaps 20 or 30 years to reflecting on the problems and implications of his stand) anticipated those difficulties" (page 6). Curiously, the reader gives not a single example to substantiate this charge. Nor did the reader acknowledge what others have found, namely, that Hartshorne's interpretations sometimes bring refreshingly new perspectives that can change one's understanding of the achievements of a given philosopher. Doubtless the reader was correct that Hartshorne was not endeavoring to write a Copleston-style history of philosophy, and Hartshorne took this to heart. The original subtitle of the book was "An Evaluative History of Philosophy." The reader suggested changing the subtitle to "An Evaluation of Western Philosophy," which he said better reflected Hartshorne's purpose (page 11). Whatever Hartshorne may have thought of the reader's snide remarks about his scholarship, he followed the suggestion. He also paid attention to the reader's objection that there was no discussion of Descartes, Heidegger, Sartre, Dewey, Wilfrid Sellars, and Quine (page 14). The published version of *Insights and Oversights* includes chapters on Descartes (ch. 10), Heidegger (ch. 27), and Sartre (ch. 28). Of course, Dewey, Sellars, and Quine were Americans, so they are discussed in *Creativity in American Philosophy* in chs. 8, 21, and 22, respectively.

3   William James, *The Principles of Psychology*, Vol. II (New York: Dover, 1950 [1890]): 573 [ch. 26, "The Question of Free Will"]. Hartshorne often mentioned Lequyer, citing his work in the last sixteen books that he wrote. Hartshorne and Reese included an excerpt from one of Lequyer's works in PSG (pp.227–30). Apart from this, Hartshorne's most extensive comments on Lequyer are in CAP 60 and in *Charles Hartshorne's Letters to a Young Philosopher*: 29, 33–34, 43–44 [Letters of May 21, 1986, July 9, 1988, and April

25, 1991]. For a fuller treatment see, Donald Wayne Viney, "The American Reception of Lequyer: From James to Hartshorne," *American Journal of Theology and Philosophy* 36/3 (September 2015): 260–277. For other English translations of Lequyer's works see *Translations of Works of Jules Lequyer,* ed. and trans. Donald Wayne Viney (Lewiston: Edwin Mellen Press, 1998) and Jules Lequyer's *Abel and Abel followed by Incidents in the Life and Death of Jules Lequyer,* trans. Mark West, biography by Donald Wayne Viney (Lewiston: Edwin Mellen Press, 1999). For a summary statement of Lequyer's philosophical and religious views see, Donald Wayne Viney, "Jules Lequyer (Lequier) (1814–1862)" *Internet Encyclopedia of Philosophy,* http://www.iep.utm.edu/lequyer/ (September 18, 2013).

4   See Barry A. Woodbridge, *Alfred N. Whitehead: A Primary-Secondary Bibliography* (Bowling Green, KY: Philosophy Documentation Center, 1977). Also of interest is the productivity of Hartshorne's students. John B. Cobb, Jr. has thirty-seven entries and his name is mentioned in forty-six other entries; Schubert Ogden has eighteen entries and his name is mentioned in sixteen other entries: Lewis Ford has thirty-one entries and his name is mentioned in twelve others.

5   We have in mind the following: Ivor Leclerc, *Whitehead's Metaphysics: An Introductory Exposition* (1958), William A. Christian, *An Interpretation of Whitehead's Metaphysics* (1959), Victor Lowe, *Understanding Whitehead* (1962), and Dorothy Emmet, *Whitehead's Philosophy of Organism,* 2nd ed. (1966).

6   Two scholars who agree with Hartshorne that Plato anticipated neoclassical theism are Leonard J. Eslick, "Plato as Dipolar Theist," *Process Studies* 12/4 (1982): 243–51 and Daniel A. Dombrowski, *A Platonic Philosophy of Religion: A Process Perspective* (Albany: SUNY Press, 2005). Don Viney makes the case for Plato's anticipation of neoclassical ideas in "Process, Parturition, and Perfect Love: Diotima's Rather Non-Platonic Metaphysic of Eros" in *The Many Facets of Love: Philosophical Explorations,* ed. Thomas Jay Oord (New Castle, UK: Cambridge Scholars Publishing, 2007), 41–49.

7   A good example of this treatment (and lack of treatment) of Whitehead is in *The Oxford Illustrated History of Western Philosophy,* ed. Anthony Kenny (New York: Oxford University Press, 2001 [1994]). In an article by David Pears and Anthony Kenny, titled "Mill to Wittgenstein," the only mention of Whitehead is as the coauthor

of *Principia Mathematica,* with Russell seeming to be the first author (see pages 250 and 378). The only other mention of Whitehead is in another article where he and the school of process philosophers are said to have been inspired by Bergson (see page 225). The book makes no mention whatsoever of C. S. Peirce, William James, Josiah Royce, John Dewey, or George Santayana. Even Quine is ignored. This blindness to philosophy in America in a book that is supposed to cover the history of Western philosophy confirms Hartshorne's complaint about the "European provincialism" that so often marginalizes the genius of American philosophy (see Hartshorne's "From Colonial Beginnings to Philosophical Greatness," the first chapter of CAP). In Kenny's later book, *Philosophy in the Modern World: A New History of Philosophy,* Vol. 4 (New York: Oxford University Press, 2008), he pays attention to Peirce, James, and Quine but continues the treatment of Whitehead, mentioning only *Principia* as "the work of Russell and Whitehead," 51, 110.

8   Steven Shaviro asks what postmodern philosophy would look like had Whitehead rather than Heidegger set the agenda. See Shaviro's fascinating fantasy, *Without Criteria: Kant, Whitehead, Deleuze, and Aesthetics* (Cambridge, MA: MIT Press, 2009). Other works that should revive interest in Whitehead include: George W. Shields, ed., *Process and Analysis: Whitehead, Hartshorne, and the Analytic Tradition* (Albany: SUNY Press, 2003); David Ray Griffin, *Whitehead's Radically Different Postmodern Philosophy: An Argument for its Contemporary Relevance* (Albany: SUNY Press, 2007); Leemon B. McHenry, *The Event Universe: The Revisionary Metaphysics of Alfred North Whitehead* (Edinburgh: Edinburgh University Press, 2015); Leemon B. McHenry and George W. Shields, "Analytical Critiques of Whitehead's Metaphysics," *Journal of the American Philosophical Association* 2/3 (Fall 2016); and Daniel Dombrowski, *Whitehead's Religious Thought* (Albany: SUNY Press, 2017).

9   Bowman L. Clarke, *Language and Natural Theology* (The Hague/ Paris: Mouton & Co., 1966).

10   Cobb, "The Philosophy of Charles Hartshorne," 83.

11   Huston Smith, "The Death and Rebirth of Metaphysics" in *Process and Divinity, The Hartshorne Festschrift,* ed. William L. Reese and Eugene Freeman, (La Salle, IL: Open Court, 1964), 43.

12   Wright spoke of the gratification he felt in discovering his "far

reaching agreement with Charles Hartshorne." Sewall Wright, "Biology and the Philosophy of Science" in *Process and Divinity,* ed. Reese and Freeman, 118.

13   Hartshorne, "Darwin and Some Philosophers," *Process Studies* 30/2 (2001): 276-288. See also LP 205f and OO 67-72.

14   See Daniel Dombrowski, "Beyond the Impasse? Classical and Neoclassical Theism in Richards and Viney" in *Metaphysics, Analysis, and the Grammar of God,* ed. Randy Ramal (Tübingen: Mohr Siebeck, 2010), 159. See also James F. Ross, "An Impasse on Competing Descriptions of God," *International Journal for Philosophy of Religion* 8 (1977): 233–49.

15   Carol P. Christ, *She Who Changes: Re-Imagining the Divine in the World* (New York: Palgrave Macmillan, 2003).

16   Albert William Levi, "Bergson or Whitehead?" in *Process and Divinity,* ed. Reese and Freeman, 139.

17   Barry L. Whitney, *Evil and the Process God,* Toronto Studies in Theology, Vol. 19 (Lewiston, NY: Edwin Mellen Press, 1985), 75–81. In February 1981, Hartshorne gave some credit to Teilhard de Chardin for making Catholics more willing to consider the process alternative. Hartshorne remarked, "His main importance is in opening the eyes of many Roman Catholics who might otherwise have remained within the Thomistic tradition, to a growing God." Donald Wayne Viney, "Talks and Meetings with Charles Hartshorne" (page 10) PSU Digital Commons: http://digitalcommons.pittstate.edu/cgi /viewcontent.cgi?article=1041&context=phil_faculty

18   W. Norris Clarke, S. J., *The Philosophical Approach to God: A Neo-Thomist Perspective* (Winston-Salem, NC: Wake Forest University 1979), 93. In the revised edition of this book, Clarke deleted his statement about God as "Supreme Receiver," and he considerably toned down his concession to Hartshorne. In the later book he says, "And if we examine the matter more fully, we realize that God's 'receiving' from us, being delighted at our response to His love, is really His original delight in sharing with us in His eternal Now His own original power of loving and infinite goodness which has come back to Him in return." Clarke continues, "Could we not then possibly agree with the Whiteheadians in saying, in a very carefully qualified way, that God is not only the universe's great Giver, but also thereby its great Appreciator, its great Receiver? This

is stretching the language indeed for a Thomist, but perhaps not beyond the bounds of what is really, truly the case?" W. Norris Clarke, S. J., *The Philosophical Approach to God: A New Thomistic Perspective*, 2nd rev. ed. (New York: Fordham University Press, 2007), 137.

19 Clarke, T*he Philosophical Approach to God* (1979), 92.

20 David Tracy, *Blessed Rage for Order: The New Pluralism in Theology* (New York: Seabury Press, 1975), re-published by the University of Chicago Press in 1996. See especially ch. 8, "The Meaning, Meaningfulness, and Truth of God-Language," 172–203.

21 David Tracy, "Analogy, Metaphor and God Language: Charles Hartshorne," *The Modern Schoolman* 62/4 (May 1985): 259.

22 Hartshorne's mention of the "openness of God" dates to 1963 or 1964 (in the article reprinted in WM). The book that put Open Theism or the Open View of God on the radar of Evangelicals was co-authored by five scholars, all of whom are well-known to other Evangelical scholars: Clark Pinnock, Richard Rice, John Sanders, William Hasker, and David Basinger, *The Openness of God: A Biblical Challenge to the Traditional Understanding of God* (Downers Grove, IL: InterVarsity Press, 1994). Each author has written one or more books in defense of the open view of God. See, for example: Clark H. Pinnock, *Most Moved Mover: A Theology of God's Openness* (Grand Rapids, MI: Baker Academic, 2001); Richard Rice, *The Openness of God: The Relationship of Divine Foreknowledge and Human Free Will* (Nashville: Review and Herald Publishing Association, 1980); John Sanders, *The God Who Risks: a Theology of Divine Providence* (Downers Grove, IL: IVP Academic, 2007 [1998]); William Hasker, *God, Time, and Knowledge* (Ithaca, NY: Cornell University Press, 1989); David Basinger, *The Case for Freewill Theism: A Philosophical Assessment* (Downers Grove, IL: IVP Academic, 1996). See also: Gregory A. Boyd, *God of the Possible: A Biblical Introduction to the Open View of God* (Grand Rapids, MI: Baker, 2000).

For an analysis and assessment of the relation of Hartshorne's dipolar theism and Evangelical openness theology see Donald Wayne Viney, "The Varieties of Theism and the Openness of God: Charles Hartshorne and Free Will Theism," *The Personalist Forum* 14/2 (Fall 1998): 199–238. Available at the PSU Digital Commons site: http://digitalcommons.pittstate.edu/cgi/viewcontent

.cgi?article=1000&context=phil_faculty. See also Julia Enxing's very thorough and more recent treatment of the same topic in *Gott im Werden: Di Prozesstheologie Charles Hartshornes* (Regensberg: Verlag-Friedrich Pustet, 2013), ch. 5, pp. 240–94. Enxing does not flinch in calling out the uncharitable response to the proponents of open theism (especially Pinnock and Sanders) from some of their critics. For a defense of the idea that Jules Lequyer is a forerunner of open theism see Donald Wayne Viney, "Jules Lequyer and the Openness of God," *Faith and Philosophy* 14/2 (April 1997): 212–35.

23 See John B. Cobb, Jr. and Clark H. Pinnock, eds., *Searching for an Adequate God: A Dialogue Between Process Theists and Free Will Theists* (Grand Rapids, MI: William B. Eerdmans, 2000).

24 Richard Rice, *The Openness of God* (1980) was republished without the Appendix as *God's Foreknowledge and Man's Free Will* (Minneapolis: 1985). The Appendix of the earlier version specifically targets the interests of Seventh Day Adventists by examining the views of Ellen G. White as they bear on the question of human freedom and divine foreknowledge.

25 Gregory Boyd, *Trinity and Process: A Critical Evaluation of Hartshorne's Di-Polar Theism Towards a Trinitarian Metaphysics* (New York: Peter Lang, 1992), Preface.

26 Oord has edited and written many books. The clearest statement to date of his version of open theism, which he calls "Essential Kenosis," is in his book *The Uncontrolling Love of God: An Open and Relational Account of Providence* (Downers Grove, IL: IVP Academic, 2015).

27 John B. Cobb, Jr., "The Philosophy of Charles Hartshorne," *Process Studies* 21/2 (Summer 1992): 81.

28 Cobb, "The Philosophy of Charles Hartshorne," 84.

Primary Bibliography
of Philosophical Works

Compiled by Dorothy C. Hartshorne

Revised and Updated by Donald Wayne Viney and Randy Ramal

This bibliography is a corrected version of the one that appeared in *Process Studies* 30, 2 (2001): 374–409; in Santiago Sia's *Religion, Reason and God* (Frankfurt am Main: Peter Lang, 2004): 195–223; and in Herbert F. Vetter (ed.), *Hartshorne: A New World View* (Cambridge, Massachusetts: Harvard Square Library, 2007): 129–60. Earlier versions appeared in *Process and Divinity*, the Hartshorne Festschrift, eds. William L. Reese and Eugene Freeman (La Salle, Illinois: Open Court, 1964): 579–91; *Process Studies* 6, 1 (1973): 73–93 [Addenda published in issue 11, 2 (1981): 108–13]; and in *The Philosophy of Charles Hartshorne*, the Library of Living Philosophers, volume XX, ed. Lewis Hahn (La Salle, Illinois: Open Court, 1991): 735–66. Randy Ramal, while at the Center for Process Studies, added material to these earlier works in his alphabetically ordered bibliographies of Hartshorne's works posted on the CPS web site. Don Viney, working independently, was also adding items to the LLP bibliography. The following combines these separate efforts and is more than what either Viney or Ramal produced individually. Since the last version of this bibliography appeared, Viney has seen to the publication of several articles and a book that Hartshorne never published; those items have now been included. Typographical mistakes have been corrected and cross references for articles that later appeared in

Hartshorne's books have been added. There have also been added some items originally missed. We are especially grateful to Professor Yasuto Murota at St. Mary's College of Nagoya, Japan, for providing us with a copy of item number 470.

Although Viney and Ramal followed Dorothy Hartshorne's practice of listing items in chronological order, they diverged from her lead by (1) listing Hartshorne's abstracts of his books and articles under the same item as the book or article itself; (2) listing reviews and articles, including translations, that appeared in more than one place—but not in one of Hartshorne's books—under a single heading; (3) listing multiple replies in a single volume under a single item (Dorothy did this, but inconsistently). Thus, forty-eight items that she listed separately are consolidated here under other entries.

This bibliography revises and updates Dorothy's original, but it is in one respect less than what she compiled, for no attempt is made to list Hartshorne's ornithological works unless they include philosophical content. Moreover, Viney and Ramal make no claim to being exhaustive; for example, a complete bibliography would include Hartshorne's many letters to the editor, but none of those are listed here (nor are they listed in the bibliographies mentioned above). It is worth noting that there are over sixty unpublished articles in the Hartshorne archives as well as an extensive correspondence. Thus, what is offered here, though more extensive than previous bibliographies, remains a work in progress.

Books

1. *Collected Papers of Charles Sanders Peirce*. Edited by Charles Hartshorne and Paul Weiss. Cambridge: Harvard UP.

    Vol. 1, *Principles of Philosophy*, 1931.

    Vol. 2, *Elements of Logic*, 1932.

    Vol. 3, *Exact Logic*, 1933.

    Vol. 4, *The Simplest Mathematics*, 1933.

    Vol. 5, *Pragmatism and Pragmaticism*, 1934.

    Vol. 6, *Scientific Metaphysics*, 1935.

2. *The Philosophy and Psychology of Sensation*. Chicago: U of Chicago P, 1934. Reissued in Port Washington, New York: Kennikat P,

1968.

3   *Beyond Humanism: Essays in the New Philosophy of Nature.* Chicago: Willet, Clark and Company, 1937. Reprinted as a Bison Book Edition, with new Preface. Lincoln: U of Nebraska P, 1968. Also reprinted in Gloucester, Massachusetts: Peter Smith, 1975.

4. *Man's Vision of God and the Logic of Theism.* Chicago: Willet, Clark and Company, 1941. After 1948 published by Harper and Brothers, New York. Reprinted by Hamden, Connecticut: Archon Books, 1964.

5. *The Divine Relativity: A Social Conception of God.* The Terry Lectures, 1947. New Haven: Yale UP, 1948.

6. *Whitehead and the Modern World: Science, Metaphysics, and Civilization, Three Essays on the Thought of Alfred North Whitehead.* By Victor Lowe, Charles Hartshorne, and A.H. Johnson. Boston: the Beacon P, 1950. "Whitehead's Metaphysics" by Charles Hartshorne, 25-41. Reprinted by Books for Libraries P, 1972. "Whitehead's Metaphysics" reprinted as chapter 2 of *Whitehead's Philosophy.* See abstract in Program of the American Philosophical Association, Western Division (May 6-8, 1948): 13-14.

7. *Reality as Social Process: Studies in Metaphysics and Religion.* Foreword by William Ernest Hocking. Glencoe: The Free P and Boston: The Beacon P, 1953. Reprinted in New York: Hafner Publishing Co., 1971.

8. *Philosophers Speak of God* (with William L. Reese). Chicago: U of Chicago P, 1953, reprinted in 1969. Reissued by Chicago: Midway Reprints, 1976. Reprinted by Amherst, New York: Humanity Books, 2000, with an addendum to the Preface by William L. Reese.

9. *The Logic of Perfection and Other Essays in Neoclassical Metaphysics.* La Salle, Illinois: Open Court, 1962. Author's abstract in *The Monist* 59, 4 (1976): 596.

10. *Anselm's Discovery: A Re-Examination of the Ontological Proof for God's Existence.* La Salle, Illinois: Open Court, 1965.

11. The Social Conception of the Universe [Three chapters from Reality as Social Process]. Edited by Keiji Matsunobu. Tokyo: Aoyama, and New York: Macmillan, 1967.

12. *A Natural Theology for Our Time*. La Salle, Illinois: Open Court, 1967. Author's abstract in *The Monist* 59, 4 (1976): 594.

13. *Creative Synthesis and Philosophic Method*. London: SCM P Ltd., and La Salle, Illinois: Open Court, 1970. Reprinted in 1983 by Lanham, Maryland: UP of America. Chinese translation in process (The China Project, Center for Process Studies, Claremont, California). Author's abstract in *The Monist* 56, 4 (1972): 626-27.

14. *Whitehead's Philosophy: Selected Essays, 1935-1970*. Lincoln: U of Nebraska P, 1972. [Japanese translation by Keiji Matsunobu and Minoru Otsuka, Kyoto: Korosha, 1989.]

15. *Born to Sing: An Interpretation and World Survey of Bird Song*. Bloomington: Indiana UP, 1973. Author's abstract in *The Monist* 59, 2 (1976): 299.

16. *Aquinas to Whitehead: Seven Centuries of Metaphysics of Religion. The Aquinas Lecture, 1976*. Milwaukee: Marquette U Publications, 1976.

17. *Whitehead's View of Reality* (with Creighton Peden). New York: Pilgrim P, 1981. "Whitehead in Historical context" by Charles Hartshorne, 2-24.

18. *Insights and Oversights of Great Thinkers: An Evaluation of Western Philosophy*. Albany: State U of New York P, 1983.

19. *Omnipotence and other Theological Mistakes*. Albany: State U of New York P, 1984. [Japanese translation by Minoru Otsuka. Kyoto: Korosha, 1991.] Author's abstract in *The Monist* 69, 4 (1986): 633.

20. *Creativity in American Philosophy*. Albany: State U of New York P, 1984. [Spanish translation by Mari Luz Caso as *Creatividad en la Filosofia Estadonnidense* (Mexico: Edamex, 1987).]

21. *Wisdom as Moderation: A Philosophy of the Middle Way*. Albany: State U of New York P, 1987. [Japanese translation by Minoru Otsuka, with a preface by Charles Hartshorne.]

22. *The Darkness and the Light: A Philosopher Reflects Upon His Fortunate Career and Those Who Made It Possible*. Albany: State U of New York P, 1990.

23. *The Zero Fallacy and Other Essays in Neoclassical Philosophy*. Edited and Introduced by Mohammad Valady. Peru, Illinois: Open

Court, 1997.

24. *Hartshorne and Brightman on God, Process, and Persons: The Correspondence, 1922-1945*. Edited by Randall E. Auxier and Mark Y. A. Davies. Nashville: Vanderbilt UP, 2001.

25. *Charles Hartshorne's Letters to a Young Philosopher: 1979-1995*. Edited by Donald Wayne Viney. *Logos-Sophia: The Journal of the Pittsburg State University Philosophical Society*, Volume 11 (Fall 2001). Available at http://digitalcommons.pittstate.edu/phil_faculty/40/

26. *Hartshorne: A New World View, Essays by Charles Hartshorne*. Edited by Herbert F. Vetter. Cambridge, Massachusetts: Harvard Square Library, 2007. http://www.harvardsquarelibrary.org/Hartshorne/index.html.

27. *Creative Experiencing: A Philosophy of Freedom*. Edited by Donald Wayne Viney and Jincheol O. Albany: State University of New York Press 2011. [Hartshorne completed work on this manuscript in the late 1980s or early 1990s.]

28. *The Unity of Being*. [Original title: *An Outline and Defense of the Argument for the Unity of Being in the Absolute or Divine Good*]. Doctoral Dissertation, Harvard University. (May 1923). Edited by Randall E. Auxier and Hyatt Carter. Scheduled for publication from Open Court.

Articles, Reviews, and Discussions

1. "Memory, Youth, and Age." *The Haverfordian* 37, 8 (1916): 323.

2. "Barriers to Progress: Or Some Superstitions of Modernism." *The Gad-Fly* [Student Liberal Club of Harvard University] (1923): 1-15.

3. Review of A.N. Whitehead. *Symbolism, Its Meaning and Effect* (New York: Macmillan, 1927). *Hound and Horn* 1 (1927): 148-52.

4. Reviews of Martin Heidegger. *Sein und Zeit*; Oskar Becker, *Mathematische Existenz* (from *Jahrbuch für Philosophie und Phanomenologische Forschung*, Herausgegeben von Edmund Husserl) [Achter Band. Halle: Max Niemeyer, 1927, xxi, 809]. *Philosophical Review* 38, 3 (1929): 284-93. Incorporated into chapter 17 of *Beyond Humanism*.

5.   "Continuity, the Form of Forms, in Charles Peirce." *The Monist* 39, 4 (1929): 521-34.

6.   Review of Etienne Souriau. *L'Avenir de l'esthétique* (Paris: Félix Alcan, 1929). *International Journal of Ethics* 40, 1 (1929): 132-33

7.   "Ethics and the Assumption of Purely Private Pleasures." *International Journal of Ethics* 40, 4 (1930): 496-515.

8.   "Sense Quality and Feeling Tone." *Proceedings of the Seventh International Congress of Philosophy*, ed. Gilbert Ryle (London: Oxford UP, 1931): 168-72.

9.   "Contingency and the New Era in Metaphysics, I." *Journal of Philosophy* 29, 16 (1932): 421-31; "Contingency and the New Era in Metaphysics, II." *Journal of Philosophy* 29, 17 (1932): 457-69.

10.   Review of André Lalande. *Les Illusions évolutionnistes* (Paris: Félix Alcan, 1930). *International Journal of Ethics* 43, 1 (1932): 94-97.

11.   "Four Principles of Method—with Applications." *The Monist* 43, 1 (1933): 40-72.

12.   Review of G. Watts Cunningham. *The Idealistic Argument in Recent British and American Philosophy* (New York: Century, 1933). *International Journal of Ethics* 43, 4 (1933): 447-49.

13.   Foreword to *The Categories of Charles Peirce* by Eugene Freeman (Chicago: Open Court, 1934).

14.   Review of R. G. Collingwood. *An Essay on Philosophical Method* (Oxford: Clarendon, 1933). *International Journal of Ethics* 44, 3 (1934): 357-58.

15.   "The Intelligibility of Sensations." *The Monist* 44, 2 (1934): 161-85.

16.   Reviews of Ernest W. Barnes. *Scientific Theory and Religion* (New York: Macmillan, 1933); J. E. Turner. *Essentials in the Development of Religion* (New York: Macmillan, 1934); T. V. Seshagiro Row. *New Light on Fundamental Problems* (Madras: UP, 1932). *International Journal of Ethics* 44, 4 (1934): 465-71.

17.   Reviews of Gerhard Kraenzlin. *Max Schelers' Phaenomenologische Systematik*; Adolph Sternberger, *Der verstandene Tod: Eine Untersuchung zu Martin Heideggers Existenzilontologie* (Leipzig: S. Hirzel, 1934). *International Journal of Ethics* 44, 4 (1934): 478-80.

18.   "Redefining God." *New Humanist* 7, 4 (1934): 8-15. Reprinted in *Contemporary American Protestant Thought: 1900-1970*, ed. William

R. Miller (Indianapolis, Indiana: Bobbs-Merrill Co., 1973): 315-322. Also reprinted in *American Journal of Theology and Philosophy* 22, 2 (2001): 107-13.

19. "The New Metaphysics and Current Problems, I." *New Frontier* I, I (1934): 24-31; "The New Metaphysics and Current Problems, II." *New Frontier* I, 5 (1934): 8-14.

20. "Ethics and the New Theology." *International Journal of Ethics* 45, I (1934): 90-101.

21. Review of Louis Vialle. *Le Désir du néant* (Paris: Félix Alcan, 1933). *International Journal of Ethics* 45, I (1934): 116-117.

22. Review of William Pepperell Montague. *The Chances of Surviving Death* (Cambridge: Harvard UP, 1934). *International Journal of Ethics* 45, I (1934): 120-21

23. Reviews of John Nibb. *Christianity and Internationalism* (London: Elliot Stock, 1934); Georges Lakhovsky. *Le Racisme et l'orchestre universelle* (Paris: Félix Alcan, 1934). *International Journal of Ethics* 45, I (1934): 121-22.

24. "The Parallel Development of Method in Physics and Psychology." *Philosophy of Science* I, 4 (1934): 446-59.

25. "Pattern and Movement in Art and Science." *Comment* (The U of Chicago) 3, 2 (1935): 1-2, 11. Chapter 2 of *Reality as Social Process*.

26. Discussion: "Flexibility of Scientific Truth." *Philosophy of Science* 2 (1935): 255-56.

27. Review of D. Draghicesco. *Vérité et Revelation*, Vol. I. (Paris: Félix Alcan, 1934). *International Journal of Ethics* 45, 2 (1935): 248-249. [cf. item 36] Incorporated into chapter 4 of *Beyond Humanism*.

28. Review of Adolphe Ferrière. *Der Primat des Geistes als Grundlage einer aufbauenden Erziehung*, Translated by Emmi Hirschberg (Berlin: Julius Beltz, n.d.). *International Journal of Ethics* 45, 2 (1935): 250.

29. Review of Henry C. Simons. *A Positive Program for Laissez Faire* (Chicago: U of Chicago P, 1935). *Christian Century* 52, 23 (1935): 761-62.

30. "Metaphysics for Positivists." *Philosophy of Science* 2, 3 (1935): 287-303.

31. "On Some Criticisms of Whitehead's Philosophy." *Philosophical*

Review 44, 4 (1935): 323-44. [cf. item 50]. Chapter 3 of *Whitehead's Philosophy*.

32.   Reviews of John Wisdom. *Problems of Mind and Matter* (Cambridge: Cambridge UP, 1934); Thomas Whittaker. *Reason* (Cambridge: Cambridge UP, 1934); Julius W. Friend and James Feibleman. *Science and the Spirit of Man* (London: Allen and Unwin, 1933). *International Journal of Ethics* 45, 4 (1935): 461-65.

33.   Review of Gajanan Wasudeo Kaveeshwar. *The Metaphysics of Berkeley Critically Examined in the Light of Modern Philosophy* (Mandleshwar, India: A. Kaveeshwar, 1933). *International Journal of Ethics* 45, 4 (1935): 494.

34.   "The Compound Individual." *Philosophical Essays for Alfred North Whitehead*, ed. Otis H. Lee (New York: Longmans Green, 1936): 193-220. Chapter 4 of *Whitehead's Philosophy*.

35.   "The New Pantheism, I." *Christian Register* 115, 8 (1936): 119-20; "The New Pantheism, II." *Christian Register* 115, 9 (1936): 141-43.

36.   Review of D. Draghicesco. *Vérité et Revelation*, Vol. 2, (Paris: Félix Alcan, 1934). *International Journal of Ethics* 47, 1 (1936): 133-35. [cf. item 27].

37.   "The Philosophical Limitations of Humanism." *University Review* 3, 4 (1937): 240-42. Chapter 11 of *Reality as Social Process*.

38.   Abstract: "Positivism as Anthropomorphism." *The Journal of Philosophy* 34, 25 (1937): 685.

39.   Review of André Cresson. *La Representation*. (Paris: Boivin, 1936). *Philosophical Review* 47, 1 (1938): 90-91.

40.   Review of G. P. Adams, W. R. Dennes, J. Loewenberg, D. S. Mackay, P. Marhenke, S. C. Pepper, and E. W. Strong. *Knowledge and Society* (New York: Appleton-Century, 1938). *Christian Century* 55, 30 (1938): 917.

41.   Reply to [R. H., Jr.] Randall's review of *Beyond Humanism*, in *Journal of Philosophy* 35, 5 (1938): 131-33.

42.   Review of Jacques Maritain. *The Degrees of Knowledge* (New York: Scribner's, 1938). *Christian Century* 55 (1938): 1195. Also in *Journal of Religion* 19, 3 (1939): 267-69.

43.   "The Reality of the Past, the Unreality of the Future." *Hibbert Journal* 37, 2 (1939): 246-57.

44. Review of Wilhelm Keller. *Der Sinnbegriff als Kategorie der Geisteswissenschaften* (Munich: Ernst Reinhardt, 1937). *Philosophical Review* 48, 1 (1939): 95.

45. Review of Rasvihari Das. *The Philosophy of Whitehead* (London: James Clarke and Co., 1964). *Philosophical Review* 48, 2 (1939): 230-31.

46. Notes: Letter (Reply to Roger Holmes). *Philosophical Review* 68, 2 (1939): 243.

47. "The Method of Imaginative Variations," in "Notes Concerning Husserl." *Journal of Philosophy* 36, 9 (1939): 233-34.

48. "Are All Propositions about the Future either True or False?" *Program of the American Philosophical Association* (April 20-22, 1939): 26-32.

49. Review of A.N. Whitehead. *Modes of Thought* (New York: Macmillan, 1938). *Review of Religion* 3, 4 (1939): 494-496.

50. Discussion: "The Interpretation of Whitehead (Reply to John W. Blyth)." *Philosophical Review* 48, 4 (1939): 415-23. [cf. item 31].

51. Review of James Bissett Pratt. *Naturalism* (New Haven: Yale UP, 1939). *Journal of Religion* 19, 3 (1939): 234-35.

52. Review of Ralph Barton Perry. *In the Spirit of William James* (New Haven: Yale UP, 1938). *Journal of Religion* 19, 3 (1939): 247-48.

53. Review of A. Campbell Garnett. *Reality and Value* (New Haven: Yale UP, 1937). *The Scroll* 37, 3 (1939): 93-95.

54. "Husserl and the Social Structure of Immediacy." *Philosophical Essays in Memory of Edmund Husserl*. Marvin Farber, ed. (Cambridge: Harvard UP, 1940): 219-30.

55. "Santayana's Doctrine of Essence." *The Philosophy of George Santayana*, ed. Paul Arthur Schilpp. The Library of Living Philosophers, Vol. 2 (Evanston and Chicago: Northwestern UP, 1940): 135-82.

56. "The Three Ideas of God." *Journal of Liberal Religion* 1, 3 (1940): 9-16. Chapter 9 of *Reality as Social Process*.

57. Review of Justus Buchler. *Charles Peirce's Empiricism* (New York: Harcourt, Brace, 1939). *Ethics* 50, 2 (1940): 248.

58. Review of Josef Maier. *On Hegel's Critique of Kant* (New York:

Columbia UP, 1939). *Journal of Religion* 20, 1 (1940): 106.

59. Review of Paul Arthur Schilpp, ed. *The Philosophy of John Dewey*. Library of Living Philosophers (Evanston: Northwestern UP, 1939). *Christian Century* 42, 10 (1940): 313-15. Chapter 12 of *Reality as Social Process*.

60. Review of Irwin Edman. *Arts and the Man* (New York: Norton, 1939). *Ethics* 50, 3 (1940): 369-70.

61. Reviews of Arthur Hazard Dakin. *Man the Measure* (Princeton, N. J.: Princeton UP, 1939); Archibald Allan Bowman, *A Sacramental Universe*. (Princeton, N. J.: Princeton UP, 1939). *Ethics* 50, 3 (1940): 363-66.

62. Review of Milton Karl Munitz. *The Moral Philosophy of Santayana* (New York: Columbia UP, 1939). *Journal of Religion* 20, 2 (1940): 196-98.

63. Review of Charles M. Perry. *Toward a Dimensional Realism* (Norman: U of Oklahoma P, 1939). *Journal of Religion* 20, 2 (1940): 214.

64. Review of Theodore Meyer Greene. *The Arts and the Art of Criticism* (Princeton, N. J.: Princeton UP, 1940). *Ethics* 51, 1 (1940): 116-17.

65. "Whitehead's Idea of God." *The Philosophy of Alfred North Whitehead*, ed. Paul Arthur Schilpp. The Library of Living Philosophers, Vol. 3 (Evanston and Chicago: Northwestern UP, 1941): 513-59. Chapter 5 of *Whitehead's Philosophy*.

66. "Charles Sanders Peirce's Metaphysics of Evolution." *New England Quarterly* 14, 1 (1941): 49-63.

67. "Anthropomorphic Tendencies in Positivism." *Philosophy of Science* 8, 2 (1941): 184-203.

68. Review of Frederick J. E. Woodbridge. *An Essay on Nature* (New York: Columbia UP, 1940). *Ethics* 51, 4 (1941): 488-90.

69. Review of DeWitt H. Parker. *Experience and Substance* (Ann Arbor: U of Michigan P, 1940). *Christian Century* 48, 27 (1941): 864. Also published in *Philosophical Review* 51, 5 (1942): 523-26.

70. "A Critique of Peirce's Idea of God." *Philosophical Review* 50, 5 (1941): 516-23. See also, "Abstracts of Papers to be Read at the Joint Meeting of the Eastern and Western Divisions of the American

Philosophical Association, Columbia U, December, 1939." *Journal of Philosophy* 36, 25 (1939): 683-84.

71. Review of Ledger Wood. *The Analysis of Knowledge* (Princeton, N. J.: Princeton UP, 1941). *Philosophy and Phenomenological Research* 2, 1 (1941): 104-08.

72. Review of Gustaf Stromberg. *The Soul of the Universe* (Philadelphia: David McKay P, 1940). *Review of Religion* 5, 3 (1941): 357-60.

73. "A Philosophy of Democratic Defense." *Science, Philosophy, and Religion: Second Symposium* (New York: Conference on Science, Philosophy, and Religion in their Relation to the Democratic Way of Life, Inc. 1942): 130-72.

74. Review of Justus Buchler, ed. *The Philosophy of Peirce: Selected Writings* (New York: Harcourt Brace, 1940). *Philosophical Review* 51, 1 (1942): 92.

75. Review of Etienne Gilson. *God and Philosophy* (New Haven: Yale UP, 1941). *Journal of Religion* 22, 2 (1942): 221-24.

76. "Elements of Truth in the Group-Mind Concept." *Social Research* 9, 2 (1942): 248-65. Chapter 3 of *Reality as Social Process.*

77. Review of Paul Arthur Schilpp, ed. *The Philosophy of Alfred North Whitehead* (Evanston: Northwestern UP, 1941). *Religion in Life* 11, 3 (1942): 469-70. Also published in *Thought* 17, 66 (1942): 545-47.

78. Review of Stephen C. Pepper. *World Hypotheses* (Berkeley: U of California P, 1942). *Ethics* 53, 1 (1942): 73-75.

79. "Organic and Inorganic Wholes." *Philosophy and Phenomenological Research* 3, 2 (1942): 127-136. Notice in *Program of the Fiftieth Anniversary Symposia* (Chicago: U of Chicago P, 1941): 12. Published as "A World of Organisms," chapter 7 of *Logic of Perfection*. Republished in *Process Philosophy: Basic Writings*, eds. Jack R. Sibley and Pete A.Y. Gunter (Washington D.C.: UP of America, 1978): 275-96.

80. Comment on "Democracy and the Rights of Man." *Science, Philosophy, and Religion: Second Symposium* (New York: Conference on Science, Philosophy, and Religion, Inc. 1942): 292.

81. Review of John Blyth. *Whitehead's Theory of Knowledge* (Providence: Brown UP, 1941). *Philosophy and Phenomenological Research* 3, 3 (1943): 372-75.

82. "Is Whitehead's God the God of Religion?" [Suggested by Ely's book, cf. item 85]. *Ethics* 53, 3 (1943): 219-27. Chapter 6 of *Whitehead's Philosophy*.

83. Review of Lewis Edwin Hahn. *A Contextualistic Theory of Perception* (Berkeley: U of California P, 1942). *Ethics* 53, 3 (1943): 233.

84. Review of Campbell Garnett. *A Realistic Philosophy of Religion* (Chicago: Willett Clark, 1942). *Journal of Religion* 23, 1 (1943): 70-71. Also published in *Ethics* 54, 1 (1943): 62-63.

85. Review of Stephen Lee Ely. *The Religious Availability of Whitehead's God* (Madison: U of Wisconsin P, 1942). *Journal of Liberal Religion* 5, 1 (1943): 55.

86. Communication, Rejoinder: "Ely on Whitehead." *Journal of Liberal Religion* 5, 2 (1943): 97-100.

87. Discussion: "Reflections on the Strength and Weakness of Thomism." *Ethics* 54, 1 (1943): 53-57.

88. "A Mathematical Analysis of Theism." *Review of Religion* 8, 1 (1943): 20-38. Revised as epilogue of *Philosophers Speak of God*, 499-514.

89. Radio Discussion: "How Christians Should Think About Peace." By Edwin Aubrey, Charles Hartshorne, and Bernard Loomer. Pamphlet. Chicago: U of Chicago Round Table (April 9, 1944): 20 pages.

90. Review of K. R. Sreenivasa Iyengar. *The Metaphysics of Value*, Vol. I. (Mysore: U of Mysore, 1942). *Ethics* 54, 3 (1944): 230-31.

91. Review of John Elof Boodin. *Religion of Tomorrow* (New York: Philosophical Library, 1943). *Ethics* 54, 3 (1944): 233-34.

92. "The Formal Validity and Real significance of the Ontological Argument." *Philosophical Review* 53, 3 (1944): 225-45. [cf. items 100 and 106].

93. "Philosophy and Orthodoxy." *Ethics* 54, 4 (1944): 295-98.

94. Review of Werner Jaeger. *Humanism and Theology* (Milwaukee: Marquette UP, 1943). *Journal of Religion* 24, 3 (1944): 230.

95. "God and Man not Rivals." *Journal of Liberal Religion* 6, 2 (1944): 9-13.

96. Abstract: "Beauty as Balance of Unity and Variety." In *Proceedings*

of The American Society for Aesthetics. First Annual Meeting. Cleveland, Ohio (Sept. 11-13, 1944): 29-30.

97. Comments on "Philosophical Ideas and Enduring Peace," 557; on "Philosophical Ideas and World Peace," 597; on "In Quest of Worldly Wisdom," 719-721. *Approaches to World Peace, Fourth Symposium*, eds. Lyman Bryson, Louis Finkelstein, and Robert M. MacIver (New York: Conference on Science, Philosophy, and Religion, 1944).

98. Review of Henry Alonzo Myers. *The Spinoza-Hegel Paradox* (Ithaca: Cornell UP, 1944). *Ethics* 55, 1 (1944): 71-72.

99. Review of Adhar Chandra Das. *Negative Fact, Negation, and Truth* (Calcutta: Calcutta UP, 1942). *Ethics* 55, 1 (1944): 77.

100. Discussion: "On Hartshorne's Formulation of the Ontological Argument: A Rejoinder [to Elton]." *Philosophical Review* 54, 1 (1945): 63-65. [cf. items 92 and 106].

101. Entries in *An Encyclopedia of Religion*, ed. Vergilius Ferm (New York: Philosophical Library, 1945): acosmism; analogy; anthropopathism; Aristotle and Aristotelianism; axiom; Berkeley, George; Carneades; cause; Copernican astronomy; eternal; eternity; ether; etiology, aetiology; foreknowledge, Divine; Gerson, Levi ben; God, as personal; Hume; infinite; Kant, Immanuel; omnipotence; omnipresence; omniscience; panentheism; panlogism; pantheism; Peirce, Charles Sanders; perfect, perfection; Ptolemaic astronomy; Renouvier, Charles; Spencer, Herbert; Spinoza, Benedict; time; transcendence; Whitehead, Alfred North.

102. Review Article: "Efficient Causality in Aristotle and St. Thomas" by Francis X. Meehan's book of the same title (Washington: Catholic UP, 1940). *Journal of Religion* 25, 1 (1945): 25-32. [cf. item 111].

103. Review of Rudolf Jordan. *Homo Sapiens Socialis* (South Africa: Central News Agency, 1944). *Ethics* 55, 4 (1945): 312-13.

104. Review of Jacques Maritain. *The Dream of Descartes* (New York: Philosophical Library, 1944). *Ethics* 55, 4 (1945): 321.

105. Review of *Vladimir Soloviev's Lectures on Godmanhood* (with Introduction by Peter Zouboff) (New York: International UP, 1944). *Ethics* 55, 4 (1945): 322.

106. "Professor Hartshorne's Syllogism: Rejoinder [to Elton]." *Philosophical Review* 54, 5 (1945): 506-08. [cf. items 92 and 100].

107. Review of K. F. Reinhardt. *A Realistic Philosophy* (Milwaukee: Bruce, 1944). *Philosophical Review* 54, 5 (1945): 521-22.

108. "A New Philosophic Conception of the Universe." *Hibbert Journal* 44, 1 (1945): 14-21. Chapter 1 of *Reality as Social Process*.

109. Review of Paul Arthur Schilpp, ed. *The Philosophy of Bertrand Russell*. Library of Living Philosophers, Vol. 5. (Evanston: Northwestern UP, 1944). *Journal of Religion* 25, 4 (1945): 280-84. Chapter 13 of *Reality as Social Process*.

110. Communication: "Reply to Father Meehan." *Journal of Religion* 26, 1 (1946): 54-57. [cf. item 103].

111. Review of Erich Frank. *Philosophical Understanding and Religious Truth* (London: Oxford UP, 1945). *Review of Religion* 10, 2 (1946): 182-89.

112. Review of William Ernest Hocking. *Science and the Idea of God* (Chapel Hill: U of North Carolina P, 1944). *Philosophy and Phenomenological Research* 6, 3 (1946): 453-57.

113. "Relative, Absolute, and Superrelative: A Formal Analysis." *Philosophical Review* 55, 3 (1946): 213-28. Chapter 6 of *Reality as Social Process*.

114. "The Common Good and the Value Receptacle." *Program of the American Philosophical Association, Western Division* (May 9-11, 1946): 10-11.

115. "Tragic and Sublime Aspects of Christian Love." *Journal of Liberal Religion* 8, 1 (1946): 36-44. Chapter 8 of *Reality as Social Process*.

116. "Theological Values in Current Metaphysics." *Journal of Religion* 26, 3 (1946): 157-67. Chapter 7 of *Reality as Social Process*.

117. "Leibniz's Greatest Discovery." *Journal of the History of Ideas* 7, 4 (1946): 411-21.

118. "Ideal Knowledge Defines Reality: What Was True in Idealism." *Journal of Philosophy* 43, 21 (1946): 573-82. See also: Correction of "Ideal Knowledge Defines Reality." *Journal of Philosophy* 43, 26 (1946): 724.

119. Review of Henri Bergson. *The Creative Mind*. Trans. Mabelle L. Andison (New York: Philosophy Library, 1946). *Journal of Religion*

27, 1 (1947): 64-65.

120. Review of José Ortega y Gasset. *Concord and Liberty* (New York: Norton, 1946). *Christian Century* 64, 7 (1947): 207.

121. Review of Gustav Theodor Fechner. *Religion of a Scientist: Selections from Fechner*, ed. and trans. Walter Lowrie (New York: Pantheon, 1946). *Journal of Religion* 27, 2 (1947): 126-28.

122. Review of Nels F. S. Ferré. *Faith and Reason* (New York: Harper, 1946). *Review of Religion* 11, 4 (1947): 409-13.

123. Review of Martin Foss. *The Idea of Perfection in the Western World* (Princeton, N. J.: Princeton UP, 1946). *Journal of Modern History* 19, 2 (1947): 15.

124. "God as Absolute, Yet Related to All." *Review of Metaphysics* 1, 1 (1947): 24-51.

125. Review of Henry N. Wieman et al. *Religious Liberals Reply* (Boston: Beacon P, 1947). *Christian Register* 126, 9 (1947): 412-13.

126. Review of A. H. Johnson. *The Wit and Wisdom of Whitehead* (Boston: Beacon P, 1947). *Christian Register* 126, 10 (1947): 446.

127. "Two Levels of Faith and Reason." *Journal of Bible and Religion* 16, 1 (1948): 30-38. See also *Program of Week of Work of the National Council on Religion in Higher Education* (1947): 16. Chapter 10 of *Reality as Social Process*.

128. Review of Paul Weiss. *Nature and Man* (New York: Henry Holt, 1947). *Ethics* 58, 2 (1948): 143-44.

129. Review of Campbell Garnett. *God in Us: A Liberal Christian Philosophy of Religion for the General Reader* (Chicago: Willett Clark, 1945). *Ethics* 58, 2 (1948): 151.

130. "The Rationalistic Criterion in Metaphysics." *Philosophy and Phenomenological Research* 8, 3 (1948): 436-47.

131. "Existential Propositions and the Law of Categories." *Fascicule 1, Proceedings of the Tenth International Congress of Philosophy*, eds. E. W. Beth et al. (Amsterdam: North-Holland Publishing Company, 1948): 342-44.

132. "Aesthetics of Color." *Program: Research in Textiles, Clothing, and Related Art* (March 19-20, 1948): 2.

133. Review of Jean Wahl. *The Philosopher's Way* (New York: Oxford

UP, 1948). *Philosophical Review* 57, 5 (1948): 509-11.

134. "Ein theologisches Paradoxon. I Die Wissensform des Paradoxons. II Die Willensform des Paradoxons." *Philosophisches Jahrbuch* 59, 2 (1949): 250-51.

135. "Noch einmal die Zufälligkeit der Welt und Notwendigkeit Gottes: Erwiderung an Dr. Ferdinand Bergenthal." *Philosophisches Jahrbuch* 59, 2 (1949): 355-56.

136. "Ob Göttliches Wissen um die weltliche Existenz notwendig sein kann: Eine Erwiderung." *Philosophisches Jahrbuch* 60, 4 (1950): 469-71.

137. "The Synthesis of Idealism and Realism." *Theoria* (Sweden) 15 (1949): 90-107. Chapter 4 of *Reality as Social Process*; chapter 8, section B of *Zero Fallacy*.

138. "Chance, Love, and Incompatibility." Presidential Address, Western Division of the American Philosophical Association meeting at Columbus, Ohio, April 29, 1949. *Philosophical Review* 58, 5 (1949): 429-50. Chapter 5 of *Reality as Social Process*.

139. Review of Otis Lee. *Existence and Inquiry* (Chicago: U of Chicago P, 1949). *Review of Metaphysics* 3, 1 (1949): 107-14.

140. "Panpsychism." *A History of Philosophical Systems*, ed. Vergilius Ferm (New York: Philosophical Library, 1950): 442-53.

141. "Le Principe de relativité philosophique chez Whitehead." *Revue de Métaphysique et de Morale* 55, 1 (1950): 16-29. Lecture originally delivered at the Sorbonne, Feb. 4, 1949, announced in Bulletin. EC 1959. Translation by D. W. Viney, "The Philosophical Principle of Relativity in Whitehead" in *Process Studies* 40/1 (Spring/Summer 2011): 91-103.

142. "The Divine Relativity and Absoluteness: A Reply [to John Wild]." *Review of Metaphysics* 4, 1 (1950): 31-60.

143. "God in General Philosophical Thought." [article in Hebrew] *The Encyclopedia Hebraica* 3 (1951) [Jewish Calendar 5711], Jerusalem: Encyclopedia Publishing Company, 1951: 467-78.

144. "Strict and Genetic Identity: An Illustration of the Relations of Logic to Metaphysics." *Structure, Method, and Meaning: Essays in Honor of Henry M. Sheffer*, eds. Horace M. Kallen et al. (New York: Liberal Arts P, 1951): 242-54.

145. "Philosophy of Religion in the United States." *Philosophy and Phenomenological Research* 11, 3 (1951): 406-10. French translation, "La Philosophie de la religion aux Etats-Unis," in *Les Etudes Philosophiques* 7, 1-2 (1952): 50-56.

146. Discussion: "Arthur Berndtson on Mystical Experience." *Personalist* 32, 2 (1951): 191-93.

147. Review of Kelvin Van Nuys. *Science and Cosmic Purpose* (New York: Harper, 1949). *Review of Religion* 16, 1-2 (1951): 79-84.

148. "The Relativity of Nonrelativity: Some Reflections on Firstness." *Studies in the Philosophy of Charles Sanders Peirce*, eds. Philip P. Wiener and Frederic H. Young (Cambridge: Harvard UP, 1952): 215-24.

149. "Radhakrishnan on Mind, Matter, and God." *The Philosophy of Saevepalli Radhakrishnan*, ed. Paul Arthur Schilpp. The Library of Living Philosophers, Vol. 8. (New York: Tudor, 1952): 315-22.

150. "Tillich's Doctrine of God." *The Theology of Paul Tillich*. The Library of Living Theology, Vol. 1, eds. Charles W. Kegley and Robert W. Bretall (New York: Macmillan, 1952): 164-95.

151. "Time, Death, and Eternal Life." *Journal of Religion* 32, 2 (1952): 97-107. Reprinted in *Classical and Contemporary Readings in the Philosophy of Religion*. 2nd ed. John Hick (Englewood Cliffs, New Jersey: Prentice-Hall, 1970): 357-69. Incorporated into chapter 10 of *Logic of Perfection*.

152. Review of Georg Siegmund. *Naturordnung als Quelle der Gotteserkenntnis: Neubegründung des theologischen Gottesbeweises* (Freiburg: Herder, 1950). *Philosophy and Phenomenological Research* 12, 4 (1952): 584-85.

153. "Politics and the Metaphysics of Freedom." *Enquête sur la liberté, Fédération internationale des sociétés de philosophie*. Publié avec le concours de l'u.n.e.s.c.o (Paris: Hermann, 1953): 79-85. Chapter 13 of *Creative Experiencing*.

154. "Noch einmal, das Wissen Gottes." *Philosophisches Jahrbuch* 62, 2 (Freiburg-München: Verlag Karl Alber, 1953): 409-11.

155. "Spirit as Life Freely Participating in Life." *Biosophical Review* 10, 2 (1953): 31-32.

156. "The Monistic Theory of Expression." *Journal of Philosophy* 50, 14

(1953): 425-34.

157. Review of John Wisdom. *Philosophy and Psycho-Analysis* (New York: Philosophical Library, 1953). *Ethics* 63, 4 (1953): 317-18.

158. Discussion: "The Immortality of the Past: Critique of a Prevalent Misinterpretation." *Review of Metaphysics* 7, 1 (1953): 98-112.

159. Symposium: "Are Religious Dogmas Cognitive and Meaningful?" *Journal of Philosophy* 51, 5 (1954): 148-50.

160. Review of Risieri Frondizi. *The Nature of the Self* (New Haven: Yale UP, 1953). *Philosophy and Phenomenological Research* 14, 3 (1954): 419-20.

161. "The Kinds of Theism: A Reply [to Taubes]." *Journal of Religion* 34, 2 (1954): 127-31.

162. "Mind, Matter, and Freedom." *Scientific Monthly* 78, 5 (1954): 314-20. Chapter 8 of *Logic of Perfection*.

163. Review Article: "Whitehead's Philosophy of Reality as Socially-Structured Process" (apropos *Alfred North Whitehead: An Anthology*, selected by F.S.C. Northrop and Mason Gross [New York: Macmillan, 1953]). *Chicago Review* 8, 2 (1954): 60-77. Chapter 7 of *Whitehead's Philosophy*.

164. Review of F. W. Eggleston. *Reflections of an Australian Liberal* (Melbourne: Cheshire, 1953). *Ethics* 64, 4 (1954): 332.

165. "Biology and the Spiritual View of the World: A Comment on Dr. Birch's Paper." *Christian Scholar* 37, 3 (1954): 408-09.

166. "Russian Metaphysics: Some Reactions to Zenkovsky's History." *Review of Metaphysics* 8, 1 (1954): 61-78. Incorporated into chapter 11 of *Logic of Perfection*.

167. "Causal Necessities: An Alternative to Hume." *Philosophical Review* 63, 4 (1954): 479-99.

168. Review of J. Defever, S. J. *La Preuve réelle de Dieu* (Paris: Desclée de Brouwer, 1953). *Philosophy and Phenomenological Research* 15, 2 (1954): 285-86.

169. Review of Brand Blanshard. *The Nature of Thought* (London: Allen and Unwin, 1959). *Philosophische Rundschau* 3, 1-2 (1955): 119-20.

170. "Process as Inclusive Category: A Reply [to John E. Smith]." *Journal of Philosophy* 52, 4 (1955): 94-102.

171. Review of Eranos et al. *Spirit and Nature, Papers from the Eranos Yearbooks*, vol. 1. (New York: Pantheon, 1954). *Journal of Religion* 35, 2 (1955): 106-07.

172. Review of Wilmon Henry Sheldon. *God and Polarity* (New Haven: Yale UP, 1954). *Philosophical Review* 64, 2 (1955): 312-16. Chapter 15 of *Creativity in American Philosophy*.

173. Panel Discussion: 1955 Edward Gallahue Seminar in Religion and Psychology at the Menninger Foundation. *Passim.* [Mimeographed.]

174. "Some Empty Though Important Truths: A Preface to Metaphysics." *Review of Metaphysics* 8, 4 (1955): 553-68. Reprinted in *American Philosophers at Work: The Philosophic Scene in the United States*, ed. Sidney Hook (New York: Criterion Books, 1956): 225-35. Chapter 12 of *Logic of Perfection*.

175. "The Unity of Man and the Unity of Nature." *Emory University Quarterly* 11, 3 (1955): 129-41. Chapter 13 of *Logic of Perfection*.

176. "Royce's Mistake and Achievement." *Journal of Philosophy* 53, 3 (1956): 123-30. Chapter 6 of *Creativity in American Philosophy*.

177. Panel Discussion: 1956 Edward Gallahue Seminar in Religion and Psychology at the Menninger Foundation. *Passim.* [Mimeographed.]

178. "Comments on Stallknecht's Theses." (Colloquium No. 8). *Review of Metaphysics* 9, 3 (1956): 464-65.

179. Review of Robert Leet Patterson. *Irrationalism and Rationalism in Religion* (Durham: Duke UP, 1954). *Review of Religion* 20, 3-4 (1956): 211-13.

180. "The Idea of God—Literal or Analogical?" *Christian Scholar* 29, 2 (1956): 131-36. Chapter 3 of *Logic of Perfection*.

181. Discussion: "New Propositions and New Truths." *Review of Metaphysics* 9, 4 (1956): 656-61.

182. "Two Strata of Meaning in Religious Discourse." *Symposium on Philosophy of Religion, Southern Philosopher* 5, 3 (1956): 4-7. Expanded in *Logic of Perfection* as chapter 4, "Three Strata of Meaning of Religious Discourse." [cf. item 282].

183. "Some Reflections Suggested by H. Wolfson's *Philosophy of the Church Fathers, Vol. I: Faith, Trinity, Incarnation*." (Cambridge:

Harvard UP, 1956). *Collection of Reviews*, Southern Society for Philosophy of Religion, J. R. Cresswell, Bibliographer (1957): 1-10. [Mimeographed]

184. "Whitehead and Berdyaev: Is there Tragedy in God?" *Journal of Religion* 37, 2 (1957): 71-84. Chapter 13 of *Whitehead's Philosophy*.

185. Review of William Ernest Hocking. *The Coming World Civilization* (New York: Harper, 1956). *Chicago Theological Seminary Register* 47, 5 (1957): 21-22. Also published in *Philosophy and Phenomenological Research* 17, 4 (1957): 562-63.

186. Review of Gerda Walter. *Phänomenologie der Mystik* (Olten und Freiburg im Breisgau: Walter-Verlag, 1955). *Philosophy and Phenomenological Research* 18, 1 (1957): 140-41.

187. "Charles Peirce, Philosopher-Scientist." Charles Sanders Peirce Symposium, No.1. *Journal of Public Law* 7, 1 (1958): 2-12.

188. "Whitehead on Process: A Reply to Professor Eslick." *Philosophy and Phenomenological Research* 18, 4 (1958): 514-20.

189. "Science, Insecurity, and the Abiding Treasure." *Journal of Religion* 38, 3 (1958): 168-74. Abridged version in *The Spirit of American Philosophy: An Anthology*, selected, edited, and introduced by Gerald E. Myers (New York: Capricorn Books, 1971): 327-32. Incorporated into chapter 9 of *Logic of Perfection*.

190. "Outlines of a Philosophy of Nature, Part I." *Personalist* 39, 3 (1958): 239-48. "Outlines of a Philosophy of Nature, Part II." *Personalist* 39, 4 (1958): 380-91.

191. "Freedom Requires Indeterminism and Universal Causality." *Journal of Philosophy* 55, 19 (1958): 793-811. Chapter 6 of *Logic of Perfection*.

192. "Metaphysical Statements as Nonrestrictive and Existential." *Review of Metaphysics* 12, 1 (1958): 35-47. Chapter 8 of *Creative Synthesis*.

193. "The Logical Structure of Givenness." *Philosophical Quarterly* [Scotland] 8, 33 (1958): 307-16.

194. "The Philosophy of Creative Synthesis." *Journal of Philosophy* 55, 22 (1958): 944-53. Reprinted in *Americana: A Monthly Journal of Humanities, Social Sciences, and Natural Sciences* [Tokyo] 5, 8 (1959): 80-90. Tokyo, U.S.I.S. In Japanese. EC 1968. Part of

chapter 1 of *Creative Synthesis*. [cf. items 219, 220, and 414]

195. Discussion: "The Structure of Metaphysics: A Criticism of Lazerowitz's Theory." *Philosophy and Phenomenological Research* 19, 2 (1958): 226-40. Incorporated into chapter 5 of *Wisdom as Moderation*.

196. "Four Unrefuted Forms of the Ontological Argument." *Journal of Philosophical Studies* [Kyoto, Japan] 40, 1 (1959): 1-15. In Japanese, with English Summary. [Summer 1958, Kyoto American Studies Seminar—in English.]

197. "A Philosopher's Assessment of Christianity." *Religion and Culture: Essays in Honor of Paul Tillich*, ed. Walter Leibrecht (New York: Harper, 1959): 167-80.

198. "John Wisdom On 'Gods': Two Views of the Logic of Theism." *Downside Review* [Bath, England] (1958-1959): 5-17. Chapter 5 of *Logic of Perfection*.

199. "The Principle of Shared Creativity." *Unitarian Symposia No. 6, What Can Religion Offer Modern Man?* (1959): 1-8.

200. "Freedom, Individuality, and Beauty in Nature." *Snowy Egret* 24, 2 (1960): 5-14. [Mimeographed] Chapter 9 of *Hartshorne: A New World View*.

201. "Equalitarianism and the Great Inequalities." *Emory Alumnus* 36, 7 (1960): 24-25, 49.

202. "Jinsei no mokuteki" ("The Aim of Life.") Trans. Toshio Mikoda, *Tetsugaku Kenkyu* [Journal of Philosophical Studies, Japan] 41, 2 (1960): 1-13.

203. "The Buddhist-Whiteheadian View of the Self and the Religious Traditions." *Proceedings of the Ninth International Congress for the History of Religions* (Tokyo and Kyoto: Maruzen, 1960 [1958]): 298-302.

204. "Whitehead and Contemporary Philosophy." *The Relevance of Whitehead: Philosophical Essays in Commemoration of the Centenary of the Birth of Alfred North Whitehead*, ed. Ivor Leclerc (London: Allen and Unwin, 1961): 21-43. Chapter 10 of *Whitehead's Philosophy*.

205. "Metaphysics and the Modality of Existential Judgments." *The Relevance of Whitehead: Philosophical Essays in Commemoration*

of the Centenary of the Birth of Alfred North Whitehead, ed. Ivor Leclerc (London: Allen and Unwin, 1961): 107-21.

206. "Hume's Metaphysics and Its Present-Day Influence." *New Scholasticism* 35, 2 (1961): 152-71. Chapter 13 of *Insights and Oversights*.

207. "The Social Structure of Experience." *Philosophy* 36, 137 (1961): 97-111.

208. "The Structure of Givenness." *Philosophical Forum* 18 (1960-1961): 22-39. Chapter 16 of *Creativity in American Philosophy*. Reprinted as Appendix 2 of *Hartshorne and Brightman on God*.

209. "God's Existence: A Conceptual Problem." *Religious Experience and Truth: A Symposium*, ed. Sidney Hook (New York University Press, 1961): 211-19.

210. Discussion: "Professor Hall on Perception." *Philosophy and Phenomenological Research* 21, 4 (1961): 563-71.

211. "Tillich and the Other Great Tradition." *Anglican Theological Review* 43, 3 (1961): 245-59. Part of chapter 7 in *Creative Synthesis*.

212. "The Logic of the Ontological Argument." *Journal of Philosophy* 58, 17 (1961): 471-73.

213. Discussion: "Absolute Objects and Relative Subjects: A Reply [to F. H. Parker]." *Review of Metaphysics* 15, 1 (1961): 174-88.

214. "Man in Nature." *Experience, Existence, and the Good: Essays in Honor of Paul Weiss*, ed. Irwin C. Lieb (Carbondale: Southern Illinois UP, 1961): 89-99.

215. "Whitehead, the Anglo-American Philosopher-Scientist." *Proceedings of the American Catholic Philosophical Association* (Washington: Catholic U of America, 1961): 163-71. Chapter 9 of *Whitehead's Philosophy*.

216. Introduction to Second Edition, *Saint Anselm: Basic Writings*. Trans. S. W. Deane (La Salle, Illinois: Open Court Publishing Company, 1962): 1-19.

217. "The Modern World and a Modern View of God." *Crane Review* 4, 2 (1962): 73-85. Also in *Philosophy of Religion: Contemporary Perspectives*, ed. Norbert O. Schedler (New York: Macmillan Publishing Co., Inc., 1974): 469-79. Chapter 5 of *Hartshorne: A New World View*.

218. "What Did Anselm Discover?" *Union Seminary Quarterly Review* 17, 3 (1962): 213-222. An expanded version published in *The Many-Faced Argument*, eds. John Hick and Arthur C. McGill (New York: Macmillan, 1967): 321-33. The 1962 version of the paper is reprinted as chapter 8 of *Insights and Oversights*.

219. "La Creatividad Participada." Trans. Sira Jaén. *Revista de Filosofía de la Universidad de Costa Rica* 3, 11 (1962): 237-44. Spanish version of most of chapter 1 of *Creative Synthesis*. [cf. items 194, 220, and 414]

220. "Religion and Creative Experience." *Darshana, an International Quarterly of Philosophy, Psychology, Psychical Research, Religion, Mysticism, and Sociology* [India] 2, 1 (1962): 47-52. Also in *Unitarian Register and Universalist Leader* 141, 6 (1962): 9-11. Part of Chapter 1 of *Creative Synthesis*. Chapter 3 of *Hartshorne: A New World View*. [cf. items 194, 219, and 414]

221. "Mind as Memory and Creative Love." *Theories of the Mind*, ed. Jordan M. Scher (New York: The Free Press of Glencoe, 1962): 440-63.

222. Discussion: "How Some Speak and Yet Do Not Speak of God." *Philosophy and Phenomenological Research* 23, 2 (1962): 274-76. Part of chapter 5 of *Wisdom as Moderation*.

223. "Individual Differences and the Ideal of Equality." *New South* 18, 2 (1963): 3-8. Chapter 14 of *Zero Fallacy*.

224. "Alternative Conceptions of God." *Religious Belief and Philosophical Thought*. ed. William P. Alston (New York: Harcourt, Brace, & World, 1963): 320-37. Reprinted from *Man's Vision of God*.

225. "Further Fascination of the Ontological Argument: Replies to Richardson." *Union Seminary Quarterly Review* 18, 3 [Part I] (1963): 244-45.

226. "Whitehead's Novel Intuition." *Alfred North Whitehead: Essays On His Philosophy*, ed. George L. Kline (Englewood Cliffs, New Jersey: Prentice-Hall, 1963): 18-26. Chapter 11 of *Whitehead's Philosophy*.

227. "Sensation in Psychology and Philosophy." *Southern Journal of Philosophy* 1, 2 (1963): 3-14.

228. "Rationale of the Ontological Proof" [Reply to John Hick].

Theology Today 20, 2 (1963): 278-83.

229. "Whitehead's Conception of God" and "Whitehead's Theory of Prehension." In *Actas: Segundo Congreso Extraordinario Interamericano de Filosofía, 22-26 Julio, 1961* (San José, Costa Rica: Imprenta Nacional, 1963 [misprinted 1962]): 163-170.

230. Communication: "Finite or Finite-Infinite?" *Philosophy and Phenomenological Research* 24, 1 (1963): 149.

231. "Real Possibility." *Journal of Philosophy* 60, 21 (1963): 593-605.

232. "Present Prospects for Metaphysics." *The Monist* 47, 2 (1963): 188-210. Reprinted in *Process Philosophy: Basic Writings*, eds. Jack R. Sibley and Pete A. Y. Gunter (Washington D.C.: UP of America, 1978): 199-212. Chapter 3 of *Creative Synthesis*.

233. "Man's Fragmentariness." *Wesleyan Studies in Religion* 41, 6 (1963-1964): 17-28. Chapter 6 of *Wisdom as Moderation*.

234. "Abstract and Concrete in God: A Reply [to Julian Hartt]." *Review of Metaphysics* 17, 2 (1963): 289-95.

235. "Santayana's Defiant Eclecticism." *Journal of Philosophy* 61, 1 (1964): 35-44. Reprinted in *Animal Faith and Spiritual Life*, ed. John Lachs (New York: Appleton-Century-Crofts, 1967): 33-43. Chapter 10 of *Creativity in American Philosophy*.

236. "Thinking About Thinking Machines." *Texas Quarterly* 7, 1 (1964): 131-40.

237. Discussion: "What the Ontological Proof Does Not Do." *Review of Metaphysics* 17, 4 (1964): 608-09.

238. "From Colonial Beginnings to Philosophical Greatness." *The Monist* 48, 3 (1964): 317-31. Chapter 1 of *Creativity in American Philosophy*. Chapter 7 of *Hartshorne: A New World View*.

239. Comments and Criticism: "Deliberation and Excluded Middle." *Journal of Philosophy* 61, 16 (1964): 476-77.

240. Replies to "Interrogation of Charles Hartshorne, conducted by William Alston." *Philosophical Interrogations*, eds. Sydney and Beatrice Rome (New York: Holt, Rinehart, and Winston, 1964): 321-54. Questions to: John Wild, 158-160; Brand Blanshard, 205; Paul Tillich, 374-375.

241. "Is God's Existence a State of Affairs?" *Faith and the Philosophers*, ed. John Hick (New York: St. Martin's Press, 1964): 26-33.

242. "El valor como disfrute del contraste y la teoría acumulativa del proceso." Trans. J. L. González, *Dianoia, Annuario de Filosofía* 10 (1964): 182-194.

243. "Charles Peirce's 'One Contribution to Philosophy' and His Most Serious Mistake." *Studies in the Philosophy of Charles Sanders Peirce. Second Series*, eds. Edward G. Moore and Richard S. Robin (Amherst: U of Massachusetts P, 1964): 455-74.

244. "Negative Facts and the Analogical Inference to 'Other Mind'." *Dr. S. Radhakrishan Souvenir Volume*, eds. Prof. J. P. Atreya et al. (Moradabad [India]: Darshana International, 1964): 147-52. Chapter 3 of *Creative Experiencing*.

245. "The Idea of a Worshipful Being." *Southern Journal of Philosophy* 2, 4 (1964): 165-67.

246. "God as the Supreme Relativity." *Japanese Religions* 4, 1 (1964): 30-33.

247. "The Necessarily Existent." *The Ontological Argument*, ed. Alvin Plantinga (New York: Anchor Books, Doubleday, 1965): 123-35. Reprinted in *Philosophy of Religion*, eds. George L. Abernethy and Thomas A. Langford, 2nd ed. (New York: Macmillan, 1968): 238-47. Chapter 9 of *Man's Vision of God*.

248. "The Meaning of 'Is Going to Be'." *Mind* 74, 293 (1965): 46-58. Reprinted in John Martin Fischer and Patrick Todd (eds.), *Freedom, Fatalism, and Foreknowledge* (New York: Oxford University Press, 2015): 305-16. Chapter 8 of *Creative Experiencing*.

249. "The Theistic Proofs." *Union Seminary Quarterly Review* 20, 2 (1965): 115-29. Chapter 2 of *Natural Theology*.

250. "Abstract and Concrete Approaches to Deity." *Union Seminary Quarterly Review* 20, 3 (1965): 265-70.

251. "A Metaphysics of Individualism." *Innocence and Power: Individualism in Twentieth-Century America,* ed. Gordon Mills (Austin: U of Texas P, 1965): 131-46.

252. "Determinism, Memory, and the Metaphysics of Becoming." *Pacific Philosophy Forum* 4, 4 (1965): 81-85.

253. "The Social Theory of Feelings." *Southern Journal of Philosophy* 3, 2 (1965): 87-93. Reprinted in *Persons, Privacy, and Feeling: Essays in the Philosophy of Mind*, ed. Dwight Van de Vate, Jr. (Memphis:

Memphis State UP, 1970): 39-51.

254. "The Development of Process Philosophy." Introduction to *Philosophers of Process*, ed. Douglas Browning (New York: Random House, 1965): v-xii. Also published in *Process Theology: Basic Writings*, ed. Ewert H. Cousins (New York: Newman P, 1971): 47-64. Chapter 11 of *Hartshorne: A New World View*.

255. "Religious Aspects of Necessity and Contingency." *Great Issues Concerning Theism*, ed. Charles H. Manson, Jr. (Salt Lake City: U of Utah P, 1965): 147-64. Reprinted in *And More About God*, eds. Lewis M. Rogers and Charles H. Monson, Jr. (Salt Lake City: U of Utah P, 1969): 145-61.

256. "Criteria for Ideas of God." *Rice University Studies* 51, 4 (1965): 85-95. Also in *Insight and Vision: Essays in Philosophy in Honor of Radoslav Andrea Tsanoff*, ed. Konstantin Kolenda (San Antonio: Principia P of Trinity University, 1966): 85-95.

257. "Comment." *The Creative Advance*, by Eugene H. Peters (St. Louis: Bethany P, 1966): 133-43.

258. "The Two Possible Philosophical Definitions of God." In *Actas: XIII Congreso Internacional de Filosofía*, volumen 9 (Mexico City: Universidad Nacional Autonoma de Mexico, 1966): 121.

259. "A New Look at the Problem of Evil." *Current Philosophical Issues: Essays in Honor of Curt John Ducasse*, ed. Frederick C. Dommeyer (Springfield, Illinois: Charles C. Thomas, 1966): 201-12.

260. "Idealism and Our Experience of Nature." *Philosophy, Religion, and the Coming World Civilization: Essays in Honor of William Ernest Hocking*, ed. Leroy S. Rouner (The Hague: Martinus Nijhoff, 1966): 70-80. Chapter 12 of *Creativity in American Philosophy*.

261. "Tillich and the Non-theological Meaning of Theological Terms." *Religion in Life* 35, 5 (1966): 674-85. Reprinted in *Paul Tillich: Retrospect and Future* [pamphlet]. (Nashville: Abingdon P, 1966): 19-30.

262. "Some Reflections on Metaphysics and Language." *Foundations of Language: International Journal of Language and Philosophy* 2, 1 (1966): 20-32.

263. "Is the Denial of Existence Ever Contradictory?" *Journal of Philosophy* 63, 4 (1966): 85-93. Author's abstract in *The Review of*

Metaphysics 19, 4 (1966): 836.

264. "The Idea of Creativity in American Philosophy." *Journal of Kamatak University* [India]: *Social Sciences II* (1966): 1-13. Chapter 8 of *Hartshorne: A New World View*.

265. Review of N. S. Srivastava. *Contemporary Indian Philosophy* (Delhi: M.R.M. Lal, 1965). *Research Journal of Philosophy* (Ranchi University [India]) 1, 1 (1966): 110-11.

266. "Religion in Process Philosophy." *Religion in Philosophical and Cultural Perspective*, eds. J. Clayton Feaver and William Horosz (Princeton, New Jersey: D. Van Nostrand Co, 1967): 246-58.

267. "Royce and the Collapse of Idealism." *Revue internationale de philosophie* 23, 79-80 (1967, Fasc. 1-2): 46-59.

268. "Kagaku, Geijyutsu, Shukyo-Kofuku no Gensen to shite no." ("Science, Art, and Religion as Sources of Happiness.") Trans. Matao Noda. *Japan-American Forum* 13, 3 (1967): 47-66.

269. "God and the Social Structure of Reality," "The Significance of Man in the Life of God," and Answers to Questions. *Theology in Crisis: A Colloquium on 'The Credibility of God'* (New Concord, Ohio: Muskingum College, 1967): 19-32, 40-43, 44-50.

270. "Pantheism." *Encyclopedia Britannica*, Vol. 17 (1967): 233-34.

271. "Psychology and the Unity of Knowledge." *Southern Journal of Philosophy* 5, 2 (1967): 81-90.

272. "The Dipolar Conception of Deity." *Review of Metaphysics* 21, 2 (1967): 273-89.

273. "Necessity." *Review of Metaphysics* 21, 2 (1967): 290-96.

274. "Rejoinder to Purtill." *Review of Metaphysics* 21, 2 (1967): 308-09.

275. "Martin Buber's Metaphysics." *The Philosophy of Martin Buber*, eds. Paul Arthur Schilpp and Maurice Friedman. The Library of Living Philosophers, Vol. 12 (La Salle, Illinois: Open Court, 1967): 49-68. Also published as "Martin Buber's Metaphysik" in *Martin Buber*, herausgegeben von Schilpp u. Friedman (Stuttgart: Kohlhammer Verlag, 1963): 42-61.

276. "What Metaphysics Is." *Journal of Kamatak University: Social Sciences III* (1967): 1-15. Chapter 2 of *Creative Synthesis*; Chapter 6 of *Zero Fallacy*.

277. "The Irreducibly Modal Structure of the Argument." *The Many-Faced Argument*, eds. John Hick and Arthur C. McGill (New York: Macmillan, 1967): 334-40. Reprinted from chapter 2, part VI of *Logic of Perfection*.

278. "Process Philosophy as a Resource for Christian Thought." *Philosophical Resources for Christian Thought*, ed. Perry LeFevre (Nashville: Abingdon P, 1968): 44-66.

279. "The Divine Relativity." *Philosophy of Religion*, eds. George L. Abernethy and Thomas A. Langford. 2nd ed. (New York: Macmillan, 1968): 321-29. From *Divine Relativity*.

280. "Order and Chaos." *The Concept of Order*, ed. Paul G. Kuntz (Seattle: U of Washington P, 1968): 253-67.

281. "Three Strata of Meaning in Religious Discourse." *Philosophy and Religion: Some Contemporary Perspectives*, ed. Jerry H. Gill (Minneapolis: Burgess, 1968): 173-82. Chapter 4 of *Logic of Perfection*. [cf. item 183].

282. "The Aesthetics of Birdsong." *Journal of Aesthetics and Art Criticism* 26, 3 (1968): 311-15.

283. "Kant's Refutation Still Not Convincing: A Reply [to W. H. Baumer]." *The Monist* 52, 2 (1968): 312-16.

284. "Lewis's Treatment of Memory." *The Philosophy of C. I. Lewis*, ed. Paul Arthur Schilpp. The Library of Living Philosophers, Vol. 13 (La Salle, Illinois: Open Court, 1968): 395-414. Chapter 13 of *Creativity in American Philosophy*.

285. "Armchair and Laboratory: A Philosopher Looks at Psychology." *Newsletter, Division 24 of the American Psychological Association* 2, 3 (1968): 1-4. [Excerpt from an address given as president of the Southern Society for Philosophy and Psychology, 1963.]

286. "Born Equal: The Importance and Limitations of an Ideal." *Parables and Problems* (Winona, Minnesota: College of St. Teresa, 1968): 59-71. [Mimeographed]

287. "The Case for Idealism." *Philosophical Forum* 1, 1 (1968): 7-23. Chapter 6 of *Creative Experiencing*.

288. "The God of Religion and the God of Philosophy." *Talk of God: Royal Institute of Philosophy Lectures, Vol. Two¾1967-1968* (London: Macmillan, 1969): 152-67. Originally Broadcast Monday, June 10,

1968, BBC London Third Programme, *The Listener.*

289. "Duality versus Dualism and Monism." *Japanese Religions* 5, 1 (1969): 51-63.

290. "Leibniz und das Geheimnis der Materie." *Studia Leibnitiana: Akten des Internationalen Leibniz-Kongresses, Hannover, 14-19 November 1966, Band II: Mathematik-Naturwissenschaften* (Wiesbaden: Franz Steiner Verlag GMBH, 1969): 166-75.

291. "Whitehead in French Perspective: A Review Article." [Review of Alix Parmentier, *La Philosophie de Whitehead et le problème de Dieu* (Paris: Beauchesne, 1968)]. *Thomist* 33, 3 (1969): 573-81.

292. Response to *Directives from Charles Hartshorne and Henry Nelson Wieman Critically Analyzed: Philosophy of Creativity Monograph Series*, Vol. 1, ed. William S. Minor (Carbondale: The Foundation for Creative Philosophy, Inc., 1969): 33-42.

293. "Divine Absoluteness and Divine Relativity." *Transcendence*, eds. Herbert W. Richardson and Donald R. Cutler (Boston: Beacon P, 1969): 164-71.

294. "Metaphysics in North America." *Contemporary Philosophy: A Survey*, ed. Raymond Klibansky (Florence: La Nuova Italia Editrice, 1969): 36-49.

295. "Whitehead and Ordinary Language." *Southern Journal of Philosophy* 7, 4 (1969-1970): 437-45. Chapter 12 of *Whitehead's Philosophy.*

296. Preface of *Berdyaev's Philosophy of History*, ed. David Bonner Richardson (The Hague: Martinus Nihjoff, 1970): ix-xiii.

297. "Why Study Birds?" *Virginia Quarterly Review* 46, 1 (1970): 133-40.

298. "Recollections of Famous Philosophers and Other Important Persons." *Southern Journal of Philosophy* 8, 1 (1970): 67-82. Chapter 13 of *Darkness and Light.*

299. "Two Forms of Idolatry." *International Journal for Philosophy of Religion* 1, 1 (1970): 3-15.

300. "Six Theistic Proofs." *Monist* 54, 2 (1970): 159-80. Chapter 14 of *Creative Synthesis.*

301. "Equality, Freedom, and the Insufficiency of Empiricism." *Southern Journal of Philosophy* 1, 3 (1970): 20-27.

302. "Eternity," "Absolute," "God." *Prophetic Voices: Ideas and Words on Revolution*, ed. Ned O'Gorman (New York: Random House, 1969; New York: Vintage Books, 1970): 130-48.

303. "The Development of My Philosophy." *Contemporary American Philosophy: Second Series*, ed. John E. Smith (London: Allen & Unwin, 1970): 211-28.

304. "Ontological Primacy: A Reply to Buchler." *Journal of Philosophy* 67, 23 (1970): 979-86. Reprinted in *Explorations in Whitehead's Philosophy*, eds. Lewis S. Ford and George L. Kline (New York: Fordham UP, 1983): 295-303.

305. "Charles Hartshorne's Recollections of Editing the Peirce Papers." *Transactions of the Charles S. Peirce Society* 6, 3-4 (1970): 149-59.

306. "Deity as the Inclusive Transcendence." *Evolution in Perspective: Commentaries in Honor of Pierre Lecomte du Noüy*, eds. George N. Shuster and Ralph E. Thorson (Notre Dame and London: U of Notre Dame P, 1970): 155-60.

307. "The Formally Possible Doctrines of God." *Classical and Contemporary Readings in the Philosophy of Religion*, ed. John Hick. Second Edition. (Englewood Cliffs, New Jersey: Prentice-Hall, 1970): 336-57. Also printed in *Process Philosophy and Christian Thought*, eds. Delwin Brown, Ralph E. James, Jr., and Gene Reeves (Indianapolis: Bobbs-Merrill, 1971): 188-214. Chapter 1 of *Man's Vision of God*.

308. "Mind and Matter in Ryle, Ayer, and C. I. Lewis." *Idealistic Studies* 1, 1 (1971): 13-32. Chapter 24 of *Insights and Oversights*.

309. "Are There Absolutely Specific Universals?" *Journal of Philosophy* 68, 3 (1971): 76-78.

310. "Can Man Transcend His Animality?" *The Monist* 55, 2 (1971): 208-217. Chapter 7 of *Wisdom as Moderation*.

311. "Selfishness in Man." *PHP* [Peace Happiness Prosperity] 1, 8 (1971): 24-25.

312. "Could There Have Been Nothing? A Reply [to Houston Craighead]." *Process Studies* 1, 1 (1971): 25-28.

313. "Expression and Association." *Artistic Expression*, ed. John Hospers (New York: Appleton-Century-Crofts, 1971): 204-17. Chapter 5, Section 23 of *Philosophy and Psychology of Sensation*.

314. "Obligability and Determinism." *Journal of Social Philosophy* 2, 2 (1971): 1-2. Reprinted in *Philosophy for a Changing Society*, ed. Creighton Peden (Reynoldsburg, Ohio: Advocate Publishing Co., 1982): 95-96.

315. "Philosophical and Religious Uses of 'God'." *Process Theology: Basic Writings*, ed. Ewert H. Cousins (New York: Newman P, 1971): 101-18. Chapter 1 of *Natural Theology*.

316. "Can There Be Proofs for the Existence of God?" *Religious Language and Knowledge*, eds. Robert H. Ayers and William T. Blackstone (Athens: U of Georgia P, 1972): 62-75. Chapter 10 of *Hartshorne: A New World View*.

317. "Mortimer Adler as Philosopher: A Criticism and Appreciation." *American Scholar* 41, 2 (1972): 269-74. Chapter 19 of *Creativity in American Philosophy*.

318. "A Conversation with Charles Hartshorne at Hiram College." Edited by Eugene Peters. *Eclectic: A Journal of Ideas* 1, 1 (1972): 1-18.

319. Review of Paul Ramsay. *Fabricated Man* (New Haven: Yale UP, 1970). *Philosophy Forum* 12, 1 & 2 (1972): 149-52.

320. Review of Paul Weiss. *The God We Seek* (Carbondale: Southern Illinois P, 1964). *Review of Metaphysics* 25 [supplement] (1972): 108-16. Chapter 19 of *Creativity in American Philosophy*.

321. "Personal Identity from A to Z." *Process Studies* 2, 3 (1972): 209-15.

322. Feature Book Review: "Some Thoughts Suggested by [Irwin C.] Lieb's *Four Faces of Man*." (Philadelphia: U of Pennsylvania P, 1971). *International Philosophical Quarterly* 13, 1 (1973): 131-34.

323. "Some Thoughts on 'Souls' and Neighborly Love." *Anglican Theological Review* 55, 2 (1973): 144-47.

324. "Analysis and Cultural Lag in Philosophy." *Southern Journal of Philosophy* 11, 2-3 (1973): 105-12.

325. "Being and Becoming: Review of Harold N. Lee. *Percepts, Concepts, and Theoretic Knowledge*." *Review of Books and Religion* 2, 9 (1973): 7.

326. "Process and the Nature of God." *Traces of God in a Secular Culture*, ed. George F. McLean, O.M.I (New York: Alba House, 1973): 117-41.

327. "Creativity and the Deductive Logic of Causality." *Review of*

Metaphysics 27, 1 (1973): 62-74. Chapter 7 of *Creative Experiencing*.

328.   "Pensées sur ma vie," 26-32; "Thoughts on my Life," 60-66. *Bilingual Journal, Lecomte du Noüy Association* 5 (1973).

329.   "Charles Peirce and Quantum Mechanics." *Transactions of the Charles S. Peirce Society* 9, 4 (1973): 191-201. See also *Abstracts of Communications Sent to the XVth World Congress of Philosophy*. Varna, Sept. 17-22, 1973. Bulgarian Organizing Committee, International Federation of Philosophical Societies.

330.   "Husserl and Whitehead on the Concrete." *Phenomenology: Continuation and Criticism—Essays in Memory of Dorion Cairns*, eds. F. Kersten and R. Zaner (The Hague: Martinus Nijhoff, 1973): 90-104. Chapter 23 of *Insights and Oversights*.

331.   "Ideas and Theses of Process Philosophers." *Two Process Philosophers: Hartshorne's Encounter with Whitehead*. AAR Studies in Religion Number Five (Tallahassee, Florida: American Academy of Religion, 1973): 100-03.

332.   "Science and Quality." *Sound Seminars: Tapes in Philosophy*. New York: McGraw-Hill, 1954, 1973.

333.   "Contribuciones Permanentes de Spinoza." [Spanish translation of "Spinoza's Permanent Contributions."] *Folia humanistica: ciencias, artes, letras* 12 (1974): 121-29.

334.   "Twelve Elements of My Philosophy." *Southwestern Journal of Philosophy* 5, 1 (1974): 7-15.

335.   Abstract: "Do Philosophers Know That They Have Bodies?" *Abstracts of Papers, 1974. Annual Conference of the Australasian Association of Philosophy* (Canberra: Australian National U, 1974): 7-8.

336.   "Philosophy after Fifty Years." *Mid-Twentieth Century American Philosophy: Personal Statements*, ed. Peter A. Bertocci (New York: Humanities P, 1974): 140-54.

337.   "The Environmental Results of Technology." *Philosophy and Environmental Crisis*, ed. William T. Blackstone (Athens: U of Georgia P, 1974): 69-78.

338.   "Beyond Enlightened Self-Interest: A Metaphysics of Ethics." *Ethics* 84, 3 (1974): 201-16. Reprinted in *Religious Experience and Process Theology*, eds. Harry James Cargas and Bernard Lee

(New York: Paulist P, 1976): 301-322. Also published in *Process Philosophy: Basic Writings*, eds. Jack R. Sibley and Pete A. Y. Gunter (Washington, D.C.: UP of America, 1978): 395-416. Chapter 12 of *Zero Fallacy*.

339. "Perception and the Concrete Abstractness of Science." *Philosophy and Phenomenological Research* 34, 4 (1974): 465-76. Chapter 9 of *Zero Fallacy*. Chapter 4 of *Creative Experiencing*.

340. "The Nature of Philosophy." *Philosophy in Context: An Experiment in Teaching*, Vol. 4, ed. Leslie Armour (Cleveland State UP, 1975): 7-16.

341. "Love and Dual Transcendence." *Union Seminary Quarterly Review* 30, 2-4 (1975): 94-100.

342. "Whitehead's Differences from Buddhism." *Philosophy East and West* 25, 4 (1975): 407-13.

343. "Whitehead and Leibniz: A Comparison." *Contemporary Studies in Philosophical Idealism*, eds. John Howie and Thomas O. Buford (Cape Cod, Massachusetts: Claude Starke, 1975): 95-115.

344. "Do Birds Enjoy Singing? (An Ornitho-Philosophical Discourse)." *Bulletin of the Texas Ornithological Society* 8 (1975): 2-5. Chapter 2 of *Zero Fallacy*.

345. "The Centrality of Reason in Philosophy (Replies to Questions for Charles Hartshorne)." *Philosophy in Context*, Supplement to Volume 4 (1975): 5-11.

346. Discussion: "Synthesis as Polyadic Inclusion: A Reply to Sessions." *Southern Journal of Philosophy* 14, 2 (1976): 245-55.

347. "Mysticism and Rationalistic Metaphysics." *The Monist* 59, 4 (1976): 463-69. Also published in *Understanding Mysticism*, ed. Richard Woods (Garden City, New York: Image, 1980): 415-21.

348. "Psychicalism and the Leibnizian Principle." *Studia Leibnitiana* 8, 2 (1976): 154-59. Chapter 8 of *Zero Fallacy*.

349. "Why Psychicalism? Comments on Keeling's and Shepherd's Criticisms." *Process Studies* 6, 1 (1976): 67-72.

350. "Additional Reflections." [On Jean-Marie Breuvart's *Les Directives de la Symbolisation et les Modeles de Référence dans la Philosophie d'A. N. Whitehead*]. *Process Studies* 7, 4 (1977): 271-74.

351. "Bell's Theorem and Stapp's Revised View of Space-time." *Process*

Studies 7, 3 (1977): 183-91.

352. "The Books That Shape Lives: Book Choices of Charles Hartshorne." *Christian Century* 44, 30 (1977): 860.

353. "Cobb's Theology of Ecology." *John Cobb's Theology in Process*, eds. David Ray Griffin and Thomas J. J. Altizer (Philadelphia: Westminster P, 1977): 112-15.

354. "The Duty to Happiness." *Catalyst Tape Talk* 9, 5 (1977): 4.

355. "John Hick on Logical and Ontological Necessity." *Religious Studies* 13, 2 (1977): 155-65.

356. "The Neglect of Relative Predicates in Modern Philosophy." *American Philosophical Quarterly* 14, 4 (1977): 309-18. Chapter 14 of *Insights and Oversights*.

357. "Physics and Psychics: The Place of Mind in Nature." *Mind in Nature: Essays on the Interface of Science and Philosophy*, eds. John B. Cobb, Jr. and David Ray Griffin (Washington, D.C.: UP of America, 1977): 89-96; also in this volume, "Response to Arthur Koestler's 'Free Will in a Hierarchic Context'," 66 and "Response to Bernhard Rensch's 'Arguments for Panpsychistic Identism'," 78.

358. "Whitehead's Metaphysical System." Trans. Schubert M. Ogden (from "Das metaphysische System Whiteheads"). *A Rational Faith: Essays in Honor of Rabbi Levi A. Olan*, ed. Jack Bemporad (New York: KTAV Publishing House, Inc., 1977): 107-123. German original in *Zeitschrift für philosophische Forschung* 3, 4 (1949): 566-575. German version also in *Whitehead: Einführung in seine Kosmologie*. Beiträge von Gernot Bohme, Charles Hartshorne, u.s.w. Herausgegeben von Ernest Wolf-Gazo (Freiburg/München: Verlag Karl Albers, 1980): 28-44.

359. "The Acceptance of Death." *Philosophical Aspects of Thanatology*, Vol. 1. eds. Florence M. Hetzler and Austin H. Kutscher (New York: MSS Information Corporation, 1978): 83-87. Chapter 1 of *Hartshorne: A New World View*.

360. "Can We Understand God?" *Louvain Studies* 7, 2 (1978): 75-84. Reprinted in *Framing a Vision of the World: Essays in Philosophy, Science and Religion*, eds. André Cloots and Santiago Sia (Leuven UP, 1999): 87-97.

361. Foreword to *The Ontological Argument of Charles Hartshorne* by

George L. Goodwin (Missoula, MT: Scholars P, 1978): xi-xviii.

362. "Foundations for a Humane Ethics: What Human Beings Have in Common with Other Higher Animals." *On the Fifth Day: Animal Rights and Human Ethics*, eds. Richard K. Morris and Michael W. Fox (Washington, DC: Acropolis Books, 1978): 154-72.

363. "The Individual is a Society." *The Individual and Society: Essays Presented to David L. Miller on His Seventy-fifth Birthday*, eds. Michael P. Jones, Patricia O.F. Nobo, Jorge L. Nobo, and Yenling Chang. *Southwestern Journal of Philosophy* (1978): 73-88.

364. "A New World and a New World View." *The Life of Choice*, ed. Clark Kucheman (Boston: Beacon P, 1978): 82-92. Chapter 6 of *A New World Order*. (First given as a speech at University of Texas graduation convocation, 1976.)

365. "The Organism According to Process Philosophy." *Organism, Medicine, and Metaphysics: Essays in Honor of Hans Jonas on his 75th Birthday, May 10th, 1978*, ed. Stuart Spicker (Dordrecht, Holland: D. Reidel, 1978): 137-54. Also in *Process in Context: Essays in Post-Whiteheadian Perspectives*, ed. Ernest Wolf-Gazo (New York: Peter Lang Publishing, Inc., 1988): 69-92.

366. "Panpsychism: Mind as Sole Reality." *Ultimate Reality and Meaning* 1, 2 (1978): 115-29.

367. "A Philosophy of Death." *Philosophical Aspects of Thanatology*, Vol. 2. eds. Florence M. Hetzler and A. H. Kutscher (New York: MSS Information Corporation, 1978): 81-89.

368. Preface to *Process Philosophy: Basic Writings*, eds. Jack R. Sibley and Pete A. Y. Gunter (Washington D.C.: UP of America, 1978): 1-7.

369. "Reply to Eugene H. Peters." *Ultimate Reality and Meaning* 1, 3 (1978): 233-34.

370. "Theism in Asian and Western Thought." *Philosophy East and West* 28, 4 (1978): 401-11.

371. "The Mystery of Omnipotence is Too Deep for Human Reason." *The Power of God: Readings on Omnipotence and Evil*, eds. Linwood Urban and Douglas N. Walton (New York: Oxford UP, 1978): 249-251. Retitled excerpt from *Natural Theology*, 116-20.

372. "'Emptiness' and Fullness in Asiatic and Western Thought."

Journal of Chinese Philosophy 6 (1979): 411-20.

373.   "Charles Morris." *Semiotica* 28, 3-4 (1979): 193-94.

374   "God and Nature." *Anticipation* 25 (1979): 58-64.

375.   "The Rights of the Subhuman World." *Environmental Ethics: An Interdisciplinary Journal Dedicated to the Philosophical Aspects of Environmental Problems* 1, 1 (1979): 49-60. German translation by Dr. Ilse Tödt: "Rechte¾nicht nur für die Menschen" published in *Zeitschrift für Evangelische Ethik* 22, 1 (1978): 3-14. English original published as chapter 9 of *Wisdom as Moderation*.

376.   "Metaphysics Contributes to Ornithology." *Theoria to Theory* 13, 2 (1979): 127-40. Chapter 8 of *Wisdom as Moderation*.

377.   "Whitehead's Revolutionary Concept of Prehension." *International Philosophical Quarterly* 19, 3 (1979): 253-63. Hartshorne used the same title for chapter 9 of *Creativity in American Philosophy* but it is a different article.

378.   "Process Themes in Chinese Thought." *Journal of Chinese Philosophy* 6 (1979): 323-36.

379.   Interview with Charles Hartshorne [conducted by Santiago Sia]. *Miltown Studies* 4 (1979): 1-23.

380.   "Philosophy and Religion." *Program of the International Congress of Philosophy* on "Contemporary Problems of Philosophy and Religion" at Fu Jen Catholic University, Taipei, Taiwan (Dec. 28, 1979-Jan. 4, 1980): 26.

381.   "James' Empirical Pragmatism." *American Journal of Theology and Philosophy* 1, 1 (1980): 14-20. Chapter 5 of *Creativity in American Philosophy*.

382.   "My Neoclassical Metaphysics." *Tijdschrift voor Philosophie* 42, 1 (1980): 3-10.

383.   "In Defense of Wordsworth's View of Nature." *Philosophy & Literature* 4, 1 (1980): 80-91.

384.   Review of Karol Wojtyla. *The Acting Person* (Dordrecht: D. Reidel Publishing Co., 1979). *Philosophy and Phenomenological Research* 40, 3 (1980): 443-44.

385.   "Ethics and the Process of Living." *Man and His Conduct: Philosophical Essays in Honor of Risieri Frondizi*, ed. Jorge J. E. Garcia (Rio Piedras, Puerto Rico: Editorial Universitaria, 1980):

191-202.

386. "Pepper's Approach to Metaphysics." *Root Metaphor: The Live Thought of Stephen C. Pepper.* PAUNCH #53-54 (1980): 80-81.

387. "Understanding Freedom and Suffering." *Catalyst Tape Talk* 12, 9 (1980): 4-5 [cut and edited without consultation with author. Also, recorded tape available.]

388. "A Revision of Peirce's Categories." *The Monist* 63, 3 (1980): 277-89. Reprinted in *The Relevance of Charles Peirce*, ed. Eugene Freeman (La Salle, Illinois: Monist Library of Philosophy, 1983): 80-92. Chapter 7 of *Creativity in American Philosophy*.

389. "Understanding as Seeing to be Necessary." *The Philosophy of Brand Blanshard*, ed. Paul Arthur Schilpp. The Library of Living Philosophers, Vol. 15 (La Salle, Illinois: Open Court, 1980): 629-35.

390. "Response to Robert Neville's *Creativity and God.*" *Process Studies* 10, 3-4 (1980): 93-97.

391. "A Conversation between Charles Hartshorne and Jan Van der Veken." *Louvain Studies* VII, 2 (1980): 129-42.

392. "Concerning Abortion: An Attempt at a Rational View." *The Christian Century* 98, 2 (1981): 42-45. Reprinted in *Speak Out Against the New Right*, ed. Herbert F. Vetter (Boston: Beacon P, 1982): 152-157. Also reprinted in *The Ethics of Abortion*, first edition, eds. Robert M. Baird and Stuart E. Rosenbaum (Buffalo, New York: Prometheus Books, 1989): 109-14. Chapter 2 of *Hartshorne: A New World View*.

393. "The Ethics of Contributionism." *Responsibilities to Future Generations: Environmental Ethics*, ed. Ernest Partridge (Buffalo: Prometheus P, 1981): 103-07.

394. "Critical Study: A Neglected Nonacademic Philosopher" [on Rudolf Jordan]. *Process Studies* 11, 3 (1981): 213-15.

395. "Neoclassical Metaphysics." *Philosophers on Their Own Work*, Vol. 8. Bern, Frankfurt, Las Vegas: Peter Lang, 1981): 63-104. In French and English. Includes a list of publications.

396. "Science as the Search for the Hidden Beauty of the World." *The Aesthetic Dimension of Science* 1980 Nobel Conference, Number 16, ed. Deane W. Curtin (New York: Philosophical Library, 1982): 85-106. See also pp. 107, 108, 117, 119-120, 123-125, 128-129, 130, 131,

137, 140, 143.

397. "Creative Interchange and Neoclassical Metaphysics." *Creative Interchange*, eds. John A. Broyer and Wm. S. Minor (Carbondale and Edwardsville: Southern Illinois U P, 1982): 107-21.

398. "Grounds for Believing in God's Existence." *Meaning, Truth, and God*, ed. Leroy S. Rouner (Notre Dame and London: U of Notre Dame P, 1982): 17-33.

399. "Interview with Charles Hartshorne," *Unitarian Universalist World* (November 15, 1982): 1, 6-7.

400. Review of Daniel A. Dombrowski. *Plato's Philosophy of History* (Washington, D.C.: UP of America, 1981). *Process Studies* 12, 3 (1982): 201-02.

401. "Anselm and Aristotle's First Law of Modality." *Anselm Studies: An Occasional Journal* 1 (1983): 51-58.

402. Review of George R. Lucas, Jr. *The Genesis of Modern Process Thought: A Historical Outline with Bibliography* (Metuchen, N. J. and London: Scarecrow P, 1983). *Process Studies* 13, 2 (1983): 176-79.

403. "Categories, Transcendentals, and Creative Experiencing." *The Monist* 66, 3 (1983): 319-35. Chapter 11 of *Creative Experiencing*.

404. "Peirce's Fresh Look at Philosophical Problems." *Krisis* 1, 1 (1983): 1-5.

405. "Taking Freedom Seriously." Lowell Lecture, 1983. Cambridge Forum, taped lecture # 471 (June 25, 1983) (3 Church Street, Cambridge, Massachusetts, 02138). Unpublished paper that was also presented as a sermon at the First Unitarian Church in Oklahoma City on February 22, 1981.

406. "God and the Meaning of Life." [Reflections on Robert Nozick's *Philosophical Explanations*.] *On Nature*, ed. Leroy S. Rouner. Boston U Studies in Philosophy and Religion, Vol. 6 (Notre Dame, Indiana: U of Notre Dame P, 1984): 154-68.

407. "Toward a Buddhist-Christian Religion." *Buddhism and American Thinkers*, eds. Kenneth K. Inada and Nolan P. Jacobson (Albany: State U of New York P, 1984): 1-13.

408. "Indeterministic Freedom as Universal Principle." *Journal of Social Philosophy* 15 (1984): 5-11.

409. "Marcel on God and Causality." *The Philosophy of Gabriel Marcel*,

eds. Paul Arthur Schilpp and Lewis Edwin Hahn. The Library of Living Philosophers, Vol. 17 (La Salle, Illinois: Open Court, 1984): 353-66.

410. "How I got that way," *Existence and Actuality: Conversations with Charles Hartshorne*, eds. John B. Cobb, Jr., and F. I. Gamwell (Chicago: U of Chicago P, 1984). Responses to: Eugene H. Peter, 12-15; Schubert M. Ogden, 37-42; Richard M. Martin, 66-77; William P. Alston, 98-102; John E. Smith, 109-12; Paul Weiss, 121-29; Manley Thompson, 143-48; John B. Cobb, Jr., 164-66; George Wolf, 184-88.

411. "Whitehead as Central but not Sole Philosopher of Process." *Whitehead und der Prozessbegriff*, eds. Harold Holz and Ernest Wolf-Gazo (Freiburg, Nunchen: Karl Alber, 1984): 34-38. From *Proceedings of the First International Whitehead Symposium*, eds. Harold Holz and Ernest Wolf-Gazo, 1981.

412. Foreword to *Divine Omniscience and Human Freedom: Thomas Aquinas and Charles Hartshorne* by John Moskop (Georgia: Mercer UP, 1984): ix-xi.

413. "Theistic Proofs and Disproofs: The Findlay Paradox." *Studies in the Philosophy of J. N. Findlay*, eds. Robert S. Cohen, Richard M. Martin, and Merold Westphal (Albany: State U of New York P, 1985): 224-34.

414. "Creativity as a Value and Creativity as a Transcendental Category." *Creativity in Art, Religion, and Culture*, ed. Michael H. Mitias ([*Elementa: Schriften Zur Philosophie und Ihrer Problemgeschichte*, ed. Rudolph Berlinger and Wiebke Schrader. Band 42 – 1985] Amsterdam: Rodopi, 1985): 3-11.

415. "A Philosophy of Shared Creative Experience." *American Philosophy: A Historical Anthology*, ed. with commentary, Barbara McKinnon (Albany: State U of New York P, 1985): 414-27. Chapter 1 of *Creative Synthesis*. [cf. items 194, 219, and 220]

416. Foreword to *Charles Hartshorne and the Existence of God* by Donald Wayne Viney (Albany: State U of New York P, 1985): viii-x.

417. "Process Theology in Historical and Systematic Contexts." *Modern Schoolman* 62, 4 (1985): 221-31.

418. Postscript to *God in Process Thought, A Study in Charles Hartshorne's Concept of God* by Santiago Sia (Dordrecht: Martinus Nijoff

Publishing, 1985): 113-23.

419. "Scientific and Religious Aspects of Bioethics." *Theology and Bioethics*, ed. E. E. Schelp (Dordrecht, Boston, Lancaster, Tokyo: D. Reidel Publishing Co., 1985): 27-44.

420. "Our Knowledge of God." *Knowing Religiously*. Boston U Studies in Philosophy and Religion, Vol. 7, ed. Leroy S. Rouner (Notre Dame, Indiana: U of Notre Dame P, 1985): 52-63.

421. "Reeves and Stearns on My Idealism." *American Journal of Theology and Philosophy* 7, 1 (1986): 45-50.

422. "Some Perspectives on Chinese Philosophy." *Journal of Chinese Philosophy* 13 (1986): 267-70. Also published in *Philosophie et Culture* Actes du XVIIe Congrès Mondial de Phillosophie. Édition Montmorency, Montréal, 1988: 249-51.

423. "Metaphysics and the Dual Transcendence of God." *Tulane Studies in Philosophy*, "Hartshorne's Neoclassical Theology," eds. Forrest Wood, Jr. and Michael DeArmey, 34 (1986): 65-72. Chapter 9 of *Creative Experiencing*.

424. Review of Stephen Toulmin. *Return to Cosmology* (Berkeley, California: U of California P, 1982). *Philosophy and Rhetoric* 19, 4 (1986): 266-269.

425. "Argument in Metaphysics of Religion." *Process Theology and the Christian Doctrine of God*, ed. Santiago Sia. Special edition of *Word and Spirit, A Monastic Review*, 8 (Petersham, Massachusetts: St. Bede's, Publications, 1986): 44-47.

426. "Wisdom as Moderation: A Philosophy of the Golden Mean." Cambridge Forum, taped lecture # 716 (April 9, 1986) (3 Church Street, Cambridge, Massachusetts, 02138). Chapter 2 of *Wisdom as Moderation* followed by audience discussion.

427. "Some Theological Mistakes and Their Effects on Literature." *Journal of Speculative Philosophy*, New Series 1, 1 (1987): 55-72. Chapter 3 of *Zero Fallacy*.

428. Response to resurrection debate in *Did Jesus Rise From the Dead? The Resurrection Debate, Gary Habermas and Antony G. N. Flew*, ed. Terry L. Miethe (San Francisco: Harper & Row, 1987): 137-42.

429. "Pantheism and Panentheism." *The Encyclopedia of Religion*, Senior Ed., Mircea Eliade (New York: Macmillan Publishing

Co.; London: Collier Macmillan, Vol. 11, 1987): 165-71.

430. "Transcendence and Immanence." *The Encyclopedia of Religion*, Senior Ed. Mircea Eliade (New York: Macmillan Publishing Co.; London: Collier Macmillan, Vol. 15, 1987): 16-21.

431. "An Anglo-American Phenomenology: Method and Some Results." *Pragmatism Considers Phenomenology*, eds. R. S. Corrington, Carl Hausman, and T. M. Seebohn (Washington: Center for Advanced Research in Phenomenology and UP of America, 1987): 59-71.

432. "Bergson's Aesthetic Creationism Compared to Whitehead's." *Bergson & Modern Thought: Toward a Unified Science*, eds. A.C. Papanicolaou and Pete A. Gunter (Chur, Switzerland and New York: Harwood Academic Publishers, 1987): 369-82.

433. "Weiss After Sixty Years." *Creativity and Common Sense: Essays in Honor of Paul Weiss*, ed. Thomas Krettek (Albany: State U of New York P, 1987): 262-69.

434. "Mind and Body: A Special Case of Mind and Mind." *A Process Theory of Medicine: Interdisciplinary Essays*, ed. Marcus Ford (Lewiston, New York: Edwin Mellen P, 1987): 77-88.

435. "A Metaphysics of Universal Freedom." *Faith and Creativity: Essays in Honor of Eugene H. Peters*, eds. George Nordgulen and George W. Shields (St. Louis, Missouri: CBP Press, 1987): 27-40.

436. "Reflecting on the Existence [and] Meaning of God." [Interview with Monty Jones]. *The Austin-American Stateman* (Sunday, Jan. 31, 1988): B8.

437. "Can Peirce's Categories Be Retained?" *Philosophie et Culture*, Actes du XVIIe Congrès Mondial de Philosophie. Montréal: Éditions Montmorency, 1988: 140-42.

438. "Some Principles of Procedure in Metaphysics." *The Nature of Metaphysical Knowledge*, eds. G. F. McLean and Hugo Meynell. International Society for Metaphysics (Lanham, New York: UP of America, 1988): 69-75.

439. "Sankara, Nagarjuna, and Fa Tsang, with some Western Analogues." *Interpreting Across Boundaries: New Essays in Comparative Philosophy*, eds. G. J. Larson and Eliot Deutsch (Princeton, New Jersey: Princeton UP, 1988): 98-115.

440. "In Dispraise of Empiricism." *American Journal of Theology and*

Philosophy 10, 2 (1989): 123-26.

441. "A Dual Theory of Theological Analogy." *American Journal of Theology and Philosophy* 10, 3 (1989): 171-78. Also in *God, Values, and Empiricism, Issues in Philosophical Theology*, eds. Creighton Peden and Larry Axel (Macon, Georgia: Mercer UP, 1989): 85-91.

442. "Metaphysical and Empirical Aspects of the Idea of God." *Witness and Existence: Essays in Honor of Schubert M. Ogden*, eds. Philip E. Devenish and George L. Goodwin (Chicago: U of Chicago P, 1989): 177-89.

443. "General Remarks." *Hartshorne, Process Philosophy, and Theology*, eds. Robert Kane and Stephen H. Phillips (Albany: State U of New York P, 1989). Replies to David Griffin, 181-83; Jan Van der Veken, 183-84; Barry Whitney, 184-85; Donald Wayne Viney, 186; Daniel Dombrowski, 186-88, Stephen Phillips, 188-90; Kenneth Ketner, 190-92; Lewis S. Ford, 192-94; Robert Kane, 194-95; Jorge L. Nobo, 195-96.

444. "Von Wright and Hume's Axiom." *The Philosophy of Georg Henrik von Wright*, eds. Paul Arthur Schilpp and Lewis Edwin Hahn. The Library of Living Philosophers, Vol. 19 (La Salle, Illinois: Open Court, 1989): 59-76.

445. Foreword and Postscript to *Benevolent Living: Tracing the Roots of Motivation to God* by Richard Hazelett and Dean Turner (Pasadena: Hope Publishing House, 1990): xi-xiv; 313-17.

446. "Charles Hartshorne on Metaphilosophy, Person and Immortality, and Other Issues." An interview with Charles Hartshorne by John Kennedy and Piotr Gutowski [on May 20-21, 1989]. *Process Studies* 19, 4 (1990): 256-78.

447 Review of *The Philosophical Theology of Jonathan Edwards* by Sang Hyun Lee (Princeton: Princeton UP, 1988). *Transactions of the Charles S. Peirce Society* 26, 2 (1990): 249-52.

448. "Response to Piotr Gutowski's 'Charles Hartshorne's Rationalism'." *Process Studies* 19, 1 (1990): 10-14.

449. "Hegel, Logic, and Metaphysics." *CLIO* 19, 4 (1990): 347-52.

450. Critical Response by Charles Hartshorne. *Charles Hartshorne's Concept of God, Philosophical and Theological Responses*, ed. Santiago Sia (Hingam, Massachusetts: Kluwer Publishers, 1990): 241-321.

Responses to: [Theodore] Walker on Afro-American and African Theology, 241-42; [Peter] Phan on Liberation Theology, 243-50; [Randall] Morris on Political Philosophy, 251-55; [Sheila Greeve] Devaney on God, Power, and Liberation, 256-62; Arabindu Basu on Indian Thought, 263-65; [Fr. Joseph] Bracken on the God-world Issue, 266-68; [Fr. W. Norris] Clarke's Thomistic Critique, 269-79; [André] Cloots and [Jan] Van der Veken on Panentheism, 280-83; [Hiroshi] Endo's Comparative Study, 284-89; [Piotr] Gutowski on Philosophical Theology, 290-93; [John S.] Ishihara on Buddhism, 294-98; [Rabbi William] Kaufman on Judaism's Idea of God, 299-303; [Martin] McNamara on Biblical Theology, 304-09; [David] Pailin on Rigor, Reason, and Moderation, 310-20; Concluding Remarks [in appreciation of Santiago Sia and the contributors], 320-21.

451.   "An Open Letter to Carl Sagan." *The Journal of Speculative Philosophy*, 5, 4 (1991): 227-32.

452.   "Communication from Charles Hartshorne" [concerning the history of the Central Division of the American Philosophical Association]. *Proceedings and Addresses of the American Philosophical Association* 65, 3 (1991): 69-70.

453.   "Some Causes of My Intellectual Growth." *The Philosophy of Charles Hartshorne*, ed. Lewis Edwin Hahn. The Library of Living Philosophers, Vol. 20 (La Salle, Illinois: Open Court, 1991): 3-45. "A Reply to My Critics," 569-731: Preliminaries and Principles: Reply to Everybody, 569-89; [Charles L.] Birch on Darwin, Chance, and Purpose, 584-86; [Alexander K.] Skutch on Bird Song and Philosophy, 586-89; [Lucio] Chiaraviglio on Song, Evolution, and Theism, 589-98; [Wayne] Viney on Psychology of Sensation, 598-600; [John] Hospers on the Aesthetics of Sensation, 600-06; [Robert] Kane on Freedom and Sufficient Reason, 606-13; Englehardt on Theism and Bioethics, 613-14; [John B.] Cobb [Jr.] on My Theology, 614-16; [William L.] Reese on Panentheism and God's Goodness, 616-17; [Jan] Van der Veken on God and the Ultimate, 617-19; [Jacquelyn Ann] Kegley on Royce and Community, 620-23; [Sallie B.] King on Buddhism, Hierarchy, and Reason, 624-27; [John G.] Arapura on My Response to Vedantism, 627-30; [James P.] Devlin on Metaphysical Asymmetry, 630-33; [Nancy] Frankenberry on Method in Metaphysics, 633-39;

[Lewis S.] Ford on Whitehead's and My Philosophy, 640-56; [Norman M.] Martin on the Logic of My Metaphysics, 656-64; [Hubertus G.] Hubbeling on the Ontological Argument, 664-69; [Robert C.] Neville on Temporality and God, 669-72; [T. L. S.] Sprigge on Past, Future, and Eternity, 672-80; [Paul G.] Kuntz on Order and Orderliness, 680-84; [Sterling M.] McMurrin on Neoclassical Metaphysics, 684-88; [Reiner] Wiehl on Whitehead's and My Psychicalism, 688-702; [Daniel A.] Dombrowski on My Platonism, 703-04; [John E.] Smith on the History of Philosophy, 704-12; [George R.] Lucas [Jr.] on Sources of Process Philosophy, 712-14; Donald Lee on My Pragmatism, 714-21; [Matao] Noda on My Atomism, 721-26; [Keiji] Matsunobu on Philosophy in the Kyoto School, 726-31.

454. "Peirce, Whitehead und die sechzehn Ansichten über Gott." [translated by Helmut Maaßen] *Die Gifford Lectures und ihre Deutung: Materialien zu Whiteheads ›Prozeß und Realität‹ 2*, eds. Michael Hampe und Helmut Maaßen (Frankfurt am Main: Suhrkamp, 1991): 194-216. English original, "Peirce, Whitehead, and the Sixteen Views About God" published in *Process Studies* 40/1 (Spring/Summer 2011): 104-121.

455. "The Aesthetic Dimensions of Religious Experience." *Logic, God and Metaphysics*, ed. J. F. Harris (Dordrecht: Kluwer Academic Publishers, 1992): 9-18.

456. "Some Not Ungrateful But Perhaps Inadequate Comments About Comments on My Writings and Ideas." *Process Studies* 21, 2 (1992): 123-29.

457. "Some Comments on Randall Morris' *Process Philosophy and Political Ideology*." *Process Studies* 21, 3 (1992): 149-51.

458. "Some Under- and Over-rated Great Philosophers [Plato, Bergson, Aristotle, Kant, and others]." *Process Studies* 21, 3 (1992): 166-74.

459. "Hartshorne's Response [to D. Haugen and L. G. Keeling's 'Hartshorne's Process Theism and Big Bang Cosmology']." *Process Studies* 22, 3 (1993): 172.

460. "Can Philosophers Cooperate Intellectually: Metaphysics as Applied Mathematics." *The Midwest Quarterly* 35, 1 (1993): 8-20.

461. "Reminiscences of Charles Hartshorne (member since 1942)." *Journal of Aesthetics and Art Criticism* 51 (1993): 286-89.

462. "God, Necessary and Contingent; World, Contingent and Necessary; and the Fifteen Other Options in Thinking about God: Necessity and Contingency as Applied to God and the World." *Metaphysics as Foundation: Essays in Honor of Ivor Leclerc,* eds. Paul A. Bogaard and Gordan Treash (Albany: State U of New York P, 1993): 296-311.

463. "Interview with Hartshorne, December 1, 1993" (with Randall Auxier). *Hartshorne and Brightman on God, Process, and Persons: The Correspondence, 1922-1945,* eds. Randall E. Auxier and Mark Y. A. Davies (Nashville: Vanderbilt UP, 2001): 88-99.

464. "Three Important Scientists on Mind, Matter, and the Metaphysics of Religion." *The Journal of Speculative Philosophy* 8, 3 (1994): 211-27.

465. "Buddhism and the Theistic Question." *Buddhism and the Emerging World Civilization: Essays in Honor of Nolan Pliny Jacobson,* eds. Ramakrishna Puligandla and David Lee Miller (Carbondale, Illinois: Southern Illinois UP, 1994): 62-72.

466. "Peirce's Philosophy on Religion: Between Two Forms of Religious Belief." *Peirce and Contemporary Thought: Philosophical Inquiries,* ed. Denneth Laine Ketner (New York: Fordham UP, 1995): 339-55.

467. "Rorty's Pragmatism and Farewell to the Age of Faith and Enlightenment." *Rorty & Pragmatism: The Philosopher Responds to His Critics,* ed. Herman J. Saatkamp, Jr. (Nashville & London: Vanderbilt UP, 1995): 16-28. Chapter 24 of *Creativity in American Philosophy.*

468. "Freedom as Universal." *Process Studies* 25 (1996): 1-9.

469. "The Meaning of Life." *Process Studies* 25 (1996): 10-18.

470. "Theism as Radical Positivism: Minds, Bodies, Yes, Mindless Matter, No; Causality, Yes, Determinism, No." *Process Thought: The Japan Society for Process* Studies (1996): 1-5.

471. "Reminiscences of Charles Hartshorne" (excerpted from an unpublished paper: "Importance, Families, Religions, Darwin: A Case Study From the Inside," written in 1994). *Process Perspectives* 20, 3. *Newsletter of the Center for Process Studies,* Special Hartshorne edition (Spring 1997): 8-11.

472. "A Philosopher at 99." [Interview by Steven Vita]. *Austin American*

Statesman. (Sunday, April 13, 1997): D1, D7.

473. "A hundred years of thinking about God: a philosopher soon to be rediscovered." [Interview by Greg Easterbrook]. *US News and World Report* (Feb. 23, 1998): 61, 65.

474. "Philosophy (at) 101: Centenarian Charles Hartshorne is Austin's Preeminent Man of Ideas." [Interview by Dayna Finet]. *The Good Life* [published in Austin, Texas] (Oct. 1998): 15-18.

475. "Twenty Opinions from Five Times Twenty Years." *The Personalist Forum*, Special Issue: The Hartshorne Centennial Conference, 14, 2 (1998): 75-76.

476. "Thoughts on the Development of My Concept of God." *The Personalist Forum*, Special Issue: The Hartshorne Centennial Conference, 14, 2 (1998): 77-82.

477. "A Psychologist's Philosophy Evaluated After Fifty Years: Troland's Psychical Monism." Ed. Donald Wayne Viney. *Process Studies* 30, 2 (2001): 237-41. [Originally presented April 1, 1983 at the Southern Society of Philosophy and Psychology, Atlanta, Georgia.]

478. "God as Composer-Director and Enjoyer, and in a Sense Player, of the Cosmic Drama." Ed. Donald Wayne Viney. *Process Studies* 30, 2 (2001): 242-53. [Presented April 7, 1987 at Central State University, Edmund, Oklahoma.]

479. Audience Discussion of "God as Composer-Director and Enjoyer, and in a Sense Player, of the Cosmic Drama" [Transcription of a video tape from April 7, 1987, Central State U, Edmond, Oklahoma]. Ed. Donald Wayne Viney. *Process Studies* 30, 2 (2001): 254-60.

480. "Thomas Aquinas and Three Poets Who Do Not Agree With Him." Ed. Donald Wayne Viney. *Process Studies* 30, 2 (2001): 261-75. [Written in the late 1980s or early 1990s.]

481. "Darwin and Some Philosophers [Review of *Charles Darwin: A New Life* by John Bowlby]." Ed. Donald Wayne Viney. *Process Studies* 30, 2 (2001): 276-88. [Manuscript indicates that Hartshorne worked on this review as late 1993.]

482. "Charles Hartshorne's Handwritten Notes on A. N. Whitehead's Harvard-Lectures 1925-1926." Ed. Roland Faber. *Process Studies* 30, 2 (2001): 289-73.

483. "Theistic Humanism." *Hartshorne: A New World View*, chapter 4, previously unpublished. [Written in 1950.]

484. "Some Formal Criteria of Good Metaphysics." *Creative Experiencing*, chapter 1, previously unpublished.

485. "My Eclectic Approach to Phenomenology." *Creative Experiencing*, chapter 2, previously unpublished.

486. "Metaphysical Truth by Systematic Elimination of Absurdities." *Creative Experiencing*, chapter 5, previously unpublished.

487. "The Ontological Argument and the Meaning of Modal Terms." *Creative Experiencing*, chapter 10, previously unpublished.

488. "The Higher Levels of Creativity: Wieman's Theory." *Creative Experiencing*, chapter 12, previously unpublished.

489. "Determinate Views about the Indeterminate Future." *Process Studies* 40/1 (2011): 122-130. [Originally written in the 1970s as a response to two articles in *The Review of Metaphysics*, but never previously published.]

490. "Response to Zycinski." *Process Studies* 40/1 (2011): 144-149. [Response to Joseph Zycinski, "How to Naturalize Theology?" *Process Studies* 40/1 (2011): 131-143; see also in the same number Zycinski's response to Hartshorne: 150-153. The exchange occurred in the 1990s.]

491. "My Religious Beliefs." *Process Studies* 40/1 (2011): 154-161. [Presented as a sermon at a Unitarian church on August 23, 1992.]

Miscellaneous Hartshorne Correspondence and Letters to the Editor

"Recollections of Leo Szilard by Charles Hartshorne" (6 pages) Hartshorne sent this document to William Lanouette for his biography of Szilard on January 10, 1986. On file at the Claremont School of Theology at the Center for Process Studies in the Hartshorne Archives.

Letter from Charles Hartshorne to David Basinger (August 4, 1988) and letter from Basinger to Hartshorne (August 24, 1988). Shared by Basinger with Don Viney.

Letter from Charles Hartshorne to Robert S. Corrington (July 10, 1992), http://users.drew.edu/rcorring/downloads

/APPRAISAL&CRITIQUECOPYRight.pdf, accessed June 13, 2017.

Letter from Carl Sagan to Hartshorne (Feb. 27, 1992) and Hartshorne's response (Jan. 23, 1995). On file at the Claremont School of Theology at the Center for Process Studies in the Hartshorne Archives in "Professional Correspondence to Hartshorne" #1155). Hartshorne's response is in "Professional Correspondence from Hartshorne," #186.

Hartshorne's letter to the editor of the *Austin American Statesman* concerning "creation science" opposing May 23, 1981; February 1, 1984 and May 11, 1989; concerning abortion, April 26, 1971, February 6, 1973, February 15, 1973, February 26, 1973, September 17, 1990, and July 5, 1991.

Name Index

Subject Index

Abortion, 322-28, 341, 385, 474, 476; and birth control, 475; Chancey's critique of Hartshorne, 326-27; and infanticide, 325; moral v. legal questions, 327; most substantive argument against, 325; and the mother's right to self-determination, 327-28; Roe v. Wade, 132, 326, 328, 341, 385

actual entities (see also dynamic singulars), 46, 72, 84, 87, 89, 91, 111, 125, 160, 161, 162, 179, 289, 290, 410; their objective immortality and perishing, 86; 179, 221, 410, 421

actuality: atomic v. continuous, 11, 88-91

affective continuum, 14, 37-49, 84, 95, 98, 102, 140, 141, 280

afterlife beliefs (see also immortality and contributionism), 4-7; Auxier's views, 128-29, 423, heaven and hell, 224; karma and reincarnation, 224; limited afterlife, 5, 129, 425; resurrection of the body, 126, 422; Suchocki's views, 126-28, 422-23

angels, 157, 225-26, 448

animal (nonhuman) ethics, vii, 314-15, 335, 477

Anselm's Discovery, vi, 21, 193, 195, 204, 224

asymmetry; of entailment, 61; inclusive, vi, 11, 53, 58-61, 118, 156; of temporal relations, 134-38, 171; in quantum events, 293, 294

Made in the USA
Middletown, DE
16 May 2023

30697312R00325